T0181964

# Lecture Notes in Computer Science     13021

More information about this subseries at http://www.springer.com/series/7412

Huimin Ma · Liang Wang · Changshui Zhang ·
Fei Wu · Tieniu Tan · Yaonan Wang ·
Jianhuang Lai · Yao Zhao (Eds.)

# Pattern Recognition and Computer Vision

4th Chinese Conference, PRCV 2021
Beijing, China, October 29 – November 1, 2021
Proceedings, Part III

Springer

*Editors*
Huimin Ma (iD)
University of Science and Technology Beijing
Beijing, China

Changshui Zhang
Tsinghua University
Beijing, China

Tieniu Tan
Chinese Academy of Sciences
Beijing, China

Jianhuang Lai
Sun Yat-Sen University
Guangzhou, Guangdong, China

Liang Wang
Chinese Academy of Sciences
Beijing, China

Fei Wu (iD)
Zhejiang University
Hangzhou, China

Yaonan Wang
Hunan University
Changsha, China

Yao Zhao (iD)
Beijing Jiaotong University
Beijing, China

ISSN 0302-9743          ISSN 1611-3349  (electronic)
Lecture Notes in Computer Science
ISBN 978-3-030-88009-5          ISBN 978-3-030-88010-1  (eBook)
https://doi.org/10.1007/978-3-030-88010-1

LNCS Sublibrary: SL6 – Image Processing, Computer Vision, Pattern Recognition, and Graphics

# Preface

Welcome to the proceedings of the 4th Chinese Conference on Pattern Recognition and Computer Vision (PRCV 2021) held in Beijing, China!

PRCV was established to further boost the impact of the Chinese community in pattern recognition and computer vision, which are two core areas of artificial intelligence, and further improve the quality of academic communication. Accordingly, PRCV is co-sponsored by four major academic societies of China: the China Society of Image and Graphics (CSIG), the Chinese Association for Artificial Intelligence (CAAI), the China Computer Federation (CCF), and the Chinese Association of Automation (CAA).

PRCV aims at providing an interactive communication platform for researchers from academia and from industry. It promotes not only academic exchange but also communication between academia and industry. In order to keep track of the frontier of academic trends and share the latest research achievements, innovative ideas, and scientific methods, international and local leading experts and professors are invited to deliver keynote speeches, introducing the latest advances in theories and methods in the fields of pattern recognition and computer vision.

PRCV 2021 was hosted by University of Science and Technology Beijing, Beijing Jiaotong University, and the Beijing University of Posts and Telecommunications. We received 513 full submissions. Each submission was reviewed by at least three reviewers selected from the Program Committee and other qualified researchers. Based on the reviewers' reports, 201 papers were finally accepted for presentation at the conference, including 30 oral and 171 posters. The acceptance rate was 39.2%. PRCV took place during October 29 to November 1, 2021, and the proceedings are published in this volume in Springer's Lecture Notes in Computer Science (LNCS) series.

We are grateful to the keynote speakers, Larry Davis from the University of Maryland, USA, Yoichi Sato from the University of Tokyo, Japan, Michael Black from the Max Planck Institute for Intelligent Systems, Germany, Songchun Zhu from Peking University and Tsinghua University, China, and Bo Xu from the Institute of Automation, Chinese Academy of Sciences, China.

We give sincere thanks to the authors of all submitted papers, the Program Committee members and the reviewers, and the Organizing Committee. Without their contributions, this conference would not have been possible. Special thanks also go to all of the sponsors and the organizers of the special forums; their support helped to make the conference a success. We are also grateful to Springer for publishing the proceedings.

October 2021

Tieniu Tan  
Yaonan Wang  
Jianhuang Lai  
Yao Zhao  
Huimin Ma  
Liang Wang  
Changshui Zhang  
Fei Wu

# Organization

## Steering Committee Chair

Tieniu Tan            Institute of Automation, Chinese Academy of Sciences, China

## Steering Committee

Xilin Chen            Institute of Computing Technology, Chinese Academy of Sciences, China
Chenglin Liu        Institute of Automation, Chinese Academy of Sciences, China
Yong Rui            Lenovo, China
Hongbing Zha       Peking University, China
Nanning Zheng      Xi'an Jiaotong University, China
Jie Zhou            Tsinghua University, China

## Steering Committee Secretariat

Liang Wang          Institute of Automation, Chinese Academy of Sciences, China

## General Chairs

Tieniu Tan            Institute of Automation, Chinese Academy of Sciences, China
Yaonan Wang       Hunan University, China
Jianhuang Lai       Sun Yat-sen University, China
Yao Zhao           Beijing Jiaotong University, China

## Program Chairs

Huimin Ma          University of Science and Technology Beijing, China
Liang Wang          Institute of Automation, Chinese Academy of Sciences, China
Changshui Zhang    Tsinghua University, China
Fei Wu             Zhejiang University, China

## Organizing Committee Chairs

Xucheng Yin         University of Science and Technology Beijing, China
Zhanyu Ma          Beijing University of Posts and Telecommunications, China
Zhenfeng Zhu       Beijing Jiaotong University, China
Ruiping Wang       Institute of Computing Technology, Chinese Academy of Sciences, China

## Sponsorship Chairs

Nenghai Yu          University of Science and Technology of China, China
Xiang Bai           Huazhong University of Science and Technology, China
Yue Liu             Beijing Institute of Technology, China
Jinfeng Yang        Shenzhen Polytechnic, China

## Publicity Chairs

Xiangwei Kong       Zhejiang University, China
Tao Mei             JD.com, China
Jiaying Liu         Peking University, China
Dan Zeng            Shanghai University, China

## International Liaison Chairs

Jingyi Yu           ShanghaiTech University, China
Xuelong Li          Northwestern Polytechnical University, China
Bangzhi Ruan        Hong Kong Baptist University, China

## Tutorial Chairs

Weishi Zheng        Sun Yat-sen University, China
Mingming Cheng      Nankai University, China
Shikui Wei          Beijing Jiaotong University, China

## Symposium Chairs

Hua Huang           Beijing Normal University, China
Yuxin Peng          Peking University, China
Nannan Wang         Xidian University, China

## Doctoral Forum Chairs

Xi Peng             Sichuan University, China
Hang Su             Tsinghua University, China
Huihui Bai          Beijing Jiaotong University, China

## Competition Chairs

Nong Sang           Huazhong University of Science and Technology, China
Wangmeng Zuo        Harbin Institute of Technology, China
Xiaohua Xie         Sun Yat-sen University, China

## Special Issue Chairs

| | |
|---|---|
| Jiwen Lu | Tsinghua University, China |
| Shiming Xiang | Institute of Automation, Chinese Academy of Sciences, China |
| Jianxin Wu | Nanjing University, China |

## Publication Chairs

| | |
|---|---|
| Zhouchen Lin | Peking University, China |
| Chunyu Lin | Beijing Jiaotong University, China |
| Huawei Tian | People's Public Security University of China, China |

## Registration Chairs

| | |
|---|---|
| Junjun Yin | University of Science and Technology Beijing, China |
| Yue Ming | Beijing University of Posts and Telecommunications, China |
| Jimin Xiao | Xi'an Jiaotong-Liverpool University, China |

## Demo Chairs

| | |
|---|---|
| Xiaokang Yang | Shanghai Jiaotong University, China |
| Xiaobin Zhu | University of Science and Technology Beijing, China |
| Chunjie Zhang | Beijing Jiaotong University, China |

## Website Chairs

| | |
|---|---|
| Chao Zhu | University of Science and Technology Beijing, China |
| Zhaofeng He | Beijing University of Posts and Telecommunications, China |
| Runmin Cong | Beijing Jiaotong University, China |

## Finance Chairs

| | |
|---|---|
| Weiping Wang | University of Science and Technology Beijing, China |
| Lifang Wu | Beijing University of Technology, China |
| Meiqin Liu | Beijing Jiaotong University, China |

## Program Committee

| | |
|---|---|
| Jing Dong | Chinese Academy of Sciences, China |
| Ran He | Institute of Automation, Chinese Academy of Sciences, China |
| Xi Li | Zhejiang University, China |
| Si Liu | Beihang University, China |
| Xi Peng | Sichuan University, China |
| Yu Qiao | Chinese Academy of Sciences, China |
| Jian Sun | Xi'an Jiaotong University, China |
| Rongrong Ji | Xiamen University, China |
| Xiang Bai | Huazhong University of Science and Technology, China |
| Jian Cheng | Institute of Automation, Chinese Academy of Sciences, China |
| Mingming Cheng | Nankai University, China |
| Junyu Dong | Ocean University of China, China |
| Weisheng Dong | Xidian University, China |
| Yuming Fang | Jiangxi University of Finance and Economics, China |
| Jianjiang Feng | Tsinghua University, China |
| Shenghua Gao | ShanghaiTech University, China |
| Maoguo Gong | Xidian University, China |
| Yahong Han | Tianjin University, China |
| Huiguang He | Institute of Automation, Chinese Academy of Sciences, China |
| Shuqiang Jiang | Institute of Computing Technology, China Academy of Science, China |
| Lianwen Jin | South China University of Technology, China |
| Xiaoyuan Jing | Wuhan University, China |
| Haojie Li | Dalian University of Technology, China |
| Jianguo Li | Ant Group, China |
| Peihua Li | Dalian University of Technology, China |
| Liang Lin | Sun Yat-sen University, China |
| Zhouchen Lin | Peking University, China |
| Jiwen Lu | Tsinghua University, China |
| Siwei Ma | Peking University, China |
| Deyu Meng | Xi'an Jiaotong University, China |
| Qiguang Miao | Xidian University, China |
| Liqiang Nie | Shandong University, China |
| Wanli Ouyang | The University of Sydney, Australia |
| Jinshan Pan | Nanjing University of Science and Technology, China |
| Nong Sang | Huazhong University of Science and Technology, China |
| Shiguang Shan | Institute of Computing Technology, Chinese Academy of Sciences, China |
| Hongbin Shen | Shanghai Jiao Tong University, China |
| Linlin Shen | Shenzhen University, China |
| Mingli Song | Zhejiang University, China |
| Hanli Wang | Tongji University, China |
| Hanzi Wang | Xiamen University, China |
| Jingdong Wang | Microsoft, China |

| | |
|---|---|
| Nannan Wang | Xidian University, China |
| Jianxin Wu | Nanjing University, China |
| Jinjian Wu | Xidian University, China |
| Yihong Wu | Institute of Automation, Chinese Academy of Sciences, China |
| Guisong Xia | Wuhan University, China |
| Yong Xia | Northwestern Polytechnical University, China |
| Shiming Xiang | Chinese Academy of Sciences, China |
| Xiaohua Xie | Sun Yat-sen University, China |
| Jufeng Yang | Nankai University, China |
| Wankou Yang | Southeast University, China |
| Yang Yang | University of Electronic Science and Technology of China, China |
| Yilong Yin | Shandong University, China |
| Xiaotong Yuan | Nanjing University of Information Science and Technology, China |
| Zhengjun Zha | University of Science and Technology of China, China |
| Daoqiang Zhang | Nanjing University of Aeronautics and Astronautics, China |
| Zhaoxiang Zhang | Institute of Automation, Chinese Academy of Sciences, China |
| Weishi Zheng | Sun Yat-sen University, China |
| Wangmeng Zuo | Harbin Institute of Technology, China |

## Reviewers

Bai Xiang
Bai Xiao
Cai Shen
Cai Yinghao
Chen Zailiang
Chen Weixiang
Chen Jinyu
Chen Yifan
Cheng Gong
Chu Jun
Cui Chaoran
Cui Hengfei
Cui Zhe
Deng Hongxia
Deng Cheng
Ding Zihan
Dong Qiulei
Dong Yu
Dong Xue
Duan Lijuan
Fan Bin
Fan Yongxian
Fan Bohao
Fang Yuchun

Feng Jiachang
Feng Jiawei
Fu Bin
Fu Ying
Gao Hongxia
Gao Shang-Hua
Gao Changxin
Gao Guangwei
Gao Yi
Ge Shiming
Ge Yongxin
Geng Xin
Gong Chen
Gong Xun
Gu Guanghua
Gu Yu-Chao
Guo Chunle
Guo Jianwei
Guo Zhenhua
Han Qi
Han Linghao
He Hong
He Mingjie
He Zhaofeng

He Hongliang
Hong Jincheng
Hu Shishuai
Hu Jie
Hu Yang
Hu Fuyuan
Hu Ruyun
Hu Yangwen
Huang Lei
Huang Sheng
Huang Dong
Huang Huaibo
Huang Jiangtao
Huang Xiaoming
Ji Fanfan
Ji Jiayi
Ji Zhong
Jia Chuanmin
Jia Wei
Jia Xibin
Jiang Bo
Jiang Peng-Tao
Kan Meina
Kang Wenxiong

Lei Na
Lei Zhen
Leng Lu
Li Chenglong
Li Chunlei
Li Hongjun
Li Shuyan
Li Xia
Li Zhiyong
Li Guanbin
Li Peng
Li Ruirui
Li Zechao
Li Zhen
Li Ce
Li Changzhou
Li Jia
Li Jian
Li Shiying
Li Wanhua
Li Yongjie
Li Yunfan
Liang Jian
Liang Yanjie
Liao Zehui
Lin Zihang
Lin Chunyu
Lin Guangfeng
Liu Heng
Liu Li
Liu Wu
Liu Yiguang
Liu Zhiang
Liu Chongyu
Liu Li
Liu Qingshan
Liu Yun
Liu Cheng-Lin
Liu Min
Liu Risheng
Liu Tiange
Liu Weifeng
Liu Xiaolong
Liu Yang
Liu Zhi

Liu Zhou
Lu Shaoping
Lu Haopeng
Luo Bin
Luo Gen
Ma Chao
Ma Wenchao
Ma Cheng
Ma Wei
Mei Jie
Miao Yongwei
Nie Liqiang
Nie Xiushan
Niu Xuesong
Niu Yuzhen
Ouyang Jianquan
Pan Chunyan
Pan Zhiyu
Pan Jinshan
Peng Yixing
Peng Jun
Qian Wenhua
Qin Binjie
Qu Yanyun
Rao Yongming
Ren Wenqi
Rui Song
Shen Chao
Shen Haifeng
Shen Shuhan
Shen Tiancheng
Sheng Lijun
Shi Caijuan
Shi Wu
Shi Zhiping
Shi Hailin
Shi Lukui
Song Chunfeng
Su Hang
Sun Xiaoshuai
Sun Jinqiu
Sun Zhanli
Sun Jun
Sun Xian
Sun Zhenan

Tan Chaolei
Tan Xiaoyang
Tang Jin
Tu Zhengzheng
Wang Fudong
Wang Hao
Wang Limin
Wang Qinfen
Wang Xingce
Wang Xinnian
Wang Zitian
Wang Hongxing
Wang Jiapeng
Wang Luting
Wang Shanshan
Wang Shengke
Wang Yude
Wang Zilei
Wang Dong
Wang Hanzi
Wang Jinjia
Wang Long
Wang Qiufeng
Wang Shuqiang
Wang Xingzheng
Wei Xiu-Shen
Wei Wei
Wen Jie
Wu Yadong
Wu Hong
Wu Shixiang
Wu Xia
Wu Yongxian
Wu Yuwei
Wu Xinxiao
Wu Yihong
Xia Daoxun
Xiang Shiming
Xiao Jinsheng
Xiao Liang
Xiao Jun
Xie Xingyu
Xu Gang
Xu Shugong
Xu Xun

Xu Zhenghua
Xu Lixiang
Xu Xin-Shun
Xu Mingye
Xu Yong
Xue Nan
Yan Bo
Yan Dongming
Yan Junchi
Yang Dong
Yang Guan
Yang Peipei
Yang Wenming
Yang Yibo
Yang Lu
Yang Jinfu
Yang Wen
Yao Tao
Ye Mao
Yin Ming
Yin Fei

You Gexin
Yu Ye
Yu Qian
Yu Zhe
Zeng Lingan
Zeng Hui
Zhai Yongjie
Zhang Aiwu
Zhang Chi
Zhang Jie
Zhang Shu
Zhang Wenqiang
Zhang Yunfeng
Zhang Zhao
Zhang Hui
Zhang Lei
Zhang Xuyao
Zhang Yongfei
Zhang Dingwen
Zhang Honggang
Zhang Lin

Zhang Mingjin
Zhang Shanshan
Zhang Xiao-Yu
Zhang Yanming
Zhang Yuefeng
Zhao Cairong
Zhao Yang
Zhao Yuqian
Zhen Peng
Zheng Wenming
Zheng Feng
Zhong Dexing
Zhong Guoqiang
Zhou Xiaolong
Zhou Xue
Zhou Quan
Zhou Xiaowei
Zhu Chaoyang
Zhu Xiangping
Zou Yuexian
Zuo Wangmeng

# Contents – Part III

**Biomedical Image Processing and Analysis**

# Low-Level Vision and Image Processing

# SaliencyBERT: Recurrent Attention Network for Target-Oriented Multimodal Sentiment Classification

Jiawei Wang[1], Zhe Liu[1(✉)], Victor Sheng[2], Yuqing Song[1], and Chenjian Qiu[1]

[1] Jiangsu University, Zhenjiang 212013, China
lzhe@ujs.edu.cn
[2] Texas Tech University, Lubbock, TX, USA

**Abstract.** As multimodal data become increasingly popular on social media platforms, it is desirable to enhance text-based approaches with other important data sources (e.g. images) for the Sentiment Classification of social media posts. However, existing approaches primarily rely on the textual content or are designed for the coarse-grained Multimodal Sentiment Classification. In this paper, we propose a recurrent attention network (called SaliencyBERT) over the BERT architecture for Target-oriented Multimodal Sentiment Classification (TMSC). Specifically, we first adopt BERT and ResNet to capture the intra-modality dynamics with the textual content and the visual information respectively. Then, we design a recurrent attention mechanism, which can derive target-sensitive visual representations, to capture the inter-modality dynamics. With recurrent attention, our model can progressively optimize the alignment of target-sensitive textual features and visual features and produce an output after a fixed number of time steps. Finally, we combine the loss of all-time steps for deep supervision to prevent converging slower and overfitting. Our empirical results show that the proposed model consistently outperforms single modal methods and achieves an indistinguishable or even better performance on several highly competitive methods on two multimodal datasets from Twitter.

**Keywords:** Target-oriented multimodal sentiment classification · BERT architecture · Recurrent attention

## 1 Introduction

With the increasing popularity of social media, a large number of multimodal posts containing images and text are generated by users on social media platforms such as Twitter, Facebook, and Flickr to express their attitudes or opinion. It is quite valuable to analyze such large-scale multimodal data to study the user's emotional orientation toward certain events or topics. Target-oriented Sentiment Classification (TSC) is a fine-grained sentiment classification task, which identifies sentiment polarities through individual opinion targets hidden inside each input sentence. For example, "More on this dramatic bus fire on Haight Street by @Evan", the polarity of the sentence towards the "Haight Street" is neutral while the polarity is negative in terms of "bus" in Fig. 1.b.

© Springer Nature Switzerland AG 2021
H. Ma et al. (Eds.): PRCV 2021, LNCS 13021, pp. 3–15, 2021.
https://doi.org/10.1007/978-3-030-88010-1_1

(a)   Congratulations to Shelby County Sheriff [ **Bill Oldham** ]$_{positive}$ on his re-election.

(b) More on this dramatic [ **bus** ]$_{negative}$ fire on [ **Haight Street** ]$_{neutral}$ by @Evan

**Fig. 1.** Representative examples for Target-oriented Multimodal Sentiment Classification in our Twitter datasets. The target words and corresponding sentiment are highlighted and show that different target opinions in the same sentence may express different sentiment polarities.

Since TSC was proposed, this problem of fine-grained Sentiment Classification has been receiving the attention and research of the academic community. Early research uses statistical methods, such as support vector machines [1, 2], which require carefully designed manual features. In recent years, neural network models [3, 4] have been widely used to automatically learn the representation of target words and their context. Attention mechanisms [5, 6] have also been studied to strengthen the target characteristics' attention to important words in the context. However, most existing target-oriented sentiment classification methods are only based on text content and ignore other associated data sources. Multimodal posts usually come with images, and these images often provide valuable insights into users' sentiment (e.g., the smile of the man is a sign of positive sentiment in Fig. 1.a). In a word, due to the shortness and informality of the text in a post, the sentiment classification of a target sometimes depends largely on its associated images. Especially for sentences with multiple targets, the textual content often only expresses the subjective feelings of a certain target but ignores other targets. The introduction of related pictures can help supplement additional sentiment information. Therefore, Target-oriented Multimodal Sentiment Classification (TMSC) with text and images will be meaningful. A tensor fusion network [8] and a memory fusion network [9] was designed to better capture the interactions between different modalities. However, these methods are designed for the coarse-grained dialogue multimodal sentiment classification and do not explore the relationship between the individual opinion target and the multi-modal content.

As the aforementioned previous causes are, in this paper, we propose to use a soft, sequential, top-down attention mechanism on top of the recent BERT [10] architecture. Through the enhancement of visual modality, we can more accurately capture sentiment polarities of individual opinion target in each input sentence. Specifically, a stand-alone BERT can be used at each time step to obtain rich target-sensitive textual representations. Then, the attention mechanism learns appropriate attention weights for different regions in the associated image to induce the alignment of target-sensitive textual representations and visual representations. Furthermore, we adopt a feed-forward network and two-layer norms with residual connections to obtain the output of the current time step. By deconvoluting the output of the current time step, the rich interactive information between target-sensitive textual features and visual features is propagated to the higher resolution layer as the input of the next time step. Through multiple time steps, to progressively optimize the alignment of the target-sensitive textual representation and the visual representation. It is sort of analogous to the cognition procedure of a person, who might first notice part of the important information at the beginning, then notices more as she reads through. Finally, we combine the loss of each time step for deep supervise to prevent converging slower and overfitting.

The main contributions of this paper can be concluded as follows: (1) We propose a recurrent attention network for Target-oriented Multimodal Sentiment Classification, which uses the BERT architecture. Its input consists of two modalities (i.e., text, image). (2) We further develop a soft, sequential, top-down attention mechanism to effectively capture the intra-modality and inter-modality dynamics. The core idea is to obtain the saliency feature of a certain modal through the enhancement of another modal. (3) We also present a deep supervision method to overcome the problems caused by the number of unrolling steps, which makes the back-propagation convergence rate slower and easy to overfit.

To investigate the performance of the proposed model, we conduct comprehensive experiments in a supervised setting on two benchmark multimodal datasets. The proposed model can achieve an indistinguishable or even better performance over several highly competitive multimodal approaches.

## 2 Related Work

Early sentiment classification was usually performed using machine learning [11] and lexical-based methods [12]. These technologies are inseparable from a lot of manual work, such as data preprocessing and manually designing a set of task-specific features. The preprocessing becomes difficult as the number of data increases. Deep Learning is a relatively new approach that has been employed to carry out sentiment analysis [13]. Deep Learning has been found to perform better than traditional machine learning or lexical-based approaches when an enormous amount of training data is available. Target-oriented Sentiment Classification (TSC) has been extensively studied in recent years [14]. Target-oriented sentiment classification is a branch of sentiment classification, which requires considering both the sentence and opinion target. Unlike the previous coarse-grained dialogue sentiment classification, target-oriented fine-grained sentiment classification [7, 15] is more challenging. Because different target words in the same sentence may express different sentiment polarities. Inspired by the advantages of attention mechanisms in capturing long-range context information in other NLP tasks [10, 16, 17], many recent studies have devised different attention mechanisms to model the interactions between the target entity and the context [18, 19].

With the increasing popularity of social media, a large number of multimodal posts are generated by users on social media platforms to express their attitudes or opinion. People began to study the use of information from different modalities (visual, auditory, etc.) to provide additional emotional information for traditional text features. Early work was designed for coarse-grained sentiment analysis for multimodal dialogue and focused on how integrating other relevant information with text features. Bertero et al. [20] proposed a hierarchical CNN method, which classifies the emotions and emotions of each utterance in the interactive speech dialogue system. But their work is designed for coarse-grained sentence-level sentiment analysis, whereas our work targets at fine-grained target-level sentiment analysis. In recent years, the majority of these studies learned to effectively model the interactions between the target entity, the textual context, and the associated image context. A tensor fusion network [8] and a memory fusion network [9] was designed to better capture the interactions between different modalities. Attention mechanisms [21, 23] are studied to enhance the influence of target opinion on the final representation for prediction. Yu et al. [22] proposed an entity-sensitive attention and fusion network, which uses the single attention mechanism to perform target-image matching to derive target-sensitive visual representations. However, these single-attention-based methods may hide the characteristics of each attended word when attending multiple scattered words with one attention.

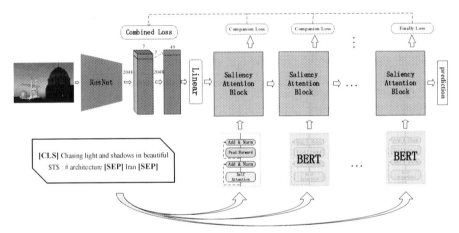

**Fig. 2.** Overview of our multimodal model for TMSC. The final decision of sentiment classification is obtained after a fixed time step.

## 3   Proposed Model

In this section, we first formulate our task and introduce visual encoder and textual encode respectively. Then, we will discuss our multimodal recurrent attention network in detail, which is end-to-end trainable.

### 3.1   Task Definition

Our task is to learn a target-oriented multimodal sentiment classifier so that it can use both textual modal data and visual modal data to predict the sentiment label of the opinion target in an unseen sample. Specifically, given a sentence $X = \{x_1, x_2, \ldots, x_n\}$ containing an opinion target T (a sub-sequence of words in X) and an associated image V. For the opinion target T, it has a sentiment label Y, which can be 2 for positive, 1 for negative, or 0 for neutral.

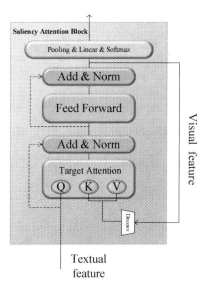

**Fig. 3.** Overview of Saliency Attention Block. By deconvoluting the output of the current time step, the rich interactive information between target-sensitive textual features and visual features is propagated to the higher resolution layer as the input of the next time step.

### 3.2   Recurrent Attention Network

**Visual Feature Encode.** Unlike other models that use only single modal data, information from visual modalities is leveraged to provide additional feature information to traditional textual features in our model. As illustrated in Fig. 2, for the associated image V, we first resize it to 224 × 224 pixels and adopt one of state-of-the-art pre-trained image recognition models ResNet-152 [24] to obtain the output of the last convolutional layer.

$$\text{ResNet}(V) = \left\{ R_i | R_i \in R^{2048}, i = 1, 2, \ldots, 49 \right\} \tag{1}$$

Which essentially divides the original image into $7 \times 7 = 49$ regions and each region consists of the vector $R_i$ of 2048 dimensions. Next, we adjust the output through linear transformation to project the visual features to the same space of textual features.

$$G = W_v \text{ResNet}(V) \tag{2}$$

Where $W_v \in R^{d \times 2048}$ is the learnable parameter and d is the latitude of the word vector. Finally, the visual features $G \in R^{d \times 49}$ are fed into the Saliency Attention Block.

**Textual Feature Encode.** We input the personal opinion target words and the remaining context words as two sentences into stand-alone BERT at each time step to obtain target-sensitive textual representations. For example, the BERT input is given in Fig. 2. The preprocessing method is to convert each sentence X into two sub-sentences: the opinion target and the remaining context and connect them as the input sequence of BERT [25]. Different from the most of existing recurrent models [27], the data are encoded once, and the same underlying features are input, our model uses a stand-alone textual encoder in each time step t. Using stand-alone textual encode can produce a target-sensitive textual representation in each step to allow the target to attend to different parts of the sentence during each pass. Because when paying attention to multiple scattered words at once, the characteristics of each word of attention may be hidden. Finally, we will obtain rich target-sensitive textual representations S for the recurrent attention mechanism.

$$S = BERT_t(X) \tag{3}$$

Where $S \in R^{d \times N}$, d is the vector dimensions and N is the maximum length of the sentences.

**Saliency Attention Block.** The recurrent attention mechanism contains two key components: the Saliency Attention Block and the sequential nature of the model. As illustrated in Fig. 3, the Saliency Attention Block, which we improve over the BERT architecture, can select the regions where the input sequence is closely related to the target, and other irrelevant regions are ignored. Specifically, we regard visual feature G as a sequence of 49 items, each of which is a vector of d-dimensions. Then visual feature G is used as the input sequence, and the textual feature is used as the target. Different from the existing model [25], which only inputs a single target word for matching, our method makes full use of the target word and its context. Because we believe that the single target word without its context cannot provide good textual in-formation for the visual representations.

Following the BERT architecture, we use the m-head target attention mechanism to match the target-sensitive textual representations and the image to obtain a visual representation that is sensitive to the target-sensitive textual representations. Specifically, we process the S as the target to generate the query Q and the G is used as the input sequence to generate the key K and value V. So as to use the target to guide the model to align it with the appropriate area, which is the image areas closely related to the target-sensitive textual representations, and to assign high attention weights. Then, the i-th head target attention $ATT_i$ is defined as follow.

$$ATT_i(G, S) = softmax\left(\left[W_{Qi}S\right]^T [W_{Ki}G]/\sqrt{d/m}\right) \times [W_{Vi}G]^T \tag{4}$$

Where $\{W_{Qi}, W_{Ki}, W_{Vi}\} \in R^{d/d \times m}$ are learnable parameters corresponding to queries, keys, and values respectively. After that, we adopt the same structure as the standard BERT. The outputs of the m attention mechanisms (MATT) are concatenated together followed by a linear transformation. Then, using the feedforward network (MLP) and the two-layer norms (LN) with residual connections to obtain the target-sensitive visual output TI.

$$MATT(G, S) = W_m[ATT_1(G, S), \dots, ATT_m(G, S)]^T \tag{5}$$

$$TI(G, S) = LN(S + MLP(LN(S + MATT(G, S)))) \tag{6}$$

Where $W_m \in R^{d \times d}$ is the learnable parameter. Then, we stack such TI(G, S) to obtain the final target-sensitive visual output H, where $H \in R^{d \times m}$ and the first token of H is essentially a weighted sum of the textual features and the 49 regions image features. Furthermore, We provide a pool function to obtain the first token: $O = H_0$, and then feed the softmax function to the classification at time step $t$.

$$p(y|O) = \text{softmax}(W^T O) \tag{7}$$

Where $W \in R^{d \times 3}$ is the learnable parameter. Similar to the RNN, the sequential nature of the model can connect the information $H_{t-1}$ of the previous time step to the current time step for learning, and actively process the interactive information related to the multimodal data at each time step to refine its estimate of the correct label. Specifically, the rich interactive information between target-sensitive textual features and visual features is propagated to the higher resolution layer as the input of the next time step by deconvoluting the output of the current time step. We feed the $H_{t-1}$ to a deconvolution to get the input $H_t$ at the next time.

$$H_t = \text{Deconv1D}(H_{t-1}) \tag{8}$$

Finally, Due to the number of unrolling steps, the model may have more and more parameters, which makes the back-propagation convergence rate slower and easy to overfit. To overcome this problem, we introduce the method of deep supervision where auxiliary classifiers are added at all Saliency Attention Blocks and their companion losses are added to the loss of the final layer. At training time, we use the standard cross-entropy loss function to obtain companion losses after auxiliary classifiers.

$$\mathcal{J} = -\frac{1}{|D|} \sum_{j=1}^{|D|} \log(y^{(j)}|o^{(j)}) \tag{9}$$

Then, we optimize a loss function that is a sum of the final loss and companion losses with all Saliency Attention Blocks.

$$\mathcal{L} = \sum_{1}^{t} \mathcal{J}_t \tag{10}$$

## 4   Experiments

In this section, the data set, baseline method, and experimental setup are described. Then, we empirically studied the performance of SaliencyBERT on several multimodal data sets and discussed important parameters.

### 4.1   Experiment Settings

**Datasets.**  To evaluate the effect of SaliencyBERT, we adopt two multimodal publicly available named entity recognition datasets TWITTER-15 and TWITTER-17 respectively collected by Zhang et al. [14] and Lu et al. [26]. However, they only provide annotated target opinions, textual contents, and their associated images in each Twitter. Yu et al. [25] annotated the sentiment (positive, negative, and neutral) towards each target by three domain experts and all the entities belong to four types: Person, Location, Organization, and Miscellaneous. Finally, a total of 5288 tweets in TWITTER-15 and 5972 tweets in TWITTER-17 are retained. Then, we randomly separate all image-text pairs in each dataset into a training set, a development set, and a test set with the proportion of 60%, 20%, and 20% respectively. Each sentence has an average of 1.3 targets at TWITTER-15 and 1.4 targets at TWITTER-17.

**Baselines.** In this paper, we will investigate the performance of our model by comparing it with baseline models. The baseline models can be categorized into three groups: models using only the visual modality, models using only the text modality, and models with multiple modalities. The models are listed as follows: ResNet-Target: a pre-trained image recognition model and concatenating the target word; AE-LSTM [22]: incorporating aspect embeddings and target-specific attention mechanism; MGAN [20]: building up a multi-grained attention network for fusing the target and the context; BERT [10]: adding a pooling layer and the softmax function on top of $BERT_{base}$; Res-MGAN-TFN [8]: using Tensor Fusion Network (TFN) to fuse the textual and visual representations; Res-BERT: replacing the textual encoder in Res-MGAN-TFN with BERT; ESAFN [23]: fusing the entity-sensitive textual representations and the entity-sensitive visual representations with a bilinear interaction layer; mPBERT [26]: a multimodal BERT architecture that directly concatenates the image features with the final hidden states of the input sequence, followed by multimodal attention mechanism; Propose Model: For convenience, we denote SaliencyBERT-k to be our model that is unrolled for k-time steps. We select three representatives Proposed Model-1, Proposed Model-3, and Proposed Model-6 to compare with baseline models.

**Detailed Parameters.** We build a textual encoder model on top of the pre-trained cased $BERT_{base}$ model, and the parameters are both initialized from the pre-trained opinion model. The images with size $224 \times 224$ and channel RGB are used as the visual input, and pre-trained ResNet-152 are used to encode the visual features. Finally, like the $BERT_{base}$ model, we set the learning rate as $5e-5$, the number of attention heads m $= 12$, and the dropout rate as 0.1 for our SaliencyBERT. All the models are fine-tuned between 15 and 45 epochs, depending on the number of unrolling steps.

**Table 1.** Experimental results on our two Twitter datasets for TMSC.

| Modality | Method | TWITTER-15 | | TWITTER-17 | |
|---|---|---|---|---|---|
| | | ACC | Mac-F1 | ACC | Mac-F1 |
| Visual | ResNet-Target | 59.88 | 46.48 | 58.59 | 53.98 |
| Text | AE-LSTM | 70.30 | 63.43 | 61.67 | 57.97 |
| | MGAN | 71.17 | 64.21 | 64.75 | 64.46 |
| | BERT | 74.02 | 68.86 | 67.74 | 65.66 |
| Text+Visual | Res-MGAN-TFN | 70.30 | 64.14 | 64.10 | 59.13 |
| | Res-BERT | 75.89 | 69.00 | 67.82 | 65.26 |
| | ESAFN | 73.38 | 67.37 | 67.83 | 64.22 |
| | mPBERT | 75.79 | 71.07 | 68.80 | 67.06 |
| | SaliencyBERT-1 | 75.60 | 69.88 | 67.66 | 65.54 |
| | SaliencyBERT-3 | **77.03**(76.08) | **72.36**(71.00) | **69.69**(68.23) | **67.19**(65.55) |
| | SaliencyBERT-6 | 73.76(63.19) | 65.36(60.56) | 68.62(52.37) | 65.51(48.64) |

**Table 2.** Breakdown of accuracy with single opinion target and multiple opinion targets.

| Method | TWITTER-15 | | TWITTER-17 | |
|---|---|---|---|---|
| | Target $= 1$ | Target $\geq 2$ | Target $= 1$ | Target $\geq 2$ |
| BERT | 77.40 | 73.42 | 68.64 | 66.25 |
| ESAFN | 73.14 | 73.76 | 68.16 | 67.53 |
| mPBERT | 76.50 | 73.88 | **68.88** | 68.37 |
| SaliencyBERT-3 | **79.27** | **75.64** | 68.81 | **69.89** |

## 4.2 Results and Analysis

**Main Metrics.** We report the accuracy (ACC) and Macro-F1 score of the single modal methods and the highly competitive multimodal methods on all the two multimodal datasets in Table 1. The results show that the proposed model outperforms all of the above baseline methods. We can observe that the single visual modal method (ResNet-Target) is the worst among all the methods. Since the single visual model classifies sentiment with only visual data, this means that related images cannot handle goal-oriented emotion prediction independently. The simple method (e.g. Res-MG-TFN) of splicing visual modalities and textual modalities is inferior to BERT models that only use the textual modality. These results show that the introduction of multimodal data brings more abundant features, but also produces a lot of redundant information and noise. Simple fusion methods have difficulty in directly capturing the interactions between the two modalities. Worse still, it may negatively affect the final results. By observing BERT, Res-BERT, and mPBERT, we can know that the BERT model pays attention to the text representation in fine granularity and achieves good results, but the image can enhance the text-based method on the whole. Finally, when we use SaliencyBERT-3 with deep supervision, the model consistently achieves the best results on the two datasets. As time steps increase, the results without the deep supervision method get worse. These results appear to be in alignment with our hypothesis that using Saliency Attention Block in multiple time steps can well capture intra-modality and inter-modality dynamics. However, the number of unrolling steps makes the back-propagation convergence rate slower and easy to overfit.

**Table 3.** The accuracy rates for all models discussed so far.

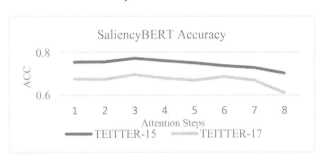

**Auxiliary Metrics.** To further analyze the advantages of SaliencyBERT over other strong baseline methods, we divided the test set of the two datasets into a single target and multiple targets. Our experimental results are shown in Table 2. From Table 2, we can see that our model performs better than BERT, ESAFN, and mPBERT in dealing with multiple target sentences. These results are consistent with what we observed before. For single target sentences, our model can progressively optimize target-text encoding and the alignment of target-sensitive textual features and the visual features. through multiple time steps, and for multiple target sentences, our model can capture accurate and diverse target-sensitive textual features and progressively optimize the alignment of the target-sensitive textual features and the visual features.

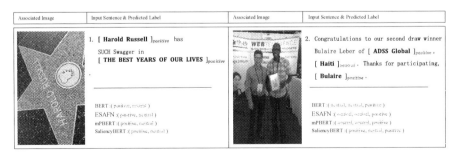

**Fig. 4.** Representative examples for Target-oriented Multimodal Sentiment Classification in our Twitter datasets.

Moreover, Table 3 shows the accuracy rates for all models discussed so far. The results show that more attention steps weaken accuracy rates during our task. Considering that we have no more than 6 targets in the same sentence, too many attention steps make it difficult for the model to optimize.

**Case Study.** We can see that the test sample of Fig. 4 shows the input sentence, associated image, and predicted label of different methods. First, in Fig. 4, because the user-posted by the correlated image contains a smiley face, the multimodal approach completely correctly predicts the sentiment of the three target views. However, in Fig. 4, we can see that the multimodal approach makes the same incorrect prediction as the unimodal approach, although it utilizes the relevant images. This may be due to the fact that the relevant images posted by the users failed to provide valid information. These examples further confirm that our multimodal approach combining images and text can somewhat enhance the validity of the text-based approach, but relies on the relevant images posted by the users.

## 5   Conclusion

In this paper, we studied Target-oriented Multimodal Sentiment Classification (TMSC) and proposed a multimodal BERT architecture to effectively capture the intra-modality and inter-modality dynamics and progressively optimize the alignment of target-sensitive textual features and the visual features. Extensive evaluations on two datasets for TMSC demonstrated the effectiveness of our model in detecting the sentiment polarity for individual opinion targets.

## References

1. Wagner, J., et al.: DCU: aspect-based polarity classification for semeval task 4. In: Proceedings of the 8th International Workshop on Semantic Evaluation (SemEval 2014), pp. 223–229 (2014)
2. Kiritchenko, S., Zhu, X., Cherry, C., Mohammad, S.: Nrc-canada-2014: detecting aspects and sentiment in customer reviews. In: Proceedings of the 8th International Workshop on Semantic Evaluation (SemEval 2014), pp. 437–442 (2014)
3. Dong, L., Wei, F., Tan, C., Tang, D., Zhou, M., Xu, K.: Adaptive recursive neural network for target-dependent twitter sentiment classification. In: Proceedings of the 52nd Annual Meeting of the Association for Computational Linguistics (volume 2: Short papers), pp. 49–54 (2014)
4. Nguyen, T. H., & Shirai, K.: PhraseRNN: phrase recursive neural network for aspect-based sentiment analysis. In: Proceedings of the 2015 Conference on Empirical Methods in Natural Language Processing, pp. 2509–2514 (2015)
5. Ma, D., Li, S., Zhang, X., Wang, H.: Interactive attention networks for aspect-level sentiment classification. In: Twenty-Sixth International Joint Conference on Artificial Intelligence, pp. 4068–4074 (2017)
6. Li, C., Guo, X., Mei, Q.: Deep memory networks for attitude identification. In: Proceedings of the Tenth ACM International Conference on Web Search and Data Mining, pp. 671–680 (2017)

7. Xue, W., Li, T.: Aspect based sentiment analysis with gated convolutional networks. In: Proceedings Annual Meeting Association for Computational Linguistics, pp. 2514–2523 (2018)
8. Zadeh, A., Chen, M., Poria, S., Cambria, E., Morency, L.P.: Tensor fusion network for multimodal sentiment analysis. In: Empirical Methods in Natural Language Processing, pp. 1103–1114 (2017)
9. Zadeh, A., Liang, P.P., Mazumder, N., Poria, S., Cambria, E., Morency, L.P.: Memory fusion network for multi-view sequential learning. In: AAAI, pp. 5634–5641 (2018)
10. Vaswani, A., et al.: Attention is all you need. In: Proceedings Neural Information Processing System, pp. 5998–6008 (2017)
11. Li, J., Qiu, L.: A Sentiment Analysis Method of Short Texts in Microblog. A Sentiment Analysis Method of Short Texts in Microblog. IEEE Computer Society (2017)
12. Fan, X., Li, X., Du, F., Li, X., Wei, M.: Apply word vectors for sentiment analysis of APP reviews. In: 2016 3rd International Conference on Systems and Informatics, ICSAI 2016, 2017, no. Icsai, pp. 1062–1066 (2016)
13. Tang, D., Wei, F., Qin, B., Liu, T., Zhou, M.: Coooolll: a deep learning system for twitter sentiment classification. In: Proceedings of the 8th International Workshop on Semantic Evaluation (SemEval 2014), pp. 208–212 (2014)
14. Zhang, L., Wang, S., Liu, B.: Deep learning for sentiment analysis: a survey. WIREs Data Mining Knowl. Discov. **8**(4), e1253 (2018)
15. Tang, D., Qin, B., Feng, X., and Liu, T.: Effective LSTMs for target-dependent sentiment classification. In: Computer Conference, pp. 3298–3307 (2015)
16. Bahdanau, D., Cho, K., Bengio, Y.: Neural machine translation by jointly learning to align and translate. In: Proceedings International Conference Learning Representation, pp. 1–15 (2014)
17. Yang, Z., Yang, D., Dyer, C., He, X., Smola, A., Hovy, E.: Hierarchical attention networks for document classification. In: Proceedings Conference North American Chapter Association Computational Linguistics: Human Language Technologies, pp. 1480–1489 (2016)
18. Majumder, N., Poria, S., Gelbukh, A., Akhtar, M.S., Ekbal, A.: IARM: inter-aspect relation modeling with memory networks in aspect-based sentiment analysis. In: Proceedings of the 2018 Conference on Empirical Methods in Natural Language Processing, pp. 3402–3411 (2018)
19. Fan, F., Feng, Y., Zhao, D.: Multi-grained attention network for aspect level sentiment classification. In: Proc. Conf. Empir. Methods Nat. Lang. Process, pp. 3433–3442 (2018)
20. Bertero, D., Siddique, F.B., Wu, C.S., Wan, Y., Chan, R.H.Y., Fung, P.: Real-time speech emotion and sentiment recognition for interactive dialogue systems. In: Proceedings of the 2016 Conference on Empirical Methods in NLP, pp. 1042–1047 (2016)
21. Wang, Y., Huang, M., Zhu, X., Zhao, L.: Attention-based LSTM for aspect-level sentiment classification. In: Proceedings of the 2016 Conference on Empirical Methods in Natural Language Processing, pp. 606–615 (2016)
22. Yu, J., Jiang, J., Xia, R.: Entity-sensitive attention and fusion network for entity-level multimodal sentiment classification. IEEE/ACM Trans. Audio Speech Lang. Process. **28**, 429–439 (2019)
23. Kumar, A., Irsoy, O., Ondruska, P., Iyyer, M., Bradbury, J., Gulrajani, I.: Ask me anything: dynamic memory networks for natural language processing. arXiv:1506.07285 (2015)
24. He, K., Zhang, X., Ren, S., Sun, J.: Deep residual learning for image recognition. In: Proceedings of the IEEE Conference on Computer Vision and Pattern Recognition, pp. 770–778 (2016)
25. Yu, J., Jiang, J.: Adapting BERT for target-oriented multimodal sentiment classification. In: Twenty-Eighth International Joint Conference on Artificial Intelligence IJCAI-19 (2019)

26. Lu, D., Neves, L., Carvalho, V., Zhang, N., Ji, H.: Visual attention model for name tagging in multimodal social media. In: The Association for Computational Linguistics, pp. 1990–1999 (2018)

27. Zoran, D., Chrzanowski, M., Huang, P.S., Gowal, S., Mott, A., Kohli, P.: Towards robust image classification using sequential attention models. In: Proceedings of the IEEE/CVF Conference on Computer Vision and Pattern Recognition, pp. 9483–9492 (2020)

# Latency-Constrained Spatial-Temporal Aggregated Architecture Search for Video Deraining

Zhu Liu[1], Long Ma[1], Risheng Liu[2], Xin Fan[2], Zhongxuan Luo[2(✉)], and Yuduo Zhang[3]

[1] School of Software, Dalian University of Technology, Dalian 116024, China
[2] DUT-RU International School of Information Science and Engineering, Dalian University of Technology, Dalian 116024, China
zxluo@dlut.edu.cn
[3] Dalian Minzu University, Dalian 116024, China

**Abstract.** Existing deep learning-based video deraining techniques have achieved remarkable processes. However, there exist some fundamental issues including plentiful engineering experiences for architecture design and slow hardware-insensitive inference speed. To settle these issues, we develop a highly efficient spatial-temporal aggregated video deraining architecture, derived from the architecture search procedure under a newly-defined flexible search space and latency-constrained search strategy. To be specific, we establish an inter-frame aggregation module to fully integrate temporal correlation according to a set division perspective. Subsequently, we construct an intra-frame enhancement module to eliminate the residual rain streaks by introducing rain kernels that characterize the rain locations. A flexible search space for defining architectures of these two modules is built to avert the demand for expensive engineering skills. Further, we design a latency-constrained differentiable search strategy to automatically discover a hardware-sensitive high-efficient video deraining architecture. Extensive experiments demonstrate that our method can obtain best performance against other state-of-the-art methods.

**Keywords:** Latency-constrained neural architecture search ·
Spatial-temporal aggregation · Video deraining

## 1 Introduction

The degradation of rain streaks is a common imaging factor of severe weather, which leads to the visual-unpleasant quality for human visual system and brings

This work is partially supported by the National Natural Science Foundation of China (Nos. 61922019, 61733002, and 61672125), LiaoNing Revitalization Talents Program (XLYC1807088), and the Fundamental Research Funds for the Central Universities. The first author is a student.

H. Ma et al. (Eds.): PRCV 2021, LNCS 13021, pp. 16–28, 2021.
https://doi.org/10.1007/978-3-030-88010-1_2

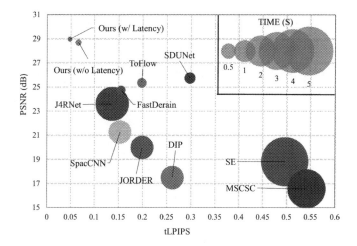

**Fig. 1.** Numerical performance, temporal consistency and inference speed comparisons on the *RainSynComplex25* [12]. We plotted our schemes (i.e., w/ and w/o latency versions) with other video deraining approaches including JORDER [28], SE [25], DIP [6], MSCSC [9], ToFlow [26], SDUNet [27], FastDerain [7], SpacCNN [1] and J4RNet [12]. We can illustrate the superiority in the aspects of visual quality, temporal preservation and inference speed.

occlusions with blurred objects for a series of high-level vision tasks. Therefore, the extreme urgency of removing rain streaks accurately has been recognized in recent years [13,18,19]. To recover the clear background from rain corrupted observations, numerous methods have been proposed in past decades. We can roughly divide these methods into single image deraining and video deraining.

Recently, single image deraining methods have attracted widespread attentions. Extracting the video as successive frames, these methods can be applied for the video deraining task. The basic formulation of rainy images can be considered as the superimposition of rain streaks and clear background. Based on this principle, conventional model-based schemes were proposed to characterize the rain streaks by exploiting inhere features. For instance, sparse coding methods [9] utilize the high frequency features to learn the rain streaks. A great pile of prior-based methods construct prior knowledge measures such as low rank representation [8], dictionary learning [5], guided filters [33] and Gaussian mixture model [10] to restore the rain-free images. These model-driven methods achieve comparable deraining performance. However, these schemes have high computational burdens and are time-consuming. With the emergence of CNN-based methods, plentiful handcrafted CNN architectures [14,15,17] have been designed for single image deraining. For example, Yang *et al.* [28] proposed a dilated convolution network to capture different properties of rain streaks. Furthermore, attention mechanisms [24] are introduced for image deraining.

In contrast to the single-image deraining schemes, video sequences can provide more contextual compensation and more effective information to discover and eliminate rain streaks from temporal correlated frames. The classic methods exploited the intrinsic temporal and photometric characteristics of videos to estimate rain streaks. For instance, the directional property of rain streaks [6], the correlation between spatial and temporal information in local patches [2], the shape and size of rain streaks [23] have been investigated widely. The inhere prior knowledge are formulated by Gaussian mixture models, low-rank regularization, sparse coding and tensor models to explore the property of rain streaks for rain detection and removal. Lately, CNN-based schemes have achieved remarkable performances to address the video deraining task. Specifically, a sparse coding method with multi-scale convolution [9] is proposed. Recently, a semi-supervised method [29] is proposed to construct a dynamic generator of rain streaks to explore insightful characteristics of frames.

Different from aforementioned handcrafted architecture construction schemes, Neural Architecture Search (NAS) methodology provides an insightful viewpoint to discover the desired architecture automatically. Especially, differentiable gradient-based schemes [11] utilize the continuous weight relaxation to composite a super-network, reducing the search time effectively. Various gradient-based schemes are performed for low-level vision tasks. In details, Zhang *et al.* [30] proposed a hierarchical search strategy with channel width for image denosing using a series of primitive operators (e.g., 3×3 convolution). Liu *et al.* [16] presented a collaborative search strategy by unrolling architecture for image enhancement. However, the ignorance of exploring task characteristics (e.g., degradation formation) creates limitations of the flexibility for addressing different scenarios. Actually, current CNN-based video deraining methods produce clearer backgrounds since the relevant temporal information from consecutive frames can help the rain removal implicitly. However, there exist several fundamental issues in these existing approaches. Firstly, the temporal correlated information is leveraged as one part of black-box networks. Secondly, the network architectures are based on manual design and relied on heuristic architecture engineering, which needs abundant handcrafted experiences and dedicated adjustment of hyper-meters (e.g., setting different convolution layers and connections). Last but not least, most of existing CNN methods for video deraining do not consider the deployment on hardware, which have huge computation costs.

To mitigate the above issues, we first formulate the video deraining task via investigating the temporal and spatial characteristics aggregation. In detail, we analyze the inner relationships between consecutive frames from the perspective of set division. Based on this principle, we propose an inter-frame aggregation module to fully integrate temporal correlation explicitly for initial rain streak estimation, that breaks down the black-box of temporal information utilization. Furthermore, we construct an intra-frame enhancement module to further eliminate the rain streaks and enhance the details, assisted by one group of learnable rain kernels. Subsequently, we introduce the latency-constrained architecture search strategy to discover the entire structure to avoid lots of manual labor for designing networks. Targeting to establish different principled modules, we introduce diverse operators to construct the specific search space. Constrained by the

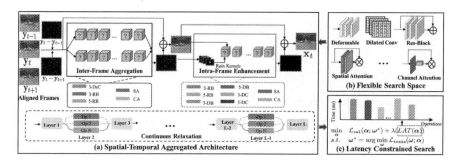

**Fig. 2.** Overview of main components in the proposed method. We first illustrate the entire architecture that is comprised by the inter-frame aggregation module and intra-frame enhancement module in the subfigure (a). We also illustrate the corresponding search spaces and relaxation formulation. We then demonstrate the concrete details of these operators and the latency constrained search in subfigure (b) and (c).

latency of hardware devices, we can obtain an effective architecture with fast inference speed. The superiority of our method can be demonstrated in Fig. 1. In brief, our contributions can be summarized as three-folds:

- Different from manually designed network-based video deraining schemes, we propose a latency constrained search strategy and a flexible task-specific search space to discover an efficient video deraining architecture.
- We fully explore the intrinsic characteristics of video deraining from the temporal aggregation and spatial enhancement perspectives, to establish a search-based spatial-temporal aggregated macro-structure.
- Comprehensive experiments compared with various state-of-the-art methods on three benchmarks fully reveal the superiority of our method. A series of evaluative experiments demonstrate the effectiveness of our scheme.

## 2   The Proposed Method

### 2.1   Spatial-Temporal Aggregated Architecture

**Inter-Frame Aggregation Module.** We first propose an Inter-Frame Aggregation Module (IFAM) to estimate the major rain streaks by investigating the explicit temporal information from set division perspective. In detail, the current rainy frame (denoted as $\mathbf{y}_t$) can be considered as the union set based on background set ($\Phi_{\mathbf{x}}$) and rain set ($\Phi_{\mathbf{r}}$), i.e., $\Phi_{\mathbf{y}_t} = \Phi_{\mathbf{x}_t} \cup \Phi_{\mathbf{r}_t}$ and $\Phi_{\mathbf{x}_t} \cap \Phi_{\mathbf{r}_t} = \emptyset$, where $\Phi$ denotes the set of pixel locations. Leveraging aligned consecutive frames, we can decouple the rain streaks into two parts, $\Phi_{\mathbf{r}_t} = (\sum_{i,i\neq t} \Phi_{\mathbf{r}_t} \cap \Phi_{\mathbf{r}_i}) \cup \widehat{\Phi}_{\mathbf{r}_t}{}^1$. $\sum_{i,i\neq t} \Phi_{\mathbf{r}_t} \cap \Phi_{\mathbf{r}_i}$ denotes the rain streaks that contain in the adjacent frames and $\widehat{\Phi}_{\mathbf{r}_t}$ denotes the unique rain streaks generated in current $t$-th frame or the

---

[1] We leverage the latest optical flow method RAFT [22] to align the frames.

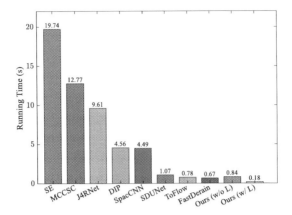

**Fig. 3.** The average running time calculated on *RainSynComplex25*. "L" denotes the latency constraint.

residual moved rain streaks. In other words, the rain streaks $\mathbf{r}_t$ can be captured by the shared regions in other frames and residue streaks in current frames.

The mentioned intrinsic principle motivates us to design one module for capturing the main rain streaks by utilizing the concatenation of current frames and the coarse rain streaks contained in $\mathbf{y}_t - \mathbf{y}_{t\pm i}$. In this paper, we only utilize three-frames temporal information as the inputs. As shown in the subfigure (a) of Fig. 2, we extract the rain streaks based on two parallel layers with $\mathbf{N}_T$ blocks and obtain the final streaks by the $3 \times 3$ convolution.

**Intra-Frame Enhancement Module.** Subsequently, the residue rain streaks $\widehat{\Phi}$ cannot be removed exactly based on the above formulation. Thus, we propose an Intra-Frame Enhancement Module (IFEM) to perform single-frame deraining and estimate the partial rain streaks. To enhance the spatial structure, we first introduce the successive architecture with $\mathbf{N}_S$ blocks. Then, aiming to focus on the location of rain streaks, we introduce the convolutional dictionary learning mechanism to learn a series of rain kernels (denoted as $\mathbf{C}$). Based on this mechanism, we can obtain the accurate locations and size of residual rain streaks with obvious rain region, i.e., $\widehat{\mathbf{r}}_t = \mathbf{C} \otimes \mathbf{r}_t$. Then we concatenate $\widehat{\mathbf{r}}_t$ and estimated frame as the inputs. The whole module aims to learn the residue streaks.

### 2.2  Architecture Search

**Flexible Search Space.** Establishing a task-specific search space is the vital component to perform architecture search. In contrast to adopting the primitive operators (e.g., separable *conv* $3 \times 3$) directly, which maybe not suitable for video deraining tasks. Therefore we explore more effective operations to composite our search space. Thus, we list the ten operators that are included in the search space in following: $3 \times 3$ Deformable Convolution (i.e., 3-DeC) [4],

$3 \times 3/5 \times 5$ Dilated Convolution with dilation rate of 2 (3-DC, 5-DC), $3 \times 3/5 \times 5$ Residual Blocks (3-RB, 5-RB), $3 \times 3/5 \times 5$ Dense Blocks (3-DB, 5-DB), Channel Attention (CA) and Spatial Attention (SA). The structure details of some operators are shown in subfigure (b) of Fig. 2. Considering the different peculiarity of blocks, we divide these operators into two sub search spaces for each module. In detail, only deformable convolution, residual blocks and attention mechanisms are constituted as the search space of IFAM, which have the better ability to extract or align the features. For instance, deforamble convolution blocks are used widely to represent the shared information across aligned frames. On the other hand, the dilated convolution, residual blocks, dense blocks and attentions are considered in the search of IFEM. These operators are widely used for deraining tasks. Furthermore, we remove the pooling and skip connections from the search space. In order to keep the fair comparison, each operation has three layers of convolutions. Constructing this flexible search space, the performance of searched architecture can be guaranteed.

**Latency-Constrained Search.** In order to speed up of the inference time on diverse hardware scenarios, we introduce the hardware latency as a regularization term, aiming to discover a architecture with low latency. The search process based on the differentiable search framework [11] can be formulated as:

$$\min_{\alpha} \mathcal{L}_{\text{val}}(\alpha; \omega^{\star}) + \lambda(LAT(\alpha))$$
$$s.t. \quad \omega^{*} = \arg \min_{\omega} \mathcal{L}_{\text{train}}(\omega; \alpha), \tag{1}$$

where $\alpha$ and $\omega$ denote the architecture and network weights. The formulation of super-net (i.e., continuous relaxation by $\alpha$) is shown in the bottom row of subfigure (a) in Fig. 2. More concretely, the $LAT$ term can be obtained by the weighted linear sum of operations:

$$LAT(\alpha) = \sum_{k} \sum_{i} \alpha_{i}^{k} LAT(op_{i}), op_{i} \in \mathcal{O}, \tag{2}$$

where we denote that $\alpha_{i}^{k}$ is the i-th operation weight of k-th cell and $\mathcal{O}$ is the search space. In this manuscript, we only calculate the inference time on GPU.

## 3  Experimental Results

### 3.1  Experiment Preparation

**Datasets.** We utilize three mainstream benchmarks to evaluate our method with various state-of-the-arts. *RainSynLight25*, *RainSynComplex25* are two synthetic datasets, proposed in [12], used to simulate the light rain and heavy rain scenarios of real world. *NTURain* datasets [1] includes the synthetic and real rainy videos. Additionally, several real-world rainy videos are collected from Youtube and mixkit[2] websites for the evaluation.

---

[2] https://www.youtube.com, https://mixkit.co.

Rain Frame    SPANet    FastDerain    MSCSC    J4RNet    Ours

**Fig. 4.** Visual Comparison among various remarkable approaches on the $NTU$ dataset.

**Baselines and Metrics.** We compare our method with competitive deraining methods: three single frame deraining methods (JORDER [28], SE [25] and SPANet [24]) and eight multi-frame methods (DIP [6], MSCSC [9], ToFlow [26], SDUNet [27], FastDerain [7], SpacCNN [1] and J4RNet [12]). Two widely used numerical metrics, Peak Signal-to-Noise Ratio (PSNR) and Structure Similarity Index (SSIM) are calculated as the criterion terms. Several perceptual metrics are also introduced: Visual Information Fidelity (VIF) [21], Feature SIMilarity (FSIM) [31], Natural Image Quality Evaluator (NIQE) [20], Learned Perceptual Image Patch Similarity (LPIPS) [32] and temporal LPIPS (tLPIPS) [3].

**Search Configurations.** We define the basic hyper-parameters empirically in our search process. The supernet have only one IFAM and one IFEM. Each of modules has four candidate layers (i.e., $N_T = N_S = 4$). We randomly selecte ten video sequences from $RainSynComplex25$ to composite the dataset in search phase. We divide it equally to be used for updating the network weights and architecture weights. The loss term is composited by two parts, which is leveraged for the training and validation:

$$\mathcal{L} = \mathcal{L}_{L1}(\mathbf{x}_t, \mathbf{x}_{gt}) + \mathcal{L}_{SSIM}(\mathbf{x}_t, \mathbf{x}_{gt}) + \gamma \mathcal{L}_{L1}(\mathbf{x}_a, \mathbf{x}_{gt}), \quad (3)$$

where the first part composited by previous two term is to restraint the final output $\mathbf{x}_t$. The last term is utilized to restraint the output $\mathbf{x}_a$ of IFAM. We set the $\gamma$ as 0.1 in our search and training phase. We utilize SGD optimizer with the cosine annealing strategy to perform the search with 150 epochs, where the initial learning rate is 0.0005 and $\lambda = 0.05$. We only reserve the layers with the maximum values in $\alpha$. Derived from the search phase, we can obtain the final architecture. IFAM consists of $5 \times 5$ residual block, deformable block, channel attention and $3 \times 3$ residual block. IFEM consists of $3 \times 3$ dilated convolution, $3 \times 3$ residual block, $3 \times 3$ residual block and channel attention.

**Training Configurations.** We propose a stage-wise training strategy to train our searched architecture, rather than adopting end-to-end training straightforwardly. At the first stage, we first train the IFAM with 50 epochs, using L1 and SSIM losses to enforce for utilizing reasonable temporal information and generating rain streaks exactly. Then at the second stage, we train the entire

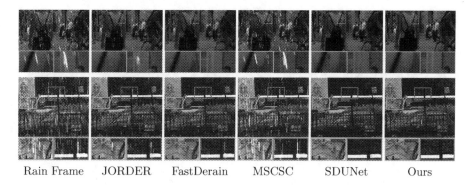

Rain Frame      JORDER      FastDerain      MSCSC      SDUNet      Ours

**Fig. 5.** Visual Comparison among deraining schemes on the synthetic datasets.

architecture (including IFEM) end to end with 200 epochs. We leverage the similar training losses of search phase to constrain the whole training process. Data augmentation, such as the random flipping and shape changing are performed in our training phase. We use Adam as the optimizer and set $\beta_1$, $\beta_2$ as 0.9, 0.999 respectively. Furthermore, we set the initial learning rate as 0.0005 and perform the cosine annealing strategy to decay the learning rates. Our method is based on the PyTorch framework and runs on a NVIDIA GTX1070 GPU.

### 3.2   Running Time Evaluation

Figure 3 reports the average running time of various multi-frame deraining methods, which were calculated on *RainSynComplex25*. In detail, we plot the concrete inference speed in Fig. 3 and make a bubble diagram (Fig. 1) to show the performance and inference time simultaneously. Compared with deep learning based methods, our approach significantly reduce the inference time. At the same time, our method also can guarantee the best performance on the challenging *RainSynLight25*. On the other hand, we can obtain faster inference time than existing fastest multi-frame video deraining methods. Both two figures demonstrated the superiority of our method, which obtain the comparable inference time and remarkable performance improvement.

### 3.3   Quantitative Comparison

We compare our method with a series of remarkable deraining schemes on three mainstream datasets in Table 1. We can observe the remarkable improvement to previous schemes. It is worth noting that we only trained our models on *RainSynLight25* and *RainSynComplex25* and used the model for light video raining to solve the *NTURain* dataset. Compared with S2VD, which is the latest method training on *NTURain*, our method gain 0.69 dB in PSNR and 0.0057 in SSIM on this dataset. Compared on *RainSynLight25* and *RainSynComplex25*, we can observe the consistent improvement than either single-frame deraining schemes, low-rank based methods or deep learning based multi-frame deraining approaches. Furthermore, compared with multi-frame video deraining methods (e.g., SDUNet and J4RNet), which utilizes the temporal information implicitly, we can gain 4.47 dB and 5.46 dB improvements. That also verifies the effectiveness of our proposed intra-frame aggregation.

**Table 1.** Quantitative comparison with a series of single image deraining and video deraining methods on *RainSynLight25*, *RainSynComplex25* and *NTURain* benchmarks.

| Methods | RainSynLight25 | | RainSynComplex25 | | NTURain | |
|---|---|---|---|---|---|---|
| | PSNR | SSIM | PSNR | SSIM | PSNR | SSIM |
| JORDER | 31.0298 | 0.9142 | 19.9904 | 0.6085 | 33.3922 | 0.9410 |
| SPANet | 27.3924 | 0.8816 | 18.1857 | 0.5819 | 31.6594 | 0.9388 |
| DIP | 28.0723 | 0.8526 | 17.8974 | 0.5316 | 30.7583 | 0.8970 |
| SE | 25.4435 | 0.7550 | 18.8258 | 0.5897 | 25.4151 | 0.7548 |
| MSCSC | 24.4424 | 0.7310 | 16.5653 | 0.4810 | 26.1984 | 0.7630 |
| ToFlow | 32.3821 | 0.9208 | 25.3418 | 0.7695 | 35.1296 | 0.9636 |
| FastDerain | 29.2038 | 0.8745 | 24.7442 | 0.7434 | 29.5142 | 0.9303 |
| SDUNet | 29.8117 | 0.8803 | 25.7357 | 0.7594 | 26.5602 | 0.8604 |
| SpacCNN | 31.6704 | 0.8997 | 21.2634 | 0.5863 | 33.0235 | 0.9465 |
| J4RNet | 30.5339 | 0.9071 | 23.6075 | 0.7506 | 31.0203 | 0.9373 |
| Ours | **35.2668** | **0.9540** | **28.6975** | **0.8660** | **36.7337** | **0.9698** |

In Table 2, we also report the perceptual quality evaluation on the *RainSynComplex25* benchmark, using various perceptual metrics. VIF and FSIM are two essential metrics to measure the perceptual quality for human visual system by the low-level features and information fidelity. We can obtain the best results on the both reference-based metrics. Our method has the smallest value under the NIQE metric, which measures the distance to natural images. Moreover, LPIPS and tLPIPS are constructed by the feature distances of AlexNet. tLPIPS

**Table 2.** Perceptual quality comparison and temporal consistency evaluation on the *RainSynComplex25* benchmark.

| Methods | VIF | FSIM | NIQE | LPIPS | tLPIPS |
|---|---|---|---|---|---|
| JORDER | 0.242 | 0.738 | 5.270 | 0.407 | 0.199 |
| SpacCNN | 0.198 | 0.759 | 4.933 | 0.386 | 0.153 |
| FastDeRain | 0.335 | 0.861 | 8.708 | 0.454 | 0.155 |
| J4RNet | 0.275 | 0.824 | 3.804 | 0.274 | 0.137 |
| Ours | **0.485** | **0.915** | **3.181** | **0.188** | **0.066** |

measures the inter-frame temporal loss. Similarly, the results verify the excellent performance of our scheme for human visual system and temporal consistency.

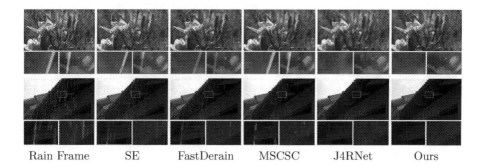

Rain Frame     SE     FastDerain     MSCSC     J4RNet     Ours

**Fig. 6.** Visual comparison on two real-world rainy videos.

**Table 3.** Ablation study on the *RainSynComplex25*. The underlined results are generated by the final configuration of this manuscript.

| λ | w/IFAM | w/IFEM | 3 frames | 5 frames | 7 frames | PSNR | Time (s) |
|------|--------|--------|----------|----------|----------|-------|----------|
| 0.05 | ✓ | ✓ | ✓ | ✗ | ✗ | <u>28.70</u> | <u>0.18</u> |
| 0.05 | ✓ | ✗ | ✓ | ✗ | ✗ | 27.46 | 0.12 |
| 0    | ✓ | ✓ | ✓ | ✗ | ✗ | 28.57 | 0.84 |
| 0.5  | ✓ | ✓ | ✓ | ✗ | ✗ | 25.17 | 0.15 |
| 0.05 | ✓ | ✓ | ✗ | ✓ | ✗ | 29.04 | 0.34 |
| 0.05 | ✓ | ✓ | ✗ | ✗ | ✓ | 26.23 | 0.76 |

### 3.4 Qualitative Comparison

We also carry out the qualitative experiment to evaluate the visual quality from the subjective perspective. As for the synthesized videos, we conduct the visual comparisons in Fig. 4 and Fig. 5. As shown in Fig. 4, one can see that our method preserves more texture details (e.g., the streetlight and fences). Obviously, other methods may consider the streetlight as rain streaks and eliminate it wrongly. MSCSC introduces much blurred objects in the frame. Compared on the heavy rainy video, shown in Fig. 5, our method removes the most of rain streaks and keeps regionally consistent with rich details. We also collected two real world rainy videos to evaluate the generation ability for challenging scenarios, which is shown in Fig. 6. The result in the top row depicts the effectiveness of our method to remove the long rain streaks. While other methods still remain the residue rain to some extent or are failed to remove this kind of rain streaks. As shown in the last row, this frame also contains different types of rain streaks. Our method can preserve the structure well and remove all types of rain streaks.

### 3.5   Ablation Study

The results of a series of ablation study are reported in Table 3. First, we verify the role of proposed modules respectively. We can conclude that IFAM plays the essential role to estimate the rain streaks and IFEM can remove the residual rain streaks effectively. Moreover, with the increase of $\lambda$, the latency can be reduced. However, we need to adjust $\lambda$ carefully to improve performance and reduce latency. Three-frame video deraining schemes obtain the best balance between numerical results and inference time, which is shown in the first row. Large frames cannot obtain the best numerical results. The possible reason is that the fast movement of rain streaks cannot be captured entirely and the temporal information cannot be utilized sufficiently in seven frames.

## 4   Conclusions

In this paper, we settled the video deraining by investigating the inhere characteristics from temporal correlation and spatial structure perspectives. A novel temporal and spatial aggregation architecture was proposed and constructed by the automatic architecture search. Leveraging an efficient and compact search space and coupling with the hardware constraint, the architecture can guarantee outstanding performance for video deraining and fast inference time. Consistent improvements of numerical and visual performances demonstrate the superiority of our method against various state-of-the-art deraining schemes.

## References

1. Chen, J., Tan, C.H., Hou, J., Chau, L.P., Li, H.: Robust video content alignment and compensation for rain removal in a cnn framework. In: CVPR (2018)
2. Chen, Y.L., Hsu, C.T.: A generalized low-rank appearance model for spatio-temporally correlated rain streaks. In: IEEE ICCV, pp. 1968–1975 (2013)
3. Chu, M., Xie, Y., Mayer, J., Leal-Taixé, L., Thuerey, N.: Learning temporal coherence via self-supervision for gan-based video generation. ACM TOG 39(4), 75–1 (2020)
4. Dai, J., et al.: Deformable convolutional networks. In: CVPR (2017)
5. Deng, L.J., Huang, T.Z., Zhao, X.L., Jiang, T.X.: A directional global sparse model for single image rain removal. Appl. Math. Model. 59, 662–679 (2018)
6. Jiang, T.X., Huang, T.Z., Zhao, X.L., Deng, L.J., Wang, Y.: A novel tensor-based video rain streaks removal approach via utilizing discriminatively intrinsic priors. In: IEEE CVPR, pp. 4057–4066 (2017)
7. Jiang, T., Huang, T., Zhao, X., Deng, L., Wang, Y.: Fastderain: a novel video rain streak removal method using directional gradient priors. IEEE TIP 28(4), 2089–2102 (2019)

8. Kim, J.H., Sim, J.Y., Kim, C.S.: Video deraining and desnowing using temporal correlation and low-rank matrix completion. IEEE Trans. Image Process. **24**(9), 2658–2670 (2015)
9. Li, M., et al.: Video rain streak removal by multiscale convolutional sparse coding. In: IEEE CVPR, pp. 6644–6653 (2018)
10. Li, Y., Tan, R.T., Guo, X., Lu, J., Brown, M.S.: Rain streak removal using layer priors. In: IEEE CVPR, pp. 2736–2744 (2016)
11. Liu, H., Simonyan, K., Yang, Y.: Darts: differentiable architecture search. In: ICLR (2019)
12. Liu, J., Yang, W., Yang, S., Guo, Z.: Erase or fill? deep joint recurrent rain removal and reconstruction in videos. In: IEEE CVPR, pp. 3233–3242 (2018)
13. Liu, R., Cheng, S., He, Y., Fan, X., Lin, Z., Luo, Z.: On the convergence of learning-based iterative methods for nonconvex inverse problems. IEEE TPAMI (2019)
14. Liu, R., Liu, J., Jiang, Z., Fan, X., Luo, Z.: A bilevel integrated model with data-driven layer ensemble for multi-modality image fusion. IEEE Trans, Image Process (2020)
15. Liu, R., Liu, X., Yuan, X., Zeng, S., Zhang, J.: A hessian-free interior-point method for non-convex bilevel optimization. In: ICML (2021)
16. Liu, R., Ma, L., Zhang, J., Fan, X., Luo, Z.: Retinex-inspired unrolling with cooperative prior architecture search for low-light image enhancement. In: IEEE CVPR (2021)
17. Liu, R., Mu, P., Chen, J., Fan, X., Luo, Z.: Investigating task-driven latent feasibility for nonconvex image modeling. IEEE TIP **29**, 7629–7640 (2020)
18. Liu, R., Mu, P., Yuan, X., Zeng, S., Zhang, J.: A generic first-order algorithmic framework for bi-level programming beyond lower-level singleton. In: ICML (2020)
19. Liu, R., Zhong, G., Cao, J., Lin, Z., Shan, S., Luo, Z.: Learning to diffuse: A new perspective to design pdes for visual analysis. IEEE TPAMI (2016)
20. Mittal, A., Soundararajan, R., Bovik, A.C.: Making a "completely blind" image quality analyzer. IEEE SPL, pp. 209–212 (2012)
21. Sheikh, H.R., Bovik, A.C.: Image information and visual quality. IEEE TIP
22. Teed, Z., Deng, J.: Raft: Recurrent all-pairs field transforms for optical flow. IEEE ECCV (2020)
23. Wang, H., Xie, Q., Zhao, Q., Meng, D.: A model-driven deep neural network for single image rain removal. In: IEEE CVPR, pp. 3103–3112 (2020)
24. Wang, T., Yang, X., Xu, K., Chen, S., Zhang, Q., Lau, R.W.: Spatial attentive single-image deraining with a high quality real rain dataset. In: IEEE CVPR, pp. 12270–12279 (2019)
25. Wei, W., Yi, L., Xie, Q., Zhao, Q., Meng, D., Xu, Z.: Should we encode rain streaks in video as deterministic or stochastic? In: IEEE ICCV, pp. 2516–2525 (2017)
26. Xue, T., Chen, B., Wu, J., Wei, D., Freeman, W.T.: Video enhancement with task-oriented flow. IJCV **127**(8), 1106–1125 (2019)
27. Xue, X., Ding, Y., Mu, P., Ma, L., Liu, R., Fan, X.: Sequential deep unrolling with flow priors for robust video deraining. In: IEEE ICASSP, pp. 1813–1817 (2020)
28. Yang, W., Tan, R.T., Feng, J., Liu, J., Guo, Z., Yan, S.: Deep joint rain detection and removal from a single image. IEEE CVPR, pp. 1685–1694 (2017)
29. Yue, Z., Xie, J., Zhao, Q., Meng, D.: Semi-supervised video deraining with dynamic rain generator. CVPR (2021)
30. Zhang, H., Li, Y., Chen, H., Shen, C.: Memory-efficient hierarchical neural architecture search for image denoising. In: IEEE CVPR, pp. 3657–3666 (2020)

31. Zhang, L., Zhang, L., Mou, X., Zhang, D.: Fsim: a feature similarity index for image quality assessment. IEEE TIP
32. Zhang, R., Isola, P., Efros, A.A., Shechtman, E., Wang, O.: The unreasonable effectiveness of deep features as a perceptual metric. In: IEEE CVPR, pp. 586–595 (2018)
33. Zheng, X., Liao, Y., Guo, W., Fu, X., Ding, X.: Single-Image-Based Rain and Snow Removal Using Multi-guided Filter. In: Lee, M., Hirose, A., Hou, Z.-G., Kil, R.M. (eds.) ICONIP 2013. LNCS, vol. 8228, pp. 258–265. Springer, Heidelberg (2013). https://doi.org/10.1007/978-3-642-42051-1_33

# Semantic-Driven Context Aggregation Network for Underwater Image Enhancement

Dongxiang Shi[1], Long Ma[1], Risheng Liu[2], Xin Fan[2], and Zhongxuan Luo[1(✉)]

[1] School of Software, Dalian University of Technology, Dalian 116024, China
zxluo@dlut.edu.cn
[2] DUT-RU International School of Information Science and Engineering,
Dalian University of Technology, Dalian 116024, China

**Abstract.** Recently, underwater image enhancement has attracted broad attention due to its potential in ocean exploitation. Unfortunately, limited to the hand-crafted subjective ground truth for matching low-quality underwater images, existing techniques are less robust for some unseen scenarios and may be unfriendly to semantic-related vision tasks. To handle these issues, we aim at introducing the high-level semantic features extracted from a pre-trained classification network into the image enhancement task for improving robustness and semantic-sensitive potency. To be specific, we design an encoder-aggregation-decoder architecture for enhancement, in which a context aggregation residual block is tailored to improve the representational capacity of the original encoder-decoder. Then we introduce a multi-scale feature transformation module that transforms the extracted multi-scale semantic-level features, to improve the robustness and endow the semantic-sensitive property for the encoder-aggregation-decoder network. In addition, during the training phase, the pre-trained classification network is fixed to avoid introducing training costs. Extensive experiments demonstrate the superiority of our method against other state-of-the-art methods. We also apply our method into the salient object detection task to reveal our excellent semantic-sensitive ability.

**Keywords:** Underwater image enhancement · Semantic feature · Context aggregation network · Feature transformation module

## 1 Introduction

Underwater images often suffer from severe color casting and contrast decreasing caused by light absorption and scattering. This degradation not only disturbs

This work is partially supported by the National Natural Science Foundation of China (Nos. 61922019, 61733002, and 61672125), LiaoNing Revitalization Talents Program (XLYC1807088), and the Fundamental Research Funds for the Central Universities. D. Shi—Author is a student.

| Input | EUIVF [1] | Water-Net [16] | Ours |

**Fig. 1.** Underwater image enhancement results and the corresponding saliency maps predicted by a salient object detection method $F^3$Net [26] on USOD dataset [13]. Obviously, our method performs better than other state-of-the-art methods, especially without noise or artifact. The superior salient object detection result further reveals semantic-sensitive property of the proposed method in high-level vision tasks.

visual quality of images but also has negative impact on visual tasks, *e.g.*, salient object detection and instance segmentation. Moreover, it is hard for submarine robotic explorers equipped with visual system to autonomously explore underwater environment. Therefore, underwater image enhancement has drawn much attention in recent years.

Underwater image enhancement aims to generate clear and natural images against several degradations (e.g., color cast, low contrast and even detail loss). The existing image underwater enhancement methods can be roughly divided into three categories: non-physical model-based methods, physical model-based methods and data-driven methods. In early enhancement methods, some are directly used to enhance underwater images regardless of underwater imaging model. [12,28] enhanced image contrast by expanding the dynamic range of the image histogram. [6,24] corrected color cast based on color assumption of natural images. To enhance contrast and correct color cast simultaneously, Ancuti *et al.* [1] proposed a fusion-based method to fuse several kinds of enhancement images. From the perspective of underwater physical imaging model, underwater image enhancement is regarded as an inverse problem. As He *et al.* [10] proposed Dark Channel Prior (DCP) which achieved an outstanding performance in single image dehazing, several DCP variants [2,9] were proposed by exploring different underwater prior. However, these methods might be restricted with some assumptions and simple physical imaging model. When the assumption and prior are less adaptive to unseen scene, these methods may generate severe artifacts, as shown in Fig. 1(b).

With the success of deep learning in various vision tasks [4,18,20,21] some learning-based underwater image enhancement methods are proposed. Wang *et al.* [25] proposed UIE-Net, which is composed of two branches to estimate attenuation coefficient and transmission map respectively. Li *et al.* [15] directly reconstructed the clear latent natural images from inputs instead of estimating the parameters of underwater imaging model. Recently, some methods [14,17] adopted the generative and discriminative mechanism to improve the capability of network.

However, existing methods for underwater image enhancement still suffer from color distortion and unclear background details in some unknown scenarios, and these algorithms may be adverse to the high-level vision tasks. To settle these issues, we propose a semantic-driven context aggregation network that utilizes multi-scale semantic features to guide detail restoration and color correction. As shown in Fig. 1, our method realizes a stronger adaptation on the unknown scenario and performs a better semantic-sensitive property than other state-of-the-art methods. To be specific, we first build an encoder-aggregation-decoder enhancement network to establish the map between underwater low-quality observations and high-quality images. Then we introduce an encoder-type classification network that has been pre-trained on ImageNet [3], to provide semantic cues for better enhancement. We further construct a multi-scale feature transformation module to convert semantic features to the desired features of the enhanced network. Concretely, our main contributions can be concluded as the following three-folds:

- We successfully incorporate semantic information into a context aggregation enhancement network for underwater image enhancement to achieve robustness towards unknown scenarios and be friendly to semantic-level vision tasks.
- We construct a multi-scale feature transformation module to extract and convert effective semantic cues from the pre-trained classification network to assist in enhancing the low-quality underwater images.
- Extensive experiments demonstrate that our method is superior to other advanced algorithms. Moreover, the application on salient object detection further reveals our semantic-sensitive property.

## 2   Method

The overall architecture of our proposed method is shown in Fig. 2. In this section, we begin with describing the overall architecture in Sect. 2.1, then introduce the semantic feature extractor in Sect. 2.2, the proposed multi-scale feature transformation module in Sect. 2.3, and finally the context aggregation enhancement network and the loss function in Sect. 2.4.

### 2.1   The Overall Architecture

Semantic information extracted from high-level network has potential to facilitate underwater image enhancement with more accurate and robust predictions. Thus, we propose a semantic-driven context aggregation network for underwater image enhancement, as illustrated in Fig. 2. Our whole architecture includes a semantic feature extractor, a multi-scale feature transformation module, and a context aggregation enhancement network. Specifically, we adopt a general VGG16 classification network to extract the semantic features, then the extracted multi-scale semantic features with abundant information are fed into the enhancement network through the multi-scale feature transformation

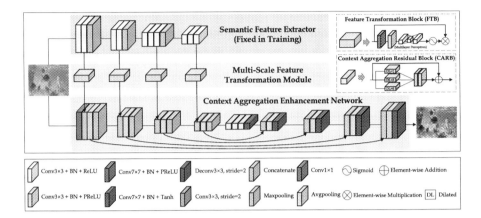

**Fig. 2.** Overview of the proposed semantic-driven context aggregation network for underwater image enhancement. Our network is composed of three basic modules. a) Semantic feature extractor, which consists of a pre-trained VGG16 classification network to extract semantic features. b) Multi-scale feature transformation module, which is used to concentrate on beneficial semantic features to guide underwater image enhancement. c) Context aggregation enhancement network, which integrates semantic features and enhancement features to generate clear and natural underwater images.

module. The feature transformation blocks process the affluent features in an attentive way, which benefit the enhancement network in restoring details and correcting color casts for underwater images.

## 2.2   Semantic Feature Extractor

A common perception is that the shallower features from backbone network of high-level task consider texture and local information, while the deeper features focus more on semantic and global information. This motivates us to explore the ability of multi-scale semantic features. Specifically, we extract features of the first four scales (denoted as $F_n$, $n \in [1, 4]$) from a VGG16 network pre-trained on ImageNet [3]. To avoid information loss caused by pooling operation, we select features before pooling layers of each stage. The abundant use of guidance information from multi-scale features allows us to better handle the challenges in low-quality underwater images. Besides, in order to avoid introducing the training costs, semantic feature extractor is fixed during training phase.

## 2.3   Multi-scale Feature Transformation Module

With the extracted multi-scale semantic features, we aim at incorporating the abundant semantic information into the enhancement network. A straightforward method is directly combining semantic features with the features in the enhancement network, *e.g.*, addition or concatenation. However, this may ignore the distinguishability of semantic features and introduce redundant information into the enhancement network. Inspired by the attention mechanism in [11], we propose a feature transformation block (FTB) to attentively select and incorporate the key prior for the enhancement network. We first adopt a 1×1 convolution block to match the channel dimensions of features, then exploit the inter-channel dependences and reweight the importance of each channel to highlight the vital information and suppress the unnecessary ones. The process can be formulated as the following equation:

$$F_o^n = S(MLP(Avgpool(Conv_{1\times1}(F^n)))) \odot F^n, n = 1, 2, 3, 4 \qquad (1)$$

where $Conv_{1\times1}(\cdot)$ denotes a convolution block consisting of $1 \times 1$ Conv, BN and PReLU. $Avgpool(\cdot)$ and $MLP(\cdot)$ denote global average pooling and multilayer perceptron respectively, and $S(\cdot)$ denotes a sigmoid function. $\odot$ is pixel-wise multiplication, and $F_o^n$ is the output of feature transformation block.

Through the multi-scale feature transformation module, we can suppress and balance the comprehensive information to guide the enhancement network to achieve finer predictions. The extensive experiments in Sect. 3.3 also demonstrate the effectiveness of our proposed FTB.

### 2.4  Context Aggregation Enhancement Network and Loss Function

For the enhancement network, we employ an encoder-aggregation-decoder network. On the one hand, in the encoder part, the multi-scale semantic features are attentively incorporated into the corresponding level through FTB. On the other hand, with the goal of extracting global contextual information from the combined features, we adopt Context Aggregation Residual Block (CARB) to further enlarge the respective field following [4]. Finally, the comprehensive and attentive features are fed into the decoder to generate clearer and more natural predictions for underwater images.

In order to apply an appropriate loss function, there are two key factors needed to be considered. First, the widely-used $\mathcal{L}_2$ loss usually leads to over-smoothed results. Thus, we choose to adopt $\mathcal{L}_1$ loss function as a pixel-wise objective function. Second, considering that pixel-wise loss function is not sensitive to image structure characteristics (e.g., luminance, contrast), we simultaneously adopt MS-SSIM [27] to guide the network to focus on image structure information. As a result, the overall loss function can be formulated as

$$\mathcal{L}_{total} = \lambda\mathcal{L}_1 + (1 - \lambda)\mathcal{L}_{MS-SSIM}, \qquad (2)$$

where $\lambda$ is a balance parameter. In our experiment, $\lambda$ was empirically set as 0.2.

## 3  Experiments

In this section, we first introduce the adopted datasets and implementation details. Next we comprehensively compare the performance of our approach with other state-of-the-art methods. We also perform ablation experiments to analyze the effect of main components in our proposed network. Finally, we evaluate our method in the application of underwater salient object detection.

**Table 1.** Quantitative evaluation on two underwater benchmark datasets. The best two results are shown in red and **blue** fonts, respectively.

| Dataset | Metric | EUIVF | TSA | UDCP | UWCNN | Water-Net | F-GAN | Ours |
|---|---|---|---|---|---|---|---|---|
| UIEB | PSNR ↑ | 18.300 | 14.119 | 12.320 | 14.891 | **19.492** | 18.300 | 21.611 |
| | SSIM ↑ | 0.824 | 0.631 | 0.539 | 0.733 | **0.850** | 0.812 | 0.894 |
| | UIQM ↑ | **2.757** | 1.996 | 1.772 | 2.428 | 2.307 | 2.740 | 2.893 |
| | NIQE ↓ | **4.049** | 4.166 | 4.304 | 4.488 | 4.485 | 4.393 | 3.923 |
| | TM ↑ | **1.120** | 0.747 | 0.640 | 0.439 | 0.912 | 0.789 | 1.184 |
| UCCS | UIQM↑ | **3.073** | 2.512 | 2.098 | 2.536 | 3.150 | 2.982 | 2.983 |
| | NIQE↓ | 4.542 | 4.842 | 5.131 | **4.411** | 5.696 | 4.543 | 3.574 |
| | TM ↑ | **0.598** | 0.432 | 0.086 | 0.173 | 0.527 | 0.326 | 0.613 |

### 3.1  Experimental Setup

**Datasets.** To evaluate the performance and generalization ability of our model, we conduct experiments on two underwater benchmark datasets: Underwater Image Enhancement Benchmark (UIEB) [16] and Underwater Color Cast Set (UCCS) [19]. The UIEB dataset includes 890 raw underwater images with corresponding high-quality reference images. The UCCS dataset contains 300 real underwater no-reference images in blue, green and blue-green tones. In order to achieve a fair comparison, we randomly selected 712 paired images from 890 paired images on UIEB as the training set. The remaining 178 paired images on UIBE and the UCCS dataset are used for testing.

**Implementation Details.** We implemented our network using Pytorch toolbox on a PC with an NVIDIA GTX 1070 GPU. The training images were all uniformly resized to 640×480 and then randomly cropped into patches with the size of 256×256. During the training phase, we used the ADAM optimizer and set the parameter $\beta_1$ and $\beta_2$ as 0.9 and 0.999, respectively. The initial learning rate was set as 5e−4 and decreased by 20% every 10k iterations.

**Evaluation Metrics.** To comprehensively evaluate the performance of various underwater image enhancement methods, we adopt five evaluation metrics, including two widely-used evaluation metrics for data with reference, *i.e.*, Peak Signal to Noise Ratio (PSNR) and Structure Similarity Index Measure (SSIM); and three reference-free metrics, *i.e.*, Naturalness Image Quality Evaluator (NIQE) [22], Underwater Image Quality Measure (UIQM) [23], and Twice-Mixing (TM) [8].

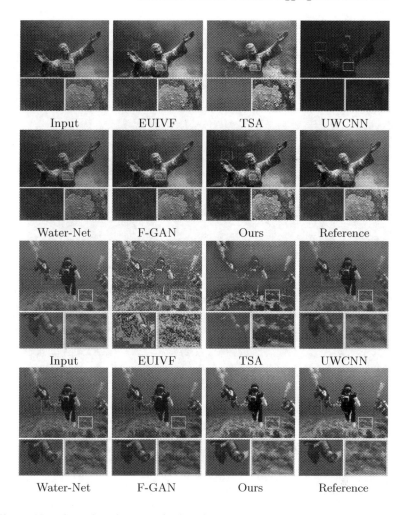

Input          EUIVF          TSA          UWCNN

Water-Net          F-GAN          Ours          Reference

Input          EUIVF          TSA          UWCNN

Water-Net          F-GAN          Ours          Reference

**Fig. 3.** Visual results of our method and top-ranking methods on UIBE dataset.

## 3.2 Comparison with the State-of-the-Arts

To fully evaluate the performance of our method, we compare our method with other six state-of-the-art underwater image enhancement methods. There are three conventional methods, *i.e.*, EUIVF [1], TSA [7] and UDCP [5], and three learning-based methods, *i.e.*, UWCNN [15], Water-Net [16] and F-GAN [14].

**Quantitative Evaluation.** Table 1 shows the validation results of all the competing methods on the UIEB dataset and the UCCS dataset. It is noted that our method outperforms other advanced methods in terms of all the evaluation metrics across the two datasets except the Top-3 UIQM on UCCS dataset. Specially, our method respectively boosts the PSNR and SSIM by 10.87% and 5.17%, compared to the suboptimal method Water-Net on the UIEB dataset.

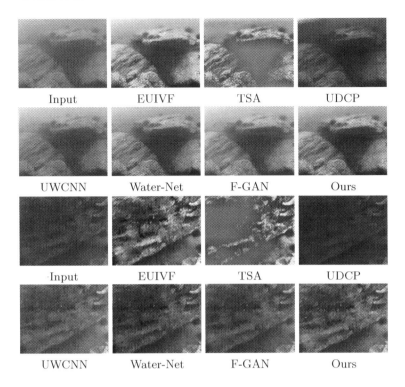

**Fig. 4.** Visual results of our method and top-ranking methods on UCCS dataset.

**Qualitative Evaluation.** From a more intuitive view, we visualize some representative results generated from our method and other top-ranking approaches across UIBE and UCCS datasets in Figs. 3 and 4, respectively. It can be easily seen from Fig. 3 that our method can simultaneously restore clearer details of the background and more natural color. Moreover, we can observe from the visual results in Fig. 4 that our method achieves more visually pleasing results on UCCS dataset. For instance, other methods have trouble in restoring natural images (*e.g.*, the reddish color of row 1, column 4, and the yellowish color of row 2, column 1 in Fig. 4), while our results are closer to the real scenarios with lighter color casts.

### 3.3    Ablation Study

In this section, we conduct ablation studies to validate the effectiveness of the key components proposed by our method.

**Effectiveness of Semantic Features and FTB.** First, we apply the encoder-aggregation-decoder network as our baseline (denoted as "M1" in Table 2). For the sake of investigating the effectiveness of introducing semantic features into the underwater image enhancement task, we directly concatenate the semantic features from the pre-trained VGG16 network and the enhancement features

**Table 2.** Ablation study of our method on UIEB dataset. "w/" means with the corresponding experimental setting. The best result is shown in **bold** font.

| Method | Baseline | w/F1, F2 | w/F3, F4 | w/FTB | PSNR/SSIM |
|--------|----------|----------|----------|-------|-----------|
| M1 | ✓ | | | | 20.519/0.883 |
| M2 | ✓ | ✓ | ✓ | | 20.846/0.887 |
| M3 | ✓ | ✓ | | ✓ | 21.014/0.884 |
| M4 | ✓ | | ✓ | ✓ | 21.056/0.887 |
| Ours | ✓ | ✓ | ✓ | ✓ | **21.611/0.894** |

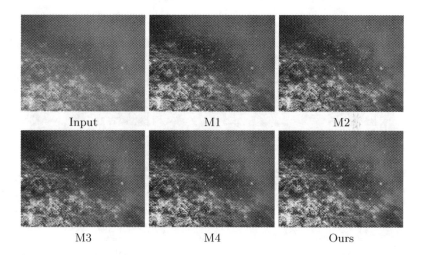

**Fig. 5.** Visual results of ablation study on UIEB dataset.

(denoted as "M2"). The comparison results of "M1" and "M2" in Table 2 demonstrate that directly introducing semantic features can bring 0.33dB performance gains towards PSNR on the UIEB dataset. Moreover, we further employ our proposed FTB to attentively extract and transmit the semantic features (denoted as "Ours"). We can see from the comparison results of "M2" and "Ours" that after applying the proposed FTB, our network obtains consistent performance gains (*e.g.*, 0.76dB towards PSNR). In addition, the corresponding visual results shown in Fig. 5 also demonstrate that our FTB is beneficial for color correction and detail restoration.

**Effectiveness of Multi-scale Features.** In order to further study the effectiveness of multi-scale semantic features, we carefully divide the multi-scale features into two groups and specified a series of experimental settings, *i.e.*, the shallower group (denoted as "M3") with the $1^{st}$ scale and the $2^{nd}$ scale features, and the deeper group (denoted as "M4") with the $3^{th}$ scale and the $4^{th}$ scale features. The comparison results of "M3", "M4" and "Ours" in Table 2 indicate that the incorporation of deeper-scale features and shallower-scale features both obtain

**Table 3.** Application of the top-ranking image enhancement methods and ours to the saliency detection task evaluated on USOD dataset. The best result is shown in **bold** font.

| Method | F-measure↑ | S-measure↑ | MAE↓ |
|---|---|---|---|
| Original F$^3$Net | 0.837 | 0.822 | 0.085 |
| + EUIVF | 0.850 | 0.833 | 0.081 |
| + Water-Net | 0.852 | 0.833 | 0.080 |
| + F-GAN | 0.851 | 0.830 | 0.082 |
| + Ours | **0.860** | **0.843** | **0.078** |

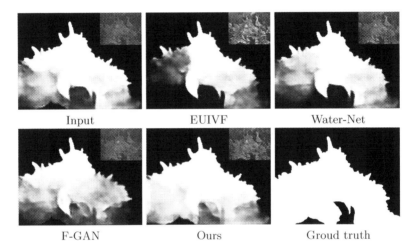

Input          EUIVF          Water-Net

F-GAN          Ours          Groud truth

**Fig. 6.** Visualization of the application of the top-ranking image enhancement methods and ours to the saliency detection task evaluated on the USOD dataset. The corresponding enhanced images are shown in the upper right corner.

much performance gains. And when the multi-scale features are fully incorporated, we achieve the best results. Besides, the visual comparisons shown in Fig. 5 also present the consistent performance.

## 3.4 Application on Salient Object Detection

To further verify the effectiveness and applicability of our proposed network, we also apply our method to the underwater salient object detection task. Specifically, we first adopt the pre-trained salient object detection network F$^3$Net [26] and evaluate it on an underwater salient object detection dataset (USOD) [13] (denoted as "Original input" in Table 3). We employ several top-ranking image enhancement networks and our proposed network to conduct image enhancement on the inputs and made saliency predictions through the F$^3$Net. The quantitative results of the predicted saliency maps are tabulated in Table 3. It is obvious that our method shows performance gains against other image enhancement methods. Meanwhile, we can note that after applying our method, the images achieve finer details and more natural colors, and further facilitate F$^3$Net to predict saliency maps with superior consistence and improved robustness in Fig. 6.

## 4 Conclusion

In this paper, we presented a semantic-driven context aggregation network to cooperatively guide detail restoration and color correcting. Multi-scale semantic features extracted from a pre-trained VGG16 network are fused into the encoder-aggregation-decoder architecture to explore the ability of semantic features. We further proposed a multi-scale feature transformation module which attentively concentrates on the key priors and suppresses the unhelpful ones. Moreover, experimental results conducted on two real datasets demonstrate that our method outperforms the state-of-the-art methods. Additionally, our method can also help salient object detection to achieve better performance.

## References

1. Ancuti, C., Ancuti, C.O., Haber, T., Bekaert, P.: Enhancing underwater images and videos by fusion. In: Proceedings of the IEEE Conference on Computer Vision and Pattern Recognition, pp. 81–88 (2012)
2. Chiang, J.Y., Chen, Y.C.: Underwater image enhancement by wavelength compensation and dehazing. IEEE Trans. Image Process. **21**(4), 1756–1769 (2011)
3. Deng, J., Dong, W., Socher, R., Li, L.J., Li, K., Fei-Fei, L.: Imagenet: a large-scale hierarchical image database. In: Proceedings of the IEEE Conference on Computer Cision and Pattern Recognition, pp. 248–255 (2009)
4. Deng, S., et al.: Detail-recovery image deraining via context aggregation networks. In: Proceedings of the IEEE Conference on Computer Vision and Pattern Recognition, pp. 14560–14569 (2020)
5. Drews, P.L., Nascimento, E.R., Botelho, S.S., Campos, M.F.M.: Underwater depth estimation and image restoration based on single images. IEEE Comput. Graphics Appl. **36**(2), 24–35 (2016)
6. Ebner, M.: Color constancy, vol. 7. John Wiley & Sons (2007)
7. Fu, X., Fan, Z., Ling, M., Huang, Y., Ding, X.: Two-step approach for single underwater image enhancement. In: 2017 International Symposium on Intelligent Signal Processing and Communication Systems, pp. 789–794 (2017)
8. Fu, Z., Fu, X., Huang, Y., Ding, X.: Twice mixing: a rank learning based quality assessment approach for underwater image enhancement. arXiv preprint arXiv:2102.00670 (2021)
9. Galdran, A., Pardo, D., Picón, A., Alvarez-Gila, A.: Automatic red-channel underwater image restoration. J. Vis. Commun. Image Represent. **26**, 132–145 (2015)
10. He, K., Sun, J., Tang, X.: Single image haze removal using dark channel prior. IEEE Trans. Pattern Anal. Mach. Intell. **33**(12), 2341–2353 (2010)
11. Hu, J., Shen, L., Sun, G.: Squeeze-and-excitation networks. In: Proceedings of the IEEE Conference on Computer Vision and Pattern Recognition, pp. 7132–7141 (2018)

12. Hummel, R.: Image enhancement by histogram transformation. Comput. Graph. Image Process. **6**(2), 184–195 (1977)
13. Islam, M.J., Wang, R., de Langis, K., Sattar, J.: Svam: saliency-guided visual attention modeling by autonomous underwater robots. arXiv preprint arXiv:2011.06252 (2020)
14. Islam, M.J., Xia, Y., Sattar, J.: Fast underwater image enhancement for improved visual perception. IEEE Robot. Automation Lett. **5**(2), 3227–3234 (2020)
15. Li, C., Anwar, S., Porikli, F.: Underwater scene prior inspired deep underwater image and video enhancement. Pattern Recogn. **98**, 107038 (2020)
16. Li, C., Guo, C., Ren, W., Cong, R., Hou, J., Kwong, S., Tao, D.: An underwater image enhancement benchmark dataset and beyond. IEEE Trans. Image Process. **29**, 4376–4389 (2019)
17. Li, C., Guo, J., Guo, C.: Emerging from water: underwater image color correction based on weakly supervised color transfer. IEEE Signal Process. Lett. **25**(3), 323–327 (2018)
18. Liu, R., Fan, X., Hou, M., Jiang, Z., Luo, Z., Zhang, L.: Learning aggregated transmission propagation networks for haze removal and beyond. IEEE Trans. Neural Networks Learn. Syst. **30**(10), 2973–2986 (2018)
19. Liu, R., Fan, X., Zhu, M., Hou, M., Luo, Z.: Real-world underwater enhancement: challenges, benchmarks, and solutions under natural light. IEEE Trans. Circuits Syst. Video Technol. **30**(12), 4861–4875 (2020)
20. Liu, R., Ma, L., Zhang, J., Fan, X., Luo, Z.: Retinex-inspired unrolling with cooperative prior architecture search for low-light image enhancement. In: Proceedings of the IEEE Conference on Computer Vision and Pattern Recognition, pp. 10561–10570 (2021)
21. Ma, L., Liu, R., Zhang, X., Zhong, W., Fan, X.: Video deraining via temporal aggregation-and-guidance. In: 2021 IEEE International Conference on Multimedia and Expo (ICME), pp. 1–6. IEEE (2021)
22. Mittal, A., Soundararajan, R., Bovik, A.C.: Making a "completely blind" image quality analyzer. IEEE Signal Process. Lett. **20**(3), 209–212 (2012)
23. Panetta, K., Gao, C., Agaian, S.: Human-visual-system-inspired underwater image quality measures. IEEE J. Oceanic Eng. **41**(3), 541–551 (2015)
24. Van De Weijer, J., Gevers, T., Gijsenij, A.: Edge-based color constancy. IEEE Trans. Image Process. **16**(9), 2207–2214 (2007)
25. Wang, Y., Zhang, J., Cao, Y., Wang, Z.: A deep cnn method for underwater image enhancement. In: IEEE International Conference on Image Processing, pp. 1382–1386 (2017)
26. Wei, J., Wang, S., Huang, Q.: F$^3$net: Fusion, feedback and focus for salient object detection. In: Proceedings of the AAAI Conference on Artificial Intelligence, vol. 34, pp. 12321–12328 (2020)
27. Zhao, H., Gallo, O., Frosio, I., Kautz, J.: Loss functions for image restoration with neural networks. IEEE Trans. Comput. Imaging **3**(1), 47–57 (2016)
28. Zuiderveld, K.: Contrast limited adaptive histogram equalization. Graphics gems, pp. 474–485 (1994)

# A Multi-resolution Medical Image Fusion Network with Iterative Back-Projection

Chang Liu and Bin Yang[✉]

College of Electric Engineering, University of South China, Hengyang 421001, CO, China
changliu0286@163.com, yangbin01420@163.com

**Abstract.** The aim of medical image fusion is to integrate complementary information in multi-modality medical images into an informative fused image which is pivotal for assistance in clinical diagnosis. Since medical images in different modalities always have great variety of characteristics (such as resolution and functional information), the fused images obtained from traditional methods would be blurred in details or loss of information in some degree. To solve these problems, we propose a novel deep learning-based multi-resolution medical image fusion network with iterative back-projection (IBPNet) in this paper. In our IBPNet, up-projection and down-projection blocks are designed to achieve feature maps alternation between high- and low-resolution images. The feedback errors generated in the alternation process are self-corrected in the reconstruction process. Moreover, an effective combined loss function is designed, which can adapt to multi-resolution medical image fusion task. High spatial resolution magnetic resonance imaging (MRI) images and low spatial resolution color Positron emission tomography (PET) images are used to demonstrate the validation of the proposed method. Experimental results show that our method is superior to other state-of-the-art fusion methods in terms of visual perception and objective evaluation.

**Keywords:** Medical image fusion · Deep learning · Back-projection · Multi-modality medical images · Multi-resolution

## 1 Introduction

With different medical imaging equipment, various medical images of internal tissues in human body can be obtained by mean of non-invasive way. Medical images in different modalities provide different information. For example, computed tomography (CT) and magnetic resonance imaging (MRI) mainly reflect high-resolution structure information of internal tissues. Positron emission tomography (PET) and single-photon emission computed tomography (SPECT) provide functional and metabolic information [1]. At present, high-precision diagnosis of diseases needs to consider various medical images from different imaging modalities cooperatively. The emergence of multi-modality medical image fusion technology saves human resources to a certain extent, while retaining the specific characteristics of different modal images.

© Springer Nature Switzerland AG 2021
H. Ma et al. (Eds.): PRCV 2021, LNCS 13021, pp. 41–52, 2021.
https://doi.org/10.1007/978-3-030-88010-1_4

In the past few decades, many image fusion methods have been proposed. These methods are mainly composed of two categories: spatial and transform domain. Spatial domain methods use the pixels or patches in the source images to construct the fusion image, which makes full use of the characteristics of spatial information. They have very well fusion results for multi-focus and multi-exposure images. However, it is not suitable for multi-modality medical images fusion due to that the spatial domain methods may produce artificial or loss of contrast in fused image. By contrast, transform domain methods are widely used in medical image fusion. In transform domain methods, original images are decomposed into coefficients with different resolution firstly. Then the coefficients of different source images are fused and inversely transformed into a fused image. In the field of medical image fusion, the combination of pulse coupled neural network (PCNN) and transform decomposition algorithm is also popular [2, 3]. PCNN is mainly used to extract the activity level of decomposition coefficients obtained by a certain multi-scale transformation for image fusion [4]. In recent years, sparse representation is widely used in fusion algorithms due to that sparse representation can represent the significant information of an image [5, 6]. However, conventional sparse representation-based fusions are sensitivity to image misregistration and inefficient. Although these methods achieve promising results, very complex fusion rules and higher computational costs are needed to achieve better fusion results.

Recently, deep learning (DL) methods have attracted more and more attentions, which promote the development of medical image fusion technology [7]. However, there are still some disadvantages for most deep learning-based methods. On the one hand, most of the deep learning attempts are only applied to feature extraction, and the entire learning process is still included in the traditional framework. For example, Fayez et al. [8] adopt the convolutional neural network preprocessing model to extract the deep features of the source images. Fusion rules are still needed to carefully design to achieve promising fusion. On the other hand, the training process of the fusion method based on GAN network is unstable. The dual discriminator conditional generation confrontation network (DDcGAN) proposed by Ma et al. [9] has achieved good results, but the use of dual discriminators makes it difficult to obtain stable results in the process of generating confrontation, and the information loss in the fusion process is also difficult to control. In addition, compared with images that characterize structural information such as MRI, medical images that characterize functional information such as PET are usually affected by problems such as low resolution and multiple channels, which are not conducive to the further development of medical clinics.

To address the above challenges, an end-to-end medical image fusion network is developed in this paper. The network can realize the fusion of medical images in multi-resolution without any fusion rules. The idea of iterative back-projection is adopted in this network, short for IBPNet. High-resolution MRI and low-resolution PET images are taken as example to introduce the proposed method. Upsampling of low-resolution images directly can easily lead to loss of information. Therefore, research on a multi-resolution medical image fusion method that does not lose information is of great significance to medical clinical applications. The characteristics and contributions of this paper are summarized as follows:

- We propose an end-to-end multi-resolution medical image fusion network, which makes the fused images structure clear and the information remains intact.
- Motivated by back-projection algorithms, the proposed deep learning network successfully combines the idea of image reconstruction algorithms. We construct up-projection and down-projection blocks that alternate the feature map between high and low resolution. Feedback error between alternate steps realizes the self-correction function, which guides the network to produce better results.
- We design an effective combination of loss functions, and the task of multi-resolution medical image fusion can be completed by adjusting the weight of the loss item. Compared with state-of-the-art alternatives, the results demonstrate the superiority of the proposed methods in terms of both subjective visual perception and objective evaluation metrics.

## 2   Proposed Approach

### 2.1   Overall Framework

Generally, the input high-resolution medical MRI image provides rich texture details and structural information. On the contrary, low-resolution pseudo-color PET images are regarded as color images, and different color distributions provide different functional information. Therefore, we need to choose an appropriate de-correlation color model. In our framework, we choose the YUV model to solve the color de-correlation problem. Y represents the luminance component, which indicates the structure and luminance changes. U and V reflect the chromaticity information. We mainly use the Y-channel component of PET for fusion with MRI images. The overall framework of our method is shown in Fig. 1 in which the resolution of MRI images is uniformly defined as $4 \times 4$ of the PET image resolution.

Firstly, the low-resolution PET images are converted from RGB space to YUV space. Then, high-resolution MRI image and Y-channel component of low-resolution PET images are fed into IBPNet to obtain high-resolution Y-channel fused image $Y_f$. U and V channel components which are $4 \times 4$ up-sampled by bicubic interpolation are reverse converted with the fused Y channel components. Finally, new RGB fused image is obtained by inverse color space conversion.

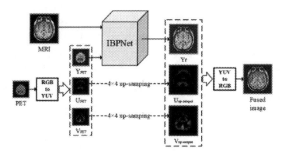

**Fig. 1.** The overall framework of the proposed method.

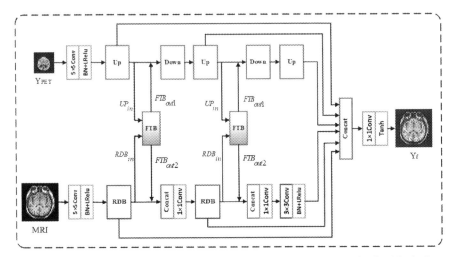

**Fig. 2.** Network architecture of the proposed IBPNet. Up represents up-projection block; Down represents down-projection block; RDB represents residual-dense blocks and FTB represents feature transmission blocks.

## 2.2  Network Architecture

The proposed IBPNet architecture is shown in Fig. 2 which consists of two branches corresponding to low-resolution Y-channel luminance component of PET image and high-resolution MRI image. The Y-channel component of PET images and the high-resolution (HR) MRI images are first passed through a $5 \times 5$ convolution block with an activation function combination of "BN + LReLU" to obtain shallow features. In the upper Y-channel component branch, iterative up-projection and down-projection blocks are interconnected to get the HR features. It is worth noting that the feature map is scaled up by $4 \times 4$ after the up-projection block and the opposite after the down-projection block. In the MRI image branch, residual dense blocks (RDBs) [10] are used to extract deeper features of MRI images. The sequentially network block "Concat+ $1 \times 1$ Conv" is used to integrate the previous features while reducing the computational cost. In addition, there are two intersecting network blocks in the middle of the network denoted as feature transfer blocks (FTBs) which are used to fuse the features from the two branches and to enhance the information processing at the next level. Features extracted from modules at different stages are globally fused through jump connection, which involves six feature maps of two paths. Finally, the concatenated feature maps are passed through a $1 \times 1$ convolution block with a tanh activation function to obtain the fusion result $Y_f$.

**Feature Transmission Blocks (FTB).** The input $UP_{in}$ and $RDB_{in}$ of the feature transmission block (FTB) are derived from the up-projection block (Up) and the residual dense block (RDB), which are assembled into a combined feature map in a concatenation way as shown in Fig. 3. Then, the combined feature map is inputted into two $1 \times 1$ convolutional layers with combination of "BN + LReLU" convolutional layer which improves the speed of the network. It is worth noting that the output $FTB_{out1}$ is the input to the down-projection and the output $FTB_{out2}$ is the feature map required for the lower branch of the network. FTB fuses and passes on the features of the two branches of the network. Pre-processing and post-processing are closely linked together, which reflects the concept of functional reuse.

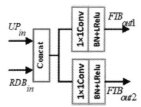

**Fig. 3.** Feature transmission block (FTB) architecture.

**Back-projection.** Back-projection is an iterative algorithm to minimize the reconstruction error [11], which starts to be designed for multiple LR image inputs. Subsequently, Dai et al. [12] extended the back-projection idea to a single LR image and achieved better results. For a single LR image, multiple up-sampling operators are used to update the iterative reconstruction error. Many studies have demonstrated that the back-projection algorithm can improve the quality of images [13]. However, these methods are susceptible to predefined parameters as well as the number of iterations.

Meanwhile, most methods for reconstruction tasks are built on a one-way mapping from LR to HR space, which has limited LR spatial information for larger scaled images. Inspired by DBPN [14], we design the alternating pattern of up-projection and down-projection to realize the mutual process from LR to HR. The idea can overcome the above problems and makes full use of the information between them. The architecture of up- and down-projection is shown in the following Fig. 4, which embodies the idea of back projection.

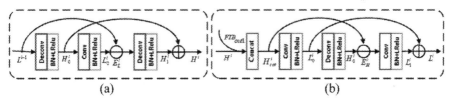

**Fig. 4.** Proposed up- and down-projection block architecture. (a) represents up-projection block; (b) represents down-projection block.

In the up-projection block, we take the previously extracted shallow LR feature map $L^{i-1}$ as input and map it to the HR map $H_0^i$. Subsequently, $H_0^i$ is mapped back to the LR map $L_0^i$, which is a back-projection process. The error $E_L^i$ between $L_0^i$ and $L^{i-1}$ is mapped to generate a new HR error $H_1^i$. Finally, the HR results generated by the mapping are subjected to a summation operation to obtain a new feature map $H_1^i$.

Process of the down-projection block is also very similar, the difference is that we use the output $H^i$ of the up-projection block and the output $FTB_{out1}$ of the feature transmission block as input in a concatenation way, ultimately in order to map the input HR image $H^i_{cat}$ to the LR image $L^i$. Definition of the up- and down-projection blocks is shown in the following Table 1.

**Table 1.** Definition of the up- and down-projection blocks

| Up-projection block | | Down-projection block | |
|---|---|---|---|
| Steps | Formulas | Steps | Formulas |
| $\times$ | $\times$ | Concatenation | $H^i_{cat} = H^i + FTB_{out1}$ |
| Scale up | $H^i_0 = L^{i-1} \uparrow_s$ | Scale down | $L^i_0 = H^i_{cat} \downarrow_s$ |
| Scale down | $L^i_0 = H^i_0 \downarrow_s$ | Scale up | $H^i_0 = L^i_0 \uparrow_s$ |
| Error | $E^i_L = L^i_0 - L^{i-1}$ | Error | $E^i_H = H^i_0 - H^i_{cat}$ |
| Scale error up | $H^i_1 = E^i_L \uparrow_s$ | Scale error down | $L^i_1 = E^i_H \downarrow_s$ |
| Output feature map | $H^i = H^i_1 + H^i_0$ | Output feature map | $L^i = L^i_1 + L^i_0$ |

where $\uparrow_s$ and $\downarrow_s$ represent up-sampling or down-sampling operations with scale factor s, respectively.

Iterative projection block lets the feature map to alternate between HR and LR. In addition, iterative projection errors are fed back to the sampling layer for self-correction. Each sampled convolution block comes with a combination of "BN + LReLU" activation functions, which alleviates the gradient disappearance problem. Compared to other networks, the use of large size filters such as $8 \times 8$ does not slow down the convergence speed during the iterations.

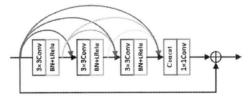

**Fig. 5.** Residual dense block (RDB) architecture.

**Residual Dense Block (RDB).** We use the residual dense block (RDB) [10] to extract the deep features of MRI images, as shown in Fig. 5. The RDBs consists mainly of $3 \times 3$ convolutional layers with "BN + LReLU" activation functions, which are connected by dense connections. Finally, a $1 \times 1$ convolutional layer is introduced to adaptively control the output information, which improves the information flow by performing residual learning with the features introduced by the skip connection.

## 2.3   Loss Function

Loss function is used to evaluate the extent to which the predicted value of the model is different from the true value. The loss function of our network consists of three types of loss terms as:

$$L(\theta, D) = \alpha(L_{\text{ssim}}(\theta, D) + kL_{mse}(\theta, D) + L_{Grad}(\theta, D)) \tag{1}$$

where structural similarity $L_{\text{ssim}}(\theta, D)$ and intensity distribution $L_{mse}(\theta, D)$ are used to implement adaptive similarity constraints, and gradient loss $L_{Grad}(\theta, D)$ ensures rich texture details. The symbol $\theta$ represents the parameters in the network and $D$ denotes the training dataset. $k$ is used to balance the mean square error with other terms. $\alpha$ represents the total loss coefficient which is conducive to the convergence of the loss function.

Structural similarity index metric (SSIM) combines brightness, structure, and contrast, which is widely used for structural similarity between two images. Mean square error (MSE) is to maintain the intensity distribution of the source image. Similarity constraints is defined by (2) and (3) as:

$$L_{\text{ssim}}(\theta, D) = \mathrm{E}\left[\omega_1 \cdot \left(1 - \text{SSIM}_{\text{MRI}, Y_f}\right) + \omega_2 \cdot \left(1 - \text{SSIM}_{Y_{\text{PET}}, \gamma Y_f}\right)\right] \tag{2}$$

$$L_{\text{mse}}(\theta, D) = \mathrm{E}\left[\omega_1 \cdot \left(1 - \text{MSE}_{\text{MRI}, Y_f}\right) + \omega_2 \cdot \left(1 - \text{MSE}_{Y_{\text{PET}}, \gamma Y_f}\right)\right] \tag{3}$$

where the weights $\omega_1$ and $\omega_2$ control the degree of retention of similar information. Considering the low-resolution case of PET images, we downsample the fused image before participating in the calculation of the relevant similarity constraint terms, where $\gamma$ denotes the down-sampling operation, which is realized by the averaging pooling operation.

The gradient loss constraints is calculated by (4).

$$L_{Grad}(\theta, D) = \lambda_1 \left[\frac{1}{\text{HW}} \left\| \nabla Y_f - \nabla \text{MRI} \right\|_F^2 \right] + \lambda_2 \left[\frac{1}{\text{HW}} \left\| \nabla Y_f - \nabla Y_{\text{PET\_HR}} \right\|_F^2 \right] \tag{4}$$

where $\lambda_1$ and $\lambda_2$ represent the gradient weights of MRI and PET images associated with the fused images. It is worth noting that the high-resolution image $Y_{PET\_HR}$ that has not been processed by the degradation model participates in the calculation of the gradient loss. Because the gradient information at low resolution is not obvious. $\nabla$ represents the gradient operator.

## 3   Experiments

### 3.1   Dataset and Training Details

We validate the proposed IBPNet on the publicly available Harvard dataset[1] for the MRI and PET image fusion. All the source images in this dataset have been registered previously. 30 MRI and PET image pairs are selected from the dataset and crop them

---

[1] http://www.med.harvard.edu/AANLIB/home.html.

into 5070 patch pairs with $120 \times 120$ pixels. Their original image size is $256 \times 256$. To fuse multi-resolution images, we downsample each channel of the PET images to a quarter of the resolution. Thus, the MRI image patch size is $120 \times 120$ and the PET image patch size is $30 \times 30$.

In the training process, our network mainly learns texture information in MRI images and metabolic intensity information in PET images. Y-component pixel intensity of PET images after color channel space transformation is much larger than that of MRI, and we need to apply equal similarity constraints to PET and MRI. It is also necessary to ensure that the fused image has clear texture details. Therefore, we need to ensure that the conditions for the coefficients in Eqs. (2), (3) and (4) are: $\omega_1 = \omega_2$ and $\lambda_1 > \lambda_2$. Our parameters in both (2), (3) and (4) are set as $\omega_1 = 1$, $\omega_2 = 1$, $\lambda_1 = 300$, and $\lambda_2 = 5$. The mean square error factor $k$ is set to 20 and the total loss coefficient $\alpha$ is set to 50. Our experiments run on NVIDIA Geforce RTX 2080 GPU and 3.60 GHz Intel Core i9-9900K CPU.

## 3.2    Results and Analysis of IBPNet

To indicate the effectiveness of the proposed IBPNet, we compare it with six state-of-the-art image fusion methods including adaptive sparse representation method (ASR, Liu et al. 2015) [5], convolutional sparsity based morphological component analysis method (CSMCA, 2019) [6], NSST-MSMG-PCNN method (NMP, Tan et al. 2020) [2], zero-learning fusion method (ZLF, Lahoud et al. 2020) [8], dual-discriminator conditional generative adversarial network (DDcGAN, Ma et al. 2020) [9], and proportional maintenance of gradient and intensity method (PMGI, Hao et al. 2020) [16]. ZLF, PMGI, and DDcGAN are all deep learning-based methods, while the others belong to traditional methods. In particular, DDcGAN can directly process medical images with multi-resolution. For other methods, the low-resolution PET images are unsampled into the same resolution as the MRI images. In all six methods, all parameters are the same as the original paper settings.

In our experiments, 20 pairs of MRI and PET images from the Harvard dataset are selected to test. Figure 6 and Fig. 7 show the fusion results of the two sets of images. To facilitate observation, we have selected arbitrary local areas of the images for magnification by a red box and a green box. It is worth noting that the IHS color conversion model adopted by the DDcGAN and PMGI methods, and the YUV color conversion model used by others. From the two sets of experiments, it can be observed that there is no significant distortion in the color distribution for all methods.

In the Fig. 6 and Fig. 7, the results of the ZLF method shows many artifact-like detailed textures that are not present in the source image MRI. At the same time, missing texture detail information can be observed in the local magnified region in the ZLF method. For the DDcGAN and PMGI methods, the overall visual effect is poor and the texture is unclear. ASR, CSMCA and NMP methods have better visual results, but they still have some defects compared with our method. For example, in the Fig. 6, the fused image of CSMCA method is missing part of the brain sulcus in the local magnification area. In the Fig. 7, there is a significant loss of information in the part of the skull enlarged in red, but the information obtained by our method is richer especially in the locally magnified part. The lower part of the skull becomes darker after fusion of the

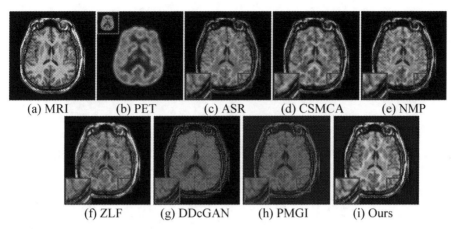

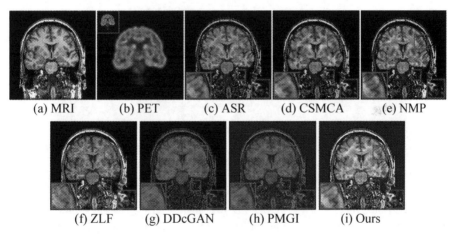

**Fig. 6.** The first set of MRI and PET image fusion results obtained by different methods (Color figure online).

ASR, CSMCA and NMP methods, and the dense structural information of our method is relatively complete. Overall, our method clearly characterizes the functional information of PET images and retains rich textural details from the MRI images.

**Fig. 7.** The second set of MRI and PET image fusion results obtained by different methods (Color figure online).

Five popular fusion metrics such as entropy mutual information (MI), image feature based metrics ($Q^{AB/F}$) [17], image structural similarity based metrics ($Q_W$ and $Q_E$) [18], and universal quality index ($Q_0$) [19] are used to objectively evaluate our method and others. MI reflects the amount of information that the fused image inherits from the source images. $Q^{AB/F}$ is a gradient-based evaluation metric proposed by Xydeas et al. [17] to measure the degree of retention of gradient information of the source image in the fused image. $Q_W$ and $Q_E$ are quality assessment metrics based on structural similarity, which are closely related to image quality, edges, and clarity. $Q_0$ is a general quality index which can comprehensively evaluate the quality of the fusion image. For the above indicators, the higher the value, the better the fusion effect.

**Table 2.** Objective metrics of MRI-PET image fusion with multi-resolution

| Images | Metrics | Methods | | | | | | |
|---|---|---|---|---|---|---|---|---|
| | | ASR | CSMCA | NMP | ZLF | DDcGAN | PMGI | Ours |
| Figure 6 | MI | 2.8199 | 2.8459 | 2.7918 | 3.2176 | 3.0831 | **3.3425** | 2.9929 |
| | $Q^{AB/F}$ | 0.6417 | 0.6472 | 0.6234 | 0.6536 | 0.5369 | 0.6613 | **0.7258** |
| | $Q_W$ | 0.7675 | 0.8307 | 0.7963 | 0.8580 | 0.7491 | 0.8469 | **0.9002** |
| | $Q_E$ | 0.6318 | 0.7190 | 0.6739 | 0.7349 | 0.5726 | 0.7463 | **0.8239** |
| | $Q_0$ | 0.4111 | 0.4295 | 0.4118 | 0.4127 | 0.3756 | 0.4042 | **0.4314** |
| Figure 7 | MI | 2.5492 | 2.6248 | 2.6804 | **3.0756** | 2.7709 | 2.9965 | 2.7029 |
| | $Q^{AB/F}$ | 0.6869 | 0.6979 | 0.6850 | 0.7199 | 0.5944 | 0.7078 | **0.7258** |
| | $Q_W$ | 0.7744 | 0.8266 | 0.8207 | 0.8846 | 0.8166 | 0.8789 | **0.9238** |
| | $Q_E$ | 0.6493 | 0.7252 | 0.7234 | 0.7824 | 0.6858 | 0.7902 | **0.8592** |
| | $Q_0$ | 0.4958 | 0.5026 | 0.5159 | 0.5082 | 0.4568 | 0.4734 | **0.5198** |
| Average | MI | 2.6052 | 2.6344 | 2.7117 | **3.0845** | 2.8319 | 3.0441 | 2.7529 |
| | $Q^{AB/F}$ | 0.6631 | 0.6741 | 0.6673 | 0.6917 | 0.5519 | 0.6833 | **0.7025** |
| | $Q_W$ | 0.7560 | 0.8158 | 0.8323 | 0.8758 | 0.7729 | 0.8628 | **0.9086** |
| | $Q_E$ | 0.6133 | 0.6958 | 0.7233 | 0.7608 | 0.5976 | 0.7605 | **0.8273** |
| | $Q_0$ | 0.4217 | 0.4358 | 0.4479 | 0.4336 | 0.3802 | 0.4151 | **0.4518** |

Table 2 shows the objective evaluation results of image fusion, including Fig. 6, Fig. 7 and the average objective evaluation results obtained from 20 pairs of MRI-PET images. The best largest results are labeled in bold in each row, while the second ones are underlined. All our objective metrics are the best except the MI metric. For metric MI, our method ranks fourth. However, the top three methods of MI value are not effective in subjective evaluation. For example, non-existent artifacts appear in the fusion result of the ZLF method, DDcGAN and PMGI methods have the phenomenon of information loss. In addition, most of the PMGI and ZLF metrics ranked second but showed blurred details. On the whole, our method can retain structural and functional information to a large extent, and obtain the best fusion performance.

## 4   Conclusions

In this paper, we propose a new deep learning-based fusion method, which is applied to multi-resolution medical images. The idea of iterative back projection is applied to our network, so it is called IBPNet. Up-projection and down-projection blocks are designed to correct the errors in the reconstruction process. At the same time, the reconstruction process does not affect the features of the other fused image. Our method can obtain high-quality results in terms of visual quality and objective measurement. The proposed deep learning network successfully combines the idea of image reconstruction, which will further stimulate the great potential of image fusion in the field of deep learning.

**Acknowledgments.** This paper is supported by the National Natural Science Foundation of China (Nos.61871210), Chuanshan Talent Project of the University of South China.

# References

1. Yousif, A.S., Omar, Z.B., Sheikh, U.U.: A survey on multi-scale medical images fusion techniques: brain diseases. J. Biomed. Eng. Med. Imaging **7**(1), 18–38 (2020)
2. Wei, T., Tiwari, P., Pandey, H.M., Moreira, C., Jaiswal, A.K.: Multimodal medical image fusion algorithm in the era of big data. Neural Comput. Appl. **3**, 1–21 (2020)
3. Das, S., Kundu, M.K.: A neuro-fuzzy approach for medical image fusion. IEEE Trans. Biomed. Eng. **60**(12), 3347–3353 (2013)
4. Yin, M., Liu, X., Liu, Y., Chen, X.: Medical image fusion with parameter-adaptive pulse coupled neural network in nonsubsampled shearlet transform domain. IEEE Trans. Instrum. Meas. **68**(1), 49–64 (2018)
5. Liu, Y., Wang, Z.: Simultaneous image fusion and denoising with adaptive sparse representation. IET Image Proc. **9**(5), 347–357 (2014)
6. Liu, Y., Chen, X., Ward, K.R., Wang, Z.J.: Medical image fusion via convolutional sparsity based morphological component analysis. IEEE Signal Process. Lett. **26**(3), 485–489 (2019)
7. Huang, J., Le, Z., Ma, Y., Fan, F., Yang, L.: MGMDcGAN: medical image fusion using multi-generator multi-discriminator conditional generative adversarial network. IEEE Access **8**, 55145–55157 (2020)
8. Lahoud, F., Sabine S.: Zero-learning fast medical image fusion. In: The Proceedings of 22th International Conference on Information Fusion, Ottawa, ON, Canada, pp. 1–8. IEEE (2019)
9. Ma, J., Xu, H., Jiang, J., Mei, X., Zhang, X.P.: DDcGAN: a dual-discriminator conditional generative adversarial network for multi-resolution image fusion. IEEE Trans. Image Process. **29**, 4980–4995 (2020)
10. Zhang, Y., Tian, Y., Kong, Y., Zhong, B., Fu, Y.: Residual dense network for image super-resolution. In: Proceedings of International Conference on Computer Vision and Pattern Recognition, Salt Lake City, UT, USA (2018)
11. Irani, M., Peleg, S.: Improving resolution by image registration. GVGIP: Graph. Models Image Process. **53**(3), 231–239 (1991)
12. Dai, S., Mei, H., Ying, W., Gong, Y.: Bilateral back-projection for single image super resolution. In the Proceedings of International Conference on Multimedia and Expo, Beijing, China, pp. 1039–1042. IEEE (2008)
13. Dong, W., Zhang, L., Shi, G., Wu, X.: Nonlocal back-projection for adaptive image enlargement. In: Proceedings of International Conference on Image Processing, Piscataway, NJ, pp. 348–352. IEEE (2010)
14. Haris, M., Shakhnarovich, G., Ukita, N.: Deep back-projection networks for super-resolution. In: Proceedings of CVF Conference on Computer Vision and Pattern Recognition, UT, Salt Lake City, pp. 1664–1673. IEEE (2018)
15. Timofte, R., Rothe, R., Gool, L.V.: Seven ways to improve example-based single image super resolution. In the Proceedings of International Conference on Computer Vision and Pattern Recognition, Las Vegas, USA, pp. 1865–1873. IEEE (2016)

16. Zhang, H., Xu, H., Xiao, Y., Guo, X., Ma, J.: Rethinking the image fusion: a fast unified image fusion network based on proportional maintenance of gradient and intensity. In the Proceedings of 34th AAAI Conference on Artificial Intelligence, New York, USA, pp. 12797–12804 (2020)
17. Xydeas, C.S., Petrovic, V.: Objective image fusion performance measure. Electron. Lett. **36**(4), 308–309 (2000)
18. Piella, G., Heijmans, H.: A new quality metric for image fusion. In: The Proceedings of International Conference on Image Processing, pp. 173–176. Barcelona, Spain. IEEE (2003)
19. Zhou, W., Bovik, A.C.: A universal image quality index. IEEE Signal Process. Lett. **9**(3), 81–84 (2002)

# Multi-level Discriminator and Wavelet Loss for Image Inpainting with Large Missing Area

Junjie Li and Zilei Wang[✉]

University of Science and Technology of China, Hefei, China
hnljj@mail.ustc.edu.cn, zlwang@ustc.edu.cn

**Abstract.** Recent image inpainting works have shown promising results thanks to great advances of generative adversarial networks (GANs). However, these methods would still generate distorted structures or blurry textures for the situation of large missing area, which is mainly due to the inherent difficulty to train GANs. In this paper, we propose a novel multi-level discriminator (MLD) and wavelet loss (WT) to improve the learning of image inpainting generators. Our method does not change the structure of generator and only works in the training phase, which thus can be easily embedded into sophisticated inpainting networks and would not increase the inference time. Specifically, MLD divides the mask into multiple subregions and then imposes an independent discriminator to each subregion. It essentially increases the distribution overlap between the real images and generated images. Consequently, MLD improves the optimization of GANs by providing more effective gradients to generators. In addition, WT builds a reconstruction loss in the frequency domain, which can facilitate the training of image inpainting networks as a regularization term. Consequently, WT can enforce the generated contents to be more consistent and sharper than the traditional pixel-wise reconstruction loss. We integrate WLD and WT into off-the-shelf image inpainting networks, and conduct extensive experiments on CelebA-HQ, Paris StreetView, and Places2. The results well demonstrate the effectiveness of the proposed method, which achieves state-of-the-art performance and generates higher-quality images than the baselines.

**Keywords:** Image inpainting · Generative Adversarial Network (GAN) · Multi-level discriminator · Wavelet transform · Loss function

---

J. Li—Student.

---

**Electronic supplementary material** The online version of this chapter (https://doi.org/10.1007/978-3-030-88010-1_5) contains supplementary material, which is available to authorized users.

# 1   Introduction

For image inpainting, it is unnecessary to require the generated image to be exactly same as the groundtruth image, but the generated content to fill the hole is expected to be natural and consistent with the surrounding content. Generative Adversarial Network (GAN) [7] is an excellent generative model and has shown powerful ability to generate natural and high-quality images. Therefore, a lot of works [9,11,19,20,24] introduce GAN to the image inpainting task. Typically, the networks in these methods consist of two main components, namely, generator and discriminator. Most of the methods [9,19,20,24] focus on how to construct a better generator, and rarely concern the design of discriminator. According to the structure of generators, we can divide these methods into two broad categories: one-stage model and two-stage model. The one-stage methods adopt one encoder-decoder as a generator, e.g., CE [19] and GMCNN [20]. They usually cannot work well for complex images (such as the Places2 dataset [27]) due to limited capacity to express complicated patterns of image contents. Differently, the two-stage models, e.g., EdgeConnect (EC) [9] and HighFill [23], employ two encoder-decoder networks to generate natural results. However, either one-stage or two-stage models still would suffer from serious artifacts, especially for the images with large missing area, as shown in Fig. 1.

According to [2], an important reason why large-area missing images is difficult to repair is that the distribution of generated images and the distribution of real images are difficult to overlap, which leads to optimization difficulties. We will explain it in detail in Sect. 3.1. In addition, the pixel-wise $\ell_1$ or $\ell_2$ loss can not capture high-frequency information, which can easily produce blurred results. Based on the above

**Fig. 1.** Inpainting results of different methods. *-O means that our proposed method is applied. It can be seen that the current methods have great difficulties in the case of large area missing. On the contrary, our method can handle this situation well.

two issues, we mainly focus on how to better learn a generator, i.e., designing an method to more effectively train image inpainting networks. Our method is only involved in the training phase and thus would not increase the time of forward inference.

In this paper, we propose a new discriminator and loss function to address the aforementioned challenges of image inpainting. First, we propose a multi-level discriminator (MLD) to increase the overlap between the generated and real distributions so that the generator can be more effectively trained. MLD partitions the missing regions into multiple parts, and then we separately build the adversarial loss for each of them. Consequently, a discriminator for larger missing area is decomposed into multiple sub-discriminators with smaller missing area.

Second, we propose to use wavelet coefficients to represent image contents and then wavelet loss (WT) to enforce the content consistency between the generated image and raw image. Different from the $\ell_1$ and $\ell_2$ loss, WT is to compute the reconstruction loss in the frequency domain, in which each component represents the information of regions rather than pixels. For example, the low-frequency component can describe the global topology information and the high-frequency one can describe the local texture details [10]. Note that our proposed method in this work are orthogonal to existing image inpainting generators, and thus can be integrated into off-the-shelf networks. Particularly, we would investigate the combinations with GMCNN [20] and CA [24] in this paper due to their good performance. To our best knowledge, this work is the first attempt to handle the large-hole problem of image inpainting from the perspective of distribution overlap.

We experimentally evaluate the proposed method on three benchmark datasets: CelebA-HQ [13], Paris StreetView [4], and Places2 [27]. The results well demonstrate the effectiveness of our proposed method, which can produce much higher-quality images than the corresponding baseline.

The main contributions of this work are summarized as follows:

- We propose a multi-level discriminator, which increases the overlap between the generated and real distributions and thus can aid the generator networks to be more effectively trained.
- We propose wavelet loss for image inpainting networks to improve the constraints of content consistency. As a result, the artifact and blur of generated images can be greatly alleviated.
- We integrate the proposed method into representative inpainting networks, and experimentally show the effectiveness of our method on different types of images.

## 2   Related Work

### 2.1   Image Inpainting

There are two broad types of approaches in previous works, *i.e.*, traditional matching methods [3,17] and deep convolutional neural network (DCNN) based methods [9,11,16,19–22,25,26]. Traditional image inpainting methods like [3,5,6] work well for the images with small holes and consistent textures. However, these methods [5,6,14] are generally time-consuming due to iteratively searching for the most similar patch in surrounding areas. In sharp contrast, the DCNN-based method can better capture high-level information of images and efficiently synthesize images in an end-to-end manner. Wang *et al.* [20] proposed a Generative Multi-column Convolutional Neural Network (GMCNN) to capture different levels of information to generate more plausible synthesized content. CA [24] takes a coarse-to-fine structure with contextual attention module for image inpainting. Particularly, contextual attention can borrow the information from distant spatial location and thus overcomes the limitation of convolutional

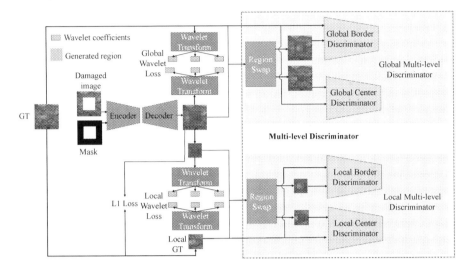

**Fig. 2.** Illustration of our proposed method. For an encoder-decoder image inpainting network, *multi-level discriminator* and *wavelet loss* are appended to the outputs of network to guide the training of generator. Here the global and local versions are used.

layers that only integrate local information. More recently, EdgeConnect (EC) [9] further improves the quality of generated images by a two-stage model, in which an edge generator is inserted before image completion network. However, these methods still suffer from serious artifacts, especially for the situation of large missing area. The work most similar to ours is PGN [25]. It proposes to progressively complete the masked area from edge to center, where multiple generators are introduced to take charge of generating different areas. Evidently, PGN would involve large memory consumption and high computational complexity, so even an image of $256 \times 256$ size is difficult to process. Our method only needs an additional discriminator during the training phase, so it does not increase the burden of memory too much.

## 2.2   Adversarial Training

Essentially, GAN acts as a min-max two-player game, which utilizes the adversarial loss to train the generator $g_\theta$ and the discriminator $D$ alternatively [7]. Here the discriminator $D$ is targeted to distinguish the generated images $I^g$ and real images $I^r$, and the generator $g_\theta$ is targeted to produce an image $I^g$ from a latent code $z$ or a corrupted image $I^c$, to cheat the discriminator $D$. In practice, the training of GANs contains two main steps. The first one is to fix the generator $g_\theta$ and train a discriminator $D$ with maximizing

$$L_D(I^r, I^g) = E_{x \sim P_r}[\log D(x)] + E_{x \sim P_g}[\log(1 - D(x))]. \qquad (1)$$

The second one is to fix the discriminator $D$ and train a generator $g_\theta$ with minimizing

$$L_g(I^g) = E_{g_\theta(x) \sim P_g}[\log(1 - D(g_\theta(x)))]. \tag{2}$$

Here $P_r$ and $P_g$ represent the distributions of the real images and generated images, respectively. Ideally, after iterative training, the distributions of generated images and real images would be nearly same. However, GANs still face huge challenge in generating high-resolution images due to unstable training procedure [13]. A similar issue actually exists for image inpainting with large missing area [20], which consequently will generate sharp artifacts. In this work, we particularly propose a multi-level discriminator and wavelet loss to alleviate the unstable optimization of GANs and meanwhile capture local details.

## 3   Our Approach

In this work, we propose a novel multi-level discriminator and wavelet loss to facilitate the training of generator networks from two different perspectives. MLD is to improve the stability of adversarial training by increasing the distribution overlap between generated and real images, and the WT loss is to improve the regularization of content consistency and generator optimization by constructing a reconstruction loss in frequency domain. Figure 2 illustrates the overall architecture of our proposed method. Note that MLD and WT are only employed in the training phase and thus do not increase the inference time.

### 3.1   Multi-level Discriminator

Before elaborating on MLD, we first briefly explain the underlying reason of GANs to produce artifacts for image inpainting with large missing area. According to [2], when the generator $g_\theta$ is fixed, the optimal discriminator is

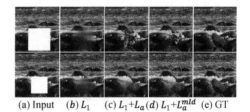

(a) Input   (b) $L_1$   (c) $L_1+L_a$ (d) $L_1+L_a^{mld}$ (e) GT

$$D^*(x) = \frac{P_r(x)}{P_r(x) + P_g(x)}. \tag{3}$$

As proven in [2], if $P_g$ and $P_r$ have no overlap (*i.e.*, are too easy to tell apart), the optimal discriminator $D^*$ cannot provide effective gradients to guide the optimization of the generator $g_\theta$. Here we provide a brief explanation. We define $U = \{x : P_r(x) > 0\}$, $\bar{U} = \{x : P_r(x) = 0\}$,

**Fig. 3.** Visual comparison of different loss functions to guide the learning of generator, where GMCNN is particularly used as the base model. $L_1$ and $L_a$ represent the $\ell_1$ loss and the global and local adversarial loss, respectively. $L_a^{mld}$ denotes our proposed MLD adversarial loss. Compared to a small area missing, a large area missing is more likely to lead to sharp artifacts and MLD can make the generated images more natural.

$V = \{x : P_g(x) > 0\}$, and $\bar{V} = \{x : P_g(x) = 0\}$. Then $D^*$ can be redefined as

$$D^*(x) = \begin{cases} 1, & \text{for } x \in U \cap \bar{V}, \\ 0, & \text{for } x \in \bar{U}, \\ \dfrac{P_r(x)}{P_r(x) + P_g(x)}, & \text{for } x \in U \cap V. \end{cases} \tag{4}$$

If $P_g$ and $P_r$ have no overlap, which means $U \cap V = \varnothing$, $D^*$ would equal to either 1 or 0. Obviously, the gradient $\nabla_x D^*(x)$ would always be zero. According to the chain rule, we have

$$\nabla_\theta L_g = \nabla_D L_g \cdot \nabla_{g_\theta(x)} D^*(g_\theta(x)) \cdot \nabla_\theta g_\theta(x) = 0. \tag{5}$$

That is, the discriminator $D^*$ cannot provide effective gradients to guide the optimization of the generator $g_\theta$. Thus $P_g$ and $P_r$ need have enough overlap so that the generator can be effectively optimized.

For image inpainting, the difference of the generated image $I^g$ and corresponding real image $I^r$ is exactly the missing region represented by a mask. When the missing area is larger, therefore, it is difficult to effectively learn a generator since the gradients provided by the discriminator would have more or less random direction [2,18]. As a result, the generated images often present some artifacts, as shown in Fig. 3(c). In this work, we exploit the information of original images to improve the optimization of generators. The key idea is to increase the overlap of $P_r$ and $P_g$ by reducing the differential area between the generated image $I^g$ and real image $I^r$. To be specific, we propose a multi-level discriminator, which decomposes the missing regions of an image into multiple parts and then separately imposes a discriminator for each part. Consequently, compared with the original discriminator over the whole missing regions, one single discriminator in MLD would possess an increased overlap between generated and real distributions due to smaller missing area to handle. Figure 3(d) shows the effect of MLD, which usually can generate more natural images, especially for the case of large missing area.

Formally, assume the generated image $I^g$ corresponds to the real image $I^r$, and the missing mask is $M$. We divide the masked region into $K$ subregions (e.g., from border to center), as shown in Fig. 4. Then we build one discriminator for each

**Fig. 4.** Illustration of the MLD masks for different shapes. Here two levels are particularly used.

subregion, i.e., $K$ discriminators would be constructed. Considering the computational complexity and inpainting performance, $K = 2$ is particularly used throughout our experiments. For such a setting, we define two virtual synthesized images $\bar{I}_c$ and $\bar{I}_b$ as

$$\bar{I}_c = M_c \odot I^g + (1 - M_c) \odot I^r, \tag{6}$$

$$\bar{I}_b = M_b \odot I^g + (1 - M_b) \odot I^r, \tag{7}$$

where $M_c$ is the central mask (we set its area as a quarter of that of the original mask $M$ in our implementation), $M_b$ is the border mask with $M = M_b \vee M_c$, and $\odot$ denotes the spatially element-wise multiplication. Note that the division from border to center is particularly used for simplicity and we can also adopt other division strategy.

Evidently, the area of different regions between $\bar{I}_c(\bar{I}_b)$ and $I^r$ is smaller than that between $I^g$ and $I^r$, implying that the distributions of $I^r$ and $\bar{I}_c(\bar{I}_b)$ have a larger overlap than that of $I^g$ and $I^r$. We use $\bar{I}_c$ and $\bar{I}_b$ to replace $I^g$ in the traditional adversarial loss separately. Then we can build a two-level discriminator. The adversarial loss functions become $L_D^{mld}$ and $L_g^{mld}$ for discriminator and generator, $i.e.$,

$$L_D^{mld} = L_D(I^r, \bar{I}_b) + L_D(I^r, \bar{I}_c), \tag{8}$$

$$L_g^{mld} = L_g(I^r, \bar{I}_b) + L_g(I^r, \bar{I}_c). \tag{9}$$

To better understand our proposed MLD, here we particularly compare MLD and GLD (Global and Local discriminator). The main difference is that GLD uses different discriminators to focus on multiple images with different scales, while MLD uses different discriminators to focus on multiple regions of the same image with different overlaps. To be specific, GLD targets to utilize multi-scale background contents, while MLD targets to increase the overlap of the distributions between generated and real images. From the perspective of implementation, GLD operates on the background regions to construct multi-scale contents, while MLD operates on the missing regions to construct different synthesized images. Therefore, GLD cannot alleviate the optimization difficulties caused by non-overlapping distributions. It often causes sharp artifacts in the case of large areas, as shown in Fig. 3(c). However, MLD can greatly alleviate this problem, as shown in Fig. 3(d). In addition, due to the existence of local discriminator, GLD is not applicable for irregular masks. But our MLD can still work well for such masks, as shown in Fig. 4.

### 3.2   Wavelet Loss

Wavelet transform can extract multi-frequency signals of images [1,10,15], and thus can model the consistency for different details. Here we introduce wavelet transform into image inpainting networks to explicitly model high frequency components, and it is shown in our experiments to work well in preventing image blurring. Note that we do not change the discriminator which still works in image space, and our proposed WT serves as a reconstruction loss to guide the optimization of generator together with adversarial loss. In our implementation, we particularly adopt the Harr wavelet for the sake of simplicity.

Formally, given an image $I$, wavelet transform decomposes it with $L$ levels, and each level $l$ consists of four types of coefficients with $C = \{C_1, C_2, C_3, C_4\}$ [10]. Then we define the wavelet loss as

$$L_{wt} = \sum_{l=1}^{L} \sum_{m \in C} \left\| \bar{w}_m^l - w_m^l \right\|_1, \tag{10}$$

where $\bar{w}_m^l$ and $w_m^l$ represent the wavelet transform coefficients of the $m$-th component in the $l$-th level for the completed image and raw one, respectively.

## 4 Experiments

In this section, we evaluate the proposed method on three challenging datasets, including CelebA-HQ faces [13], Paris StreetView [4], and Places2 [27]. In particular, we adopt the one-stage model GMCNN [20] and two-stage model CA [24] as the baseline networks due to their excellent image inpainting performance. We directly add the WT and MLD modules to CA and GMCNN, resulting in

**Table 1.** Performance comparison of different methods on the Places2 dataset. Here ↓ means the lower is better, and ↑ means the higher is better. ∗ represents our retrained model.

| | | Thin Irregular | | Thick Irregular | | Center |
|---|---|---|---|---|---|---|
| | Method | 30–40% | 40–50% | 30–50% | 50–70% | Rectangle |
| PSNR↑ | HighFill [23] | 25.839 | 24.337 | 22.488 | 21.198 | 17.142 |
| | CA [24] | – | – | | – | 18.145 |
| | EC [9] | 26.565 | 25.046 | **23.707** | 22.428 | **19.069** |
| | GMCNN [20] | 26.732 | 25.294 | 21.869 | 20.656 | – |
| | CA* [24] | – | – | | – | 17.974 |
| | CA-O | – | – | – | – | 18.931 |
| | GMCNN* [20] | 26.665 | 24.793 | 22.291 | 20.751 | 17.998 |
| | GMCNN-O | **27.146** | **25.569** | 23.679 | **22.503** | 18.877 |
| SSIM↑ | HighFill [23] | 0.877 | 0.835 | 0.802 | 0.740 | 0.459 |
| | CA [24] | – | – | – | – | 0.537 |
| | EC [9] | 0.883 | 0.847 | 0.824 | 0.771 | 0.548 |
| | GMCNN [20] | 0.891 | 0.860 | 0.813 | 0.764 | – |
| | CA* [24] | – | – | | – | 0.523 |
| | CA-O | – | – | – | – | 0.553 |
| | GMCNN* [20] | 0.889 | 0.851 | 0.820 | 0.771 | 0.549 |
| | GMCNN-O | **0.895** | **0.863** | **0.835** | **0.791** | **0.578** |
| FID↓ | HighFill [23] | 12.802 | 19.224 | 27.525 | 47.526 | 22.845 |
| | CA [24] | – | – | – | – | **7.696** |
| | EC [9] | 7.190 | 11.402 | 13.994 | 24.227 | 9.288 |
| | GMCNN [20] | 5.476 | 8.409 | 16.509 | 27.885 | – |
| | CA* [24] | – | – | | – | 9.149 |
| | CA-O | – | – | – | – | 8.231 |
| | GMCNN* [20] | 5.293 | 9.087 | 18.336 | 33.918 | 8.958 |
| | GMCNN-O | **5.122** | **7.872** | **11.703** | **18.560** | 8.011 |

GMCNN-O and CA-O. Both GMCNN and CA use the global and local discriminators for the rectangular masks, and correspondingly we replace them with the global-MLD and local-MLD. CA does not support the irregular masks due to using local discriminator, while GMCNN supports the irregular masks by adopting PatchGAN [12] as discriminator. Hence we conduct the experiments on the irregular masks only using GMCNN. For the irregular masks, we use a $16 \times 16$ kernel to corrode the masks to produce the $M_b$ and $M_c$, as shown in Fig. 4. For comparison and fairness, in all experiments, we keep the loss function of the original method unchanged.

## 4.1 Experimental Settings

## 4.2 Performance Evaluation

In this section, we evaluate our proposed method by comparing with five representative baseline methods, including High-Fill [23], GMCNN [20], EC [9] and CA [24]. For fair comparison, we retrain the baseline CA and GMCNN using our data

Fig. 5. Compared to the thick masks, the center of the thin masks is closer to the existing regions.

besides testing the models provided by authors. The retrained models are marked by $*$ in the experimental results.

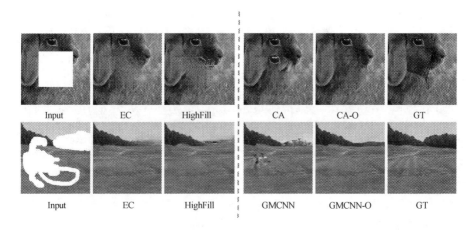

Fig. 6. Example inpainting results of different methods on Places2 with the rectangle masks.

*Quantitative  Comparison.*
We measure the quality of inpainting results using the following metrics: peak signal-to-noise ratio (PSNR), structural similarity index (SSIM), and Frchet Inception Distance (FID) [8]. For PSNR and SSIM, higher values indicate better performance, while for FID, the

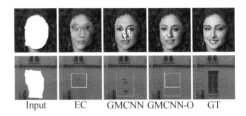

Input    EC    GMCNN  GMCNN-O    GT

**Fig. 7.** Performance of different combinations of MLD and wavelet loss.

lower the better. For Places2, 10,000 images randomly selected from the validation set for test. For Paris StreetView and CelebA-HQ, we follow GMCNN [20] to construct test set.

In order to comprehensively evaluate various methods, we test on both the rectangular masks and irregular masks. All images are resized to $256 \times 256$. For the rectangular masks, all masked holes are placed at the center of images with the size of $128 \times 128$. For the irregular masks, as shown in Fig. 5, we use the thin masks and thick masks separately. For the thin mask, the hole-to-image ratio ranges from 0.3 to 0.5. For the thick mask, the hole-to-image ratio ranges from 0.3 to 0.7.

Table 1 gives the results of different methods on the Places2 dataset, where PSNR and SSIM are computed on the hole regions for the rectangular masks and on the whole images for the irregular masks. From the results, we have the following observations. First, compared with the baseline GMCNN* and CA* using the same data, our GMCNN-O and CA-O can bring significant performance improvement, especially for the thick masks. Because in this case, the problem of non-overlapping distribution is more serious, and it can better reflect the advantages of our method. Second, GMCNN-O achieves better performance than the current state-of-the-art methods including two-stage method EC and HighFill for almost all settings of irregular masks, which shows the ability of our method to boost the advanced methods. In particular, HighFill [23] is a good method to recover the image with large-missing area. However, the key for High-Fill to reduce artifacts is that on the reduced image ($256 \times 256$), the missing area is small enough to be easily repaired. Finally, a super-resolution module can be used to obtain a inpaited image of the original size. Therefore, it requires that the proportion of the missing area on the original image cannot be large (generally not more than 25%), otherwise the reduced missing area will still be large, resulting in artifacts, as shown in Fig. 6.

*Qualitative  Comparison.* For the image inpainting task, there is no a comprehensive metric that can accurately measure the quality of completed images. Here we qualitatively compare our model with the baselines. Figure 6, Fig. 7 give some examples of different methods with different image masks. It can be seen that most of existing methods usually suffer from discontinuous structure and mutant color (black or white). Our proposed method can effectively reduce the artifacts and improve the quality of the generated images. For more results, please refer to the supplementary material.

## 4.3   Ablation Study

**Fig. 8.** Performance of different combinations of MLD and wavelet loss.

In this section, we investigate the effects of the main components of our proposed methods. Since the rectangle masks with a large hole are very challenging, we particularly use such masks with a size of 128 × 128 to conduct ablation experiments. We use the metrics PSNR, SSIM, and FID to quantitatively compare different methods. All the metrics are reported on the test set. For convenience, we put the SSIM, PSNR, and FID together with the example generated images. For fair comparison, we use retrained CA* and GMCNN* as the baseline. In the case of no ambiguity, we omit * here.

***Effect of MLD and Wavelet Loss.*** Here we evaluate the effect of our proposed MLD and wavelet loss by comparing their combinations with the baseline GMCNN and CA. To be specific, we separately impose MLD and wavelet loss to the baselines (denoted by *-MLD and *-WT respectively), and then use both of them (denoted by *-O). Particularly, we use the Place2 dataset due to its challenge. Figure 8 provides the results for different models. It can be seen that MLD and wavelet loss both contribute to the performance of image inpainting. In particular, GMCNN may produce some black and red regions, wavelet loss can provide more details, and MLD can make the images more natural. Finally, the combination of our proposed MLD and WT performs best, which can generate high-quality images.

***Number of MLD Levels.*** Here we set the level of MLD $K$ from $\{1, 2, 3, 4\}$ to analysis the impact of different MLD levels. We adopt CA with the rectangle masks as the baseline model and CelebA-HQ is used for evaluation. Figure 9 give the results of different MLD levels. Compared with the original CA (*i.e.*, $K = 1$), the MLD can significantly increase the quantity of generated images. Considering the computational complexity, we particularly adopt $K = 2$ in our experiments that actually can produce satisfactory results.

***Level of Wavelet Transform.*** In this section, we analyze the impact of each wavelet decomposition level. Here $w/o$ $WT$ represents the baseline model without wavelet loss, $w/o$ $WT$-$n$ represents the baseline model which uses 3 wavelet levels but removes the results of the $n$-th level, and $WT$-$all$ represents the baseline model with all the 3 wavelet decomposition levels. Figure 10 gives the results of different settings on CelebA-HQ. It can be seen that each wavelet level contributes to the quality of inpainting results.

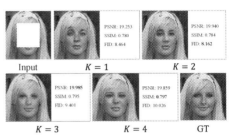

**Fig. 9.** Results of different MLD levels on CelebA-HQ.

## 5 Conclusion

In this paper, we proposed two novel techniques to improve the training of GANs for image inpainting, namely multi-level discriminator. Specifically, MLD can improve the stability of network training by increasing the distribution overlap between the generated images and real images. WT can achieve a good

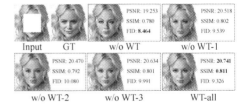

**Fig. 10.** Results of removing single wavelet level on CelebA-HQ.

trade-off between the sharpness and naturalness of generated images by exploiting the frequency-domain information as the reconstruction loss. We experimentally verified the effectiveness of the proposed MLD and WT, which can generate high-quality images for both the rectangle and irregular masks.

**Acknowledgments.** This work is supported by the National Natural Science Foundation of China under Grant 61836008 and 61673362, Youth Innovation Promotion Association CAS (2017496).

## References

1. Antonini, M., Barlaud, M., Mathieu, P., Daubechies, I.: Image coding using wavelet transform. TIP (1992)

2. Arjovsky, M., Bottou, L.: Towards principled methods for training generative adversarial networks. In: ICLR (2017)
3. Barnes, C., Shechtman, E., Finkelstein, A., Goldman, D.B.: Patchmatch: a randomized correspondence algorithm for structural image editing. TOG (2009)
4. Doersch, C., Singh, S., Gupta, A., Sivic, J., Efros, A.A.: What makes paris look like paris? TOG (2012)
5. Efros, A.A., Freeman, W.T.: Image quilting for texture synthesis and transfer. In: SIGGRAPH (2001)
6. Ghorai, M., Samanta, S., Mandal, S., Chanda, B.: Multiple pyramids based image inpainting using local patch statistics and steering kernel feature. TIP (2019)
7. Goodfellow, I., et al.: Generative adversarial nets. In: NeurIPS (2014)
8. Heusel, M., Ramsauer, H., Unterthiner, T., Nessler, B., Hochreiter, S.: Gans trained by a two time-scale update rule converge to a local nash equilibrium. In: NeurIPS (2017)
9. Hu, J., Shen, L., Sun, G.: Edgeconnect: Generative image inpainting with adversarial edge learning. In: ICCV Workshop (2019)
10. Huang, H., He, R., Sun, Z., Tan, T.: Wavelet-srnet: a wavelet-based cnn for multi-scale face super resolution. In: ICCV (2017)
11. Iizuka, S., Simo-Serra, E., Ishikawa, H.: Globally and locally consistent image completion. TOG (2017)
12. Isola, P., Zhu, J.Y., Zhou, T., Efros, A.A.: Image-to-image translation with conditional adversarial networks. In: ICCV (2017)
13. Karras, T., Aila, T., Laine, S., Lehtinen, J.: Progressive growing of gans for improved quality, stability, and variation. In: ICLR (2018)
14. Kwatra, V., Essa, I., Bobick, A., Kwatra, N.: Texture optimization for example-based synthesis. In: TOG (2005)
15. Lewis, A.S., Knowles, G.: Image compression using the 2-d wavelet transform. TIP (1992)
16. Liu, G., Reda, F.A., Shih, K.J., Wang, T.C., Tao, A., Catanzaro, B.: Image inpainting for irregular holes using partial convolutions. In: ECCV (2018)
17. Liu, J., Yang, S., Fang, Y., Guo, Z.: Structure-guided image inpainting using homography transformation. TMM (2018)
18. Odena, A., Olah, C., Shlens, J.: Conditional image synthesis with auxiliary classifier gans. In: ICML (2017)
19. Pathak, D., Krahenbuhl, P., Donahue, J., Darrell, T., Efros, A.A.: Context encoders: Feature learning by inpainting. In: CVPR (2016)
20. Wang, Y., Tao, X., Qi, X., Shen, X., Jia, J.: Image inpainting via generative multi-column convolutional neural networks. In: NeurIPS (2018)
21. Xie, J., Xu, L., Chen, E.: Image denoising and inpainting with deep neural networks. In: NeurIPS (2012)
22. Yang, Y., Guo, X.: Generative landmark guided face inpainting. In: PRCV (2020)
23. Yi, Z., Tang, Q., Azizi, S., Jang, D., Xu, Z.: Contextual residual aggregation for ultra high-resolution image inpainting. In: CVPR (2020)
24. Yu, J., Lin, Z., Yang, J., Shen, X., Lu, X., Huang, T.S.: Generative image inpainting with contextual attention. In: CVPR (2018)
25. Zhang, H., Hu, Z., Luo, C., Zuo, W., Wang, M.: Semantic image inpainting with progressive generative networks. In: ACM MM (2018)
26. Zheng, C., Cham, T.J., Cai, J.: Pluralistic image completion. In: CVPR (2019)
27. Zhou, B., Lapedriza, A., Khosla, A., Oliva, A., Torralba, A.: Places: a 10 million image database for scene recognition. TPAMI (2018)

# 3D²Unet: 3D Deformable Unet for Low-Light Video Enhancement

Yuhang Zeng, Yunhao Zou, and Ying Fu$^{(\boxtimes)}$

Beijing Institute of Technology, Beijing, China
fuying@bit.edu.cn

**Abstract.** Video recording suffers from noise, artifacts, low illumination, and weak contrast under low-light conditions. With such difficulties, it is challenging to recover a high-quality video from the corresponding low-light one. Previous works have proven that convolutional neural networks perform well on low-light image tasks, and these methods are further extended to the video processing field. However, existing video recovery methods fail to fully exploit the long-range spatial and temporal dependency simultaneously. In this paper, we propose a 3D deformable network based on Unet-like architecture (3D²Unet) for low-light video enhancement, which recovers RGB formatted videos from RAW sensor data. Specifically, we adopt a spatial temporal adaptive block with 3D deformable convolutions to better adapt the varying features of videos along spatio-temporal dimensions. In addition, a global residual projection is employed to further boost learning efficiency. Experimental results demonstrate that our method outperforms state-of-the-art low-light video enhancement works.

**Keywords:** Low-light · Video enhancement · Video processing

## 1  Introduction

Ranging from object detection to surveillance system, videos are involved in many research fields and practical applications. However, due to the limitation of the acquisition device and constrained illumination conditions, videos captured in low-light conditions always suffer from extremely low Signal-to-Noise Ratio (SNR) and cannot be directly used in downstream applications including segmentation, detection, *etc.* Thus, it is highly demanded to recover high-quality videos by enhancing low-light ones. An ideal low-light video enhancement method is supposed to recover buried details and obtain videos with normal brightness from dynamic scenes in the dark. Nevertheless, in the dark environment, due to

---

Y. Fu—Student.

**Electronic supplementary material** The online version of this chapter (https://doi.org/10.1007/978-3-030-88010-1_6) contains supplementary material, which is available to authorized users.

© Springer Nature Switzerland AG 2021
H. Ma et al. (Eds.): PRCV 2021, LNCS 13021, pp. 66–77, 2021.
https://doi.org/10.1007/978-3-030-88010-1_6

low photon counts and unwanted artifacts, low-light video enhancement turns out to be a challenging task and becomes a widely discussed topic in signal processing and computer vision communities.

Researchers have been devoted to investigating low-light imaging problems for decades. A series of traditional model-based methods have been proposed to solve this problem. These methods are generally divided into two categories: histogram equalization (HE) based methods [1,9,16,20,21,25] and Retinex theory [15] based methods [8,13,17,18,33,34]. HE based approaches aim to adjust the brightness of images to a uniform distribution while the latter one is based on the assumption that observation can be decomposed into illumination and reflection. Recently, learning-based methods have achieved better results for both low-light image and video enhancement [4,6,19,26,30]. However, these methods either train their model from the synthetic dataset or fail to fully exploit the temporal correlation between frames. More recently, researchers tend to reconstruct high-quality RGB images directly from low-light RAW sensor data [2,35], since the 8-bit RGB data fails to keep fidelity in a low-light environment compared with 14-bit RAW data. Despite significant improvement, the above works are trained on static videos or videos captured in a frame-by-frame pattern which cannot well represent real dynamic scenes.

In this paper, we propose a network named 3D$^2$Unet to solve the problem of underutilization of spatio-temporal information in low-light video enhancement tasks. To achieve this, A spatial temporal adaptive block with residual projection (RSTAB) is customized to adapt geometric transformations in dynamic videos. Inside RSTAB module, we adopt 3D deformable convolutions [32] to better capture the spatial information and temporal relationship in and between neighboring frames. Finally, we combine the RSTAB and 3D ResBlock into a Unet-shape structure [24], which performs excellent results in denoising aspects. Quantitative and qualitative experimental results on the dynamic video dataset prove that our method outperforms current algorithms in terms of metrics, visual effects and achieves state-of-the-art performance.

## 2  Related Work

In this section, we provide a brief review of related work on the low-light enhancement from aspects of image and video methods.

### 2.1  Low-Light Image Enhancement

In early explorations of low-light imagery, researchers try to recover high-quality images from the images obtained in insufficiently illuminated environments. In general, existing low-light image enhancement methods can be divided into three categories: histogram equalization (HE) based methods, retinex theory based methods, and learning based methods.

Different algorithms have been proposed to solve low-light problems, some of which are based on histogram equalization. The main idea of the HE algorithm is to balance the histogram of the entire image and adjust the intensity of the image to satisfy the uniform distribution. However, HE method always causes local oversaturation artifacts and HE-based methods [1,9,16,21,25] suffer the reduction of application scope and the increase of computational expenses.

Another series of low-light image enhancement methods are derived from retinex theory [15]. Classically, Jobson *et al.* [13] uses the Gaussian convolution function to estimate the brightness and then calculates the reflection from the known image for low-light enhancement. To obtain better performance, ASMR [17], LIME [8], BIMEF [33] are proposed based on the SSR [13] thesis. More recently, Ying *et al.* [34] utilize a camera response model to adjust each pixel in the exposure ratio map. Li *et al.* [18] take intensive noise into account to improve the performance of enhancing and proposes a robust retinex model. Generally speaking, the traditional modeling methods are limited by certain preconditions and conditions to ensure the low-light enhancement effect under specific tasks.

With the rapid development of deep learning, neural networks such as CNNs and GANs have achieved remarkable results in many low-level vision fields, including low-light enhancement. LLNet [19] shows a stacked-sparse denoising autoencoder to adaptively enhance and denoise from images while PMRID [27] designed an encoder-decoder architecture for denoise tasks. Ren *et al.* [23] propose a hybrid network with two distinct streams to simultaneously learn the global content and the salient structures of the clear image. Zero-DCE [7] formulates low-light enhancement as a task of image-specific curve estimation with a deep network. Chen *et al.* [3] proposes a low-light dataset and introduce a well-accepted U-shape network to solve low-light problems. However, these methods lack adaptability to image content and they can not tackle video tasks as well.

## 2.2 Low-Light Video Enhancement

Recently, the focus of researchers has shifted from images to more complex video data. Since videos can be regarded as composed of frames, image enhancement methods can be directly employed on videos. However, video frames are consecutive and interrelated, directly applying low-light image enhancement methods to video scenes may cause severe problems, like flickering effects and shape inconsistency. To handle these unwanted artifacts, researchers attempt to propose video-specific enhancement methods. HE based methods and retinex theory based methods are utilized to enhance video quality. Dong *et al.* [31], Jiang *et al.* [11], and Pang *et al.* [12] proposed dehazing based enhancement methods since the intensity distribution of the inverted dark video is similar to its hazy counterpart. Moreover, recent approaches prefer to use deep learning [2] to solve the problem. Though progress has been made in low-light video enhancement, the above methods omit temporal information which can be crucial and beneficial for this task. In order to solve the problem, some of the existing works, such as MBLLVEN [6], RViDeNet [35] and, Jiang *et al.* [10], use 3D convolution or multiple frames at once in their network to better capture temporal information. Even though these methods extract information in both temporal and spatial dimensions, they only focus on local feature maps

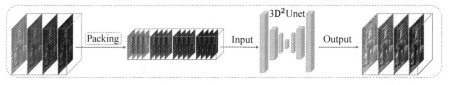

Overview of PipeLine

**Fig. 1.** An overview of our proposed low-light video enhancement pipeline.

and discard to exploit longer-range spatio-temporal dependencies. In contrast, Our method tries to adaptively extract knowledge from various videos in a more flexible manner to achieve better restoration performance.

## 3    Method

In this section, we first formulate the task of this study, then provide the overview of our RGB video generation pipeline and finally perform a detailed analysis of the proposed components.

### 3.1    Problem Formulation

Given video RAW data $I_{RAW}$ captured from an imaging sensor under low-light conditions and the ideal latent high-quality video $O_{RGB}$, our goal is to find a mapping $F(\cdot)$ that can achieve the $I_{RAW}$ to $O_{RGB}$ conversion accurately. The problem can be formulated as

$$O_{RGB} = F(I_{RAW}). \tag{1}$$

Generally, $F(\cdot)$ aims to adjust the video's dynamic range, denoise it to an acceptable level and further improve the visibility of the underlying scene details. In this work, we propose a 3D deformable convolution based architecture to enhance videos captured in the dark, which exploit features from both spatial and temporal dimensions.

### 3.2    Overview of the Pipeline

The pipeline of our proposed method is pictured in Fig. 1. It can be divided into two steps: RAW video packing and RGB video generating. RAW video packing separates different color filter arrays of RAW data into different tensor channels before sending it into the network. The video generating process is done by our proposed network. For input RAW video captured with Bayer filters, We first pack it from shape $F \times H \times W \times 1$ to shape $F \times H/2 \times W/2 \times 4$. This procedure is meant to split mixed GRBG pixels into 4 separated channels. Next, our proposed 3D Deformable UNet (3D$^2$Unet) maps the input to the RGB domain. Our model accomplishes demosaicing, white balance, gamma correction, and other

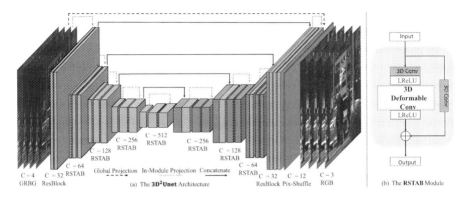

**Fig. 2.** The architecture of our proposed $3D^2$Unet network(a) and RSTAB module(b).

procedures of image signal processing pipeline, together with denoising, detail recovery, and low-light video enhancement in an end-to-end manner.

In our low-light video enhancement model, packed RAW videos are sent into an Unet-like architecture, which contains two stages, *i.e.*, the contracting path and the expansive path. In the contracting path, we use our designed spatial temporal adaptive block with residual projection (RSTAB) to better extract features from a larger receptive field. Then, in the expansive path, we also adopt our RSTAB to remove noise, reconstruct boundaries and textures, and enhance the brightness and contrast of the video. Furthermore, we introduce a long residual projection to fuse input features and output of the last convolution. Finally, a pixel-shuffle layer helps to adjust the space size and channel number of each frame to $H \times W \times 3$.

The following sections present detailed descriptions and explanations of the important network components in our architecture.

### 3.3    RSTAB Module

In this section, we introduce deformable convolution and corresponding 3D version, then, we give a detailed description of our RSTAB module.

The motivation of deformable convolution [5] is to make up the limitation of traditional convolution kernels, *i.e.*, operating at a fixed location. Given input feature map $x$, the output of a traditional convolution is calculated by the following formula

$$y(p_0) = \sum_{p_n \in R} w(p_n) \cdot x(p_0 + p_n),\tag{2}$$

where $p_0$ means a location in the output feature and $p_n$ are neighboring positions in field $R = \{(-1,-1),(-1,0),...,(0,1),(1,1)\}$. Besides, function $w(\cdot)$ denotes the weight at $p_n$. By analyzing the above formula, we can know that the traditional convolution can only sample in a fixed area $(p_0 + p_n)$, where $p_n \in R$. However, this geometry-fixed sampling method is naturally not robust to variable

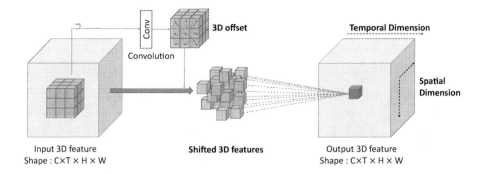

**Fig. 3.** An illustration of 3D deformable Convolution.

data, especially for videos, since the geometry of video content varies spatially and temporally.

Derived from traditional convolution, deformable convolution introduces learnable offsets to expand the sampling area. Therefore, a larger spatial receptive field and adaptive sampling grid help to improve image restoration ability. Deformable convolution is formulated as

$$y(p_0) = \sum_{p_n \in R} w(p_n) \cdot x(p_0 + p_n + \Delta p_n), \tag{3}$$

where $\Delta p_n$ is the offset value, which is learned by a parallel convolution from input features. Since $\Delta p_n$ is usually a float number, a bilinear interpolation step is adopted to generate the value at fractional positions.

However, videos are sequences of images, and different frames of the same video are highly correlated and share similar features. Thus, we are motivated to take the advantage of this characteristic to achieve better temporal continuity. Taking temporal dimension into consideration, 3D deformable convolution samples both spatially and temporally. In contrast to 2D deformable convolution, the corresponding sampling area of 3D version extends from $R$ to $G = \{(-1, -1, -1), (-1, 0, -1), ..., (0, 1, 1), (1, 1, 1)\}$ (Fig. 3).

Generally, our RSTAB process can be divided into three steps as shown in Fig. 2(b). First, the input features are fed into a 3D convolution layer with Leaky ReLU activation, while channels are simultaneously expanded or contracted. Next, a 3D deformable convolution is applied. Finally, similar to Res-Block, a residual projection is implemented to enhance the expression ability of our model. Different from ResBlock, a $1 \times 1$ 3D convolution is adopted to adapt channel changes. The process of RSTAB can be expressed as follows

$$F_{RSTAB}(x) = F_{Act}(F_{DeConv}(F_{Act}(F_{Conv_1}(x)))) + F_{Conv_2}(x), \tag{4}$$

where $F_{DeConv}(\cdot)$ is 3D deformable convolution and $F_{Conv_{1,2}}(\cdot)$ means 3D convolutions with different settings. $F_{Act}(\cdot)$ is the activation function. In our module, Leaky ReLU is used.

### 3.4   Unet Architecture with Global Projection

Previous work [2,3,29] has shown that multi-scale context aggregation networks like Unet [24] can achieve fast and effective denoising and low-light enhancement since Unet has a large receptive field and the expansive path properly fuses both low-level and high-level feature. Here, we use an Unet-like architecture to build our network. Different from the original Unet, our 3D$^2$Unet utilizes RSTAB as basic modules in both contracting path and expansive path. Moreover, a global projection from input to the feature from the last convolution layer is adopted to ease network learning.

In the last part of the network is a pixel-shuffle layer following the last convolution. Our target output is videos of size $F \times H \times W \times C$, where $C$ equals 3 for RGB videos. A 2D pixel-shuffle operation helps to expand the spatial resolution to $H \times W$.

## 4   Experiment

In this section, we first introduce training details about our experiment. Then, we compare our 3D$^2$Unet with state-of-the-art low-light video enhancement methods. Finally, we conduct a set of ablation experiments to validate the effectiveness of the proposed components.

### 4.1   Experimental Setting

We use See Moving Objects in the Dark (SMOID [10]) dataset since it consists of dynamic paired low-light RAW videos and the corresponding ground truth RGB videos. Specifically, SMOID collected 179 paired videos of street views with moving vehicles and pedestrians under different conditions, i.e., Gains from 0 to 20 at intervals of 5. Gain is the amplification factor of the signal in the analog-to-digital converter, which affects the quality of the collected image. For example, larger gain value indicates higher brightness. 125 of the video sequences are chosen as the training set, while 27 videos are served as the validation set and the rest 27 as the testing set. We randomly crop the training video with a spatial size of $256 \times 256$ (while the patch size of the corresponding gt video is $512 \times 512$), and the number of successive frames is set as 16. For data augmentation, there is only a single frame shift between consecutive input sequences, which means an original video with 200 frames is split into $200 - (16 - 1) = 185$ sub-videos. At the same time, these sub-videos are randomly flipped.

Our network is trained using ADAM optimizer [14] with mini-batch 1 and initial learning rate $5e^{-5}$. We adopt $L_1$ loss to accurately calculate errors in fine granularity. In addition, our model is implemented by using PyTorch [22] and trained with an RTX 3090 GPU. Peak Signal-to-Noise Ratio (PSNR) and Structural Similarity (SSIM [28]) are selected to measure the model's performance.

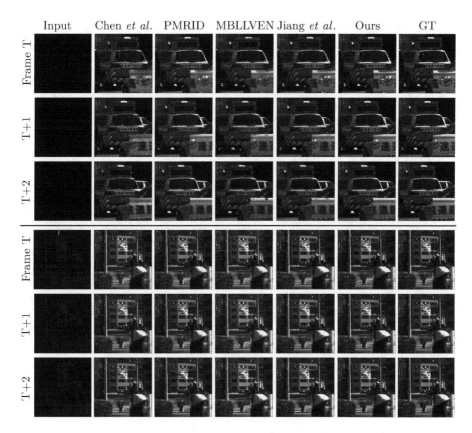

**Fig. 4.** Qualitative reconstruction results on SMOID data. The upper 3 frames are tested at Gain = 0 while the lower 3 frames are tested at Gain = 20.

## 4.2    Comparison with State-of-the-art Methods

In order to prove the effectiveness of our method, we compare with state-of-the-art low-light video enhancement approaches, including MBLLVEN [6], models proposed by Jiang *et al.* [10] and Chen *et al.* [3]. Moreover, we also compare our method with denoising method PMRID [27]. As the method proposed by Chen *et al.* [2] uses static videos in their training stage and needs customized training data, we cannot conduct it with other dataset. For fair comparison, we modify and retrained all competing methods according to the settings in Sect. 4.1. Noting that we try our best to get the best results of all compared methods. Specifically, since the original MBLLVEN [6] recover videos from RGB format input, we change the parameters of MBLLVEN's first layer to adapt our 4 channel inputs. As models in Chen *et al.* [3] and PMRID [27] are used to process single images, we train and test them in a frame-by-frame way. And we adaptively modified the last layer of the PMRID model to a pixel-shuffle layer to generate RGB output.

**Table 1.** Comparison with state-of-the-art methods. Results are measured with PSNR and SSIM. The best results are highlighted in **Bold**.

| Gain | Chen et al. [3] | | PMRID [27] | | MBLLVEN [6] | | Jiang et al. [10] | | Ours | |
|------|------|------|------|------|------|------|------|------|------|------|
| | PSNR | SSIM | PSNR | SSIM | PSNR | SSIM | PSNR | SSIM | PSNR | SSIM |
| 0 | 27.99 | 0.9147 | 27.86 | 0.9020 | 29.10 | 0.9291 | 29.64 | 0.9255 | **31.46** | **0.9462** |
| 5 | 26.82 | 0.9054 | 27.83 | 0.8996 | 26.13 | 0.9002 | 28.99 | 0.9085 | **29.05** | **0.9137** |
| 10 | 27.81 | 0.9103 | 31.05 | 0.9319 | 28.66 | 0.9330 | 31.00 | 0.9396 | **33.32** | **0.9546** |
| 15 | 28.04 | 0.8879 | 29.52 | 0.8897 | 28.81 | **0.9067** | 29.07 | 0.8992 | **29.69** | 0.9017 |
| 20 | 28.93 | 0.9181 | **30.79** | 0.9328 | 26.32 | 0.9165 | 30.55 | **0.9421** | 30.75 | 0.9408 |

The test results of the comparison method and our method under different Gain values are listed in Table 1. Generally, the proposed 3D$^2$Unet outperforms the competing methods under Gain = 0, 5, 10, 15 and finishes a close second under Gain = 20. Compared with Jiang et al. [10] and Chen et al. [3], which also utilize Unet shape architecture, our method achieves 1.82/0.06/2.30/0.62/0.20 dB, and 3.47/2.23/5.51/1.65/1.82 dB improvement (Gain 0/5/10/15/20). Compared with MBLLVEN [6], our method is 2.36/2.92/4.66/1.59/4.43 dB higher. Since the test set of Gain = 20 consists of a large series of dark and almost static scenes, PMRID [27] outperforms 0.05 dB better than ours.

Figure 4 shows a visual example of the low-light enhancement results by different methods under different Gain values. It can be observed that compared with other methods, our method has significant advantages in removing low-light video noise, recovering object shape, boundary, texture, and other details, and improving visual perception. For example, MBLLVEN [6] and PMRID [27] cannot accurately restore the color of the video. Methods of Jiang et al. [10] and Chen et al. [3] cannot remove the noise in the video and flickering artifacts appear in Chen et al. [3], since it does not take the temporal information into account. On the contrary, our method recovers the texture well and introduces temporal features to avoid discontinuity between adjacent frames. More visual comparisons are presented in the *supplementary material*.

### 4.3   Ablation Study

To verify the effectiveness of components in our model, we conduct a series of ablation experiments and all of them follow settings in Sect. 4.1. In each experiment, we independently verify the effectiveness of specific components by removing them from our complete version. The experimental results are shown in Table 2 and Fig. 5. More detailed information about the ablation experiments is in the text below.

**Residual Spatial-Temporal Adaptive Block.** In order to test the importance of RSTAB module and specify the proper location for this module, we perform four relative ablation experiments. For the first one, we replace RSTAB

**Table 2.** Ablation study of different components based on Gain values 0. Results are measured with PSNR and SSIM. The best results are highlighted in **Bold**.

| Experiment | Settings | PSNR | SSIM |
|---|---|---|---|
| RSTAB | None | 30.12 | 0.9331 |
| | Contracting path | 31.34 | 0.9426 |
| | Expansive path | 30.36 | 0.9333 |
| | Both | **31.46** | **0.9462** |
| Feature extraction | 3D conv | 30.74 | 0.9430 |
| | 3D Deformable conv | **31.46** | **0.9462** |

(a)      (b)      (c)      (d)      Ours      GT

**Fig. 5.** Qualitative reconstruction results of our ablation study on SMOID dataset with Gain = 0. Figures (a), (b), (c) and (d) correspond to the visual results of a typical scene under different settings: (a) None; (b) Contracting Path; (c) Expansive Path; (d) 3D Conv.

in the final model with two 3D convolutional layers and Leaky ReLU activation. Take it as a benchmark, we apply RSTAB to the contracting path, expansive path, and both sizes. The contrast ablation studies are either not as good as our method in denoising effect, or it will produce a variety of artifacts. In consequence, we achieve better performance by using RSTAB module on both sizes.

**Feature Extraction.** In order to prove the effectiveness of our 3D deformable convolution module in feature extraction, we replace the deformable convolution in RSTAB module with ordinary 3D convolution. Compared with the latter one, deformable convolutions do make a significant improvement qualitatively and quantitatively because spatial and temporal information is adaptively captured, as shown in Fig. 5.

## 5   Conclusion

In this paper, we propose a 3D Deformable neural network ($3D^2$Unet) for low-light video enhancement. In each step of feature extraction, $3D^2$Unet adopts 3D deformable convolution to enlarge the receptive field and adaptively extract features in both spatial and temporal dimensions. Given a RAW formatted low-light video, $3D^2$Unet outputs restored RGB video without any extra ISP. Experimental results demonstrate that our $3D^2$Unet performs better than the competing state-of-the-art methods. Nevertheless, in many application scenarios, the computing resources are limited or the process is required to be real-time, so it is necessary to design a lightweight, real-time low-light video processing model. We will explore how to extend our work to more practical applications in the future.

**Acknowledgements.** This work was supported by the National Natural Science Foundation of China under Grant No. 61827901 and No. 62088101.

# References

1. Celik, T., Tjahjadi, T.: Contextual and variational contrast enhancement. IEEE Trans. Image Process. **20**(12), 3431–3441 (2011)
2. Chen, C., Chen, Q., Do, M.N., Koltun, V.: Seeing motion in the dark. In: Proceedings of International Conference on Computer Vision (ICCV) (2019)
3. Chen, C., Chen, Q., Xu, J., Koltun, V.: Learning to see in the dark. In: Proceedings of Conference on Computer Vision and Pattern Recognition (CVPR) (2018)
4. Chen, W., Wenjing, W., Wenhan, Y., Liu, J.: Deep retinex decomposition for low-light enhancement. In: Proceedings of British Machine Vision Conference (BMVC) (2018)
5. Dai, J., et al.: Deformable convolutional networks. In: Proceedings of International Conference on Computer Vision (ICCV) (2017)
6. Lv, F., Lu, F., Wu, J., Lim, C.: Mbllen: low-light image/video enhancement using cnns. Proceedings of British Machine Vision Conference (BMVC) (2018)
7. Guo, C., et al.: Zero-reference deep curve estimation for low-light image enhancement. In: Proceedings of Conference on Computer Vision and Pattern Recognition (CVPR) (2020)
8. Guo, X., Li, Y., Ling, H.: Lime: low-light image enhancement via illumination map estimation. IEEE Trans. Image Process. **26**(2), 982–993 (2017)
9. Ibrahim, H., Pik Kong, N.S.: Brightness preserving dynamic histogram equalization for image contrast enhancement. IEEE Trans. Consum. Electron. **53**(4), 1752–1758 (2007)
10. Jiang, H., Zheng, Y.: Learning to see moving objects in the dark. In: Proceedings of International Conference on Computer Vision (ICCV) (2019)
11. Jiang, X., Yao, H., Zhang, S., Lu, X., Zeng, W.: Night video enhancement using improved dark channel prior. In: Proceedings of International Conference on Image Processing (ICIP), pp. 553–557 (2013)
12. Pang, J., Zhang, S., Bai, W.: A novel framework for enhancement of the low lighting video. In: 2017 IEEE Symposium on Computers and Communications (ISCC), pp. 1366–1371 (2017)
13. Jobson, D.J., Rahman, Z., Woodell, G.A.: Properties and performance of a center/surround retinex. IEEE Trans. Image Process. **6**(3), 451–462 (1997)
14. Kingma, D.P., Ba, J.: Adam: a method for stochastic optimization (2017)
15. Land, E.H.: The retinex theory of color vision. Sci. Am. **237**(6), 108–129 (1977)
16. Lee, C., Lee, C., Kim, C.: Contrast enhancement based on layered difference representation of 2d histograms. IEEE Trans. Image Process. **22**, 5372–5384 (2013)
17. Lee, C., Shih, J., Lien, C., Han, C.: Adaptive multiscale retinex for image contrast enhancement. In: International Conference on Signal-Image Technology Internet-Based Systems, pp. 43–50 (2013)
18. Li, M., Liu, J., Yang, W., Sun, X., Guo, Z.: Structure-revealing low-light image enhancement via robust retinex model. IEEE Trans. Image Process. **27**(6), 2828–2841 (2018)

19. Lore, K.G., Akintayo, A., Sarkar, S.: Llnet: a deep autoencoder approach to natural low-light image enhancement. Pattern Recogn. **61**, 650–662 (2017)
20. Nakai, K., Hoshi, Y., Taguchi, A.: Color image contrast enhacement method based on differential intensity/saturation gray-levels histograms. In: International Symposium on Intelligent Signal Processing and Communication Systems, pp. 445–449 (2013)
21. Ooi, C.H., Pik Kong, N.S., Ibrahim, H.: Bi-histogram equalization with a plateau limit for digital image enhancement. IEEE Trans. Consum. Electron. **55**(4), 2072–2080 (2009)
22. Paszke, A., et al.: Pytorch: an imperative style, high-performance deep learning library (2019)
23. Ren, W., et al.: Low-light image enhancement via a deep hybrid network. IEEE Trans. Image Process. **28**(9), 4364–4375 (2019)
24. Ronneberger, O., Fischer, P., Brox, T.: U-Net: convolutional networks for biomedical image segmentation. In: Navab, N., Hornegger, J., Wells, W.M., Frangi, A.F. (eds.) MICCAI 2015. LNCS, vol. 9351, pp. 234–241. Springer, Cham (2015). https://doi.org/10.1007/978-3-319-24574-4_28
25. Sheet, D., Garud, H., Suveer, A., Mahadevappa, M., Chatterjee, J.: Brightness preserving dynamic fuzzy histogram equalization. IEEE Trans. Consum. Electron. **56**(4), 2475–2480 (2010)
26. Tao, L., Zhu, C., Xiang, G., Li, Y., Jia, H., Xie, X.: Llcnn: a convolutional neural network for low-light image enhancement. In: Proceedings of Visual Communications and Image Processing (VCIP), pp. 1–4 (2017)
27. Wang, Y., Huang, H., Xu, Q., Liu, J., Liu, Y., Wang, J.: Practical deep raw image denoising on mobile devices. In: Proceedings of European Conference on Computer Vision (ECCV), pp. 1–16 (2020)
28. Wang, Z., Bovik, A., Sheikh, H., Simoncelli, E.: Image quality assessment: from error visibility to structural similarity. IEEE Trans. Image Process. **13**(4), 600–612 (2004)
29. Wei, K., Fu, Y., Yang, J., Huang, H.: A physics-based noise formation model for extreme low-light raw denoising. In: Proceedings of Conference on Computer Vision and Pattern Recognition (CVPR) (2020)
30. Xiang, Y., Fu, Y., Zhang, L., Huang, H.: An effective network with convlstm for low-light image enhancement. In: Pattern Recognition and Computer Vision, pp. 221–233 (2019)
31. Dong, X., et al: Fast efficient algorithm for enhancement of low lighting video. In: IEEE International Conference on Multimedia and Expo, pp. 1–6 (2011)
32. Ying, X., Wang, L., Wang, Y., Sheng, W., An, W., Guo, Y.: Deformable 3d convolution for video super-resolution. IEEE Signal Process. Lett. **27**, 1500–1504 (2020)
33. Ying, Z., Li, G., Ren, Y., Wang, R., Wang, W.: A new image contrast enhancement algorithm using exposure fusion framework. In: Felsberg, M., Heyden, A., Krüger, N. (eds.) CAIP 2017. LNCS, vol. 10425, pp. 36–46. Springer, Cham (2017). https://doi.org/10.1007/978-3-319-64698-5_4
34. Ying, Z., Li, G., Ren, Y., Wang, R., Wang, W.: A new low-light image enhancement algorithm using camera response model. In: Proceedings of the IEEE International Conference on Computer Vision (ICCV) Workshops (2017)
35. Yue, H., Cao, C., Liao, L., Chu, R., Yang, J.: Supervised raw video denoising with a benchmark dataset on dynamic scenes. In: Proceedings of Conference on Computer Vision and Pattern Recognition (CVPR) (2020)

# Single Image Specular Highlight Removal on Natural Scenes

Huaian Chen[1], Chenggang Hou[1], Minghui Duan[1], Xiao Tan[1], Yi Jin[1(✉)], Panlang Lv[2], and Shaoqian Qin[2]

[1] University of Science and Technology of China, Hefei, China
{anchen,wukong,dmhustc,tx2015}@mail.ustc.edu.cn, jinyi08@ustc.edu.cn
[2] FuHuang AgileDevice Co., Ltd., Hefei, China
https://www.gaosuxiangji.com/

**Abstract.** Previous methods of highlight removal in image processing have exclusively addressed images taken in specific illumination environments. However, most of these methods have limitations in natural scenes and thus, introduce artifacts to nature images. In this work, we propose a specular highlight removal method that is applicable to natural scene image. Firstly, we decompose the input image into a reflectance image and an illumination image based on Retinex theory, and show that the illumination image of natural scene is obviously different from that of commonly used experimental scene. Then, the smooth features of the input image are extracted to help estimate the specular reflection coefficient in chromaticity space. Finally, the space transformation is used to calculate the specular components and the highlight removal is achieved by subtracting the specular reflection component from the original image. The experimental results show that our method outperforms most of existing methods on natural scene images, especially in some challenging scenarios with saturated pixels and complex textures.

**Keywords:** Specular highlight removal · Natural scenes · Reflection coefficient estimation

## 1 Introduction

Recovering a high quality image from a corrupted image [1–3] plays an essential role in the follow-up visual tasks [4,5]. In these techniques, specular highlight removal, which aims at separating the specular and diffuse components from the corrupted image, is one of the key problems. To address this problem, early methods [6,7] use additional hardware outside the camera. However, these approaches usually cause serious measurement distortion. Therefore, current research tends

This research was supported in part by the National Natural Science Foundation of China 61727809 and in part by the Special Fund for Key Program of Science and Technology of Anhui Province 201903a05020022 and 201903c08020002. The first two authors contribute equally to this work.

ⓒ Springer Nature Switzerland AG 2021
H. Ma et al. (Eds.): PRCV 2021, LNCS 13021, pp. 78–91, 2021.
https://doi.org/10.1007/978-3-030-88010-1_7

to remove highlights directly from a single image using an image processing algorithm without the assistance of additional hardware. Typically, many works have been developed from the dichromatic reflection model that retains scene physical information for better results.

According to the physical properties of objects, the observed image intensity I(p) at pixel p can be represented by a dichromatic reflection model, and then can be decomposed into a diffuse reflection component D(p) representing object surface information and a specular reflection component S(p) representing light source information:

$$I(p) = D(p) + S(p) = m_d(p)\Lambda(p) + m_s(p)\Gamma(p), \tag{1}$$

where $m_d(p)$ and $m_s(p)$ denote the corresponding diffuse and specular reflection coefficients that represent the reflection ability of the object at position p. $\Lambda(p)$ and $\Gamma(p)$ denote the diffuse and specular chromaticity; the latter is usually regarded as the illumination chromaticity of ambient light.

Currently, many existing specular highlight remove algorithms [8–12] are derived from the artificial controlled experimental scenes, in which the background and specular highlight are usually unnatural. In contrast, the nature scenes are captured under a non-controlled environment, where objects are exposed to natural light. Therefore, the highlights usually emerge irregularly. As a result, the performance of the aforementioned methods on nature scenes dramatically decrease.

In this paper, in contrast to the aforementioned methods addressing artificial experimental scenes, we take natural scenes as our research object and propose a single natural scene image highlight removal method, focusing on the estimate of specular reflection coefficients based on the accurately estimated illumination chromaticity. The proposed method shows the different characteristics of highlight areas in natural scene images and experimental scene images often used in past methods. Our model provides the key smooth feature information, which is used in the specular reflection coefficient estimation in chromaticity space after normalization, and combines the intensity information with color information to avoid color distortion, thus achieving highlight removal with the dichromatic reflection model. The contributions of this paper are summarized as follows:

1. We propose a highlight removal method for natural scene image, which separates the specular reflection by fully considering the distribution characteristic of ambient light.
2. We explain the difference between the natural scene images and artificial experimental scene images often used in past methods, and propose using smooth feature information of nature scene images to estimate the specular reflection coefficient matrix.
3. The proposed model achieves very competitive highlight removal results in natural scenes. It greatly preserves the details and structural information of the original image in some challenging scenarios containing complex textures or saturated pixels.

## 2   Related Works

Specular highlight removal is a challenging problem in low level vision task. To tackle this problem, many methods have been proposed. Typically, Tan and Ikeuchi [13] proposed a method of iterating the specular component until only the diffuse component is left. They gave the concept of specular free (SF) images for the first time. The SF image contains only the diffuse component and its scene geometry is the same as the original image. By comparing pixel values of the highlight area and the adjacent regions, the maximum value of the pixel is converted to match the neighboring pixel values to achieve highlight removal. Assuming that the camera is highly sensitive, Tan and Ikeuchi [14] further discovered a method to separate the reflection components with a large number of linear equations. However, the color of objects is also affected by the material, roughness and texture. To address this problem, Shen *et al.* [15] proposed modified specular free (MSF) images. They assumed that there were only two types of pixels in MSF images, normal pixels and highlighted pixels, and then calculated the reflection components of two types of pixels using chrominance. The main disadvantage of the MSF image is that it suffers from hue-saturation ambiguity which exists in many natural images.

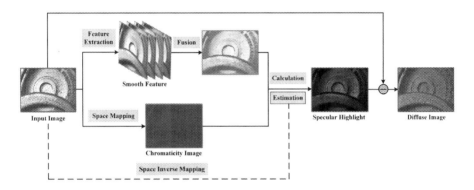

**Fig. 1.** Single natural scene image highlight removal pipeline.

Recently, the dichromatic reflection model, which fully considers the physical properties of the scene, has become the most widely used method. Klinker *et al.* [16] found that the diffusion and specularity showed T-shaped distribution in the RGB color space images and used them to remove highlights. However, it has been proven that this T-shaped distribution is susceptible to noise in practical applications and is prone to cause deformation in real images. Yang *et al.* [8,9] proposed a fast bilateral filter for estimating the maximum diffuse chrominance value in the local block of images, which caused the diffuse pixels to propagate to the specular pixels. Shen and Zheng [10] proposed the concept of pixel intensity ratio and constructed a pseudo-chrominance space to address the problem of texture surface, classifying pixels into clusters and robustly estimating the intensity ratio of each cluster. Ren *et al.* [12] introduced a color-lines constraint into the dichromatic reflection model, but it is limited to objects with dark or impure color surfaces and accurate pixel clustering cannot be achieved. Jie *et al.* [17] transformed reflection separation into a solution of a low-rank and sparse matrix on the assumption that the highlight part is sparse in images. In [18], Fu *et al.* proposed a specular highlight removal method for real-world images, but it cannot achieve well result in large white specular highlight regions because this method is based on the assumption that the specular highlight is sparse in distribution and small in size.

More recently, some deep learning based methods have been proposed to tackle this problem. Wu *et al.* [19] built a dataset in a controlled lab environment and proposed a specular highlight removal network. Fu *et al.* [20] proposed a multi-task network that jointly performs specular highlight detection and removal. These methods have achieved great performance in the man-made datasets. However, deep learning based methods rely on the training data and cannot achieve general performance in the natural scene images whose distribution are different from man-made images.

## 3   Proposed Method

In this work, we propose a single image highlight removal method for natural scenes by estimating the specular reflection coefficients:

$$D = I - E(M(I), F(T(I_c)))\Gamma, \tag{2}$$

where I represents a highlight image, $I_c$ is the input image from different channels of I, $\Gamma$ is the specular chromaticity, and D is the output diffuse image. $T(\cdot)$ denotes the low-frequency information extraction based on image decomposition. $F(\cdot)$ is the feature fusion function of all channels. $M(\cdot)$ represents the space mapping from color space to chromaticity space. $E(\cdot)$ denotes the estimation function of specular reflection coefficients. An overview of the proposed method is shown in Fig. 1. First, we extract the smooth feature components of an image by $T(\cdot)$. Simultaneously, considering the effect of colors, the decomposition is implemented in the intensity and the three color channels. The information from the four channels is normalized and combined with $F(\cdot)$ to estimate the specular reflection coefficients by our derivation $E(\cdot)$. This process also uses the transformed input image, which is generated by transforming the input image into chromaticity space using $M(\cdot)$. Finally, highlight removal is achieved by subtracting the specular reflection component from the original image I.

### 3.1   Scene Illumination Evaluation

To illustrate the difference between natural scene images and experimental scene images with highlight areas, we focus on their light distribution characteristics.

According to Retinex theory [21], a digital image can be represented as the product of reflectance and illumination. The former represents the detailed information of an image, and the latter represents the ambience light. It can be simply written as:

$$I_c(x, y) = R_c(x, y) \cdot L_c(x, y), \tag{3}$$

where $I_c(x, y)$ is the pixel intensity value at $(x, y)$ and $c$ represents color channel R, G or B. $R_c(x, y)$ and $L_c(x, y)$ are the reflectance and illumination of channel $c$, respectively. Gaussian filters are usually used to calculate $L_c(x, y)$.

In Fig. 2, we present the illuminance histogram of $L_c(x, y)$ for the experimental and natural images. The illuminance histogram counts the number of pixels in each gray level. As shown in Fig. 2, the illumination distribution in the natural scene is brighter than that in the experimental scene. The ground truth illumination should be natural and provide the best visual quality for the panorama. Related study [22] has proofed that images with an average gray value of 128 are close to the best visual effects for humans. For the given images, the average values of experimental and natural scenes are 24 and 103, respectively. For the experimental scene, a large number of pixels in the captured images are in the dark interval, and their neighboring pixels are mostly dark. This distribution is usually nonexistent in natural lighting conditions.

## 3.2  Smooth Feature Extraction

We first start with the dichromatic reflection model presented in Eq. (1). We denote $I(p) = [I_r(p), I_g(p), I_b(p)]^T$ as the intensity value of the image pixel at $p = [x, y]$. $m_d(p)$ and $m_s(p)$ are diffuse and specular reflection coefficients, respectively, which are related to surface geometry. $\Lambda(p) = [\Lambda_r(p), \Lambda_g(p), \Lambda_b(p)]^T$ is the diffuse chromaticity, and its value usually remains the same in a continuous surface with the same color. Therefore, many studies estimate diffuse chromaticity based on the assumption that it is piecewise constant. However, the surface of the object is sometimes rough with irregularities in a nature scene, and the

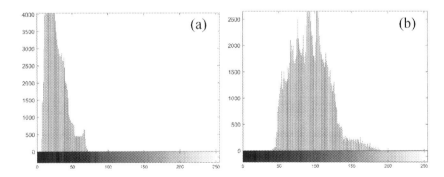

**Fig. 2.** Illuminance histograms of images from different surroundings. (a) presents the illuminance histogram of experimental scenes and (b) shows the illuminance histogram of natural scenes.

assumption is not suitable in all cases. By contrast, the illumination chromaticity $\Gamma(p) = [\Gamma_r(p), \Gamma_g(p), \Gamma_b(p)]^T$ can be estimated accurately via the color constancy algorithm in [23] or color-lines constraint in [12]. After normalization, the illumination is a white color, i.e., $\Gamma_r(p) = \Gamma_g(p) = \Gamma_b(p) = 1/3$. Thus, we focus on the estimate of the specular reflection coefficient $m_s(p)$.

In general, the observed image can be decomposed into two components: a low-frequency component called illumination and a high-frequency detail component called reflectance [24]. The former represents the ambient illumination and the later represents the details of objects [21]. In addition, in the dichromatic reflection model, the specular reflection component represents the information of ambient illumination and the diffuse reflection component represents the information of objects. Thus, the low-frequency information extracted from an image can truly reflect the intensity of the specular reflection at each pixel. The low-frequency information is the smooth feature. Moreover, the coefficient $m_s(p)$ precisely encodes the position and intensity of the specular reflection. For the low-frequency image at a certain position p, the larger the luminance value, the stronger the specular reflection, which accurately represents the intensity of the specular reflection. Therefore, we attempt to employ a low-frequency component to estimate the specular reflection coefficient $m_s(p)$. At the same time, we do not make any changes to the texture detail information.

To achieve accurate separation of the low- and high-frequency parts, we utilize the method proposed in [25]. The process of image robust sparse decomposition is shown in Fig. 3. The robust sparse representation improves the robustness to non-Gaussian noise. We first implement decomposition for the grayscale map. It can be written as follows:

$$I = W + H \quad \text{and} \quad W = NZ, \tag{4}$$

where I is an input image with highlight and N is the dictionary we construct, which mainly contains the extracted luminance information. Z is a sparse coefficient matrix in which very few element values are nonzero. NZ composes the low-frequency intensity information image W. H is the error matrix, containing edge and texture detail information. To construct a dictionary, we slide a small patch with a fixed step on the input image to obtain image blocks. Then, after vectorizing each block, all vectors form a vectorization matrix. Finally, the dictionary N is obtained by normalizing the vectorization matrix. We set the size of the patch to 1/10 of the image size through a large number of experiments. For an image of size $150 \times 150$, the patch size is set to $15 \times 15$. Thus, the sparse decomposition problem can be transformed into the following optimization problem with an equality constraint:

$$\min_{Z,H} \ \|Z\|_0 + \lambda\|H\|_{2,0} \quad \text{s.t. } I = NZ + H, \tag{5}$$

in which $\|\cdot\|_0$ denotes the $l_0$ norm of the matrix Z, which counts the number of nonzero entries in the matrix. $\|\cdot\|_{2,0}$ denotes the $l_2$ norm of the matrix H, which describes sample specific error terms and outliers. The parameter $\lambda$ is used to

**Fig. 3.** The process of image robust sparse decomposition. The former denotes the low-frequency area, and the latter denotes the high-frequency area, which is rescaled for visualization.

balance the effect of different components. We can adjust the proportion of the two components by changing $\lambda$. While $\lambda$ is larger, matrix H has less texture detail information, and more illuminance information is contained in matrix NZ. The appropriate value of $\lambda$ is discussed in our experiment section.

However, the $l_0$ norm is highly nonconvex, and there is no efficient solution available. To make the optimization tractable, we relax it via replacing $\|\cdot\|_0$ with $\|\cdot\|_1$ and $\|\cdot\|_{2,0}$ with $\|\cdot\|_{2,1}$, and Eq. (5) can be formulated as the following convex optimization problem:

$$\min_{Z,H} \|Z\|_1 + \lambda\|H\|_{2,1} \quad \text{s.t. } I = NZ + H, \tag{6}$$

where $\|\cdot\|_1$ denotes the $l_1$ norm of the matrix, which can be calculated as follows:

$$\|Z\|_1 = \sum_k \sum_j |Z(j,k)|$$
$$\|H\|_{2,1} = \sum_k \sqrt{\sum_j H(j,k)^2}, \tag{7}$$

where $(j,k)$ denotes the position of an element in matrix Z and H. Many efficient algorithms have been developed to solve this convex optimization problem, among which the linearized alternating direction method with the adaptive penalty (LADMAP) [26,27] is widely used. Then Z and H can be obtained, and W can be calculated by multiplying matrix N and Z.

### 3.3   Coefficient Estimation and Highlight Removal

We first decompose the grayscale map into the low-frequency part and the high-frequency part. However, the grayscale map contains only luminance information without any color information. It causes color distortion in the diffuse reflection part after separation when we use only the luminance to estimate the specular reflection coefficient $m_s(p)$. To preserve the original color of the input image, robust sparse decomposition is implemented in three color channels: R, G, and B. Then, the information of these channels is combined as the final low-frequency component. At the same time, we assign weights to each W of the three color channels to fully consider the contribution of different colors at each pixel, which benefits from that our estimation of the reflection coefficient is based on global information. The weight can be calculated as:

$$\omega_c(\mathrm{p}) = \frac{I_c(\mathrm{p})}{I_r(\mathrm{p}) + I_g(\mathrm{p}) + I_b(\mathrm{p})}, \tag{8}$$

where $c$ represents color channel R or G or B. The final W can be written as follows:

$$\mathrm{W} = \frac{\mathrm{W}_U + \omega_R \cdot \mathrm{W}_R + \omega_G \cdot \mathrm{W}_G + \omega_B \cdot \mathrm{W}_B}{4}. \tag{9}$$

where $\mathrm{W}_U$, $\mathrm{W}_R$, $\mathrm{W}_G$, $\mathrm{W}_B$ denote the low-frequency information extracted in grayscale and three color channels, respectively. For the final low-frequency intensity image W at a certain position, the larger the value, the stronger the specular reflection, and the larger the value of $m_s(\mathrm{p})$. However, it is difficult to determine the specific interval of $m_s(\mathrm{p})$. Therefore, we use chromatic space to solve this problem. Chromaticity is usually defined as the function of component $C(\mathrm{p})$:

$$C(\mathrm{p}) = \frac{I(\mathrm{p})}{\sum_{c \in \{r,g,b\}} I_c(\mathrm{p})}. \tag{10}$$

Substituting (1) into (10), $C(\mathrm{p})$ can be written as follows:

$$C(\mathrm{p}) = \frac{m_d(\mathrm{p})}{\sum_{c \in \{r,g,b\}} I_c(\mathrm{p})} \Lambda(\mathrm{p}) + \frac{m_s(\mathrm{p})}{\sum_{c \in \{r,g,b\}} I_c(\mathrm{p})} \Gamma(\mathrm{p}). \tag{11}$$

Then, chromaticities $\Lambda(\mathrm{p})$ and $\Gamma(\mathrm{p})$ are normalized, i.e., $\sum_{c \in \{r,g,b\}} \Lambda_c(\mathrm{p}) = 1$ and $\sum_{c \in \{r,g,b\}} \Gamma_c(\mathrm{p}) = 1$. After that, combining with Eq. (1), the sum of the pixel intensities of the three channels can be expressed as:

$$\sum_{c \in \{r,g,b\}} I_c(\mathrm{p}) = m_d(\mathrm{p}) + m_s(\mathrm{p}). \tag{12}$$

As a result, chromaticity can be written as the following:

$$C(\mathrm{p}) = \frac{m_d(\mathrm{p})}{m_d(\mathrm{p}) + m_s(\mathrm{p})} \Lambda(\mathrm{p}) + \frac{m_s(\mathrm{p})}{m_d(\mathrm{p}) + m_s(\mathrm{p})} \Gamma(\mathrm{p}). \tag{13}$$

This process can be deemed as normalizing the reflection coefficient to the $[0, 1]$ interval. $m_s(\mathrm{p})$ has strong relationship with the W. To simplify the estimation of $m_s(\mathrm{p})$, we directly use W to approximate $m_s(\mathrm{p})$. Moreover, to avoid over separation or incomplete separation of the specular reflection, the estimation is written as:

$$\frac{m_s(\mathrm{p})}{m_d(\mathrm{p}) + m_s(\mathrm{p})} = \alpha\, \mathrm{W}, \tag{14}$$

where $\alpha$ is an adjustable parameter, whose range is $[0, 1]$. In this work, we empirically set the value of $\alpha$ to 0.6, and present the detailed discussion in the experiment section. Thus, the specular reflection component $S(\mathrm{p})$ can be obtained with Eq. (12), (13) and (14). The image after highlight removal can be obtained by subtracting the specular component from the original image.

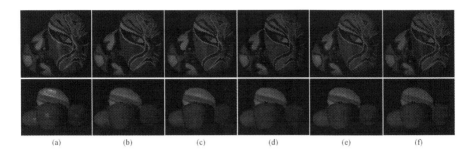

**Fig. 4.** Diffuse components of experimental scene images *Masks* and *Fruits*. (a) Input highlight images, (b) ground truths, (c) results of [10], (d) results of [12], (e) results of [17], (f) ours. (Color figure online)

**Table 1.** Quantitative comparison in terms of PSNR and SSIM for the images in Fig. 4

| Image | Method | | | | | | | |
|-------|--------|------|------|------|------|------|------|------|
|       | PSNR   |      |      |      | SSIM |      |      |      |
|       | [10]   | [12] | [17] | Ours | [10] | [12] | [17] | Ours |
| *Masks*  | 33.9 | 30.0 | 34.4 | **34.5** | 0.941 | 0.913 | 0.955 | **0.968** |
| *Fruits* | **39.2** | 37.5 | 36.4 | 37.1 | 0.960 | 0.952 | 0.930 | **0.976** |

**Table 2.** Quantitative comparison in terms of PSNR and SSIM for the images from SPEC database.

| Image | Method | | | | | | | |
|-------|--------|------|------|------|------|------|------|------|
|       | PSNR   |      |      |      | SSIM |      |      |      |
|       | [9]    | [10] | [12] | Ours | [9]  | [10] | [12] | Ours |
| *Woodlego* | 20.3 | 19.0 | 21.3 | **25.9** | 0.508 | 0.463 | 0.472 | **0.601** |
| *Vase* | 13.5 | 14.6 | 14.9 | **26.0** | 0.053 | 0.134 | 0.114 | **0.550** |
| *Wire* | 15.2 | 16.7 | 17.2 | **24.2** | 0.142 | 0.246 | 0.288 | **0.701** |
| *Key*  | 14.5 | 12.8 | 12.9 | **21.7** | 0.169 | 0.176 | 0.175 | **0.478** |

## 4    Experiments

In this section, we evaluate the highlight removal performance of our method compared with currently effective methods. Following methods in [12,17], we first use some commonly used laboratory images to perform quantitative comparisons. Then, some typical natural images, which include some challenging scenarios with rough surfaces, saturated pixels, and complex textures, are used to perform visual comparisons. Note that, real-world natural images have no ground truth. Therefore, we do not provide the quantitative results. In addition, the related state-of-the-art methods [1,18] do not release their codes. Therefore, it is hard for us to provide the comparison results of these methods.

## 4.1   Quantitative Comparison on Laboratory Images

We first show the separation results of experimental scene images under a black background, which was often used in past methods. Figure 4 shows *Masks* with pure and multicolored surfaces. The methods proposed in [10], [12], and [17] all create new artifacts while removing highlights on the yellow region of the mask on the left. The method in [12] makes the result darker due to over separation of the specular component. In contrast, our method removes highlights better in the yellow and blue regions that are closer to the ground truth. The captured surface of our result looks smoother and more continuous, which is why our method produces the highest PSNR and SSIM values as shown in Table 1. For the *Fruits* image, our method does not achieve the best separation results but produces the highest SSIM, which demonstrates our competitiveness compared with other methods in that we retain the original structure of the image to the greatest extent.

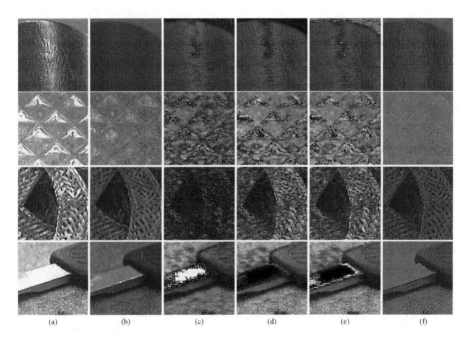

**Fig. 5.** Diffuse components of images close to natural scene *Woodlego, Vase, Wire,* and *Key.* (a) Input highlight images, (b) ground truths, (c) results of [8], (d) results of [10], (e) results of [12], (f) ours.

Moreover, we use the challenging images from the SPEC database to perform quantitative and qualitative comparisons. These images are taken under ambient light conditions created in the laboratory, which is closer to the natural scene but somewhat extreme. As shown in Fig. 5, the methods of *bilateral filtering* [8] and *intensity ratio* [10] introduce a large number of black and white noise points to the images during highlight removal, impairing the original image structure even in a single-color surface. The *color-lines constraint* method [12] tends to generate blur images because it is based on diffuse reflection pixel clustering. For scenes with unclear color or some metal surfaces, it is difficult to cluster pixels through only the chromaticity, and most of the image details are lost. In contrast, our method achieves good results in all these scenarios. Specifically, the proposed method can preserve the original structure and retain more edge details. For the severely overexposed scenes, the proposed method can still remove the specular highlight without introducing any artifacts and impairing image structure. For these challenging scenes, the proposed method produces the highest PSNR and SSIM values and is far better than other methods, as shown in Table 2.

### 4.2   Visual Effect Comparison on Natural Scene Images

Finally, we show the performance in natural scenes to further validate the superiority of our method. These images are taken under natural illumination from [12] and [17]. As ground truth results are unavailable, we provide a visual appearance comparison in Fig. 6. The method in [17] always achieves better highlight removal results than others. However, they are all inclined to degrade details and introduce additional artifact noise as shown in the red boxes. As illustrated in the first row of Fig. 6, the proposed method achieves more natural highlight removal, and the words on the *plate* are the clearest. For multicolored surfaces shown in the second row, our method produces pleasing visual result. The transition between highlight and nonhighlight regions is very natural, without the blurry edge that exists in other methods. In the third row, we not only remove highlights on the main object lock, but also on the background. The texture details in the background are optimally recovered through our method. Moreover, as shown in the fourth row, compared with other methods, the leaves recovered by the proposed method are more nature and colorful. In summary, the proposed method can produce better highlight removal results for nature scene images, which demonstrates its superiority.

### 4.3   Discussion of Important Parameters

*The Effect of Balance Parameter* $\lambda$. Parameter $\lambda$ is used to balance the effect of low-frequency and high-frequency components. When $\lambda$ is larger, less high-frequency information and more low-frequency information are separated. In Fig. 7(a), we observe the trend of PSNR when $\lambda$ changes. Generally, PSNR shows an upward tendency with increasing $\lambda$, and there are few fluctuations between them. When $\lambda > 1.5$, the PSNR values are slightly downward. Intuitively, when $\lambda$ is small, high-frequency is excessively separated, resulting in a lack of information used for estimation; the image after separation is partially blurred. However, when $\lambda > 1.5$, very few high-frequency parts are separated, and low-frequency estimation does not preserve texture details very well. The maximum PSNR

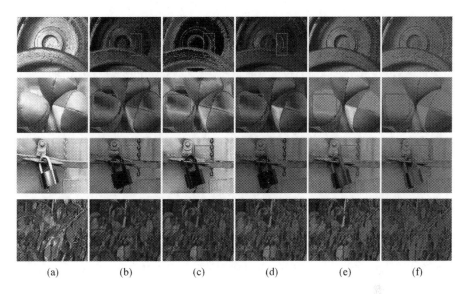

|  (a)  |  (b)  |  (c)  |  (d)  |  (e)  |  (f)  |

**Fig. 6.** Highlight removal results for natural scene image. (a) Input highlight images, (b) results of [8], (c) results of [10], (d) results of [12], (e) results of [17], (f) ours. (Color figure online)

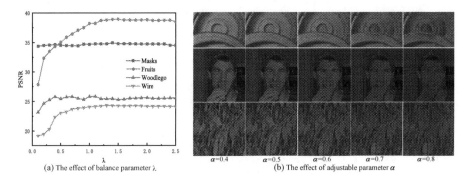

(a) The effect of balance parameter λ.      (b) The effect of adjustable parameter $\alpha$

**Fig. 7.** Discussion of important parameters

values appear in $\lambda \in [1.1, 1.5]$. In this work, $\lambda$ is set to 1.4 and this value works well for most of the highlight images.

*The Effect of Adjustable Parameter $\alpha$.* Figure 7(b) shows the visual comparisons of natural images with different $\alpha$. Larger $\alpha$ makes the image darker, while smaller $\alpha$ makes the specular reflection cannot be completely separated. When $\alpha$ is 0.6, the proposed method achieves relatively better visual result. Although $\alpha = 0.6$ may not be very accurate, it has little impact on the final result.

## 5    Conclusion

In this paper, we proposed an effective method for removing specular highlights focusing on captured natural scene images. The background and the distribution characteristics of ambient light are fully considered and the difference between the natural scene and the experimental scene is explained. We first constructed smooth feature images based on robust sparse decomposition. Then, we combined the smooth feature information with three color channels' information, and assigned different weights according to the contributions of different colors at each pixel to ensure that the color is not distorted. Finally, we converted the image into the chromaticity space, where the normalized smooth feature can be used as an accurate estimate of the specular reflection coefficient. Our method achieved very pleasing highlight removal results in natural scene images. It can preserve the original structure information and details of images. However, our method could not detect subtle bright spots or recover information that has been damaged by highlights, which will be addressed in future work.

## References

1. Son, M., Lee, Y., Chang, H.S.: Toward specular removal from natural images based on statistical reflection models. IEEE Trans. Image Process. **29**, 4204–4218 (2020)
2. Chen, H., Jin, Y., Duan, M., Zhu, C., Chen, E.: DOF: a demand-oriented framework for image denoising. IEEE Trans. Industr. Inform. **17**(8), 5369–5379 (2021)
3. Chen, H., Jin, Y., Xu, K., Chen, Y., Zhu, C.: Multiframe-to-multiframe network for video denoising. IEEE Trans. Multimedia, 1–15 (2021)
4. Zhu, T., Xia, S., Bian, Z., Lu, C.: Highlight removal in facial images. In: Proceedings of the Chinese Conference on Pattern Recognition and Computer Vision (PRCV), pp. 422–433 (2020)
5. Chen, H., Jin, Y., Jin, G., Zhu, C., Chen, E.: Semisupervised semantic segmentation by improving prediction confidence. IEEE Trans. Neural Netw. Learn. Syst., 1–13 (2021)
6. Umeyama, S., Godin, G.: Separation of diffuse and specular components of surface reflection by use of polarization and statistical analysis of images. IEEE Trans. Pattern Anal. Mach. Intell. **26**(5), 639–647 (2004)
7. Wang, F., Ainouz, S., Petitjean, C., Bensrhair, A.: Specularity removal: a global energy minimization approach based on polarization imaging. Comput. Vis. Image Underst. **158**, 31–39 (2017)
8. Yang, Q., Wang, S., Ahuja, N.: Real-time specular highlight removal using bilateral filtering. In: Daniilidis, K., Maragos, P., Paragios, N. (eds.) ECCV 2010. LNCS, vol. 6314, pp. 87–100. Springer, Heidelberg (2010). https://doi.org/10.1007/978-3-642-15561-1_7
9. Yang, Q., Tang, J., Ahuja, N.: Efficient and robust specular highlight removal. IEEE Trans. Pattern Anal. Mach. Intell. **37**(6), 1304–1311 (2015)
10. Shen, H.-L., Zheng, Z.-H.: Real-time highlight removal using intensity ratio. Appl. Opt. **52**(19), 4483–4493 (2013)
11. Suo, J., An, D., Ji, X., Wang, H., Dai, Q.: Fast and high quality highlight removal from a single image. IEEE Trans. Image Process. **25**(11), 5441–5454 (2016)

12. Ren, W., Tian, J., Tang, Y.: Specular reflection separation with color-lines constraint. IEEE Trans. Image Process. **26**(5), 2327–2337 (2017)
13. Tan, R., Ikeuchi, K.: Separating reflection components of textured surfaces using a single image. IEEE Trans. Pattern Anal. Mach. Intell. **27**(2), 178–193 (2005)
14. Tan, R., Ikeuchi, K.: Reflection components decomposition of textured surfaces using linear basis functions. In: Proceedings of the IEEE Conference on Computer Visual Pattern Recognition (CVPR), vol. 1, pp. 125–131 (2005)
15. Shen, H.-L., Zhang, H.-G., Shao, S.-J., Xin, J.H.: Chromaticity-based separation of reflection components in a single image. Pattern Recognit. **41**(8), 2461–2469 (2008)
16. Klinker, G.J., Shafer, S.A., Kanade, T.: The measurement of highlights in color images. Int. J. Comput. Vis. **2**(1), 309–334 (1992)
17. Guo, J., Zhou, Z., Wang, L.: Single image highlight removal with a sparse and low-rank reflection model. In: Ferrari, V., Hebert, M., Sminchisescu, C., Weiss, Y. (eds.) ECCV 2018. LNCS, vol. 11208, pp. 282–298. Springer, Cham (2018). https://doi.org/10.1007/978-3-030-01225-0_17
18. Fu, G., Zhang, Q., Song, C., Lin, Q., Xiao, C.: Specular highlight removal for real-world images. Comput. Graph. Forum. **38**(7), 253–263 (2019)
19. Wu, Z., Zhuang, C., Shi, J., Xiao, J., Guo, J.: Deep specular highlight removal for single real-world image. In: SIGGRAPH Asia, pp. 1–2. ACM (2020)
20. Fu, G., Zhang, Q., Zhu, L., Li, P., Xiao, C.: A multi-task network for joint specular highlight detection and removal. In: Proceedings of the IEEE/CVF Conference on Computer Visual Pattern Recognition (CVPR), pp. 7752–7761 (2021)
21. Wang, S., Zheng, J., Hu, H.-M., Li, B.: Naturalness preserved enhancement algorithm for non-uniform illumination images. IEEE Trans. Image Process. **22**(9), 3538–3548 (2013)
22. Yefeng, H., Bo, L., Jin, Z., Bai, Y.: An adaptive image enhancement based on the vector closed operations. In: Proceedings of the International Conference on Image and Graphics (ICIG), pp. 75–80 (2007)
23. Tan, T., Nishino, K., Ikeuchi, K.: Illumination chromaticity estimation using inverse-intensity chromaticity space. In: Proceedings of the IEEE Conference on Computer Visual Pattern Recognition (CVPR), vol. 1, pp. 673–680 (2003)
24. Cai, J., Gu, S., Zhang, L.: Learning a deep single image contrast enhancer from multi-exposure images. IEEE Trans. Image Process. **27**(4), 2049–2062 (2018)
25. Wright, J., Yang, A., Ganesh, A., Sastry, S., Ma, Y.: Robust face recognition via sparse representation. IEEE Trans. Pattern Anal. Mach. Intell. **31**(2), 210–227 (2009)
26. Lin, Z., Liu, R., Su, Z.: Linearized alternating direction method with adaptive penalty for low-rank representation. In: Proceedings of the Advances in Neural Information Processing Systems (NeurIPS), pp. 612–620 (2011)
27. Zhang, Y., Jiang, Z., Davis, L.S.: Learning structured low-rank representations for image classification. In: Proceedings of the IEEE Conference on Computer Vision and Pattern Recognition (CVPR), pp. 676–683 (2013)

# Document Image Binarization Using Visibility Detection and Point Cloud Segmentation

Jianhong Li[1]([✉]), Yan Chen[2], and Siling Liu[2]

[1] Guangzhou Key Laboratory of Multilingual Intelligent Processing,
Guangzhou 510006, China
[2] School of Information Science and Technology,
Guangdong University of Foreign Studies, Guangzhou 510006, China

**Abstract.** In order to solve the problems of degradation, uneven illumination, and shadows in the process of binarization of document images, two approaches were proposed. In this paper, many state of the art were deeply studied and an improved scheme were proposed. According to position and intensity information of each pixel in the document image, the image was mapped into 3D space. The visibility detection technology of 3D point cloud combined with convex hull calculation was used to extract background of the image and enhance the input image of any binarization algorithm. Based on this, the authors proposed another new binarization algorithm to remove shadows, in which does not need special illumination uniformity solution or shadow removal algorithm. The algorithm can generate binary images in one step. Document images with shadows were mapped into 3D space, the characteristic of the point cloud was distinctly hierarchical. The idea used its hierarchy in 3D space to calculate the set of points at convex hull several times, then selected the non-text points and segmented them from the text, and then obtained the binary image. The experimental results demonstrated the effectiveness of the two algorithms.

**Keywords:** Document image · Binarization · Shadow removing · Visibility detection · Point cloud segmentation

## 1 Introduction

In OCR (Optical Character Recognition), the characters of the color document image are difficult to recognize, due to the sheer volume of information contained in the color image, so image binarization is required. Binary images greatly reduce the amount of information contained in the original image, highlight the contours of the target, thus improve the efficiency and accuracy of recognition processing.

This research was financially supported by Guangdong university students' scientific and technological innovation training project (No.pdjh2021b0178).

ⓒ Springer Nature Switzerland AG 2021
H. Ma et al. (Eds.): PRCV 2021, LNCS 13021, pp. 92–104, 2021.
https://doi.org/10.1007/978-3-030-88010-1_8

In daily life, researchers encounter books, newspapers, leaflets, and other document images that containing a lot of text regularly. These realistic document images generally include different degrees of defects, such as stains, spots, ink bleeding, and various degradations [3,6,14,15,23]. Document images captured with cameras are prone to be uneven illumination due to the presence of multiple light sources, such as sunlight, indoor lighting, and shadows caused by various occlusions [1,5,16]. These problems lead to great obstacles in the binarization process of document images. The appearance and nature of these problems are different. In previous processing methods, each problem was solved by a special algorithm.

In previous binarization approaches, Su et al. [23] described a adaptive local thresholding binarization method by constructing local contrast images and text handwriting edge detection. The authors of [20,21] proposed a local adaptive binarization method that used local information to compute thresholds. Subsequently, Bukhari et al. [2] improved the method proposed in [21] by introducing an automatic parameter adjustment algorithm that used local information. Howe et al. [6] classified text pixels from background pixels by automatically adjusting the parameters and used the global energy function as a loss function. Kligler et al. [12] used the visibility information of point clouds to enhance document images. They used the *TPO (Target-Point Occlusion)* operator [9] to optimize the input image so that the background of the input image is cleaner, and they created a low-light map that gives better results to other binarization algorithms.

For document images with shadows, the usual approach is to remove the shadows using a shadow removal algorithm [1,5,7,12,13,16] before binarization. [1,16] created a shadow mask based on the global and local intensity information of the image, and combined the shadow mask with the image to remove the shadow through certain calculations. In [12], both TPO operator and *HPR (Hidden Point Removal)* operator [9–11] were used to improve the algorithm of [1] by generating shadow masks that contain only intensity information.

In this paper, two binarization approaches were proposed, which were applicable to the vast majority of document images with different defects. Our approach captured the characteristics of document images in 3D space. The first idea added a loop to the algorithm of [12]. The addition of the loop to the original algorithm allowed it to select more valid background points, it's not the same as repeating the original algorithm multiple times, the algorithm in this paper is more efficient and achieves better results. The second idea was to segment the background from the image by a surface. The surface which obtained by adding a target point to the 3D point cloud of the image and computing the convex hull of the point cloud several times.

In summary, the main contributions of this paper are: 1) The characteristics of document images in 3D space were grasped, and an improved scheme was proposed for the previous algorithm. 2) A new document image binarization method based on point cloud segmentation was proposed, which revealed the new characteristics of document image in 3D space and provided new ideas for the combination of visibility detection and document image processing.

## 2    TPO(Target-Point Occlusion)

TPO is a dual operator of HPR, in this paper we only use the TPO operator. The TPO operator is used to detect Occluding Points [9] of a point cloud. As shown in Fig. 1, given a point cloud $P$ (gray) and a target point $C$ (red), the TPO operator finds a subset of $P$ (black). The observer (blue) observes $C$ from infinity, and the black points are the points occluding $C$. TPO operator consists of two parts. 1) Point cloud transformation and deformation. 2) Calculation of convex hull.

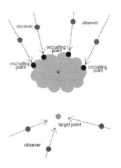

**Theorem 1.** *Given a point set $P$ and a target point $C$, a point $P_i \in P$ is an occluding point to $C$, if $P_i$ is visible to some observer located in $O = C + u\frac{P_i-C}{|P_i-C|}$ where $u > sup_{p_j \in P}\langle p_j - C, \frac{P_i-C}{|P_i-C|}\rangle$.*

**Fig. 1.** TPO schematic. (Color figure online)

### 2.1    Point Cloud Transformation

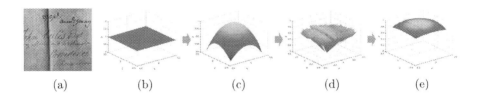

| (a) | (b) | (c) | (d) | (e) |

**Fig. 2.** Point cloud transformation 1.

To apply TPO operator in 2D images requires the transformation from 2D image to 3D point cloud. As shown in Fig. 2, Fig. 2(a) shows the gray-scale document image to be transformed. Create a 3D planar point cloud in Fig. 2(b) and match the position of this planar point cloud with each pixel of the document image, then restrict the length and width of this plane to a range. The plane is mapped to the polar coordinate system $(r_i, \theta_i, \phi_i)$, such that all $r_i = 1$ obtain $(1, \theta_i, \phi_i)$, i.e. Figure 2(c). Based on the gray value of each pixel of the gray-scale image $I_i$ calculate the new radius $r_i$:

$$r_i = \alpha_1 * I_i + \alpha_0 \tag{1}$$

where $\alpha_0$ and $\alpha_1$ are parameters. The transformed point cloud is in the shape of a mountain range in Fig. 2(d). When the value of $\alpha_0$ is large, the low intensity pixel points i.e. the points at bottom of the valley are far away from the origin. When the value of $\alpha_1$ is large, the concave and convex of the point cloud are more obvious, the difference between the height of mountains increases. In different applications, value settings for $\alpha_0$ and $\alpha_1$ vary, $\alpha_0$ and $\alpha_1$ are generally fixed in the same dataset.

Based on Fig. 2(d), the point cloud is squeezed upward using *spherical flipping* [8]. The transformation formula is:

$$F_\gamma(P_i) = P_i||P_i||^{\gamma-1} \tag{2}$$

where $P_i$ is coordinate of the point, and $\gamma$ is parameter. When $\gamma > 0$ Eq. 2 presents the TPO operator, and when $\gamma < 0$ the HPR operator is presented. Only the TPO operator is used in this paper, so we set $\gamma > 0$. $\gamma$ determines the degree to which the point cloud is squeezed by the algorithm. As $\gamma$ approaches 0, the point cloud approaches a surface with no thickness, and the more occluding points can be detected. The point cloud in Fig. 2(d) is calculated by Eq. 2, then the target point (red point) is added to obtain Fig. 2(e).

## 2.2 Convex Hull

The Convex Hull is a concept in computational geometry. Let $D$ be an arbitrary subset of Euclidean space $R^n$. The smallest convex set containing $D$ is called a convex hull of $S$. The convex hull of point cloud $D$ refers to a minimum convex polygon that satisfies the point in $D$ or on or within the polygon edge. For a 2D point cloud, convex hull can be vividly described as a convex polygon encasing the point cloud.

**Fig. 3.** 2D convex hull in TPO.

**Theorem 2.** *For a set $D$, all convex combinations of any finite points in $D$ are called convex hull of $D$.*

Figure 3 shows the application of TPO operator in a 2D point cloud. The red one is the target point, and the blue points are the detected occluding points after spherical flipping. Only the back side points of the rabbit are detected. The same principle applies to 3D point clouds. Figure 4(c) is obtained by calculating its convex hull on Fig. 4(b). The result obtained in a 3D point cloud is a polyhedron that has the smallest surface area in the polyhedron wrapping all the points. In Fig. 4(c), the intersection of many black lines at the top is the point needed for the algorithm. In order to facilitate the display and understanding, only a small number of points are selected in Fig. 4. Because in practical applications, too

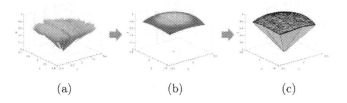

(a)                    (b)                    (c)

**Fig. 4.** 3D convex hull in TPO

many black lines make it difficult for human visual senses to identify them. Only when the curvature of the point at that place is higher than the threshold $k$, the point will be detected as an occluding point.

$$k > \frac{\gamma(1-\gamma)sin(\beta)(cos^2(\beta) - \gamma sin^2(\beta))}{d(\gamma^2 sin^2(\beta) + cos^2(\beta))^{\frac{3}{2}}} \tag{3}$$

where $\gamma$ is the parameter in Eq. 2, $\beta$ is the angle between the surface normal and the line of sight, $d$ is the distance between the surface and the target point.

## 3    Algorithm

### 3.1    Binarization

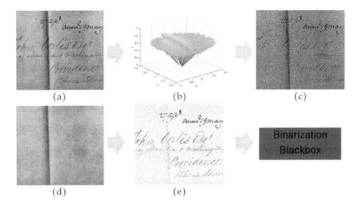

(a)    (b)    (c)

(d)    (e)

**Fig. 5.** Binarization process.

The first binarization algorithm is an improvement of the previous binarization algorithm. The idea of it is to use the coordinate information of the image pixels to spread each pixel evenly onto a 3D unit sphere. Then the distance of each pixel point to the center of the sphere is set according to the intensity of them. Points with lower intensity are seted closer to the center of the sphere, while points with higher intensity are seted further away from the center of the sphere. The transformed 3D point cloud is in the shape of uneven mountains, with the pixel points corresponding to the text located in the low valley area and the background pixels with higher intensity at the top of the mountain peaks. Figure 5(a) is the input image, and Fig. 5(b) is the transformed 3D point cloud. Clearly, the creases in the original image correspond to the canyon portion of the 3D point cloud. The yellow part, the top of the point cloud, is distributed with most of the background points. Using the spherical flipping (Eq. 2), the point cloud is squeezed upward so that the whole 3D point cloud is close to the top. The purpose of this is to push the points in the middle (green part) to the top as much as possible. The extruded point cloud shape will approach a curved surface, with a smoother top than the origin cloud. The background points easier to be selected, the convex hull calculating can select these background points at a lower time cost. Since the points corresponding to the text are generally not pushed to the top, the selection of the foreground points can be easily avoided by adding a target point (defaulted to the origin).

Calculating its convex hull, the red points in Fig. 5(c) can be selected, which barely contain the position where the text is located. Applying the natural-neighbor interpolation [22] on the selected red points to generate the smooth background image Fig. 5(d), and subtracting Fig. 5(d) from the original Fig. 5(a) and then normalizing it to obtain the *lowlights map* [12], which is Fig. 5(e). The crease has become not obvious. Lowlights map has a cleaner background and can be used as the input to any other binarization algorithm to obtain better results than the original input.

The original algorithm yields good results, and we extended it. We add a parameter $T$ to the calculation of the set of convex hull points, which determines the number of times the convex hull is calculated. In Eq. 2, $\gamma$ determines the number of points selected by the convex hull calculation. The smaller the $\gamma$ is, the more background points will be detected, but it is also tend to damage the text. When fuzzy texts are included, these text pixels may be detected as the background. In this situation, the parameter $T$ works. We set $\gamma$ to a slightly larger and then increase $T$, so that text pixels can be kept at a lower position and more background pixels can be detected. The calculated convex hull point set $K_i$ is merged into the background point set $V$ ( initial $V$ is empty ), and then $K_i$ is removed from the point cloud P. In the new point cloud, convex hull algorithm is used to select the $K_{i+1}$. After $T$ times, we can get a new background point set $V$:

$$V = K_1 \cup K_2 \cup ... \cup K_{T-1} \cup K_T \tag{4}$$

where $K_i$ is a subset of P.

$$K_i = ConvexHull[P - (K_1 \cup ... \cup K_{i-1})] \tag{5}$$

$P$ is the 3D point cloud transformed from the original image. The following steps are the same as [12]. The improved algorithm can get better output.

### 3.2   Unshadow Binarization

The idea of the unshadow bina-rization algorithm is similar to that of the first binarization algo-rithm. We have a basic obser-vation about document images. The intensity of text pixels in document images are generally lower than that of nearby pixels.

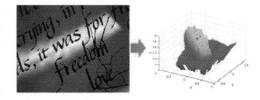

**Fig. 6.** Point cloud transformation 2.

Regardless of what the ambient lighting is, it is also true, even when the text is in shadows or at the edge of shadows. A document image is mapped to a 3D space based on the coordinates and intensity values of each pixel in Fig. 6. And then, a surface is used to segment the text from the background including shadows. The key of this proposal is how to find the surface. It is difficult to find the surface exactly, but we can find the points falling on the surface in the 3D point cloud. Using convex hull algorithm helps to find them, and with these points we can segment the point cloud. The TPO operator calculates convex hull to find the occluding points, which contain most of the background points (non-text points) in the image. Simply using TPO operator cannot find all the background points. Similar to the first algorithm, taking the union set $V$ of the repeatedly calculated convex hull point set as the background point set, as Eq. 4 and Eq. 5. It should be noted that different from the first algorithm, this $V$ is almost a complete background point set rather than a part of the background. By setting the gray value of the pixels corresponding to the point set $V$ in the original image as 1, i.e., pure white, a new image that nearly completes binarization can be obtained. Set the normalized grayscale image as $G(x, y)$, then the new image $G'$ is:

$$G'(x, y) = \begin{cases} 1, & (x, y) \in V \\ G(x, y), & (x, y) \notin V \end{cases} \tag{6}$$

Different from the application scope of the first algorithm, this algorithm is mainly applied to a variety of document images with soft shadows. Document images with soft shadows are converted into 3D point clouds, which are usually divided into three layers. As shown in Fig. 6, the background with high intensity is at the top, the shadow with slightly low intensity is at the middle, and the text is at the bottom. Since the layers of the 3D point cloud are cleaner, it is more difficult to detect text pixels when using convex hull algorithm.

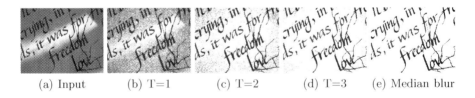

(a) Input     (b) T=1     (c) T=2     (d) T=3     (e) Median blur

Fig. 7. Unshadowing binarization process

Figure 7(a) is the input image, and Fig. 7(b-d) are the new images generated by corresponding changes with the increase of T. Since the foreground point set (text point set) may contain a little salt and pepper noise, and the text edges may have sawtooth, we use median filter as an option of the algorithm. Median filter defines a sliding window of $2N + 1$. The sample value at the center of the window is selected, and the median value calculated using the $y_i$ replacing that center sample value, for $y_i$:

$$y_i = Med[x_{j-N}, ...x_j, ...x_{j+N}] \tag{7}$$

where $i$ is the serial number of the sliding window and $x_j$ is the sample value in the center of the window. The results after median filtering are shown in Fig. 7(d) and Fig. 7(e), where Fig. 7(d) represents the image with noise, and Fig. 7(e) represents the image after median filtering. It effectively filters out the noise of the image. Finally, a complete binary image can be obtained by setting the gray value of pixels whose gray value is not 1 to 0:

$$Result(x,y) = \begin{cases} 1, & G'(x,y) = 1 \\ 0, & G'(x,y) \neq 1 \end{cases} \tag{8}$$

Algorithm process:

---

**Algorithm 1.** Binarization.

---

**Input:** Document image; $\gamma$; T;
**Output:** Binary image;
 1: GayImage = RGBToGray(Document image);
 2: G = Normalize(GayImage);
 3: P = ImageTo3DPointset(G);
 4: P = SphericalFlipping(P,$\gamma$);
 5: P = P ∪ TargetPoint; // Add the target point (default is origin).
 6: V = empty;
 7: **for** i **do** = 1 → T
 8:     K = ConvexHull(P);
 9:     P = P - K;
10:     V = V ∪ K;
11: **end for**
12: S = NaturalNeighborInterpolation(V); // Generate a smooth background image.
13: L = GayImage - S;
14: L = Normalize(L); // Obtain lowlights map.
15: **return** AnyBinarizationAlgorithm(L);

---

**Algorithm 2.** Unshadow Binarization.

---

**Input:** Document image; $\gamma$; T;
**Output:** Binary image;
 1: V is obtained from lines 1 to 11 of algorithm 1.
 2: Set the grayscale value of all $G_i$ in G that can be indexed by V to 1;
 3: G = MedianFilter(G); // Median blur (optional).
 4: Set the grayscale value of $G_i$ in G that is not 1 to 0;
 5: **return** G;

---

## 4    Experiment

To verify the effectiveness of the algorithms, for the first algorithm, the experiments in this paper used printed documents from the document image binarization competition DIBCO 2009 [4] and the handwritten document dataset provided by DIBCO 2011 [19] to evaluate the results. As a control algorithm, the low lights maps generated by Kligler's and our algorithm were used as input to Howe's three binarization algorithms for comparison. The performance metrics were used as F-Measure (FM), pseudo F-measure (Fps), peak signal-to-noise ratio (PSNR), distance reciprocal distortion (DRD). F-measure is the weighted average of Precision and Recall, the higher the F-measure is, the closer the binary image is to ground truth. Pseudo F-measure is described in [18]. PSNR is an objective standard for image evaluation. The larger the PSNR value is, the less distortion it represents. DRD is used to measure visual distortion in images of binary documents, and the lower the score, the better.

|  (a) Input  |  (b) Howe's-3  |  (c) Kligler's  |  (d) Our  |

**Fig. 8.** Binarization results

Figure 8(a) are the input images from the DIBCO 2011 dataset. Figure 8(b) are the results of Howe's-3 [6] with F-Measure of 92.06% and 72.33%. Figure 8(c) use Kligler's low lights map as the input of Howe's-3 with F-Measure of 93.28% and 89.91%. Figure 8(d) use the low lights map generated by the improved algorithm of this paper as the input, and the F-Measure improves to 93.87% and 94.97%, respectively. Compared with the original algorithm in [12], the results of our proposed method have significantly improved the quality of the binary image.

**Table 1.** Average of DIBCO 2009 and DIBCO 2011.

| Algorithm | FM | Fps | PSNR | DRD |
|---|---|---|---|---|
| Howe's-1 | 91.84 | 93.28 | 19.15 | 3.59 |
| Kligler's | 93.18 | 94.83 | 19.63 | 2.27 |
| Our | **94.02** | **95.89** | **20.07** | **1.83** |
| Howe's-2 | 91.28 | 92.38 | 19.49 | 2.50 |
| Kligler's | 94.45 | 95.67 | 20.37 | 1.69 |
| Our | **94.97** | **96.37** | **20.72** | **1.45** |
| Howe's-3 | 91.94 | 92.81 | 19.28 | 3.60 |
| Kligler's | 94.33 | 95.58 | 20.29 | 1.75 |
| Our | **95.02** | **96.32** | **20.73** | **1.44** |

Table 1 demonstrates the average of the metrics when applying the algorithm to DIBCO 2009 and DIBCO 2011 dataset. We used the three binarization algorithms of Howe [6] as the baseline, and we used the tuned low lights map generated by Kligler [12] and this paper as input respectively. The statistical results manifest that the algorithm in this paper outperforms the original algorithm, with significant improvement in all metrics.

For unshadow binarization algorithm proposed in this paper, we used the partially document images with shadows from [1, 12] as experimental input data. So it lacks the ground truth image. The OTSU method [17] was used to generate a binary image after removing the image shadows by the algorithm of [12]. It was compared to the output of our algorithm. Figure 9 shows the comparison.

Figure 9(a) are the input images, Fig. 9(b) are the results of Kligler& Otsu method, and Fig. 9(c) are the results of our algorithm. The algorithm in this paper had excellent output for document images containing various shadows. Unexpectedly, we found that this algorithm can effectively remove the grid if the input image contains light color or blurred grid. It can be seen clearly in the last row of Fig. 9. For all the experimental data in this paper, we set $\alpha_0 = 0.05$ and $\alpha_1 = 1$. $\gamma$ and $T$ are the tuning parameters.

For space cost, the convex hull algorithm can directly operate on the original data, and the space complexity is $O(1)$. In addition, both algorithms require an auxiliary storage space of the same size as the original data, so the overall space complexity is $O(n)$. In terms of time cost, since sorting is required before scanning the convex hull, the time complexity is at least $O(nlgn)$, and the subsequent scanning process is $O(n)$, and a total of $T$ times are calculated. The remaining calculations can be completed in $O(n)$. Therefore, the overall time complexity of the two algorithms is $O(Tnlgn)$.

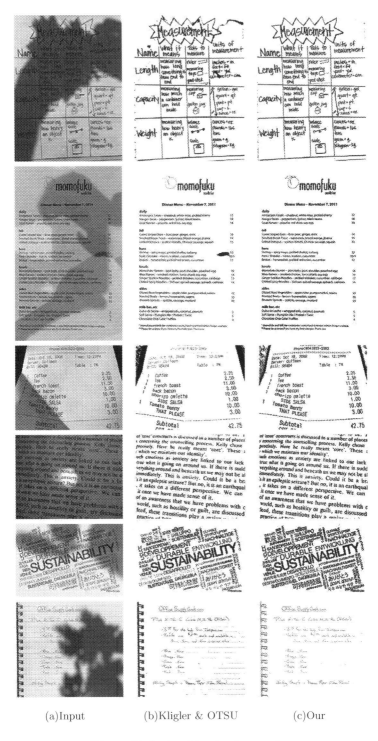

(a)Input                    (b)Kligler & OTSU                    (c)Our

**Fig. 9.** Unshadow binarization results

# 5   Conclusion

This paper improved the previous algorithm and combined its ideas to propose a new binarization algorithm for document images, which provided a new idea for the combination of visibility detection and document image processing that makes a positive contribution to the field of image enhancement. The algorithms proposed in this paperl had shortcomings. Although we obtained excellent results by manually tuning the parameters, the operation was too complicated in the practical application. As a follow-up study of this paper, we shall combine character size detection, character stroke width detection, deep learning, and other technologies to summarize the rules of tuning parameters and refine formulas to achieve automatic parameter adjustment.

# References

1. Bako, S., Darabi, S., Shechtman, E., Wang, J., Sunkavalli, K., Sen, P.: Removing shadows from images of documents. In: Lai, S.-H., Lepetit, V., Nishino, K., Sato, Y. (eds.) ACCV 2016. LNCS, vol. 10113, pp. 173–183. Springer, Cham (2017). https://doi.org/10.1007/978-3-319-54187-7_12
2. Bukhari, S., Shafait, F., Breuel, T.: Foreground-background regions guided binarization of camera-captured document images. In: Proceedings of the 3rd International Workshop on Camera-Based Document Analysis and Recognition, CBDAR 2009 (01 2009)
3. Chaki, N., Shaikh, S.H., Saeed, K.: A comprehensive survey on image binarization techniques. In: Exploring Image Binarization Techniques. SCI, vol. 560, pp. 5–15. Springer, New Delhi (2014). https://doi.org/10.1007/978-81-322-1907-1_2
4. Gatos, B., Ntirogiannis, K., Pratikakis, I.: Icdar 2009 document image binarization contest (dibco 2009). In: DBLP (2009)
5. Gryka, M., Terry, M., Brostow, G.J.: Learning to remove soft shadows. Acm Trans. Graph. **34**(5), 1–15 (2015)
6. Howe, N.R.: Document binarization with automatic parameter tuning. Int. J. Doc. Anal. Recogn. (ijdar) **16**(3), 247–258 (2013)
7. Jung, S., Hasan, M.A., Kim, C.: Water-filling: an efficient algorithm for digitized document shadow removal. In: Jawahar, C.V., Li, H., Mori, G., Schindler, K. (eds.) ACCV 2018. LNCS, vol. 11361, pp. 398–414. Springer, Cham (2019). https://doi.org/10.1007/978-3-030-20887-5_25
8. Katz, S., Leifman, G., Tal, A.: Mesh segmentation using feature point and core extraction. Vis. Comput. **21**(8), 649–658 (2005)
9. Katz, S., Tal, A.: Improving the visual comprehension of point sets. In: 2013 IEEE Conference on Computer Vision and Pattern Recognition (CVPR) (2013)
10. Katz, S., Tal, A.: On the visibility of point clouds. In: IEEE International Conference on Computer Vision (2015)
11. Katz, S., Tal, A., Basri, R.: Direct visibility of point sets. In: ACM, pp. 24.1-24.11 (2007)
12. Kligler, N., Katz, S., Tal, A.: Document enhancement using visibility detection. In: 2018 IEEE/CVF Conference on Computer Vision and Pattern Recognition (CVPR) (2018)

13. Lin, Y.H., Chen, W.C., Chuang, Y.Y.: Bedsr-net: a deep shadow removal network from a single document image. In: 2020 IEEE/CVF Conference on Computer Vision and Pattern Recognition (CVPR) (2020)
14. Mesquita, R.G., Mello, C., Almeida, L.: A new thresholding algorithm for document images based on the perception of objects by distance. Integr. Comput. Aided Eng. **21**(2), 133–146 (2014)
15. Ntirogiannis, K., Gatos, B., Pratikakis, I.: A combined approach for the binarization of handwritten document images. Pattern Recogn. Lett. **35**(1), 3–15 (2014)
16. Oliveira, D.M., Lins, R.D., Silva, G.D.F.P.E.: Shading removal of illustrated documents. In: International Conference Image Analysis and Recognition (2013)
17. Otsu, N.: A threshold selection method from gray-level histograms. IEEE Trans. Syst. Man Cybern. **9**(1), 62–66 (1979)
18. Pratikakis, I., Gatos, B., Ntirogiannis, K.: H-dibco 2010 - handwritten document image binarization competition. In: International Conference on Frontiers in Handwriting Recognition, ICFHR 2010, Kolkata, India, 16–18 November 2010 (2010)
19. Pratikakis, I., Gatos, B., Ntirogiannis, K.: Icdar 2011 document image binarization contest (dibco 2011). IEEE (2011)
20. Rais, N.B., Hanif, M.S., Taj, I.A.: Adaptive thresholding technique for document image analysis. In: International Multitopic Conference (2004)
21. Sauvola, J., Pietikäinen, M.: Adaptive document image binarization. Pattern Recogn. **33**(2), 225–236 (2000)
22. Sibson, R.: A brief description of natural neighbor interpolation. In: Interpreting Multivariate Data (1981)
23. Su, B., Lu, S., Tan, C.L.: Robust document image binarization technique for degraded document images. IEEE Trans. Image Process. **22**(4), 1408–1417 (2013)

# LF-MAGNet: Learning Mutual Attention Guidance of Sub-Aperture Images for Light Field Image Super-Resolution

Zijian Wang[1], Yao Lu[1(✉)], Yani Zhang[2], Haowei Lu[1], Shunzhou Wang[1], and Binglu Wang[3]

[1] Beijing Laboratory of Intelligent Information Technology, School of Computer Science and Technology, Beijing Institute of Technology, Beijing 100081, China
vis_yl@bit.edu.cn
[2] School of Marine Electrical Engineering, Dalian Maritime University, Dalian 116026, China
[3] School of Artificial Intelligence, Optics and Electronics (iOPEN), Northwestern Polytechnical University, Xi'an 710072, China

**Abstract.** Many light field image super-resolution networks are proposed to directly aggregate the features of different low-resolution sub-aperture images (SAIs) to reconstruct high-resolution sub-aperture images. However, most of them ignore aligning different SAI's features before aggregation, which will generate sub-optimal light field image super-resolution results. To handle this limitation, we design a mutual attention mechanism to align the SAI's features and propose a Light Field Mutual Attention Guidance Network (LF-MAGNet) constructed by multiple Mutual Attention Guidance blocks (MAGs) in a cascade manner. MAG achieves the mutual attention mechanism between center SAI and any surrounding SAI with two modules: the center attention guidance module (CAG) and the surrounding attention guidance module (SAG). Specifically, CAG first aligns the center-SAI features and any surrounding SAI features with the attention mechanism and then guides the surrounding SAI feature to learn from the center-SAI features, generating refined-surrounding SAI features. SAG aligns the refined-surrounding SAI feature and the original surrounding SAI feature and guides the refined surrounding SAI feature to learn from the original surrounding SAI features, generating the final outputs of MAG. With the help of MAG, LF-MAGNet can efficiently utilize different SAI features and generate high-quality light field image super-resolution results. Experiments are performed on commonly-used light field image super-resolution benchmarks. Qualitative and quantitative results prove the effectiveness of our LF-MAGNet.

---

This is a student paper.
This work is supported by the National Natural Science Foundation of China (No. 61273273), by the National Key Research and Development Plan (No. 2017YFC0112001), and by China Central Television (JG2018-0247).

H. Ma et al. (Eds.): PRCV 2021, LNCS 13021, pp. 105–116, 2021.
https://doi.org/10.1007/978-3-030-88010-1_9

**Keywords:** Light-field image super-resolution · Visual attention mechanism · Feature alignment · Sub-aperture image

# 1    Introduction

Light field image super-resolution (LFSR) is a newly emerging computer vision task which aims to enlarge the spatial resolution of sub-aperture images of light field image. It is a basic technology for many applications, such as virtual reality [5,29], depth sensing [15,16], 3D reconstruction [37,38] and so on.

Benefited from the development of deep learning, LFSR has achieved significant progress recently. LFCNN [28] is the first LFSR network that employs the bicubic interpolation to enlarge the sub-aperture images' spatial size and applies the convolution neural network to learn the angular information of LF image. After that, many LFSR networks are proposed for efficiently utilizing the spatial-angular information of LF images. For example, Yeung *et al.* [27] propose a spatial-angular separable convolution to extract the spatial-angular features. Wang *et al.* [21] formulate the different sub-aperture images into a macro-pixel image and propose an LF-InterNet to process the generated macro-pixel image to learn spatial-angle information for LFSR. Although they obtain promising LFSR performance, the features of SAIs are not efficiently utilized due to lack of feature alignment, resulting in sub-optimal results. Thus, we should align different SAI's features before the aggregation operation to improve the LFSR performance.

Recently, visual attention mechanism has been successfully applied to many computer vision tasks [2,4,12,20,25,32]. It can help the model to focus on more task-relevant feature representations and suppress the irrelevant features. In this paper, we want to use the visual attention mechanism to highlight the similar feature representations of different SAIs for aligning features, and the aligned features are subsequently processed for learning the complementary information of different SAIs. Based on this motivation, we propose a Mutual Attention Guidance Network (namely LF-MAGNet). Specifically, we propose a Mutual Attention Guidance block (MAG) to align the features of different SAIs. Each MAG includes two modules: the Center Attention Guidance module (CAG) and the Surrounding Attention Guidance module (SAG). Given two SAIs (*i.e.*, the center SAI (c-SAI) and its any surrounding SAI (s-SAI)), CAG first uses the attention module to align the feature of c-SAI and s-SAI, and then extract the complementary information from them to guide the s-SAI feature learning and generate the refined s-SAI feature. SAG uses the attention module to align the refined s-SAI and s-SAI features and then extract the complementary information from them to guide refined s-SAI feature learning. With the help of MAG, LF-MAGNet can fully utilize all SAIs and suppress the irrelevant representations for final LFSR. Extensive experiments are performed on five commonly-used LFSR benchmarks. Compared with the other advanced LFSR models, LF-MAGNet achieves new state-of-the-art results, which demonstrate the effectiveness of our model.

To summarize, our contributions are two-fold:

– We propose a new Mutual Attention Guidance block (MAG) to efficiently learn the complementary representations of different SAIs for final LFSR.
– Based on the proposed MAG block, we build an LF-MAGNet which achieves new state-of-the-art results on five commonly-used LFSR benchmarks.

The rest of this paper is organized as follows. We will review the related works in Sect. 2. Section 3 illustrates the details of our LF-MAGNet. Experiment and implementation details are illustrated in Sect. 4. We give a conclusion of this paper in Sect. 5.

## 2    Related Work

### 2.1    Light Field Image Super-Resolution

With the renaissance of deep learning, many CNN-based LFSR networks are proposed in recent years. Early CNN-based methods can be mainly divided into two categories: two-stage methods and one-stage methods. Two stages methods usually enlarge the spatial size of sub-aperture images firstly and then learn the LF angular information. For example, Yoon et al. [28] applied the bicubic interpolation to enlarge the spatial size of sub-aperture Images and employ a convolution neural network to reconstruct final LFSR results. Yuan et al. [30] first applied the SISR network to super-resolved the sub-aperture images and then used the designed epipolar plane image network to learn the LF structure information. One-stage methods simultaneously learn the spatial and angular information of LF images for LFSR. For instance, Yeung et al. [27] proposed a spatial-angular separable convolution to learn the spatial-angular information of LF images for LFSR. Recently, the research interests of LFSR are mainly about how to utilize the different views of sub-aperture images for LFSR efficiently. They employ part [23,31] or all [6,22] of Sub-Aperture Images to learn the complementary information of each other for final LFSR. Although the above methods achieve satisfactory performance, the complementary information of different sub-aperture images is not explicitly modeled to improve super-resolution results. Different from the above methods, we propose a mutual attention guidance mechanism to efficiently learn the similar representations of different sub-aperture images to align features for improving the LFSR performance.

### 2.2    Visual Attention Mechanism

Visual attention mechanism aims to enhance the task-relevant feature representations of a network, and has been successfully applied to various computer vision tasks, such as image or video classification [4,12,20,25], video object segmentation [11,33,35], human parsing [19,34,36], temporal action localization [18,26], single image super-resolution [2,32] and so on. There are some representative attention blocks among them. For example, Hu et al. [4] proposed a Squeeze-and-Excitation block to enhance the feature representations of different channels.

Woo *et al.* [12,25] modeled channel attention and spatial attention respectively to highlight the task-relevant feature representations. Wang *et al.* [20] designed a non-local block to extract the long-range context information for efficiently suppressing the irrelevant features. There are few works to explore the visual attention mechanism for LFSR. To this end, we propose a Mutual Attention Guidance block to efficiently align the features of different sub-aperture images for generating high-quality LF images.

## 3   Proposed Method

Following [21,22,31], we convert the input LF image from the RGB space to the YCbCr space. Given an LF image, only the Y channel of the image is super-resolved, and the bicubic interpolation is used to process the Cb and Cr channel of the images. We don't consider the channel dimension and denote the LF image as a 4-D tensor $L \in \mathbb{R}^{U \times V \times H \times W}$, where $U$ and $V$ stand for the LF angular resolution, and $H$ and $W$ represent the spatial resolution of each SAI. Given a low-resolution LF image $L_{lr} \in \mathbb{R}^{U \times V \times H \times W}$, LFSR aims to generate high-resolution SAIs while maintaining the angular resolution of LF image unchanged. We denote the LFSR result as $L_{sr} \in \mathbb{R}^{U \times V \times sH \times sW}$, where $s$ $(s > 1)$ represents the upsampling scale factor. In this paper, we only explore LFSR with the square array distributed (*i.e.*, $U = V = A$).

LF-MAGNet is illustrated in Fig. 1. It consists of three modules: Shallow Feature Extraction $\mathcal{F}_{\text{feat}}$, Hierarchical Feature Extraction $\mathcal{F}_{\text{sa}}$, and LF Image Reconstruction $\mathcal{F}_{\text{up}}$. Given a low resolution LF image $L_{lr} \in \mathbb{R}^{U \times V \times H \times W}$, the feature process of LF-MAGNet is as follows:

$$\text{Shallow Feature Extraction: } F = \mathcal{F}_{\text{feat}}(L_{lr}) \in \mathbb{R}^{A^2 \times H \times W}, \tag{1}$$

$$\text{Hierarchical Feature Extraction: } S = \mathcal{F}_{\text{sa}}(F) \in \mathbb{R}^{A^2 \times H \times W}, \tag{2}$$

$$\text{LF Image Reconstruction: } L_{sr} = \mathcal{F}_{\text{up}}(S) \in \mathbb{R}^{A \times A \times sH \times sW}. \tag{3}$$

In the rest of this paper, we will introduce the $\mathcal{F}_{\text{feat}}$, $\mathcal{F}_{\text{sa}}$ and $\mathcal{F}_{\text{up}}$ in detail.

### 3.1   Shallow Feature Extraction

Residual learning has been successfully applied to single image super-resolution and achieved promising progresses [9,32]. To obtain efficient feature representations of each SAI, we also construct $\mathcal{F}_{\text{feat}}$ with multiple residual blocks for learning efficient shallow feature representations. The structure of $\mathcal{F}_{\text{feat}}$ is shown in Fig. 1(b). It consists of four residual blocks in a cascaded way. Each residual block is constructed with two $3 \times 3$ convolutions in a residual manner. We denote the center SAI of the low-resolution LF image as $I_c \in \mathbb{R}^{H \times W}$, and the surrounding SAI of the low-resolution LF image as $I_s^i \in \mathbb{R}^{H \times W}$, where $i \in [1, \cdots, A^2 - 1]$. Thus, the low-resolution LF image can be denoted as $L_{lr} = \{I_c, I_s^1, \cdots, I_s^{A^2-1}\}$. We use the same $\mathcal{F}_{\text{feat}}$ to separately process $I_c$ and $I_s^i$, and obtain shallow feature $F_c$ and $F_s^i$ as follows:

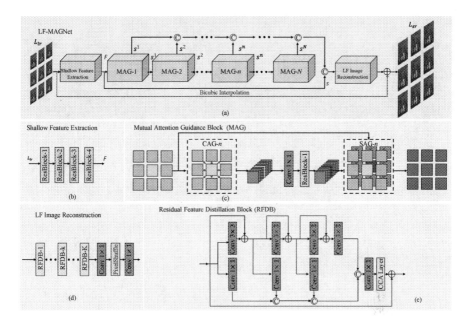

**Fig. 1.** Overview of LF-MAGNet. Given LR SAIs input, *Shallow Feature Extraction* module first processes the input. Then, multiple *MAG* blocks process the extracted feature to learn from each others. Finally, the output features are fed to *LF Image Reconstruction* module to generate the final LFSR results.

$$F_c = \mathcal{F}_{\text{feat}}(I_c) \in \mathbb{R}^{C \times H \times W}, F_s^i = \mathcal{F}_{\text{feat}}(I_s^i) \in \mathbb{R}^{C \times H \times W}, \tag{4}$$

where $C$ denotes the feature channel number. The shallow features can be denoted as $F = [F_c, F_s^1, \cdots, F_s^{A^2-1}]$, and $[\cdot, \cdot]$ represents the feature concatenate operation.

## 3.2 Mutual Attention Guidance

Shallow Feature Extraction module $\mathcal{F}_{\text{feat}}$ extracts features $\boldsymbol{F}$ from input SAIs, but it does not efficiently utilize the complementary information between different SAIs, which is important for the network to reconstruct the high-quality LFSR image. The SAIs in an LF image share a similar appearance and vary slightly due to the view disparity of LF structure. Thus, to efficiently obtain the complementary information, we should first align different SAI's features and then aggregate them for LFSR. Inspired by the success of the visual attention mechanism, we propose a hierarchical feature extraction module $\mathcal{F}_{\text{sa}}$, which is constructed with $N$ mutual attention guidance blocks (MAGs), to process different SAIs. The MAG block includes two modules: The Center Attention Guidance module (CAG) and the Surrounding Attention Guidance module (SAG). Given a center SAI feature $F_c$ and the $i$th surrounding SAI feature $F_s^i$, CAG obtains the aligned feature $A_{CAG}^i$ between $F_c$ and $F_s^i$, and use the $A_{CAG}^i$ to guide the $F_s^i$

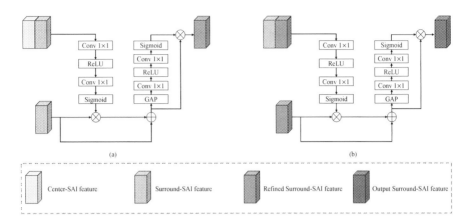

**Fig. 2.** illustration of MAG block. (a) Center attention guidance module. (b) Surrounding attention guidance module.

to learn the complementary information to generate the refined surrounding-SAI feature $\hat{F}_s^i$. While SAG learns the aligned feature $A_{SAG}^i$ between the $\hat{F}_s^i$ and the $F_s^i$, and guide the $\hat{F}_s^i$ to learn the complementary representations from $F_s^i$. The above two attention guidance modules construct our proposed MAG, and the detailed illustrations of each module are as follows. For simplicity, we take the $n$-th MAG as an example.

**Center Attention Guidance Module.** The structure of CAG is illustrated in Fig. 2(a). Given the center-SAI feature $F_c$ and the $i$th surrounding feature $F_s^i$, we first use the spatial attention $\mathcal{F}_{\mathcal{SA}}$, which is implemented with conv $1 \times 1 \rightarrow$ReLU$\rightarrow$conv$1 \times 1 \rightarrow$Sigmoid, to process the concatenated feature of $F_c$ and $F_s^i$ for extracting the complementary information between $F_c$ and $F_s^i$, and obtain the aligned feature $A_{CAG}^i$ as follows:

$$A_{CAG}^i = \mathcal{F}_{\mathcal{SA}}([F_c, F_s^i]). \tag{5}$$

Then, the surrounding-SAI feature $F_s^i$ multiplies with $A_{CAG}^i$ to receive the supplementary information from $F_c$, and adds with the original feature $F_s^i$ to obtain the refined surrounding-SAI feature $\overline{F}_s^i$ as follows:

$$\overline{F}_s^i = (F_s^i \otimes A_{CAG}^i) \oplus F_s^i, \tag{6}$$

where $\otimes$ denotes the element-wise multiplication, $\oplus$ represents the element-wise summation. Finally, to further enhance the feature representations, the refined surrounding-SAI feature $\overline{F}_s^i$ is further processed by the channel attention $\mathcal{F}_{\mathcal{CA}}$ which is implemented with Global Average Pooling (GAP)$\rightarrow$conv $1 \times 1 \rightarrow$ReLU$\rightarrow$conv$1 \times 1 \rightarrow$Sigmoid as follows:

$$\hat{F}_s^i = \mathcal{F}_{\mathcal{CA}}(\overline{F}_s^i) \otimes \overline{F}_s^i. \tag{7}$$

Both $\mathcal{F}_{\mathcal{S}\mathcal{A}}$ and $\mathcal{F}_{\mathcal{C}\mathcal{A}}$ adopt the same channel dimension reduction ratio $r$ to highlight the relevant representations. The effect of different settings of reduction ratio $r$ for final performance are explored in Sect. 4.2.

**Surrounding Attention Guidance Module.** CAG helps $F_s^i$ to align with $F_c$, learn the complementary information from $F_c$ and the feature representations of the surrounding SAI $F_s^i$ are refined. However, CAG only considers the center-SAI features while ignoring the surrounding SAI features, generating sub-optimal results. We also need to utilize the surrounding SAI features to improve the final LFSR performance. To this end, we propose a SAG module to guide the $F_s^i$ to learn from the $\hat{F}_s^i$. The structure of SAG is illustrated in Fig. 2(b). The whole feature process is the same with CAG, and the major difference is that the input of $\mathcal{F}_{\mathcal{S}\mathcal{A}}$. The detail processes of SAG are as follows:

$$A_{SAG}^i = \mathcal{F}_{\mathcal{S}\mathcal{A}}([\hat{F}_s^i, F_s^i]), \tag{8}$$

$$\widetilde{F}_s^i = \hat{F}_s^i \otimes A_{SAG}^i \oplus \hat{F}_s^i, \tag{9}$$

$$\dot{F}_s^i = \mathcal{F}_{\mathcal{C}\mathcal{A}}(\widetilde{F}_s^i) \otimes \widetilde{F}_s^i. \tag{10}$$

The refined center and surrounding SAI features construct the $n$-th MAG output $S^n = [\dot{F}_s^1, \cdots, \dot{F}_s^n]$, and different MAG outputs are concatenated to generate the hierarchical spatial-angular features $S = [S^1, \cdots, S^n]$ for LF image reconstruction.

### 3.3 LF Image Reconstruction

After getting the hierarchical features processed by the cascade MAGs, we need to fuse and upsample the extracted features for LFSR. Thus, we propose an LF Image Reconstruction module as illustrated in Fig. 1(d). It mainly consists of two components: the feature fusion part and the feature upsampling part. Feature fusion part is constructed by multiple lightweight residual feature distillation blocks (RFDBs) [10], which are illustrated in Fig. 1(e). With the help of RFDB, the feature fusion part can efficiently obtain the complementary information of different SAIs with fewer network parameters and computational resources. Afterward, the fused features are sent to $1 \times 1$ convolutions and PixelShuffle layer to enlarge the spatial size of each SAI for LFSR.

## 4 Experiment

### 4.1 Dataset and Implementation Details

Following [22], we select five commonly-used LFSR datasets (*i.e.*, EPFL [13], HCInew [3], HCIold [24], INRIA [8], and STFgantry [17]) to train and evaluate the performance of our LF-MAGNet on them. The angular resolution of LF images from the above datasets are all $9 \times 9$. For the training stage, we crop

**Table 1.** Performance comparisons of different numbers of MAG in LF-MAGNet on INRIA dataset for ×4 SR. MAG-$n$ indicates the $n$th MAG block in LF-MAGNet.

| MAG-1 | MAG-2 | MAG-3 | MAG-4 | MAG-5 | PSNR | SSIM |
|---|---|---|---|---|---|---|
| ✓ | | | | | 30.34 | 0.9418 |
| ✓ | ✓ | | | | 30.48 | 0.9429 |
| ✓ | ✓ | ✓ | | | 30.88 | 0.9478 |
| ✓ | ✓ | ✓ | ✓ | | **30.94** | **0.9489** |
| ✓ | ✓ | ✓ | ✓ | ✓ | 30.84 | 0.9480 |

$64 \times 64$ patch from each SAI and use the bicubic interpolation to generate ×2 and ×4 LR patch. Random horizontal rotation, vertical rotation, and 90° rotation are employed to augment the training data. Spatial and angular resolution all needs to be processed simultaneously for maintaining the LF image structure.

We only process $5 \times 5$ angular resolution for ×2 and ×4 SR. LF-MAGNet is optimized with *L1* loss, and we select Adam to optimize the network. All experiments are performed on a single NVIDIA RTX 2080Ti GPU card with the Pytorch framework. The batch size is set to 8, and the initial learning rate is set to $2 \times 10^{-4}$. We train LF-MAGNet with a total of 50 epochs, and the learning rate is decreased to half after every 15 epochs.

Following [21, 22], we choose PSNR and SSIM to evaluate the LFSR performance on the Y channel. To obtain the performance score of $M$ scenes with angular resolution $A \times A$, we first calculate the performance score of each SAI. Then, we average the performance score of $A^2$ SAIs to get the performance score of one scene. Finally, The performance score of $M$ scenes are averaged to obtain the final performance score.

### 4.2    Ablation Studies

**Number of MAG.** We explore the number of MAG from LF-MAGNet for final LF-SR performance. The results are displayed in Table 1. We can see that with the increase of the number of MAG, the LFSR performances are improved. LF-MAGNet achieves the best result when $N = 4$. After that, the performance is decreased when the number becomes large. The reason is that large network parameters hinder the network optimization. Thus, we set $N = 4$ in our LF-MAGNet.

**Table 2.** Performance comparisons of different attention guidance on INRIA dataset for ×4 SR.

| Variants | PSNR | SSIM |
|---|---|---|
| LF-MAGNet w/o CAG and SAG | 30.61 | 0.9480 |
| LF-MAGNet w/o CAG | 30.72 | 0.9486 |
| LF-MAGNet w/o SAG | 30.79 | 0.9484 |
| LF-MAGNet | **30.94** | **0.9489** |

**Table 3.** Performance comparisons of different reduction ratio $r$ settings in MAG block on INRIA dataset for ×4 SR.

| $r$ | 1 | 2 | 4 | 8 |
|---|---|---|---|---|
| LF-MAGNet | 30.69 | 30.80 | **30.94** | 30.88 |

**Table 4.** Performance comparison of different methods for ×2 and ×4 SR. The best and the second best results are marked with bold and italic.

| Method | Scale | EPFL | HCInew | HCIold | INRIA | STFgantry |
|---|---|---|---|---|---|---|
| Bicubic | ×2 | 29.50/0.9350 | 31.69/0.9335 | 37.46/0.9776 | 31.10/0.9563 | 30.82/0.9473 |
| VDSR | ×2 | 32.50/0.9599 | 34.37/0.9563 | 40.61/0.9867 | 34.43/0.9742 | 35.54/0.9790 |
| EDSR | ×2 | 33.09/0.9631 | 34.83/0.9594 | 41.01/0.9875 | 34.97/0.9765 | 36.29/0.9819 |
| RCAN | ×2 | 33.16/0.9635 | 34.98/0.9602 | 41.05/0.9875 | 35.01/0.9769 | 36.33/0.9825 |
| LFBM5D | ×2 | 31.15/0.9545 | 33.72/0.9548 | 39.62/0.9854 | 32.85/0.9695 | 33.55/0.9718 |
| GB | ×2 | 31.22/0.9591 | 35.25/0.9692 | 40.21/0.9879 | 32.76/0.9724 | 35.44/0.9835 |
| resLF | ×2 | 32.75/0.9672 | 36.07/0.9715 | 42.61/0.9922 | 34.57/0.9784 | 36.89/0.9873 |
| LFSSR | ×2 | 33.69/0.9748 | 36.86/0.9753 | 43.75/0.9939 | 35.27/0.9834 | 38.07/0.9902 |
| LF-InterNet | ×2 | *34.14/0.9761* | 37.28/0.9769 | *44.45/0.9945* | *35.80/0.9841* | 38.72/0.9916 |
| LF-DFnet | ×2 | **34.44/0.9766** | *37.44/0.9786* | 44.23/0.9943 | **36.36/0.9841** | *39.61/0.9935* |
| LF-MAGNet | ×2 | **34.44**/0.9761 | **37.62**/*0.9783* | **44.62/0.9946** | **36.36/0.9846** | **39.66**/*0.9931* |
| Bicubic | ×4 | 25.14/0.8311 | 27.61/0.8507 | 32.42/0.9335 | 26.82/0.8860 | 25.93/0.8431 |
| VDSR | ×4 | 27.25/0.8782 | 29.31/0.8828 | 34.81/0.9518 | 29.19/0.9208 | 28.51/0.9012 |
| EDSR | ×4 | 27.84/0.8858 | 29.60/0.8874 | 35.18/0.9538 | 29.66/0.9259 | 28.70/0.9075 |
| RCAN | ×4 | 27.88/0.8863 | 29.63/0.8880 | 35.20/0.9540 | 29.76/0.9273 | 28.90/0.9110 |
| LFBM5D | ×4 | 26.61/0.8689 | 29.13/0.8823 | 34.23/0.9510 | 28.49/0.9137 | 28.30/0.9002 |
| GB | ×4 | 26.02/0.8628 | 28.92/0.8842 | 33.74/0.9497 | 27.73/0.9085 | 28.11/0.9014 |
| resLF | ×4 | 27.46/0.8899 | 29.92/0.9011 | 36.12/0.9651 | 29.64/0.9339 | 28.99/0.9214 |
| LFSSR | ×4 | 28.27/0.9080 | 30.72/0.9124 | 36.70/0.9690 | 30.31/0.9446 | 30.15/0.9385 |
| LF-InterNet | ×4 | 28.67/0.9143 | 30.98/0.9165 | 37.11/0.9715 | 30.64/0.9486 | 30.53/0.9426 |
| LF-DFnet | ×4 | *28.77/0.9165* | **31.23/0.9196** | *37.32/0.9718* | *30.83/0.9503* | **31.15/0.9494** |
| LF-MAGNet | ×4 | **29.03/0.9170** | *31.09/0.9162* | **37.40/0.9721** | **30.94**/*0.9489* | *30.71/0.9428* |

**Ablation of LF-MAGNet Design.** To explore the effectiveness of our MAG block, we design three variants of LF-MAGNet, which are LF-MAGNet w/o CAG and SAG, LF-MAGNet w/o CAG, and LF-MAGNet w/o SAG. The results are presented in Table 2. Without the assistance of MAG, LF-MAGNet achieves the lowest LFSR performance. Only CAG or SAG can improve the LFSR results, but they don't obtain the best results. LF-MAGNet with full implementation of MAG achieves the best performance, which demonstrates the effectiveness of our proposed mutual attention guidance mechanism. We also explore the reduction ratio settings in each MAG block. The performance comparisons are displayed in Table 3. We can see that LF-MAGNet achieves the best result when $r = 4$. Thus, we select $r = 4$ in our final model.

## 4.3   Comparisons with the State-of-The-Arts

We compare our LF-MAGNet with other image super-resolution (SISR) methods, including single image super-resolution methods (*i.e.*, VDSR [7], EDSR [9],

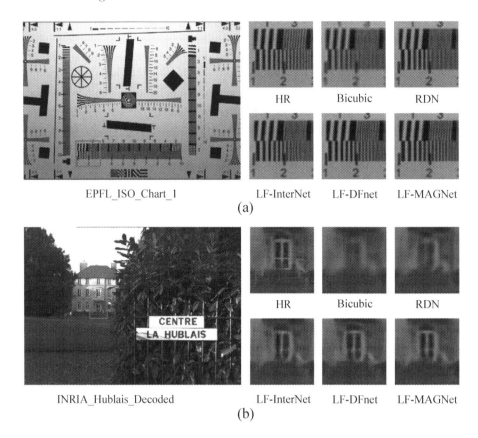

**Fig. 3.** Visual results of different methods for (a) ×2 SR and (b) ×4 SR.

and RCAN [32]), and LFSR methods (*i.e.*, LFBM5D [1] GB [14] LFSSR [27] resLF [31] LF-InterNet [21] LF-DFNet [22]). We also select bicubic interpolation as the baseline method for performance comparisons.

Table 4 reports the results on 5 × 5 LF images for ×2 and ×4 SR. We can see that LF-MAGNet achieves new state-of-the-art results on all LFSR benchmarks. Compared with SISR methods, LF-MAGNet achieves a significant performance improvement by efficiently utilizing the complementary information from different SAIs. Compared with the other LFSR methods, LF-MAGNet also outperforms them, demonstrating the effectiveness of our network.

Figure 3 present the qualitative results of different super-resolution methods. We can see that LF-MAGNet outputs more clear LF images with abundant textures and details compared with other methods, which further proves the superiority of LF-MAGNet.

# 5    Conclusion

In this paper, we propose a Mutual Attention Guidance Network (namely LF-MAGNet) for LFSR. LF-MAGNet is mainly constructed by multiple MAGs, which helps the center-SAI and surrounding SAIs of an LF image learn from each other efficiently. Extensive experiments are performed on commonly-used light filed image super-resolution benchmarks. Our LF-MAGNet achieves new state-of-the-art results compared with other advanced light filed image super-resolution networks.

# References

1. Alain, M., Smolic, A.: Light field super-resolution via lfbm5d sparse coding. In: ICIP, pp. 2501–2505 (2018)
2. Dai, T., Cai, J., Zhang, Y., Xia, S.T., Zhang, L.: Second-order attention network for single image super-resolution. In: CVPR, pp. 11065–11074 (2019)
3. Honauer, K., Johannsen, O., Kondermann, D., Goldluecke, B.: A dataset and evaluation methodology for depth estimation on 4D light fields. In: ACCV, pp. 19–34 (2016)
4. Hu, J., Shen, L., Sun, G.: Squeeze-and-excitation networks. In: CVPR, pp. 7132–7141 (2018)
5. Huang, F.C., et al.: The light field stereoscope-immersive computer graphics via factored near-eye field displays with focus cues. SIGGRAPH (2015)
6. Jin, J., Hou, J., Chen, J., Kwong, S.: Light field spatial super-resolution via deep combinatorial geometry embedding and structural consistency regularization. In: CVPR, pp. 2260–2269 (2020)
7. Kim, J., Lee, J.K., Lee, K.M.: Accurate image super-resolution using very deep convolutional networks. In: CVPR, pp. 1646–1654 (2016)
8. Le Pendu, M., Jiang, X., Guillemot, C.: Light field inpainting propagation via low rank matrix completion. IEEE TIP **27**(4), 1981–1993 (2018)
9. Lim, B., Son, S., Kim, H., Nah, S., Mu Lee, K.: Enhanced deep residual networks for single image super-resolution. In: CVPRW, pp. 136–144 (2017)
10. Liu, J., Tang, J., Wu, G.: Residual feature distillation network for lightweight image super-resolution. arXiv preprint arXiv:2009.11551 (2020)
11. Lu, X., Wang, W., Danelljan, M., Zhou, T., Shen, J., Van Gool, L.: Video object segmentation with episodic graph memory networks. In: ECCV, pp. 661–679 (2020)
12. Park, J., Woo, S., Lee, J.Y., Kweon, I.S.: Bam: Bottleneck attention module. arXiv preprint arXiv:1807.06514 (2018)
13. Rerabek, M., Ebrahimi, T.: New light field image dataset. In: 8th International Conference on Quality of Multimedia Experience. No. CONF (2016)
14. Rossi, M., Frossard, P.: Geometry-consistent light field super-resolution via graph-based regularization. IEEE TIP **27**(9), 4207–4218 (2018)
15. Sheng, H., Zhang, S., Cao, X., Fang, Y., Xiong, Z.: Geometric occlusion analysis in depth estimation using integral guided filter for light-field image. IEEE TIP **26**(12), 5758–5771 (2017)
16. Shi, J., Jiang, X., Guillemot, C.: A framework for learning depth from a flexible subset of dense and sparse light field views. IEEE TIP **28**(12), 5867–5880 (2019)
17. Vaish, V., Adams, A.: The (new) stanford light field archive. Computer Graphics Laboratory, Stanford University 6(7) (2008)

18. Wang, B., Yang, L., Zhao, Y.: POLO: learning explicit cross-modality fusion for temporal action localization. IEEE Signal Process. Lett. **28**, 503–507 (2021)
19. Wang, W., Zhou, T., Qi, S., Shen, J., Zhu, S.C.: Hierarchical human semantic parsing with comprehensive part-relation modeling. IEEE TPAMI (2021)
20. Wang, X., Girshick, R., Gupta, A., He, K.: Non-local neural networks. In: CVPR, pp. 7794–7803 (2018)
21. Wang, Y., Wang, L., Yang, J., An, W., Yu, J., Guo, Y.: Spatial-angular interaction for light field image super-resolution. In: ECCV, pp. 290–308 (2020)
22. Wang, Y., Yang, J., Wang, L., Ying, X., Wu, T., An, W., Guo, Y.: Light field image super-resolution using deformable convolution. IEEE TIP **30**, 1057–1071 (2020)
23. Wang, Y., Liu, F., Zhang, K., Hou, G., Sun, Z., Tan, T.: LFNet: a novel bidirectional recurrent convolutional neural network for light-field image super-resolution. IEEE TIP **27**(9), 4274–4286 (2018)
24. Wanner, S., Meister, S., Goldluecke, B.: Datasets and benchmarks for densely sampled 4D light fields. Vis. Modell. Visual. **13**, 225–226 (2013)
25. Woo, S., Park, J., Lee, J.Y., Kweon, I.S.: CBAM: convolutional block attention module. In: ECCV, pp. 3–19 (2018)
26. Yang, L., Peng, H., Zhang, D., Fu, J., Han, J.: Revisiting anchor mechanisms for temporal action localization. IEEE TIP **29**, 8535–8548 (2020)
27. Yeung, H.W.F., Hou, J., Chen, X., Chen, J., Chen, Z., Chung, Y.Y.: Light field spatial super-resolution using deep efficient spatial-angular separable convolution. IEEE TIP **28**(5), 2319–2330 (2018)
28. Yoon, Y., Jeon, H.G., Yoo, D., Lee, J.Y., Kweon, I.S.: Light-field image super-resolution using convolutional neural network. IEEE Signal Process. Lett. **24**(6), 848–852 (2017)
29. Yu, J.: A light-field journey to virtual reality. IEEE Multimedia **24**(2), 104–112 (2017)
30. Yuan, Y., Cao, Z., Su, L.: Light-field image superresolution using a combined deep CNN based on EPI. IEEE Signal Process. Lett. **25**(9), 1359–1363 (2018)
31. Zhang, S., Lin, Y., Sheng, H.: Residual networks for light field image super-resolution. In: CVPR, pp. 11046–11055 (2019)
32. Zhang, Y., Li, K., Li, K., Wang, L., Zhong, B., Fu, Y.: Image super-resolution using very deep residual channel attention networks. In: ECCV, pp. 286–301 (2018)
33. Zhou, T., Li, J., Wang, S., Tao, R., Shen, J.: MATNet: motion-attentive transition network for zero-shot video object segmentation. IEEE TIP **29**, 8326–8338 (2020)
34. Zhou, T., Qi, S., Wang, W., Shen, J., Zhu, S.C.: Cascaded parsing of human-object interaction recognition. IEEE TPAMI (2021)
35. Zhou, T., Wang, S., Zhou, Y., Yao, Y., Li, J., Shao, L.: Motion-attentive transition for zero-shot video object segmentation. In: AAAI, pp. 13066–13073 (2020)
36. Zhou, T., Wang, W., Liu, S., Yang, Y., Van Gool, L.: Differentiable multi-granularity human representation learning for instance-aware human semantic parsing. In: CVPR, pp. 1622–1631 (2021)
37. Zhu, H., Wang, Q., Yu, J.: Occlusion-model guided antiocclusion depth estimation in light field. IEEE J. Selected Top. Signal Process. **11**(7), 965–978 (2017)
38. Zhu, H., Zhang, Q., Wang, Q.: 4D light field superpixel and segmentation. In: CVPR, pp. 6384–6392 (2017)

# Infrared Small Target Detection Based on Weighted Variation Coefficient Local Contrast Measure

YuJie He[1(✉)], Min Li[1], ZhenHua Wei[1], and YanCheng Cai[2]

[1] Xi'an Research Institute of Hi-Tech, Xi'an, China
[2] Fudan University, Shanghai, China
19307140030@fudan.edu.cn

**Abstract.** Infrared small target detection is one of the key technologies in IR guidance systems. In order to obtain high detection performance and low false alarm rates against intricate backgrounds with heavy clutters and noises, an infrared small target detection method based on weighted variation coefficient local contrast measure is proposed in this paper. For the raw infrared image, the variation coefficient local contrast map is calculated firstly, which can extract the local contrast features of different background regions better. Then, the modified local entropy is used as weights for the contrast map to enhance the target further. After that, a simple adaptive threshold is applied to segment the target. Experimental results on four sequences compared with seven baseline methods demonstrate that our method not only has better detection performance even if with strong clutters, but also can suppress the interference simultaneously.

**Keywords:** Infrared target detection · Local contrast measure · Local information entropy · Weighted variation coefficient local contrast measure (WVCLCM)

## 1 Introduction

Infrared (IR) small target detection under low signal-to-clutter ratio (SCR) and complex background conditions is one of the most important techniques in terminal precision guidance and early warning systems, which has attracted significant research attention and been research focus in recent years [11]. However, due to the difference between infrared and visible imaging mechanism, target in infrared image usually appears as a dim point which does not have concrete texture, shape and color features. Little information can be extracted for the detection system. In addition, small targets are usually submerged in the complex background edges or highlight background areas because of the transmitting and scattering of the atmospheric with long observation distance [7]. All these

Supported by National Natural Science Foundation of China (Grant No. 62006240).

H. Ma et al. (Eds.): PRCV 2021, LNCS 13021, pp. 117–127, 2021.
https://doi.org/10.1007/978-3-030-88010-1_10

factors make infrared small target detection more difficult to be solved and a challenging task.

Recently, various infrared small target detection methods has been developed, which can be classified into two categories: detection based on single frame and multi-frame. The multi-frame detection algorithms usually need more prior information which can not be acquired on many high-speed motion detection platforms in advance. In addition, the multi-frame detection methods are built on single frame detection in many cases. So, high-performance single-frame algorithms have attracted considerable attention from researchers, which can be divided into two classes. The first class methods consider the target as singular point in image and use image filtering to suppress background clutters [1,4]. However, this kind of method loses the effective information of target, and its performance depends on the manually selected background template. The second class methods transform the detection task into an machine learning problem using some pattern classification models, such as IPI [7], LRSR [11] and SR [6]. Nevertheless, these methods have high computational complexity and can not meet the real-time requirements of practical application.

A series of infrared small target detection algorithms based on human visual system (HVS) currently have achieved awesome results, which can use local contrast mechanism to segment the target point efficiently. Chen [2] proposed the local contrast measure (LCM) to suppress background using directional information; ILCM [9] adopt mean operation based on LCM, which can effectively cope with the impact of PNHB; RLCM [10] considered the relationship between target and background; MPCM [14] can not only detect the bright target, but also detect the dark target; MLHM [12] and HWLCM [5] used homogeneity characteristics of the surrounding regions to enhance the target, and so on. However, these methods do not consider the difference among background cells when obtaining the contrast information, which causes the background noise points being regarded as targets and inaccurate detection in the case of complex background and heavy clutter.

In order to improve the detection performance, a new method named weighted variation coefficient local contrast measure is proposed in this paper. It takes the difference among background cells into account by using the variability of difference between target and background cells in eight directions and then the modified local entropy is used as pixel weight to enhance the target effectively. Experimental results demonstrate that, against the heavy noise and serious clutters, our method is effective with respect to detection accuracy.

## 2   The Proposed Algorithm

In this section, we introduce a new approach for the detection of infrared small target under complex background. The flow chart of the proposed approach is shown in Fig. 1. Considering the difference characteristics of background regions, this approach weights a variation coefficient based local contrast measure using the modified adaption local entropy. Then an effective threshold method is used to gain the target in the contrast map.

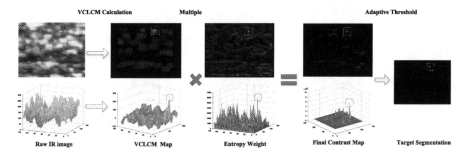

**Fig. 1.** The flow chart of the proposed WVCLCM algorithm

## 2.1 Variation Coefficient Local Contrast Measure

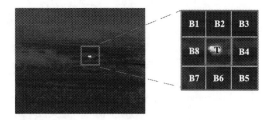

**Fig. 2.** The nested structure of the sliding window

The Local Contrast Measure (LCM) and its improvements usually use a nested structure of sliding window shown as Fig. 2, which is divided into nine cells. The central cell is used to represent the target defined as $T$ and the eight surrounding cells are used to represent the background denoted by $B_i, i = 1, 2, \ldots, 8$. The local contrast map is calculated using several methods based on LCM, which could enhance target signal and suppress background clutter. Nevertheless, because the background is relatively homogeneous in local region, the variation of the difference between target and background at eight surrounding cells is not obvious. That is to say, the difference among background cells in eight directions is very tiny. With these considerations in mind, the proposed variation coefficient local contrast measure is given by

$$\text{VCLCM} = I_\text{T}(\frac{I_\text{T} - \text{mean}(I_B)}{\sigma_\text{D} + \alpha}) \tag{1}$$

$$I_T = \frac{1}{N_T} \sum_{j=1}^{N_T} G_T^j \tag{2}$$

$$\text{mean}(I_\text{B}) = \frac{1}{8} \sum_{i=1}^{8} (\frac{1}{N_\text{B}} \sum_{j=1}^{N_\text{B}} G_\text{Bi}^j) \tag{3}$$

where $I_T$ denotes the average gray of the $N_T$ maximum gray pixels in target cell; $I_{Bi}$ denotes the average gray of the $N_B$ maximum gray pixels in the $i$-th background cell; $\sigma_D$ is the gray standard deviation among the eight directions of differences between $T$ and $B_i$ as given in (4)–(6). We use this parameter to measure the homogeneity of different background cells; $\alpha$ is the prior parameter with value 6 to avoid singular points. $G_T^j$ denotes the $j$-th maximal gray value in the target cell T and $G_{Bi}^j$ is the $j$-th maximal gray value in the $i$th background cell $B_i$. Generally, the $N_T$ is set to smaller than $N_B$ to reduce the impact of isolated noise. We first compute the average grays $I_T$ and $I_B$, then calculate the standard deviations of difference between $T$ and $Bi$ as follows:

$$\sigma_D = \sqrt{\frac{1}{8}\sum_{i=1}^{8}[di - M_{di}]^2} \tag{4}$$

$$d_i = I_T - I_{Bi} \tag{5}$$

$$M_{di} = \frac{1}{8}\sum_{i=1}^{8} di \tag{6}$$

where $di$ denotes the difference between $I_T$ and the $I_{Bi}$. $M_{di}$ is the mean of $di$. In this way, the VCLCM map can be obtained for each pixel of the raw IR image by sliding the window from left to right and top to bottom pixel by pixel. Obviously, the larger the pixel value of the VCLCM map is, the more likely a target appears.

As a matter of fact, there are several different situations, which could cause interferences to the detection, such as complex background edges, high brightness backgrounds, pixel-sized noise with high brightness (PNHB). So it is necessary to discuss the VCLCM results for different situations. Equation 1 can be transformed as VCLCM $= I_T w$, and the $w$ can be treated as variation coefficient. This variation coefficient not only represents the relationship between the target and background, but also shows the the severity of the pixel gray's change among different background cells. In other words, the variation coefficient directly reflects the background homogeneity and the local contrast features of different background regions, that is why the proposed method is named as VCLCM.

1. For a target pixel (denoted by $T$) which is conspicuous in a local region, its gray value is much larger than the surrounding cells. So $I_T$ is much lager than $mean(I_B)$ . In addition, the surrounding area of target is often homogeneous and the difference of background pixel's gradient is tiny. So the gray standard deviation $\{\sigma_D\}^T$ is very small and we can easily get $w \gg 1$. Then the target region is enhanced.
2. For a background pixel (denoted by $B$), the value of $I_T$ is similar to its surrounding value $I_{Bi}$ and the numerator and denominator of $w$ approaches 0. In this ideal case, the prior parameter $\alpha$ makes the variation coefficient $w < 1$, which can suppress the background.

3. For a background edge pixel (denoted by $E$), since the similarity of background is broken by the boundaries, $\{\sigma_D\}^E > \{\sigma_D\}^T$ and $\text{VCLCM}_T > \text{VCLCM}_E$.
4. For a PNHB which is also bright in local region, the $I_T$ is smaller than the real target's by adjusting the $N_T$. So $\text{VCLCM}_T > \text{VCLCM}_{\text{PNHB}}$.

## 2.2  Weighted Variation Coefficient Local Contrast Measure

The VCLCM map can be obtained using Eq. (1) which can enhance the small target while suppressing the background as shown in Fig. 1. Consider that the target usually is discontinuous with its neighboring areas, the weighted method can be used to enhance the isolated points again for gaining a better detection performance. Since the information entropy can illustrate the complex degree of gray value distribution upon the raw image, which can emphasize high frequency component of the infrared image [13]. That is to say, the brighter target has more information and higher entropy than uniform background. Consequently, the modified local information entropy is adopted as weights for VCLCM map to eliminate the clutters and noise residual.

Assume that $I(x, y)$ is the gray value at the position $(x, y)$ in the raw image with a size of $M \times N$. Its neighborhood is defined as

$$\Omega_k = \{(p, q) | max(|p - x|, |q - y|) \leqslant k\} \tag{7}$$

where $k$ is size of the neighborhood (local window) which has $s$ kinds of gray values, $f_i$, $i = 1, 2, \ldots, s$, the weight map will be given as

$$W(x, y) = -\sum_{i=1}^{s} (f_i - I(x, y))^2 p_i \log_2 p_i, \ p_i = \frac{ni}{M \times N} \tag{8}$$

where $p_i$ is the probability density function of the $i$th gray level in the whole image. As shown in Fig. 1, It is obvious that the detection performance is improved using entropy weight which can enhance the target effectively. Accordingly, the WVCLCM is proposed and the formula is given as

$$\text{WVCLCM} = W(x, y) \times \text{VCLCM}(x, y) \tag{9}$$

where $W(x, y)$ and $\text{VCLCM}(x, y)$ denote entropy weight map and VCLCM map at pixel $(x, y)$ respectively. The final salient map can be achieved by traversing the whole image and replacing the value of the central pixel with the $\text{WVCLCM}(x, y)$. As shown in Fig. 1, the WVCLCM can improve the adaptability and robustness of the variation coefficient local contrast measure.

**Table 1.** Details of four sequences

| Seq | Length | Target | Details |
|-----|--------|--------|---------|
| Seq.1 | 100 | Ship | Bright spot, heavy clutters |
| Seq.2 | 70 | Plane | Disturbing by cloud clutter |
| Seq.3 | 200 | Plane | Distractor, low SNR |
| Seq.4 | 200 | Plane | Small target, complex background |

### 2.3   Target Detection

As mentioned before, the WVCLCM can enlarge the discontinuity of the target region from its neighboring areas and therefore the true target has the most salient in the scene. A simple threshold operation on salient map can be used to extract the true target, and the threshold $Th$ is defined as

$$Th = \mu_{\text{WVCLCM}} + k \times \sigma_{\text{WVCLCM}} \tag{10}$$

where $\mu_{\text{WVCLCM}}$ and $\sigma_{\text{WVCLCM}}$ denote the mean and standard deviation of the final salient map, respectively. $k$ is an empirical parameter ranging from 15 to 25 and is set to 18 in our experiments. The pixel is target if its value is larger than $Th$, otherwise it should be seen as background.

## 3   Experimental Results

We evaluate the target detection performance on four public-available infrared image sequences. These sequences have lots of difficult conditions, such as heavy noises and distractor in Seq.3, cloud edges and cover in Seq.2 and Seq.4, high brightness background in Seq.1 and Seq.3. The details are shown in Table 1. In our experiments, based on the consideration of computational cost, the size of cell and the local entropy neighborhood are experimentally determined as 9 and 4. Different scales are considered by using three pairs of $N_T$ and $N_B$ values, $(N_T, N_B) = (2, 4), (5, 9), (9, 16)$. We also test the conventional single-frame detection methods for comparison such as ILCM, RLCM, HWLCM, MLHM, MPCM, WLDM [3] and TLLCM [8]. All experiments are implemented by MAT-LAB 2015a on a laptop with 8 GB RAM, and 2.46 GHz Intel i7 processor.

### 3.1   Enhancement Performance Comparison

For the four sequences, Fig. 3 denotes the 3-D gray distributions of enhanced results obtained by using different base line methods (Target is indicated by red circle). It can be seen that there are heavy background noise, clutters and large bright spots in Seq.1. Moreover, the brightness of the target is weak compared with the surrounding backgrounds, which causing the target to be submerged easily. Figure 3 shows that only our method has outstanding detection performance while the detection results of other seven algorithms are unsatisfactory.

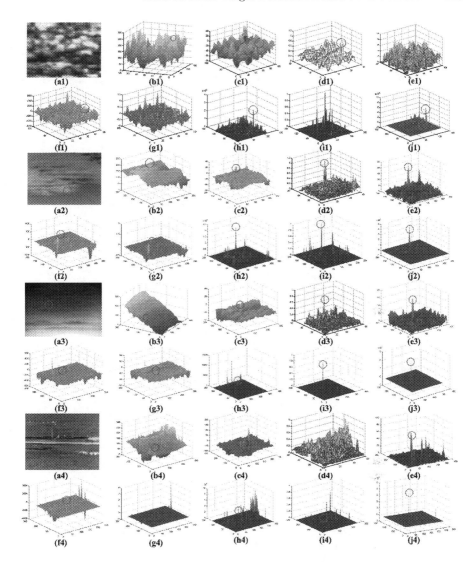

**Fig. 3.** 3-D mesh view of Salient Map of different methods. The figures (a1)–(j1), (a2)–(j2), (a3)–(j3) and (a4)–(j4) correspond to the four sequences, respectively. (a1)–(a4) Raw images, (b1)–(b4) 3-D mesh of the original images, (c1)–(c4) RLCM, (d1)–(d4) ILCM, (e1)–(e4) HWLCM, (f1)–(f4) MPCM, (g1)–(g4) MLHM, (h1)–(h4) WLDM, (i1)–(i4) TLLCM and (j1)–(j4) Ours (Color figure online)

This is because our method considers the difference among background cells which can availably suppress diverse complex and noisy background.

Seq.2 and Seq.3 have diverse intricate and brighter cloudy-sky backgrounds, which cause impact to target detection. All eight algorithms can detect the target with suppress the background, but our method produces less clutters and noise residual for complex cloudy-sky backgrounds which can reduce False Alarm Rate. Seq.4 have various complex mechanical noises which have almost the same brightness as target and the target size is only $2 \times 1$. So the noise points is enhanced by all methods except WVCLCM which can achieve the target correctly. Thus, our method can efficiently discriminate the target from background clutters and noise.

## 3.2    Detection Performance Comparison

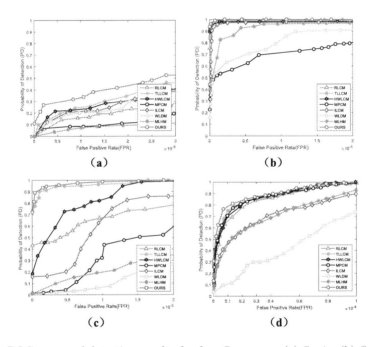

**Fig. 4.** ROC curves of detection results for four Sequences. (a) Seq1. (b) Seq2. (c) Seq3. (d) Seq4.

To illustrate the effectiveness of the WVCLCM algorithm further, the SCR-gain (SCRG), background suppression factor (BSF) and receiver operating characteristic (ROC) are used to be as the objective metrics, where the ROC curve is the curve of detection probability PD and false positive rate FPR. The SCRG and BSF are given as

$$\mathrm{SCRG} = \frac{\mathrm{SCR_{out}}}{\mathrm{SCR_{in}}} \text{ and } \mathrm{BSF} = \frac{\sigma_{\mathrm{in}}}{\sigma_{\mathrm{out}}} \tag{11}$$

where $\mathrm{SCR}_{out}$ and $\mathrm{SCR}_{in}$ are the values of SCR after and before WVCLCM calculation, respectively. $\sigma_{in}$ and $\sigma_{out}$ denote the standard deviation of the raw image and final salient map, respectively. PD and FPR are defined by

$$PD = \frac{\text{number of detected true targets}}{\text{total number of real targets}} \tag{12}$$

$$FPR = \frac{\text{number of detected false targets}}{\text{total number of pixels in the whole image}} \tag{13}$$

The ROC curve represents the relationship between PD and FPR. The larger area under the curve, the better the detection performance is. In this paper, the judgment threshold is selected as 3 pixels. That is to say, if the distance between ground truth and detected result is smaller than 3 pixels, the result is correct.

ROC curves of the eight methods for the four real small target image sequences are given in Fig. 4. It can be seen that our method has better detection performance than the others, especially for Seq.1 and Seq.4 which have heavy clutters and noises. We also can see that most methods can rise to 1 (100%) quickly when FPR $< 0.3$ for Seq.2 and the TLLCM, HWLCM, ILCM and MLHM methods performed better than the other three baseline methods. For Seq.3, the results of the eight algorithms are quite different due to the complex sky background with bright and dark cloud region. Only TLLCM and our algorithm can achieve better detection results which can reach 1 (100%) gradually when FPR $> 1.5$. However, our algorithm displays superior performance than that of the others with the same FPR.

**Table 2.** The SCRG of different methods

| Sequence | RLCM | ILCM | MPCM | MLHM | HWLCM | WLDM | TLLCM | Ours |
|----------|------|------|------|------|-------|------|-------|------|
| Seq.1 | 1.5172 | 1.6478 | 2.5471 | 4.3214 | 7.3547 | 15.3219 | 10.2541 | **23.5637** |
| Seq.2 | 3.0124 | 7.1254 | 3.2451 | 3.1425 | 21.3543 | 7.6574 | **32.2478** | 28.3578 |
| Seq.3 | 13.3715 | 21.8345 | 3.0349 | 2.5957 | 39.3279 | 45.2477 | 175.3247 | **180.3548** |
| Seq.4 | 10.2537 | 15.2367 | 10.2576 | 9.3247 | 78.3685 | 38.9578 | 65.3278 | **136.8519** |

Table 2 and Table 3 show the SCRG and BSF evaluations of eight methods on the four sequences and the highest value is marked in bold. It can be seen that the proposed method shows superiority over the baseline methods in terms of the SCRG values and BSF values for all sequences except for Seq.2 about SCRG. Therefore, our method our method works more robustly for various clutter and noisy backgrounds.

In order to measure the computational complexity of different methods quantitatively, we also compared the average computational cost of the eight detection algorithms for a single image as shown in Table 4. It can be seen that the RLCM achieves the fastest detection results, and the running time of our method is mediocre. There is still some room for improvement due to our method is made up of two steps. For instance, parallel computation can be used for the proposed method to improve the computation speed.

**Table 3.** The BSF of different methods

| Sequence | RLCM | ILCM | MPCM | MLHM | HWLCM | WLDM | TLLCM | Ours |
|----------|------|------|------|------|-------|------|-------|------|
| Seq.1 | 3.214 | 10.2531 | 1.3574 | 1.5628 | 15.9871 | 75.3245 | 125.3698 | **358.2146** |
| Seq.2 | 6.5784 | 25.284 | 0.5478 | 0.9741 | 1.8523E3 | 135.147 | 1.7532E3 | **1.9624E3** |
| Seq.3 | 32.5246 | 65.3244 | 0.1785 | 0.1425 | 1.3225E3 | 235.5789 | 4.5671E5 | **4.9852E5** |
| Seq.4 | 26.3547 | 12.3542 | 1.3254 | 2.4578 | 789.1475 | 685.1475 | 1.1471E3 | **1.4257E3** |

**Table 4.** The average running time of different methods (in seconds)

| Sequence | Resolution | RLCM | ILCM | MPCM | MLHM | HWLCM | WLDM | TLLCM | Ours |
|----------|-----------|------|------|------|------|-------|------|-------|------|
| Seq.1 | $118 \times 119$ | 0.0137 | 0.0235 | 0.752 | 0.8024 | 0.0213 | 1.125 | 0.0153 | 0.792 |
| Seq.2 | $250 \times 200$ | 0.0279 | 0.0354 | 1.1255 | 1.2337 | 0.0308 | 1.596 | 0.0292 | 1.145 |
| Seq.3 | $320 \times 180$ | 0.0241 | 0.0392 | 1.3125 | 1.3597 | 0.0336 | 1.783 | 0.0281 | 1.343 |
| Seq.4 | $256 \times 256$ | 0.0229 | 0.0376 | 1.3026 | 1.3382 | 0.0324 | 1.692 | 0.0269 | 1.298 |

## 4    Conclusion

This paper presents an effective small infrared target method based on WVCLCM in which the variance of difference between target and background in eight directions is considered. In addition, the method weights the variation coefficient local contrast measure using modified local entropy and obtains target by a simple adaptive threshold operation. The proposed method can eliminate complex background clutters and noise by enhancing the target. Experimental results show that the proposed method significantly outperforms the baseline methods and is more robust to different backgrounds and targets.

## References

1. Bai, X., Zhou, F.: Analysis of new top-hat transformation and the application for infrared dim small target detection. Pattern Recognit. **43**(6), 2145–2156 (2010)
2. Chen, C.L.P., Li, H., Wei, Y.T., Xia, T., Tang, Y.Y.: A local contrast method for small infrared target detection. IEEE Trans. Geosci. Remote Sens. **52**(1), 574–581 (2014)
3. Deng, H., Sun, X., Liu, M., Ye, C.H., Zhou, X.: Small infrared target detection based on weighted local difference measure. IEEE Trans. Geosci. Remote Sens. **54**(7), 4204–4214 (2016)
4. Dong, X., Huang, X., Zheng, Y., Shen, L., Bai, S.: Infrared dim and small target detecting and tracking method inspired by human visual system. Infr. Phys. Technol. **62**, 100–109 (2014)
5. Du, P., Hamdulla, A.: Infrared small target detection using homogeneity weighted local contrast measure. IEEE Geosci. Remote Sens. Lett. **17**(3), 514–518 (2020)
6. Gao, C.Q.: Small infrared target detection using sparse ring representation. Aerosp. Electron. Syst. Mag. IEEE **27**(3), 21–30 (2012)
7. Gao, C.Q., Meng, D.Y., Yang, Y., et al.: Infrared patch-image model for small target detection in a single image. IEEE Tans. Image Process. **22**(12), 4996–5009 (2013)

8. Han, J., Moradi, S., Faramarzi, I., Liu, C., Zhang, H., Zhao, Q.: A local contrast method for infrared small-target detection utilizing a tri-layer window. IEEE Geosci. Remote Sens. Lett. **17**, 1822–1826 (2020)
9. Han, J.H., Ma, Y., Zhou, B., Fan, F., Kun, L., Fang, Y.: A robust infrared small target detection algorithm based on human visual system. IEEE Geosci. Remote Sens. Lett. **11**(12), 2168–2172 (2014)
10. Han, J., Liang, K., Zhou, B., Zhu, X., Zhao, J., Zhao, L.: Infrared small target detection utilizing the multiscale relative local contrast measure. IEEE Geosci. Remote Sens. Lett. **15**(4), 612–616 (2018)
11. He, Y.J., Li, M., Zhang, J.L., An, Q.: Small infrared target detection based on low-rank and sparse representation. Infr. Phys. Technol. **68**, 98–109 (2015)
12. Nie, J., Qu, S., Wei, Y., Zhang, L., Deng, L.: An infrared small target detection method based on multiscale local homogeneity measure. Infr. Phys. Technol. **90**, 186–194 (2018)
13. Qu, X.J., Chen, H., Peng, G.H.: Novel detection method for infrared small targets using weighted information entropy. J. Syst. Eng. Electron. **23**(6), 838–842 (2012)
14. Wei, Y., You, X., Li, H.: Multiscale patch-based contrast measure for small infrared target detection. Pattern Recogn. **58**, 216–226 (2016)

# Scale-Aware Distillation Network for Lightweight Image Super-Resolution

Haowei Lu, Yao Lu[✉], Gongping Li, Yanbei Sun, Shunzhou Wang,
and Yugang Li

Beijing Laboratory of Intelligent Information Technology, School of Computer Science
and Technology, Beijing Institute of Technology, Beijing 100081, China
vis_yl@bit.edu.cn

**Abstract.** Many lightweight models have achieved great progress in single image super-resolution. However, their parameters are still too many to be applied in practical applications, and it still has space for parameter reduction. Meanwhile, multi-scale features are usually underutilized by researchers, which are better for multi-scale regions' reconstruction. With the renaissance of deep learning, convolution neural network based methods has prompted many computer vision tasks (e.g., video object segmentation [21,38,40], human parsing [39], human-object interaction detection [39]) to achieve significant progresses. To solve this limitation, in this paper, we propose a lightweight super-resolution network named scale-aware distillation network (SDNet). SDNet is built on many stacked scale-aware distillation blocks (SDB), which contain a scale-aware distillation unit (SDU) and a context enhancement (CE) layer. Specifically, SDU enriches the hierarchical features at a granular level via grouped convolution. Meanwhile, the CE layer further enhances the multi-scale feature representation from SDU by context learning to extract more discriminative information. Extensive experiments are performed on commonly-used super-resolution datasets, and our method achieves promising results against other state-of-the-art methods with fewer parameters.

**Keywords:** Image super-resolution · Lightweight network · Multi-scale feature learning · Context learning

## 1 Introduction

Single image super-resolution (SISR) is a classical low-level computer vision task. It aims to reconstruct a high-resolution (HR) image from its corresponding degraded low-resolution (LR) one. It has been widely used in security and surveillance imaging [41], medical imaging [26], and image generation [12]. It is an ill-posed problem that many HR images can be degraded to the same LR image. To

---

This is a student paper.

This work is supported by the National Natural Science Foundation of China (No. 61273273), by the National Key Research and Development Plan (No. 2017YFC0112001), and by China Central Television (JG2018-0247).

© Springer Nature Switzerland AG 2021
H. Ma et al. (Eds.): PRCV 2021, LNCS 13021, pp. 128–139, 2021.
https://doi.org/10.1007/978-3-030-88010-1_11

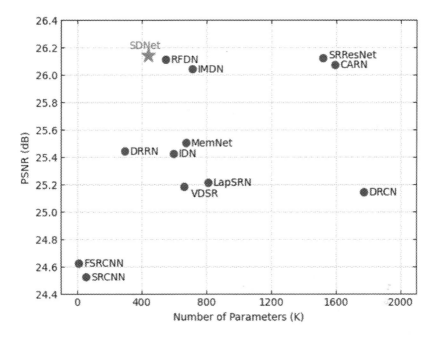

**Fig. 1.** Trade-off between performance *vs.* parameters on Urban100 for ×4 SR. Our proposed model achieves promising performance against state-of-the-art approaches with fewer parameters.

solve the inverse problem, many effective methods [3,13,18,20,31,35,36] based on deep learning have been proposed and shown their capability. Benefited from the residual learning, networks tend to be designed deeper and wider for better image super-resolution performance. However, these methods bring huge parameters and computation costs, which are not suitable for edge devices with limited memory and high execution speed requirements.

To solve this limitation, researchers propose some lightweight methods to reduce the parameters and computation costs, such as recursive method [14,28, 29], parameter sharing strategy [1,15], group convolution methods [1], neural architecture search [16], knowledge distillation [5,17], and feature enhancement method [22,37]. However, they do not fully utilize the multi-scale features, which are useful for reconstruction in some regions with multi-scale objects [4]. As mentioned in the Inception module [27], different receptive fields can provide multi-scale features. It can enrich the hierarchical features and expressive capabilities of the network for computer vision tasks (*e.g.* image classification, object detection, and so on). Some works [10,11,19] in SR employ the information distillation method to extract multi-scale features with different receptive fields. Although they have achieved good performance, they are not efficient enough due to a large number of parameters.

To obtain abundant multi-scale features with fewer parameters, we devise a more efficient block named scale-aware distillation block (SDB). Unlike the PRM in IMDB [10] which uses all channels in every step, the proposed SDB splits the features into four groups at first in scale-aware distillation unit (SDU) and only processes a small number of features in every step. Moreover, SDU can obtain multi-scale features through information transfer between adjacent groups step by step. Furthermore, we devise a context enhancement (CE) layer following to reweight different regions of the multi-scale features. Based on SDB, we build a lightweight model named SDNet to learn more abundant hierarchical features for image super-resolution (SR). Experiments show that our method can achieve promising performance against other state-of-the-art methods on five benchmark datasets with fewer parameters. As shown in Fig. 1.

To summarize, the contributions of this work are as follows:

– We propose a scale-aware distillation block (SDB) to learn multi-scale features for better SR performance with fewer parameters. Specifically, it extracts multi-scale features in scale-aware distillation unit (SDU) and reweights different regions to learn more discriminative information for SR via the context enhancement (CE) layer.
– We propose a lightweight network named SDNet with stacked SDBs. It can achieve promising performance on commonly-used benchmark datasets with fewer parameters and multi-add operations.

## 2    Related Work

Many effective methods have been proposed to solve the super-resolution (SR) problem these years. Dong *et al.* [3] first introduces the deep learning method into SISR. Early works [3,13] usually use interpolated images as their input. Later works always use LR images as their input and upsample the features at the end of the network, in order to reduce parameters and computation cost. As the rapid development of deep learning, convolution neural network with residual learning [18], dense connection learning [30], back-projection [7], and attention mechanism [20,35] promotes the rapid development of SR. EDSR [18] uses residual learning and removed the batch normalization layer to achieve good results while avoiding producing artifacts, and it has about 43M parameters with 69 layers. RCAN promotes the result by a large margin with channel attention, and it has about 16M parameters with more than 400 layers. However, networks tend to be deeper and wider for better performance [10], and it is unavoidable to bring huge parameters and computation costs.

Meanwhile, lightweight models have attracted researchers' attention with practical SR applications' demand. In the literature, various methods have made meaningful attempt, including neural architecture search [16], knowledge distillation [5,17], channel grouping [1], the pyramid network [15], the recursive methods [14,28] and feature enhancement [22,37]. Unlike the above methods, some works [10,11,19] explore to utilize multi-scale features by an information distillation method. IDN [11] divides the features into two parts. One part is retained, and the other part is further processed. IMDN [10] conducts multiple information distillations based on IDN. RFDN [19] proposes a more powerful

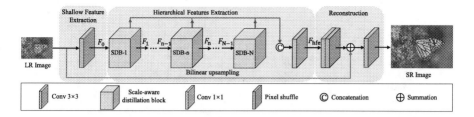

**Fig. 2.** Network architecture of our proposed SDNet. Our hierarchical feature extraction module enriches the hierarchical features via a cascade of Scale-aware distillation blocks (Sect. 3.2). All the intermediate features are processed by $1 \times 1$ convolution respectively, and then aggregated by $1 \times 1$ convolution to obtain more comprehensive information.

network based on IMDN by replacing the channel split operation with convolution layers. Although they achieve good performance, they still have too many parameters. To further reduce the parameters, our method focuses on extracting multi-scale features in a more parameter-economic way.

## 3 Proposed Method

### 3.1 Network Architecture

As shown in Fig. 2, the network structure we proposed has three components: shallow feature extraction module (SFE), hierarchical feature extraction module (HFE) with stacked SDBs, and reconstruction module. Let's denote the $I_{\mathrm{LR}}$ and $I_{\mathrm{SR}}$ as the input and output of SDNet.

**Shallow Feature Extraction.** We use a $3 \times 3$ convolution layer to extract shallow features $F_0$ from the LR input. It can be formulated as

$$F_0 = H_0 \left( I_{\mathrm{LR}} \right), \tag{1}$$

where $H_0$ denotes the convolutional operation.

**Hierarchical Feature Extraction.** Then $F_0$ is used for HFE to learn abundant hierarchical features, which is composed of SDBs. We denote $H_{\mathrm{SDB}}$ as the proposed SDB given by

$$F_N = H_{SDB}^n(H_{SDB}^{n-1}(\dots H_{SDB}^1(F_0)\dots)), \tag{2}$$

where $H_{SDB}^i(i = 1, 2, \dots, N)$ denotes the $i_{th}$ SDB, $F_N$ is the output features of $N_{th}$ SDB.

After that, all the intermediate features are processed by a set of $1 \times 1$ convolution for channel reduction, respectively. Then they are concatenated together and further processed by a $1 \times 1$ convolution to aggregate these hierarchical features from different blocks. It can be denoted as,

$$F_{\mathrm{hfe}} = H_{1 \times 1}([H_{1 \times 1}^1(F_1), H_{1 \times 1}^2(F_2), \dots, H_{1 \times 1}^N(F_N)]), \tag{3}$$

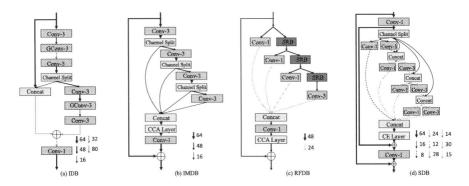

**Fig. 3.** Information distillation methods comparison. (a) Information distillation block (IDB) [11], (b) Information multi-distillation block (IMDB) [10], (c) Residual feature distillation block (RFDB) [19], (d) Our scale-aware distillation block (SDB).

where $F_{\mathrm{hfe}}$ is the output of HFE.

**Reconstruction Module.** For accelerating training and preserving original information, we use skip connection to transmit the LR input for the final reconstruction. Through the final reconstruction module, we can obtain

$$I_{\mathrm{SR}} = H_{3\times 3}(H_{\mathrm{pix}}(H_{3\times 3}(F_{\mathrm{hfe}})) + H_{\mathrm{up}}(I_{\mathrm{LR}})), \tag{4}$$

where $H_{\mathrm{pix}}$ and $H_{\mathrm{up}}$ denotes the pixel shuffle operation and bilinear upsampling operation.

## 3.2   Scale-Aware Distillation Block

Scale-aware distillation block (SDB) aims to learn abundant hierarchical features for the reconstruction module. It mainly consists of SDU and CE layer, as shown in Fig. 3.

**Scale-Aware Distillation Unit.** Multi-scale features are superior to reconstruct high-frequency details, especially in some regions with multi-scale object [4]. Like the multi-branch with different receptive fields in Inception module [27], it can get multi-scale features with different receptive fields, which are important for computer vision tasks. Inspired by [10,33], We devise a scale-aware distillation unit (SDU) to obtain multi-scale features for better SR performance. For lightweight design, we use the channel grouping method in our SDU. Given an input feature $f$, we split it evenly into four groups, denoted by $f_j(j = 1, 2, 3, 4)$. Take the first group as example, $f_1$ will be sent to distillation layer $DL_1$ and refinement layer $RL_1$, respectively. And the outputs are denoted as $\hat{f}_{1,1}$ and $\hat{f}_{1,2}$, respectively. Then, $\hat{f}_{1,1}$ remains, $\hat{f}_{1,2}$ is concatenated with the next group $f_{j+1}$, and further fed to $RL_2$ and $DL_2$. This process repeats several times until the remaining features are processed. This procedure can be described as

$$\hat{f}_{1,1}, \hat{f}_{1,2} = DL_1(f_1), RL_1(f_1),$$
$$\hat{f}_{2,1}, \hat{f}_{2,2} = DL_2(f_2 \oplus \hat{f}_{1,2}), RL_2(f_2 \oplus \hat{f}_{1,2}),$$
$$\hat{f}_{3,1}, \hat{f}_{3,2} = DL_3(f_3 \oplus \hat{f}_{2,2}), RL_3(f_3 \oplus \hat{f}_{2,2}),$$ (5)
$$\hat{f}_{4,1}, \hat{f}_{4,2} = DL_4(f_4 \oplus \hat{f}_{3,2}), RL_4(f_4 \oplus \hat{f}_{3,2}).$$

After that, we use channel concatenate operation to fuse all features as follows

$$\hat{f} = [\hat{f}_{1,1}, \hat{f}_{2,1}, \hat{f}_{3,1}, \hat{f}_{4,1}, \hat{f}_{4,2}],$$ (6)

where $\hat{f}$ is the output of SDU. By this operation, we can get multi-scale features. Specifically, to make sure the input and output features of SDU have the same channels, we set the channels of $\hat{f}_{j,1}$ and $\hat{f}_{j,2}$ is half of $f_j \oplus \hat{f}_{j-1,2}$.

**Context Enhancement Layer.** Although the multi-scale features give a flexible choice for SR, it does not consider that different scales may have different contributions to different regions. So we devise an attention layer based on context learning to make the network focus more on its interest regions. A large receptive field is essential for the attention layer to focus on sufficient information. Thus, to enlarge the receptive field with fewer parameters, we devise a context enhancement (CE) layer based on enhanced spatial attention mechanism [20].

The structure of the CE layer is shown in Fig. 4. We use a $1 \times 1$ convolution layer first to reduce the channel dimension for lightweight design. Then a max-pooling layer (kernel size 7, stride 3) and a $3 \times 3$ convolution layer are followed to enlarge the receptive field. After that, a bilinear upsampling layer is used to recover spatial size, and a $1 \times 1$ convolution layer is used to recover channel dimension. Finally, the attention map is generated by a sigmoid operation. Benefited from the CE layer, our SDB can learn more discriminative information for further process and reconstruction.

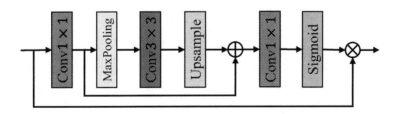

**Fig. 4.** Context enhancement layer.

### 3.3 Comparisons with Other Information Distillation Methods

We compare SDB with other information distillation methods from [10, 11, 19], as shown in Fig. 3. They [10, 11, 19] use all channels to distill information in each step, which brings huge parameters. To further reduce the parameters while obtaining similar multi-scale features, we use the channel grouping method and transmit information between adjacent groups to enlarge the receptive field step by step.

Moreover, IDN [11], IMDN [10], and RFDN [19] can be considered global information distillation methods. However, there exist many redundancy features in standard convolution [6] and is no need to use the global features to distill information in every step [34]. In other words, it is costly to distill information on all channels. Our SDB distills information on a small number of features, and it can be considered a local information distillation method. By transmitting information between adjacent groups, we can get comprehensive information like these global information distillation methods while saving parameters.

## 4     Experiments

### 4.1     Implementation Details

Following [10,11,19,22,25], we use DIV2K as the training dataset. It has 800 training images and 100 validation images. For evaluation, we use five standard benchmark datasets to evaluate the performance of our method: Set5 [2], Set14 [32], B100 [23], Urban100 [9], and Manga109 [24]. All SR results are evaluated by PSNR and SSIM on the Y channel of transformed YCbCr space. We also summarize the parameters and multi-adds, which are commonly-used metrics for a lightweight network.

During the training, the HR image patch sizes are set to $128 \times 128$, $192 \times 192$, $256 \times 256$ for $\times 2$ SR, $\times 3$ SR and $\times 4$ SR. We augment the training dataset with flipping and random rotation. We use the $L1$ loss function and Adam optimizer to train our model. The minibatch size is 32. The learning rate is updated by cosine annealing learning scheme with the period set to $250k$ iterations. And its initial maximum learning rate $1e-3$, and the minimum learning rate $1e-7$. All the experiments are implemented under the PyTorch framework on a single NVIDIA GTX 2080Ti GPU. Our model has 16 SDBs ($N = 16$). The channel number in the main network structure is 64.

### 4.2     Ablation Study

**Multi-scale Features in SDU.** As mentioned in Sect. 3, SDU aims to obtain multi-scale features related to the receptive field's size [27]. In this experiment, SDU has five different fields $(1, 3, 5, 7, 9)$. To verify multi-scale features are useful, we change the receptive field by changing the kernel size of convolution in extraction operations in different steps. When all the kernel size is $1 \times 1$ in all steps' extraction operation, the receptive field is $(1, 1, 1, 1, 1)$. Then change the kernel size to $3 \times 3$ in the extraction operation of the final step, and others remain unchanged, so the receptive field of SDU is $(1, 1, 1, 1, 3)$. And so on, we can obtain different receptive field combinations shown in Table 1.

From this table, we can see that multi-scale features are essential in SDU intuitively. We can obtain more useful information for further proceedings based on SDU.

**Table 1.** Performances of multiple receptive fields combination on Urban100 for ×4 SR.

| Receptive field | Params | Multi-adds | PSNR/SSIM |
|---|---|---|---|
| [1, 1, 1, 1, 1] | 284K | 14.2G | 25.31/0.7590 |
| [1, 1, 1, 1, 3] | 342K | 17.5G | 25.95/0.7817 |
| [1, 1, 1, 3, 5] | 392K | 20.4G | 26.02/0.7838 |
| [1, 1, 3, 5, 7] | 429K | 22.6G | 26.10/0.7865 |
| [1, 3, 5, 7, 9] | 445K | 23.5G | 26.14/0.7879 |

**Table 2.** Average PSNR/SSIM for scale factor 2, 3 and 4 on datasets Set5, Set14, BSD100, Urban100, and Manga109. '−' denotes the results are not provided. The best and second best results are highlighted in **bold** and *italic* respectively.

| Scale | Method | Params | Multi-adds | Set5 PSNR/SSIM | Set14 PSNR/SSIM | B100 PSNR/SSIM | Urban100 PSNR/SSIM | Manga109 PSNR/SSIM |
|---|---|---|---|---|---|---|---|---|
| ×2 | SRCNN | 57K | 52.7G | 36.66/0.9542 | 32.45/0.9067 | 31.36/0.8879 | 29.50/0.8946 | 35.60/0.9663 |
| | DRRN [28] | 298K | 6,796.9G | 37.74/0.9591 | 33.23/0.9136 | 32.05/0.8973 | 31.23/0.9188 | 37.88/0.9749 |
| | MemNet [29] | 678K | 2,662.4G | 37.78/0.9597 | 33.28/0.9142 | 32.08/0.8978 | 31.31/0.9195 | 37.72/0.9740 |
| | CARN-M [1] | 412K | 91.2G | 37.53/0.9583 | 33.26/0.9141 | 31.92/0.8960 | 30.83/0.9233 | −/− |
| | IDN [11] | 579K | 124.6G | 37.83/0.9600 | 33.30/0.9148 | 32.08/0.8985 | 31.27/0.9196 | 38.01/0.9749 |
| | IMDN [10] | 694K | 158.8G | 38.00/*0.9605* | *33.63*/0.9177 | *32.19*/0.8996 | *32.17*/*0.9283* | **38.88/0.9774** |
| | RFDN [19] | 534K | 120.9G | **38.05/0.9606** | **33.68**/*0.9184* | 32.16/0.8994 | 32.12/0.9278 | **38.88**/*0.9773* |
| | **SDNet (ours)** | 443K | 93.3G | *38.02*/**0.9606** | **33.68/0.9186** | **32.20/0.9000** | **32.24/0.9294** | *38.69*/*0.9773* |
| ×3 | SRCNN | 57K | 52.7G | 32.75/0.9090 | 29.30/0.8215 | 28.41/0.7863 | 26.24/0.7989 | 30.48/0.9117 |
| | DRRN [28] | 298K | 6,796.9G | 34.03/0.9244 | 29.96/0.8349 | 28.95/0.8004 | 27.53/0.8378 | 32.71/0.9379 |
| | MemNet [29] | 678K | 2,662.4G | 34.09/0.9248 | 30.00/0.8350 | 28.96/0.8001 | 27.56/0.8376 | 32.51/0.9369 |
| | CARN-M [1] | 412K | 46.1G | 33.99/0.9236 | 30.08/0.8367 | 28.91/0.8000 | 26.86/0.8263 | −/− |
| | IDN [11] | 588K | 56.3G | 34.11/0.9253 | 29.99/0.8354 | *28.95*/0.8013 | 27.42/0.8359 | 32.71/0.9381 |
| | IMDN [10] | 703K | 71.5G | 34.36/*0.9270* | 30.32/0.8417 | **29.09**/0.8046 | *28.17*/*0.8519* | *33.61*/*0.9445* |
| | RFDN [19] | 541K | 54.3G | *34.41*/**0.9273** | *30.34*/*0.8420* | **29.09**/*0.8050* | **28.21/0.8525** | **33.67/0.9449** |
| | **SDNet (ours)** | 444K | 41.5G | **34.42/0.9273** | **30.36/0.8426** | **29.09/0.8053** | 28.14/*0.8519* | 33.53/0.9443 |
| ×4 | SRCNN | 57K | 52.7G | 30.48/0.8628 | 27.49/0.7503 | 26.90/0.7101 | 24.52/0.7221 | 27.66/0.8505 |
| | DRRN [28] | 297K | 6,796.9G | 31.68/0.8888 | 28.21/0.7720 | 27.38/0.7284 | 25.44/0.7638 | 29.46/0.8960 |
| | MemNet [29] | 677K | 2,662.4G | 31.74/0.8893 | 28.26/0.7723 | 27.40/0.7281 | 25.50/0.7630 | 29.42/0.8942 |
| | CARN-M [1] | 412K | 32.5G | 31.92/0.8903 | 28.42/0.7762 | 27.44/0.7304 | 25.63/0.7688 | −/− |
| | IDN [11] | 600K | 32.3G | 31.82/0.8928 | 28.25/0.7730 | 27.41/0.7297 | 25.42/0.7632 | 29.41/0.8942 |
| | IMDN [10] | 715K | 40.9G | 32.21/0.8948 | *28.58*/0.7811 | 27.56/0.7353 | 26.04/0.7838 | 30.45/0.9075 |
| | RFDN [19] | 550K | 31.1G | **32.24**/*0.8952* | **28.61**/*0.7819* | *27.57*/*0.7360* | *26.11*/*0.7858* | **30.58**/*0.9089* |
| | **SDNet (ours)** | 445K | 23.5G | *32.23*/**0.8953** | **28.61/0.7822** | **27.57/0.7371** | **26.14/0.7879** | *30.56*/**0.9098** |

**Different Attention Mechanism.** To prove the effectiveness of the context enhancement (CE) layer, we implement some different lightweight attention mechanisms like SE Layer [8], CCA Layer [10] in our model. From Table 3, we find that SDNet *w/o* CE Layer achieves the lowest reconstruction accuracy, demonstrating the effectiveness of the CE Layer. We can also find that the CE layer performs better than others. The parameters of the CE layer are increased, but the PSNR is improved by about 0.1 dB on the Manga109 dataset.

**Table 3.** Performances of different attention mechanism on Manga109 for ×4 SR.

| Attention mechanism | Params | Multi-adds | PSNR/SSIM |
|---|---|---|---|
| SDNet *w/o* CE Layer | 374K | 21.4G | 30.40/0.9074 |
| SDNet *w.* SE Layer | 383K | 21.4G | 30.44/0.9084 |
| SDNet *w.* CCA Layer | 383K | 21.4G | 30.47/0.9075 |
| SDNet | 445K | 23.5G | 30.56/0.9098 |

### 4.3   Comparisons with the State-of-the-Arts

We compare our method with the other lightweight state-of-the-art SR methods, including SRCNN [3], DRRN [28], MemNet [29], CARN-M [1], IDN [11], IMDN [10], and RFDN [19]. Table 2 shows the quantitative comparison results on five benchmark datasets. Our method can achieve promising results against other state-of-the-art methods with fewer parameters and multi-adds. RFDN is the winning solution of the AIM 2020 efficient super-resolution challenge. Our method can achieve comparable results to RFDN and only has 80.9% networks parameters of RFDN. For visual comparison, Fig. 5 shows the visualization of different super-resolution networks on Urban100 for ×4 SR. Compared with other methods, our method performs better on reconstructing multi-scale regions while avoiding producing artifacts.

We also report the running time of some methods in Table 4. It is tested on a single NVIDIA GTX 2080Ti GPU. Although our SDNet costs more time than IMDN and RFDN, it achieves better image super-resolution performance, especially on images with rich details and textures like Urban100 with fewer parameters.

**Table 4.** Running time on Urban100 for ×4 SR

| Method | Params | Multi-adds | Runtime | PSNR/SSIM |
|---|---|---|---|---|
| IMDN | 715K | 40.9G | 0.039 s | 26.04/0.7838 |
| RFDN | 550K | 31.1G | 0.039 s | 26.11/0.7858 |
| SDNet | 442K | 23.2G | 0.080 s | 26.14/0.7879 |

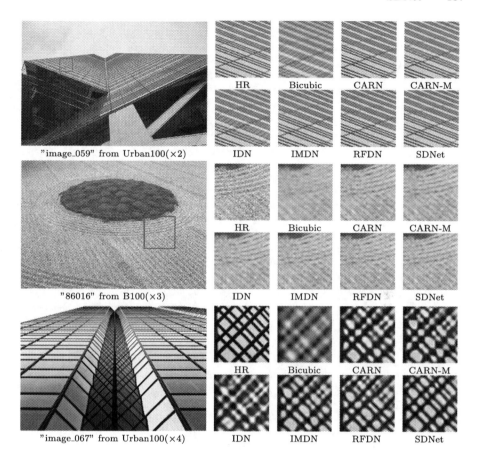

**Fig. 5.** Visual qualitative comparison for ×4 SR on Urban100 and B100 datasets.

## 5    Conclusion

In this paper, we propose a novel SDNet for lightweight image super-resolution. To design a lightweight and efficient model, we introduce SDU to learn multi-scale features. Meanwhile, we devise a context enhancement layer to reweight different regions of the multi-scale features from SDU. Extensive experiment results have shown that our method has achieved promising performance against other state-of-the-art methods with fewer parameters and multi-add operations.

## References

1. Ahn, N., Kang, B., Sohn, K.-A.: Fast, accurate, and lightweight super-resolution with cascading residual network. In: Ferrari, V., Hebert, M., Sminchisescu, C., Weiss, Y. (eds.) ECCV 2018. LNCS, vol. 11214, pp. 256–272. Springer, Cham (2018). https://doi.org/10.1007/978-3-030-01249-6_16

2. Bevilacqua, M., Roumy, A., Guillemot, C., Alberi-Morel, M.L.: Low-complexity single-image super-resolution based on nonnegative neighbor embedding. In: BMVC, pp. 1–10 (2012)
3. Dong, C., Loy, C.C., He, K., Tang, X.: Learning a deep convolutional network for image super-resolution. In: Fleet, D., Pajdla, T., Schiele, B., Tuytelaars, T. (eds.) ECCV 2014. LNCS, vol. 8692, pp. 184–199. Springer, Cham (2014). https://doi.org/10.1007/978-3-319-10593-2_13
4. Feng, R., Guan, W., Qiao, Y., Dong, C.: Exploring multi-scale feature propagation and communication for image super resolution. arXiv preprint arXiv:2008.00239 (2020)
5. Gao, Q., Zhao, Y., Li, G., Tong, T.: Image super-resolution using knowledge distillation. In: Jawahar, C.V., Li, H., Mori, G., Schindler, K. (eds.) ACCV 2018. LNCS, vol. 11362, pp. 527–541. Springer, Cham (2019). https://doi.org/10.1007/978-3-030-20890-5_34
6. Han, K., Wang, Y., Tian, Q., Guo, J., Xu, C., Xu, C.: GhostNet: more features from cheap operations. In: CVPR, pp. 1580–1589 (2020)
7. Haris, M., Shakhnarovich, G., Ukita, N.: Deep back-projection networks for super-resolution. In: CVPR, pp. 1664–1673 (2018)
8. Hu, J., Shen, L., Sun, G.: Squeeze-and-excitation networks. In: CVPR, pp. 7132–7141 (2018)
9. Huang, J.B., Singh, A., Ahuja, N.: Single image super-resolution from transformed self-exemplars. In: CVPR, pp. 5197–5206 (2015)
10. Hui, Z., Gao, X., Yang, Y., Wang, X.: Lightweight image super-resolution with information multi-distillation network. In: ACM MM, pp. 2024–2032 (2019)
11. Hui, Z., Wang, X., Gao, X.: Fast and accurate single image super-resolution via information distillation network. In: CVPR, pp. 723–731 (2018)
12. Karras, T., Aila, T., Laine, S., Lehtinen, J.: Progressive growing of GANs for improved quality, stability, and variation. arXiv preprint arXiv:1710.10196 (2017)
13. Kim, J., Kwon Lee, J., Mu Lee, K.: Accurate image super-resolution using very deep convolutional networks. In: CVPR, pp. 1646–1654 (2016)
14. Kim, J., Kwon Lee, J., Mu Lee, K.: Deeply-recursive convolutional network for image super-resolution. In: CVPR, pp. 1637–1645 (2016)
15. Lai, W.S., Huang, J.B., Ahuja, N., Yang, M.H.: Deep Laplacian pyramid networks for fast and accurate super-resolution. In: CVPR, pp. 624–632 (2017)
16. Lee, R., et al.: Journey towards tiny perceptual super-resolution. In: Vedaldi, A., Bischof, H., Brox, T., Frahm, J.-M. (eds.) ECCV 2020. LNCS, vol. 12371, pp. 85–102. Springer, Cham (2020). https://doi.org/10.1007/978-3-030-58574-7_6
17. Lee, W., Lee, J., Kim, D., Ham, B.: Learning with privileged information for efficient image super-resolution. In: Vedaldi, A., Bischof, H., Brox, T., Frahm, J.-M. (eds.) ECCV 2020. LNCS, vol. 12369, pp. 465–482. Springer, Cham (2020). https://doi.org/10.1007/978-3-030-58586-0_28
18. Lim, B., Son, S., Kim, H., Nah, S., Mu Lee, K.: Enhanced deep residual networks for single image super-resolution. In: CVPR, pp. 136–144 (2017)
19. Liu, J., Tang, J., Wu, G.: Residual feature distillation network for lightweight image super-resolution. arXiv:2009.11551 (2020)
20. Liu, J., Zhang, W., Tang, Y., Tang, J., Wu, G.: Residual feature aggregation network for image super-resolution. In: CVPR, pp. 2359–2368 (2020)
21. Lu, X., Wang, W., Danelljan, M., Zhou, T., Shen, J., Van Gool, L.: Video object segmentation with episodic graph memory networks. In: Vedaldi, A., Bischof, H., Brox, T., Frahm, J.-M. (eds.) ECCV 2020. LNCS, vol. 12348, pp. 661–679. Springer, Cham (2020). https://doi.org/10.1007/978-3-030-58580-8_39

22. Luo, X., Xie, Y., Zhang, Y., Qu, Y., Li, C., Fu, Y.: LatticeNet: towards lightweight image super-resolution with lattice block. In: Vedaldi, A., Bischof, H., Brox, T., Frahm, J.-M. (eds.) ECCV 2020. LNCS, vol. 12367, pp. 272–289. Springer, Cham (2020). https://doi.org/10.1007/978-3-030-58542-6_17

23. Martin, D., Fowlkes, C., Tal, D., Malik, J.: A database of human segmented natural images and its application to evaluating segmentation algorithms and measuring ecological statistics. In: ICCV, vol. 2, pp. 416–423 (2001)

24. Matsui, Y., et al.: Sketch-based manga retrieval using Manga109 dataset. Multimedia Tools Appl. **76**(20), 21811–21838 (2017)

25. Muqeet, A., Hwang, J., Yang, S., Kang, J., Kim, Y., Bae, S.H.: Multi-attention based ultra lightweight image super-resolution. arXiv:2008.12912 (2020)

26. Shi, W., et al.: Cardiac image super-resolution with global correspondence using Multi-Atlas PatchMatch. In: Mori, K., Sakuma, I., Sato, Y., Barillot, C., Navab, N. (eds.) MICCAI 2013. LNCS, vol. 8151, pp. 9–16. Springer, Heidelberg (2013). https://doi.org/10.1007/978-3-642-40760-4_2

27. Szegedy, C., et al.: Going deeper with convolutions. In: CVPR, pp. 1–9 (2015)

28. Tai, Y., Yang, J., Liu, X.: Image super-resolution via deep recursive residual network. In: CVPR, pp. 3147–3155 (2017)

29. Tai, Y., Yang, J., Liu, X., Xu, C.: MemNet: a persistent memory network for image restoration. In: ICCV, pp. 4539–4547 (2017)

30. Tong, T., Li, G., Liu, X., Gao, Q.: Image super-resolution using dense skip connections. In: ICCV, pp. 4799–4807 (2017)

31. Xu, Y.S., Tseng, S.Y.R., Tseng, Y., Kuo, H.K., Tsai, Y.M.: Unified dynamic convolutional network for super-resolution with variational degradations. In: CVPR, pp. 12496–12505 (2020)

32. Yang, J., Wright, J., Huang, T.S., Ma, Y.: Image super-resolution via sparse representation. IEEE TIP **19**(11), 2861–2873 (2010)

33. Yuan, P., et al..: HS-ResNet: hierarchical-split block on convolutional neural network. arXiv:2010.07621 (2020)

34. Zhang, Q., et al.: Split to be slim: an overlooked redundancy in vanilla convolution. arXiv preprint arXiv:2006.12085 (2020)

35. Zhang, Y., Li, K., Li, K., Wang, L., Zhong, B., Fu, Y.: Image super-resolution using very deep residual channel attention networks. In: Ferrari, V., Hebert, M., Sminchisescu, C., Weiss, Y. (eds.) ECCV 2018. LNCS, vol. 11211, pp. 294–310. Springer, Cham (2018). https://doi.org/10.1007/978-3-030-01234-2_18

36. Zhang, Y., Tian, Y., Kong, Y., Zhong, B., Fu, Y.: Residual dense network for image super-resolution. In: CVPR, pp. 2472–2481 (2018)

37. Zhao, H., Kong, X., He, J., Qiao, Y., Dong, C.: Efficient image super-resolution using pixel attention. arXiv:2010.01073 (2020)

38. Zhou, T., Li, J., Wang, S., Tao, R., Shen, J.: MATNet: motion-attentive transition network for zero-shot video object segmentation. IEEE TIP **29**, 8326–8338 (2020)

39. Zhou, T., Qi, S., Wang, W., Shen, J., Zhu, S.C.: Cascaded parsing of human-object interaction recognition. IEEE TPAMI (2021)

40. Zhou, T., Wang, S., Zhou, Y., Yao, Y., Li, J., Shao, L.: Motion-attentive transition for zero-shot video object segmentation. In: AAAI, pp. 13066–13073 (2020)

41. Zou, W.W., Yuen, P.C.: Very low resolution face recognition problem. IEEE TIP **21**(1), 327–340 (2011)

# Deep Multi-Illumination Fusion
# for Low-Light Image Enhancement

Wei Zhong[1]($\boxtimes$), Jie Lin[2], Long Ma[2], Risheng Liu[1], and Xin Fan[1]

[1] DUT-RU International School of Information Science and Engineering,
Dalian University of Technology, Dalian 116024, China
zhongwei@dlut.edu.cn
[2] School of Software, Dalian University of Technology, Dalian 116024, China

**Abstract.** In recent years, improving the visual quality of low-light images has attracted tremendous attention. Most of the existing deep learning approaches estimate the single illumination and then obtain the enhanced result according to the Retinex theory. However, only estimating the single illumination limits the solution space of the enhanced result, causing the unideal performance, e.g., color distortion, details loss, etc. To overcome the issues, we design a new Deep Multi-Illumination Fusion (denoted as DMIF) network to effectively handle low-light image enhancement. Specifically, we first construct an illumination estimation module to generate multiple illuminations to enlarge the solution space. We fuse these illuminations and aggregate their advantages by an illumination fusion algorithm to produce a final illumination. Finally, the enhanced result is obtained according to the Retinex theory. Plenty of experiments are conducted to fully indicate our effectiveness and superiority against other state-of-the-art methods.

**Keywords:** Low-light image enhancement · Image fusion · Deep network

## 1 Introduction

As for many computer vision and multimedia applications, high visibility images with clear targets are urgent. Limited to the adverse imaging conditions, the low-quality images with low illumination are frequent and inevitable. In recent years, there emerge many algorithms to enhance low-light images.

A common method is histogram equalization, which enlarges the dynamic range and increases the image contrast, but its limitations are obvious and the results tend to be over enhancement. Based on the Retinex theory [13], there exists an assumption, i.e., the low-light image can be decomposed into two parts, illumination and reflectance, where illumination represents the intensity of light

This work is partially supported by National Natural Science Foundation of China (NSFC) under Grant 61906029, the Fundamental Research Funds for the Central Universities.

H. Ma et al. (Eds.): PRCV 2021, LNCS 13021, pp. 140–150, 2021.
https://doi.org/10.1007/978-3-030-88010-1_12

Input                                           SSIENet [24]

DeepUPE [19]                                    Ours

**Fig. 1.** Visual comparison of low-light image enhancement.

exposure, reflectance denotes the physical properties of the object itself. This model can be formulated as: $\mathbf{S} = \mathbf{I} \odot \mathbf{R}$, where $\mathbf{S}$ denotes the low-light input and "$\odot$" is the pixel-wise multiplication. $\mathbf{I}, \mathbf{R}$ are illumination and reflectance, respectively. Numerous approaches are currently aimed at removing or adjusting the illumination map to reduce the impact of the illumination. Early attempts include Single-scale Retinex [11] and Multi-scale Retinex [10]. Their results tend to look unnatural, and over-exposure in some cases. In RRM [15], the procedure of noises suppression was also considered in the designed model derived from the Retinex theory. In LIME [7], the illumination was estimated by the structure-aware prior and the reflectance was further obtained by utilizing the Retinex theory. SRIE [5] and JIEP [2] built their model by defining the physical priors of different components, to simultaneously estimate the reflectance and illumination. In [20], an enhancement algorithm for inhomogeneous illumination images was proposed, to balance the details and naturalness. Although these traditional methods get better results in some cases, they are limited since the regularization capacity. The reason is that the exact distribution of these potential components (especially the illumination) is hard to certain by a simple regularization constraint.

Recently, many approaches based on CNN have been proposed to solve low-light image enhancement task. LightenNet [14] is an early method utilized CNN to estimate the illumination from low-light image and remove it to obtain the

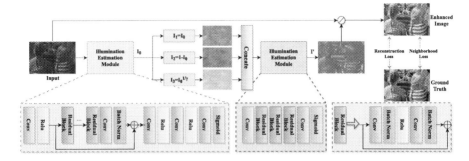

**Fig. 2.** The overall flowchart of DMIF. The basic illumination $I_0$ is predicted from the low-light image by the illumination estimation module, $I_1$, $I_2$ and $I_3$ are obtained by different formulas, and their concatenation is used as the input of the illumination fusion network to predict the final illumination. Finally, the final result is obtained by dividing the input by the $I'$. Below the flowchart are the illumination estimation networks, illumination fusion networks and residual blocks.

enhanced result. RetinexNet [21] estimated both illumination and reflectance in a two-stage way that consists of decomposition and enhancement. However, this work did not take into account the different effects of noise on different areas of light. DeepUPE [19] increased network complexity, taking samples on a bilateral grid and presenting multiple loss functions. However, it also estimated single illumination which is lacked complementary information. Chen *et al.*, solved the extremely low light imaging problem by using the new data set to directly manipulate the original sensor data [3]. Jiang *et al.*, proposed Enlightening GAN [9], which can be trained without low/normal light image pairs. In SSIENet [23] the result of histogram equalization is used as reference, and the reflection and illumination images are decomposed simultaneously. In [22], a deep recursive band network (DRBN) is proposed to recover a linear band representation of an enhanced normal-light image with paired low normal-light images.

In summary, most of existing methods only estimate the single illumination, which limits its solution space to influence the enhanced performance. To settle this issue, we in this paper design an end-to-end Deep Multi-Illumination Fusion (DMIF) network. We provide a group of visual comparison in Fig. 1. Obviously, The result of SSIENet shows excessive brightness while DeepUPE produces color deviation. In contrast, our method addresses the color distortion and non-uniform brightness, providing a more comfortable visual expression. In brief, our contributions can be described as three-folds:

- We devote ourselves to estimate multiple illuminations to provide a larger range of solution space for more effectively handling low-light image enhancement.
- We design a deep multi-illumination fusion network to cater to our demands of estimating multiple illuminations and fuse these outputs by a simple fusion module.

- Comprehensive and elaborate experiments are conducted to illustrate our effectiveness and superiority against existing state-of-the-art approaches.

## 2  Deep Multi-Illumination Fusion

In this section, we clearly introduce our proposed algorithm (DMIF), including network architecture and training loss functions. The flow chart is shown in Fig. 2.

### 2.1  Network Structure

In fact, the issue of existing Retinex-based methods (maybe iterative algorithms, maybe deep networks) lies in the inaccurate illumination estimation. This is to say, we need to make sure that the illumination estimation module can generate an effective enough illumination map. Otherwise, the model inference based on illumination brings about the deviates. Hence, we first carefully design the illumination estimation module. In order to preserve more details in the illumination, we keep the resolution of the illumination map without down sampling. Specifically, 16 residual blocks are applied which contains Convolutional layer (Conv), Batch Normalization (BN), Rectified Linear Units (ReLU) and a skip connection, and the kernel size of the Conv is $3 \times 3$, 64 channels. A sigmoid is added at the end of the module to normalize the value. This module outputs a basic illumination $I_0$.

Subsequently, we generate multiple illumination with different meanings to learn complementary information of the basic illumination. We empirically explore three explicit forms. The following three models are calculated based on $I_0$: $I_1 = I_0$, $I_2 = 1 - I_0$, $I_3 = I_0^{1/\gamma}$, where $I_1$, $I_2$ and $I_3$ represent different illumination maps. It is worth noting that these three formulas have three characteristics: 1) they can normalize the illumination value to 0–1; 2) the curve these formulas should be monotonous to preserve the differences local region; 3) they should be differentiable in the process of gradient backpropagation. To be specific, we first preserve the basic illumination map. Moreover, we consider the second formula. As we all know, low-light images have extremely low pixel values. From this formula, we obtain the inverse illumination map, which looks like the image with fog. What's more, with this illumination, we can address the problem of overexposure to a certain extent. The third formula is inspired by the gamma correction, we utilize the third formula, and we set $\gamma$ as 2.2. Gamma correction is used for smooth extended dark details. To increase the nonlinearity and contrast of illumination, we perform gamma correction on the illumination. We find that the quality of the final illumination map could be improved by fusing the gamma corrected illumination map.

In order to aggregate the above three illumination advantages, we integrate and optimize illumination maps to generate the better illumination. The concatenation operation is utilized for integration. Then, we develop a network to optimize the fusion result and further aggregate their advantages. As showed in

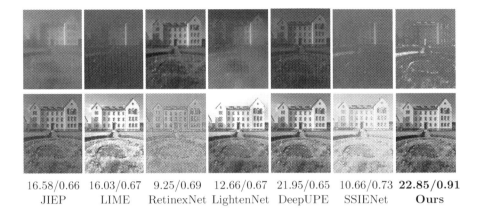

| 16.58/0.66 | 16.03/0.67 | 9.25/0.69 | 12.66/0.67 | 21.95/0.65 | 10.66/0.73 | **22.85/0.91** |
| JIEP | LIME | RetinexNet | LightenNet | DeepUPE | SSIENet | **Ours** |

**Fig. 3.** Comparison of illumination components and the enhanced results. The top row is the estimated illumination, and the bottom row is the enhanced result. PSNR/SSIM scores are reported below each image.

Fig. 2, we only use three residual blocks but still be able to predict the desired results. the kernel size of the Conv is also $3 \times 3$, 64 channels. This module outputs a final illumination $\mathbf{I}'$. It's worth noting that, the pixel values of $\mathbf{I}'$ are in definitely ranges, $\{\mathbf{I}'|\mathbf{S}_i \leq \mathbf{I}'_i \leq 1, i = 1, ..., N\}$, thus preventing colors from going beyond the range indicated.

## 2.2 Loss Function

Our loss function $\mathcal{L}$ contains two parts, i.e., the reconstruction loss $\mathcal{L}_{recon}$ and neighborhood loss $\mathcal{L}_{nb}$ formulated as:

$$\mathcal{L} = \mathcal{L}_{recon} + \lambda\mathcal{L}_{nb}. \tag{1}$$

We empirically set $\lambda = 0.5$. Since we have low light/normal paired images, a following reconstruction loss is defined:

$$\mathcal{L}_{recon} = \sum_{i,j} \|\mathbf{R}(i,j) - \widetilde{\mathbf{R}}(i,j)\|^2, \tag{2}$$

where $\mathbf{R}$ represents the final enhanced result, and $\widetilde{\mathbf{R}}$ is the ground truth, $i$ and $j$ represent pixel position in $x$ and $y$ direction, respectively. Note that restoring an illumination map from a single low-light image is a highly ill-posed problem, and hence the final enhanced result, that is, the reflection map is unideal. Without the guidance of the illumination ground truth, it is necessary to add additional loss constraints on reflection map. Hence, inspired by EPS [4], we also put forward a following neighborhood loss to explicitly encourage the network to learn the local information:

$$\mathcal{L}_{nb} = \sum_{i,j} \sum_{(p,q)\in\mathcal{N}(i,j)} \|(f(i,j) - f(p,q)\|_1, \tag{3}$$

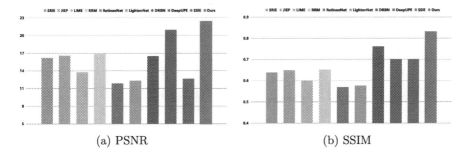

(a) PSNR                                    (b) SSIM

**Fig. 4.** Quantitative results of low-light image enhancement.

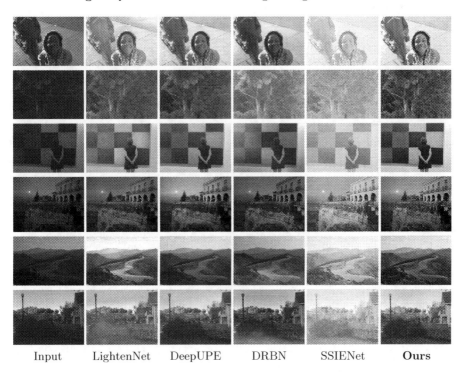

Input      LightenNet      DeepUPE      DRBN      SSIENet      **Ours**

**Fig. 5.** More visual results. The first three lines are the results of MIT-Adobe FiveK dataset, the last three lines are the results of LIME, MEF and NPE datasets.

where $f(x,y) = \mathbf{R}(x,y) - \widetilde{\mathbf{R}}(x,y)$ and $\mathcal{N}_{i,j}$ denotes the $5 \times 5$ neighborhood centered at pixel $(i,j)$. This term explicitly penalizes deviations in the gradient domain and enhances the image contrast. We add this neighborhood term to the weighted $\ell_1$ loss since smoothing involves evident gradient changes. It also can prevent color deviation and improve the generalization ability of the model.

## 3   Experimental Results

### 3.1   Implementation Details

We utilize the MIT-Adobe FiveK dataset [1] as the training dataset with 5000 low/normal image pairs, each with five retouched images produced by different experts (A/B/C/D/E). We follow previous methods [6,8,18] to use only the output by Expert C, randomly select 500 images for testing, and train on the remaining 4500 images. We randomly cropped the image to a small size of $48 \times 48$ and used the Adam optimizer to iterate at a rate of 500. The learning rate was 0.001 for the first 50 epoched and 0.0001 for the next. Our code is implemented on a NVIDIA Titan X GPU based on tensorlfow.

### 3.2   Performance Evaluation

We compared our algorithm with advanced low-light enhancement methods including LIME [7], JIEP [2], SRIE RRM [15], LightenNet [14], RetinexNet [21], DeepUPE [19], SSIENet [23] and DRBN [22]. We evaluated them in five widely-used datasets, including MIT-Adobe FiveK [1], LIME [7], MEF [16], NPE [20], and VV[1] datasets.

**Results on MIT-Adobe FiveK Dataset.** We first evaluate our approach in this dataset including quantitative and qualitative results. We calculate the PSNR and SSIM in 500 testing. As is shown in Fig. 4, obviously our approach has the best PSNR/SSIM. To evaluate the performance of the illumination map, we choose six representative methods for comparison. As is shown in Fig. 3, LIME and SSIENet have the sensible issues, causing some details cannot be recovered. In addition, Fig. 5 provides more visual comparisons with other better performing methods, it is not difficult to find that these methods are deficient in brightness and color restoration, but our method can address these problems well. Our results have more comfortable brightness and saturation.

**Results on Other Datasets.** We directly test the trained model in other datasets to verify the generalization ability of our method. Through quantitative and qualitative comparison, it is found that our method also performs well in other datasets. Then we show more visual comparisons in LIME, MEF and NPE datasets, and the result is shown in Fig. 5, In these data sets, some methods have similar problems. For example, SSIENet still has uneven brightness, and DeepUPE's results are significantly less bright in these datasets (Table 1).

---

[1] https://sites.google.com/site/vonikakis/datasets.

**Table 1.** Quantitative comparison in terms of NIQE.

| Methods | LIME | MEF | VV | NPE | AVG |
|---|---|---|---|---|---|
| SRIE | 4.0502 | 3.4513 | 3.0164 | 3.1845 | 3.4251 |
| JIEP | **3.7192** | 3.4351 | 2.9704 | 3.2415 | **3.3406** |
| LIME | 4.1291 | 3.7663 | 3.2012 | 3.6384 | 3.6844 |
| RRM | 4.8661 | 5.0626 | 3.8002 | 3.2473 | 4.2437 |
| RetinexNet | 4.5923 | 4.4104 | 4.0776 | 4.2126 | 4.3231 |
| LightenNet | 3.7312 | **3.3823** | *2.9524* | 3.3884 | 3.3631 |
| DRBN | 3.9645 | 4.0579 | 3.2036 | **2.8772** | 3.4839 |
| SSIENet | 4.8260 | 4.3510 | 4.2368 | 2.9609 | 4.0936 |
| DeepUPE | 3.9282 | 3.5342 | 3.0082 | 3.7977 | 3.5668 |
| Ours | *3.6124* | *3.3731* | **2.9530** | *2.6322* | *3.1430* |

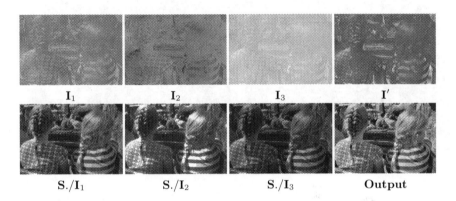

$I_1$                $I_2$                $I_3$                $\mathbf{I'}$

$\mathbf{S./I_1}$          $\mathbf{S./I_2}$          $\mathbf{S./I_3}$          **Output**

**Fig. 6.** Visual comparison of different illumination maps and the corresponding enhanced results.

## 3.3   Ablation Analysis

To analyze the effect of each illumination, we show the visual comparison of different illumination in our designed network. In the Fig. 6, the first row shows three illuminations and the fused illumination, and the second row shows the corresponding enhancement results. This experiment reflects that the necessity and effectiveness of our designed multiple illumination estimation module.

We also conduct the ablation study to verify our effectiveness about the main components. According to the different combinations of the three formulas, we consider four networks and evaluated their quantitative results in the MIT-Adobe FiveK dataset. All the cases include "$I_1 + I_2 + I_3$", "$I_1 + I_2$", "$I_1 + I_3$", and the original single illumination "$I_1$". For "$I_1$", since they only have single illumination, we removed the illumination fusion algorithm. In the experiment, we find that the result of "$I_1$" is slightly brighter than that of "$I_1 + I_2 + I_3$",

**Table 2.** Ablation study of different cases of our DMIF.

| Methods | $\mathbf{I}_1$ | $\mathbf{I}_1 + \mathbf{I}_2$ | $\mathbf{I}_1 + \mathbf{I}_3$ | $\mathbf{I}_1 + \mathbf{I}_2 + \mathbf{I}_3$ |
|---------|------|---------|---------|---------------|
| PSNR | 20.3170 | 21.0910 | 20.5995 | **21.9697** |
| SSIM | 0.8017 | 0.8210 | 0.8116 | **0.8315** |

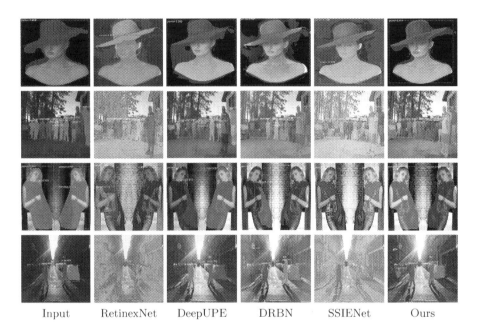

Input        RetinexNet        DeepUPE        DRBN        SSIENet        Ours

**Fig. 7.** Visual comparison of instance segmentation (**Best viewed with zoom**).

but the overall image quality is reduced. The results in Table 2 show that the complete three models improve the enhancement.

### 3.4    Object Instance Segmentation

In order to further demonstrate our superiority, we directly apply our trained models to enhance low-light images of some real-world scenes. We enhance the low-light image in UFDD dataset [17] by utilizing our method without any fine-tuning and then execute Mask-RCNN [12] to achieve the object instance segmentation. We consider the segmentation results of the original low-light image RetinexNet, DeepUPE, DRBN and SSIENet for comparison. The visual comparison is shown in Fig. 7. Obviously, the results of other methods have the problems of unsatisfactory segmentation and inaccurate object detection, but our proposed algorithm realizes a more superior performance with high accuracy, since it recovers more semantic information in the image.

# 4   Conclusion

In this paper, we proposed a deep multi-illumination fusion network for low-light enhancement. We applied different formulas and well-designed network to predict multiple illumination with different meanings. We developed a fusion module to fuse them, to overcome details loss and color deviation caused by using single illumination. The low/normal image pairs and the proposed loss function are used to train the whole network. Experimental results showed that our method was superior to advanced low-light enhancement methods. In the future, we will incorporate more illumination maps to further improve performance.

# References

1. Bychkovsky, V., Paris, S., Chan, E., Durand, F.: Learning photographic global tonal adjustment with a database of input/output image pairs. In: Proceedings of the IEEE Conference on Computer Vision and Pattern Recognition (2011)
2. Cai, B., Xu, X., Guo, K., Jia, K., Hu, B., Tao, D.: A joint intrinsic-extrinsic prior model for retinex. In: Proceedings of the IEEE Conference on Computer Vision and Pattern Recognition (2017)
3. Chen, Q., Xu, J., Koltun, V.: Learning to see in the dark. In: Proceedings of the IEEE Conference on Computer Vision and Pattern Recognition (2018)
4. Zhu, F., Liang, Z., Jia, X., Zhang, L., Yu, Y.: A benchmark for edge-preserving image smoothing. IEEE Trans. Image Process. **28**, 3556–3570 (2019)
5. Fu, X., Zeng, D., Huang, Y., Zhang, X.P., Ding, X.: A weighted variational model for simultaneous reflectance and illumination estimation. In: Proceedings of the IEEE Conference on Computer Vision and Pattern Recognition (2016)
6. Gharbi, M., Chen, J., Barron, J.T., Hasinoff, S.W., Durand, F.: Deep bilateral learning for real-time image enhancement. ACM Trans. Graph. **36**(4), 118 (2017)
7. Guo, X., Li, Y., Ling, H.: LIME: low-light image enhancement via illumination map estimation. IEEE Trans. Image Process. **26**(2), 982–993 (2017)
8. Hu, Y., He, H., Xu, C., Wang, B., Lin, S.: Exposure: a white-box photo post-processing framework. ACM Trans. Graph. (TOG) **37**(2), 1–17 (2018)
9. Jiang, Y., et al.: EnlightenGAN: deep light enhancement without paired supervision. arXiv preprint arXiv:1906.06972 (2019)
10. Jobson, D.J., Rahman, Z., Woodell, G.: A multiscale retinex for bridging the gap between color images and the human observation of scenes. IEEE Trans. Image Process. **6**(7), 965–976 (1997)
11. Jobson, D.J., Rahman, Z.U., Woodell, G.A.: Properties and performance of a center/surround retinex. IEEE Trans. Image Process. **6**(3), 451–462 (1997)
12. Kaiming He, Georgia Gkioxari, P.D., Girshick, R.: Mask R-CNN. In: IEEE International Conference on Computer Vision, pp. 2961–2969 (2017)
13. Land, E., McCann, J.: Lightness and retinex theory. J. Opt. Soc. Am. **61**, 1–11 (1971). https://doi.org/10.1364/JOSA.61.000001
14. Li, C., Guo, J., Porikli, F., Pang, Y.: LightenNet: a convolutional neural network for weakly illuminated image enhancement. Pattern Recogn. Lett. **104**, 15–22 (2018)
15. Li, M., Liu, J., Yang, W., Sun, X., Guo, Z.: Structure-revealing low-light image enhancement via robust retinex model. IEEE Trans. Image Process. **27**(6), 2828–2841 (2018)

16. Ma, K., Zeng, K., Wang, Z.: Perceptual quality assessment for multi-exposure image fusion. IEEE Trans. Image Process. **24**(11), 3345–3356 (2015)
17. Nada, H., Sindagi, V.A., Zhang, H., Patel, V.M.: Pushing the limits of unconstrained face detection: a challenge dataset and baseline results. In: IEEE International Conference on Biometrics Theory, Applications and Systems, pp. 1–10. IEEE (2018)
18. Park, J., Lee, J.Y., Yoo, D., So Kweon, I.: Distort-and-recover: color enhancement using deep reinforcement learning. In: Proceedings of the IEEE Conference on Computer Vision and Pattern Recognition, June 2018
19. Wang, R., Zhang, Q., Fu, C.W., Shen, X., Zheng, W.S., Jia, J.: Underexposed photo enhancement using deep illumination estimation. In: Proceedings of the IEEE Conference on Computer Vision and Pattern Recognition, June 2019
20. Wang, S., Zheng, J., Hu, H.M., Li, B.: Naturalness preserved enhancement algorithm for non-uniform illumination images. IEEE Trans. Image Process. **22**(9), 3538–3548 (2013)
21. Wei, C., Wang, W., Yang, W., Liu, J.: Deep retinex decomposition for low-light enhancement. In: British Machine Vision Conference (2018)
22. Yang, W., Wang, S., Fang, Y., Wang, Y., Liu, J.: From fidelity to perceptual quality: a semi-supervised approach for low-light image enhancement. In: IEEE/CVF Conference on Computer Vision and Pattern Recognition, June 2020
23. Zhang, Y., Di, X., Zhang, B., Wang, C.: Self-supervised image enhancement network: training with low light images only (2020)

# Relational Attention with Textual Enhanced Transformer for Image Captioning

Lifei Song[1(✉)], Yiwen Shi[2], Xinyu Xiao[3], Chunxia Zhang[4], and Shiming Xiang[3]

[1] School of Artificial Intelligence, University of Chinese Academy of Sciences,
Beijing 100049, China
songlifei2018@ia.ac.cn
[2] Beijing City University Intelligent Electronic Manufacturing Research Center,
Beijing 101309, China
[3] National Laboratory of Pattern recognition, Institute of Automation of Chinese
Academy of Sciences, Beijing 100190, China
{xinyu.xiao,smxiang}@nlpr.ia.ac.cn
[4] School of Computer Science and Technology, Beijing Institute of Technology,
Beijing 100081, China
cxzhang@bit.edu.cn

**Abstract.** Image captioning has attracted extensive research interests in recent years, which aims to generate a natural language description of an image. However, many approaches focus only on individual target object information without exploring the relationship between objects and the surrounding. It will greatly affect the performance of captioning models. In order to solve the above issue, we propose a relation model to incorporate relational information between objects from different levels into the captioning model, including low-level box proposals and high-level region features. Moreover, Transformer-based architectures have shown great success in image captioning, where image regions are encoded and then attended into attention vectors to guide the caption generation. However, the attention vectors only contain image-level information without considering the textual information, which fails to expand the capability of captioning in both visual and textual domains. In this paper, we introduce a Textual Enhanced Transformer (TET) to enable addition of textual information into Transformer. There are two modules in TET: text-guided Transformer and self-attention Transformer. The two modules perform semantic and visual attention to guide the decoder to generate high-quality captions. We extensively evaluate model on MS COCO dataset and it achieves 128.7 CIDEr-D score on Karpathy split and 126.3 CIDEr-D (c40) score on official online evaluation server.

This research was supported by the National Key Research and Development Program of China under Grant No. 2020AAA0104903, and the National Natural Science Foundation of China under Grants 62072039, 62076242, and 61976208.

H. Ma et al. (Eds.): PRCV 2021, LNCS 13021, pp. 151–163, 2021.
https://doi.org/10.1007/978-3-030-88010-1_13

**Keywords:** Relational information · Attention · Textual enhanced transformer

# 1 Introduction

Image captioning [1–3] aims to automatically describe an image with natural language. It is a task at the intersection connecting computer vision and nature language processing. It is particularly challenging because it requires to simultaneously capture information of target objects as well as their relationships. Inspired by the development of neural machine translation [4], existing research on image captioning usually employs a encoder-decoder architecture with a Convolutional Neural Network (CNN) used for image feature extraction and a Recurrent Neural Network (RNN) for caption generation. The attention mechanism [5–7] also plays a crucial role in image captioning task, instead of transferring an entire image to a single representation, visual attention allows to focus on features relevant for captions.

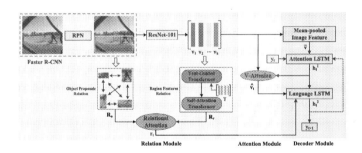

**Fig. 1.** The overall architecture of RA-TET. Our model consists of three modules. (1) In relation module, object proposals and region features are detected, then explores relational matrix $\mathbf{R_o}$ and $\mathbf{R_r}$ based on low-level and high-level information. (2) In attention module, V-attention is designed to obtain attended visual features $\hat{\mathbf{v}}_t$ based on image features $\mathbf{V}$. (3) In LSTM decoder, decoding word by word $y_t$ based on attended visual features and attended relational features so as to generate the final caption.

Despite impressive successes, there are still limitations in the current captioning frameworks. In fact, understanding inter relationships between objects facilitate a major component in visual understanding. Current methods focus on obtaining information of each object individually, but overlook existing relationships with other objects or the environment. Although some methods [8,9] based on exploring the connections between objects have been proposed, but these methods only employ Graph Convolutional Networks (GCN) [10] to integrate object relationships into image encoder, completely replace the previous image input, and the performance of the result is limited. Considering that the structure of CNN is hierarchical and features are propagated through the network layer by layer, more efficient relational features can be derived from the hierarchical information of the network. As shown in Fig. 1, a relational attention network is proposed in our paper, aiming at extracting relevant relations from two levels of information (low-level object proposals, high-level region features). For object proposals, location and size information of each object proposal (generated by a Region Proposal Network, RPN) are extracted to generate low-level features. For region features, the TET encourages our model to explore the relations between image regions and detected texts to generate high-level features. Afterwards, low-level and high-level features processed by a relational attention network to obtain attended relational features. Finally, the attended relational features combined with attended visual features which is obtained by visual attention(V-Attention) model to decoder model to guide the final caption generation.

In summary, our contributions are as follows:

- To address the issue of relation information missing, a novel relation model is proposed to explore relations from two levels of image information, i.e. low-level object proposals and high-level image region features.
- To expand the capability of complex multi-modal reasoning in image captioning, TET is designed to model interactions between image regions and detected texts.
- Experiments show that the proposed method can achieve competitive performance in MS COCO dataset compared with other state-of-the-art models, e.g. 128.7 CIDEr-D score on Karpathy split and 126.3 CIDEr-D (c40) score on official online evaluation server.

## 2 Related Work

### 2.1 Relationship Exploration

Recently, a few works have attempted to utilize relations between objects from images to improve the performance of image captioning. For example, Kim et al. [8] introduced a relational captioning, which aims to generate multiple captions about relational information between objects. To explore the relationship between objects and semantic attributes, Yao et al. [11] applied two kinds of graph convolution neural networks in the encoding stage. Moreover, Yang et al. [9] leveraged an image scene graph and a semantic scene graph which incorporate the language inductive bias into the image captioning framework. Wang et al. [28] proposed a hierarchical attention network that enables attention to be calculated on pyramidal hierarchy of features. Our method explores relations based on low-level and high-level image information, adding more relationship information to improve the performance of the model.

### 2.2 Transformer Architecture

The Transformer architecture is introduced in [12], which is based solely on attention mechanisms, dispensing with recurrence and convolutions entirely. It has advantages of low computational complexity, parallel computing and better learning about long-range distance dependence. For example, Li et al. [13] developed EnTangled Attention (ETA) that enables the transformer to exploit semantic and visual information simultaneously. In addition, Simao et al. [14] proposed a Object Relation Transformer, which incorporates information about the spatial relationship between detected objects through geometric attention. Our ETE seeks to model textual and visual information based on the input of detected texts and image features, which could be more comprehensive for caption generation.

# 3   The Proposed Approach

As illustrated in Fig. 1, our model consists of three modules: a Relation Module, an Attention Module, and a Decoder Module. In relation module, Faster R-CNN [15] with ResNet-101 [16] is used for object detection and feature extraction. Specially, RPN is leveraged to generates $m$ object bounding boxes (non-maximum suppression with an intersection-over-union threshold is used to select the top box proposals), the location and size information of each object proposal can be obtained. Then, we take outputs of the $pool5$ layer from ResNet-101 as image region features $\mathbf{V} = \{\mathbf{v_i}\}_{i=1}^{m}$, where $\mathbf{v_i} \in \mathbb{R}^{d_v}$ denotes the $d_v$-dimensional feature vector. Moreover, two relation modules are designed to extract relational information based on the above two sources of information. Finally, additional relational attention networks are proposed to extract attended relational features. In attention module, V-Attention is proposed to predict attended visual features based on image region features. In decoder module, two-layer LSTMs decoder is designed to generate the caption, which is based on attended relational features and attended visual features.

## 3.1   Relation Module

**Object Proposals Relation.** Each box proposal predicted by RPN is described by its location and size information: the center coordinates of bounding box $c_i = (x_i, y_i)$, width $w_i$ and height $h_i$, with $i = 1, 2, ..., m$. For two object proposals $i$ and $j$, the relational vector $o_{ij}$ can be defined as:

$$\mathbf{o_{ij}} = [\frac{|x_i - x_j|}{H}, \frac{|y_i - y_j|}{W}, \frac{h_i}{h_j}, \frac{w_i}{w_j}], \tag{1}$$

where $W$ and $H$ are the width and height of the image. By stacking these vectors together, a low-level feature relational matrix $\mathbf{R_o} \in \mathbb{R}^{m(m-1) \times 4}$ of object proposals can be created.

**Region Features Relation.** To process high-level region features, we employ TET to convert fixed number of image features into the unified relational feature representation. The Transformer module includes self-attention and multi-head attention. For self-attention, inputs consist of queries $\mathbf{Q} = (\mathbf{q_1}, ..., \mathbf{q_m})$,

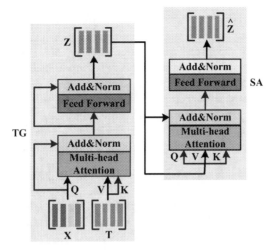

**Fig. 2.** The structure of TET. Two basic units with different types of inputs. Firstly, the TG unit takes the input of image features **V** and text features **T**, and outputs the features **Z**. Then, the SA unit takes the input of attended features **Z** and outputs the attended features **Ẑ**.

keys $\mathbf{K} = (\mathbf{k_1}, ..., \mathbf{k_m})$ and values $\mathbf{V} = (\mathbf{v_1}, \mathbf{v_2}..., \mathbf{v_m})$, $\mathbf{q_i}, \mathbf{k_i}, \mathbf{v_i} \in \mathbb{R}^{d_v}$. The dot products of the query is computed with all keys, divided each by $\sqrt{d_v}$. Finally, a softmax function is applied to obtain the weights, the process can be seen as follows:

$$Attention(\mathbf{Q}, \mathbf{K}, \mathbf{V}) = Softmax(\frac{\mathbf{Q}\mathbf{K^T}}{\sqrt{d}})\mathbf{V}. \tag{2}$$

To extend the capacity of exploring subspaces, the multi-head attention which consists of $h$ parallel scaled dot-product attentions is adopted. The inputs include queries, keys, and values which are projected into $h$ subspaces, and the attention is performed in the subspaces separately. Then, $h$ heads are concatenated and linearly projected to the feature set:

$$MultiHead(\mathbf{Q}, \mathbf{K}, \mathbf{V}) = Concat(\mathbf{H_1}, ..., \mathbf{H_h})\mathbf{W^O}, \tag{3}$$

$$\mathbf{H_i} = Attention(\mathbf{Q}\mathbf{W_i^Q}, \mathbf{K}\mathbf{W_i^K}, \mathbf{V}\mathbf{W_i^V}), \tag{4}$$

where $\mathbf{W^O} \in \mathbb{R}^{d_v \times d_v}$ denotes the linear transformation. $\mathbf{W_i^Q}, \mathbf{W_i^K}, \mathbf{W_i^V} \in \mathbb{R}^{\frac{d_v}{h} \times d_v}$ are independent head projection matrices, $i = 1, 2, ..., h$. In addition to attention sub-layers, each of attention layer contains a point-wise feed-forward network ($\mathcal{FFN}$), which consists of two linear transformations with a ReLU activation.

$$\mathcal{FFN}(\mathbf{x}) = max(0, \mathbf{x}\mathbf{W_1} + \mathbf{b_1})\mathbf{W_2} + \mathbf{b_2}, \tag{5}$$

where $\mathbf{W_1} \in \mathbb{R}^{d_v \times m}$, $\mathbf{W_2} \in \mathbb{R}^{m \times d_v}$, $\mathbf{b_1}$ and $\mathbf{b_2}$ are weights and biases of two fully connected layers.

Different from the original Transformer model, the ETE model is guided by detected texts, in order to associate text features with image features. As illustrated in Fig. 2, there are two units in our ETE: text-guided Transformer (TG) and self-attention Transformer (SA). In the TG unit, the input of image features $\mathbf{V} = (\mathbf{v_1}, \mathbf{v_2}..., \mathbf{v_m})$ is transformed into queries matrix $\mathbf{Q_v}$, and text features $\mathbf{T} = \{\mathbf{t_1}, \mathbf{t_2}, ..., \mathbf{t_n}\}$ which are detected by the method [17], is transformed into keys matrix $\mathbf{K_t}$ and values matrix $\mathbf{V_t}$. The calculation is as follows:

$$\mathbf{Q_v}, \mathbf{K_t}, \mathbf{V_t} = Linear(\mathbf{V}, \mathbf{T}, \mathbf{T}). \tag{6}$$

Then, with focusing on relevant image regions through detected texts, multi-head attention is applied. And the output is computed by residual connection, which is followed by layer normalization:

$$\mathbf{F_{t \to v}} = \mathcal{LN}(\mathbf{V} + MultiHead(\mathbf{Q_v}, \mathbf{K_t}, \mathbf{V_t})), \tag{7}$$

where $\mathbf{F_{t \to v}}$ is the output features of images guided by text features, $\mathcal{LN}$ represents layer normalization. Then, $\mathcal{LN}$ layer and residual connection are used to obtain the attended image features $\widetilde{\mathbf{V}}$:

$$\mathbf{F'_{t \to v}} = \mathcal{FFN}(\mathbf{F_{t \to v}}), \tag{8}$$

$$\widetilde{\mathbf{V}} = \mathcal{LN}(\mathbf{F_{t \to v}} + \mathbf{F'_{t \to v}}). \tag{9}$$

In the SA unit, given the attended image features $\widetilde{\mathbf{V}}$ guided by text features, then transformed into queries matrix $\mathbf{Q_{\widetilde{v}}}$, keys matrix $\mathbf{K_{\widetilde{v}}}$ and values matrix $\mathbf{V_{\widetilde{v}}}$ through linear layers:

$$\mathbf{Q_{\widetilde{v}}}, \mathbf{K_{\widetilde{v}}}, \mathbf{V_{\widetilde{v}}} = Linear(\widetilde{\mathbf{V}}, \widetilde{\mathbf{V}}, \widetilde{\mathbf{V}}). \tag{10}$$

Specially, residual connection followed by layer normalization is applied to the multi-head attention as follows:

$$\mathbf{F_{\widetilde{v} \to \widetilde{v}}} = \mathcal{LN}(\widetilde{\mathbf{V}} + MultiHead(\mathbf{Q_{\widetilde{v}}}, \mathbf{K_{\widetilde{v}}}, \mathbf{V_{\widetilde{v}}})). \tag{11}$$

Then, with the optimization mentioned above, the relational matrix $\mathbf{R_r}$ of image regions are obtained as follows:

$$\mathbf{F'_{\widetilde{v} \to \widetilde{v}}} = \mathcal{FFN}(\mathbf{F_{\widetilde{v} \to \widetilde{v}}}), \tag{12}$$

$$\mathbf{R_r} = \mathcal{LN}(\mathbf{F_{\widetilde{v} \to \widetilde{v}}} + \mathbf{F'_{\widetilde{v} \to \widetilde{v}}}), \tag{13}$$

the final output is $\mathbf{R_r} \in \mathbb{R}^{m \times d_v}$.

Based on two kinds of relational features, we adopt relational attention networks $Att_{obj}$ and $Att_{reg}$ to transform relational feature matrix outputs into two attended relational feature vectors:

$$\hat{\mathbf{r}}_{\mathbf{ot}} = Att_{obj}(\mathbf{R_o}, \mathbf{h_t^1}), \tag{14}$$

$$\hat{\mathbf{r}}_{\mathbf{rt}} = Att_{reg}(\mathbf{R_r}, \mathbf{h_t^1}), \tag{15}$$

where $\mathbf{h_t^1}$ represents the hidden state of attention LSTM, the calculation of $Att_{obj}$ and $Att_{reg}$ is consistent with the following calculation process of V-Attention, which is shown as the Eqs. (17) and (18).

After obtaining two attended relational feature vectors, the final attended relational feature vector can be concatenated as:

$$\mathbf{r_t} = Concat(\hat{\mathbf{r}}_{\mathbf{ot}}, \hat{\mathbf{r}}_{\mathbf{rt}}), \tag{16}$$

the final output $\mathbf{r_t}$ will be sent to language LSTM as input.

## 3.2    Attention Module

The V-Attention, which is widely used in other attention methods, could focus on the image features that are most relevant to words at the current time step. Specially, given the image region features $\mathbf{v_i}$ and hidden state $\mathbf{h_t^1}$ of attention LSTM, a single-layer neural network followed by a softmax layer is applied as V-Attention to obtain attention weights $\alpha_t$:

$$\mathbf{a_{it}} = \omega_\mathbf{h}^\mathbf{T} \tanh\left(\mathbf{W}_v \mathbf{v_i} + \mathbf{W_h} \mathbf{h_t^1}\right), \tag{17}$$

$$\alpha_t = softmax(\mathbf{a_t}), \tag{18}$$

where $\mathbf{W_v} \in \mathbb{R}^{H \times d_v}$, $\mathbf{W_h} \in \mathbb{R}^{H \times d_h}$, and $\omega_\mathbf{h} \in \mathbb{R}^H$ are parameters to be learned. Based on the weight distribution, attended image region feature $\hat{\mathbf{v}}_\mathbf{t}$ can be calculated by weighted summing at the current time step t:

$$\hat{\mathbf{v}}_\mathbf{t} = \sum_{i=1}^{m} \alpha_\mathbf{it} \mathbf{v_i}. \tag{19}$$

## 3.3    Decoder Module

Based on the final attended relational feature vector $\mathbf{r_t}$ and attended image feature vector $\hat{\mathbf{v}}_\mathbf{t}$, decoder module uses a two-layer LSTM decoder, namely attention LSTM and language LSTM, to guide the process of generating captions sequentially. The input vector of attention LSTM at each time step $\mathbf{x_t^1}$ consists of mean-pooled image feature $\overline{\mathbf{v}} = \frac{1}{m}\sum_{i=1}^{m} \mathbf{v_i}$, the encoding of the previously generated word $\mathbf{y_{t-1}}$, and the previous output $\mathbf{h_{t-1}^2}$ of language LSTM:

$$\mathbf{x_t^1} = [\overline{\mathbf{v}}, \mathbf{W_{e1}} \mathbf{y_{t-1}}, \mathbf{h_{t-1}^2}], \tag{20}$$

$$\mathbf{h_t^1} = LSTM_{att}[\mathbf{x_t^1}, \mathbf{h_{t-1}^1}], \tag{21}$$

where $\mathbf{W_{e1}}$ is a word embedding matrix for a vocabulary $\Sigma$.

Then, the output $\mathbf{h_t^1}$ of attention LSTM, attended relational features $\mathbf{r_t}$ and attended image features $\mathbf{\hat{v}_{ct}}$ are used as input to the language LSTM, given by:

$$\mathbf{x_t^2} = [\mathbf{\hat{v}_t}, \mathbf{h_t^1}, \mathbf{r_t}], \tag{22}$$

$$\mathbf{h_t^2} = LSTM_{lan}[\mathbf{x_t^2}, \mathbf{h_{t-1}^2}]. \tag{23}$$

We model hidden state $\mathbf{h_t^2}$ of language LSTM to compute the conditional probabilities on the vocabulary:

$$p(y_t) = softmax(\mathbf{W_h}\mathbf{h_t^2} + \mathbf{b_h}), \tag{24}$$

where $\mathbf{W_h} \in \mathbb{R}^{d_v \times d_h}$ is the weight parameters to be learnt and $\mathbf{b_h}$ is bias. $d_v$ is the size of whole vocabulary.

### 3.4  Training and Objectives

We first train our hierarchical relation attention captioning model by optimizing the Cross Entropy Loss:

$$L_{XE}(\theta) = -\sum_{t=1}^{T} log(p_\theta(y_t^*|y_{1:t-1}^*)), \tag{25}$$

where $y_{1:T}^*$ denotes the ground truth word sequence.

Then we directly optimize the non-differentiable metrics with self-critical sequence training [18]:

$$L_{RL}(\theta) = -E_{y_{1:T} \sim p_\theta}[r(y_{1:T})], \tag{26}$$

where the reward $r$ represents the score of CIDEr-D [19]. The gradients can be approximated:

$$\nabla_\theta L_{RL}(\theta) \approx -(r(y_{1:T}^s) - r(\hat{y}_{1:T}))\nabla_\theta log p_\theta(y_{1:T}^s), \tag{27}$$

where $y_{1:T}^s$ means its a result sampled from probability distribution, while $\hat{y}_{1:T}$ indicates a result of greedy decoding.

## 4  Experiments

### 4.1  Datasets and Evaluation Metrics

**MS COCO.** We evaluate our proposed method on the popular MS COCO dataset [20]. MS COCO dataset contains 123,287 images, including 82,783 for training and 40,504 for validation. Each image has five human-annotated captions. For offline evalution, we use the Karpathy split [21] for the performance comparison, where 5,000 images are used for validation, 5,000 images for testing, and the rest for training. We convert all sentences to lower case, drop the words that occur less than 5 times, and trim each caption to a maximum of 16 words, which results in a vocabulary of 10,369 words.

**Evaluation Metrics.** To evaluate caption quality, we use the standard automatic evaluation metrics, namely BLEU [22], METEOR [23], ROUGE-L, CIDEr-D [19], and SPICE [24], which are denoted as B@n(n=1,2,3,4), MT, R-L, C-D and SP for short respectively.

## 4.2   Implementation Details

The size of input images is $224 \times 224$. The dimension of the region vector $d_v$ and the word embedding are respectively 2048 and 1024, the hidden size $d_h$ of both two LSTM layers is set to 2048, and the dimension of attention layers $H$ is set to 512. For each image, we set the IoU thresholds for box proposal suppression to 0.7. For the training process, we train our model under cross-entropy loss for 20 epochs, ADAM optimizer is used with mini-batch size of 64, the learning rate starts from 0.01 and after 10 epochs decays by the factor of 0.8 at every five epoch. Then we use self-critical sequence training (SCST) [18] to optimize the CIDEr-D score with Reinforcement Learning for another 20 epochs with an initial learning rate of 1e−5, and annealed by 0.5 when the CIDEr-D score on the validation split has not improved.

## 4.3   Ablation Study

To show the effectiveness of different levels of relational strategies used in our framework, we conduct experiments to compare the models leveraging different image relational information, including low-level object proposals and high-level region features. The results are shown in Table 1. In the first row, we remove the attention operation and instead use two fully connected layers to get relational embedding vector. We notice that the use of region features get better performance with respect to object proposals with an improvement of 2.7% in terms of the C-D metric. The combination of the two relational information further improves the score by 2.4% compared with region features, hence demonstrating the effectiveness of using levels of relation information in our model.

To illustrate the effect of our relational attention strategy, we further carry out another ablation study and the results are exhibited in the lower column of Table 1. Compared with the previous methods that don't use relational attention, our relational attention networks all achieve an improvement in terms of the C-D metric. This is due to the ability of the relation attention mechanism to further extract object-related information on the basis of the original relational information.

We also compare the Textual Enhanced Transformer with the Original Transformer which includes no text information in Table 2. We observe a significant increase in performance when using TET, which leads to 128.7 on C-D. This is due to the semantic information added to the Transformer, and improves the language generalization ability of the model.

**Table 1.** The performance of ablation experiments on relational information with relational attention or not. The sign − means that we remove relational information from the model.

| Attention | Relation | B@4 | MT | R-L | C-D | SP |
|---|---|---|---|---|---|---|
| - | − | 34.3 | 22.9 | 53.1 | 122.1 | 18.8 |
| | Object Proposals | 35.2 | 23.1 | 53.8 | 122.8 | 19.2 |
| | Region Features | 37.3 | 27.4 | 56.3 | 125.5 | 21.1 |
| | Combination | 38.0 | 27.7 | 57.8 | 127.9 | 21.8 |
| Relational Attention | Object Proposals | 35.9 | 24.0 | 54.2 | 123.9 | 20.1 |
| | Region Features | 37.9 | 27.5 | 57.3 | 126.7 | 21.5 |
| | Combination | **38.4** | **28.3** | **58.6** | **128.1** | **22.2** |

**Table 2.** The performance of ablation experiments on Original Transformer and Textual Enhanced Transformer

| Transformer | B@4 | MT | R-L | C-D | SP |
|---|---|---|---|---|---|
| Original transformer | 38.4 | 28.3 | 58.6 | 128.1 | 22.2 |
| Textual enhanced transformer | 38.6 | 28.9 | 58.6 | 128.7 | 22.2 |

Specifically, we compared our methods with other state-of-the-art approaches, including SCST [18], Up-down [3], GCN-LSTM [11], SGAE [9], CNM [27] and ETA [13]. The experiment results on MS COCO dataset are shown in Table 3.

From the experiment results, we can observer that our RA-TET model performed significantly better than most captioning models. For instance, compared with GCN-LSTM [11] which is also the relation caption model similar to our model, our model improves the scores by a wide margin on all evaluation metrics, due to the use of relation information. Moreover, compared with CNM [27] which uses the Original Transformer, our method also has experimental result improvement due to the use of ETE.

We also submitted our RA-TET optimized with C-D score to online COCO testing server and evaluated the performance on official testing set. Table 4 shows the performance on official testing image set with 5 and 40 reference captions. Compared to other performing methods, our proposed model achieves superior performances across all the evaluation metrics on both c5 and c40 testing sets.

Figure 3 provides examples on generated captions. Compared with GCN[11], we can find that our model can have more accurate description.

## 4.4    Comparison with State-of-the-Art

**Table 3.** Performance of our model and other state-of-the-art methods on MS-COCO Karpathy test split.

| Method | Cross-Entropy Loss | | | | | Self-Critical Loss | | | | |
|---|---|---|---|---|---|---|---|---|---|---|
| | B@4 | MT | R-L | C-D | SP | B@4 | MT | R-L | C-D | SP |
| Adaptive [27] | 33.2 | 26.6 | – | 108.5 | – | – | – | – | – | – |
| SCST [18] | 30.0 | 25.9 | 53.4 | 99.4 | – | 34.2 | 26.7 | 55.7 | 114.0 | – |
| Up-Down [3] | 36.2 | 27.0 | 56.4 | 113.5 | 20.3 | 36.3 | 27.7 | 56.9 | 120.1 | 21.4 |
| GCN-LSTM [11] | 36.8 | 27.9 | 57.0 | 116.3 | 20.9 | 38.2 | 28.5 | 58.3 | 127.6 | 22.0 |
| CNM [28] | 37.1 | 27.9 | 57.3 | 116.6 | 20.8 | – | – | – | – | – |
| ETA [13] | 37.8 | 28.4 | 57.4 | 119.3 | 21.6 | 39.9 | 28.9 | 59.0 | 127.6 | 22.6 |
| Our Method | 37.0 | 28.0 | 57.2 | 117.3 | 21.1 | 38.6 | 28.9 | 58.6 | 128.7 | 22.2 |

**Table 4.** Comparision of various methods on the online MS-COCO test server.

| Method | B@1 | | B@2 | | B@4 | | MT | | R-L | | C-D | |
|---|---|---|---|---|---|---|---|---|---|---|---|---|
| | c5 | c40 | c5 | c40 | c5 | c40 | c5 | c40 | c5 | c40 | c5 | c40 |
| Adaptive [27] | 74.8 | 92.0 | 58.4 | 84.5 | 33.6 | 63.7 | 26.4 | 35.9 | 55.0 | 70.5 | 104.2 | 105.9 |
| SCST [18] | 78.1 | 93.7 | 61.9 | 86.0 | 35.2 | 64.5 | 27.0 | 35.5 | 56.3 | 70.7 | 114.7 | 116.0 |
| Up-down [3] | 80.2 | 95.2 | 64.0 | 88.8 | 36.9 | 68.5 | 27.6 | 36.7 | 57.1 | 72.4 | 117.9 | 120.5 |
| GCN-LSTM [11] | – | – | 65.5 | 89.3 | 38.7 | 69.7 | 28.5 | 37.6 | 58.5 | 73.4 | 125.3 | 126.5 |
| CNM [28] | – | – | – | – | 37.9 | 68.4 | 28.1 | 36.9 | 58.3 | 72.9 | 123.0 | 125.3 |
| ETA [13] | 81.2 | 95.0 | 65.5 | 89.0 | 38.9 | 70.2 | 28.6 | 38.0 | 58.6 | 73.9 | 122.1 | 124.4 |
| Our Method | 80.7 | 94.8 | 65.4 | 89.0 | 38.8 | 69.7 | 28.6 | 37.5 | 58.6 | 73.5 | 125.5 | 126.3 |

| Image | Captions |
|---|---|
|  bathroom shower sink jacuzzi toilet | **Ground Truth:** This is a bathroom with a jacuzzi, shower, sink, and toilet. **GCN-LSTM:** A bathroom with toilet, tub and a stand up shower. **RA-TET:** A bathroom with a jacuzzi, shower, sink, and toilet. |
|  girl bread hand | **Ground Truth:** A baby is holding onto a piece of bread. **GCN-LSTM:** A little girl is holding a piece of bread. **RA-TET:** A little girl is holding a piece of bread with her right hand. |
|  field snowy | **Ground Truth:** Five horses are roaming in a snowy field. **GCN-LSTM:** A group of horses stand together in a snowy field. **RA-TET:** A group of horses are roaming in a snowy field. |

**Fig. 3.** The example of generated captions of RA-TET.

# 5    Conclusion

In this paper, we introduce a novel captioning model, namely Relational Attention with Textual Enhanced Transformer. Our model accounts for the relationship between objects within an image. There are two relation modules that could learn dependencies from two levels of image information, including low-level object proposals and high-level region features. Moreover, a Textual Enhance Transformer is designed to infer attended information in both textual and visual domains to guide the caption generation. Extensive experiments conducted on the MS COCO dataset demonstrate the effectiveness of our framework compared to state-of-the-art approaches.

# References

1. Mao, J., Xu, W., Yang, Y., Wang, J., Yuille, A.L.: Deep captioning with multimodal recurrent neural networks (m-rnn). In: ICLR (2015)
2. Jia, X., Gavves, E., Fernando, B., Tuytelaars, T.: Guiding the long-short term memory model for image caption generation. In: ICCV (2015)
3. Anderson, P., et al.: Bottom-up and top-down attention for image captioning and visual question answering. In: CVPR (2018)
4. Sutskever, I., Vinyals, O., Le, Q.V.: Sequence to sequence learning with neural networks. NIPS (2014)
5. Yang, Z., He, X., Gao, J., Deng, L., Smola, A.J.: Stacked attention networks for image question answering. In: CVPR (2016)
6. Jiasen, L., Xiong, C., Parikh, D.: and Richard Socher. Adaptive attention via a visual sentinel for image captioning. CVPR, Knowing when to look (2017)
7. Chen, L., et al.: SCA-CNN: spatial and channel-wise attention in convolutional networks for image captioning. In: CVPR (2017)
8. Kim, D.-J., Choi, J., Tae-Hyun, O., Kweon, I.S.: Dense relational captioning: Triple-stream networks for relationship-based captioning. In: CVPR (2019)
9. Yang, X., Tang, K., Zhang, H., Cai, J.: Auto-encoding scene graphs for image captioning. In: CVPR (2019)
10. Hong, D., Gao, L., Yao, J., Zhang, B., Plaza, A., Chanussot, J.: Graph convolutional networks for hyperspectral image classification. CoRR, vol. abs/2008.02457 (2020)
11. Yao, T., Pan, Y., Li, Y., Mei, T.: Exploring visual relationship for image captioning. In: ECCV (2018)
12. Vaswani, A., Shazeer, N., Parmar, N., Uszkoreit, J., Jones, L., Gomez, A.N., Kaiser, L., Polosukhin, I.: Attention is all you need. NIPS (2017)
13. Li, G., Zhu, L., Liu, P., Yang, Y.: Entangled transformer for image captioning. In: ICCV (2019)
14. Herdade, S., Kappeler, A., Boakye, K., Soares, J.: Image captioning, Transforming objects into words. NIPS (2019)
15. Ren, S., He, K., Girshick, R.B., Sun, J.: Faster R-CNN: towards real-time object detection with region proposal networks. NIPS (2015)
16. He, K., Zhang, X., Ren, S., Sun, J.: Deep residual learning for image recognition. In: CVPR (2016)
17. Fang, H., et al.: From captions to visual concepts and back. In: CVPR (2015)

18. Steven, J.: Rennie, E.M., Mroueh, Y., Ross, J., Goel, V.: Self-critical sequence training for image captioning. In: CVPR (2017)
19. Vedantam, R., Zitnick, C.L., Cider, D.P.: Consensus-based image description evaluation. In: CVPR (2015)
20. Chen, X., et al.: Microsoft COCO captions: Data collection and evaluation server. vol. abs/1504.00325 (2015)
21. Karpathy, A., Li, F.-F.: Deep visual-semantic alignments for generating image descriptions. In: CVPR (2015)
22. Papineni, K., Roukos, S., Ward, T., Zhu, W.-J.: Bleu: a method for automatic evaluation of machine translation. ACL (2002)
23. Banerjee, S., Lavie, A.: METEOR: an automatic metric for MT evaluation with improved correlation with human judgments. ACL (2005)
24. Anderson, P., Fernando, B., Johnson, M., Gould, S.: SPICE: semantic propositional image caption evaluation. In: ECCV (2016)
25. Vinyals, O., Toshev, A., Bengio, S., Erhan, D.: Show and tell: A neural image caption generator. In: CVPR (2015)
26. Huang, L., Wang, W., Chen, J., Wei, X.: Attention on attention for image captioning. In: ICCV (2019)
27. Yang, X., Zhang, H., Cai, J.: Learning to Collocate Neural Modules for Image Captioning. In: ICCV (2019)
28. Wang, W., Chen, Z., Hu, H.: Hierarchical Attention Network for Image Captioning, AAAI (2019)

# Non-local Network Routing
# for Perceptual Image Super-Resolution

Zexin Ji[1], Xin Dong[1], Zhendong Li[1,2(✉)], Zekuan Yu[3], and Hao Liu[1,2]

[1] School of Information Engineering, Ningxia University, Yinchuan 750021, China
[2] Collaborative Innovation Center for Ningxia Big Data and Artificial Intelligence
Co-founded by Ningxia Municipality and Ministry of Education,
Yinchuan 750021, China
lizhendong13@mails.ucas.ac.cn, liuhao@nxu.edu.cn
[3] Academy for Engineering and Technology, Fudan University,
Shanghai 200433, China
yzk@fudan.edu.cn

**Abstract.** In this paper, we propose a non-local network routing (NNR) approach for perceptual image super-resolution. Unlike conventional methods which generate visually-faked textures due to exiting hand-designed losses, our approach aims to globally optimize both procedures of learning an optimal perceptual loss and routing a spatial-adaptive network architecture in a unified reinforcement learning framework. To this end, we introduce a reward function to teach our objective to pay more attention on the visual quality of the super-resolved image. Moreover, we carefully design an offset operation inside the neural architecture search space, which typically deforms the receptive field on boundary refinement in a non-local manner. Experimentally, our proposed method surpasses the perceptual performance over state-of-the-art methods on several widely-evaluated benchmark datasets.

**Keywords:** Image super-resolution · Neural architecture search · Deep learning · Reinforcement learning

## 1 Introduction

Single image super-resolution aims to recover a high-resolution (HR) image (Fig. 1(a)) for a given low-resolution (LR) image (Fig. 1(b)), which plays a key role in image enhancement [8,12,29]. Although numerous image super-resolution approaches have been proposed recently [4,9–11,25], the performance still remains unsatisfied in practice. This is because the high-frequency information from the high-resolution image is excessively missing when it degrades due to extreme illumination conditions, motion blur, etc. Hence, this motivates us to develop a robust super-resolution approach to particularly recover the high-frequency information and enhance the *visual quality* for the super-resolved static images.

This is a student paper.

© Springer Nature Switzerland AG 2021
H. Ma et al. (Eds.): PRCV 2021, LNCS 13021, pp. 164–176, 2021.
https://doi.org/10.1007/978-3-030-88010-1_14

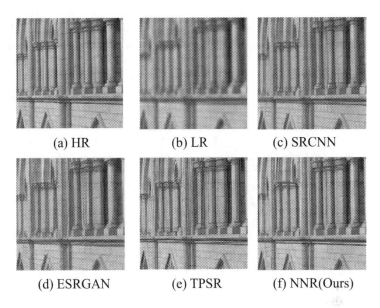

(a) HR                    (b) LR                    (c) SRCNN

(d) ESRGAN                (e) TPSR                  (f) NNR(Ours)

**Fig. 1.** Image super-resolution results of different methods. The distortion-based method SRCNN [4] generates blurred textures. The perceptual-based methods including ESRGAN [25], TPSR [10] generate unnatural artifacts. Our method achieves to recover sharper boundary and finer textures visually compared with others.

Based on different types of optimization losses, the image super-resolution methods can be roughly divided into distortion-based [11,22,31] and perceptual-based [9,10,21,25]. Specifically, the distortion-based methods aim to generate high PSNR images which typically minimize the discrepancy between the super-resolved images and the ground truth images in a pixel-wise manner. One major issue in these methods is that the pixel-level reconstruction loss likely results in blurred textures, ignoring the high-frequency details (Fig. 1(c)). To address this issue, the perceptual-based methods have been proposed to improve the visual quality of the super-resolved images. For example, Wang *et al.* [25] developed a ESRGAN method, the generative models typically use perceptual loss and adversarial loss to improve the perceptual quality. However, these methods likely generate fake textures and unnatural artifacts when recovering super-resolved images (Fig. 1(d),(e)). The underlying reason is that the discriminator likely produces bias supervision signal during the optimization process, which hardly captures texture details accurately. Moreover, the existing loss functions (*e.g.*, perceptual loss [7], pixel-wise MSE loss) are hand-crafted which provide local perceptual supervision signals.

Besides a well-defined perceptual objective function, making full use of the self-similarity information in the image itself is also effective on improving the perceptual quality [18]. For example, Yang *et al.* [27] proposed to explicitly transfer similar high-frequency features from a given reference image, so that the produced textures are more reasonable rather than the conventional fake ones. However, the performance of this method is semantically sensitive to the reference, which degrades seriously when the irrelevant reference images are given. Besides, the local features are in fixed-location neighborhoods, which cannot adapt the spatial relevant textures. To fully exploit the global cues of the input image itself, we introduce an offset learning strategy, which takes in the non-local information by utilizing the self-similarity of the inputs. By doing this, we use feature similarity to propagate between non-local pixels to explore high-frequency information (such as edges). In parallel, it reduces the geometric distortions produced by GAN-based methods [9,25].

In this work, we argue to jointly optimize both procedures of learning an optimal perceptual loss function and searching a reliable network architecture, which can further improve the perceptual quality of the super-resolved images (Fig. 1 (f)). To achieve this, we propose a non-local network routing (NNR) method for perceptual image super-resolution. Specifically, we leverage the neural architecture search which optimizes using reinforcement-based algorithm. To improve the visual quality of the super-resolved images, we develop a learnable reward to optimize an optimal perceptual loss for image super-resolution. Moreover, we design an offset learning strategy to adaptively capture spatial boundary information in a non-local manner. Extensive experiments on the widely-used datasets demonstrate the effectiveness of the proposed method quantitatively and qualitatively.

## 2    Related Work

**Single Image Super-Resolution.** Low-resolution images are affected by many degradation factors during the imaging process, such as motion blur, noise and downsampling. Shallow single image super-resolution approaches can be roughly divided into two categories: interpolation-based [13,15], reconstruction-based [6, 19]. Interpolation-based methods recover high-resolution images by interpolation algorithm. For example, bicubic interpolation. However, these methods usually undergo accuracy shortcomings. To address this limitation, reconstruction-based methods have been proposed to adopt prior knowledge to restrict the possible solution space, which can restore sharp details. Nevertheless, these methods are usually time-consuming.

Recent years have witnessed that deep learning networks have been applied to address the nonlinear issue in image super-resolution [4,9,16,18,25], which learns a set of nonlinear mapping from low-resolution to high-resolution image in an end-to-end manner. The distortion-based methods aim to improve the fidelity of images which typically minimize the mean square error between the predicted pixel and the ground-truth pixel. For example, Dong *et al.* [4] proposed SRCNN, which is the first work that applies deep learning for image super-resolution. Mao *et al.* [16] proposed to use encoder-decoder design to super-resolve the image. Although these methods have achieved the promising performance, one major issue is that the pixel-wise loss results in smooth images due to a lack of high-frequency details. To address this issue, perceptual-based methods have been proposed to improve the visual quality. For example, SRGAN [9] used an adversarial loss to restore the high-frequency details for perceptual satisfaction. However, the generative models likely produce geometric distortion textures. Besides, the hand-designed perceptual loss are not optimal for image perceptual evaluation and efficient training. To address these problems, our proposed method optimizes the procedures of learning an optimal perceptual objective function.

**Neural Architecture Search.** Recent trends have been seen that neural architecture search(NAS) [33] is gradually introduced to many computer vision applications. The coarse-grained tasks include image classification [20], object detection [34]. The fine-grained tasks include semantic segmentation [14], image super-resolution [3,10]. Auto-deeplab [14] proposed to search the network level structure in addition to the cell level structure, which aims to search the outer network structure automatically for semantic segmentation. Ulyanov *et al.* [23] argued that the structure of networks can be used as a structured image prior. Hence, Chen *et al.* [3] proposed to search for neural architectures which can capture stronger structured image priors for image restoration tasks. However, these methods mainly focus on searching for a network architecture and ignoring the image visual quality. Lee *et al.* [10] incorporated the NAS algorithm with GAN-based image super-resolution to improve the quality of perception while considering the computation cost. However, this method cannot fully exploit the global cues of image itself. To fully exploit the global cues of the input image itself, we exploit an offset learning strategy based on the self-similarity of images. Then we add the offset operation to the search space to further search for the perceptual-based super-resolution network. Besides, the GAN-based super-resolution method may likely produce fake textures duo to the unstable training. Thus our approach propose to optimize the perceptual loss function and perceptual-based super-resolution network simultaneously.

## 3    Methodology

In image super-resolution, we aim to restore a high-resolution image denoted by $I^{SR}$ based on the given low-resolution input denoted by $I^{LR}$. As demonstrated in Fig. 2, we develop a non-local network routing method. Technically, we leverage reinforcement learning algorithms and incorporate neural architecture search with the image super-resolution task. Furthermore, we design a learnable perceptual reward as loss function to produce optimal supervision signal for efficient training. Besides, we develop a search space by introducing spatial-adaptive offset operation, which aims to reason a reliable network for perceptual image super-resolution.

### 3.1    Non-local Network Routing

Although traditional perceptual-based methods can significantly improve the perceptual quality of the super-resolved images, it will produce inconsistent artifacts and false textures. Moreover, the hand-designed perceptual loss function

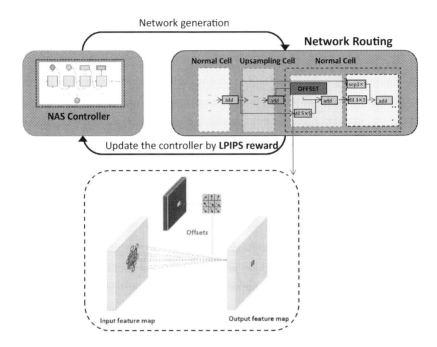

**Fig. 2.** Overall framework of our NNR method. We design a reward (LPIPS) and exploit neural architecture search algorithm (reinforcement learning-based with LSTM controller) beyond a search space. The offset operation is deployed in the search space to seek for a reliable network architecture.

is easy to fall into local optima and cannot be considered as a strong supervision signal to train the optimal super-resolution network. To address this, we introduce NAS into image super-resolution task. The search algorithm is mainly based on reinforcement learning, which incorporates with LSTM as the controller. The action $a$ specifies the generation of a neural network architecture. The state $s$ is defined by a set of observed network architecture. We design a learnable reward (LPIPS) to jointly optimize both procedures of learning an optimal perceptual loss and routing a reliable super-resolution network architecture denoted by $\boldsymbol{\omega}$. The LPIPS reward function is designed to measure the image patch similarity from feature space, which is defined as follows:

$$r(s^t, a^t) = -l_{\text{LPIPS}} \tag{1}$$

Specifically, we define the LPIPS function [30] by the following equation:

$$l_{\text{LPIPS}} = \sum_l \frac{1}{H_l W_l} \sum_{h,w} \|w_l \odot (\hat{I}_l^{\text{SR}} - \hat{I}_l^{\text{HR}})\|^2, \tag{2}$$

where $\hat{I}_l^{\text{SR}}, \hat{I}_l^{\text{HR}} \in \mathbb{R}^{H_l \times W_l \times C_l}$ is the feature from $l$ layers of the pre-trained network. $w_l \in \mathbb{R}^{C_l}$ is used to scale the channel-wise activations .

The traditional PSNR is the distortion based metric, which is insufficient for estimating the visual quality of images. This is because the pixel-wise restraint results in over-smoothed results without sufficient high-frequency details. However, the LPIPS is a perceptual-based metric to measure the image patch similarity from feature space. It is mentioned in [30] that the perceptual similarity measurement of two images is more consistent with human judgment than PSNR. Therefore, we use the LPIPS as the perceptual reward to optimize an optimal perceptual loss.

Aside from learning an optimal perceptual loss function, we introduce an offset learning strategy to fully exploit the global cues of the input image itself. Moreover, the non-local feature representation is also effective on improving the perceptual quality of the super-resolved images. We explore the boundary information by the self-similarity of images. The captured high-frequency information such as spatial textures and edges reinforces the visual quality. In this way, the boundary information further resolves the geometric distortion. The offset strategy can be written as follows:

$$y(p_0) = \sum_{p_n \in R} w(p_n) \cdot x(p_0 + p_n + \triangle p_n), \tag{3}$$

where $x$ is the input, $y$ is the output feature map, and $p_n$ enumerates the location in a regular grid $R$ respectively. $\{\triangle p_n | n = 1, ..., N\}$ is the learnable offsets and the sampling performs on the offset locations $p_n + \triangle p_n$.

To automatically search for a network architecture with promising perceptual performance, we design to plug the offset operation inside the search space. The offset operation adaptively learns a set of offsets from the input image itself. Then our search space is developed to perform micro-cell approach and the normal cell can be regarded as a feature extractor. In our approach, we aim to obtain high-frequency feature representation which is crucial for perceptual image super-resolution. As a result, our model focuses on selecting for the best architecture of the normal cell. We show the candidate operation $Op\_normal$ of the normal cell search subspace as follows:

$Op\_normal = \{$Offset,
Dilated Conv $(k, n)$ with $k = 3, 5,$
Separable Conv $(k, n)$ with $k <= 3, 5,$
Residual Channel Attention Block(RCAB),
Identity $\}$

For the normal cell, the search space is composed by the offset operation [32] and other several commonly used candidate operations including $3 \times 3$ and $5 \times 5$ dilated convolution, $3 \times 3$ and $5 \times 5$ separable convolution, residual channel attention block [31] and skip connection.

The upsampling cell is used to recover images with higher spatial resolution. We develop a search space with several upsampling operations. The candidate operation $Op\_upsampling$ of upsampling search subspace can be expressed as

---

**Algorithm 1:** NNR

---

**Input**: Training set: $(I_i^{\mathrm{LR}}, I_i^{\mathrm{HR}})_{i=1}^{N_1}$ with $N_1$ samples,
          Validation set: $(I_i^{\mathrm{LR}}, I_i^{\mathrm{HR}})_{i=1}^{N_2}$ with $N_2$ samples. $Inter = 300$.
**Output**: NNR model
1   **Require:** learning rate $\eta$, sharing parameters $\omega$, controller parameters $\theta$
2   //Initialize $\omega$ and $\theta$
3   **for** $i = 1$ *to Inter* **do**
4      **for** *each training sample* $i = 1, ... N_1$ **do**
5          //Sampling a group of network architectures;
6          //training $\omega$ on training sample
7          Sampling $s \sim \pi(s, \theta)$;
8          Compute $l_{total}(s, \omega)$ via (4)
9          $\omega \leftarrow \omega\text{-}\eta \bigtriangledown_\omega l_{total}(s, \omega)$
10     **end**
11     **for** *each validation sample* $j = 1, ... N_2$ **do**
12          //training controller parameters $\theta$
13          //compute LPIPS reward on validation samples
14          Sampling $s \sim \pi(s, \theta)$;
15          $\theta \leftarrow \theta + \eta r(s) \bigtriangledown_\theta \log \pi(s; \theta)$
16     **end**
17 **end**

---

$$\text{Op\_upsampling} = \{\text{Pixel Shuffle Layer},$$
$$\text{Deconvolution Layer}$$
$$\text{Nearest-neighbor Interpolation}$$
$$\text{Bilinear interpolation}\}$$

## 3.2 Model Learning

For our optimization, we specify a small scale of epochs and higher batch size as the proxy task. In detail, we first leverage the proxy task to search the optimal architecture. Then we exploit the weight sharing strategy, which uses the weights of step $t$ to initialize the model at step $t + 1$. We evaluate the searched network architecture by computing the LPIPS reward between the ground truth image and the super-resolved image. With the learnable perceptual reward, we exploit the policy gradient [26] to train the LSTM controller. Based on the learned policy $\pi(\cdot)$, we obtain the best-performing network architectures and the optimal reward loss function simultaneously. Finally, we apply the full task to retrain the acquired best-performing super-resolution network architecture from scratch. We also use the LPIPS loss to train the searched super-resolution network. The previous works [2] mentioned that only using perceptual quality to constrain the network may produce undesirable artifacts. Hence, we incorporate $\ell_1$ loss in our final optimization. The overall loss of training the searched network architecture can be expressed as follows:

$$l_{total} = \alpha \frac{1}{N} \sum_{i=1}^{N} |I_i^{\text{SR}} - I_i^{\text{HR}}| + \beta l_{\text{LPIPS}}, \tag{4}$$

where $\alpha$ and $\beta$ are the trade-off weights and $N$ is the total number of images respectively. Specifically, we specified the parameters $\alpha=0.8$ and $\beta=0.2$ of our model.

**Algorithm 1** details the training procedure of our NNR.

## 4   Experiments

### 4.1   Evaluation Dataset and Metric

In our experiments, we used the DIV2K dataset as the training data, and the commonly-used SR benchmarks, namely Set5 [1], Set14 [28], BSD100 [17] and Urban100 [5] as the testing datasets. All experiments were performed with a scale factor 4x between low-resolution and high-resolution images. For data augmentation, we used horizontal flip, verticle flip and rotation randomly.

We evaluated the trained model under the learned perceptual image patch similarity (LPIPS) and the peak signal-to-noise ratio (PSNR). Accordingly, we used LPIPS to measure the perceptual quality of the super-resolved images, where the lower the LPIPS value indicates better image visual quality. The PSNR is distortion-based measures that pays more attention to the fidelity of images. Obviously, the higher the PSNR value and the smaller the image distortion. Following the standard settings in [10], we evaluated PSNR and LPIPS on the Y channel and RGB image respectively.

### 4.2   Implementation Details

Our model was built based on the popular accelerated deep learning toolbox PyTorch[1]. We conducted all experiments on a NVIDIA Tesla V100 GPU with 300 epochs for searching network architectures and 300 epochs for training networks. The batch-size was set to 16. The ADAM optimizer was for searching and SGD for training. Moreover, we use sample entropy regularization for robust and fast convergence in our NAS controller.

### 4.3   Derived Architecture

Figure 3 shows the normal cell and upsampling cell searched via our method respectively. As the figure shows, each cell contains four intermediate nodes and every node has two operations from previous nodes. For each cell, the nodes represent the feature map, and the edge is the searched operation. It can be concluded that the cell structure selection is controlled by our proposed reward, which achieves the highest reward during the optimization iterations.

---

[1] https://github.com/pytorch/pytorch.

**Table 1.** Quantitative results of our method on different datasets including Set5, Set14, BSD100, and Urban100. Note that higher is better for PSNR, lower is better for LPIPS. Our method achieves compelling performance especially under the perceptual LPIPS metric.

| Model | Set5 PSNR/LPIPS | Set14 PSNR/LPIPS | BSD100 PSNR/LPIPS | Urban100 PSNR/LPIPS |
|---|---|---|---|---|
| Bicubic | 28.420/0.341 | 26.100/0.439 | 25.961/0.525 | 23.145/0.473 |
| SRGAN [9] | 29.168/0.088 | 26.171/0.166 | 25.459/0.198 | 24.397/0.155 |
| ESRGAN [25] | 30.454/0.075 | 26.276/0.133 | 25.317/0.161 | 24.360/0.123 |
| SFTGAN [24] | 29.930/0.089 | 26.223/0.148 | 25.505/0.177 | 24.013/0.143 |
| NatSR [21] | 30.991/0.094 | 27.514/0.176 | 26.445/0.211 | 25.464/0.150 |
| TPSR [10] | 29.600/0.076 | 26.880/0.110 | 26.230/0.116 | 24.120/0.141 |
| Baseline | 30.866/0.078 | 27.747/0.109 | 26.941/0.129 | 24.839/0.125 |
| w/Reward | 31.477/0.070 | 28.072/0.102 | 27.170/0.123 | 25.344/0.109 |
| NNR (Ours) | 31.427/0.065 | 28.074/0.095 | 27.183/0.117 | 25.248/0.108 |

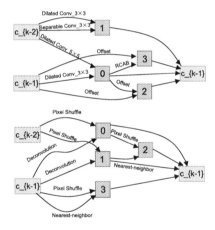

**Fig. 3.** Resulting routing of our NNR

### 4.4   Comparison with State-of-the-Art Methods

**Quantitative Comparison.** We compared our approach with folds of state-of-the-art perceptual driven super-resolution methods. In Table 1, we reported the PSNR, LPIPS on Set5, Set14, BSD100 and Urban100 under the evaluation setting. From the results, we made two-fold conclusion: (1) Our proposed learnable perceptual reward can capture sufficient high-frequency details which improves the visual quality of the super-resolved images. We also used the perceptual reward to route a reliable super-resolution network. In this manner, our method provides optimal supervision for texture recovery and trains the super-resolution network efficiently. However, the traditional perceptual loss is handcrafted which may be local for capturing high-frequency information. Meanwhile, the hand-designed super-resolution network architecture is redundant for

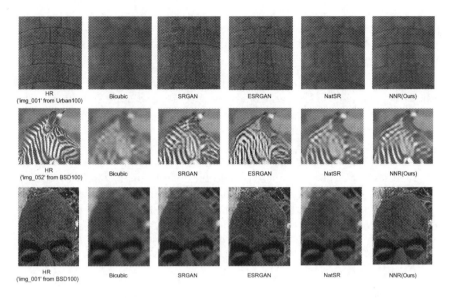

**Fig. 4.** Visualized results of our NNR versus conventional super-resolution approaches.

recovering visual quality. (2) Benefiting from the offset operation, our method can capture non-local similar feature representation and further improve the visual quality of the super-resolved images. Since the Urban100 dataset contains more building structure images, we observe that our NNR method generalizes better and gives performance gain 0.015 in LPIPS on the dataset. Unfortunately, some methods such as NatSR [21] and TPSR [10] which enforce local features, likely resulting in the inability to obtain global information. Thus, the LPIPS performance of these methods is poor than us. In addition, we figure out that our NNR achieves competitive performance on PSNR and better performance on LPIPS especially on the perceptual dimension.

Besides, we performed ablation study to validate the effectiveness for different components of our NNR method. Specifically, we only applied PSNR as the reward to search the super-resolution network as Baseline model. We first validated the importance of the designed learnable perceptual reward, which only used the LPIPS reward to constrain the network training in w/ Reward model. Then we added the offest operation to the search space based on the w/ Reward model, which further validates the effectiveness of the offset learning strategy. Table 1. presents the quantitative comparison of our ablation study.

We see that w/Reward has a significant improvement compared with Baseline model, which demonstrates the effectiveness of the learnable perceptual reward. The reason lies on that the optimal loss function efficiently dominates the optimal super-resolution network routing. Furthermore, our NNR method also indicates improvements especially on LPIPS performance over w/ Reward. With this, the offset operation adaptively captures the relevant features from complex images, especially the spatial textures and edges. In summary, our results clarify the effectiveness integrated with both the learnable perceptual reward and offset learning strategy.

**Qualitative Comparison.** Finally, we compared our NNR method with other methods qualitatively. The traditional perceptual-based super-resolution methods produce inconsistent fake textures duo to bias supervision signals. As shown in Fig. 4, our method is more realistic than others. For example, for the stone statue's head, the compared methods are accompanied with unpleasant artifacts, while our method generates sharper textures. This is mainly due to the optimal perceptual loss and reliable super-resolution network architecture. Besides, the offset learning strategy achieves the non-local edge information, which reduces the geometric distortion and enhances the discriminability of the boundary and texture information.

## 5   Conclusion

In this paper, we have proposed a non-local network routing (NNR) method for perceptual image super-resolution. We have designed a learnbale reward to select a reliable super-resolution network architecture with an offset learning strategy. Quantitative and qualitative results have shown the effectiveness of our NNR. Differential convolutions in frequency domain with NAS is a desirable direction.

**Acknowledgement.** This work was supported in part by the National Science Foundation of China under Grant 61806104 and 62076142, in part by the West Light Talent Program of the Chinese Academy of Sciences under Grant XAB2018AW05, and in part by the Youth Science and Technology Talents Enrollment Projects of Ningxia under Grant TJGC2018028.

## References

1. Bevilacqua, M., Roumy, A., Guillemot, C., Alberi-Morel, M.: Low-complexity single-image super-resolution based on nonnegative neighbor embedding. In: BMVC, pp. 1–10 (2012)
2. Chen, R., Xie, Y., Luo, X., Qu, Y., Li, C.: Joint-attention discriminator for accurate super-resolution via adversarial training. In: ACM MM, pp. 711–719 (2019)
3. Chen, Y., Gao, C., Robb, E., Huang, J.: NAS-DIP: learning deep image prior with neural architecture search. ECCV. **12363**, 442–459 (2020)
4. Dong, C., Loy, C.C., He, K., Tang, X.: Learning a deep convolutional network for image super-resolution. In: ECCV, vol. 8692, pp. 184–199 (2014)
5. Huang, J., Singh, A., Ahuja, N.: Single image super-resolution from transformed self-exemplars. In: CVPR, pp. 5197–5206 (2015)
6. Irani, M., Peleg, S.: Improving resolution by image registration. Graph. Models Image Process. **53**(3), 231–239 (1991)
7. Johnson, J., Alahi, A., Fei-Fei, L.: Perceptual losses for real-time style transfer and super-resolution. In: ECCV, vol. 9906, pp. 694–711 (2016)

8. Kouame, D., Ploquin, M.: Super-resolution in medical imaging: an illustrative approach through ultrasound. In: ISBI, pp. 249–252 (2009)
9. Ledig, C., et al.: Photo-realistic single image super-resolution using a generative adversarial network. In: CVPR, pp. 105–114 (2017)
10. Lee, R., Dudziak, L., Abdelfattah, M.S., Venieris, S.I., Kim, H., Wen, H., Lane, N.D.: Journey towards tiny perceptual super-resolution. In: ECCV, vol. 12371, pp. 85–102 (2020)
11. Lim, B., Son, S., Kim, H., Nah, S., Lee, K.M.: Enhanced deep residual networks for single image super-resolution. In: CVPRW, pp. 1132–1140 (2017)
12. Lin, F., Fookes, C., Chandran, V., Sridharan, S.: Super-resolved faces for improved face recognition from surveillance video. In: Lee, S.-W., Li, S.Z. (eds.) ICB 2007. LNCS, vol. 4642, pp. 1–10. Springer, Heidelberg (2007). https://doi.org/10.1007/978-3-540-74549-5_1
13. Lin, T., RoyChowdhury, A., Maji, S.: Bilinear CNN models for fine-grained visual recognition. In: ICCV (2015)
14. Liu, C., et al.: Auto-deeplab: hierarchical neural architecture search for semantic image segmentation. In: CVPR, pp. 82–92 (2019)
15. Loop, C.T., Schaefer, S.: Approximating catmull-clark subdivision surfaces with bicubic patches. ACM Trans. Graph. $27(1)$, 8:1–8:11 (2008)
16. Mao, X., Shen, C., Yang, Y.: Image restoration using very deep convolutional encoder-decoder networks with symmetric skip connections. In: NIPS, pp. 2802–2810 (2016)
17. Martin, D.R., Fowlkes, C.C., Tal, D., Malik, J.: A database of human segmented natural images and its application to evaluating segmentation algorithms and measuring ecological statistics. In: ICCV, pp. 416–425 (2001)
18. Mei, Y., Fan, Y., Zhou, Y., Huang, L., Huang, T.S., Shi, H.: Image super-resolution with cross-scale non-local attention and exhaustive self-exemplars mining. In: CVPR, pp. 5689–5698 (2020)
19. Patti, A.J., Sezan, M.I., Tekalp, A.M.: Superresolution video reconstruction with arbitrary sampling lattices and nonzero aperture time. IEEE Trans. Image Process. $6(8)$, 1064–1076 (1997)
20. Real, E., Moore, S., Selle, A., Saxena, S., Suematsu, Y.L., Tan, J., Le, Q.V., Kurakin, A.: Large-scale evolution of image classifiers. In: ICML, vol. 70, pp. 2902–2911 (2017)
21. Soh, J.W., Park, G.Y., Jo, J., Cho, N.I.: Natural and realistic single image super-resolution with explicit natural manifold discrimination. In: CVPR, pp. 8122–8131 (2019)
22. Tong, T., Li, G., Liu, X., Gao, Q.: Image super-resolution using dense skip connections. In: ICCV, pp. 4809–4817 (2017)
23. Ulyanov, D., Vedaldi, A., Lempitsky, V.S.: Deep image prior. In: CVPR (2018)
24. Wang, X., Yu, K., Dong, C., Loy, C.C.: Recovering realistic texture in image super-resolution by deep spatial feature transform. In: CVPR, pp. 606–615 (2018)
25. Wang, X., et al.: SRGAN: enhanced super-resolution generative adversarial networks. In: ECCVW, vol. 11133, pp. 63–79 (2018)
26. Williams, R.J.: Simple statistical gradient-following algorithms for connectionist reinforcement learning. Mach. Learn. $8$, 229–256 (1992)
27. Yang, F., Yang, H., Fu, J., Lu, H., Guo, B.: Learning texture transformer network for image super-resolution. In: CVPR, pp. 5790–5799 (2020)
28. Zeyde, R., Elad, M., Protter, M.: On single image scale-up using sparse-representations. Curves Surf. $6920$, 711–730 (2010)

29. Zhang, L., Zhang, H., Shen, H., Li, P.: A super-resolution reconstruction algorithm for surveillance images. Sig. Process. **90**(3), 848–859 (2010)
30. Zhang, R., Isola, P., Efros, A.A., Shechtman, E., Wang, O.: The unreasonable effectiveness of deep features as a perceptual metric. In: CVPR, pp. 586–595 (2018)
31. Zhang, Y., Li, K., Li, K., Wang, L., Zhong, B., Fu, Y.: Image super-resolution using very deep residual channel attention networks. In: ECCV, vol. 11211, pp. 294–310 (2018)
32. Zhu, X., Hu, H., Lin, S., Dai, J.: Deformable convnets V2: more deformable, better results. In: CVPR, pp. 9308–9316 (2019)
33. Zoph, B., Le, Q.V.: Neural architecture search with reinforcement learning. In: ICLR (2017)
34. Zoph, B., Vasudevan, V., Shlens, J., Le, Q.V.: Learning transferable architectures for scalable image recognition. In: CVPR, pp. 8697–8710 (2018)

# Multi-focus Image Fusion with Cooperative Image Multiscale Decomposition

Yueqi Tan and Bin Yang[(✉)]

College of Electric Engineering, University of South China, Hengyang 421001, CO, China

**Abstract.** Multi-focus image fusion plays an important role in the field of image processing for its ability in solving the depth-of-focus limitation problem in optical lens imaging by fusing a series of partially focused images of the same scene. The improvements on various fusion methods focus on the image decomposition methods and the fusion strategies. However, most decompositions are separately conducted on each image, which fails to sufficiently consider the nature of multiple images in fusion tasks, and insufficiently explores the consistent and inconsistent features of two source images simultaneously. This paper proposes a new cooperative image multiscale decomposition (CIMD) based on the mutually guided filter (MGF). With CIMD, two source multi-focus images are simultaneously decomposed into base layers and detailed layers through the iterative operation of MGF cooperatively. A saliency detection based on a mean-guide combination filter is adopted to guide the fusion of detailed layers and a spatial frequency-based fusion strategy is used to fuse the luminance and contour features in the base layers. The experiments are carried on 28 pairs of publicly available multi-focus images. The fusion results are compared with 7 state-of-the-art multi-focus image fusion methods. Experimental results show that the proposed method has the better visual quality and objective assessment.

**Keywords:** Multi-focus image fusion · Depth-of-focus · Mutually-guided filter · Cooperative image multiscale decomposition · Focus region detection

## 1 Introduction

Optical imaging has the limitation of the depth-of-focus, which makes it difficult to obtain an all-in-focus image with conventional digital cameras. The multi-focus image fusion technology which obtains an all-in-focus image by merging multiple optical images has an important practical significance. The fused images are widely used in the fields of human vision, computer vision, artificial intelligence, and so on.

According to the feature domains where the source images are fused, image fusion methods are roughly divided into two main categories, namely, spatial domain methods and transform domain methods. Spatial domain methods usually investigate the saliency information of pixels or regions to establish the fusion. Some of them are based on total variation, gradient optimization [4]. This type of methods is efficient. However, there may be artifacts and distortions in the fused image. Transform domain approaches are

© Springer Nature Switzerland AG 2021
H. Ma et al. (Eds.): PRCV 2021, LNCS 13021, pp. 177–188, 2021.
https://doi.org/10.1007/978-3-030-88010-1_15

consist of three steps, namely, decomposition, coefficient fusion, and reconstruction [1]. Pyramid transform [5][6], wavelet transform, and contourlet transform are commonly used to decompose the source images into different feature coefficients. These transform methods offer not only higher efficiencies but also offer greater flexibility to the fusion strategy design. The sparse representation [7] also attracts numerous researchers in image fusion applications due to its effective capability in underlying information extraction from an image. In recent years, deep learning has also been introduced to achieve multi-focus image fusion because of its potential in deep feature extraction [9].

Existing multiscale transforms have made various improvements in image fusion rules and image multiscale decomposition for resolving the problem of saliency detection and improving the fusion effect. Whereas the traditional multiscale decompositions do not sufficiently separate the consistent structure and inconsistent structure in the two images to be fused that have gradient amplitude differences. In this paper, we present a new fusion method based on the proposed cooperative image multiscale decomposition (CIMD). The CIMD is used to separate the consistent structure and the inconsistent structure in two images by the CIMD. With CIMD, two source images are decomposed into detailed layers and base layers cooperatively. The detailed layers which contain the inconsistent gradient structure of two source images are very helpful in adjusting the local clarity of two source images. Therefore, a saliency detection-based fusion rules are used to fusion the detailed layers that contain the inconsistent structure, and spatial frequency-based fusion rules are used to integrate the base layers. Finally, the fused base layers and detailed layers are merged together to obtain the final fused image. 28 pairs of publicly available multi-focus images are used to test the performances of the proposed method. The experimental results demonstrate that the proposed image fusion method demonstrates versatility across multiple types of multi-focus images.

The rest of this paper is organized as follows. we construct the CIMD-based MGF in Sect. 2. Sect. 3 describes the proposed image fusion algorithm in detail. The experiment results and discussions are presented in Sect. 4, and conclusions are given in Sect. 5.

## 2    Cooperative Image Multiscale Decomposition Based MGF

### 2.1    Mutually Guided Filter

Shen et al. [3] divided the mutual-structures of two input images into three types, including mutual structure, flat structure, and inconsistent structure. The mutual structure describes the part with both strong gradient structures, while the flat structure references the part of the consistent weak gradient structure. The two structures are collectively referred to as the consistent structure in this paper. The inconsistent structure represents the structure with divergence gradient amplitudes in two images at the same pixel position. The inconsistent structure would be vital for multi-focus image fusion applications. However traditional guide filter ignores the structural inconsistency when we need to filter two content correlative images simultaneously. To solve these problems, a mutually guided filter is proposed for the purpose to preserve the mutual structure, prevent misleading from inconsistent structure, and smooth flat regions between two input images [2]. Let $T_0$ and $R_0$ denote two input images that should be filtered simultaneously. The filtered outputs T and R from the MGF are obtained by:

$$\arg \min_{T,R} \alpha \varphi[T, R, \varepsilon] + \|T - T_0\|_2^2 + \|R - R_0\|_2^2 \qquad (1)$$

where

$$\varphi[T, R, \varepsilon] = \sum_{i \in \Omega} \sum_{d \in \{h,v\}} \left( \frac{|\nabla_d T_i|}{\max(|\nabla_d R_i|, \varepsilon)} + \frac{|\nabla_d R_i|}{\max(|\nabla_d T_i|, \varepsilon)} \right) \qquad (2)$$

represents the mutual structure discrimination indicated by the gradient ratio between two images. The symbol $\Omega$ represents the pixel sets of the source images. $T_i$ and $R_i$ indicate the pixel values at $i$ position. The symbol $\varepsilon$ is a small positive constant to avoid division by zero. $\nabla_h$ and $\nabla_r$ are the horizontal and vertical derivative operators respectively. The first term in Eq. (1) is the regularization term which is the consistent structure restraint aiming to reduce the gradient discrepancy between two images to be filtered. The second and third terms are the fidelity term. The parameter $\alpha$ is regularization parameter given by the users.

From Eq. (1), we can easily deduce that the mutual structure and flat structure from two filter outputs toward identical. Figure 1 (a) shows two images obtained with different focus settings. The upper image shows rich texture in the left area while the bottom one focuses on the right area. Figure 1 (b), (c), and (d) illustrate filters employed by the mean filter, the guide filter [12], and MGF, respectively. All filter results are blurred in different various degrees. However, only the two outputs of MGF still maintain the consistent gradient structure. It demonstrates that MGF can preserve the contour information of multi-focus images.

## 2.2   Cooperative Image Multiscale Decomposition

It is known that a good decomposition method should separate the useful information, such as contour, texture, and structure information into the different sub-band images. MGF is a novel edge-preserving filter that offered an effective way of preserving the mutual structure and flat structure. The inconsistent structure that exhibits divergence gradient amplitudes between two source images is filtered out. For multi-focus image fusion, the inconsistent gradient structure is very helpful in adjusting the clarity of two source images. In this paper, the CIMD based on MGF is proposed for multi-focus image fusion. The CIMD can separate the inconsistent structure represented by texture information.

The CIMD is achieved by

$$[B_t, B_r] = MuGuide(I_t, I_r) \qquad (3)$$

$$D_t = I_t - B_t \qquad (4)$$

$$D_r = I_r - B_r \qquad (5)$$

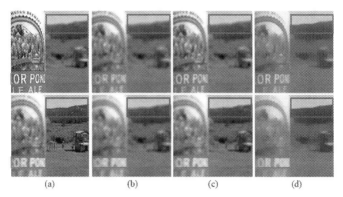

(a)                    (b)                    (c)                    (d)

**Fig. 1.** Two multi-focus images and the output results with different filters. (a) The source multi-focus images; (b) Output from mean filter; (c) Output from guide filter; (d) Output from MGF.

where $I_t$ and $I_r$ represent two source multi-focus images; $B_t$ and $B_r$ are the base layers of the multi-focus images; $D_t$ and $D_r$ represent the detailed layers. The base layers are simultaneously obtained by the mutually guided filter with two source images being employed collaborative references. The base layers contain the consistent structure such as contour, brightness, and part of details of the source images. While the detailed layers obtained by subtracting base layers from the source images show the gradient discrepancy components of the source images.

Figure 2 shows an example of the CIMD on multi-focus images. In Fig. 2, the consistent structure such as the contour features of the source images is extracted separately into the base layers, while the inconsistent structure which shows local clarity of the source images is preserved in the detailed layers. Thus, the different amplitudes of inconsistent information can accurately discriminate the focus area of the source images. In addition, the separation property of consistent structure and inconsistent structure can effectively reduce the artifacts in the fused results.

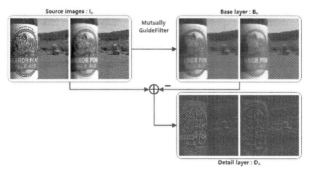

**Fig. 2.** Cooperative image multiscale decomposition on multi-focus images.

## 3   Image Fusion with CIMD

The schematic diagram of the proposed fusion strategy is illustrated in Fig. 3. Firstly, two multi-focus images are divided into the base layers and the detailed layers based on CIMD simultaneously. Then, the fused base layers and detailed layers are obtained by weight average fusion rules. Finally, the final fused image is a superimposition of the fused base and detailed layers.

### 3.1   Base Layers Fusion

Base layers images filtered by CMID preserve the consistent gradient structure of the source images. However, the consistent structure does not guarantee identical local intensity or other image features in different source images. In particular, the difference between the two base layer images manifests as weak amplitude differences, and the weak amplitude differences can be measured by the local spatial frequency (LSF). Therefore, the difference in the LSF value can be implemented to discriminate the regions of interest. This paper adopts the LSF-based fusion rule to measure the blurred features of base layers images.

The LSF of a certain sub-band image $B$ obtained by

$$LSF_B = \sqrt{Lrf_B^2 + Lcf_B^2} \tag{6}$$

where

$$Lrf_B(i,j) = \frac{1}{5}\sqrt{\sum_{a=-2}^{2}\sum_{b=-2}^{2}\left[B(i+a,j+b) - B(i+a,j+b-1)\right]^2} \tag{7}$$

$$Lcf_B(i,j) = \frac{1}{5}\sqrt{\sum_{a=-2}^{2}\sum_{b=-2}^{2}\left[B(i+a,j+b) - B(i+a-1,j+b)\right]^2} \tag{8}$$

where $B(i,j)$ is the pixel value at position $(i,j)$.

With Eq. (6), $LSF_t$ and $LSF_r$ of the base layers $B_t$ and $B_r$ are obtained respectively. Then the fusion weighted map $\overline{m}$ for $B_t$ and $B_r$ is constructed as

$$\overline{m}(i,j) = \begin{cases} 1 & if\ LSF_t(i,j) > LSF_r(i,j) + TH \\ 0.5 & elseif\ abs(LSF_t(i,j) - LSF_r(i,j)) < TH \\ 0 & Otherwise \end{cases} \tag{9}$$

where $TH$ is a predetermined threshold. To reduce the artifacts in the fused image, a threshold parameter is defined to restrict that the arithmetic mean fusion rule is used when the value of LSF difference between two images less than $TH$. In this paper, we set $TH = 0.001$ empirically. Furthermore, the guide filter defined in [12] is used to refined the weighted map as.

$$m = GuideFilter(\overline{m}, B_t) \tag{10}$$

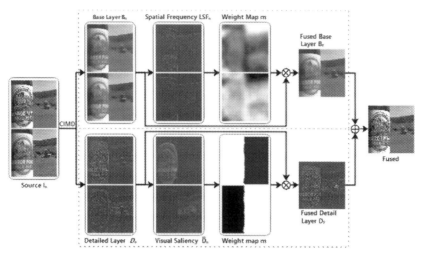

**Fig. 3.** Schematic diagram of the proposed algorithm.

The base image $B_t$ is served as the guided image.
Finally, the fused image $B_F$ is obtained by

$$B_F = mB_t + (1 - m)B_r \tag{11}$$

## 3.2  Detailed Layers Fusion

The inconsistent structure such as texture information of multi-focused images determines the clarity of the fused image. A good fused result should contain all the inconsistent structure in images obtained by different focus sets. The detailed image filtered by CIMD preserves most of the inconsistent structure such as texture features in multi-focused images. Therefore, a weighted fusion rule based on saliency detection is proposed for distinguishing the saliency of inconsistent structure in detailed layers.

The saliency information map $\overline{D}$ of a certain sub-band image $D$ is obtained by the mean-guide filter as

$$\overline{S} = |D - D * f_m| \tag{12}$$

$$\overline{D} = GuideFilter(D, \overline{S}) \tag{13}$$

where $f_m$ is a $7 \times 7$ mean filter operator and $||$ represents the absolute operator. The $*$ denotes the convolution operation. Furthermore, in order to enhance regional consistency of the map, the features saliency $\overline{D}$ are obtained by the guide filter.

With Eq. (12) and Eq. (13), the features saliency information maps $\overline{D}_t$ and $\overline{D}_r$ of the sub-band images $D_t$ and $D_r$ are obtained. The initial weight map $\overline{m}$ is determined by

$$\overline{m}(i,j) = \begin{cases} 1, & if\ \overline{D}_t(i,j) > \overline{D}_r(i,j) \\ 0, & Otherwise \end{cases} \tag{14}$$

Furthermore, to reduce artifacts or halos caused by unaligned source images or detection of edge misalignment problems, the optimized weight map $m$ is obtained by

$$m = GuideFilter(\overline{m}D_t + (1 - \overline{m})D_r, \overline{m}) \tag{15}$$

The fused detailed layers $D_F$ is obtained by

$$D_F = mD_t + (1 - m)D_r \tag{16}$$

### 3.3 Reconstruction

Finally, the fused image is constructed by

$$Fused = B_F + D_F \tag{17}$$

## 4 Experiment

### 4.1 Experiment Setup

28 pairs of publicly available multi-focus images are selected to test the proposed method. 22 pairs of images are collected from the Lytro multi-focus image dataset created by Nejati et al. in [13]. The remaining 6 pairs are collected from the website [14]. All of the source images are gray images. Figure 4 shows ten pairs of multi-focus images in the experiment dataset. All the experiments are implemented on a laptop equipped with an Intel(R) Core(TM) i5–10400 CPU (2.90GHz) and NVIDIA GeForce RTX 2070 GPU with 16GB RAM. And the software environment is MATLAB R2018b installed on Win 10 64-bit operating system.

To demonstrate the fusion effectiveness of the proposed algorithm, we quantitative compare the proposed method with 7 state-of-the-art image fusion algorithms, including guided filtering fusion (GFF) [5], sparse representation (SR) [7], gradient transfer fusion (GTF) [4], guided filter-based image detection fusion (GFDF) [6], multi-scale structural image decomposition (MSID) [10], Laplacian re-decomposition (LRD) [11], and resid-ual neural network analysis image fusion (ResNet) [9]. For SR, we use the MST-SR-Fusion-Toolbox provided by Liu et al. [8]. The remaining algorithms are implemented based on publicly available codes provided by authors. For all methods, we use the optimal default parameters reported in the related publications.

To qualitatively analyze the effectiveness of different algorithms in terms of the perspective of visual effects, we select six evaluation metrics, including the gradient-based fusion performance $Q^{AB/F}$ [15], the structural similarity-based metric $Q_S$ [19], $Q_C$ [17], $Q_Y$ [16], the human perception inspired metric $Q_{CB}$ [20], the phase congruency-based metric $Q_P$ [18].

**Fig. 4.** Ten pairs of multi-focus images were selected from the experiment dataset.

## 4.2 Comparison to Classical Fusion Method

To evaluate the sensitivities of the key parameters in the proposed method, we experimentally studied the influence of parameters $\alpha$, $\varepsilon$ in Eq. (1) and Eq. (2). Figure 5 shows the fusion quality measures with different parameter settings. The fusion performances are evaluated by the average value of $Q^{AB/F}$, $Q_S$, $Q_C$, $Q_Y$, $Q_{CB}$, and $Q_P$ on 28 pairs source images. From Fig. 5(a)–(f), we can conclude that the performance of the proposed method is comprehensively optimal when the parameter $\alpha$ is in the range of [0.05 0.1] and the parameter $\varepsilon$ is in the range of [0.01 0.02]. Moreover, we can see from Fig. 5(a) when the parameter $\varepsilon$ is larger than 0.01, the fused results are all of the good quality. Figure 5(f) shows that the fused results are all of the lower quality when the parameter $\varepsilon$ = 0.01 and the parameter $\alpha$ = 0.1. In the following experiments, the parameters are set as $\alpha$ = 0.05 and $\varepsilon$ = 0.01.

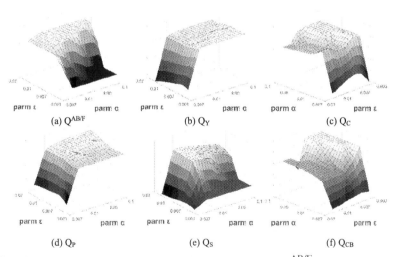

**Fig. 5.** Influence of parameters $\alpha$ and $\varepsilon$. (a)–(f) are the results of $Q^{AB/F}$, $Q_Y$, $Q_C$, $Q_P$, $Q_S$, and $Q_{CB}$.

Figure 6 shows an example of the fused images of different methods on the face image. The label regions by the blue rectangle are magnified and shown in the lower-left corner of each image. As shown in Fig. 6(a) and (h), the hair and skin texture of the

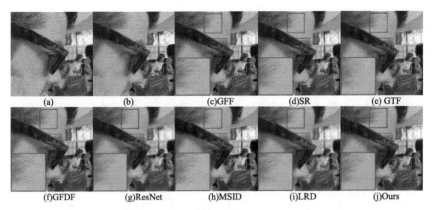

**Fig. 6.** Fusion results of the proposed and compared methods on the face image: (a) and (b) are the source images. (c)–(j) are the fusion results of GFF, SR, GTF, GFDF, ResNet, MSID, LRD, and the proposed method.

edge area are completely preserved. SR and ResNet in Fig. 6(b) and (e) preserve partial texture

(f)GFDF (g)ResNet (h)MSID (i)LRD (j)Ours.

information of the source image, but the texture of the skin disappear. Figure 6(c) generated by GTF suffers from edge clutter and texture loss. Moreover, there is a global blurring in Fig. 6(c). The edge information of hair is lost in Fig. 6(d), but the skin texture is preserved well. The person is shown in Fig. 6(f) is blurred. Figure 6(g) from LRD fails to handle white balance around the edge of the eyeglass border. The characters on the temple are overexposed caused distortions and contrast decreased surrounding pixels. As seen in Fig. 6(h), the fused image of the proposed algorithm preserves all texture details of surface skin and no blur in the fused image.

Figure 7 shows another example of fusion results of the proposed and compared methods on the game machine image. There are apparent distortions and regional blurring in the gamepads areas of the GFF in Fig. 7(a). Artifacts are visible around the wires in the green rectangle area and the buttons in the blue rectangle area in the final result generated by SR in Fig. 7(b). The GTF in Fig. 7(c) has some blurring of the whole picture due to the lack of accurate focused regions detection, especially the gamepads where there is also brightness distortion. The corresponding shadow area of the gamepads in Fig. 7(d) and (f) is not completely preserved. The whole image generated by ResNet in Fig. 7(e) has over-exposure and blurring. The corresponding red rectangle area in Fig. 7(g) generated by the LRD is blurred, and the whole picture is noisy especially around the wires and the buttons. In contrast, our proposed method can obtain a better visibility effect.

The objective evaluation metrics of Fig. 6 and Fig. 7 are shown in Table 1. For each metric, the best performance result is labeled in bold. The underlined values indicate the second-largest values. Our method provides the highest $Q^{AB/F}$ and $Q_Y$ for two experimental images. In addition, the $Q_P$ and $Q_S$ values of the proposed method are the best in Fig. 6. The $Q_C$ and $Q_{CB}$ values of the proposed method are the best in Fig. 7. The significant information in terms of gradient retention $Q^{AB/F}$, structural similarity $Q_Y$, and image phase consistency $Q_P$ are achieved maximum preservation in our algorithm.

This is mainly attributable to the fact that the complete decomposition of the consistent structure and the inconsistent structure by CIMD and the appropriate fusion rules. In our experiment, the proposed method can effectively improve the evaluation of subjective effects and the advantage of objective metrics.

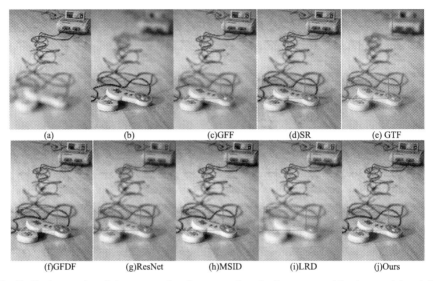

(a)          (b)          (c)GFF          (d)SR          (e) GTF

(f)GFDF          (g)ResNet          (h)MSID          (i)LRD          (j)Ours

**Fig. 7.** Fusion results of the proposed and compared methods game machine image: (a) and (b) are the source images. (c)–(j) are the fusion results of GFF, SR, GTF, GFDF, ResNet, MSID, LRD, and the proposed method.

The average metric values and standard deviations on results of 28 pairs of source images with different methods are shown in Table 2. For each metric, the best performance result is labeled in bold, and the underlined values indicate the second-largest values. The smallest standard deviation is bolded and the second smallest is underlined. It can be seen that the proposed method is always the largest in the metrics of $Q^{AB/F}$, $Q_Y$, $Q_C$, $Q_P$, and $Q_S$ for all images, which means that the proposed can well preserve the original information of different sources images. $Q_Y$ and $Q_{CB}$ have the smallest standard deviation. This means the proposed method is very stable in all experimental images.

**Table 1.** The objective metric values of fused images.

| Figures | Metrics | GFF | SR | GTF | GFDF | ResNet | MSID | LRD | Ours |
|---------|---------|-----|-----|-----|------|--------|------|-----|------|
| Figure 6 | $Q^{AB/F}$ | 0.7373 | 0.6772 | 0.5760 | 0.7260 | 0.5663 | 0.7271 | 0.5649 | **0.7403** |
| | $Q_Y$ | 0.9808 | 0.8775 | 0.9718 | 0.9847 | 0.8656 | 0.8979 | 0.8583 | **0.9853** |
| | $Q_C$ | **0.8370** | 0.7368 | 0.7093 | 0.8293 | 0.8027 | 0.7880 | 0.7454 | 0.8319 |

(*continued*)

**Table 1.** (*continued*)

| Figures | Metrics | GFF | SR | GTF | GFDF | ResNet | MSID | LRD | Ours |
|---|---|---|---|---|---|---|---|---|---|
| | $Q_P$ | 0.8650 | 0.7714 | 0.7251 | 0.8621 | 0.7774 | 0.8423 | 0.5839 | **0.8652** |
| | $Q_S$ | 0.9440 | 0.9341 | 0.8420 | 0.9428 | 0.9051 | 0.8925 | 0.9080 | **0.9444** |
| | $Q_{CB}$ | 0.7754 | 0.6887 | 0.6409 | **0.8106** | 0.6212 | 0.6994 | 0.6231 | 0.7590 |
| Figure 7 | $Q^{AB/F}$ | 0.7880 | 0.6922 | 0.7058 | 0.7801 | 0.6423 | 0.7772 | 0.5627 | **0.7891** |
| | $Q_Y$ | 0.9824 | 0.8281 | 0.9798 | 0.9834 | 0.8879 | 0.9684 | 0.8936 | **0.9848** |
| | $Q_C$ | 0.8940 | 0.7165 | 0.7467 | 0.8935 | 0.8361 | 0.8870 | 0.8144 | **0.8956** |
| | $Q_P$ | **0.8706** | 0.6376 | 0.6348 | 0.8657 | 0.7513 | 0.8388 | 0.5463 | 0.8701 |
| | $Q_S$ | 0.9459 | 0.9407 | 0.9101 | 0.9448 | 0.9304 | 0.9029 | **0.9494** | 0.9451 |
| | $Q_{CB}$ | 0.7509 | 0.6470 | 0.6254 | 0.7512 | 0.6341 | 0.7072 | 0.5878 | **0.7611** |

**Table 2.** The average metric values and standard deviations on results of 28 pairs of source images with different methods.

| Metrics | GFF | SR | GTF | GFDF | ResNet | MSID | LRD | Ours |
|---|---|---|---|---|---|---|---|---|
| $Q^{AB/F}$ | 0.7338 ± 0.0440 | 0.6705 ± 0.0558 | 0.6248 ± 0.0875 | 0.6913 ± 0.0978 | 0.5964 ± 0.0790 | 0.7329 ± 0.0314 | 0.5523 ± 0.0636 | **0.7454** ± 0.0316 |
| $Q_Y$ | 0.9699 ± 0.0183 | 0.8340 ± 0.1058 | 0.9614 ± 0.0291 | 0.9782 ± 0.0105 | 0.8659 ± 0.0402 | 0.9392 ± 0.0245 | 0.8544 ± 0.0416 | **0.9795** ± 0.0094 |
| $Q_C$ | 0.8207 ± 0.0612 | 0.6962 ± 0.1058 | 0.7252 ± 0.0855 | 0.8186 ± 0.0597 | 0.8021 ± 0.0549 | 0.8188 ± 0.0523 | 0.7465 ± 0.0627 | **0.8231** ± 0.0582 |
| $Q_P$ | 0.8231 ± 0.0880 | 0.7232 ± 0.1189 | 0.7183 ± 0.1536 | 0.8432 ± 0.0613 | 0.7451 ± 0.0667 | 0.8114 ± 0.0546 | 0.5523 ± 0.1118 | **0.8463** ± 0.0560 |
| $Q_S$ | 0.9196 ± 0.0388 | 0.9150 ± 0.0371 | 0.8576 ± 0.0632 | 0.9184 ± 0.0390 | 0.8941 ± 0.0418 | 0.9199 ± 0.0453 | 0.8764 ± 0.0398 | **0.9203** ± 0.0372 |
| $Q_{CB}$ | 0.7141 ± 0.0195 | 0.6635 ± 0.1249 | 0.6452 ± 0.0299 | **0.7703** ± 0.0111 | 0.6177 ± 0.0408 | 0.6512 ± 0.0255 | 0.6031 ± 0.0454 | 0.7306 ± 0.0102 |

## 5  Conclusions

In this paper, we have presented a novel multi-focus fusion method based on MGF. To my knowledge, the proposed method is the first to introduce CIMD into the field of image fusion to obtain the two-scale representation. Exploiting the separation feature of CIMD on the inconsistent structure, and purposely proposing a detailed layers fusion method based on the mean-guide filter and a base layers' fusion method based on the spatial frequency. Finally, the fusion result was obtained by overlaying the fused detailed layers and the base layers. The experimental part compares 28 pairs of multifocal images of three different types and validates the experimental results in terms of both subjective visual evaluation and six sets of objective metrics. The proposed method can preserve more effective information and improving the effectiveness of multi-focus image fusion compared with seven state-of-the-art methods. New advancement of introducing dual channels on the image fusion framework is achieved.

**Acknowledgments.** This paper is supported by the National Natural Science Foundation of China (No.61871210) and Chuanshan Talent Project of the University of South China.

# References

1. Li, S., Kang, X., Fang, L., Hu, J.: Pixel-level image fusion: a survey of the state of the art. Inf. Fusion **33**, 100–112 (2017)
2. Guo, X., Li, Y., Ma, J., Ling, H.: Mutually guided image filtering. IEEE Trans. Pattern Anal. Mach. Intell. **42**(3), 694–707 (2018)
3. Shen, X., Zhou, C., Xu, L., Jia, J.: Mutual-structure for joint filtering. In: ICCV, pp. 3406–3414. IEEE, Santiago (2015)
4. Ma, J., Chen, C., Li, C., Huang, J.: Infrared and visible image fusion via gradient transfer and total variation minimization. Inf. Fusion **31**, 100–109 (2016)
5. Li, S., Kang, X., Hu, J.: Image fusion with guided filtering. IEEE Trans. Image Process. **22**(7), 2864–2875 (2013)
6. Qiu, X., Li, M., Zhang, L., Yuan, X.: Guided filter-based multi-focus image fusion through focus region detection. Signal Process. Image Commun. **72**, 35–46 (2016)
7. Yang, B., Li, S.: Multifocus image fusion and restoration with sparse representation. IEEE Trans. Instrument Measur. **59**(4), 884–892 (2010)
8. Liu, Y., Liu, S., Wang, Z.: A general framework for image fusion based on multi-scale transform and sparse representation. Inf. Fusion **24**, 147–164 (2015)
9. Li, H., Wu, X.J., Durrani, T.S.: Infrared and visible image fusion with ResNet and zero-phase component analysis. Infrared Phys. Technol. **102**,103039 (2019)
10. Li, H., Qi, X., Xie, W.: Fast infrared and visible image fusion with structural decomposition. Knowl. Based Syst. **204**, 106182 (2020).
11. Li, X., Guo, X., Han, P., Wang, X., Luo, T.: Laplacian re-decomposition for multimodal medical image fusion. Trans. Instrument Measur. **69**(9), 6880–6890 (2020)
12. He, K., Sun, J., Tang, X.: Guided image filtering. IEEE Trans. Pattern Anal. Mach. Intell. **35**(6), 1397–1409 (2013)
13. Nejati M, Lytro Multi-focus Dataset (2019). https://mansournejati.ece.iut.ac.ir/content/lytro-multi-focus-dataset. Accessed 6 Jan 2019
14. Pxleyes: Multi Focus Photography. http://www.pxleyes.com/photography-contest/19726. Accessed 20 Jan 2021
15. Xydeas, C.S., Petrovic, V.: Objective image fusion performance measure. Electron. Lett. **36**(4), 308–309 (2000)
16. Yang, C., Zhang, J., Wang, X., Liu, X.: A novel similarity based quality metric for image fusion. Inf. Fusion **9**, 156–160 (2008)
17. Cvejic, N., Loza, A., Bul, D., Canagarajah, N.: A similarity metric for assessment of image fusion algorithms. Int. J. Signal Process. **2**(3), 178–182 (2005)
18. Zhao, J., Laganiere, R., Liu, Z.: Performance assessment of combinative pixel-level image fusion based on an absolute feature measurement. Int. J. Innov. Comput. Inf. Control **3**(6), 1433–1447 (2007)
19. Piella, G., Heijmans, G.: A new quality metric for image fusion. In: Proceedings International Conference Image Processing, pp. 3–173. IEEE, Barcelona (2010)
20. Chen, Y., Blum, R.S.: A new automated quality assessment algorithm for image fusion. Image Vis. Comput. **27**(10), 1421–1432 (2009)

# An Enhanced Multi-frequency Learned Image Compression Method

Lin He, Zhihui Wei[✉], Yang Xu, and Zebin Wu

Nanjing University of Science and Technology, Nanjing, China
gswei@njust.edu.cn

**Abstract.** Learned image compression methods have represented the potential to outperform the traditional image compression methods in recent times. However, current learned image compression methods utilize the same spatial resolution for latent variables, which contains some redundancies. By representing different frequency latent variables with different spatial resolutions, the spatial redundancy is reduced, which improves the R-D performance. Based on the recently introduced generalized octave convolutions, which factorize latent variables into different frequency components, an enhanced multi-frequency learned image compression method is introduced. In this paper, we incorporate the channel attention module into multi-frequency learned image compression network to improve the performance of adaptive code word assignment. By using the attention module to capture the global correlation of latent variables, complex parts of the image such as textures and boundaries can be better reconstructed. Besides, an enhancement module on decoder side is utilized to generate gains. Our method shows the great visual appearance and achieves a better grade on the MS-SSIM distortion metrics at low bit rates than other standard codecs and learning-based image compression methods.

**Keywords:** Learned image compression · Multi-frequency image coding · Channel attention · Decoder enhancement

## 1 Introduction

In the 5G era, smart terminals will see a new round of explosive growth, in which image data growth being particularly prominent. It becomes important to obtain satisfactorily compressed images based on limited hardware resources. Instead of saving the original RGB data, a lossy version of the image is stored that is as close as possible to the original in terms of visual experience. Traditional image compression methods [6,21,23,26,30] are usually composed of transform, quantization, and entropy coding, which rely on manual optimization of each module. However, hand-crafted tuning of each module may not lead to an overall performance improvement, which may limit their performance. In

© Springer Nature Switzerland AG 2021
H. Ma et al. (Eds.): PRCV 2021, LNCS 13021, pp. 189–200, 2021.
https://doi.org/10.1007/978-3-030-88010-1_16

the meanwhile, learned image compression methods [1–5, 8, 9, 12, 13, 15, 16, 18–20, 24, 25, 27–29] has attracted more and more attention. The advanced learning-based image compression methods have achieved superior performance over traditional methods(i.e. BPG [6]).

The lossy image compression methods are commonly improved in two ways: designing more efficient transformations and building more refined probabilistic statistical models of latent variables. It is experimentally demonstrated that the GDN layer can effectively Gaussianize the local joint statistical information of natural images, thus achieving local independence to a certain extent. However, latent variables are usually expressed by feature maps with no differentiation in spatial resolution, where exits some spatial redundancies. This indicates that better R-D performance can be achieved by feature maps with spatial resolution, which reduce the spatial redundancy. In [7], octave convolutions are utilized to decompose the latent variables into high-frequency and low-frequency factors . In [3], the generalized octave convolutions are proposed to accommodate image compression applications.

For the entropy modeling, in [4], the latent representations are modeled as independently identically distribution across space and channels, then in [5], the entropy model is conditional Gaussian scale mixture(GSM) and codes are modeled as conditionally independent given the hyper-prior. Most recent learned image compression techniques utilize the context-adaptive entropy method, which combines the super-priority and autoregressive models [20].

In this paper, the idea of multiple spatial frequencies is adopted, based on generalized octave convolution, a multi-frequency channel attention module is introduced to improve coding performance. Besides, the enhancement module is introduced on decoder side to enhance compression. Better image compression performance especially at a low bit rate is obtained when compared with recently advanced image compression methods.

The contributions of this paper are generalized as follows:

- We combine the channel attention technique with multi-frequency potential representations to improve coding performance.
- We apply an enhancement module on the decoder side for further compression enhancement.
- The proposed framework obtains better image compression performance at a low bit rate compared to other recently advanced methods [3, 6, 8, 20].

## 2    Related Works

Many image compression methods have been developed and some standards have been successfully established over the past decades, such as JPEG [30], JPEG2000 [23], and BPG [6]. But these existing methods rely on hand-crafted modules, which include transform, quantization, and entropy coding such as Huffman encoder. Recently, the internal prediction technique which is firstly used in video compression has also been utilized for image compression. For example, as the recently advanced technique compared with other manually designed techniques, the BPG [6] standard is based on the video compression standard HEVC/H.265 [26], which adopts the prediction-transform technique to reduce the spatial redundancy.

In learned image compression methods, some works design efficient network structures to extract more compact latent variables and rebuild high-quality images from compressed features. For example, [13,28,29] utilize recurrent networks to compress the residual signal progressively, and achieve scalable coding with binary representation in each recurrence. Although recurrent models can handle variable bit rates compression naturally, they usually take more time for encoding and decoding because the network is executed multiple times. [1,4,5,15,16,19,27] utilize full convolutional networks, which are trained under rate-distortion constraints, with a trade-off between bit rate and reconstruction quality. Since each trained model corresponds to a Lagrangian coefficient $\lambda$ which controls balance, multiple models should be trained to fit the needs of variable bit rates.

Some works establish a probability model for effective entropy coding, the modeled objects of the entropy model are divided into binary code streams and latent variables. The binary code stream is the output of the encoder, and the bitstream allocation is guided directly by modeling the binary code stream with an entropy model. The latent variables are the output of the analysis transform, which is generally a real number representation. The difference between binary code streams and latent variables is that binary code streams are the final output of the encoder, while the latent variables need to be quantized and entropy coded to obtain the bitstream which is the final output of the encoder. By modeling the entropy of the latent variables and adding end-to-end optimization, facilitates the coding network to generate a tightly compressed representation.

Based on the binary code streams, Toderici et al. [29] added an entropy model in subsequent work and used PixelRNN [22] to estimate the probability distribution of all symbols to be encoded based on the encoded symbols. Because there exist spatial redundancies in natural images, predicting the probability or coding residuals of the current target based on the context can improve the image compression performance. In addition to using contextual information to guide the encoding of the current target, Covell et al. [9] used a mask based on RNN to guide the symbol assignment, which allows compression system to adaptively change the number of bits transmitted based on the local content. Li et al. [16] used Convolutional Neural Networks (CNNs) to learn importance maps and constructed masks to indicate the length of binary codes.

Based on the latent variables, Balle [4] approximates the actual probability distribution of the symbols using a segmented linear model, with the latent variables first undergoing a GDN transformation that greatly reduces the spatial redundancy between pixels to achieve a factorized probability model of the latent variables; Agustsson [1] estimates the probability distribution of the symbols by their histograms; Theis [27] uses Laplace smoothing histograms to better estimate the probability distributions. All these models focus on learning the distribution of the representation without considering adaptivity, in other words, once the entropy model is trained, the parameters of the trained model are fixed for any input during testing. There exit large spatial dependencies in the quantified latent variables. The standard approach to modeling dependencies among a set of target variables is to introduce hidden variables, conditioned on the assumption that the target variables are independent. Balle [5] proposed a hyper-prior entropy model that introduces an additional set of random variables to capture spatial dependencies. Minnen [20] added masked convolution as a contextual model for autoregression to more fully exploit the domain relevance of the predicted pixels. Lee [15] used two types of contextual models to estimate the Gaussian distribution for each latent variable. Cheng [8] models the distribution of latent variables as a discrete Gaussian mixture model(GMM) and adds a simplified version of the Attention module, which enables the learning model to focus more on complex regions. Liu [18] adds an enhancement module at the decoder side. Hu [12] proposes a framework with a superior hierarchical framework with multi-layer superiority representation. Some methods [2,24,25] utilize generative models to learn the distribution of input signals and generalize subjectively excellent reconstructed image at extremely low bit rates.

## 3    Proposed Method

### 3.1    Formulation of Multi-frequency Learned Compression Models

The architecture of the whole scheme discussed in this paper is shown in Fig. 1. Inspired by recent advances in learned image compression [4,5,20], an autoencoder style network is performed. Specifically, the generalized octave convolutions [3] shown in Fig. 2 are utilized to reduce spatial redundancy which improves the R-D performance. The entire framework consists of five main modules, which are encoder network, decoder network, hyper encoder network, hyper decoder network, and parameter estimator network.

The encoder network transforms the original image $x$ into the corresponding latent variables $y$. Since the generalized octave convolutions are utilized, the latent variables are decomposed into high-frequency (HF) and low-frequency (LF) factors(denoted by $y^H$ and $y^L$), where the lower frequency corresponds to low spatial resolution. The internal structure of generalized octave convolution and the corresponding transposed structure is shown in Fig. 2. To further reduce spatial redundancy, channel attention modules are applied separately on $y^H$ and $y^L$, then $y^H_{at}$ and $y^L_{at}$ are obtained. The latent variables $y^H_{at}$ and $y^L_{at}$ will be quantized to $\tilde{y}^H_{at}$ and $\tilde{y}^L_{at}$. The next part is the arithmetic encoder and arithmetic decoder, where is considered as lossless entropy coding. Then the quantized latent variables $\tilde{y}^H$ and $\tilde{y}^L$ were fed to the decoder network to obtain the reconstructed image $\tilde{x}$. In this paper, the quantization strategy is the same as [4].

The hyper encoder, hyper decoder, and params estimator modules are utilized for estimation of the distribution of latent variables. Since the image compression methods aim to obtain a reconstructed image at a given bit rate, an accurate entropy model which estimates the bit rate is critical. The whole pipeline is like [20], based on the latent variables, a context model and a hyper auto-encoder are combined to exploit the probabilistic structure. The context model is a kind of autoregressive model for latent variables with different resolutions, which corrects the prediction based on the previous content. The results of the context model are denoted as $\phi^H$ and $\phi^L$. The hyper encoder module is utilized to represent side information efficiently and encode side information into latent variables. The results of the hyper autoencoder are denoted as $\psi^H$ and $\psi^L$. Since the generalized octave convolution is utilized in hyper autoencoder, we get high and low frequency latent variables $z^H$ and $z^L$. Channel attention modules are applied separately on $z^H$ and $z^L$. Similar to previous operations, $z^H_{at}$ and $z^L_{at}$ are quantized into $\tilde{z}^H$ and $\tilde{z}^L$, then sent by arithmetic coding. The statistical model of $\tilde{y}^H$ and $\tilde{y}^L$ is assumed to be conditional Gaussian entropy model [20]. To estimate the means and standard deviations of conditional Gaussian distributions for each latent variables, the params estimator module utilize the outputs of both context model ($\phi^H$,$\phi^L$) and hyper decoder($\psi^H$, $\psi^L$) for better performance.

The learned image compression network is optimized by trade-off between code rate and distortion. Rate (R) is the estimated number of consumed bits after arithmetic encoding, while distortion (D) is loss of reconstructed images. We utilize a Lagrange multiplier $\lambda$ as the trade-off parameter. The loss function is written as:

$$
\begin{aligned}
L &= R + \lambda D \\
&= R^H + R^L + \lambda d(x, \tilde{x})
\end{aligned}
\tag{1}
$$

where $R^H$ and $R^L$ are seperately the rates of high-frequency and low-frequency latent variables, which can be defined as:

$$
\begin{aligned}
R^H &= H(\tilde{y}^H) + H(\tilde{z}^H) \\
&= E(-log_2(p_{\tilde{y}^H|\tilde{z}^H}(\tilde{y}^H|\tilde{z}^H))) + E[-log_2(p_{\tilde{z}^H}(\tilde{z}^H))] \\
R^L &= H(\tilde{y}^L) + H(\tilde{z}^L) \\
&= E(-log_2(p_{\tilde{y}^L|\tilde{z}^L}(\tilde{y}^L|\tilde{z}^L))) + E[-log_2(p_{\tilde{z}^L}(\tilde{z}^L))]
\end{aligned}
\tag{2}
$$

the $p_{\tilde{y}^H|\tilde{z}^H}$ and $p_{\tilde{y}^L|\tilde{z}^L}$ are respectively the conditional Gaussian entropy model for high-frequency and low-frequency latent variables. Besides, the mean and scale parameters $\mu^H_i$, $\sigma^H_i$, $\mu^L_i$ and $\sigma^L_i$ are obtained by params estimator module $f_pe^H$ and $f_pe^L$. Then the distribution of the latent variables can be formulated as:

$$
\begin{aligned}
p_{\tilde{y}^H|\tilde{z}^H}(\tilde{y}^H|\tilde{z}^H) &= \prod_i (\mathcal{N}(\mu^H_i, \sigma^{2H}_i) * \mathcal{U}(-\frac{1}{2}, \frac{1}{2}))(\tilde{y}^H_i) \\
p_{\tilde{y}^L|\tilde{z}^L}(\tilde{y}^L|\tilde{z}^L) &= \prod_i (\mathcal{N}(\mu^L_i, \sigma^{2L}_i) * \mathcal{U}(-\frac{1}{2}, \frac{1}{2}))(\tilde{y}^L_i)
\end{aligned}
\tag{3}
$$

the $p_{\tilde{z}^H}$ and $p_{\tilde{z}^L}$ are supposed to be independent and identically distributed(i.i.d), and a non-parametric factorized model is utilized [4]. Then the distribution of the latent variables can be formulated as:

194    L. He et al.

$$p_{\tilde{z}^H|\Theta^H}(\tilde{z}^H|\Theta^H) = \prod_j (p_{\tilde{z}^H_i|\Theta^H_j}(\Theta^H_j) * \mathcal{U}(-\frac{1}{2},\frac{1}{2}))(\tilde{z}^H_j)$$

$$p_{\tilde{z}^L|\Theta^L}(\tilde{z}^L|\Theta^L) = \prod_j (p_{\tilde{z}^L_i|\Theta^L_j}(\Theta^L_j) * \mathcal{U}(-\frac{1}{2},\frac{1}{2}))(\tilde{z}^L_j)$$

$$(4)$$

where $\Theta^H$ and $\Theta^L$ denote the parameter vectors.

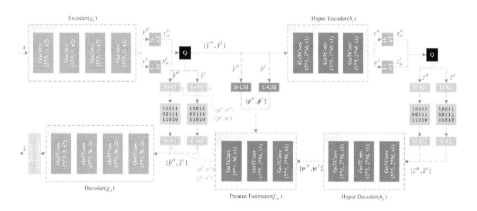

**Fig. 1.** The overall framework of the proposed learned image compression method. **H-AT** and **L-AT**: attention modules for HF and LF latent variables. **H-AE** and **H-AD**: arithmetic encoder and decoder for HF latent variables. **L-AE** and **L-AD**: arithmetic encoder and decoder for LF latent variables. **H-CM** and **L-CM**: context models for HF and LF latent variables, composed of one 5 * 5 masked convolution layer. **Q**: quantization [4]

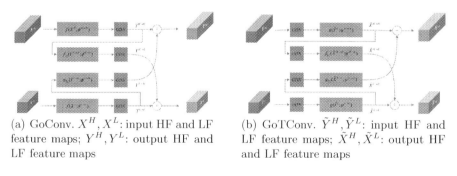

(a) GoConv. $X^H, X^L$: input HF and LF feature maps; $Y^H, Y^L$: output HF and LF feature maps

(b) GoTConv. $\tilde{Y}^H, \tilde{Y}^L$: input HF and LF feature maps; $\tilde{X}^H, \tilde{X}^L$: output HF and LF feature maps

**Fig. 2.** Architecture of the generalized octave convolution (GoConv) and transposed-convolution(GoTconv) [3]. GDN: the activation layer [4]; f: regular convolution; $f_{\downarrow 2}$: regular convolution with stride 2; g: regular transposed convolution; $g_{\uparrow 2}$: regular transposed convolution with stride 2.

## 3.2  Channel Attention Scheme

Some works have utilized spatial attention mechanisms to reduce spatial redundancy [8,18]. Inspired by [11], a channel attention model is proposed to focus on channels of outstanding local importance, and then reduce spatial redundancy. The structure of the channel attention module for latent variable with different spatial resolutions is shown in Fig. 3. By using the attention module to capture the global correlation of latent variables, complex parts of the image such as textures and boundariescan be better reconstructed.

For a feature map $X \in R^{h \times w \times c}$, first, a global average pooling is utilized to achieve statistical channel importance $t \in R^c$:

$$t_c = \frac{1}{h \times w} \sum_{i=1}^{h} \sum_{j=1}^{w} x_c(i, j) \tag{5}$$

where $x_c(i, j)$ is the value at the $(x, y)$ position in $c - th$ channel of feature map $X$. Then, several non-linear transforms are utilized to capture the channel-wise relationship, which can be denoted as:

$$s = \sigma(F_2\delta(F_1 t)) \tag{6}$$

where $F_2$ and $F_1$ are the fully connected layers, $\delta$ is the ReLU activation function, $\sigma$ is the sigmoid function. Finally, by rescaling the feature map $X$ with $s$ and adding the residual operation, a feature map with channel attention applied is obtained.

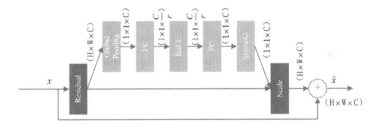

**Fig. 3.** Channel attention module on both HF and LF feature map. FC: fully connected layer. $r$ is chosen to be 16.

## 3.3  Decoder-Side Enhancement

To further enhance the quality of the reconstructed images, an enhancement module at the decoder side is introduced. Influenced by image super-resolution solutions [17], we utilize the residual block to further improve image quality.

It has been experimentally proved that the residual blocks also work in super-resolution problems. But the original ResNet was originally proposed to solve problems such as classification and detection. Since the batch normalization layer consumes the same size of memory as the convolutional layer before it, after removing this step of operation, we can stack more network layers or make more features extracted per layer, thus getting better performance. In each residual block, a constant scaling layer is placed after the final convolutional layer. These blocks greatly stabilize the training process when a large number of filters are used. The structure of the decoder-side enhancement module is shown in Fig. 4.

First, to expand the channel dimensions from 3 to 32, a convolutional layer is utilized. Then, three enhancement blocks are applied, each contains three residual blocks where remove the batch normalization operation to keep details and save computational resources. Finally, a convolution layer is applied to transfer channel dimension to 3 and apply the residual operation to get the reconstructed image.

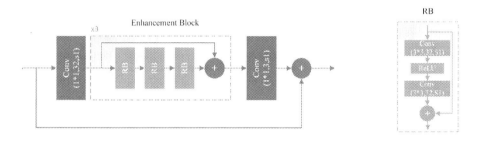

**Fig. 4.** Enhancement module on the decoder side. RB: the residual block

# 4  Experiment Results

A partial subset of ImageNet [10] is selected for training, which contains 6080 pictures in total. The size of the images is first randomly cropped into $256 \times 256 \times 3$ patches. Pixel values are normalized from $(0,255)$ to $(0,1)$. The standard Kodak dataset [14] is utilized for testing, which contains 24 high-quality uncompressed PNG images.

## 4.1  Parameter Description

In the encoder module(Fig. 1), output channel size $M = 192$, the sizes of HF and LF latent variables ($y^H$ and $y^L$) are respectively $16 \times 16 \times 96$ and $8 \times 8 \times 96$. The ratio of LF is 0.5, which means that half of the latent representations are assumed to be LF part. All modules are jointly trained over 100 epochs with Adam solver, with the batch size set as 16 and the learning rate fixed at 0.001. The trade-off parameter $\lambda$ takes values from the range $[0.0005,0.1]$.

## 4.2  Results Evaluation

The compression capability of the proposed framework is compared with the traditional image compression methods including JPEG2000 [23], WebP, BPG(4:2:0) [6], and also recently advanced learning-based image compression methods [3,5,8,20]. We utilize MS-SSIM as the evaluation indicators, which is more consistent with human eye visual perception than other evaluation metrics like PSNR and SSIM. The comparison result on the Kodak dataset is shown in Fig. 5, which is an average result over 24 images. The R-D curve is plotted based on multiple bpp points, which are corresponding to different bit rates. Several models are trained with different values of $\lambda$ to achieve different bit rates.

As shown in Fig. 5, the proposed scheme outperforms the standard codecs and most advanced methods at the low bit rates(bpp < 0.25). Compared with the recently advanced standard codecs, such as BPG (4:2:0) [6], the proposed method achieves better performance at each bit rate. Some visual examples for visualization details is shown in Fig. 6 and Fig. 7. As seen in the example, at a low bit rate, our method behaves the best compared to the others, the high-frequency details like eyelashes and curly hair are clearly expressed. While the image reconstructed by JPEG [30] faces the problems of artifacts. In particular, our method has a higher MS-SSIM score at the low bpp points compared to original framework based on GoConve [3] and Balle's method [5].

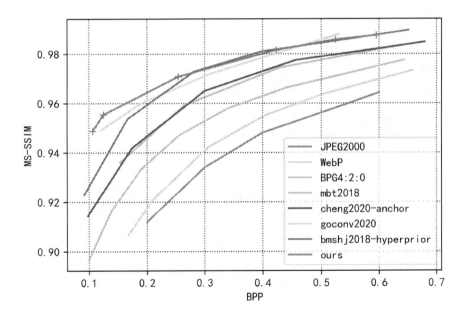

**Fig. 5.** Kodak comparison results.

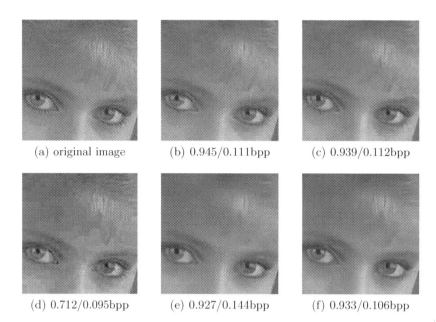

(a) original image    (b) 0.945/0.111bpp    (c) 0.939/0.112bpp

(d) 0.712/0.095bpp    (e) 0.927/0.144bpp    (f) 0.933/0.106bpp

**Fig. 6.** Visualization of partial reconstructed kodim04 from Kodak dataset, **our proposed method (b)**, GoConv2020 (c), JPEG (d), Balle et al. 2018 (e), and Cheng2020-anchor (f). We take MS-SSIM as the metrics.

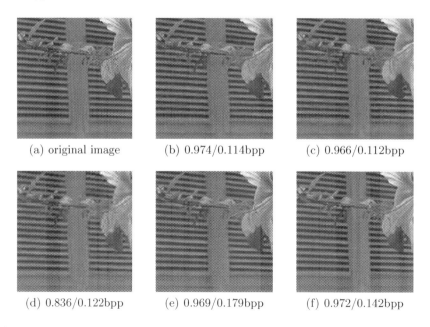

(a) original image    (b) 0.974/0.114bpp    (c) 0.966/0.112bpp

(d) 0.836/0.122bpp    (e) 0.969/0.179bpp    (f) 0.972/0.142bpp

**Fig. 7.** Visualization of partial reconstructed kodim07 from Kodak dataset, **our proposed method (b)**, GoConv2020 (c), JPEG (d), Balle et al. (2018) (e), and Cheng2020-anchor (f). We take MS-SSIM as the metrics.

# 5  Conclusion

We propose an enhanced multi-frequency learned image compression framework in this paper. Using the generalized octave convolution, the latent variables are divided into high-frequency and low-frequency components, while the high frequency part is represented by a higher spatial resolution. The channel attention modules for high-frequency and low-frequency latent variables are proposed to further reduce spatial redundancy. Finally, an enhancement module on decoder side is utilized to further enhance performance. The whole framework is trained end to end and achieves better performance at a low bite rate compared with recently advanced methods.

# References

1. Agustsson, E., et al.: Soft-to-hard vector quantization for end-to-end learning compressible representations. arXiv preprint arXiv:1704.00648 (2017)
2. Agustsson, E., Tschannen, M., Mentzer, F., Timofte, R., Gool, L.V.: Generative adversarial networks for extreme learned image compression. In: Proceedings of the IEEE/CVF International Conference on Computer Vision, pp. 221–231 (2019)
3. Akbari, M., Liang, J., Han, J., Tu, C.: Generalized octave convolutions for learned multi-frequency image compression. arXiv preprint arXiv:2002.10032 (2020)
4. Ballé, J., Laparra, V., Simoncelli, E.P.: End-to-end optimized image compression. arXiv preprint arXiv:1611.01704 (2016)
5. Ballé, J., Minnen, D., Singh, S., Hwang, S.J., Johnston, N.: Variational image compression with a scale hyperprior. arXiv preprint arXiv:1802.01436 (2018)
6. Bellard, F.: Bpg image format (http://bellard.org/bpg/). Accessed: 30 Jan 2021
7. Chen, Y., et al.: Drop an octave: reducing spatial redundancy in convolutional neural networks with octave convolution. In: Proceedings of the IEEE/CVF International Conference on Computer Vision, pp. 3435–3444 (2019)
8. Cheng, Z., Sun, H., Takeuchi, M., Katto, J.: Learned image compression with discretized gaussian mixture likelihoods and attention modules. In: Proceedings of the IEEE/CVF Conference on Computer Vision and Pattern Recognition,. pp. 7939–7948 (2020)
9. Covell, M., et al.: Target-quality image compression with recurrent, convolutional neural networks. arXiv preprint arXiv:1705.06687 (2017)
10. Deng, J., Dong, W., Socher, R., Li, L.J., Li, K., Fei-Fei, L.: Imagenet: a large-scale hierarchical image database. In: 2009 IEEE Conference on Computer Vision and Pattern Recognition, pp. 248–255. IEEE (2009)
11. Hu, J., Shen, L., Sun, G.: Squeeze-and-excitation networks. In: Proceedings of the IEEE conference on Computer Vision and Pattern Recognition, pp. 7132–7141 (2018)
12. Hu, Y., Yang, W., Liu, J.: Coarse-to-fine hyper-prior modeling for learned image compression. Proceedings of the AAAI Conference on Artificial Intelligence. **34**, 11013–11020 (2020)
13. Johnston, N., et al.: Improved lossy image compression with priming and spatially adaptive bit rates for recurrent networks. In: Proceedings of the IEEE Conference on Computer Vision and Pattern Recognition, pp. 4385–4393 (2018)
14. Kodak, E.: Kodak lossless true color image suite (photocd pcd0992). URL http://r0k.us/graphics/kodak  **6** (1993)

15. Lee, J., Cho, S., Beack, S.K.: Context-adaptive entropy model for end-to-end optimized image compression. arXiv preprint arXiv:1809.10452 (2018)
16. Li, M., Zuo, W., Gu, S., Zhao, D., Zhang, D.: Learning convolutional networks for content-weighted image compression. In: Proceedings of the IEEE Conference on Computer Vision and Pattern Recognition, pp. 3214–3223 (2018)
17. Lim, B., Son, S., Kim, H., Nah, S., Mu Lee, K.: Enhanced deep residual networks for single image super-resolution. In: Proceedings of the IEEE Conference on Computer Vision and Pattern Recognition Workshops, pp. 136–144 (2017)
18. Liu, J., Lu, G., Hu, Z., Xu, D.: A unified end-to-end framework for efficient deep image compression. arXiv preprint arXiv:2002.03370 (2020)
19. Mentzer, F., Agustsson, E., Tschannen, M., Timofte, R., Van Gool, L.: Conditional probability models for deep image compression. In: Proceedings of the IEEE Conference on Computer Vision and Pattern Recognition, pp. 4394–4402 (2018)
20. Minnen, D., Ballé, J., Toderici, G.: Joint autoregressive and hierarchical priors for learned image compression. arXiv preprint arXiv:1809.02736 (2018)
21. Ohm, J.R., Sullivan, G.J.: Versatile video coding-towards the next generation of video compression. In: Picture Coding Symposium, vol. 2018 (2018)
22. Oord, A.v.d., Kalchbrenner, N., Vinyals, O., Espeholt, L., Graves, A., Kavukcuoglu, K.: Conditional image generation with pixelcnn decoders. arXiv preprint arXiv:1606.05328 (2016)
23. Rabbani, M., Joshi, R.: An overview of the jpeg 2000 still image compression standard. Sig. Process. Image Commun. **17**(1), 3–48 (2002)
24. Rippel, O., Bourdev, L.: Real-time adaptive image compression. In: International Conference on Machine Learning. pp. 2922–2930. PMLR (2017)
25. Santurkar, S., Budden, D., Shavit, N.: Generative compression. In: 2018 Picture Coding Symposium (PCS), pp. 258–262. IEEE (2018)
26. Sullivan, G.J., Ohm, J.R., Han, W.J., Wiegand, T.: Overview of the high efficiency video coding (HEVC) standard. IEEE Trans. Circuits Syst. Video Technol. **22**(12), 1649–1668 (2012)
27. Theis, L., Shi, W., Cunningham, A., Huszár, F.: Lossy image compression with compressive autoencoders. arXiv preprint arXiv:1703.00395 (2017)
28. Toderici, G., et al.: Variable rate image compression with recurrent neural networks. arXiv preprint arXiv:1511.06085 (2015)
29. Toderici, G., et al.: Full resolution image compression with recurrent neural networks. In: Proceedings of the IEEE Conference on Computer Vision and Pattern Recognition, pp. 5306–5314 (2017)
30. Wallace, G.K.: The jpeg still picture compression standard. IEEE Trans. Consum. Electr. **38**(1), xviii-xxxiv (1992)

# Noise Map Guided Inpainting Network for Low-Light Image Enhancement

Zhuolong Jiang[1], Chengzhi Shen[2], Chenghua Li[3(✉)], Hongzhi Liu[4], and Wei Chen[1(✉)]

[1] School of Artificial Intelligence and Computer Science, Jiangnan University, Wuxi, China
wchen_jdsm@jiangnan.edu.cn
[2] Nanjing University of Aeronautics and Astronautics, Nanjing, China
[3] Institute of Automation, Chinese Academy of Sciences, Beijing 100190, China
lichenghua2014@ia.ac.cn
[4] Department of Electronic Engineering, Ocean University of China, Qingdao, China

**Abstract.** Capturing images in a low-light environment are usually bothered with problems such as serious noise, color degradation, and images underexposure. Most of the low-light image enhancement approaches cannot solve the problem of the loss of the details of the result caused by noise. Inspired by the image inpainting task, we propose a novel Noise-map Guided Inpainting Network (NGI-Net) that introduces inpainting modules to restore missing information. Specifically, the algorithm is divided into two stages. Stage I decomposes input images into a reflection map, an illumination map, and a noise map inspired by the Retinex theory. These maps are passed through Stage II to fine-tune the color and details of the images based on a designed feature enhance group and a selective kernel enhance module. Experiments on real-world and synthesized datasets demonstrate the advantages and robustness of our method. The source code of our method is public in https://github.com/JaChouSSS/NGI-Net.

**Keywords:** Low-light image enhancement · Inpainting · Retinex decomposition · Selective kernel enhance module

## 1  Introduction

Capturing images with poor illumination is an issue that people have been trying to solve for a long time, which also widely exists in other tasks such as object detection and video surveillance. Restoring visual information from such images

---

Z. Jiang—Student.

This work was supported in part by the National Key R&D Program of China under Grant 2017YFB0202303, in part by the National Natural Science Foundation of China under Grand 61602213 and 61772013.

is hard due to insufficient detail information, numerous noise, color degradation, low visibility, and low contrast.

For years, researchers have tried to handle the low-light image enhancement task. Traditionally, the histogram-equalization-based methods [1] enhance the images by expanding the dynamic range, but they ignore the distribution of image brightness. Thus, not every region in the images can be effectively improved. Retinex-based approaches [8,9,20] decompose images into reflection maps and illumination maps, but they tend to amplify noise and cause blurry edges. Recently, there are Deep Learning algorithms trained on paired data [15,26,29], unpaired data [7], and those in the zero-reference style [5].

However, the output images of these methods still have problems such as lack of detail, color deviation, and residual noise.

In this paper, we propose a two-stage Noise Map Guided Inpainting Network to enhance low-light images, and at the same time restore image details. To recover detailed information in the extremely dark images, we need to know the distribution of noise as guidance. Specifically, we use a decomposition network as Stage I to decouple the input image, from which we obtain a reflection map with preliminary restoration, as well as a noise map that contains the original noise information. In Stage II, we designed a Feature Enhancement Module (FEM) that extracts valid image features to recover the color and exposure of the reflection map. Then we use the inpainting module to combined the reflection map with the mask generated by the noise map to repair damaged image features.

The main contributions of this paper can be summarized as follows:

1) As far as we know, it is the first time that inpainting tasks are introduced for low-light image enhancement. We also design the inpainting module to recover missing information.
2) We decouple the low-light image enhancement problem into two subtasks and designed a two-stage low-light image enhancement network. Stage I is responsible for decomposing the images, while Stage II further enhances and restores the outputs from Stage I.
3) We design the Feature Enhancement Module (FEM) and the selective kernel enhance module for feature extraction and improvement.

## 2   Related Works

### 2.1   Low-Light Image Enhancement

Most of the early low-light image enhancement algorithms use histogram equalization [1] to adjust the global brightness and contrast of the images. Retinex-based algorithms decompose the images into reflection maps and illumination maps. Single-Scale Retinex (SSR) [9] methods adjust the outputs by changing single-scale Gaussian kernels, but they are prone to halo in highlight areas. To mitigate this issue, Multi-Scale Retinex (MSR) [10] methods adopt multi-scale Gaussian kernels. Multiscale Retinex With Color Restoration (MSRSR) [8] tackles color distortions by adding a non-linear restoration factor to MSR to adjust the numerical ratio of image channels. However, these methods have great limitations, and it is difficult to recover complex scenes and images with strong noise.

With the rapid development of deep learning in recent years, many data-driven low-light image enhancement approaches have been raised. Lore et al. [15] for the first time applied the deep learning method to image enhancement with a deep encoder-decoder structure. Zhang et al. [29] adopted deep neural networks based on Retinex theory to reconstruct the reflection and illumination maps respectively. Due to the scarce of paired image datasets, Jiang et al. [7] proposed an unsupervised network that can be trained on unpaired data. Yang et al. [26] proposed a semi-supervised learning framework and combined it with adversarial learning to improve the perceptual quality of images in poor illumination. Although these methods perform decently in some cases, it is still challenging to solve the problem of information loss and color deviation during recovering extremely dark images.

## 2.2   Image Inpainting

Traditional image inpainting techniques can be categorified into diffusion-based and patch-based methods. Diffusion-based algorithms [2] propagate inward the image content around the boundary to fill in the missing region. Patch-wise [3] approaches search for the most suitable patch among undamaged regions and fill in the missing one. But both of them cannot generate content with semantic information.

Among DL-based approaches, Pathak et al. [19] proposed an encoder-decoder framework and introduced Generative Adversarial Networks to assist the training process. Liu et al. [14] for the first time presented a Partial Convolution and mask update mechanism for restoring irregular holes, which improved color differences and artifacts. Yu et al. [27] proposed a Gated Convolution method based on [14]. It makes the mask update learnable, strengthens the expressive ability of the network, speeds up the training process, and improves model flexibility. Nazeri et al. [18] integrated the edge generator and the image inpainting network and introduced an image completion algorithm by using edge details as prior knowledge. Inspired by previous works, we design the Inpainting Module for detailed repairs.

## 3   Method

As illustrated in Fig. 1, our network is divided into two stages: the Decomposition Stage and the Restoration Stage. The Decomposition Stage contains a reflection branch, an illumination branch, and a noise generation branch. Among them, both the reflection branch and the noise generation branch adopt the classic encoding-decoding structure, with the noise generation branch(NB) composed of residual blocks. Through this stage, an input image will be decomposed into

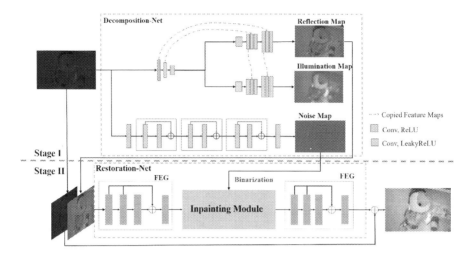

**Fig. 1.** The pipeline of our NGI-Net model, which contains a Decomposition-Net and a Restoration-Net. The Decomposition-Net contains a reflection branch, an illumination branch, and a noise map generation branch. The Restoration-Net consists of feature enhance groups (FEG) and an inpainting module. The reflection map and noise map from Stage I will be fused with the original image for better restoration.

a reflection map, an illumination map, and a noise map, while masks will be obtained.

The Restoration Stage is made of feature enhance groups and an inpainting module. The FEG is used to make the most of feature information, which can be broken down into sub-modules, named selective kernel enhance module. The inpainting module aims to repair image features with the guidance of first-stage outputs. We will further introduce our network in this section.

### 3.1   Stage I: Decomposition

In classic Retinex models, an image $M$ is decomposed into the reflection map $R$ and the illumination map $I$. But they fail in low-light image enhancement because of large amounts of noise. Thus, we adopt the robust Retinex [12] mechanism in the Decomposition Stage, which decomposes images $M$ into reflection map $R$, illumination map $I$, and noise map $N$:

$$M = R \cdot I + N \tag{1}$$

To make more effective use of feature information, the reflection branch (RB) and illumination branch (IB) share the same encoder, which contains 3 convolution layers. A max-pooling layer is added before each convolution to reduce parameters. In the RB, a bilateral upsampling layer with factor 2 is added before each decoder. Skip connections are adopted inside the RB, as well as between the RB and IB with Sigmoid layer. The NB contains 2 convolution layers and 3 Res-blocks, with LeakyReLU as the activation function.

We use the VGG [21] based perceptual loss [11] for calculating $\mathcal{L}_{vgg}$ to constrain the reconstruction error $\mathcal{L}_{rec}$, where $M_l$ and $M_h$ represent the input image and the ground-truth image. They can be decomposed into the reflection map $R_l$, $R_h$, the illumination map $I_l$, $I_h$, and the noise map $N_l$, $N_h$ respectively. $\|\cdot\|_1$ is the L1 loss. Further, the illumination map should be piece-wise smooth, thus we adopt $\mathcal{L}_{smooth}$ to minimize the error, where $\nabla_x$ and $\nabla_y$ represent first-order derivative operators in the horizontal and vertical directions, and $\epsilon$ is a non-negative minimal constant. Additionally, the SSIM loss $\mathcal{L}_{ssim}$ measures the structural similarity between two reflection maps. Since $N_h$ does not exist by default, we use a simple noise loss $\mathcal{L}_{noise}$. Finally, the loss function we use in Stage I is denoted as $\mathcal{L}_I$.

$$\mathcal{L}_I = \mathcal{L}_{rec} + 0.02\mathcal{L}_{smooth} + \mathcal{L}_{ssim} + 20\mathcal{L}_{noise}, \tag{2}$$

where

$$\begin{cases} \mathcal{L}_{ssim} = 1 - SSIM(R_l, R_h), \\[6pt] \mathcal{L}_{noise} = \|N_h\|_1, \\[6pt] \mathcal{L}_{rec} = \mathcal{L}_{vgg}((R_l \cdot I_l + N_l), M_l) + \mathcal{L}_{vgg}((R_h \cdot I_h + N_h), M_h), \\[6pt] \mathcal{L}_{smooth} = \left\| \dfrac{\nabla_{x_l}}{\max(\nabla_{x_l}, \epsilon)} + \dfrac{\nabla_{y_l}}{\max(\nabla_{y_l}, \epsilon)} \right\|_1 + \left\| \dfrac{\nabla_{x_h}}{\max(\nabla_{x_h}, \epsilon)} + \dfrac{\nabla_{y_h}}{\max(\nabla_{y_h}, \epsilon)} \right\|_1. \end{cases} \tag{3}$$

To obtain the mask corresponding to the noise map, we first convert the map into grayscale, and then use the adaptive threshold [17] for binarization.

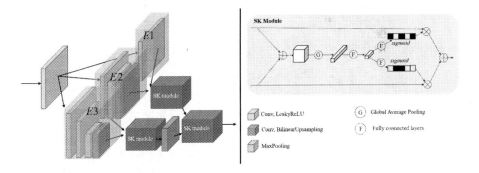

**Fig. 2.** The structure of the selective kernel enhances modules made of CNN and basic SK modules. SKEM conducts convolution in 3 branches before passing them into SK modules for fusion.

## 3.2   Stage II: Restoration

Output images from Stage I are bothered by color distortion and detail deficiency, which is analyzed in Sect. 4.3. To handle such issues, we designed the

Restoration Stage that consists of feature enhance groups and an inpainting module and inputs the original input image with a corresponding reflection map. A FEG consists of several sub-modules, named selective kernel enhance module.

**Selective Kernel Enhance Module (SKEM).** Inspired by previous works on SK [13], we propose the selective kernel enhance modules that function as the basic module to make up the FEG.

While human visual cortex neurons can change their receptive field according to different stimulations [13], CNN simulates this adaptive process by selecting and fusing multi-scale features. Such property is beneficial for the network to expand receptive fields, while in the meantime strengthening feature expression abilities.

As shown in Fig. 2, the input features first go through 1 convolution layer for preliminary extraction, and then respectively go through 3 convolution branches $E1$, $E2$, and $E3$ to obtain features of different scales, where $E1$ is composed of a convolution layer and an activation function, $E2$ adds a max-pooling layer before the convolution layer, and $E3$ adds 2 max-pooling layers to get broader receptive fields. The dimension of output features from SK modules will not be the same. Therefore, we perform channel dimensionality reduction and feature up-sampling through transposed convolution and use the SKEM to fuse them sequentially.

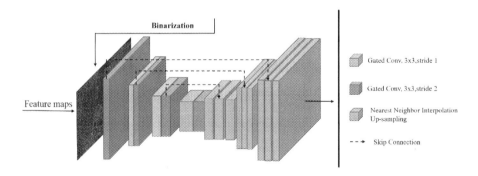

**Fig. 3.** The structure of our Inpainting Module in the encoder-decoder fashion. We feed the binarized mask and feature maps as input. Gated convolution blocks between the encoder and decoder are connected with skip connections. Nearest Neighbor Interpolation up-sampling layers are placed in the decoder.

**Feature Enhance Group (FEG).** The FEG is designed as a combination of SKEM. For two reasons, we place FEGs on both the left and right sides of the IM: i) to extract input features from Stage I in support of IM; ii) to further enhance the output of IM. Specifically, the FEG is made of 4 SKEMs, where the first two SKEMs output will be passed to the last one in terms of residual learning. It helps stabilize the training process by merging low-level and high-level semantic information.

**Inpainting Module (IM).** Traditional convolution takes each pixel as valid, which causes its failure in updating masks with empty regions. Partial convolution takes a step forward by treating input regions as "valid" or "invalid", but only updates the mask heuristically, which limits its flexibility and performance. Gated convolution, however, can learn a dynamic feature selection mechanism for each position of each channel in the feature map. We adopt Gated convolution to update the mask, which can be described as:

$$\text{Gating}_{y,x} = \Sigma\Sigma W_g \cdot I$$
$$\text{Feature}_{y,x} = \Sigma\Sigma W_f \cdot I \tag{4}$$
$$O_{y,x} = \phi(\text{Feature}_{y,x}) \odot \sigma(\text{Gating}_{y,x})$$

where $W_g$ and $W_f$ represent two different kernels for updating masks and computing input features respectively. $\sigma$ is the sigmoid activation function, and $\phi$ is the ELU activation function.

The structure of the inpainting module is illustrated in Fig. 3, which is constructed in a encoder-decoder fashion. The encoder is made of 4 Gated convolution blocks. A Gated convolution with kernel-size 3 and stride 2 is adopted in replacement of max-pooling layers, in order to make the most of information from the mask. The decoder is constructed with another 3 different Gated convolution blocks with kernel-size 3 and stride 1. Before each decoder, we use the up-sampling by nearest-neighbor interpolation.

Unlike ordinary masks, each point in the binarized mask is equivalent to a small hole area surrounded with effective boundary information, since the noise map is composed of discrete noise points and extremely small noise blocks. So we add skip connections between encoders and the decoders to pass more information for repairing these holes. The overall loss we use in Stage II is denoted as:

$$\mathcal{L}_{II} = \|\mathcal{F}(M_l, R_l, S) - M_h\|_1 + \mathcal{L}_{vgg}(\mathcal{F}(M_l, R_l, S), M_h) \tag{5}$$

where $\mathcal{F}$ denotes the function of the Stage II network, $S$ represent the noise mask.

We use the same L1 loss as in Stage I to accelerate convergence and enhance model robustness during training. We further adopt the VGG loss that strengthens the model's ability on feature perception and detail restoration.

## 4    Experiment

We use the two datasets to train and test our network. The Low-Light paired dataset (LOL [25]) contains 500 pairs of $400 \times 600$ low/high images from real scenes, of which 485 pairs are used for training and the remaining 15 pairs are used for validation. The synthesized SYN [25] dataset includes 1,000 pairs of $384 \times 384$ images, of which 950 pairs are used for training and the remaining 50 pairs are used for validation. We used data augmentation during training on the Stage II network.

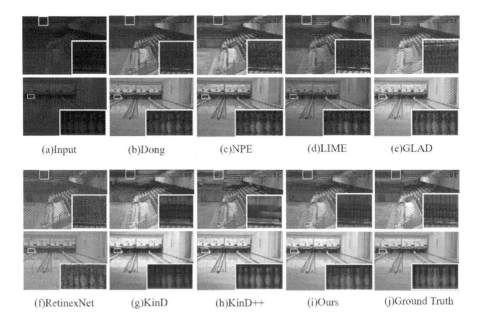

**Fig. 4.** Qualitative comparison on the output images from the LOL dataset.

## 4.1   Implementation Details

The training images are randomly cropped and rotated. The batch size is set to 10, the patch-size is set to $96 \times 96$. Stages I and II train 300 and 70 epochs respectively. We use the ADAM optimizer, with the learning rate 1e–4 and the cosine annealing learning rate scheduler [16]. Our training takes about 26 h on a single RTX2080Ti GPU.

## 4.2   Results and Analysis

We evaluate the proposed NGI-Net network and make comparisons with three traditional algorithms: Dong [4], NPE [22], LIME [6], and the state-of-the-art deep-learning methods: GLAD [23], RetinexNet [24], KinD [29], KinD++ [28] in terms of PSNR, SSIM. The quantitative results are shown in Table 1, where ours w/o stage II represents the network with and without stage II and so as to the following two lines. Our low-light enhancement model achieves the best performance among the state-of-the-art methods, with the highest PSNR and SSIM value.

In Fig. 4, we choose a few example images with severe noise and present the restoring results. Obviously, traditional methods fail to remove the noise very well, with some dark areas even remaining unimproved. DL-based methods perform better. RetinexNet has enhanced the extremely dark areas, but with serious noise. Noise also exists in outputs from GLAD, but the algorithm removes some color distortion. Although KinD and KinD++ eliminate some noise, they

**Table 1.** Experiment results on LOL and SYN dataset.

|  | LOL Dataset | | SYN Dataset | |
|---|---|---|---|---|
|  | PSNR | SSIM | PSNR | SSIM |
| Dong [4] | 16.72 | 0.4781 | 16.84 | 0.7711 |
| NPE [22] | 16.97 | 0.4835 | 16.47 | 0.7770 |
| LIME [6] | 14.22 | 0.5203 | 17.36 | 0.7868 |
| GLAD [23] | 19.72 | 0.6822 | 18.05 | 0.8195 |
| RetinexNet [24] | 16.57 | 0.3989 | 17.11 | 0.7617 |
| KinD [29] | 20.38 | 0.8240 | 18.30 | 0.8390 |
| KinD++ [28] | 21.80 | 0.8284 | 19.54 | 0.8419 |
| Ours w/o stage II | 15.68 | 0.7070 | – | – |
| Ours w/o VGG loss | 22.79 | 0.8079 | – | – |
| Ours w/o inpainting | 23.33 | 0.8319 | – | – |
| Ours | **24.01** | **0.8377** | **26.01** | **0.9366** |

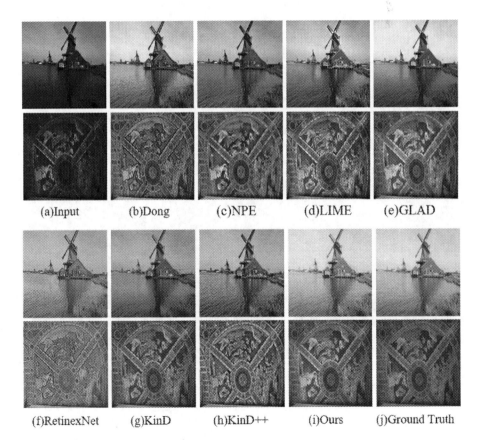

(a)Input    (b)Dong    (c)NPE    (d)LIME    (e)GLAD

(f)RetinexNet    (g)KinD    (h)KinD++    (i)Ours    (j)Ground Truth

**Fig. 5.** Qualitative comparison on the output images from the SYN dataset.

have different degrees of blurred boundaries and loss of details. In comparison, our method is more stable that simultaneously removes noise and restores details in extremely dark regions.

Figure 5 mainly illustrates some normal scenarios of low-light images. The results show that traditional algorithms generally have problems such as under-exposure and chromatic aberration. Among deep learning methods, GLAD and RetinexNet generate the most serious color deviation, while KinD and Kind++ perform well on controlling exposure. Our method has good performances on exposure and contrast at the same time, whose outputs are the most similar to ground-truth. Furthermore, Table 1 demonstrate that our network performs better on the LOL and SYN datasets in comparison to others.

### 4.3   Ablation Study

In this section, we make ablation experiments to evaluate the effectiveness of the proposed components, including the two stage structure, the VGG loss, and the inpainting module. The results of ablation experiments are summarized in Table 1. By only using stage I, we build a baseline model, which achieves 15.68 dB on PSNR and 0.7070 on SSIM. When adding the stage II module, it achieves an increase of 8.33 dB on PSNR and 0.1307 on SSIM, which means the stage II could extract better features to refine the detail information lost in stage I. The effectiveness of VGG loss and the inpainting module can be evaluated by comparing the last three rows in Table 1. It achieves better performance benefitting from the VGG loss and the inpainting process, which means the reconstruction of the detail information is very important to the low-light image enhancement task.

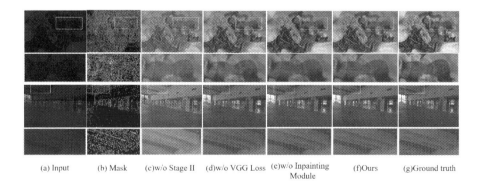

(a) Input    (b) Mask    (c)w/o Stage II    (d)w/o VGG Loss    (e)w/o Inpainting Module    (f)Ours    (g)Ground truth

**Fig. 6.** Visual comparison of the ablation study.

Figure 6 shows the visual changes of the different model structures. For example, Fig. 6(c) shows outputs from a model with/without Stage II that are influenced by severe color deviation and blurry details. After adding Stage II, color deviations can be significantly restored and high-frequency details can be enhanced. Figure 6(d) describes outputs from a network that is not trained with/without VGG loss. Sample images are of poor color and quality if VGG loss is not used. For example, the edges of the image become blurry and contain amounts of noise. VGG loss helps to restore the details and colors of the image. As mentioned earlier, the inpainting module is used to repair dark regions with information hidden in the noise map. We simply remove inpainting module in Stage II for comparisons. As shown in Fig. 6(e), texture details on the glove drop significantly when the inpainting module is removed, which verifies IM's effectiveness. Moreover, the effectiveness of the feature enhancing group is justified by comparing results from the absence of Stage II and the absence of inpainting module.

## 5  Conclusion

In this paper, we propose a Noise-map Guided Inpainting Network (NGI-Net) to restore visual information from low-light images. For the first time, we combine the low-light image enhancement task with the inpainting technique, which shows great potential and is more reasonable out of intuition. Our network has two stages. Stage I decomposes input images into the reflection map, illumination map, and noise map. Then Stage II deals with color distortion and details deficiency by feature enhancing and inpainting. The results demonstrate the advantages of our methods based on real-world datasets quantitatively and qualitatively.

However, there are still some limitations to our works. The noise map still cannot separate all the noise regions, which restrains the network's capability on detail restoration. In future works, we will focus on enhancing the semantic information of dark regions of the image to design robust approaches for more sophisticated low-light image enhancement tasks.

## References

1. Arici, T., Dikbas, S., Altunbasak, Y.: A histogram modification framework and its application for image contrast enhancement. IEEE Trans. Image Process. **18**, 1921–1935 (2009)
2. Ballester, C., Bertalmío, M., Caselles, V., Sapiro, G., Verdera, J.: Filling-in by joint interpolation of vector fields and gray levels. IEEE Trans. Image Process. Publication IEEE Signal Process. Soc. **10**(8), 1200–11 (2001)
3. Criminisi, A., Pérez, P., Toyama, K.: Region filling and object removal by exemplar-based image inpainting. IEEE Trans. Image Process. **13**, 1200–1212 (2004)
4. Dong, X., Pang, Y., Wen, J.: Fast efficient algorithm for enhancement of low lighting video. 2011 IEEE International Conference on Multimedia and Expo, pp. 1–6 (2011)
5. Guo, C., et al.: Zero-reference deep curve estimation for low-light image enhancement. 2020 IEEE/CVF Conference on Computer Vision and Pattern Recognition (CVPR), pp. 1777–1786 (2020)

6. Guo, X., Li, Y., Ling, H.: Lime: low-light image enhancement via illumination map estimation. IEEE Trans. Image Process. **26**, 982–993 (2017)
7. Jiang, Y., et al.: Enlightengan: deep light enhancement without paired supervision. IEEE Trans. Image Process. **30**, 2340–2349 (2021)
8. Jobson, D.J., Rahman, Z., Woodell, G.A.: A multiscale retinex for bridging the gap between color images and the human observation of scenes. IEEE Trans. Image Process. Publication IEEE Signal Process. Soc. **6**(7), 965–76 (1997)
9. Jobson, D.J., Rahman, Z., Woodell, G.A.: Properties and performance of a center/surround retinex. IEEE Trans. Image Process. Publication IEEE Signal Process. Soc. **6**(3), 451–62 (1997)
10. Jobson, D.J., Rahman, Z.u., Woodell, G.A.: A multiscale retinex for bridging the gap between color images and the human observation of scenes. IEEE Trans. Image Process. **6**(7), 965–976 (1997)
11. Johnson, J., Alahi, A., Fei-Fei, L.: Perceptual losses for real-time style transfer and super-resolution. ArXiv abs/1603.08155 (2016)
12. Li, M., Liu, J., Yang, W., Sun, X., Guo, Z.: Structure-revealing low-light image enhancement via robust retinex model. IEEE Trans. Image Process. **27**, 2828–2841 (2018)
13. Li, X., Wang, W., Hu, X., Yang, J.: Selective kernel networks. In: Proceedings of the IEEE/CVF Conference on Computer Vision and Pattern Recognition, pp. 510–519 (2019)
14. Liu, G., Reda, F., Shih, K.J., Wang, T., Tao, A., Catanzaro, B.: Image inpainting for irregular holes using partial convolutions. ArXiv abs/1804.07723 (2018)
15. Lore, K.G., Akintayo, A., Sarkar, S.: Llnet: a deep autoencoder approach to natural low-light image enhancement. Pattern Recogn. **61**, 650–662 (2017)
16. Loshchilov, I., Hutter, F.: Sgdr: Stochastic gradient descent with warm restarts. arXiv: Learning (2017)
17. McAndrew, A.: An introduction to digital image processing with matlab notes for scm2511 image processing. School of Computer Science and Mathematics, Victoria University of Technology **264**(1), 1–264 (2004)
18. Nazeri, K., Ng, E., Joseph, T., Qureshi, F., Ebrahimi, M.: Edgeconnect: Generative image inpainting with adversarial edge learning. ArXiv abs/1901.00212 (2019)
19. Pathak, D., Krähenbühl, P., Donahue, J., Darrell, T., Efros, A.A.: Context encoders: feature learning by inpainting. In: 2016 IEEE Conference on Computer Vision and Pattern Recognition (CVPR), pp. 2536–2544 (2016)
20. Rahman, Z., Jobson, D.J., Woodell, G.A.: Multi-scale retinex for color image enhancement. In: Proceedings of 3rd IEEE International Conference on Image Processing 3, vol. 3, pp. 1003–1006 (1996)
21. Simonyan, K., Zisserman, A.: Very deep convolutional networks for large-scale image recognition. CoRR abs/1409.1556 (2015)
22. Wang, S., Zheng, J., Hu, H., Li, B.: Naturalness preserved enhancement algorithm for non-uniform illumination images. IEEE Trans. Image Process. **22**, 3538–3548 (2013)
23. Wang, W., Wei, C., Yang, W., Liu, J.: Gladnet: low-light enhancement network with global awareness. In: 2018 13th IEEE International Conference on Automatic Face & Gesture Recognition (FG 2018), pp. 751–755 (2018)
24. Wei, C., Wang, W., Yang, W., Liu, J.: Deep retinex decomposition for low-light enhancement. In: BMVC (2018)
25. Wei, C., Wang, W., Yang, W., Liu, J.: Deep retinex decomposition for low-light enhancement. arXiv preprint arXiv:1808.04560 (2018)

26. Yang, W., Wang, S., Fang, Y., Wang, Y., Liu, J.: From fidelity to perceptual quality: a semi-supervised approach for low-light image enhancement. 2020 IEEE/CVF Conference on Computer Vision and Pattern Recognition (CVPR), pp. 3060–3069 (2020)
27. Yu, J., Lin, Z.L., Yang, J., Shen, X., Lu, X., Huang, T.: Free-form image inpainting with gated convolution. In: 2019 IEEE/CVF International Conference on Computer Vision (ICCV), pp. 4470–4479 (2019)
28. Zhang, Y., Guo, X., Ma, J., Liu, W., Zhang, J.: Beyond brightening low-light images. International Journal of Computer Vision, pp. 1–25 (2021)
29. Zhang, Y., Zhang, J., Guo, X.: Kindling the darkness: a practical low-light image enhancer. In: Proceedings of the 27th ACM International Conference on Multimedia, pp. 1632–1640 (2019)

# FIE-GAN: Illumination Enhancement Network for Face Recognition

Zhuo Wang, Weihong Deng$^{(\boxtimes)}$, and Jiancheng Ge

Beijing University of Posts and Telecommunications, Beijing 100876, China
whdeng@bupt.edu.cn

**Abstract.** Low-light face images not only are difficult to be perceived by humans but also cause errors in automatic face recognition systems. Current methods of image illumination enhancement mainly focus on the improvement of the visual perception, but less study their applications in recognition systems. In this paper, we propose a novel generative adversarial network, called FIE-GAN to normalize the lighting of face images while try to retain face identity information during processing. Besides the perceptual loss ensuring the consistency of face identity, we optimize a novel histogram controlling loss to achieve an ideal lighting condition after illumination transformation. Furthermore, we integrate FIE-GAN as data preprocessing in unconstrained face recognition systems. Experiment results on IJB-B and IJB-C databases demonstrate the superiority and effectiveness of our method in enhancing both lighting quality and recognition accuracy.

**Keywords:** Illumination enhancement · Generative adversarial networks · Face recognition

## 1 Introduction

Face images in low-light conditions are poor visibility and low contrast, which may bring challenges not only for human visual perception but also for some intelligent systems such as face recognition. Recently, deep face recognition has shown excellent performance in the normal-light range because most face datasets [1,8,33] mainly contain normal-light face images for training. Therefore, models can learn to gain a powerful capability of identity feature extraction in a normal-light environment.

However, in real uncontrolled testing scenarios [23,31], there also exist many low-light face images that may suffer mistakes during face recognition. A common strategy to solve this problem is brightening these low-light images to a normal range. To the best of our knowledge, most existing researches [13,21,26] on illumination enhancement mainly focus on promoting the visual perception of landscape images. The research on the application of illumination enhancement in face recognition has been less investigated for a long time.

© Springer Nature Switzerland AG 2021
H. Ma et al. (Eds.): PRCV 2021, LNCS 13021, pp. 214–225, 2021.
https://doi.org/10.1007/978-3-030-88010-1_18

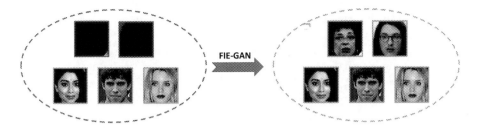

**Fig. 1.** A face recognition system may be trapped in wrong judgment when encountering low-light face images. Our FIE-GAN can brighten low-light images to a normal range, which is beneficial for unconstrained face recognition.

Furthermore, there is a major obstacle to the training data: 1) It's difficult and inefficient to collect a paired training dataset of low/normal-light images under a regular situation. 2) Synthesizing corrupted images from clean images may usually not be realistic enough. Therefore, we quit seeking paired training data, but propose a more available method of achieving face illumination enhancement in unconstrained environments with unpaired supervision.

Inspired by [35] with unsupervised image-to-image translation, we adopt the generative adversarial network (GAN) to fetch close the gap between low and normal light distribution without paired images in the wild environment. GAN is first introduced by Goodfellow et al. [6]. The training strategy is like a min-max two-player game, where the generator tries to confuse the discriminator while the discriminator tries to distinguish between generated images and real images. In our method, we utilize this adversarial thought to achieve the conversion of images from low light toward a normal range.

Therefore, we propose FIE-GAN to achieve illumination enhancement and retain identity information during transformation. FIE-GAN disentangles illumination information from content information. Then, FIE-GAN can generate enhanced face images by fusing illumination information of normal-light images and content information of low-light images. As shown in Fig. 1, brightening low-light images to a normal range is beneficial for identity information extraction due to the powerful capability of the face recognition model in the normal-light range. Lastly, to investigate the effect of illumination enhancement on face recognition, we try deploying FIE-GAN in a face recognition system as a preprocessing to convert low-light images to normal-light ones. Overall, our contributions can be summarized as follows:

- A Face Illumination Enhancement based on Generative Adversarial Network (FIE-GAN) is proposed to bright low-light face images to a normal range. To avoid overfitting, a large unpaired training set is built up and the corresponding training strategy on unpaired data is adopted.
- Histogram vector and corresponding loss function are proposed to control image illumination transformation between different light conditions by a more flexible approach. Besides, Identity information is also appropriately

preserved during this transformation. The qualitative and quantitative analysis prove the superiority of our method commonly.

- We investigate the influence of face illumination enhancement in face recognition by employing FIE-GAN as an image preprocessing step in face recognition systems. Experiment results on IJB-B and IJB-C prove the rationality and effectiveness.

## 2   Related Works

We briefly review previous works from three aspects of image illumination enhancement, image-to-image translation and deep face recognition as follow.

**Images Illumination Enhancement.** Low-light face images in unconstrained environments are difficult to be distinguished by people and also become a challenge for face recognition systems. Gamma correction [24] and histogram equalization [11] are two representative traditional methods to achieve image illumination transformation. In deep learning time, most existing research works [13,21,26] on illumination enhancement focus on the visual improvement of landscape images. However, their training data is usually required to be paired, which is difficult or even impractical to be acquired for face images in the wild.

**Image-to-Image Translation.** Generative adversarial networks (GANs) [6] have demonstrated the powerful capabilities of adversarial learning in image synthesis [7,17,18] and translation [3,12,35]. The Image-to-image translation is a more general problem for image processing such as style transfer [15,35], super resolution [14,20] and face editing [2,32]. Pix2pix[19] first defined this task and obtained impressive results on paired data. However, paired data are usually unavailable for most tasks. CycleGAN [2] proposed an unpaired image-to-image translation method to learn the mapping function between different domains.

**Deep Face Recognition.** Face recognition (FR) has been the prominent biometric technique for identity authentication [29]. This success is attributed to the development of loss function [4,27,28], network architectures [9,30] and the availability of large-scale training datasets [1,8,33]. Data cleaning [34] and data augmentation [5] can also improve the performance of FR, which proves the importance of data preprocessing in FR and the advantages of deep methods in image operation.

Therefore, in this paper, we propose an unpaired image-to-image method for illumination enhancement. Furthermore, the effectiveness of this method is investigated in an FR system.

## 3   Methodology

Our goal is to train a generator $G$ for converting low-light images to a normal-light range by using only unpaired images. Furthermore, to apply our method to face recognition, the identity information of face images should be maintained during the transformation. Therefore, the architecture and loss function will be described in detail below.

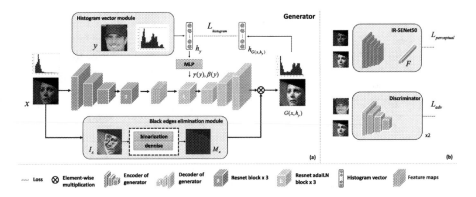

**Fig. 2.** The architecture of FIE-GAN. In part (a), the generator with integrated modules transforms low-light face images to normal ones. In part (b), the pre-trained expert network IR-SENet50 [4] is used to extract identity information, and two discriminators are applied to distinguish between the real image and generated image. All of the notations are listed at the bottom.

## 3.1 Architecture

Our framework consists of a generator $G$, two discriminators $\{D_1, D_2\}$ and an expert network. We integrate the black edges elimination module and the histogram vector module into the generator to ensure the effect of generated images.

**Generator.** The generator is shown in Fig. 2(a), where $x$ from low-light face set and $y$ from normal-light face set. Low-light face image $x$ is fed into the backbone and generate corresponding normal-light face $G(x, h_y)$ under the control of $h_y$ that is the histogram vector of normal-light image $y$.

Histogram vector is proposed to indicate the illumination distribution at pixel level. The illumination range is divided into $m$ pieces with the same interval and the histogram vector of image $y$ is defined as a $m$-dimensional vector $h_y = \left[h_y^{(1)} \cdots h_y^{(m)}\right], h_y^{(i)} = \frac{num_{I_p}}{\sum num_{I_p}}, I_i \leq I_p \leq I_{i+1}, 0 \leq i \leq m.$ $I_p$ is the illumination of a pixel. $num_{I_p}$ represents the number of pixels whose illumination is between $I_i$ and $I_{i+1}$. Therefore, the histogram vector $h_y$ represents the proportion of pixels in every piece interval.

In our method, content information of face images can be divided into face identity and illumination. Illumination is also regarded as style information. Inspired by [19], residual blocks with AdaLIN are equipped to implement style transfer while adaptively changing or keeping the content information to separate illumination information from identity information. Thus, the content information of low-light image x and the style information of normal-light image y are fused to generate corresponding normal-light image $G(x, h_y)$. Specifically, the histogram vector of normal-light face image $y$ guide this style transfer to brighten low-light image $x$ by controlling the affine transform parameters in AdaLIN: $\gamma(y), \beta(y) = MLP(h_y)$, and retaining face identity information.

Moreover, due to the defect of face alignment, low-light faces in public face datasets often contain black edges, which may affect the result of illumination enhancement. The generator will try to promote the illumination of pixels in black edges, but ignore the face region, because the former is largely darker than the latter. Therefore, we claim a mechanism of masking to ignore black edges in a pixel-wise multiplication way. As shown in Fig. 2(a), $I_x$ is the heat map of $x$, representing the illumination distribution on pixels. $M_x$ is a mask to ignore black edges in low-light face images by excluding consecutive zero-pixel regions. Furthermore, its impact is mitigated on the generated result by blocking the gradient propagation on black edges.

To sum up, our generator can convert input low-light face image $x$ to a normal range in an image-to-image way. And the transformation process is under the control of $h_y$ that is the histogram vector of normal-light face image $y$.

**Discriminator.** To better distinguish the real image $y$ and the generated images $G(x, h_y)$, we adopt a multi-scale model as the other competitor in this adversarial game, which contains two discriminators with different sizes of the convolution kernel. Especially, multi-scale discriminators possess multiple receptive fields, which means they can cover more sufficient cues to split real images and generated images.

**Expert Network.** An expert network is a model that contains abundant prior knowledge. A pre-trained face feature extraction network IR-SENet50 [4] is employed as the expert network in our pipeline to ensure the consistency of identity information during the transformation. On the other hand, to obtain continuous prior guidance, we freeze the layers of the expert network in our training and evaluating period.

### 3.2   Loss Function

The aim of FIE-GAN is to brighten the low-light face image to a normal one. Thus, besides the basic adversarial loss, there also contain additional loss functions to preserve the identity information or assist network convergence.

**Adversarial Loss.** Adversarial loss is employed to minimize the gap between the distribution of source and target domain. The least-squares loss [22] is utilized for stable training and higher generated image quality,

$$
\begin{aligned}
L_{adv}^D &= \sum_{i=1}^{2} E[D_i(G(x, h_y))^2 + (D_i(x) - 1)^2], \\
L_{adv}^G &= \sum_{i=1}^{2} E[(D_i(G(x, h_y)) - 1)^2], \\
L_{adv} &= L_{adv}^D + L_{adv}^G,
\end{aligned} \tag{1}
$$

where $x$ is the input low-light face image and $y$ represents the real normal-light face image. $h_y$ is the histogram vector of image $y$ which tries to promote the generator $G$ to transform $x$ to normal-light range and confuse the discriminator $D_1, D_2$ simultaneously.

**Perceptual Loss.** Inspired by [16], the perceptual loss is introduced to retain identity information during illumination enhancement. High-dimension feature representation $F(\cdot)$ is extracted by a pre-trained expert network. So the loss can be formulated as:

$$L_{perceptual} = \|F(G(x, h_y)) - F(x)\|_1. \tag{2}$$

**Histogram Loss.** Histogram loss is an $L2$ loss in the space of the histogram vector for ensuring the similarity in histogram distribution between generated normal-light images and real ones. $H(\cdot)$ indicates the operation of computing histogram vector,

$$L_{\text{histogram}} = \|H(G(x, h_y)) - h_y\|_2^2. \tag{3}$$

Specially, $G(x, h_y)$ is the transformation result of low-light image $x$ under the control of the histogram vector of normal-light image $y$. Thus, a similar brightness distribution at pixel level is expected between the generated normal-light image $G(x, h_y)$ and real one y.

**Reconstruction Loss.** Reconstruction loss is claimed to guarantee the input image can be reconstructed under the control of its histogram vector,

$$L_{reconstruction} = \frac{1}{W \times H \times C}\|G(y, h_y) - y\|_1, \tag{4}$$

which means that the generated result $G(y, h_y)$ under the control of histogram vector $h_y$ should retain the consistency with the input normal-light image $y$. The above description represents a reconstruction process for a real normal-light image.

**Full Objective.** Finally, we acquire the overall loss function which is defined as follows:

$$\begin{cases} L_D = \lambda_1 L_{adv}^D, \\ L_G = \lambda_1 L_{adv}^G + \lambda_2 L_{perceptual} + \lambda_3 L_{histogram} + \lambda_4 L_{reconstruction}, \end{cases} \tag{5}$$

where $\lambda_1$, $\lambda_2$, $\lambda_3$ and $\lambda_4$ are hyper-parameters to balance the importance of different loss functions. We train our discriminator and generator in turn by optimizing $L_D$ and $L_G$, respectively.

### 3.3   Deployment in Face Recognition

To explore the influence of face illumination enhancement toward face recognition (FR), we deploy FIE-GAN in the FR system, as shown in Fig. 3. FIE-GAN as an image preprocessing step is placed before the feature extraction step.

    In the training phase, the FR model can acquire a more powerful capability of feature representation for images in the normal-light range. This judgment can be explained by the following two reasons: 1) FIE-GAN brightens low-light face images into a normal range, which is equal to augment training data in normal-light range and promotes model by more learning on these adequate data; 2) This normalization operation also makes the brightness distribution of the dataset concentrated to a limited range, which means under this setting, FR model can focus its parameters to learn how to represent identity information instead of how to fit a few difficult cases such as low-light images.

Therefore, in the evaluation phase, the FR model can capture more sufficient features from brightened low-light face images. At the same time, the recognition accuracy is expected to be improved.

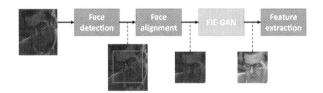

**Fig. 3.** The place of FIE-GAN in the face recognition system.

## 4    Experiments

### 4.1    Experimental Settings

In this section, we firstly train FIE-GAN to acquire a face illumination enhancement model. Then we integrate this pre-trained FIE-GAN as a preprocessing module into an unconstrained face recognition system to further evaluate its effect on face recognition (FR).

**Databases.** To train FIE-GAN in an unconstrained environment, a large-scale training set is built up, which contains unpaired low and normal light face images. Specifically, we collect 96,544 low-light face images from MS1M-RetinaFace [4] and 137,896 normal-light face images from CASIA-WebFace [33]. To exploit the effect of our method as a preprocess module in the FR system, we adopt CASIA-WebFace under different preprocessing methods as our training data to train multiple FR models. These FR models are tested on large-scale face image datasets such as IJB-B [31] and IJB-C [23], to evaluate their performance.

**Implementation Details.** We apply the $Y$ value in $YUV$ color space as the illumination of a single pixel. Image illumination is defined as the mean illumination of all pixels. Especially, images with light below 50 are regarded as low light while images with light between 80 and 120 are regarded as normal light. Therefore, illumination enhancement is equivalent to the transformation of low-light images to normal-light ones. Histogram vector guide this transformation and its dimension $m$ is set to 25 in our experiments.

Our model training is composed of FIE-GAN training and FR model training.

When training FIE-GAN, we crop and resize all face images to $112 \times 112$ as input images. We keep the learning rate equal to 0.0001, set the batch size to 16, and finish training at 10K iteration by iteratively minimizing the discriminator and generator loss function with Adam optimization. According to experimental experience, we set hyper-parameters of the optimizer as follows: $\beta_1 = 0.5$, $\beta_2 = 0.999$. The values of $\lambda_1, \lambda_2, \lambda_3$ and $\lambda_4$ are 1, 100, 100 and 10, respectively.

When training the FR model, to compare the effectiveness of different illumination enhancement methods, we utilize the dataset whose low-light face images are preprocessed by these different methods as training sets. The batch size is equal to 512. The learning rate starts from 0.1 and is divided by 10 at 100,000, 160,000 and 220,000 iterations, respectively. We employ ResNet-34 as the embedding network and arcface as the loss function. According to [4], the feature scale and angular margin $m$ are set as 64 and 0.5 respectively. SGD optimization is adopted in the training procedure of FR models.

### 4.2   Visual Perception Results

To investigate the effectiveness of our method, we compare FIE-GAN with several commonly used algorithms of illumination enhancement, including Gamma Correction [24], Histogram Equalization [11] and CycleGAN [2]. Especially, we implement histogram equalization on the Y channel of YUV. Therefore, the histogram equalization method is also marked as YUV in the paper.

**Qualitative Analysis.** As shown in Fig. 4, the results of Gamma are generally darker compared with others. The YUV method generates some over-exposure artifacts and causes some color information distorted. CycleGAN generates unsatisfactory visual results in terms of both naturalness and definition. In contrast, FIE-GAN successfully not only realizes illumination enhancement in face regions but also preserves the identity information of face images. The results demonstrate the superiority of our method to realize image-to-image illumination enhancement in the wild environment.

**Fig. 4.** Comparison of illumination enhancement results. All source images are from unconstrained dataset IJB-C.

**Quantitative Analysis.** For measuring the quality of generated images, the Inception Score (IS) [25] and the Fréchet Inception Distance (FID) [10] are adapted in our experiments. The former is applying an Inception-v3 network pre-trained on ImageNet to compare the conditional distribution of generated samples. The latter is an improvement on the IS by comparing the statistics of generated samples to real samples. As shown in Table 1, our method acquires the highest Inception score and the lowest FID, which proves the generated images by FIE-GAN are high-quality and identity-preserved again. On the other hand, it is worth noting that the Inception score of source images is even lower than generated images, which indicates low-light images are difficult for feature extraction in not only face recognition networks but also the pre-trained Inception-v3 network there. Therefore, we can conclude that illumination enhancement before identity information extraction is necessary for low-light face images.

**Table 1.** The quantitative evaluation on the quality of the generated images.

| Method | IS ↑ | FID ↓ |
|---|---|---|
| Source | 2.62 | – |
| Gamma | 3.03 | 64.94 |
| YUV | 3.05 | 64.15 |
| CycleGAN | 2.82 | 74.83 |
| **FIE-GAN** | **3.18** | **47.74** |

### 4.3    Face Recognition Results

We further try employing our FIE-GAN in a complete face recognition (FR) system as a preprocess module and explore its effect on face recognition.

**Table 2.** The 1:1 verification TAR (@FAR = 1e-5, 1e-4, 1e-3) on the IJB-B and IJB-C dataset.

| Method | IJB-B | | | IJB-C | | |
|---|---|---|---|---|---|---|
| | 1e-5 | 1e-4 | 1e-3 | 1e-5 | 1e-4 | 1e-3 |
| Baseline | 0.6432 | 0.7860 | 0.8771 | 0.7354 | 0.8273 | 0.9034 |
| Gamma | 0.6314 | 0.7862 | 0.8754 | 0.7211 | 0.8317 | 0.9044 |
| YUV | 0.6465 | 0.7835 | 0.8707 | 0.7290 | 0.8236 | 0.8988 |
| CycleGAN | 0.6369 | 0.7826 | 0.8692 | 0.7249 | 0.8248 | 0.8959 |
| **FIE-GAN** | **0.6608** | **0.7899** | **0.8844** | **0.7372** | **0.8360** | **0.9082** |

**Results on IJB-B and IJB-C.** To evaluate the performance of different FR models comprehensively, we apply IJB-B [31] and IJB-C [23] as test sets. They are significantly challenging benchmarks in unconstrained face recognition.

We employ CASIA-WebFace as training data and the ResNet34 as the embedding network. Different illumination enhancement methods, shown in Table 2 are applied as a pretreatment to brighten low-light images in training and testing data. The baseline model is trained by source images without any preprocessing. The experiment results shown in Table 2 prove the effectiveness of our method on illumination enhancement and identity information preservation. However, other methods fail to exceed the baseline model completely, which may be due to the loss of identity information during illumination enhancement.

## 4.4  Ablation Study

To verify the superiority of FIE-GAN as well as the contribution of each component, we train two incomplete models in terms of without the black edges elimination module and without the histogram vector module. Figure 5 illustrates their visual perception for a comparison. The second-row results prove black edges may cause the model to enhance the illumination of black background mistakenly, but ignore more significant face regions. From the third row results, we can conclude the importance of the histogram vector and corresponding loss on the guiding model to achieve illumination enhancement.

**Fig. 5.** Ablation study of the contribution of each component: (a) Source images, (b) Results w/o black edge elimination, (c) Results w/o histogram vector guidance, (d) Results with complete FIE-GAN.

## 5  Conclusion

In this paper, we propose a novel FIE-GAN model to achieve face image illumination enhancement in the condition of an unconstrained environment. The histogram vector we defined can guide image illumination transformation more flexibly and precisely. Multiple loss functions are utilized to ensure the effectiveness of illumination enhancement and the consistency of identity information during the transformation. After acquiring excellent visual perception results, we further investigate our FIE-GAN model as preprocessing in face recognition systems. As future work, illumination enhancement based on GAN can be assigned to other face-related missions to further test its validity.

# References

1. Cao, Q., Shen, L., Xie, W., Parkhi, O.M., Zisserman, A.: Vggface2: a dataset for recognising faces across pose and age. In: 2018 13th IEEE International Conference on Automatic Face & Gesture Recognition (FG 2018), pp. 67–74. IEEE (2018)
2. Chang, H., Lu, J., Yu, F., Finkelstein, A.: Pairedcyclegan: asymmetric style transfer for applying and removing makeup. In: Proceedings of the IEEE Conference on Computer Vision and Pattern Recognition, pp. 40–48 (2018)
3. Choi, Y., Choi, M., Kim, M., Ha, J.W., Kim, S., Choo, J.: Stargan: unified generative adversarial networks for multi-domain image-to-image translation. In: Proceedings of the IEEE Conference on Computer Vision and Pattern Recognition, pp. 8789–8797 (2018)
4. Deng, J., Guo, J., Zafeiriou, S.: Arcface: Additive angular margin loss for deep face recognition (2018)
5. Fang, H., Deng, W., Zhong, Y., Hu, J.: Generate to adapt: resolution adaption network for surveillance face recognition. In: Vedaldi, A., Bischof, H., Brox, T., Frahm, J.-M. (eds.) ECCV 2020. LNCS, vol. 12360, pp. 741–758. Springer, Cham (2020). https://doi.org/10.1007/978-3-030-58555-6_44
6. Goodfellow, I., et al.: Generative adversarial nets. In: Advances in Neural Information Processing Systems, pp. 2672–2680 (2014)
7. Gulrajani, I., Ahmed, F., Arjovsky, M., Dumoulin, V., Courville, A.: Improved training of wasserstein gans. arXiv preprint arXiv:1704.00028 (2017)
8. Guo, Y., Zhang, L., Hu, Y., He, X., Gao, J.: MS-Celeb-1M: a dataset and benchmark for large-scale face recognition. In: Leibe, B., Matas, J., Sebe, N., Welling, M. (eds.) ECCV 2016. LNCS, vol. 9907, pp. 87–102. Springer, Cham (2016). https://doi.org/10.1007/978-3-319-46487-9_6
9. He, K., Zhang, X., Ren, S., Sun, J.: Deep residual learning for image recognition. In: Proceedings of the IEEE Conference on Computer Vision and Pattern Recognition, pp. 770–778 (2016)
10. Heusel, M., Ramsauer, H., Unterthiner, T., Nessler, B., Hochreiter, S.: Gans trained by a two time-scale update rule converge to a local nash equilibrium. arXiv preprint arXiv:1706.08500 (2017)
11. Hum, Y.C., Lai, K.W., Mohamad Salim, M.I.: Multiobjectives bihistogram equalization for image contrast enhancement. Complexity $20(2)$, 22–36 (2014)
12. Isola, P., Zhu, J.Y., Zhou, T., Efros, A.A.: Image-to-image translation with conditional adversarial networks. In: Proceedings of the IEEE Conference on Computer Vision and Pattern Recognition, pp. 1125–1134 (2017)
13. Jenicek, T., Chum, O.: No fear of the dark: image retrieval under varying illumination conditions. In: Proceedings of the IEEE International Conference on Computer Vision, pp. 9696–9704 (2019)
14. Jo, Y., Yang, S., Kim, S.J.: Investigating loss functions for extreme super-resolution. In: Proceedings of the IEEE/CVF Conference on Computer Vision and Pattern Recognition Workshops, pp. 424–425 (2020)
15. Johnson, J., Alahi, A., Fei-Fei, L.: Perceptual losses for real-time style transfer and super-resolution. In: Leibe, B., Matas, J., Sebe, N., Welling, M. (eds.) ECCV 2016. LNCS, vol. 9906, pp. 694–711. Springer, Cham (2016). https://doi.org/10.1007/978-3-319-46475-6_43
16. Johnson, J., Alahi, A., Fei-Fei, L.: Perceptual losses for real-time style transfer and super-resolution. In: European Conference on Computer Vision (2016)

17. Karras, T., Aila, T., Laine, S., Lehtinen, J.: Progressive growing of gans for improved quality, stability, and variation. arXiv preprint arXiv:1710.10196 (2017)
18. Karras, T., Laine, S., Aila, T.: A style-based generator architecture for generative adversarial networks. In: Proceedings of the IEEE/CVF Conference on Computer Vision and Pattern Recognition, pp. 4401–4410 (2019)
19. Kim, J., Kim, M., Kang, H., Lee, K.: U-gat-it: unsupervised generative attentional networks with adaptive layer-instance normalization for image-to-image translation. arXiv preprint arXiv:1907.10830 (2019)
20. Ledig, C., et al.: Photo-realistic single image super-resolution using a generative adversarial network. In: Proceedings of the IEEE Conference on Computer Vision and Pattern Recognition, pp. 4681–4690 (2017)
21. Lore, K.G., Akintayo, A., Sarkar, S.: Llnet: a deep autoencoder approach to natural low-light image enhancement. Pattern Recogn. **61**, 650–662 (2017)
22. Mao, X., Li, Q., Xie, H., Lau, R.Y.K., Wang, Z., Smolley, S.P.: Least squares generative adversarial networks (2016)
23. Maze, B., et al.: Iarpa janus benchmark-c: Face dataset and protocol. In: 2018 International Conference on Biometrics (ICB), pp. 158–165. IEEE (2018)
24. Poynton, C.: Digital video and HD: Algorithms and Interfaces. Elsevier (2012)
25. Salimans, T., Goodfellow, I., Zaremba, W., Cheung, V., Radford, A., Chen, X.: Improved techniques for training gans. arXiv preprint arXiv:1606.03498 (2016)
26. Shen, L., Yue, Z., Feng, F., Chen, Q., Liu, S., Ma, J.: Msr-net: Low-light image enhancement using deep convolutional network. arXiv preprint arXiv:1711.02488 (2017)
27. Wang, F., Cheng, J., Liu, W., Liu, H.: Additive margin softmax for face verification. IEEE Signal Process. Lett. **25**(7), 926–930 (2018)
28. Wang, H., et al.: Cosface: Large margin cosine loss for deep face recognition. In: Proceedings of the IEEE Conference on Computer Vision and Pattern Recognition, pp. 5265–5274 (2018)
29. Wang, M., Deng, W.: Deep face recognition: a survey. CoRR abs/1804.06655 (2018). http://arxiv.org/abs/1804.06655
30. Wang, Q., Guo, G.: Ls-cnn: characterizing local patches at multiple scales for face recognition. IEEE Trans. Inf. Forensics Secur. **15**, 1640–1653 (2019)
31. Whitelam, C., et al.: Iarpa janus benchmark-b face dataset. In: Proceedings of the IEEE Conference on Computer Vision and Pattern Recognition Workshops, pp. 90–98 (2017)
32. Wu, R., Zhang, G., Lu, S., Chen, T.: Cascade ef-gan: progressive facial expression editing with local focuses. In: Proceedings of the IEEE/CVF Conference on Computer Vision and Pattern Recognition, pp. 5021–5030 (2020)
33. Yi, D., Lei, Z., Liao, S., Li, S.Z.: Learning face representation from scratch. arXiv preprint arXiv:1411.7923 (2014)
34. Zhang, Y., et al.: Global-local gcn: Large-scale label noise cleansing for face recognition. In: Proceedings of the IEEE/CVF Conference on Computer Vision and Pattern Recognition, pp. 7731–7740 (2020)
35. Zhu, J.Y., Park, T., Isola, P., Efros, A.A.: Unpaired image-to-image translation using cycle-consistent adversarial networks. In: Proceedings of the IEEE International Conference on Computer Vision, pp. 2223–2232 (2017)

# Illumination-Aware Image Quality Assessment for Enhanced Low-Light Image

Sigan Yao[1], Yiqin Zhu[1], Lingyu Liang[1,2,3,5(✉)], and Tao Wang[2,4(✉)]

[1] South China University of Technology, Guangzhou, China
eelyliang@scut.edu.cn
[2] Fujian Provincial Key Laboratory of Information Processing and Intelligent Control, Minjiang University, Fuzhou, China
twang@mju.edu.cn
[3] Sino-Singapore Joint Research Institute, Guangzhou, China
[4] The Key Laboratory of Cognitive Computing and Intelligent Information Processing of Fujian Education Institutions, Wuyi University, Wuyishan, China
[5] Key Laboratory of Computer Network and Information Integration (Southeast University), Ministry of Education, Nanjing, China

**Abstract.** Images captured in a dark environment may suffer from low visibility, which may degrade the visual aesthetics of images and the performance of vision-based systems. Extensive studies have focused on the low-light image enhancement (LIE) problem. However, we observe that even though the state-of-the-art LIE methods may oversharpen the low-light image and introduce visual artifacts. To reduce the overshoot effects of LIE, this paper proposes an illumination-aware image quality assessment, called LIE-IQA, for the enhanced low-light images. Since directly using the IQA of degraded image may fail to perform well, the proposed LIE-IQA is an illumination-aware and learnable metric. At first, the reflectance and shading components of both the enhanced low-light image and reference image are extracted by intrinsic image decomposition. Then, we use the weighted similarity between the VGG-based feature of enhanced low-light image and reference image to obtain LIE-IQA, where the weight of the measurement can be learned from pairs of data on benchmark dataset. Qualitative and quantitative experiments illustrate the superiority of the LIE-IQA to measure the image quality of LIE on different datasets, including a new IQA dataset built for LIE. We also use the LIE-IQA as a regularization of a loss function to optimize an end-to-end LIE method, and the results indicate the potential of the optimization framework with LIE-IQA to reduce the overshoot effects of low-light enhancement.

**Keywords:** Image quality assessment · Intrinsic image decomposition · Low-light image enhancement · Image quality perception optimization

ⓒ Springer Nature Switzerland AG 2021
H. Ma et al. (Eds.): PRCV 2021, LNCS 13021, pp. 226–237, 2021.
https://doi.org/10.1007/978-3-030-88010-1_19

# 1   Introduction

Images captured in a dark environment may suffer from low visibility or loss of significant details. Low-light image enhancement (LIE) not only improves image visual aesthetics [6,21], but also guarantees the performance of visual recognition systems requiring high-quality image inputs.

Extensively methods have been proposed to tackle LIE [19,35,37], which contains two lines of research. One aims to use intensity transform or spatial filtering operations to directly amplify intensity of images, including histogram equalization (HE) or histogram specification (matching) [19,35], unsharp masking [37], edge-aware filtering [25], or the recent learning-based operations by deep neural networks (DNN) [4,23,26]. The other one aims to utilize intrinsic properties of scene or objects to obtain better LIE based on Retinex theory [17], including constructing a new low-light imaging model [32,39], estimating illumination by different operations [8,9,13,44] or deep neural networks [11,16,31,34].

Despite the effectiveness of previous methods, eventhough the algorithms proposed recently, like Guo et al., [11] or Kwon et al. [16], may under/over-sharpen the image and cause visual artifacts, as shown in Fig. 1. The results indicate that it would be significant to assess the image quality of the sharpened low-light image. Therefore, this paper aims to propose an illumination-aware image quality assessment method for LIE to reduce the overshoot effects shown in Fig. 1.

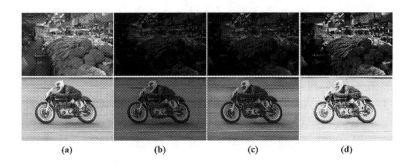

(a)                    (b)                    (c)                    (d)

**Fig. 1.** Visual artifacts caused by under/over-sharpening of two recent LIE methods. (a) Reference images (Ground-Truth). (b) Low-light image. (c) Results of DALE [16]. (d) Results of Zero-DCE [11].

Unlike the previous IQA of degraded image, like peak signal-to-noise ratio(PSNR) [14] or structural similarity (SSIM) index [33], IQA of LIE is a new sub-problem in the realm of image quality assessment (IQA) of sharpened image [5,15]. In this paper, we design a specific metric, called LIE-IQA, to measure the image quality of enhanced low-light images.

At first, the reflectance ($R$) and shading ($S$) components of both the enhanced low-light image ($I_{ell}$) and reference image ($I_{ref}$) are extracted by intrinsic image decomposition. Then, we use the weighted similarity between the VGG-based coarse-to-fine feature of $\{I_{ell}, S_{ell}, R_{ell}\}$ and $\{I_{ref}, S_{ref}, R_{ref}\}$ to obtain LIE-IQA, where the weight of the measurement can be learned from pairs of data on benchmark dataset.

Qualitative and quantitative experiments illustrate the superiority of the LIE-IQA to measure the image quality of LIE on different datasets, including a new IQA dataset built for LIE. We also use the LIE-IQA as a regularization of a loss function to optimize an end-to-end LIE method, and the results indicate the potential of optimization framework with LIE-IQA to reduce the overshoot effects of low-light enhancement.

## 2   Illumination-Aware Quality Assessment of Enhanced Low-Light Image

To reduce the overshoot effects shown in Fig. 1, we propose an illumination-aware image quality assessment method, called LIE-IQA, to further improve the performance of low-light enhancement algorithm. Let $I_{ell}$ denotes the enhanced low-light image, $I_{ref}$ denotes the reference image with good perceptual image quality, $R$ denotes the reflectance component, and $S$ denotes the shading component. The proposed LIE-IQA consists of three main stages, as shown in Fig. 2. Firstly, intrinsic image decomposition is performed to obtain $R_{ell}, R_{ref}$ and $S_{ell}, S_{ref}$ of $I_{ell}$ and $I_{ref}$, respectively. Secondly, CNN is used to obtain the VGG-based feature of $\{I_{ell}, S_{ell}, R_{ell}\}$ and $\{I_{ref}, S_{ref}, R_{ref}\}$. Finally, the LIE-IQA score is just the weighted similarity of the extracted feature between $I_{ell}$ and $I_{ref}$. Note that the weight of the proposed metric is adaptive, which can be learned from pairs of data. Furthermore, the LIE-IQA can be used as a regularization in a loss function of an end-to-end network of LIE algorithm, whose results can be further improved, as shown in Fig. 5. Then, we give more details of the proposed LIE-IQA in the following subsections.

### 2.1   Intrinsic Decomposition Module

Intrinsic image recovers the color, texture and other intrinsic information from the intensity of an image, which separates the image into reflectance and shading components [22]. The reflectance component contains the intrinsic color, or albedo, of surface points independent of the illumination environment, which is light-invariance, while the shading component consists shadows and specular hightlights caused by illumination and environment. Let $I$ denotes the observed image, $R$ denotes the reflectance component, and $S$ denotes the shading component, then we have $I = R \circ S$, where $\circ$ is a point-wise multiplication operation. Since intrinsic image decomposition (IID) is an ill-posed inverse problem, priors or regularization should be introduced into the process.

In this paper, we use the recently proposed method with unsupervised learning [22] to achieve IID.

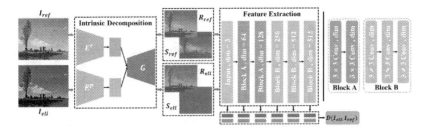

**Fig. 2.** The framework of illumination-aware image quality assessment method(**LIE-IQA**). It mainly consists of two modules, Intrinsic Decompisition Module and Feature Extraction Module. **(1) Intrinsic Decompisition Module** is a structure of encoder-decoder with some constraint conditions, which is utilized to decompose the reference image (Ground-Truth) $I_{ref}$ and the enhanced low-light image $I_{ell}$ into reflectance and shading image. **(2) Feature Extraction Module** is a VGG-based convolutional network with two main different blocks (Block A & B) including different number of convolutional filters and dimensions. **(3) Learnable Perceptual Distance Measurement** $D(I_{ell}, I_{ref})$ is the weighted similarity of the extracted feature between $I_{ell}$ and $I_{ref}$, which can be used as a regularization in a loss function of an end-to-end network of LIE algorithm.

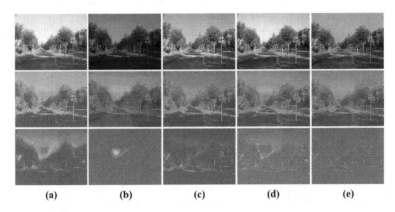

**Fig. 3.** Visual results of the intrinsic decomposition model USI$^3$D [22]. The first row of images are the input of the intrinsic decomposition model, the second row of images are their reflectance image and the third row images are their shading image. (a) Reference image (Ground-Truth). (b) Low-light image. (c) Result of OpenCE [38]. (d) Result of KinD [43]. (e) Result of Zero-DCE [11].

This method designed an image-to-image (encoder-decoder) framework, called USI$^3$D, to decompose the image into reflectance and shading image, which is similar to image style transformation. They assumed such object property can be latent coded and shared amount domains, so a content-sharing encoder was designed to extract the image content codes. With another assumption that the prior codes of reflectance and shading are domain-variant and independent to each other, the another encoder was designed to extract the image prior codes.

Finally, they utilized the image content codes and image prior codes to generate the reflectance and shading image with a generator. In this paper, we choose the intrinsic decomposition model trained on the Intrinsic Images in the Wild (IIW) benchmark [2] and the rendered dataset CGIntrinsics [20]. The results of $R$ and $S$ are shown in Fig. 3.

## 2.2    CNN-based Feature Extraction Module

Intrinsic decomposition preliminarily separates texture details, colors and lighting effects of low-light enhanced image. However, the intrinsic information of low-light enhanced image is still coupled in the intrinsic image. [7] find that measurements from early CNN layers appear to capture basic intensity and color information, and those from later layers summarize the shape and structure information. To this end, after the intrinsic image decomposition, we utilize the convolutional neural network to finely extract the higher-level fundamental image features of the reflectance and shading image, which can effectively reduce interference between different image features.

The full reference IQA algorithm requires that the feature representations can contain the information of the original image as much as possible. However, VGG Network [28] discards image information at each stage of transformation. Therefore, to ensure injective transformation, we add the original input image of intrinsic decomposition module to the VGG as the additional feature map. The original input image $I$ and its corresponding reflectance $R$ and shading $S$ are converted as follows:

$$\mathcal{F}(I, R, S) = \{\tilde{I}^{(ij)}, \tilde{R}^{(ij)}, \tilde{S}^{(ij)}; i = 0, ..., m; j = 1, ..., n_i\} \tag{1}$$

where $m = 5$ denotes the number of convolutional blocks, $n_i$ is the dimension of feature representation in the $i - th$ convolutional block, and $\tilde{I}^{(0)} = I, \tilde{R}^{(0)} = R, \tilde{S}^{(0)} = S$.

## 2.3    Learnable Perceptual Distance Measurement

After extracting image features from coarse to fine, we directly compute $L_2$ distance of image representations at different network layers between the reference image and the low-light enhanced image:

$$D_X^{(ij)}(\tilde{X}_{ell}^{(ij)}, \tilde{X}_{ref}^{(ij)}) = \|\tilde{X}_{ell}^{(ij)} - \tilde{X}_{ref}^{(ij)}\|_2^2 \tag{2}$$

where $i = 0, ..., m$ and $j = 1, ..., n_i$ donate the same meaning as mentioned-above, $X$ donates images of input image $(I)$, reflectance image $(R)$ and shading image $(S)$. We finally propose a low-light enhanced image quality assessment model that is a weighted sum of the global quality measurements at different convolutional layers:

$$D(I_{ell}, I_{ref}; \gamma, \alpha, \beta) = \sum_{i=0}^{m} \sum_{j=1}^{n_i} (\gamma_{ij} D_I^{(ij)} + \alpha_{ij} D_R^{(ij)} + \beta_{ij} D_S^{(ij)}) \tag{3}$$

where $\gamma_{ij}, \alpha_{ij}, \beta_{ij}$ are weights to balance the terms, and $\sum_{i=0}^{m} \sum_{j=1}^{n_i} (\gamma_{ij} + \alpha_{ij} + \beta_{ij}) = 1$. Note that the weights can be set manually, but it can also be learned adaptively from benchmark dataset.

**Parameter Learning from Data.** In this paper, we set the weight parameters $\{\gamma, \alpha, \beta\}$ by learning from data to obtain the adaptive LIE-IQA metric. When training the LIE-IQA, we fixed the layers of the intrinsic decomposition module and VGG-16 convolution kernel pre-trained on ImageNet, where both these module can be regarded as a pre-processing of extracting feature. Then, the weights are jointly optimized to simulate the human perception of low-light enhanced image quality. Finally, we minimize the $L_1$ loss functional between IQA score of the model prediction and the score from the benchmark:

$$E(x, y; \gamma, \alpha, \beta) = \|\mathcal{S}(x, y; \gamma, \alpha, \beta) - q(x)\|_1 \tag{4}$$

where $x$ donates the enhanced low-light image, $y$ donates reference image, $q(x)$ denotes the normalized ground-truth quality score of $x$ collected from psychophysical experiments. We train our proposed network on a synthetic low-light enhanced image assessment dataset that contains over 20,000 images to optimize the perceptual weights.

The training is carried out by optimizing the objective function in Eq. (4) to learn the perceptual weights $\{\gamma, \alpha, \beta\}$, using Adam optimizer with a batch size of 32 and an initial learning rate of $1 \times 10^{-4}$. After every 5K iterations, we reduce the learning rate by a factor of 2. We train LIE-IQA model for 20K iterations on an NVIDIA RTX 2080Ti GPU. We set up a low-light enhanced image quality assessment test dataset with subjective ranking to evaluate the performance of our proposed model.

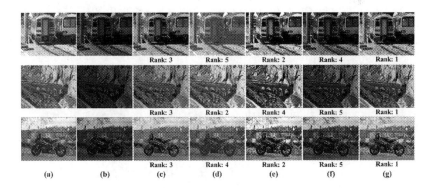

**Fig. 4.** Subjective ranking of the proposed LIE-IQA Dataset. (a) Reference image (Ground-Truth). (b) Low-light image. (c) Result of GC [10]. (d) Result of HE [10]. (e) Result of LIME [12]. (f) Result of SRIE [8]. (g) Result of OpenCE [38].

**LIE-IQA Dataset.** The large scale low-light synthetic dataset [24] which includes 97, 030 images with 3 different types (synthesized dark images, synthesized low-light with noise images, and contrast-enhanced images), is chosen as the benchmark dataset. Firstly, we employ quality assessment for the test dataset of the chosen dataset [24] with an NR-IQA method, hyperIQA [29], to screen out images with a high-quality score. Therefore, we can obtain 230 images with high quality from the chosen test dataset. Secondly, we utilize the classic image processing methods, histogram equalization (HE), gamma correction (GC) [10], SRIE [8], LIME [12] and OpenCE [38] to enhance the synthesized dark images to obtain 1, 150 enhanced images. Finally, for each image group which includes a reference image, a synthesized dark image with 5 different enhanced images, we employ a subjective experiment to compare each 5 different enhanced images with the reference image and record the similarity rank (from 1 to 5) of each image. The enhanced low-light image with lower-ranking is more similar to the reference image. Some subjective ranking results of our LIE-IQA Dataset are shown in Fig. 4.

## 3   Experiments

### 3.1   Basic Evaluations

**Ablation Studies.** We verify the effectiveness of the intrinsic decomposition module in LIE-IQA via ablation studies. We removed the intrinsic decomposition module (the result "Org" shown in Table 1) and replace it with image color space conversion (RGB to YCbCr), and compared the performance in low-light enhanced image quality assessment, as shown in Table 1. The results demonstrate that the quality evaluation performance of the network integrated with the intrinsic decomposition module is better than the other components. On the contrary, we add the intrinsic decomposition module to the natural image quality assessment models (*e.g.*, Deep-IQA [3], LPIPS [42]) to explore the contribution of intrinsic decomposition module. Results, shown in the Table 1, prove that the intrinsic decomposition module can effectively improve the performance on the low-light enhanced image quality assessment.

**Table 1.** Experiment to explore intrinsic decomposition module contribution. Larger PLCC, SROCC, KROCC, and smaller RMSE values indicate better performance.

| Method | LIE-IQA dataset | | | |
|---|---|---|---|---|
| | PLCC | SROCC | KROCC | RMSE |
| Org | 0.734 | 0.684 | 0.586 | 0.960 |
| YCbCr | 0.733 | 0.704 | 0.606 | 0.962 |
| IID+FSIM | 0.746($\uparrow$) | 0.739($\uparrow$) | 0.638($\uparrow$) | 0.942($\downarrow$) |
| IID+DeepIQA | 0.765($\uparrow$) | 0.760($\uparrow$) | 0.661($\uparrow$) | 0.911($\downarrow$) |
| LIE-IQA(*ours*) | **0.802** | **0.797** | **0.703** | **0.844** |

**Table 2.** Performance comparison on LIVE, MDID, CSIQ. Larger PLCC, SROCC, KROCC, and smaller RMSE values indicate better performance.

| Method | LIVE | | | | MDID | | | | CSIQ | | | |
|---|---|---|---|---|---|---|---|---|---|---|---|---|
| | PLCC | SROCC | KROCC | RMSE | PLCC | SROCC | KROCC | RMSE | PLCC | SROCC | KROCC | RMSE |
| SSIM [33] | 0.937 | 0.948 | 0.797 | 9.575 | 0.846 | 0.833 | 0.645 | 1.174 | 0.852 | 0.865 | 0.680 | 0.138 |
| VSI [40] | 0.948 | 0.952 | 0.806 | 8.682 | 0.854 | 0.837 | 0.649 | 1.147 | 0.928 | 0.942 | 0.786 | 0.098 |
| MAD [18] | 0.968 | 0.967 | 0.842 | **6.907** | 0.830 | 0.815 | 0.618 | 1.229 | **0.950** | 0.947 | 0.797 | **0.082** |
| FSIMc [41] | 0.961 | 0.965 | 0.836 | 7.530 | 0.900 | 0.890 | 0.712 | 0.961 | 0.919 | 0.931 | 0.769 | 0.103 |
| GMSD [36] | 0.957 | 0.960 | 0.827 | 7.948 | 0.877 | 0.861 | 0.679 | 1.057 | 0.945 | **0.950** | **0.804** | 0.086 |
| DeepIQA [3] | 0.940 | 0.947 | 0.791 | 9.305 | 0.849 | 0.832 | 0.640 | 1.163 | 0.901 | 0.909 | 0.732 | 0.114 |
| LPIPSvgg [42] | 0.934 | 0.932 | 0.765 | 9.735 | 0.932 | 0.930 | 0.764 | 0.798 | 0.896 | 0.876 | 0.689 | 0.117 |
| DISTS [7] | 0.954 | 0.954 | 0.811 | 8.214 | 0.946 | 0.943 | 0.790 | 0.716 | 0.928 | 0.929 | 0.767 | 0.098 |
| LIE-IQA(*ours*) | **0.972** | **0.974** | **0.870** | 7.351 | **0.955** | **0.953** | **0.808** | **0.655** | 0.948 | 0.933 | 0.775 | 0.084 |

**Table 3.** Performance comparison on low-light enhanced image quality assessment test dataset. Larger PLCC, SROCC, KROCC, and smaller RMSE values indicate better performance.

| Method | LIE-IQA dataset | | | |
|---|---|---|---|---|
| | PLCC | SROCC | KROCC | RMSE |
| SSIM [33] | 0.608 | 0.563 | 0.474 | 1.123 |
| VSI [40] | 0.636 | 0.595 | 0.497 | 1.091 |
| MAD [18] | 0.460 | 0.383 | 0.308 | 1.256 |
| FSIMc [41] | 0.581 | 0.551 | 0.454 | 1.151 |
| GMSD [36] | 0.709 | 0.682 | 0.584 | 0.997 |
| DeepIQA | 0.759 | 0.750 | 0.652 | 0.921 |
| LPIPSvgg [42] | 0.777 | 0.752 | 0.653 | 0.891 |
| DISTS [7] | 0.750 | 0.712 | 0.615 | 0.935 |
| LIE-IQA(*ours*) | **0.802** | **0.797** | **0.703** | **0.844** |

## 3.2 Evaluations of LIE-IQA with Related Methods

We made comparison with a set of full-reference IQA methods, including SSIM, VSI [40], MAD [18], FSIMc [41], GMSD [36], Deep-IQA [3], LPIPS [42] and DISTS [7] on different dataset. In the evaluations, the Spearman rank correlation coefficient (SROCC), the Kendall rank correlation coefficient (KROCC), the Pearson linear correlation coefficient (PLCC), and the root mean square error (RMSE) are used to measure the performance of different metrics for IQA.

Firstly, since there have been no open benchmark datasets specifically for IQA of LIE, evaluations were performed on three standard IQA databases, including CSIQ dataset [18], MDID dataset [30] and LIVE dataset [27]). The quantitative results were shown in Fig. 2. Note that even through our method is designed specifically for LIE, it is superior to others methods on MDID dataset and LIVE dataset; it also obtain competitive performance on CSIQ dataset. The results indicates the superiority of our methods and the potential for more general IQA task.

**Fig. 5.** The image with LIE-IQA score generated by optimized low-light enhancement algorithm. Smaller $D_{lie-iqa}$ values indicate better quality. (a) Ground-Truth; (b) Low-light image; (c) Low-light image enhanced by Zero-DCE [11]; (d) Image generated by the optimized Zero-DCE algorithm.

Secondly, we verify the proposed method for the task of low-light enhanced image quality prediction on LIE-IQA dataset. The comparison results are shown in Table 3, which demonstrate that LIE-IQA method has the best performance in low-light enhanced image quality assessment compared to other natural FR-IQA methods. The result of this comparison experiment proves that LIE-IQA can better capture the quality characteristics of low-light enhanced images and has high specificity to low-light enhanced image assessment, which is highly consistent with subjective ranking.

### 3.3  LIE-IQA for Low-Light Enhancement

Since the final goal of LIE-IQA is for low-light enhancement, we also use the optimization as a regularization of a loss function and optimize an end-to-end LIE method, called Zero-DCE [11]. The results show that better perceptual quality can be obtain after optimization, as shown in Fig. 5.

Our proposed LIE-IQA method can assist the LIE method in adjusting the exposure level of the image adaptively, enhancing the under-exposed image, reducing the brightness of the over-exposed image, and making the enhanced image closer to the ground-truth. The enhenced low-light image after optimization is more similar to the ground-truth with balanced brightness, abundant detail and vivid color. The results indicate the potential of the optimization framework with LIE-IQA to reduce the overshoot effects of low-light enhancement.

## 4  Conclusion

This paper proposes an illumination-aware image quality assessment, called LIE-IQA, to reduce the overshoot effects of low-light image enhancement. The LIE-IQA uses intrinsic image decomposition to extract the reflectance and shading components of both the enhanced low-light image and reference image; then use the weighted similarity between the VGG-based feature of enhanced low-light image and reference image to obtain LIE-IQA score. Since the weight of the LIE-IQA metric can be learned from data, the proposed metric is adaptive. Qualitative and quantitative experiments show the superiority of the LIE-IQA to measure the image quality. LIE-IQA can also be used the as a regularization of a loss function to optimize an end-to-end LIE method, and the results indicate the potential of the optimization framework with LIE-IQA to reduce the overshoot effects of low-light enhancement. In the future, we would extend the IQA-based optimization framework for more image enhancement tasks and implement these algorithms on Mindspore, which is a new deep learning platform [1].

**Acknowledgements.** This research is supported by Science and Technology Program of Guangzhou (202102020692), Guangdong NSF (2019A1515011045), Fujian NSF (2019J01756), the Open Fund of Fujian Provincial Key Laboratory of Information Processing and Intelligent Control (Minjiang University) (Grant No. MJUKF-IPIC202102), the Open Fund of The Key Laboratory of Cognitive Computing and Intelligent Information Processing of Fujian Education Institutions (Wuyi University) (KLCCIIP2020202), the Open Fund of Ministry of Education Key Laboratory of Computer Network and Information Integration (Southeast University) (K93-9-2021-01) and CAAI-Huawei MindSpore Open Fund.

## References

1. Mindspore (2020). https://www.mindspore.cn/

2. Bell, S., Bala, K., Snavely, N.: Intrinsic images in the wild. ACM Trans. Graph. **33**(4), 1–12 (2014)
3. Bosse, S., Maniry, D., Müller, K.R., Wiegand, T., Samek, W.: Deep neural networks for no-reference and full-reference image quality assessment. IEEE Trans. Image Process. **27**(1), 206–219 (2017)
4. Chen, C., Chen, Q., Xu, J., Koltun, V.: Learning to see in the dark. In: Proceedings of CVPR, pp. 3291–3300 (2018)
5. Cheon, M., Vigier, T., Krasula, L., Lee, J., Le Callet, P., Lee, J.S.: Ambiguity of objective image quality metrics: a new methodology for performance evaluation. Signal Process. Image Commun. **93**, 116150 (2021)
6. Deng, Y., Loy, C.C., Tang, X.: Image aesthetic assessment: an experimental survey. IEEE Signal Process. Mag. **34**(4), 80–106 (2017)
7. Ding, K., Ma, K., Wang, S., Simoncelli, E.P.: Image quality assessment: unifying structure and texture similarity. arXiv preprint arXiv:2004.07728 (2020)
8. Fu, X., Zeng, D., Huang, Y., Zhang, X.P., Ding, X.: A weighted variational model for simultaneous reflectance and illumination estimation. In: Proceedings of CVPR, pp. 2782–2790 (2016)
9. Gao, Y., Hu, H.M., Li, B., Guo, Q.: Naturalness preserved nonuniform illumination estimation for image enhancement based on retinex. IEEE Transa. Multimedia **20**(2), 335–344 (2018)
10. Gonzalez, R.C., Woods, R.E.: Digital Image Processing, 3rd edn. Pearson International Edition, Boston (2007)
11. Guo, C., et al.: Zero-reference deep curve estimation for low-light image enhancement. In: Proceedings of CVPR, pp. 1780–1789 (2020)
12. Guo, X., Li, Y., Ling, H.: Lime: low-light image enhancement via illumination map estimation. IEEE Trans. Image Process. **26**(2), 982–993 (2016)
13. Guo, X., Li, Y., Ling, H.: LIME: low-light image enhancement via illumination map estimation. IEEE Trans. Image Process. **26**(2), 982–993 (2017)
14. Huynh-Thu, Q., Ghanbari, M.: Scope of validity of psnr in image/video quality assessment. Electron. Lett. **44**(13), 800–801 (2008)
15. Krasula, L., Le Callet, P., Fliegel, K., Klíma, M.: Quality assessment of sharpened images: challenges, methodology, and objective metrics. IEEE Trans. Image Process. **26**(3), 1496–1508 (2017)
16. Kwon, D., Kim, G., Kwon, J.: Dale: dark region-aware low-light image enhancement. arXiv preprint arXiv:2008.12493 (2020)
17. Land, E.H., McCann, J.J.: Lightness and retinex theory. JOSA **61**(1), 1–11 (1971)
18. Larson, E.C., Chandler, D.M.: Most apparent distortion: full-reference image quality assessment and the role of strategy. J. Electron. Imaging **19**(1), 011006 (2010)
19. Lee, C., Lee, C., Kim, C.S.: Contrast enhancement based on layered difference representation of 2d histograms. IEEE Trans. Image Process. **22**(12), 5372–5384 (2013)
20. Li, Z., Snavely, N.: Cgintrinsics: better intrinsic image decomposition through physically-based rendering. In: Proceedings ECCV (2018)
21. Liang, L., Jin, L., Liu, D.: Edge-aware label propagation for mobile facial enhancement on the cloud. IEEE Trans. Circ. Syst. Video Technol. **27**(1), 125–138 (2017)
22. Liu, Y., Li, Y., You, S., Lu, F.: Unsupervised learning for intrinsic image decomposition from a single image. In: Proceedings CVPR, pp. 3248–3257 (2020)
23. Lore, K.G., Akintayo, A., Sarkar, S.: Llnet: a deep autoencoder approach to natural low-light image enhancement. Pattern Recogn. **61**, 650–662 (2017)
24. Lv, F., Li, Y., Lu, F.: Attention guided low-light image enhancement with a large scale low-light simulation dataset. Int. J. Comput. Vision **129**, 1–19 (2021)

25. Paris, S., Kornprobst, P., Tumblin, J., Durand, F., et al.: Bilateral filtering: theory and applications. Found. Trends® Comput. Graph. Vision **4**(1), 1–73 (2009)
26. Ren, W., Liu, S., Ma, L., Xu, Q., Xu, X., Cao, X., Du, J., Yang, M.: Low-light image enhancement via a deep hybrid network. IEEE Trans. Image Process. **28**(9), 4364–4375 (2019)
27. Sheikh, H.R., Sabir, M.F., Bovik, A.C.: A statistical evaluation of recent full reference image quality assessment algorithms. IEEE Trans. Image Process. **15**(11), 3440–3451 (2006)
28. Simonyan, K., Zisserman, A.: Very deep convolutional networks for large-scale image recognition. arXiv preprint arXiv:1409.1556 (2014)
29. Su, S., Yet al.: Blindly assess image quality in the wild guided by a self-adaptive hyper network. In: Proceedings CVPR (2020)
30. Sun, W., Zhou, F., Liao, Q.: Mdid: a multiply distorted image database for image quality assessment. Pattern Recogn. **61**, 153–168 (2017)
31. Wang, R., Zhang, Q., Fu, C., Shen, X., Zheng, W., Jia, J.: Underexposed photo enhancement using deep illumination estimation. In: Proceedings of CVPR, pp. 6842–6850 (2019)
32. Wang, Y.F., Liu, H.M., Fu, Z.W.: Low-light image enhancement via the absorption light scattering model. IEEE Trans. Image Process. **28**(11), 5679–5690 (2019)
33. Wang, Z., Bovik, A.C., Sheikh, H.R., Simoncelli, E.P.: Image quality assessment: from error visibility to structural similarity. IEEE Trans. Image Process. **13**(4), 600–612 (2004)
34. Wei, C., Wang, W., Yang, W., Liu, J.: Deep retinex decomposition for low-light enhancement. In: BMVC, pp. 127–136 (2018)
35. Xiao, B., Tang, H., Jiang, Y., Li, W., Wang, G.: Brightness and contrast controllable image enhancement based on histogram specification. Neurocomputing **275**, 2798–2809 (2018)
36. Xue, W., Zhang, L., Mou, X., Bovik, A.C.: Gradient magnitude similarity deviation: a highly efficient perceptual image quality index. IEEE Trans. Image Process. **23**(2), 684–695 (2013)
37. Ye, W., Ma, K.K.: Blurriness-guided unsharp masking. IEEE Trans. Image Process. **27**(9), 4465–4477 (2018)
38. Ying, Z., Li, G., Ren, Y., Wang, R., Wang, W.: A new low-light image enhancement algorithm using camera response model. In: Proceedings ICCVW, pp. 3015–3022 (2017)
39. Yu, S., Zhu, H.: Low-illumination image enhancement algorithm based on a physical lighting model. IEEE TCSVT **29**(1), 28–37 (2019)
40. Zhang, L., Shen, Y., Li, H.: VSI: a visual saliency-induced index for perceptual image quality assessment. IEEE Trans. Image Process. **23**(10), 4270–4281 (2014)
41. Zhang, L., Zhang, L., Mou, X., Zhang, D.: FSIM: a feature similarity index for image quality assessment. IEEE Trans. Image Process. **20**(8), 2378–2386 (2011)
42. Zhang, R., Isola, P., Efros, A.A., Shechtman, E., Wang, O.: The unreasonable effectiveness of deep features as a perceptual metric. In: Proceedings CVPR, pp. 586–595 (2018)
43. Zhang, Y., Zhang, J., Guo, X.: Kindling the darkness: a practical low-light image enhancer. In: Proceedings ACM MM, pp. 1632–1640 (2019)
44. Zhu, D., Chen, G., Michelini, P.N., Liu, H.: Fast image enhancement based on maximum and guided filters. In: Proceedings of ICIP, pp. 4080–4084 (2019)

# Smooth Coupled Tucker Decomposition for Hyperspectral Image Super-Resolution

Yuanyang Bu[1,2], Yongqiang Zhao[1,2(✉)], Jize Xue[1,2], and Jonathan Cheung-Wai Chan[3]

[1] School of Automation, Northwestern Polytechnical University, Xi'an, China
{buyuanyang,xuejize900507}@mail.nwpu.edu.cn, zhaoyq@nwpu.edu.cn
[2] Research and Development Institute of Northwestern, Polytechnical University in Shenzhen,
Xi'an, China
[3] Department of Electronics and Informatics, Vrije, Universiteit Brussel, 1050 Brussel, Belgium
jcheungw@etrovub.be

**Abstract.** Hyperspectral image processing methods based on Tucker decomposition by utilizing low-rank and sparse priors are sensitive to the model order, and merely utilizing the global structural information. After statistical analysis on hyperspectral images, we find that the smoothness underlying hyperspectral image encoding local structural information is ubiquity in each mode. Based on this observation, we propose a novel smooth coupled Tucker decomposition scheme with two smoothness constraints imposed on the subspace factor matrices to reveal the local structural information of hyperspectral image. In addition, efficient algorithms are designed and experimental results demonstrate the effectiveness of selecting optimal model order for hyperspectral image super-resolution due to the integration of the subspace smoothness.

**Keywords:** Hyperspectral image · Super-resolution · Smoothness · Tucker decomposition

## 1 Introduction

Recently, hyperspectral image (HSI) super-resolution [1–7] has attracted considerable attentions from the signal processing community, such as multi-modal fusion [8], which consists in fusing a multispectral image with high spatial resolution (HR-MSI) and a hyperspectral image with low spatial resolution (LR-HSI) to recover the desired HIS with high spatial resolution (HR-HSI).

Advances in tensor decomposition techniques have triggered extensive research efforts to solve the problem of HSI super-resolution. Existing HSI super-resolution methods are roughly classified into two branches: sparsity-based methods [3, 4] and low-rank based methods [5–7].

HSI illustrates strong correlations that redundant information is contained in each mode. A coupled Tucker decomposition method is proposed to impose the sparsity penalty on core tensor and to optimize the multi-modes dictionaries simultaneously [4]. Besides, HSI is high-dimensional and yet the intrinsic information is often preserved in

© Springer Nature Switzerland AG 2021
H. Ma et al. (Eds.): PRCV 2021, LNCS 13021, pp. 238–248, 2021.
https://doi.org/10.1007/978-3-030-88010-1_20

a lower dimensional space, which motivates to utilize low-rank property to characterize the correlations across different modes of HSI. More recently, a promising coupled CPD (canonical polyadic decomposition) method and a coupled Tucker decomposition with approximately low multilinear rank that takes the advantage of the inherent low-rankness underlying HSI are proposed in [5] and [6, 7]. Though the competitive recovery performances of the above-mentioned methods can be achieved compared with the state-of-the-art, they still have several common deficiencies: the appropriate model order[1] of the CPD and Tucker decomposition is unknown in practice and needs to be preset carefully; CPD and Tucker decomposition are reliable models merely revealing the global structural information of tensor data based on strong interactions among each mode, yet it may interpret local structural information inadequately [1].

In this study, after statistical analysis on HSI, we find that the smoothness underlying HSI encoding local structural information is ubiquity in each mode. Based on this observation, we propose a novel **S**mooth **C**oupled **T**ucker **D**ecomposition (SCTD) scheme with two smoothness constraints imposed on the subspace factor matrices to encode the local structural information. Instead of imposing the smoothness constraints on the surface reflecting intuitional structures, we impose the novel smoothness constraints on the subspace factor matrices to reveal latent smooth structural information. In addition, efficient algorithms are designed and experimental results demonstrate the effectiveness of our models for HSI super-resolution in terms of both visual comparison and numerical analysis. The proposed method admits significant advantages that the sensitivity of selecting optimal model order is mitigated owing to the integration of the local structural information, namely the latent smoothness.

## 2 Tensor Notations and Preliminaries

For convenience, it is necessary to introduce some definitions and preliminaries of tensors first. In the study, we follow the notations in [7]. Scalars, vectors and matrices are denoted by lowercase italics letters, lowercase letters and capital letters, respectively [1]. Then, a 3rd-order tensor is denoted by Euler script letter $\mathcal{X} \in \mathbb{R}^{I \times J \times K}$, with $x_{i,j,k}$ representing its $(i, j, k)$-th element [1]. The n-mode unfolding of a 3rd-order tensor $\mathcal{X} \in \mathbb{R}^{I \times J \times K}$ is denoted as $X_{(n)}$. We use the symbol $\otimes$ for the Kronecker product and operation $\times_n$ denotes the n-mode product. More detailed definitions of the above notations can be found in [1]. Given a 3rd-order tensor $\mathcal{X} \in \mathbb{R}^{I \times J \times K}$, its shorthand notation for the Tucker decomposition is used as follows:

$$[[\mathcal{G}; U_1, U_2, U_3]] = \mathcal{G} \times_1 U_1 \times_2 U_2 \times_3 U_3 \tag{1}$$

where $\mathcal{G} \in \mathbb{R}^{R_1 \times R_2 \times R_3}$, $U_1 \in \mathbb{R}^{I \times R_1}$, $U_2 \in \mathbb{R}^{J \times R_2}$ and $U_3 \in \mathbb{R}^{K \times R_3}$ denote the core tensor and corresponding factor matrices along column, row and spectral mode, respectively.

---

[1] In this study, the rank of CPD/Tucker decomposition and the size of dictionaries in [4] are collectively referred as model order. In our models, the size of core tensor is model order.

## 3   Problem Formulation

### 3.1   Problem Description and Degradation Model

In this study, we consider an LR-HSI, termed as $\mathcal{Y} \in \mathbb{R}^{I_M \times J_M \times K_H}$ and an HR-MSI, termed as $\mathcal{Z} \in \mathbb{R}^{I_H \times J_H \times K_M}$ acquired from different sensors of the same scene. The acquired MSI and HSI are regarded as two degraded versions of an HR-HSI, termed as $\mathcal{X} \in \mathbb{R}^{I_H \times J_H \times K_H}$. The HSI super-resolution problem amounts to recovering $\mathcal{X}$ from $\mathcal{Y}$ and $\mathcal{Z}$.

In this study, we employ the degradation model, formulated as follows:

$$\begin{cases} \mathcal{Y}_\ominus = \mathcal{X} \times_1 P_1 \times_2 P_2 + \mathcal{E}_H \\ \mathcal{Z}_\ominus = \mathcal{X} \times_3 P_M + \mathcal{E}_M \end{cases} \tag{2}$$

where $\mathcal{E}_H$ and $\mathcal{E}_M$ denote the error terms, and $P_M \in \mathbb{R}^{K_M \times K_H}$ is the spectral degradation matrix, $K_M < K_H$. $P_1 \in \mathbb{R}^{I_M \times I_H}$ and $P_2 \in \mathbb{R}^{J_M \times J_H}$, where $I_M < I_H$ and $J_M < J_H$, are the down-sampling matrices along the column and row modes, respectively. For simplicity, here we hold the hypothesis that the separability of spatial degradation, which is a solid hypothesis embraced by the Wald's protocol [9].

### 3.2   MAP Formulation

As shown in Formula (2), it is an ill-posed problem to recover the desired HR-HSI from the HR-MSI and the LR-HSI, thus the proper regularization or prior knowledge is needed to further reduce the solution space. Fortunately, the Bayes' theorem provides an intuitive inference of the HSI super-resolution process by defining an appropriate prior distribution [10]. In this paper, maximum a posteriori (MAP) method is utilized to reformulate the HSI super-resolution problem, which is formulated as

$$\begin{aligned} & \arg\max_{\mathcal{G}, U_1, U_2, U_3} p(\mathcal{G}, U_1, U_2, U_3 \ominus | \mathcal{Y}, \mathcal{Z}) \\ & = \arg\max_{\mathcal{G}, U_1, U_2, U_3} \frac{p(\mathcal{Y} | \mathcal{G}, U_1, U_2, U_3) p(\mathcal{Z} | \mathcal{G}, U_1, U_2, U_3) p(\mathcal{G}) p(U_1, U_2, U_3)}{p(\mathcal{Y}, \mathcal{Z})} \end{aligned} \tag{3}$$

$p(\mathcal{Y}, \mathcal{Z})$ is regarded as a constant, because the Gaussian error $\mathcal{E}_H$ and $\mathcal{E}_M$ are independent. Evidently, the probability density function (PDF) $p(\mathcal{Y} | \mathcal{G}, U_1, U_2, U_3)$ and $p(\mathcal{Z} | \mathcal{G}, U_1, U_2, U_3)$ are determined by the PDF of the error $\mathcal{E}_H$ and $\mathcal{E}_M$ in (3), usually assumed to be Gaussian with independent, and identically distributed. Consequently, the coherences given by the degradation model in (2) among the desired HR-HSI, input LR-HSI and HR-MSI are expressed as follows:

$$p(\mathcal{Y} | \mathcal{G}, U_1, U_2, U_3) = \frac{1}{(2\pi\sigma_y)^{I_M J_M K_H/2}} \times \exp\left\{ -\|\mathcal{Y} - [\![\mathcal{G}; P_1 U_1, P_2 U_2, U_3]\!]\|_F^2 / 2\sigma_y \right\} \tag{4}$$

$$p(\mathcal{Z} | \mathcal{G}, U_1, U_2, U_3) = \frac{1}{(2\pi\sigma_z)^{I_H J_H K_M/2}} \times \exp\left\{ -\|\mathcal{Z} - [\![\mathcal{G}; U_1, U_2, P_M U_3]\!]\|_F^2 / 2\sigma_z \right\} \tag{5}$$

where $\sigma_y$ and $\sigma_z$ are the variances of the error $\mathcal{E}_H$ and $\mathcal{E}_M$, and $\|\cdot\|_F$ denotes the Frobenius norm. As shown in Formula (3), the HSI super-resolution problem is cast as maximizing the posterior distribution with respect to $\mathcal{G}$, $U_1$, $U_2$, $U_3$. Similar to the work in [11], we assume that the PDF of core tensor $p(\mathcal{G})$ follows the spherical Gaussian distributions [12], i.e.,

$$p(\mathcal{G}) = \exp\left\{-\|\mathcal{G}\|_F^2/2\sigma_g\right\}/\left(2\pi\sigma_g\right)^{I_H J_H K_H/2} \qquad (6)$$

where $\sigma_g$ denotes the variance of the error. Note that the model order of core tensor $\mathcal{G}$ is identical to the original tensor $\mathcal{X}$ throughout the study, namely $I_H = R_1$, $J_H = R_2$, $K_H = R_3$.

The last PDF $p(U_1, U_2, U_3)$ represents some image priors characterizing the intrinsic structures of the HR-HSI such as low-rank [6, 7]. Another significant, yet less exploited, property is the smoothness [11, 13, 14]. HSI smooths, which implies that adjacent elements are similar or continuously changing. In the next subsection, we will discuss it in detail.

### 3.3 Smooth Coupled Tucker Decomposition Model

HSI illustrates the spatial-spectral continuity, which implies the spatial and spectral piecewise smooth property of HSI. That is to say, given an HSI $\mathcal{X} \in \mathbb{R}^{I_H \times J_H \times K_H}$, each element of $\mathcal{X}$ is generally similar to its adjacent elements or continuously changing with each mode, i.e., $x_{i_H, j_H, k_H}$ should be close to $x_{i_H \pm 1, j_H, k_H}$, $x_{i_H, j_H \pm 1, k_H}$ and $x_{i_H, j_H, k_H \pm 1}$.

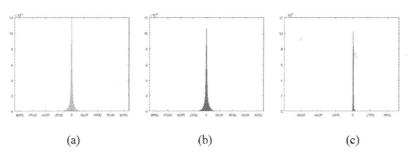

(a)      (b)      (c)

**Fig. 1.** The difference value statistics of Pavia University along (a) column, (b) row and (c) spectral mode.

As shown in the histograms in Fig. 1, most of the difference values are nearly equal to zero along column, row and spectral direction of the Pavia University dataset, which justifies the characteristics of smoothness of HSI [1]. In this study, instead of imposing the smooth constraints in image domain, which merely embodies the intuitional structures, we model the latent smoothness of $U_1$, $U_2$, $U_3$ in the multilinear space to characterize the intrinsic prior knowledge of HSI.

**Definition 1:** For a third-order tensor $\mathcal{X} \in \mathbb{R}^{I_H \times J_H \times K_H}$, we formally define the PDF of the latent smoothness of the tensor as

$$p(U_1, U_2, U_3) = \prod_{n=1}^{3} \exp\left(-\alpha_n \|D_n U_n\|_p^p\right) \tag{7}$$

where $D_1 \in \mathbb{R}^{(I_H - 1) \times I_H}$, $D_2 \in \mathbb{R}^{(J_H - 1) \times J_H}$ and $D_3 \in \mathbb{R}^{(K_H - 1) \times K_H}$. The entries of $D_n$ in the main diagonal are 1, the entries of $D_n$ in the upper secondary diagonal are -1 and the other entries are all 0. $p \in \{1, 2\}$ is a parameter to select the prior distributions of factor gradient. Particularly, when $p = 1$, the factor gradient follows Laplace distribution; when $p = 2$, then the factor gradient follows Gaussian distribution.

By taking the negative logarithmic function of the probability in (4)–(7), the MAP formulation in (3) amounts to solve an unconstrained minimization problem as follows:

$$\min_{\mathcal{G}, U_1, U_2, U_3} \|\mathcal{Y} - [\![\mathcal{G}; P_1 U_1, P_2 U_2, U_3]\!]\|_F^2 + \sum_{n=1}^{3} \alpha_n \|D_n U_n\|_p^p \tag{8}$$
$$+ \|\mathcal{Z} - [\![\mathcal{G}; U_1, U_2, P_M U_3]\!]\|_F^2 + \lambda \|\mathcal{G}\|_F^2$$

where $\alpha_n$ and $\lambda$ denote the regularization parameters. Correspondingly, Formula (8) is called the SCTD for HSI super-resolution.

## 3.4 Optimization

Optimizing Formula (8) is a non-convex problem by solving $\mathcal{G}, U_1, U_2$ and $U_3$ jointly and we can barely obtain the closed-form solutions for $\mathcal{G}, U_1, U_2$ and $U_3$ [1]. However, with respect to each block of variables, the objective function in (8) is convex while keeping the other variables fixed [1]. A hybrid framework is utilized with proximal alternating optimization [15, 16] and the alternating direction method of multipliers (ADMM) [17] to solve the objective function in (8), then the proposed models can be guaranteed to converge to a stationary point of the original NP-hard problem [1]. Based on the framework of proximal alternating optimization, the function in (8) is reformulated as four sub-problems with respect to $\mathcal{G}, U_1, U_2$ and $U_3$.

$$\begin{cases} \mathcal{G} = \arg\min_{\mathcal{G}} f(\mathcal{G}, U_1, U_2, U_3) + \beta \|\mathcal{G} - \mathcal{G}'\|_F^2 \\ U_1 = \arg\min_{U_1} f(\mathcal{G}, U_1, U_2, U_3) + \beta \|U_1 - U_1'\|_F^2 \\ U_2 = \arg\min_{U_2} f(\mathcal{G}, U_1, U_2, U_3) + \beta \|U_2 - U_2'\|_F^2 \\ U_3 = \arg\min_{U_3} f(\mathcal{G}, U_1, U_2, U_3) + \beta \|U_3 - U_3'\|_F^2 \end{cases} \tag{9}$$

where $f(\mathcal{G}, U_1, U_2, U_3)$ is implicitly defined in (8), $(\cdot)'$ denotes the estimated blocks of variables in the previous iteration and $\beta > 0$. Subsequently, we will present the optimizations for variables $\mathcal{G}, U_1, U_2$ and $U_3$ in detail.

(a)   The sub-problem with respect to $\mathcal{G}$

Fixing the variables $U_1$, $U_2$ and $U_3$, the optimization to core tensor $\mathcal{G}$ is formulated as

$$\min_{\mathcal{G}} \|\mathcal{Y} - [\![\mathcal{G}; P_1 U_1, P_2 U_2, U_3]\!]\|_F^2 + \|\mathcal{Z} - [\![\mathcal{G}; U_1, U_2, P_M U_3]\!]\|_F^2 + \lambda\|\mathcal{G}\|_F^2 + \beta\|\mathcal{G} - \mathcal{G}'\|_F^2 \tag{10}$$

By introducing two auxiliary variables $\mathcal{G}_1$ and $\mathcal{G}_2$, the problem in (10) can be efficiently solved by the ADMM framework, and then the problem in (10) turns to solving the augmented Lagrange function $\mathcal{L}(\mathcal{G}, \mathcal{G}_1, \mathcal{G}_2, \mathcal{M}_1, \mathcal{M}_2)$ as follows:

$$\mathcal{L}(\mathcal{G}, \mathcal{G}_1, \mathcal{G}_2, \mathcal{M}_1, \mathcal{M}_2) = \|\mathcal{Y} - [\![\mathcal{G}_1; P_1 U_1, P_2 U_2, U_3]\!]\|_F^2 + \|\mathcal{Z} - [\![\mathcal{G}_2; U_1, U_2, P_M U_3]\!]\|_F^2$$
$$+ \lambda\|\mathcal{G}\|_F^2 + \beta\|\mathcal{G} - \mathcal{G}'\|_F^2 + \mu\|\mathcal{G} - \mathcal{G}_1 - \mathcal{M}_1\|_F^2 + \mu\|\mathcal{G} - \mathcal{G}_2 - \mathcal{M}_2\|_F^2 \tag{11}$$

where $\mathcal{M}_1$ and $\mathcal{M}_2$ are Lagrange multipliers. $\mu$ denotes penalty parameter. Therefore, the above optimization problem is further divided into several sub-problems, which all have closed-form solutions. Here we omit the detailed derivations for lack of space.

---

**Algorithm: The SCTD model for the HSI Super-resolution**

**Input:** LR-HSI $\mathcal{Y}$, HR-MSI $\mathcal{Z}$, $P_1$, $P_2$, $P_M$, $D_n$ (n=1, 2, 3), the parameters $\lambda$, $\beta$, $\mu$, $\mu_n$ (n=1, 2, 3) and $\alpha_n$ (n=1, 2, 3).

**Output:** the factor matrices $U_1$, $U_2$, $U_3$ and the core tensor $\mathcal{G}$

**Initialize:** Generate pseudo random factor matrices $U_1$, $U_2$, $U_3$ and core tensor $\mathcal{G}$

   **While not converged do**
   a)   Solve the core tensor $\mathcal{G}$ via ADMM framework
   b.I)   Solve factor matrices $U_n$ (n=1, 2, 3) by CG method (SCTD-QV)
   b.II)   Solve factor matrices $U_n$ (n=1, 2, 3) via ADMM framework (SCTD-TV)
   **End while**

---

(b)   The sub-problem with respect to $U_1$.

Fixing the variables $\mathcal{G}$, $U_2$ and $U_3$, the optimization to $U_1$ is formulated as

$$\min_{U_1} \|\mathcal{Y} - [\![\mathcal{G}; P_1 U_1, P_2 U_2, U_3]\!]\|_F^2 + \|\mathcal{Z} - [\![\mathcal{G}; U_1, U_2, P_M U_3]\!]\|_F^2 + \alpha_1\|D_1 U_1\|_p^p + \beta\|U_1 - U_1'\|_F^2 \tag{12}$$

By operating the 1-mode unfolding of the function in (12), and we have

$$\min_{U_1} \|Y_{(1)} - \mathbf{P}_1 U_1 F_1\|_F^2 + \|Z_{(1)} - U_1 G_1\|_F^2 + \alpha_1\|D_1 U_1\|_p^p + \beta\|U_1 - U_1'\|_F^2 \tag{13}$$

where $Y_{(1)}$ is the 1-mode unfolding of LR-HSI $\mathcal{Y}$, $Z_{(1)}$ represents the 1-mode unfolding of HR-MSI $\mathcal{Z}$. $F_1 = (\mathcal{G} \times_2 P_2 U_2 \times_3 U_3)_{(1)}$, $G_1 = (\mathcal{G} \times_2 U_2 \times_3 P_M U_3)_{(1)}$.

i.  when $p = 2$, namely corresponding to the SCTD-QV model.

   The optimization problem in (13) is quadratic and its solution is equivalent to solve a general Sylvester equation [1],

$$P_1^T P_1 U_1 F_1 F_1^T + U_1 \left( G_1 G_1^T + \beta I \right) + 2\alpha_1 D_1^T D_1 U_1 = P_1^T Y_{(1)} F_1^T + \beta U_1' + Z_{(1)} G_1^T \tag{14}$$

   Here the system matrix in Eq. (14) is positive definite and symmetrical, thus, we utilize the conjugate gradient (CG) method to get the globally optimal solution for (14).

ii. when $p = 1$, namely corresponding to the SCTD-TV model.

By introducing auxiliary variables $Q_1$, the problem in (13) is efficiently solved by ADMM framework, and then the problem in (13) is transformed into the augmented Lagrangian function as follows:

$$\mathcal{L}_1(U_1, Q_1, O_1) = \left\| Y_{(1)} - \mathbf{P_1} U_1 F_1 \right\|_F^2 + \left\| Z_{(1)} - U_1 G_1 \right\|_F^2 + \alpha_1 \| Q_1 \|_1$$
$$+ \beta \left\| U_1 - U_1' \right\|_F^2 + \mu_1 \left\| Q_1 - D_1 U_1 + \frac{O_1}{2\mu_1} \right\|_F^2 \tag{15}$$

where $O_1$ is the Lagrange multiplier, and $\mu_1$ denotes penalty parameter. Therefore, the optimization problem in (11) is further divided into several sub-problems. And the sub-problems with respect to $U_2$ and $U_3$ are similar to the optimization with respect to $U_1$. Here we also omit the detailed derivations for lack of space.

In this study, two smooth constraints are employed, total variation (SCTD-TV) and quadratic variation (SCTD-QV) on factor matrices. In addition, the corresponding algorithms are invoked for model learning. **Algorithm** summarizes each step of the SCTD-QV and SCTD-TV model. However, for lack of space, a discussion of the detailed derivations of the proposed SCTD-TV and SCTD-QV algorithms are omitted and will be deferred until a later journal version.

## 4   Experimental Results

All the experiments are conducted using MATLAB R2020a on the computer with Core i7–10700 CPU with 2.90GHz and 64GB RAM. The source code will be available on the following URL: http://github.com/polwork/.

### 4.1   Experimental Settings and Implementation Issues

In this part, two HSI datasets, namely Pavia University and Pavia Centre, which are acquired by the reflective optics system imaging spectrometer [18], are used to compare the performances of our proposed SCTD-QV and SCTD-TV models with several state-of-the-art HSI super-resolution approaches, including the TenRec [5], STEREO [5], SCOTT [7] and CSTF [4].

The metrics used for assessing the quality of the recovered HSI contain reconstruction signal-to-noise ratio (R-SNR), correlation coefficient (CC), spectral angle mapper (SAM), relative dimensionless global error in synthesis (ERGAS). In this study, we follow the definitions of the above metrics in [7]. And the smaller SAM and ERGAS and the higher R-SNR and CC show better quality of the recovered HSI.

The area of $256 \times 256$ is cropped as the reference HR-HSI in two datasets. Then the corresponding LR-HSIs are simulated by averaging the $4 \times 4$ and $8 \times 8$ disjoint spatial blocks in Pavia University and Pavia Centre, respectively. Both of the simulated HR-MSIs are produced by filtering the HR-HSI with an IKONOS like reflectance spectral response [19] in two datasets.

The algorithm always converges in few iterations in our implementations.

## 4.2  Experimental Results

Table 1 and Table 2 show the quantitative results of the Pavia University and Pavia Centre dataset, respectively. It can be observed from Table 1 and Table 2 that SCTD-QV gets the best scores for R-SNR, CC and SAM. The recovered results of the 90-th and the 74-th bands and corresponding error images of two datasets are shown in Fig. 2 and Fig. 3. From Fig. 2, the error images show that the recovered results obtained by STEREO, SCOTT and TenRec have obvious artifacts whereas this problem is milder with the proposed methods leading to better recovery performance of SCTD-QV and SCTD-TV. From the error images in Fig. 3, one can observe that the recovered results produced by the proposed methods have fewer errors than the others. The experiments solidly demonstrate the effectiveness of the proposed subspace smooth priors.

**Table 1.** Quantitative results on the Pavia University

| Algorithm | Pavia University | | | | |
|---|---|---|---|---|---|
| | R-SNR | CC | SAM | ERGAS | Time/s |
| TenRec | 28.35 | 0.996 | 2.226 | 1.151 | 24.26 |
| STEREO | 28.27 | 0.996 | 2.249 | 1.163 | 26.19 |
| SCOTT | 27.86 | 0.996 | 2.044 | 1.145 | **6.735** |
| CSTF | 31.25 | 0.997 | 1.505 | **0.777** | 85.08 |
| SCTD-QV | **31.43** | **0.998** | **1.447** | 0.804 | 3639 |
| SCTD-TV | 30.41 | **0.998** | 1.712 | 0.905 | 5778 |

## 4.3  Choice of Model Order

In this part, we have a closer look at the selection of model order in the proposed SCTD-QV and SCTD-TV models. The performances of the proposed two models are analyzed (R-SNR and SAM) with respect to the model order used in the SCTD. As shown in Fig. 4, the R-SNR and SAM are optimal when the model order tends to be the size of data. This

**Table 2.** Quantitative results on the Pavia Centre

| Algorithm | Pavia Centre | | | | |
|---|---|---|---|---|---|
| | R-SNR | CC | SAM | ERGAS | Time/s |
| TenRec | 24.71 | 0.985 | 5.581 | 2.121 | 23.79 |
| STEREO | 24.53 | 0.984 | 5.686 | 2.175 | 26.35 |
| SCOTT | 27.56 | 0.991 | 3.719 | 0.846 | **7.798** |
| CSTF | 28.4 | **0.992** | 3.441 | 0.777 | 90.57 |
| SCTD-QV | **28.59** | **0.992** | **3.345** | **0.761** | 4199 |
| SCTD-TV | 28.28 | **0.992** | 3.473 | 0.793 | 4144 |

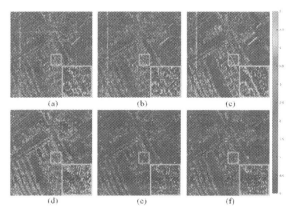

**Fig. 2.** Comparisons of the HSI super-resolution results of the 90-th band for Pavia University. (a) TenRec. (b) STEREO. (c) SCOTT. (d) CSTF. (e) SCTD-QV. (f) SCTD-TV.

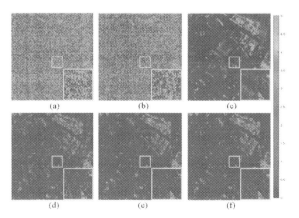

**Fig. 3.** Comparisons of the HSI super-resolution results of the 74-th band for Pavia Centre. (a) TenRec. (b) STEREO. (c) SCOTT. (d) CSTF. (e) SCTD-QV. (f) SCTD-TV.

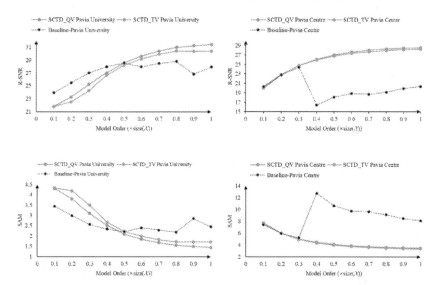

**Fig. 4.** R-SNR and SAM as functions of model order on two HSI datasets.

implies that there is no need to carefully tune the model order in our models, because we can simply preset the model order as the size of data. Because of the existing of unrecoverable area, SCOTT cannot fairly compare with our models in Fig. 4. In Fig. 4, CSTF with random initializations is compared as baseline. CSTF and SCOTT fail to constrain the variable factor matrices and core tensor respectively, hence it is necessary to preset an appropriate model order to mitigate the ill-posedness. On the contrary, due to the constraints on both the factor matrices and core tensor under MAP, the sensitivity to the model order in our models can be alleviated compared to the tensor low-rank based and sparsity-based methods.

## 5 Conclusion

In this study, a novel smooth coupled Tucker decomposition using both local and global structural information is proposed to mitigate the sensitivity of selecting optimal model order. Besides, the integration of the latent smoothness compensates for the deficiencies that traditional Tucker decomposition merely reveals the global structural information of HSI. In future work, we will investigate the effect of core tensor sparsity in the SCTD model. We expect this study can open a new perspective on smoothness with different tensor decomposition models for HSI super-resolution.

**Acknowledgements.** This work was supported in part by the National Natural Science Foundation of China under Grant 61371152 and Grant 61771391, in part by the Shenzhen Municipal Science and Technology Innovation Committee under Grant JCYJ20170815162956949 and JCYJ20180306171146740 and in part by Key R&D Plan of Shaanxi Province 2020ZDLGY07–11, by Natural Science Basic Research plan in Shaanxi Province of China 2018JM6056 and by the innovation Foundation for Doctor Dissertation of Northwestern Polytechnical University CX2021081.

# 1. References

1. Bu, Y., et al.: Hyperspectral and multispectral image fusion via graph laplacian-guided coupled tensor decomposition. IEEE Trans. Geosci. Remote Sens. **59**(1), 648–662 (2020)
2. Xue, J., Zhao, Y.Q., Bu, Y., Liao, W., Chan, J.C.W., Philips, W.: Spatial-spectral structured sparse low-rank representation for hyperspectral image super-resolution. IEEE Trans. Image Process. **30**, 3084–3097 (2021)
3. Li, H., Li, W., Han, G., Liu, F.: Coupled tensor decomposition for hyperspectral pansharpening. IEEE Access **6**, 34 206–34 213 (2018)
4. Li, S., Dian, R., Fang, L., Bioucas-Dias, J.M.: Fusing hyperspectral and multispectral images via coupled sparse tensor factorization. IEEE Trans. Image Process. **27**(8), 4118–4130 (2018)
5. Kanatsoulis, C.I., Fu, X., Sidiropoulos, N.D., Ma, W.-K.: Hyperspectral super-resolution: a coupled tensor factorization approach. IEEE Trans. Signal Process. **66**(24), 6503–6517 (2018)
6. Prevost, C., Usevich, K., Comon, P., Brie, D.: Hyperspectral super-resolution with coupled tucker approximation: Identifiability and SVD-based algorithms, November 2018, working paper or preprint. https://hal.archives-ouvertes.fr/hal-01911969
7. Prvost, C., Usevich, K., Comon, P., Brie, D.: Coupled tensor low-rank multilinear approximation for hyperspectral super-resolution. In: ICASSP 2019 - 2019 IEEE International Conference on Acoustics, Speech and Signal Processing (ICASSP), pp. 5536–5540 (2019)
8. Wang, B., Yang, L., Zhao, Y.: Polo: learning explicit cross-modality fusion for temporal action localization. IEEE Signal Process. Lett. **28**, 503–507 (2021)
9. Wald, L., Ranchin, T., Mangolini, M.: Fusion of satellite images of different spatial resolutions: assessing the quality of resulting images. Photogramm. Eng. Rem. S. **63**(6), 691–699 (1997)
10. Yokoya, N., Grohnfeldt, C., Chanussot, J.: Hyperspectral and multispectral data fusion: a comparative review of the recent literature. IEEE Geosci. Remote Sens. Mag. **5**(2), 29–56 (2017)
11. Xue, J., Zhao, Y., Liao, W., Chan, J.C., Kong, S.G.: Enhanced sparsity prior model for low-rank tensor completion. IEEE Trans. Neural Netw. Learn. Syst. 1–15 (2019)
12. Salakhutdinov, R., Mnih, A.: Probabilistic matrix factorization. In: Proceedings Advanced International Conference Neural Information Processing System, pp. 1257–1264 (2007)
13. Yokota, T., Zhao, Q., Cichocki, A.: Smooth PARAFAC decomposition for tensor completion. IEEE Trans. Signal Process. **64**(20), 5423–5436 (2016)
14. Imaizumi, M., Hayashi, K.: Tensor decomposition with smoothness, ser. Proceedings of Machine Learning Research. Precup, D., Teh, Y.W. (eds.) vol. 70. International Convention Centre, Sydney, Australia: PMLR, 06–11 Aug 2017, pp. 1597–1606 (2017). http://proceedings.mlr.press/v70/imaizumi17a.html
15. Attouch, H., Bolte, J., Redont, P., Soubeyran, A.: Proximal alternating minimization and projection methods for nonconvex problems: an approach based on the kurdyka-łojasiewicz inequality. Math. Oper. Res. **35**(2), 438–457 (2010)
16. Huang, K., Sidiropoulos, N.D., Liavas, A.P.: A flexible and efficient algorithmic framework for constrained matrix and tensor factorization. IEEE Trans. Signal Process. **64**(19), 5052–5065 (2016)
17. Boyd, S., Parikh, N., Chu, E., Peleato, B., Eckstein, J., et al.: Distributed optimization and statistical learning via the alternating direction method of multipliers. Foundat. Trends Mach. Learn. **3**(1), 1–122 (2011)
18. Dell'Acqua, F., Gamba, P., Ferrari, A., Palmason, J.A., Benediktsson, J.A., Arnason, K.: Exploiting spectral and spatial information in hyperspectral urban data with high resolution. IEEE Geosci. Remote Sens. Lett. **1**(4), 322–326 (2004)
19. Wei, Q., Dobigeon, N., Tourneret, J.-Y.: Fast fusion of multi-band images based on solving a sylvester equation. IEEE Trans. Image Process. **24**(11), 4109–4121 (2015)

# Self-Supervised Video Super-Resolution by Spatial Constraint and Temporal Fusion

Cuixin Yang[1,2,3,4,5], Hongming Luo[1,2,3,4,5], Guangsen Liao[1,2,3,4,5],
Zitao Lu[1,2,3,4,5], Fei Zhou[1,2,3,4,5(✉)], and Guoping Qiu[1,3,4,5]

[1] College of Electronics and Information Engineering, Shenzhen University,
Shenzhen, China
[2] Peng Cheng Laboratory, Shenzhen, China
[3] Guangdong Key Laboratory of Intelligent Information Processing, Shenzhen, China
[4] Shenzhen Institute for Artificial Intelligence and Robotics for Society, Shenzhen,
China
[5] Key Laboratory of Digital Creative Technology,
Shenzhen, China

**Abstract.** To avoid any fallacious assumption on the degeneration procedure in preparing training data, some self-similarity based super-
resolution (SR) algorithms have been proposed to exploit the internal
recurrence of patches without relying on external datasets. However, the
network architectures of those "zero-shot" SR methods are often shallow. Otherwise they would suffer from the over-fitting problem due to
the limited samples within a single image. This restricts the strong power
of deep neural networks (DNNs). To relieve this problem, we propose a
middle-layer feature loss to allow the network architecture to be deeper
for handling the video super-resolution (VSR) task in a self-supervised
way. Specifically, we constrain the middle-layer feature of VSR network to
be as similar as that of the corresponding single image super-resolution
(SISR) in a Spatial Module, then fuse the inter-frame information in
a Temporal Fusion Module. Experimental results demonstrate that the
proposed algorithm achieves significantly superior results on real-world
data in comparison with some state-of-the-art methods.

**Keywords:** Video super-resolution · Self-supervision · Deep learning.

## 1 Introduction

Video super-resolution (VSR) aims at recovering high-resolution (HR) video
frames from its corresponding low-resolution (LR) video sequence, which is a
classical and meaningful low-level computer vision problem. VSR has been widely
applied into many fields, such as video surveillance and display of high-definition
devices. Specifically, as the prevalence of the HR displays, such as high definition
television and ultra high definition television, VSR is under great demand in our
daily life.

© Springer Nature Switzerland AG 2021
H. Ma et al. (Eds.): PRCV 2021, LNCS 13021, pp. 249–260, 2021.
https://doi.org/10.1007/978-3-030-88010-1_21

In recent years, VSR is attracting more and more attention, and many VSR algorithms have been proposed, which can be categorized into traditional methods and deep learning based methods. The method in [11] proposed to estimate motion, blur kernel as well as noise level, and reconstruct HR frames based on the Bayesian inference. Deep neural network (DNN) was introduced into VSR in a pioneer work [8]. From then on, numerous deep learning based methods which rely on deep neural networks, such as convolutional neural networks (CNNs) [17] and recurrent convolutional neural networks (RCNNs) [7] have been proposed. However, in a supervised manner, the above deep learning based methods are trained exhaustively on large external datasets, where LR frames are downscaled from their HR counterparts with a fixed known kernel, like MATLAB bicubic. While the degradation process of real-world data is unknown and complex, the performance of those supervised methods would deteriorate notably when the degradation of test images does not match with that adopted in the training phase.

Some researchers have noticed this drawback and attempted to alleviate this simulated-to-real gap. In the field of single image super-resolution (SISR), some efforts [3,5,14] have been made to exploit the recurrence of patches across scales of a single image and utilise the internal information within a specific image to super-resolve itself without external prior, which can be seen as unsupervised "zero-shot" methods. However, there are few corresponding researches [10,13] in VSR, though such recurrence of similar patches is much more common in the spatio-temporal search space. According to our observation, the reasonable interpretation is the network architectures in the above "zero-shot" algorithms in SISR is too simple and shallow, e.g., 8 convolutional layers in [14]. It is attributed to the limited information of the internal data within a single image, which is difficult to process multiple frames in VSR. Otherwise, deep networks will result in overfitting easily in several iterations. In VSR, [13] did not take advantage of the powerful CNN and [10] produced blurry results due to the training on external datasets. Therefore, in the proposed method, to make full use of the powerful ability of CNN and the internal data, a middle-layer feature constraint is introduced to allow the VSR network architecture to be designed deep enough to handle the information from multiple frames in a specific video sequence. In general, the advantage of the added middle-layer feature constraint is two-fold: on one hand, it alleviates the over-fitting problem in a deeper network; on the other hand, it leverages the training process in case of vanishing gradient. Moreover, the contents of spatial and temporal dimensions are processed separately to take advantage of the internal data inside a video sequence.

## 2   Related Work

Due to a great drop of performance of the state-of-the-art SR networks that are trained on the ideally downsampled examples, internal data driven SR methods are appealing increasing interests among the research community. In this section, we focus on the most relevant self-similarity based SR algorithms, which can be divided into two categories: SISR and VSR.

## 2.1   SISR

A unified framework was proposed in [3] for exploiting recurrence of patches within the same scale and across different scales of a single image. [5] handled perspective distortion and additional affine transformation to enlarge the limited internal patch search space. By utilising both hierarchical random forests and self-example random forests, SRHRF+ [6] proposed to combine the benefits from external and internal examples. Taking advantage of the power of deep learning, ZSSR [14] exploited the similar patches across the same and across scales within the given image by a simple convolutional neural network. Combining the advantages of large external datasets and internal statistical prior, MLSR [1] employed meta-learning technique to finetune the externally pretrained network and adapted the meta-trained network to the test image at last. [15] also incorporated meta-learning to reduce the inference time.

## 2.2   VSR

In recent years, more and more attention has been paid to the field of VSR as SISR has obtained remarkable improvements since deep learning is introduced into SR, and the performance of state-of-the-art SISR is almost at the peak which is difficult to further improve. Although a few self-similarity based SISR methods have been proposed, there are few corresponding researches in VSR.

Observing that similar patches recur many times across space and time, [13] proposed the self-similarity based Space-Time SR method. In order to make use of external prior and internal information within a specific video sequence, DynaVSR [10] extended MLSR to the task of VSR.

However, the networks of those methods without training on external datasets are quite shallow due to the limited information from a single image or a video sequence, which constrains the powerful ability of convolutional neural network. In the meanwhile, the methods relying on external datasets often produce blurry results due to the external prior is too strong to adapt the test data at hand properly. Therefore, we propose to add a middle-layer feature constraint into the VSR network so that we are able to train a deep video-specific network to make full use of the recurrence of small patches within and across different spatio-temporal scales and take advantage of the powerful convolutional neural network.

## 3   Methodology

### 3.1   Overview

Given $(2N + 1)$ LR video frames $I_{[t-N:t+N]}^{LR}$, we denote $t$ as the moment of the current frame and $N$ as the temporal radius. By only using their internal data, our goal is to restore an HR video frame $I_t^{HR}$ in a self-supervised way. A video-specific model for VSR is depicted in Fig. 1, where LR video frames are downscaled into their lower versions (LLR), which are denoted as $I_{[t-N:t+N]}^{LLR}$

$(N = 2)$. In this way, we have two pairs of relationship: $\{I^{LR}_{t\in\mathcal{T}}, I^{HR}_{t\in\mathcal{T}}\}$ and $\{I^{LLR}_{t\in\mathcal{T}}, I^{LR}_{t\in\mathcal{T}}\}$, where $\mathcal{T} = [t - N : t + N]$. Thus, the constructed $\{I^{LLR}_{t\in\mathcal{T}}, I^{LR}_{t\in\mathcal{T}}\}$ pairs serve as the inputs and targets of the model during the training as shown in Fig. 1. After the training, it is considered to have the ability of obtaining a well-restored $\hat{I}^{LR}_t$ from $I^{LLR}_{[t-N:t+N]}$. In other words, this model represents the recovery from multiple "LR" video frames to an "HR" video frame of the given LR video frames. Therefore, once the learned recovery is applied to the LR video sequence at hand, an HR video frame would be reconstructed during the testing. This process can be depicted as

$$\hat{I}^{LR}_t = f_{SS\_VSR}(I^{LLR}_{[t-N:t+N]}) \tag{1}$$

$$\hat{I}^{HR}_t = f_{SS\_VSR}(I^{LR}_{[t-N:t+N]}) \tag{2}$$

where $f_{SS\_VSR}(\cdot)$ denotes the CNN shown in Fig. 1. In Sect. 3.3, we will embody this CNN and detail strategy to train it.

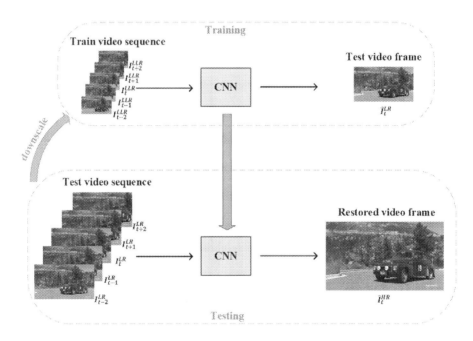

**Fig. 1.** Video-specific CNN in VSR. In the training stage, the video-specific CNN is trained on the internal spatio-temporal patches extracted from the test video sequence. The CNN learns to reconstruct the current video frame from the LLR video sequence. Then the trained CNN is applied to the test video sequence to restore the HR current video frame.

## 3.2   Internal-Data Based VSR

It is observed that there are many similar small patches across different scales within a natural image [3,18]. The key of example-based and self-similarity based methods is to learn how to add high-frequency details in HR patches to the similar LR patch in order to obtain an HR and visually pleasing image with more details. In a video sequence, the recurrence of similar small patches across spatial and temporal dimensions within a series of consecutive frames are much more abundant [13]. Therefore, it is believed that better performance can be achieved by utilizing multi-frame information in VSR. In contrast to those external-data driven methods, internal-data based VSR methods need not exhaustive training on large external datasets while are robust to various degraded data.

## 3.3   Spatio-Temporal VSR

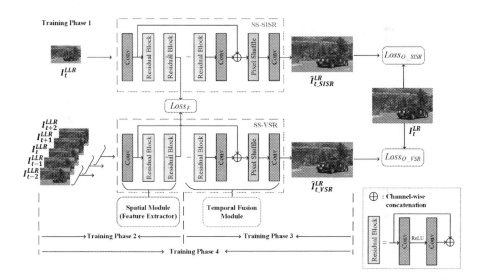

**Fig. 2.** Overall training procedure for the proposed framework. We firstly train the SS-SISR network in Training Phase 1. When training SS-VSR network, as depicted in Training Phase 2, the SM is trained under the feature loss calculated between the middle-layer features from SS-SISR and SS-VSR. In Training Phase 3, the TFM is trained while the parameters of the SM are fixed as the feature extractor. At last, the whole SS-VSR network is finetuned in Training Phase 4.

SISR has been studied for decades and features of the image SR network are excellent in representing the global information of a single image which is considered as spatial information in VSR. Therefore, it motivates us to spatially process video frames at first in the task of VSR to obtain expressive features

254 C. Yang et al.

as those in SISR. In this paper, the proposed SISR network is denoted as SS-SISR, and the proposed VSR network, i.e. the video-specific CNN in Fig. 1. Then the multiple features from the corresponding frames are fused in the following Temporal Fusion Module (TFM).

In general, we divide the whole training procedure into 4 phases shown in Fig. 2. In Training Phase 1, SS-SISR which is in the red dashed rectangle in Fig. 2 aims to super-resolve the single current frame, providing prior knowledge for the following training of SS-VSR which is in the purple dashed rectangle in Fig. 2. The training for SS-SISR, i.e., Training Phase 1, can be achieved by

$$Loss_{O\_SISR} = \left\| I_t^{LR} - f_{SS\_SISR}(I_t^{LLR}) \right\|_1 \qquad (3)$$

where $f_{SS\_SISR}(\cdot)$ denotes the network of SS-SISR, $I_t^{LLR}$ denotes the LLR current frame inputted into SS-SISR, and $Loss_{O\_SISR}$ is the loss function for Training Phase 1 which is a constraint between the predicted output $\hat{I}_{t\_SISR}^{LR}$ of SS-SISR and the "groundtruth" $I_t^{LR}$ shown in Fig. 2. Specifically speaking, in order to urge the middle-layer feature from multiple frames in SS-VSR to "learn" from the feature from the corresponding single frame in SS-SISR, we define a feature loss between these two features to constrain the former to be as closer as possible to the latter:

$$Loss_F = \left\| F_{t\_SISR} - F_{t\_VSR} \right\|_1 \qquad (4)$$

where $F_{t\_SISR}$ and $F_{t\_VSR}$ denote the middle-layer features from SS-SISR and SS-VSR for the LLR current frame, respectively, and $Loss_F$ represents the feature loss.

Then we start to train SS-VSR. In SS-VSR shown at the bottom of Fig. 2, 5 consecutive LLR frames are inputted into the network and a predicted LR frame is output at the end of the network:

$$\hat{I}_{t\_VSR}^{LR} = f_{SS\_VSR}(I_{[t-2:t+2]}^{LLR}) \qquad (5)$$

where $f_{SS\_VSR}(\cdot)$ denotes the network of SS-VSR, and $I_{[t-2:t+2]}^{LLR}$ is 5 consecutive LLR frames as the input of SS-VSR while $\hat{I}_{t\_VSR}^{LR}$ is the predicted output for the current frame of SS-VSR. Notably, as shown in the input of SS-VSR in Fig. 2, $I_{[t-2:t+2]}^{LLR}$ is divided into 3 groups, each of which includes 3 consecutive frames, and they are $I_{t-2}^{LLR} \sim I_t^{LLR}$, $I_{t-1}^{LLR} \sim I_{t+1}^{LLR}$, and $I_t^{LLR} \sim I_{t+2}^{LLR}$ respectively. As described in the Spatial Module (SM) in Fig. 2, Training Phase 2 is to train the former part of SS-VSR (one convolutional layer and two residual blocks) to urge the fusion feature of 3 central LLR frames $\{I_{t-1}^{LLR}, I_t^{LLR}, I_{t+1}^{LLR}\}$ to be "similar" as that of the single current frame $I_t^{LLR}$. The advantage of the SM is two-fold: on one hand, the spatial prior in SISR domain (source domain) is transferred to the VSR domain (target domain) to supervise how to fuse the information from 3 consecutive frames well; on the other hand, the motion among these frames is captured by the network, and thus the 2 neighbouring frames are aligned with the current frame in an implicit way. In the following Training Phase 3, the parameters of SM in SS-VSR are fixed, which act as a feature extractor to extract features. To be specific, as shown in Eq. (6), $I_{t-2}^{LLR} \sim I_t^{LLR}$, $I_{t-1}^{LLR} \sim I_{t+1}^{LLR}$ and $I_t^{LLR} \sim I_{t+2}^{LLR}$ are inputted into the trained feature extractor respectively, where $f_{SM}(\cdot)$ denotes the SM and $F_{i\_VSR}$ denotes the middle-layer feature from SS-VSR for the $i$-th frame, $i \in \{t-1, t, t+1\}$. Then $F_{t-1\_VSR}$, $F_{t\_VSR}$, and $F_{t+1\_VSR}$ are concatenated together as the input of the TFM. That is to say, the spatio-temporal features are inputted to train the remaining part of SS-VSR. The above procedures can be formulated as

$$
\begin{aligned}
F_{t-1\_VSR} &= f_{SM}(I_{t-2}^{LLR}; I_{t-1}^{LLR}; I_t^{LLR}) \\
F_{t\_VSR} &= f_{SM}(I_{t-1}^{LLR}; I_t^{LLR}; I_{t+1}^{LLR}) \\
F_{t+1\_VSR} &= f_{SM}(I_t^{LLR}; I_{t+1}^{LLR}; I_{t+2}^{LLR}).
\end{aligned}
\tag{6}
$$

$$
\hat{I}_{t\_TFM}^{LR} = f_{TFM}(F_{t-1\_VSR}; F_{t\_VSR}; F_{t+1\_VSR}).
\tag{7}
$$

In Eq. (7), $f_{TFM}(\cdot)$ denotes the TFM and $\hat{I}_{t\_TFM}^{LR}$ is the predicted output for the LR current frame of TFM. In the meanwhile, ';' denotes channel-wise concatenation in Eq. (6) and (7). In Training Phase 3, targeted at the LR current frame $I_t^{LR}$, we adopt the loss function $Loss_{O\_TFM}$ as

$$
Loss_{O\_TFM} = \left\| I_t^{LR} - \hat{I}_{t\_TFM}^{LR} \right\|_1.
\tag{8}
$$

At last, the whole VSR network is slightly finetuned in Training Phase 4 to adapt itself to the specific video sequence well. Notably, $Loss_{O\_VSR}$ in Eq. (9) is the loss function for Training Phase 4 and the target is still the LR current frame $I_t^{LR}$ which is as the same as that of Training Phase 1 and 3.

$$
Loss_{O\_VSR} = \left\| I_t^{LR} - \hat{I}_{t\_VSR}^{LR} \right\|_1
\tag{9}
$$

Moreover, to reduce the training time, we assume that the inter-frame motion patterns among neighbouring sequences are similar. Therefore, the model trained in the previous sequence can be used as a pretrained model for the next sequence. As a result, both the convergence and performance of the model would be better and better as video frames are consecutively super-resolved in sequence, because more and more data is "seen" by the model.

After the model of SS-VSR converges, we stop training the model and turn to the testing phase. During the testing, as illustrated in Eq. (2) and the bottom of Fig. 1, the 5 consecutive LR frames at hand are inputted into the already trained SS-VSR model, and a restored HR current frame would be obtained.

## 4 Experiments

### 4.1 Protocols

15 various real-world 360P video clips are downloaded from YouTube as our testing data, each of which includes 26 frames. In our experiments, 5 "LR"

frames are utilised to super-resolve a restored "HR" frame with the upscaling factor 2. The number of convolutional layers in SS-SISR and SS-VSR is 23 with 10 residual blocks as that used in [4]. The middle-layer feature is the output of the 5-th residual block. The number of channels in the former 5 residual blocks is set to 256, which is triple in the latter 5 residual blocks due to the channel-wise concatenation. In addition, the kernel size is $3 \times 3$, and both stride and padding are set to 1 in each convolutional layer. The batch size in our experiments is 16 and the training samples in an epoch are 5 batches. The terminal condition of each training phase is defined in (10):

$$\left( \left| \bar{l}_{(i-20:i]} - \bar{l}_{(i-40:i-20]} \right| < 0.01 \right) \wedge \left( \left| \bar{l}_{(i-40:i-20]} - \bar{l}_{(i-60:i-40]} \right| < 0.01 \right) \quad (10)$$

where $\bar{l}_{(i-k-20:i-k]}$ denotes the average loss from the $(i-k-20)$-th epoch (not included) to the $(i-k)$-th epoch ($k \in \{0, 20, 40\}$), '$\wedge$' is the logical operator of AND, and $|\cdot|$ calculates the absolute value of its argument. When the terminal condition is satisfied, the current training phase is stopped and it turns to the next training phase. The initial learning rate of Training Phase 1, 2, 3 for the first frame is set to be $10^{-4}$, and the learning rate of Training Phase 4 is $10^{-5}$, while the learning rate for the subsequent frames is halved, because the previous model is used as the pretrained model for the following sequence as mentioned in Sect. 3.3. The learning rate of each training phase is halved every 100 iterations. We use the Adam method [9] to optimise during the training.

## 4.2    Real-World Testing

The goal of our SS-VSR is to super-resolve a real-word LR video sequence whose degradation is unknown or non-ideal, which is more meaningful in practice. Thus, to prove the effectiveness of the proposed algorithm in real-world examples, we download 15 video clips whose resolution is $640 \times 360$ from YouTube and each video clip contains 26 frames. For these video clips, the HR video frames are not available, and their degradation methods remain unknown. We compare the proposed SS-VSR with the current state-of-the-art self-supervised or unsupervised SR networks: ZSSR [14], MLSR [1], DynaVSR [10]. In addition, we compare with a blind VSR method: Liu et al. [11]. All the codes of the competitors are official. In ZSSR and MLSR, a given or estimated kernel is needed to generate the LLR frames. For fairness, we adopt Kernel GAN [2] to estimate the degradation kernel of every LR test video frame, and use the estimated kernels to generate the corresponding LLR frames.

**Table 1.** Quantitative comparisons among other state-of-the-art SISR and VSR methods and SS-VSR with upscaling factor 2. The results of SS-VSR are shown in bold, which achieve the best performance.

| Metric | Bicubic | ZSSR | MLSR | Bayesian | DynaVSR | SS-VSR |
|--------|---------|------|------|----------|---------|--------|
| Brisque | 36.07 | 30.65 | 30.05 | 48.16 | 24.74 | **22.65** |
| CaHDC | 36.76 | 47.07 | 43.48 | 30.56 | 45.41 | **47.59** |

**Table 2.** Quantitative comparisons between SS-SISR and SS-VSR with upscaling factor 2.

| Metric | SS-SISR | SS-VSR |
|--------|---------|--------|
| Brisque | 25.47 | **22.65** |
| CaHDC | 46.44 | **47.59** |

**Quantitative Results.** Two kinds of no-reference quality assessment metrics, BRISQUE [12] and CaHDC [16], are used to compare the results of various state-of-the-art SR methods quantitatively, because no groundtruth HR frames exist. Table 1 shows quantitative comparisons with upscaling factor 2. Smaller values of BRISQUE and larger values of CaHDC imply better results. Our SS-VSR achieves the best performance among all state-of-the-art SR methods on different no-reference image quality assessment metrics.

**Visual Comparisons.** Figure. 3 is the visual results of the proposed method. Three different and representative scenarios are shown in the first row. The second and third rows are the visual results of two different patches in scenario (a), while the fourth and fifth rows are visual results of two different patches in scenario (b) and the sixth and seventh rows are visual results of two different patches in scenario (c). As illustrated in the second and sixth rows in Fig. 3, benefitting from the powerful patch-recurrence property of the internal video frames, our SS-VSR produces sharper edges and recovers more details than MLSR and DynaVSR, both of which are finetuned based on the pretrained SISR and VSR networks, because there are many similar patterns of wooden shelf, handrail and exterior wall in scenario (a) and (c), respectively. The results of ZSSR are often with much artifacts which greatly destroy the quality of the restored frames. While taking the advantage of the complementary information from neighbouring frames, our SS-VSR recovers details better and produces visually more pleasing results than ZSSR (see results in the third and the last rows). The results of conventional blind VSR method are much more blurry than those of our SS-VSR.

### 4.3   Ablation Study

To further demonstrate the effectiveness of the neighbouring frames, we compare the results of our SS-SISR and SS-VSR. Table 2 shows quantitative results of SS-SISR and SS-VSR, which demonstrate that SS-VSR surpasses SS-SISR by a large margin on quantitative evaluation metrics. Figure 4 shows that SS-VSR can recover more details and sharper edges than SS-SISR. The reasons lie in the following two aspects. On one hand, from the perspective of transfer learning, the knowledge of SISR domain is transferred to the VSR domain. That is to say, the task of VSR "learns" based on the prior knowledge of SISR. Hence, the performance of SS-VSR will be better than that of SS-SISR. On the other hand,

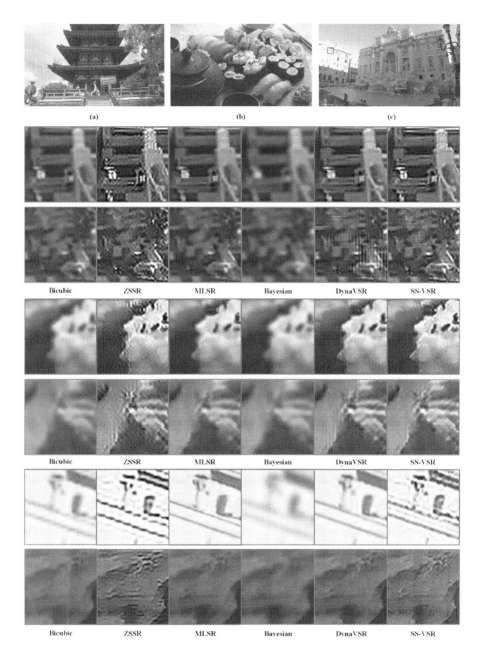

**Fig. 3.** Visual results on real-world videos from YouTube with upscaling factor 2. SS-VSR generates visually more pleasing outputs with sharper edges and more details while the other compared state-of-the-art SISR and VSR methods produce blurry results or severe artifacts.

**Fig. 4.** Visual comparisons between SS-SISR and SS-VSR. SS-VSR recovers more sharper structures and more details than SS-SISR. It demonstrates that SS-VSR benefits from the complementary information of the consecutive frames.

SS-VSR can make full use of the complementary information of multiple frames which can provide more details than a single LR image.

## 5    Conclusion

In this paper, we propose a novel self-supervised VSR algorithm. 4-stage training strategy is adopted in the proposed method, and spatial information and temporal contents are processed in the SM and the TFM respectively. In the SM, We introduce a middle-layer feature loss to permit a deeper network architecture to handle the task of VSR, learning from the prior knowledge of SISR. Subsequently, the extracted spatio-temporal features by the SM are inputted into the TFM to make full use of the complementary information from consecutive frames. In the experiments, the proposed SS-VSR outperforms the state-of-the-art SR methods, demonstrating its effectiveness in handling real-world videos.

**Acknowledgement.** This work is partially supported by Guangdong Basic and Applied Basic Reserch Foundation with No. 2021A1515011584 and No.2020 A1515110884, and supported by the Education Department of Guangdong Province, PR China, under project No. 2019KZDZX1028. The authors would like to thank the editors and reviewers for their constructive suggestions on our work. The corresponding author of this paper is Fei Zhou.

## References

1. Akyildiz, I.F., Ekici, E., Bender, M.D.: MLSR: a novel routing algorithm for multi-layered satellite IP networks. IEEE/ACM Trans. Networking **10**(3), 411–424 (2002)

2. Bell-Kligler, S., Shocher, A., Irani, M.: Blind super-resolution kernel estimation using an internal-gan. arXiv preprint arXiv:1909.06581 (2019)

3. Glasner, D., Bagon, S., Irani, M.: Super-resolution from a single image. In: 2009 IEEE 12th International Conference on Computer Vision, pp. 349–356. IEEE (2009)

4. He, K., Zhang, X., Ren, S., Sun, J.: Deep residual learning for image recognition. In: Proceedings of the IEEE Conference on Computer Vision and Pattern Recognition. pp. 770–778 (2016)

5. Huang, J.B., Singh, A., Ahuja, N.: Single image super-resolution from transformed self-exemplars. In: Proceedings of the IEEE Conference on Computer Vision and Pattern Recognition, pp. 5197–5206 (2015)

6. Huang, J.J., Liu, T., Luigi Dragotti, P., Stathaki, T.: Srhrf+: self-example enhanced single image super-resolution using hierarchical random forests. In: Proceedings of the IEEE Conference on Computer Vision and Pattern Recognition Workshops, pp. 71–79 (2017)

7. Huang, Y., Wang, W., Wang, L.: Video super-resolution via bidirectional recurrent convolutional networks. IEEE Trans. Pattern Anal. Mach. Intell. **40**(4), 1015–1028 (2017)

8. Kappeler, A., Yoo, S., Dai, Q., Katsaggelos, A.K.: Video super-resolution with convolutional neural networks. IEEE Trans. Comput. Imaging **2**(2), 109–122 (2016)

9. Kingma, D.P., Ba, J.: Adam: A method for stochastic optimization. arXiv preprint arXiv:1412.6980 (2014)

10. Lee, S., Choi, M., Lee, K.M.: Dynavsr: Dynamic adaptive blind video super-resolution. In: Proceedings of the IEEE/CVF Winter Conference on Applications of Computer Vision, pp. 2093–2102 (2021)

11. Liu, C., Sun, D.: A bayesian approach to adaptive video super resolution. In: CVPR 2011, pp. 209–216. IEEE (2011)

12. Mittal, A., Moorthy, A.K., Bovik, A.C.: Blind/referenceless image spatial quality evaluator. In: 2011 Conference Record of the Forty Fifth Asilomar Conference on Signals, Systems and Computers (ASILOMAR), pp. 723–727. IEEE (2011)

13. Shahar, O., Faktor, A., Irani, M.: Space-time super-resolution from a single video. IEEE (2011)

14. Shocher, A., Cohen, N., Irani, M.: Zero-shot super-resolution using deep internal learning. In: Proceedings of the IEEE Conference on Computer Vision and Pattern Recognition, pp. 3118–3126 (2018)

15. Soh, J.W., Cho, S., Cho, N.I.: Meta-transfer learning for zero-shot super-resolution. In: Proceedings of the IEEE/CVF Conference on Computer Vision and Pattern Recognition, pp. 3516–3525 (2020)

16. Wu, J., Ma, J., Liang, F., Dong, W., Shi, G., Lin, W.: End-to-end blind image quality prediction with cascaded deep neural network. IEEE Trans. Image Process. **29**, 7414–7426 (2020)

17. Xue, T., Chen, B., Wu, J., Wei, D., Freeman, W.T.: Video enhancement with task-oriented flow. Int. J. Comput. Vis. **127**(8), 1106–1125 (2019)

18. Zontak, M., Irani, M.: Internal statistics of a single natural image. In: CVPR 2011, pp. 977–984. IEEE (2011)

# ODE-Inspired Image Denoiser: An End-to-End Dynamical Denoising Network

Yu Bai[1,2], Meiqin Liu[1,2(✉)], Chao Yao[3], Chunyu Lin[1,2], and Yao Zhao[1,2]

[1] Institute of Information Science, Beijing Jiaotong University, Beijing 100044, China
{20125147,mqliu,cylin,yzhao}@bjtu.edu.cn
[2] Beijing Key Laboratory of Advanced Information Science and Network Technology,
Beijing Jiaotong University, Beijing 100044, China
[3] School of Computer and Communication Engineering, University of Science
and Technology Beijing, Beijing 100083, China
yaochao@ustb.edu.cn

**Abstract.** Image denoising which aims to remove noise in the given images is one of the most challenging tasks in the low level computer vision field. Especially for the real image noise, its complex distribution is difficult to be simulated by a single mathematical model. In this paper, an end-to-end dynamical denoising network (DDNet) is proposed to resolve the denoising problem of the real image. Inspired by ordinary differential equation (ODE), cascaded OI-Blocks (ODE-Inspired Blocks) are designed to iteratively approximate the distribution of noise. Moreover, non-linear affine transformation based on the attention mechanism among channels is exploited to extract the channel dependencies. Compared with the state-of-the-art works, extensive experimental results show that DDNet achieves notable improvement on both objective and subjective evaluations.

**Keywords:** Image denoising · ODE · ODE solution module ·
Convolutional neural networks

## 1 Introduction

Noise is often unavoidable in the process of image acquisition, which not only largely affects the visual quality of acquired images, but also may greatly decrease the accuracy and robustness for the subsequent high-level computer vision tasks. Therefore, as one of the most important issues, image denoising has drawn lots of research efforts from industry and academia.

Earlier image denoising works assume that noise is independent and identically distributed. For the statistical distribution-regular noise, earlier denoisers

This work is supported by the Fundamental Research Funds for the Central Universities (2019JBM018).

H. Ma et al. (Eds.): PRCV 2021, LNCS 13021, pp. 261–274, 2021.
https://doi.org/10.1007/978-3-030-88010-1_22

have been done well, such as Additive White Gaussian Noise (AWGN). Besides, most of earlier denoising methods try to model this prior knowledge over the input images, such as KSVD [1], BM3D [2] and CBM3D [3]. Although these models have achieved the competitive results, they are not adaptive and flexible enough to cope with the noise of real images. Partly because there is still a huge difference between specific noise and real-world noise.

Recently, some methods based on deep convolutional neural network (CNN) have been proposed for the real image denoising [4–7]. Especially, the residual learning is a crucial strategy in image denoising. DnCNN [4] adopted a 20 layers deep architecture with residual learning. RIDNet [8] further adopted the attention mechanism into the deep residual structure to improve the performance of real image denoising. It is noted that the residual learning strategy is very useful for boosting many denoisers' performance.

To improve the stability and approximation ability of residual structure, several latest works introduced the similarity between residual structure and the numerical ordinary differential equations (ODEs) into some low-level computer vision tasks, such as super-resolution [9] and image dehazing [10]. In these works, residual networks are interpreted as an underlying dynamical system, where the dynamics of the network are approximated by an adaptive ODE solver. These works can well explain the mathematical theory of deep network. However, directly employing numerical ODE solvers into low-level image processing does not necessarily lead to an optimal solution, moreover, time-consuming of the training is still a tough problem.

In this paper, inspired by ordinary differential equation (ODE), we propose an end-to-end dynamical denoising network(DDnet) to resolve the denoising problem of real images. We transfer the process of image denoising into the solving process of the ODE. Specifically, series of OI-Blocks are designed to iteratively approximate the distribution of noise. Moreover, a non-linear affine transformation based on the attention mechanism among channels is exploited to extract the channel dependencies. Extensive experiments based on several benchmark datasets show our proposed network can significantly improve the denoising performance on synthetic and real noisy images.

The contributions of this paper are summarized in the following aspects:

(1) We formulate image denoising process as an ODE-based dynamical system. An end-to-end dynamical denoising network(DDnet) is proposed for image noise dynamical removal.
(2) We introduce three kinds of non-linear affine transformation which are useful and necessary for solution of ODE equation. Especially, the transformation based on the attention mechanism among channels is exploited to extract channel dependencies.
(3) Our method uses lesser parameters to achieves comparable performance compared to the state-of-the-art methods.

## 2    Related Work

### 2.1    Image Denoising with CNN

With the powerful CNN, a significant performance boost for image denoising has been achieved. The first work using CNN for image denoising was proposed by Jain and Seung [11], which shows that CNN has a superior representation power compared to Markov Random Field (MRF). Later, *Zhang et al.* [4] introduced residual learning and batch normalization to predict the noise in the noisy image. Considering the long-term dependence of the deep network model, an end-to-end memory network based on residual connections was proposed by *Tai et al.* [12]. It combined long-term and short-term memory to capture different levels of information. The attention mechanism was firstly utilized in RIDnet [8], which can make full use of the dependence between channels and effectively remove the noise in the real noisy image. Compared with the traditional methods, the image denoising methods based on deep learning have stronger learning ability, which can better fit the noise distribution in the image. Furthermore, residual learning can enlarge the network scale and improve its learning ability.

### 2.2    Neural ODEs V.S. Residual Learning

Recent researches have bridged dynamical systems with neural networks, especially ResNet [13]. *Weinan et al.* [14] firstly viewed ResNet as an approximation to ODE, which explored the relations between the dynamic system and ResNet. *Chen et al.* [15] further studied the relation between CNN and ODE. *Ruseckas et al.* [16] proved that not only residual networks, but also feed-forward neural networks with small non-linearities can be related to the differential equations. All of these works treat the deep neural network as a discrete dynamical system, identifying the similarity between ResNet and the discretization of ODEs. Motivated by this, many efforts have been made to apply ODE network to computer vision tasks. For example, ODE was exploited into the design of convolutional neural network for face recognition [17]. *He et al.* [9] proposed an ODE-inspired scheme for the image super-resolution. *Shen et al.* [10] extended the explicit forward approximation to the implicit backward counterpart, and designed an end-to-end multi-level implicit network for image dehazing. Therefore, we are encouraged to take ODEs to resolve the problem of image denoising, particularly the real image denoising.

## 3    Proposed Method

In this section, we will give the details of our method. Firstly, we introduce the design of the whole framework of our method. Then, we explain how to construct the OI-Block.

## 3.1    Network Architecture

In order to remove noise of images, we build an end-to-end network which is called dynamical denoising network (DDNet) to establish the iterative mapping from the noisy image to the clean image. The network architecture of DDNet is shown in Fig. 1. Firstly, we use one convolutional layer to extract the shallow features from the input noisy image $y$. Then the shallow features are iteratively denoised by several cascaded OI-Blocks. Each OI-Block, viewed as a denoiser of the input noisy feature map, is a mapping operation that transforms the input noisy feature map to the clearer version. Each OI-Block, detailed in the following subsection, consists of an ODE solution module and a non-linear affine transformation module. Finally, the final cleaned feature map is converted into RGB space and reconstruct the final clear image $x$ through a single convolutional layer.

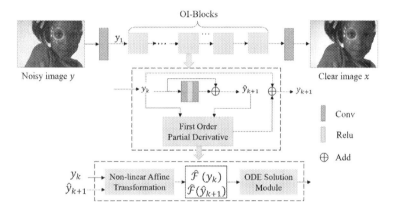

**Fig. 1.** The architecture of dynamical denoising network (DDNet).

## 3.2    Problem Formulation

In the field of image denoising, the noisy image can be treated as a combination of the clear image and the noise. Mathematically, the image denoising problem can be formulated as:

$$x = y + n, \tag{1}$$

where $x$ denotes the clear image and $y$ indicates the noisy image. Here, $n$ represents the opposite number of the synthetic or real noise.

If we can predict the precise noise of the noisy image, we can obtain the clear image by removing the noise from the noisy image in one step. However, it is difficult to predict the correct noise in one step. In this paper, we solve the image denoising problem in a multi-step strategy. We learn a mapping function $\mathcal{F}(\cdot)$ to approximate the noise $n$ iteratively as follows:

$$y_{k+1} = y_k + \mathcal{F}(y_k), \tag{2}$$

where $y_k$ denotes the noisy image in the $k^{th}$ denoising step, $y_0$ is the original noisy image. $\mathcal{F}(y_k)$ represents a one-step dynamic approximation to the noise $n$. Due to the similarity between Eq. 2 and the ODE's Euler discretization, Eq. 2 can be written as an Euler discretization:

$$\frac{1}{\triangle t}(y_{k+1} - y_k) = \mathcal{F}(y_k), \tag{3}$$

of an ODE

$$\frac{d}{dt}y(t) = \mathcal{F}(y(t)). \tag{4}$$

Through the transformation, it turns out that Eq. 4 is the neural ODE. Hence, we regard CNN-based image denoising as a dynamical system. However, neural ODEs [15] is difficult to be applied into practice with the drawback of long training time and huge computational cost of numerically integrating. Moreover, due to the fact that the real noise cannot be modeled by AWGN, the perturbation of noise will result in the decreasing of the efficiency of the learned model.

Considering that Eq. 2 is a first order differential equation, the denoising block can be seen as a differential network. On the other hand, the denoising block executes one residual learning and can also be called the residual block. The residual block is indeed to learn an approximation mapping from $y_k$ to $y_{k+1}$. The whole process of the image denoising includes several residual blocks and achieves the iterative approximation mapping. In the $k$-th Residual Block, the Taylor formula for $\mathcal{F}(y_k^i)$ is expanded as follows:

$$\mathcal{F}(y_k^i) = \mathcal{F}(y_k^{*i} + \epsilon_k^i) = \mathcal{F}(y_k^{*i}) + \epsilon_k^i \cdot \frac{\partial \mathcal{F}}{\partial y_k^{*i}} + o((\epsilon_k^i)^2), \tag{5}$$

where $y_k^{*i} + \epsilon_k^i$ represents each perturbed pixel, $i$ represents the $i$-th pixel in the image, $y_k^{*i}$ denotes the clear value of the $i$-th pixel, $\epsilon_k^i$ denotes the noise perturbation of the $i$-th pixel.

Obviously, the noise estimation of the clear pixel $y_k^{*i}$ and $o((\epsilon_k^i)^2)$ can be approximated to 0. Hence, the solution for $\mathcal{F}(y_k^i)$ can be translated into solving for the first-order partial derivative:

$$\mathcal{F}(y_k) \approx \frac{\partial \mathcal{F}}{\partial y_k^*}. \tag{6}$$

### 3.3  OI-Block

Based on ODE, the image denoising process is viewed as a dynamical system. In order to solve the ODE, we firstly introduce the ODE solution module, then describe the three proposed nonlinear affine transformations.

**ODE Solution Module.** During the solving process of ODE, an unavoidable constraint is that the function $\mathcal{F}$ in Eq. 6 must be analytic at each point. When it can not be guaranteed, it can not be solved by backward propagation. To achieve the forward solution of ODE equation, according to the definition of the derivative, $\frac{\partial \mathcal{F}}{\partial y_k^*}$ can be transformed into the form of limiting approximation:

$$\frac{\partial \mathcal{F}}{\partial y_k^*} = \lim_{y_k \to y_{k+1}} \frac{\mathcal{F}(y_{k+1}) - \mathcal{F}(y_k)}{y_{k+1} - y_k} \tag{7}$$

where $y_{k+1}$ is replaced by an approximation $\hat{y}_{k+1}$ which is estimated by one residual block.

**Non-linear Affine Transformation.** We propose three structures of non-linear affine transformation($T_1$, $T_2$ and $T_3$) to model $\mathcal{F}$.

The structures of $T_1$ and $T_2$ are shown in Fig. 2. For the structure of $T_1$, the predicted values $\hat{\mathcal{F}}(y_k)$ and $\hat{\mathcal{F}}(\hat{y}_{k+1})$ of $\mathcal{F}(y_k)$ and $\mathcal{F}(y_{k+1})$ are obtained from a residual block. Due to the model sharing operation, the model parameters are reduced greatly. For the structure of $T_2$, two residual blocks are employed to transform $y_k$ and $\hat{y}_{k+1}$ respectively, which make the transformation more flexible.

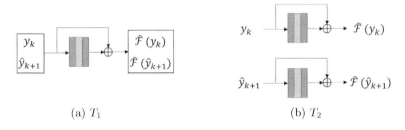

(a) $T_1$                                                    (b) $T_2$

**Fig. 2.** The structure of the non-linear affine transformation $T_1$ and $T_2$.

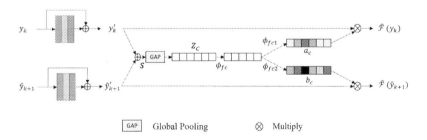

GAP  Global Pooling          ⊗  Multiply

**Fig. 3.** The structure of the non-linear affine transformation $T_3$.

Inspired by selective kernel network [18], we propose an attention module based on fusion feature, which can exploit the relationship between $y_k$ and $\hat{y}_{k+1}$

according to the channel attention weight. Firstly, features $y'_k$ and $\hat{y}'_{k+1}$ are obtained from two residual blocks. Then, features $y'_k$ and $y'_{k+1}$ are fused by the element adding operation. In this way, the process can be represented as:

$$s = W_0(y_k) + W_1(\hat{y}_{k+1}) \tag{8}$$

where $W_0$, $W_1$ represent the convolution operations, $s$ denotes the fused feature. Statistical quantity $z_c$ of channels for the fused feature is captured by the global pooling $\phi_{gp}$.

$$z_c = \phi_{gp}(s_c) = \frac{1}{H \times W} \sum_{i=1}^{W} \sum_{j=1}^{H} s_c(i,j) \tag{9}$$

where $H$ and $W$ represent the spatial dimensions, $s_c(i,j)$ represents the value of the $c$-th channel of feature $s$ with coordinates $(i,j)$. Richer features are obtained by fully-connected layers $\phi_{fc}$, and the attention weights are acquired by the sigmoid function rather than the softmax function in the selective kernel network [18]. The process can be represented as :

$$a_c = \phi_{fc}(\phi_{fc1}(z_c)), b_c = \phi_{fc}(\phi_{fc2}(z_c)) \tag{10}$$

In Eq. 10, $\phi_{fc}$, $\phi_{fc1}$ and $\phi_{fc2}$ denote fully connected ($fc$) layers. Finally, $\hat{\mathcal{F}}(y_k)$ and $\hat{\mathcal{F}}(\hat{y}_{k+1})$ are obtained by element multiplying operation, as:

$$\hat{\mathcal{F}}(y_k) = a_c \cdot y'_k, \hat{\mathcal{F}}(\hat{y}_{k+1}) = b_c \cdot \hat{y}'_{k+1} \tag{11}$$

where $\cdot$ denotes the element multiplying operation.

$\hat{\mathcal{F}}(y_k)$ and $\hat{\mathcal{F}}(\hat{y}_{k+1})$ can be obtained from any of the three non-linear affine transformations. Therefore, the denoising result of the $k$-th OI-Block can be represented as:

$$y_{k+1} = y_k + \lim_{y_k \to y_{k+1}} \frac{\hat{\mathcal{F}}(\hat{y}_{k+1}) - \hat{\mathcal{F}}(y_k)}{\hat{y}_{k+1} - y_k} \tag{12}$$

Finally, the clear image $y$ is reconstructed by $y_{k+1}$.

## 4    Experiments

In this section, we demonstrate the effectiveness of our method on both synthetic datasets and real noisy datasets.

**Dataset and Evaluation Metrics.** For the denoising of synthetic noisy images, we adopt DIV2K [19] which contains 800 images with $2K$ resolution as our training dataset. Different levels AWGN will be added to the clean images. For the training of real noisy images, we use the *SIDD* [20] Medium dataset. For test datasets, we adopt *BSD68* and *Kodak24* in the synthetic noise situation, and *SIDD* [20] validation dataset and *DnD* [7] dataset in the real noise situation. For evaluations, PSNR and SSIM are employed to evaluate the results. Best and second-best results are highlighted and underlined respectively in the following experiments.

**Experiment Setup.** We randomly rotate and flip the image horizontally and vertically for data augmentation. In each training batch, 16 patches with a size of $64 \times 64$ are input to the model in the synthetic image denoising, and 16 patches with a size of $128 \times 128$ are used for real image denoising. We train our model by the ADAM optimizer [21] with $\beta_1 = 0.9$, $\beta_2 = 0.999$ and $\epsilon = 10^{-8}$. For synthetic image denoising, The initial learning rate is $1 \times 10^{-4}$ and then halved after $1 \times 10^5$ iterations. And for real image denoising, the initial learning rate is $2 \times 10^{-4}$, which is decreased to $1 \times 10^{-6}$ in the cosine annealing strategy [22]. Our model is built in the PyTorch framework and trained with one Nvidia GeForce RTX 1080Ti.

## 4.1 Ablation Study

**Parameter Analysis.** In order to evaluate the influence of the number of OI-Blocks, we conduct a series of experiments. Here, the noise level is $\sigma = 50$ and the OI-Blocks adopts $T_2$ as the non-linear affine transformation. Experimental results are shown in Table 1.

**Table 1.** Evaluations on the number of OI-Blocks on *BSD68*

| Model | DDNet-4 | DDNet-8 | DDNet-12 | DDNet-16 |
|---|---|---|---|---|
| Parameters (M) | 1.66 | 3.29 | 4.91 | 6.54 |
| Times (ms) | 35 | 56 | 67 | 80 |
| PSNR (dB) | 28.17 | 28.27 | 28.30 | **28.32** |

**Table 2.** Comparative experiments on *BSD68*

| Model | ODE | ResNet | $T_1$ | $T_2$ | $T_3$ | OI-Block | PSNR (dB) |
|---|---|---|---|---|---|---|---|
| ODEnet [15] | $\checkmark$ | | | | | | 27.66 |
| ResNet [13] | | $\checkmark$ | | | | | 28.18 |
| DDNet-$T_1$ | | | $\checkmark$ | | | $\checkmark$ | 28.30 |
| DDNet-$T_2$ | | | | $\checkmark$ | | $\checkmark$ | 28.32 |
| DDNet-$T_3$ | | | | | $\checkmark$ | $\checkmark$ | 28.34 |

DDNet-4, DDNet-8, DDNet-12 and DDNet-16 represent that there are 4, 8, 12 and 16 OI-Blocks in DDNet respectively. Table 1 shows that the higher PSNR can be achieved by stacking more OI-Blocks. Meanwhile, the increase of OI-Blocks leads to the increase of model parameters and the inference time. For example, the parameters of DDNet-12 and DDNet-16 are increased by 3.25M and 4.88M while these two networks gain 0.05 dB and 0.15 dB over DDNet-4. The inference time of a $128 \times 128$ color image on DDNet-16 and DDNet-12 are increased by 32 ms and 45 ms over DDNet-4. Therefore, the denoising method should find a balance spot between PSNR and the model complexity in practical applications.

**Model Analysis.** Comparative experiments are implemented to compare the performance of different non-linear affine transformations. ODENet [15] and ResNet [13] are used to verify the effectiveness of our OI-Block. *BSD68* (color image with noise $\sigma = 50$) is implemented as the test dataset, and the experimental configurations and experimental results are shown in Table 2.

ODENet [15] in Table 2 consists of a set of 64-channel ODEBlocks. ResNet [13] consists of 16 convolutional blocks with the skip connection. DDNet-$T_1$, $T_2$, $T_3$ cascade 16 OI-Blocks with transformation $T_1$, $T_2$ and $T_3$ respectively. Compared with ODEnet and ResNet, the results demonstrate the superiority of DDNet. DDNet-$T_1$ improves 0.64 dB, 0.12 dB over ODEnet and ResNet. Through three sets of comparative experiments, we find that transformation $T_3$ based on fused attention is the most effective one and achieves the best result.

## 4.2   Synthetic Noisy Images

In experiments with synthetic noisy images, Koadk24 and *BSD68* datasets are used as the test datasets. They both contain gray-scale and color-scale images and we add different noise levels AWGN to clear images. In addition, 16 OI-Blocks are utilized in our model with the non-linear affine transformation $T1$ and $T_2$ respectively.

Table 3 shows the average PSNR for gray images with different noise levels. Compared with RIDNet [8], our DDNet-$T_2$ model in average gains 0.07 dB ($\sigma = 30$), 0.09 dB ($\sigma = 50$) and 0.12 dB ($\sigma = 70$) improvement on *Kodak24*, and 0.04 dB ($\sigma = 30$), 0.05 dB ($\sigma = 50$) and 0.07 dB ($\sigma = 70$) on *BSD68*. Comparative

**Table 3.** Evaluation of average PSNR (dB) on synthetic gray-scale noisy images

| Methods | *Kodak*24 | | | | *BSD*68 | | | |
|---|---|---|---|---|---|---|---|---|
| | 10 | 30 | 50 | 70 | 10 | 30 | 50 | 70 |
| BM3D [2] | 34.39 | 29.13 | 26.99 | 25.73 | 33.31 | 27.76 | 25.62 | 24.44 |
| RED [23] | 35.02 | 29.77 | 27.66 | 26.39 | 33.99 | 28.50 | 26.37 | 25.10 |
| DnCNN [4] | 34.90 | 29.62 | 27.51 | 26.08 | 33.88 | 28.36 | 26.23 | 24.90 |
| MemNet [12] | N/A | 29.72 | 27.68 | 26.42 | N/A | 28.43 | 26.35 | 25.09 |
| IRCNN [24] | 34.76 | 29.53 | 27.45 | N/A | 33.74 | 28.26 | 26.15 | N/A |
| FFDNet [5] | 34.81 | 29.70 | 27.63 | 26.34 | 33.76 | 28.39 | 26.30 | 25.04 |
| RIDNet [8] | N/A | 29.90 | 27.79 | 26.51 | N/A | 28.54 | 26.40 | 25.12 |
| DDNet-$T_1$ (ours) | 35.01 | 29.92 | 27.85 | 26.59 | 33.99 | 28.57 | 26.45 | 25.18 |
| DDNet-$T_2$ (ours) | **35.04** | **29.97** | **27.88** | **26.63** | **34.00** | **28.58** | **26.45** | **25.19** |

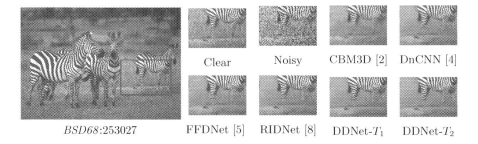

Clear    Noisy    CBM3D [2]    DnCNN [4]

*BSD68*:253027    FFDNet [5]    RIDNet [8]    DDNet-$T_1$    DDNet-$T_2$

**Fig. 4.** Visualizations of denoising results on *BSD68* with noise level $\sigma = 50$.

**Table 4.** Evaluations of average PSNR (dB) on synthetic color-scale noisy images.

| Methods | *Kodak*24 | | | | *BSD*68 | | | |
|---|---|---|---|---|---|---|---|---|
| | 10 | 30 | 50 | 70 | 10 | 30 | 50 | 70 |
| CBM3D [3] | 36.57 | 30.89 | 28.63 | 27.27 | 35.91 | 29.73 | 27.38 | 26.00 |
| RED [23] | 34.91 | 29.71 | 27.62 | 26.36 | 33.89 | 28.46 | 26.35 | 25.09 |
| DnCNN [4] | 36.98 | 31.39 | 29.16 | 27.64 | 36.31 | 30.40 | 28.01 | 26.56 |
| MemNet [12] | N/A | 29.67 | 27.65 | 26.40 | N/A | 28.39 | 26.33 | 25.08 |
| IRCNN [24] | 36.70 | 31.24 | 28.93 | N/A | 36.06 | 30.22 | 27.86 | N/A |
| FFDNet [5] | 36.81 | 31.39 | 29.10 | 27.68 | 36.14 | 30.31 | 27.96 | 26.53 |
| RIDNet [8] | N/A | 31.64 | 29.25 | 27.94 | N/A | 30.47 | 28.12 | 26.69 |
| DDNet-$T_1$ (ours) | 37.21 | 31.83 | 29.56 | 28.17 | 36.42 | 30.63 | 28.30 | 26.91 |
| DDNet-$T_2$ (ours) | **37.25** | **31.86** | **29.60** | **28.22** | **36.44** | **30.64** | **28.32** | **26.93** |

results on color images are displayed in Table 4, the performance are further improved. DDNet-$T_2$ improves 0.22 dB ($\sigma = 30$), 0.35 dB ($\sigma = 50$) and 0.28 dB ($\sigma = 70$) on Kodak24, and 0.17 dB ($\sigma = 30$), 0.20 dB ($\sigma = 50$) and 0.24 dB ($\sigma = 70$) on *BSD68*. Based on the above comparative experiments, our model achieves the best performance. Moreover, DDNet obtains better results on color images with high level noise.

The subjective results of each methods on images are visualized in Fig. 4 and Fig. 5. In particular, the zebras' stripes in Fig. 4 and the clothing textures in Fig. 5 are difficult to be separated in the heavy noise situation. The compared methods tend to remove the details along with the noise, resulting in oversmoothing artifacts. Our method can restore the vivid textures from noisy images without blurring the details.

### 4.3    Real Noisy Images

In order to evaluate the denoising performance of our method on real noisy images, we conduct a series of experiments. *DnD* [7] and *SIDD* [20] datasets are used as the test datasets. *DnD* dataset contains 50 real noisy images, and we

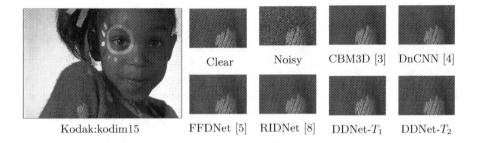

**Fig. 5.** Visualizations of denoising results on *Kodak24* with noise level $\sigma = 50$.

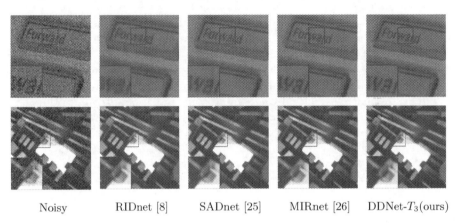

**Fig. 6.** Visualizations of two denoised images from *SIDD* and *DnD* datasets

**Table 5.** Quantitative results on *SIDD* and *DnD* datasets

| Methods | Blind/non-blind | Parameters (M) | *SIDD* dataset | | *DnD* dataset | |
|---|---|---|---|---|---|---|
| | | | PSNR (dB) | SSIM | PSNR (dB) | SSIM |
| CBM3D [2] | Non-blind | – | 25.65 | 0.685 | 34.51 | 0.8507 |
| DnCNN [4] | Blind | 0.6 | 23.66 | 0.583 | 37.90 | 0.9430 |
| CBDNet [6] | Blind | 4.3 | 30.78 | 0.801 | 38.06 | 0.9421 |
| RIDNet [8] | Blind | 1.5 | 38.71 | 0.951 | 39.26 | 0.9528 |
| SADNet [25] | Blind | 4.3 | 39.46 | 0.957 | 39.59 | 0.952 |
| MIRNet [26] | Blind | 31.8 | **39.72** | **0.958** | **39.88** | **0.959** |
| DDNet-$T_2$ (ours) | Blind | 4.1 | 39.51 | 0.957 | 39.63 | 0.9524 |
| DDNet-$T_3$ (ours) | Blind | 4.2 | 39.54 | 0.957 | 39.64 | 0.9525 |

submit the denoisd images to the *DnD* official website for testing. And *SIDD* validation dataset contains 1280 noisy-clean image pairs whose resolutions are $256 \times 256$.

Due to the fact that the increase of the number of OI-Blocks will increase the complexity of the model, we use the DDNet-$T_2$ and DDNet-$T_3$ with 10 OI-Blocks on real noisy images. In comparative experiments, we choose several outstanding works, i.e., CBM3D [2], DnCNN [4], CBDNet [6], RIDNet [8].

The objective evaluation results on two datasets are shown in Table 5. Compared to RIDNet, DDNet-$T_2$, DDNet-$T_3$ surpass 0.80 dB, 0.83 dB on *SIDD* dataset, and surpass 0.37 dB, 0.38 dB on *DnD* dataset. This indicates that our method performs better on the real noisy images than on synthetic noisy images. To be noted, the number of parameters of SADnet [25] is larger than ours, but our method obtains 0.08 dB improvement over SADnet. Although the performance of MIRNet [26] is higher than ours, its parameters are 8 times larger than that of ours. As our DDNet can achieve comparable performance with light models, it is much more flexible in the practical applications.

The subjective evaluation results are shown in Fig. 6. The image in the first row is from *SIDD* dataset, and the image in second row is from *DnD* dataset. The denoised image obtained by RIDNet [8] is very blurred and there are a lot of noise in the background. In both images, the texture restored by SADNet [25] are not clear. Our method and MIRNet [26] obtains similar denoised images. It also indicates that our method can achieve comparable performance compared to MIRNet [26]. These results show that our method can effectively remove the noise and maintain clear edges.

## 5    Conclusion

In this paper, we formulate the image denoising process as an ODE-based dynamical system and construct an end-to-end dynamical denoising network (DDNet). Specifically, series of cascaded OI-Blocks are designed to iteratively approximate the distribution of noise. OI-Block is designed to implement the forward solution of ODE equation. Experimental results show that our method achieves comparable performances with lesser parameters compared to the state-of-the-arts on both synthetic noisy images and real noisy images.

## References

1. Elad, M., Aharon, M.: Image denoising via sparse and redundant representations over learned dictionaries. IEEE Trans. Image Process. **15**(12), 3736–3745 (2006)
2. Dabov, K., Foi, A., Katkovnik, V., Egiazarian, K.: Image denoising by sparse 3d transform-domain collaborative filtering. IEEE Trans. Image Process. **16**(8), 2080–2095 (2007)
3. Dabov, K., Foi, A., Katkovnik, V., Egiazarian, K.: Color image denoising via sparse 3D collaborative filtering with grouping constraint in luminance-chrominance space. In: Proceedings of the 2007 IEEE International Conference on Image Processing, vol. 1, p. I-313. IEEE (2007)
4. Zhang, K., Zuo, W., Chen, Y., Meng, D., Zhang, L.: Beyond a Gaussian denoiser: residual learning of deep CNN for image denoising. IEEE Trans. Image Process. **26**(7), 3142–3155 (2017)
5. Zhang, K., Zuo, W., Zhang, L.: FFDNet: toward a fast and flexible solution for CNN-based image denoising. IEEE Trans. Image Process. **27**(9), 4608–4622 (2018)

6. Guo, S., Yan, Z., Zhang, K., Zuo, W., Zhang, L.: Toward convolutional blind denoising of real photographs. In: Proceedings of the IEEE/CVF Conference on Computer Vision and Pattern Recognition, pp. 1712–1722 (2019)

7. Plotz, T., Roth, S.: Benchmarking denoising algorithms with real photographs. In: Proceedings of the IEEE Conference on Computer Vision and Pattern Recognition, pp. 1586–1595 (2017)

8. Anwar, S., Barnes, N.: Real image denoising with feature attention. In: Proceedings of the IEEE/CVF International Conference on Computer Vision, pp. 3155–3164 (2019)

9. He, X., Mo, Z., Wang, P., Liu, Y., Yang, M., Cheng, J.: Ode-inspired network design for single image super-resolution. In: Proceedings of the IEEE/CVF Conference on Computer Vision and Pattern Recognition, pp. 1732–1741 (2019)

10. Shen, J., Li, Z., Yu, L., Xia, G.S., Yang, W.: Implicit Euler ode networks for single-image dehazing. In: Proceedings of the IEEE/CVF Conference on Computer Vision and Pattern Recognition Workshops, pp. 218–219 (2020)

11. Jain, V., Seung, S.: Natural image denoising with convolutional networks. Adv. Neural. Inf. Process. Syst. **21**, 769–776 (2008)

12. Tai, Y., Yang, J., Liu, X., Xu, C.: MemNet: a persistent memory network for image restoration. In: Proceedings of the IEEE International Conference on Computer Vision, pp. 4539–4547 (2017)

13. He, K., Zhang, X., Ren, S., Sun, J.: Identity mappings in deep residual networks. In: Leibe, B., Matas, J., Sebe, N., Welling, M. (eds.) ECCV 2016. LNCS, vol. 9908, pp. 630–645. Springer, Cham (2016). https://doi.org/10.1007/978-3-319-46493-0_38

14. Weinan, E.: A proposal on machine learning via dynamical systems. Commun. Math. Stat. **5**(1), 1–11 (2017)

15. Chen, R.T., Rubanova, Y., Bettencourt, J., Duvenaud, D.: Neural ordinary differential equations. arXiv preprint arXiv:1806.07366 (2018)

16. Ruseckas, J.: Differential equations as models of deep neural networks. arXiv preprint arXiv:1909.03767 (2019)

17. Sameer, G., Manasa, G.: Neural differential equations for face recognition. In: Proceedings of the 2019 International Conference on Communication and Electronics Systems, pp. 242–247. IEEE (2019)

18. Li, X., Wang, W., Hu, X., Yang, J.: Selective kernel networks. In: Proceedings of the IEEE/CVF Conference on Computer Vision and Pattern Recognition, pp. 510–519 (2019)

19. Agustsson, E., Timofte, R.: Ntire 2017 challenge on single image super-resolution: dataset and study. In: Proceedings of the IEEE Conference on Computer Vision and Pattern Recognition Workshops, pp. 126–135 (2017)

20. Abdelhamed, A., Lin, S., Brown, M.S.: A high-quality denoising dataset for smartphone cameras. In: Proceedings of the IEEE Conference on Computer Vision and Pattern Recognition. pp. 1692–1700 (2018)

21. Da, K.: A method for stochastic optimization. arXiv preprint arXiv:1412.6980 (2014)

22. Loshchilov, I., Hutter, F.: SGDR: stochastic gradient descent with warm restarts. arXiv preprint arXiv:1608.03983 (2016)

23. Mao, X.J., Shen, C., Yang, Y.B.: Image restoration using very deep convolutional encoder-decoder networks with symmetric skip connections. arXiv preprint arXiv:1603.09056 (2016)

24. Zhang, K., Zuo, W., Gu, S., Zhang, L.: Learning deep CNN denoiser prior for image restoration. In: Proceedings of the IEEE Conference on Computer Vision and Pattern Recognition, pp. 3929–3938 (2017)

25. Chang, M., Li, Q., Feng, H., Xu, Z.: Spatial-adaptive network for single image denoising. In: Vedaldi, A., Bischof, H., Brox, T., Frahm, J.-M. (eds.) ECCV 2020. LNCS, vol. 12375, pp. 171–187. Springer, Cham (2020). https://doi.org/10.1007/978-3-030-58577-8_11
26. Zamir, S.W., et al.: Learning enriched features for real image restoration and enhancement. arXiv preprint arXiv:2003.06792 (2020)

# Image Outpainting with Depth Assistance

Lei Zhang⬚, Kang Liao, Chunyu Lin(✉)⬚, Meiqin Liu, and Yao Zhao

Institute of Information Science, Beijing Jiaotong University, Beijing 100044, China
{20120324,kang_liao,cylin,mqliu,yzhao}@bjtu.edu.cn

**Abstract.** In some scenarios such as autonomous diriving, we can get a sparse point cloud with a large field of view, but an RGB image with a limited FoV. This paper studies the problem of image expansion using depth information converted from sparse point cloud projection. General image expansion tasks only use images as input for expansion. Such expansion is only carried out by RGB information, and the expanded content has limitations and does not conform to reality. Therefore, we propose introducing depth information into the image expansion task, and offering a reasonable image expansion model using the depth information of the sparse point cloud. Our model can generate more realistic and more reliable image expansion content than general image expansion. The results generated by our work must be authentic, which further enhances the practical significance of the image expansion problem. Furthermore, we also designed a variety of experimental research schemes on how to perform interactive matching between depth and RGB information further to enhance the help of depth for image expansion.

**Keywords:** Image restoration · Outpainting with depth assistance · Image extension

## 1 Introduction

As a long-standing problem in computer vision, image restoration tasks have always been highly concerned by scholars. And outpainting [12,14,18,22] is to extrapolate the edge of the specified size of the image, and predict content outside the image according to the semantic and structural information in the input image so that outpainting can generate a larger image. Undoubtedly this is more challenging for computers.

Generally speaking, the classic method of outpainting task is based on the patch method [3]. But these methods cannot generate new content from the known information. In recent years, with the popularity of deep learning methods, outpainting has also been extensively studied, and methods based on Generative Adversarial Networks (GAN) [8] have greatly improved the limitations caused by classic methods. These deep learning methods [4,7,10,12,14,18–20] can achieve relatively good expansion effects in simple scenes (such as human faces, landscapes, etc.). But in more complex scenes (such as towns, streets, etc. in Fig. 1), the results of current methods are often not believable.

ⓒ Springer Nature Switzerland AG 2021
H. Ma et al. (Eds.): PRCV 2021, LNCS 13021, pp. 275–286, 2021.
https://doi.org/10.1007/978-3-030-88010-1_23

**Fig. 1.** Image extension task (top: input image, left: the result of general outpainting model, right: ours)

When the image is acquired, lidar and camera collaboration will often be used in current. In these tasks, the camera's field of view will only have a small limited range and usually only capture narrow angles of RGB information. But the working principle of lidar allows it to have a wide field of view, even 360° full-angle data collection (see Fig. 2). Therefore, they only use the point cloud data that matches the camera's field of view, while the point cloud data outside the camera's field of view tends to have low utilization.

**Fig. 2.** The field of view difference between lidar and ordinary cameras (The blue area represents the limited field of view of the camera) (Color figure online)

Therefore, we propose using the depth of the sparse point cloud to assist the image expansion. The input of our model is not only the RGB image to be expanded but also the depth map obtained by sparse point cloud projection. This task is more reasonable and more authentic than the general image extension. The general outpainting [12,14,18] is only to expand the content of the input image without many bases, and it is difficult for the generated content to conform to the natural structure of the object. The model we proposed can better correspond to the semantic information according to the structure and depth of the object in the depth map when expanding the image, which will ensure the structure of the objects in the generated content and have a better semantic performance. It will bring great possibilities for the application of image expansion tasks in actual tasks in the future.

In summary, our contributions are as follows:

1. We propose a task goal that uses the depth map obtained from the sparse point cloud to help the image expansion. This task goal is more reasonable than the general outpainting, and it also makes the outpainting task more realistic.
2. We propose a depth model that uses depth maps and RGB images to expand the image. The model is trained and tested in complex scenes with depth information, which is greatly improved compared with general outpainting.
3. We have proposed some solutions for depth feature extraction and conducted experimental comparisons to form a better information interaction match between RGB and depth.

## 2    Related Work

Image restoration tasks have always been a research area that has attracted attention, so these studies can be roughly divided into two categories: non-parametric classical methods [1,3,5,22] and learning-based methods [4,7,10,12, 14,18–20].

**Classical Methods.** The classical methods use traditional computer vision methods, which are mainly based on the similarity and diffusion of the patch. AA Efros et al. [3] initially proposed a method of texture synthesis, which can produce a good and credible effect. M Bertalmio et al. [1] proposed a static image restoration algorithm, which automatically obtains the information of the area outside the hole area for restoration. Y Zhang et al. [22] proposed a method to extrapolate typical photos to a complete panorama using guided images. But these methods do not actually understand the semantics of the image; they cannot generate effective and credible filling content in a slightly more complicated scene.

**Learning-Based Methods.** As the learning-based method can learn the semantics of the image, these method [4,7,10,12,14,18–20] is more effective than the classical method in image restoration. They overcome the weaknesses of the non-parametric classical method. Pathak et al. [10] proposed a parametric image restoration algorithm and a context encoder for the first time. On this basis, IIZUKA et al. [4] proposed to use a full convolutional network to process images of arbitrary resolution and two discriminators of global and local to calculate the adversarial loss. Wang et al. [18] proposed a Semantic Regeneration Network (SRN), and the designed loss makes the network adapt to one-sided constraints, generating semantically meaningful structures and natural textures. P Teter-wak et al. [14] trimmed some components that are not suitable for outpainting tasks and introduced semantic conditions into the discriminator of the generated adversarial network.

These researches can only be applied to simple scenes and texture synthesis tasks. But our work is still effective in complex scenes, making the generated image more reasonable and more credible. In addition, the most important thing is to make the expanded content have authenticity and make the image expansion task more realistic.

## 3  Our Model

Our model uses the confrontational generative network [8] model commonly used in image restoration, so the network includes two parts: generator and discriminator, and the two parts are jointly trained in parallel.

The input of our generator is the RGB image $x$, which contains the hole area to be filled, the corresponding depth map $y$, and set the cropping and filling area mask $M$. It is regarded as the same size as the output image $\hat{x}$, and the pixel value of the known area in $M$ is 0, and the unknown area is 1. The image $x$ is obtained by cropping the Ground truth $z$ by the mask, as

$$x = z \odot (1 - M) \tag{1}$$

Before entering the model, the RGB image x and the depth map y will be normalized to $[-1, 1]$.

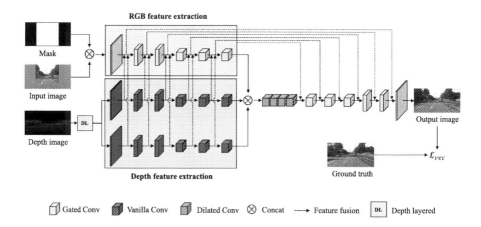

**Fig. 3.** Our framework illustration

### 3.1  Framework Design

Under the guidance of the most advanced image expansion, some parts of our model adopt the method of [14, 21] when processing RGB information and building discriminator. The complete structure of our model is shown in Fig. 3 and 4.

**RGB Feature Extraction.** We adopt the classic encoder structure to extract the features of the input $x$, and design a 6-layer convolutional layer for feature extraction, which all uses Gated Convolution [21]. It allows the model to learn to distinguish between valid pixels and invalid pixels. The dynamic feature selection mechanism for each channel and each spatial position is more in line with image restoration. Therefore, it is more in line with the goal of our research work and image restoration.

We choose to adopt ELU [2] for activation, and we use instance Norm for each layer to normalize [16], so that it can significantly reduce the number of artifacts that will appear in the generated content.

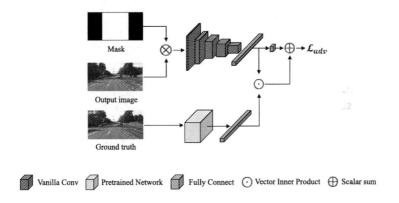

**Fig. 4.** Discriminator illustration

**Depth Feature Extraction.** Different from previous image expansion, the input of our model adds a depth map $y$, so we designed a branch of the feature extraction to process the depth information.

We propose a depth layered structure to distinguish the foreground and background information in the depth map and use the distribution of all non-zero depth values in the depth map to calculate a mean value as the layering threshold (as in Eq. 2).

$$Threshold = \frac{\sum_i \sum_j p(i,j)}{\sum_i \sum_j I} \tag{2}$$

$p(i,j)$ is the pixel value, If $p(i,j) > 0$, then $I = 1$, otherwise $I = 0$.

We divide the original depth map $y$ with this threshold to obtain the foreground and the background depth map, as in Fig. 5.

Because of the principle of depth map, that the depth value of same object or structure is often within the same range, the layered structure is used to

Foreground                          Background

**Fig. 5.** Foreground and background images divided by threshold

have a preliminary division of depth, so that different objects or structures can be distinguished. In the encoding stage, we fuse RGB, foreground, and background depth information to form a similar mechanism with attention. When the generator is processing the depth map, the foreground and background can be extracted feature separately. When filling the hole area, it will be treated as two parts for repair instead of confusing the two parts of structural information during filling. Therefore, it will make the structural distinction of the generated results more straightforward, as shown in Fig. 10.

After obtaining the layered depth, we extract the features of the two depth maps separately. The same is that the 6-layer convolutional layer is also used here as the RGB branch. The difference is that only vanilla convolution is used. The reason for this is that the depth map $y$ is a full-size image, rather than the input of the RGB branch where there are hole areas to be filled and invalid pixels. And Gated Convolution [21] requires to increase the amount of parameters twice as much as vanilla convolution. This part of the activation function also adopts ELU [2], and instance Norm [17] is used to realize normalize.

In addition, we have also tried other solutions in depth feature extraction. For example, we input the entire depth map into the encoder to get a feature map (see Fig. 6(a)). We also adopt early fusion of the depth map and RGB and increase the fusion with the RGB branch (see Fig. 6(a)). We compare these solutions in detail in 4.4.

**Feature Fusion.** We merge the RGB feature extraction branch and the depth feature extraction branch so that they can be interactively matched and realize the correspondence between the RGB and depth.

We interact the feature map of each layer of the depth feature extraction part with the RGB branch, which will enable the model to perform the correspondence between depth and RGB in the early encoding stage, and the feature map will have more detailed information. The object has more visible edges and textures, and the boundary between the object and the scene also becomes more apparent (details in Sect. 4.4).

After fusion of two branches, they will be input into a four-layer dilated convolution block, which improves the model's receptive field. There are six-layers Gated convolution in the decoder stage, two-layer of upsampling, and the last layer of the vanilla convolution. Between the encoder and decoder, we use a skip structure [11] to fuse the feature map of the encoder processing with the corresponding layer. It can bring high-frequency textures to the decoding stage, reducing the seams between the actual content and the generated content.

**Discriminator.** We stitch the generated content output by the generator with the input image $x$ as one of the inputs of the discriminator. And the discriminator adds mask $M$ together as input [14], which can make the discriminator pay more attention to the generated area. [14] proposed to adopt cGAN [9] to encourage the generated content to match the input image semantically, to avoid the phenomenon of semantic drift in long-distance expansion. It chooses to use the InceOptionv3 [13] network with the softmax layer removed and adopt its final 1000-dimensional feature vector as the condition vector. So the final discriminator is shown in Eq. 3.

$$\hat{x} = G(x, y, M) \odot M + x$$
$$D(\hat{x}, M, z) = f(f_\varphi(\hat{x}, M)) + <f_\varphi(\hat{x}, M), f_c(z)>$$

(3)

### 3.2 Training

Our model adopts a combination of a reconstruction loss and an adversarial loss during training.

The reconstruction loss intuitively reflects the difference between the generated results and the target images, so that the images consistency can be optimized, and the complete equation of L1 loss is used to achieve the following as Eq. 4.

$$\mathcal{L}_{rec} = \|z - G(x, y, M)\|_{l_1}$$

(4)

In the previous image generation tasks, it has been proved that the effectiveness of fighting adversarial loss is an indispensable measure to generate convincing details. Therefore, we use Wasserstein GAN hinge loss in our work [6,15] as Eq. 5.

$$\mathcal{L}_{adv,D} = E_{z \sim P_\chi(z)}[\text{ReLU}(1 - D(z, M, z)) + \text{ReLU}(1 + D(\hat{x}, M, z))]$$
$$\mathcal{L}_{adv,G} = E_{z \sim P_\chi(z)}[-D(\hat{x}, M, z)]$$

(5)

Finally, the model objective of our network is expressed as Eq. 6.

$$\mathcal{L} = \mathcal{L}_{rec} + \lambda \mathcal{L}_{adv,G}$$

(6)

In all our experiments, we set $\lambda = 10^{-2}$. Our models are implemented with Pytorch and an NVidia RTX 2080 GPU. The input image $x$, depth map $y$ and mask $M$ size are $512 \times 256$, batch size is set to 6, the generator and discriminator are all jointly trained with the adam optimizer [16], the parameters $\alpha = 10^{-4}$, $\beta_1 = 0.5$, $\beta_2 = 0.9$. Our dataset uses KITT's data depth annotated, but it has been screened and adjusted in size (details are described in Sect. 4.1).

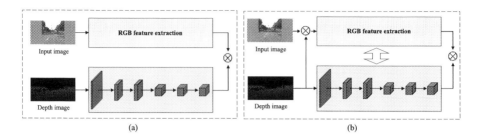

**Fig. 6.** Other solutions in depth feature extraction

## 4    Experiment

### 4.1    Dataset

Our work is based on the RGB image and depth map converted from sparse point cloud projection, and the current datasets for image restoration tasks do not contain depth map information, so we choose to adopt the datasets for depth annotation in KITT [16]. Because the collection of the datasets is carried out during the movement, we decide to select one of every four frames from the original datasets as our dataset, to prevent the scenes from being too similar. The final size of our dataset is 9864.

The selection method of the test set is to extract the middle 10% of the images from each segment of KITT, and others is as the train set. Besides, the resolution of image in KITT dataset is $1242 \times 375$, we crop the part $(512 \times 256)$ of the center position of the image as our dataset.

### 4.2    Quantitative Evaluation

The image expansion range of our model is $256 \times 256 \rightarrow 512 \times 256$. In the quantitative evaluation, we will compare with the two most advanced outpainting models [14,18] as baseline. And use the publicly available code of these models to retrain the model on the KITT dataset.

**Table 1.** Quantitative metrics on 957 test images.

|                        | PSNR        | SSIM       | FID         |
|------------------------|-------------|------------|-------------|
| Outpainting-srn [18]   | 14.8202     | 0.6315     | 34.6327     |
| Boundless [14]         | 14.6845     | 0.6295     | 31.8905     |
| Ours                   | **15.1938** | **0.6340** | **27.5007** |

In the evaluation index, we choose to adopt the most commonly used Peak Signal to Noise Ratio (PSNR) and Structural Similarity (SSIM) in image generation. In addition, Fréchet Inception Distance (FID) is also added as an evaluation

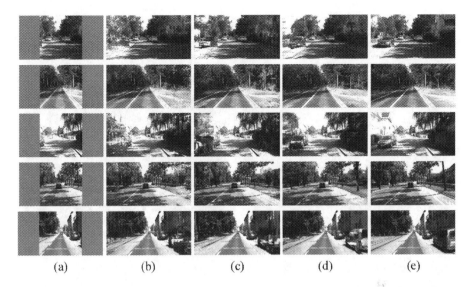

$$(a) \qquad (b) \qquad (c) \qquad (d) \qquad (e)$$

**Fig. 7.** Qualitative evaluation of model effect. (a) Input image. (b) Outpainting-srn. (c) Boundless. (d) Ours. (e) GT

index. We provide the scores of the three models on the evaluation indicators in Table 1.

### 4.3   Qualitative Evaluation

Sometimes the evaluation index cannot fully reflect the goodness of the generated image. Therefore, it is necessary to judge the image quality subjectively from the image through the human senses. We provide the test results of the three models. As shown in Fig. 7, in complex scenes such as street scenes, the generated image by [14,18] always contains many blurred areas. When objects appear at the edges of the image, the generated results are more confusing. Our method can produce more convincing structures and objects, which are reflected on the junction of the object and the road. And objects outside the input image, such as vehicles, trees, and railings, are well reflected in the newly generated content.

**Table 2.** Quantitative metrics of depth feature extraction solutions.

|  | PSNR | SSIM | FID |
|---|---|---|---|
| Encoder | 15.0102 | 0.6382 | 29.7332 |
| Encoder + EF | 15.1369 | 0.64049 | 27.7217 |
| Encoder + EF + FF | 15.1802 | **0.64409** | 28.2289 |
| Encoder + DL | 15.0523 | 0.64407 | 28.4468 |
| Encoder + DL+ FF | **15.1938** | 0.6340 | **27.5007** |

This shows that our model can reflect the actual surroundings, which makes outpainting authentic. This is an effect that general outpainting tasks cannot achieve.

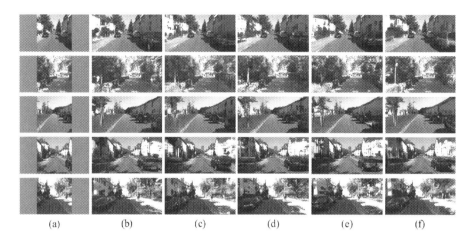

(a)          (b)          (c)          (d)          (e)          (f)

**Fig. 8.** Qualitative evaluation of depth feature extraction solutions. (a) Input image. (b) Encoder. (c) Encoder + EF. (d) Encoder + EF + FF. (e) Encoder + DL. (f) Encoder + DL + FF. (EF is early fusion, FF is fusion between features and DL is depth layered structure)

## 4.4   Comparison of Depth Feature Extraction Solutions

We also design several depth feature extraction solutions in Fig. 3, which include early fusion, fusion of features, and depth layered structure. So we design experiments to compare the impact of these three operations in Table 2.

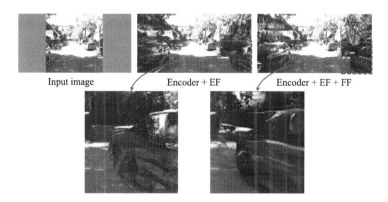

Input image          Encoder + EF          Encoder + EF + FF

**Fig. 9.** Comparison of fusion operation.

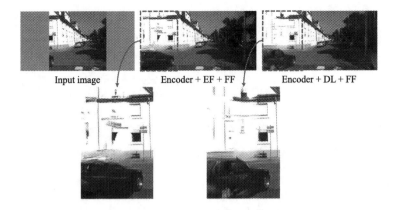

**Fig. 10.** Comparison of depth layered structure.

From the results, Joining early fusion will bring improvement to the model. And further increasing the fusion of features, the model can perform better in Fig. 8. We specifically show the details of the generated image by the model with early fusion and fusion of features and the model with only encoder in Fig. 9. The unfused result has larger blurs. But details are richer in and the structure of the generated object becomes clearer in the latter.

The depth layered structure performs best compared to others, especially in FID. Likewise, in Fig. 10, we show the details of the images generated by the model with depth layered structure and the unlayered depth model. It shows that the model with a depth layered structure can generate better edge information. As a result, the edge structure of the objects is more clearly distinguished.

## 5  Conclusion

We propose using the depth map obtained by sparse point cloud projection to help the image expansion and establish a depth model for the task. In the end, we get more credible and realistic results than general outpainting.

**Acknowledgement.** This work was supported by the National Natural Science Foundation of China (No. 61772066, No. 61972028).

## References

1. Bertalmio, M., Sapiro, G., Caselles, V., Ballester, C.: Image inpainting. In: Proceedings of the 27th Annual Conference on Computer Graphics and Interactive Techniques, pp. 417–424 (2000)
2. Clevert, D.A., Unterthiner, T., Hochreiter, S.: Fast and accurate deep network learning by exponential linear units (ELUs). arXiv preprint arXiv:1511.07289 (2015)
3. Efros, A.A., Leung, T.K.: Texture synthesis by non-parametric sampling. In: Proceedings of the Seventh IEEE International Conference on Computer Vision, vol. 2, pp. 1033–1038. IEEE (1999)

4. Iizuka, S., Simo-Serra, E., Ishikawa, H.: Globally and locally consistent image completion. ACM Trans. Graph. (ToG) **36**(4), 1–14 (2017)
5. Kopf, J., Kienzle, W., Drucker, S., Kang, S.B.: Quality prediction for image completion. ACM Trans. Graph. (ToG) **31**(6), 1–8 (2012)
6. Lim, J.H., Ye, J.C.: Geometric GAN. arXiv preprint arXiv:1705.02894 (2017)
7. Liu, G., et al.: Partial convolution based padding. arXiv preprint arXiv:1811.11718 (2018)
8. Mirza, M., Osindero, S.: Conditional generative adversarial nets. arXiv preprint arXiv:1411.1784 (2014)
9. Miyato, T., Koyama, M.: cGANs with projection discriminator. arXiv preprint arXiv:1802.05637 (2018)
10. Pathak, D., Krahenbuhl, P., Donahue, J., Darrell, T., Efros, A.A.: Context encoders: feature learning by inpainting. In: Proceedings of the IEEE Conference on Computer Vision and Pattern Recognition, pp. 2536–2544 (2016)
11. Ronneberger, O., Fischer, P., Brox, T.: U-Net: convolutional networks for biomedical image segmentation. In: Navab, N., Hornegger, J., Wells, W.M., Frangi, A.F. (eds.) MICCAI 2015. LNCS, vol. 9351, pp. 234–241. Springer, Cham (2015). https://doi.org/10.1007/978-3-319-24574-4_28
12. Sabini, M., Rusak, G.: Painting outside the box: image outpainting with GANs. arXiv preprint arXiv:1808.08483 (2018)
13. Szegedy, C., Vanhoucke, V., Ioffe, S., Shlens, J., Wojna, Z.: Rethinking the inception architecture for computer vision. In: Proceedings of the IEEE Conference on Computer Vision and Pattern Recognition, pp. 2818–2826 (2016)
14. Teterwak, P., et al.: Boundless: generative adversarial networks for image extension. In: Proceedings of the IEEE/CVF International Conference on Computer Vision, pp. 10521–10530 (2019)
15. Tran, D., Ranganath, R., Blei, D.M.: Hierarchical implicit models and likelihood-free variational inference. arXiv preprint arXiv:1702.08896 (2017)
16. Uhrig, J., Schneider, N., Schneider, L., Franke, U., Brox, T., Geiger, A.: Sparsity invariant CNNs. In: 2017 International Conference on 3D Vision (3DV), pp. 11–20. IEEE (2017)
17. Ulyanov, D., Vedaldi, A., Lempitsky, V.: Improved texture networks: maximizing quality and diversity in feed-forward stylization and texture synthesis. In: Proceedings of the IEEE Conference on Computer Vision and Pattern Recognition, pp. 6924–6932 (2017)
18. Wang, Y., Tao, X., Shen, X., Jia, J.: Wide-context semantic image extrapolation. In: Proceedings of the IEEE/CVF Conference on Computer Vision and Pattern Recognition, pp. 1399–1408 (2019)
19. Yang, C., Lu, X., Lin, Z., Shechtman, E., Wang, O., Li, H.: High-resolution image inpainting using multi-scale neural patch synthesis. In: Proceedings of the IEEE Conference on Computer Vision and Pattern Recognition, pp. 6721–6729 (2017)
20. Yu, J., Lin, Z., Yang, J., Shen, X., Lu, X., Huang, T.S.: Generative image inpainting with contextual attention. In: Proceedings of the IEEE Conference on Computer Vision and Pattern Recognition, pp. 5505–5514 (2018)
21. Yu, J., Lin, Z., Yang, J., Shen, X., Lu, X., Huang, T.S.: Free-form image inpainting with gated convolution. In: Proceedings of the IEEE/CVF International Conference on Computer Vision, pp. 4471–4480 (2019)
22. Zhang, Y., Xiao, J., Hays, J., Tan, P.: FrameBreak: dramatic image extrapolation by guided shift-maps. In: Proceedings of the IEEE Conference on Computer Vision and Pattern Recognition, pp. 1171–1178 (2013)

# Light-Weight Multi-channel Aggregation Network for Image Super-Resolution

Pengcheng Bian, Zhonglong Zheng$^{(\boxtimes)}$, and Dawei Zhang

College of Mathematics and Computer Science, Zhejiang Normal University,
Jinhua 321004, China
{cloverxl,zhonglong,davidzhang}@zjnu.edu.cn

**Abstract.** Deep convolutional neural networks (CNNs) have been extensively applied on single image super-resolution (SISR) due to the strong representation. However, since SISR is an ill-posed problem, many CNN-based methods rely heavily on excessive parameters and high computation cost, which limit the practical application on devices with limited resources. In this paper, a light-weight yet effective multi-channel aggregation network (MCAN) is proposed to improve the performance of SISR while maintaining efficiency. Specifically, the network is built upon several efficient multi-channel aggregation blocks, each of which contains a multi-channel aggregation (MCA) module and a dilated attention (DA) module. The proposed MCA module reduces network parameters considerably, moreover, the channel split and concatenation operations ensure multi-channel interaction and enrich multi-scale features effectively. Furthermore, the DA module captures multiple spatial feature correlations using multi-scale dilated convolution for a larger receptive field. Experimental results on four publicly available datasets demonstrate the superiority of the proposed MCAN in terms of accuracy and model complexity.

**Keywords:** Single image super-resolution · Multi-channel aggregation · Dilated attention · Light-weight network

## 1 Introduction

Single image super-resolution (SISR) aims at reconstructing a high-resolution (HR) image from a low-resolution (LR) observation. It has wide applications in the real world, such as medical imaging and high-definition devices. Since there are multiple HR solutions for a single LR input, SISR is a challenging ill-posed problem.

In recent years, owing to the powerful representation ability in learning a non-linear mapping between LR image and HR one, deep learning methods have been successfully applied in SISR task. The first convolutional neural network (CNN) for SISR is proposed by Dong et al. [1], namely, super-resolution using convolutional neural network (SRCNN), which is built by three key components: shallow feature extraction, nonlinear mapping, and reconstruction, each of which

© Springer Nature Switzerland AG 2021
H. Ma et al. (Eds.): PRCV 2021, LNCS 13021, pp. 287–297, 2021.
https://doi.org/10.1007/978-3-030-88010-1_24

contains one convolutional layer. Since then, various CNN-based methods have emerged to provide outstanding performance for SISR tasks, and there is a trend that designing a deeper network to pursue better performance. Very deep network for super-resolution (VDSR) [2] proposes a deep network with 20 layers. Besides, residual-learning and adaptive gradient clipping are utilized to ease the training process, however, when the number of convolutional layers further increases, the model faces the problem of gradient vanishing. To overcome this problem, enhanced deep network for super-resolution (EDSR) [3] adopts residual blocks without unnecessary modules, and further expands model size while stabilizing the training procedure. In addition to the design of novel architectures, some methods incorporate attention mechanism into SR network to capture feature inter-dependencies for discriminative representation, such as residual channel attention network (RCAN) [4], second-order attention network (SAN) [5], and residual feature aggregation network (RFANet) [6]. Despite the remarkable achievements, these networks mainly focus on performance improvement while ignoring excessive model parameters and high computation cost, resulting in the hard deployment for real-world applications. Furthermore, blindly increasing the network width and depth not only is detrimental to the interaction of feature information but also introduce redundant model parameters.

To address the above issues, some SR networks with light-weight modules and efficient strategies have been proposed. Deeply-recursive convolutional network (DRCN) [7] uses a recursive learning strategy to control the model parameters. Deep recursive residual network (DRRN) [8] combines residual learning and recursive learning to further improve performance with fewer parameters. Considering the advantage of channel-wise feature responses recalibration, Information distillation network (IDN) [9] utilizes multiple stacked information distillation blocks to distill residual information progressively. Cascading residual network (CARN) [10] designs an architecture that implements a cascading mechanism upon a residual network. ODE-inspired super-resolution network (OISR) [11] is the first attempt to apply ODE-inspired schemes to the design of SR network, and achieves a better trade-off between model accuracy and complexity. Lightweight enhanced SR CNN (LESRCNN) [12] first extracts and aggregates hierarchical LR features sequentially, and then adopts a heterogeneous architecture to remove redundant information.

Recently, a new architecture, called HS-ResNet [13], achieves the state-of-the-art performance on several tasks, such as image classification [14], object detection [15], in which multiple efficient hierarchical-split blocks are adopted to generate multi-scale feature representations. The hierarchical-split block consists of two stages of split and concatenate operation. Inspired by HS-ResNet, we revise the structure of the hierarchical-split block and propose a multi-channel aggregation network. The proposed multi-channel aggregation (MCA) module enables the interaction of multi-channel and the generation of multi-scale features without introducing extra parameters. Besides, in order to enhance the representation capability of features, dilated attention (DA) module is developed for a larger receptive field. Moreover, we design a modified up-sampling block (UB) with residual connection to further enhance the performance of the final reconstruction.

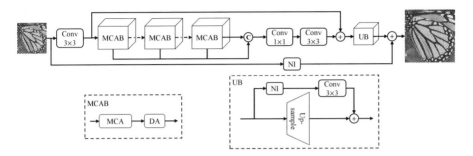

**Fig. 1.** Network architecture of the proposed multi-channel aggregation network (MCAN). Given a LR image, MCAN first extracts initial feature maps with a convolutional layer. Then a set of multi-channel aggregation blocks (MCABs) further extracts deeper features in sequence. Each of the MCABs consists of a multi-channel aggregation (MCA) module and a dilated attention (DA) module. The outputs of all MCABs are concatenated together to generate multi-scale features. Finally, an up-sampling block with a residual connection is adopted to obtain HR image. "NI" denotes nearest interpolation.

In summarize, the main contributions of this paper are as follows:

- We propose an effective and light-weight multi-channel aggregation network. The network is able to extract multi-scale features, and the split and concatenate operations ensure feature interaction at a more granular level of channels.
- To enlarge the receptive field of features and fuse representative information, we design a dilated attention module. The module contains several dilated convolution with different kernel size for exploring multi-scale feature representations.
- Extensive experiments on several benchmark datasets show that the proposed network performs favorably against the state-of-the-art methods for light-weight SISR.

## 2    Proposed Method

In this section, we first present the overall architecture of MCAN. Then we introduce the proposed MCA module, DA module in detail.

### 2.1    Network Architecture

As shown in Fig. 1, the proposed MCAN mainly consists of multiple MCABs. First of all, given a LR image $I_{LR}$ as input, a $3 \times 3$ convolutional layer is used to extract shallow features $H_0$:

$$H_0 = f_0(I_{LR}), \tag{1}$$

where $f_0(\cdot)$ denotes convolution operation.

Then the extracted features $H_0$ is further fed to the MCABs for deeper feature extraction, we will dive into the detailed modules of the MCAB in Sect. 2.2 and Sect. 2.3:

$$H_i = f_i(H_{i-1}) = f_i(f_{i-1}(\cdots f_1(H_0))), \ i \in \{1, 2, \ldots, N\} \tag{2}$$

where $f_i(\cdot)$ represents the function of the $i$-th MCAB, and $N$ is the number of MCABs, $H_i$ and $H_{i-1}$ denotes the output and input of the $i$-th MCAB, respectively.

Next, the outputs of $N$ blocks are concatenated together, and a $1 \times 1$ convolution followed by a $3 \times 3$ convolution is adopted for channel reduction:

$$H_d = H_0 + f_d(f_r([H_1, \cdots, H_n, \cdots, H_N])) \tag{3}$$

where $H_d$ is the output after channel reduction and convolution, $f_d(\cdot)$ denotes a $3 \times 3$ convolution with a parametric rectify linear unit (PReLU) activation function, $f_r(\cdot)$ denotes a $1 \times 1$ convolution, and $[\cdot]$ denotes the concatenation operation.

Subsequently, the refined features $H_d$ is up-sampled by an up-sampling block (UB), unlike previous methods [6], a residual connection with nearest interpolation and a $3 \times 3$ convolution are used in the UB, the process can be formulated as follows:

$$H_u = f_{up}(H_d) + f_e(f_{ni}(H_d)) \tag{4}$$

where $H_u$ denotes the output of UB, $f_{up}(\cdot)$ and $f_{ni}(\cdot)$ denote up-sampling with sub-pixel convolution [16] and with nearest interpolation respectively, $f_e(\cdot)$ denotes a $3 \times 3$ convolution followed by a PReLU activation function to convert the channel of feature maps to 3.

Finally, for further performance improvement, a global residual connection with nearest interpolation is adopted:

$$I_{SR} = H_u + f_{ni}(I_{LR}) \tag{5}$$

where $I_{SR}$ denotes the final super-resolved HR image.

## 2.2   MCA: Multi-Channel Aggregation Module

In order to generate stronger feature representations without increasing computational complexity, we adopt a multi-channel aggregation module, named as MCA. The module contains several split and concatenation operation, specifically, the input of the module will be split into $K$ groups, denoted by $H_1, \cdots, H_K$, each with $t$ channels. As shown in Fig. 2, the module takes a progressively hierarchical concatenation strategy, the first two groups of features $H_1$, $H_2$ are concatenated and sent to a $1 \times 1$ convolution, followed by a $3 \times$

3 convolution with a PReLU activation function, then the extracted feature is added with the original two input features:

$$S_1 = f_{cp(1)}([H_1, H_2]) + H_1 + H_2 \tag{6}$$

where $S_1$ is the output of the first split-concatenate operation, and $f_{cp(1)}(\cdot)$ denotes the function that consists of a $1 \times 1$ convolution, a $3 \times 3$ convolution and a PReLU function.

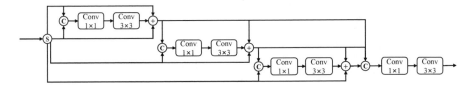

**Fig. 2.** Structure of multi-channel aggregation (MCA) module. Each $3 \times 3$ convolution followed by a PReLU activation function. "S" denotes channel split operation, "C" denotes concatenation operation.

Similarly, the next split-concatenate operation follows the same process as the first one, except that one of the inputs is the output of the previous step:

$$S_k = f_{cp(k)}([S_{(k-1)}, H_{(k+1)}]) + S_{(k-1)} + H_{(k+1)} \tag{7}$$

After several split-concatenate operation, the hierarchical features $S_k, k \in \{1, \cdots, K-1\}$ are concatenated together, and an extra convolution operation is utilized to get the final output:

$$H_{MCA(i)} = f_{cp(i)}([S_1, \cdots, S_{(K-1)}]) \tag{8}$$

where $H_{MCA(i)}$ denotes the output of the $i$-th MCA module.

Thanks to the channel split operation, the proposed MCA module can be used to extract multi-scale features without introducing an excessive number of parameters, which is effective and light-weight.

### 2.3  DA: Dilated Attention Module

The MCA module ensures the interaction of different channels, but ignores the spatial correlations. Aiming at enhance the model representation capability among spatial dimension, we design a dilated attention (DA) module. Different from the existing spatial attention block of [6] that including a pooling and an up-sapmpling layer, we adopt dilation convolution to enlarge the receptive field, for the reason that the pooling and up-sampling operation can cause the loss of information, which will be detrimental to the modeling of information.

Figure 3 illustrates the structure of our proposed DA module. In DA module, the input feature is split into $M$ branches using $M$ $1 \times 1$ convolution, then each brance is fed to a convolution with different dilation rate and kernel size are utilized to explore multi-scale spatial information:

$$H_{m(i)} = f_{e(i)}(f_{d(i)}(H_{MCA(i)}))\qquad(9)$$

where $H_{m(i)}$ denotes the output of the $i$-th part, $f_{e(i)}(\cdot)$ and $f_{d(i)}(\cdot)$ denote the $3 \times 3$ convolution and $1 \times 1$ convolution respectively.

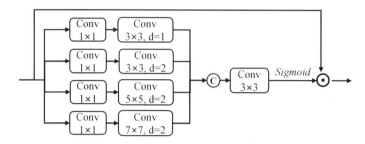

**Fig. 3.** Structure of dilated attention (DA) module. Each $3 \times 3$ convolution followed by a PReLU activation function, "d" denotes the dilation rate of convolution. "C" denotes concatenation operation.

Then the outputs of all brances are concatenated together and followed by a $3 \times 3$ convolution $f_e(\cdot)$ with PReLU function, finally, the attention map $A_i$ is generated by a Sigmoid function:

$$A_i = Sigmoid(f_e([H_{m(1)}, \cdots, H_{m(M)}]))\qquad(10)$$

where $Sigmoid(\cdot)$ denotes Sigmoid function, $H_{m(i)}, i \in \{1, \cdots, M\}$ denotes the output of the $i$-th branch.

## 3    Experiments

### 3.1    Experimental Settings

In this subsection, we present the experimental settings including datasets, evaluation metrics, and implementation details.

**Datasets.** Following [3], We choose DIV2K [17] dataset as the training set, in which 800 image pairs are used, and the LR images are generated from the corresponding HR images by bicubic interpolation with a fixed scale factor. For testing, we select four benchmark datasets: Set5 [18], Set14 [19], B100 [20], Urban100 [21].

**Evaluation Metrics.** For evaluation, images reconstructed by MCAN are first converted to YCbCr color space, then SR performance is measured with two widely used metrics, i.e., peak signal-to-noise ratio (PSNR) and structural similarity (SSIM) [22] on Y (i.e., luminance) channel only.

**Implementation Details.** In our experiment of MCAN, we adopt $N = 8$ MCABs, each block consists of a MCA module and a DA module. In each MCA module, we set the split ratio $K = 4$, and the initial channel number of input features is 64. In each DA module, input feature is split into $M = 4$ branches, the channel number of each branch after a $1 \times 1$ convolution is 16. The first branch is followed by a plain $3 \times 3$ convolution, while the other three branches are followed by a convolution with a kernel size of $3 \times 3$, $5 \times 5$, $7 \times 7$, respectively, and each convolution with a dilation rate of 2.

We set mini-batch size as 24 and initial learning rate as $10^{-4}$, which is halved at every $2 \times 10^5$ iterations. Following [3], we augment the training data with random horizontal flips and $90°$, $180°$, $270°$ rotations. We implement our network on PyTorch platform and run experiments with a NVIDIA Tesla V100 GPU. The network is trained with ADAM optimizer by setting parameters $\beta_1 = 0.9$, $\beta_2 = 0.999$, and $\epsilon = 10^{-8}$, we adopt the $L1$ loss function to optimize the network weights:

$$L(\Theta) = \frac{1}{T} \sum_{i=1}^{T} \left\| MCAN(I_{LR}^i, \Theta) - I_{HR}^i \right\|_1, \tag{11}$$

where $MCAN(\cdot)$, $T$ and $\Theta$ denote the function of the proposed MCAN, the number of training image pairs and the parameters of the MCAN, respectively.

## 3.2 Comparisons with the State-Of-The-Arts

In this part, we compare our MCAN with seven state-of-the-art light-weight SISR methods on $\times2$, $\times3$ and $\times4$ scales, including VSDR [2], DRCN [7], DRRN [8], IDN [9], CARN [10], OISR-LF-s [11], LESRCNN [12]. As shown in Table 1, our MCAN outperforms other state-of-the-art light-weight methods on all benchmarks in terms of PSNR and SSIM metrics. In addition, visual comparisons of various methods are provided in Fig. 4. It can be seen that our MCAN is able to reconstruct more clearer structure and details, compared with other methods.

Both quantitative and qualitative results show that the proposed MCAN performs favorably against the state-of-the-art light-weight methods.

## 3.3 Ablation Study

In this subsection, we conduct some ablation studies to verify the effectiveness of the proposed MCAB and two components, i.e., MCA module and DA module. Specifically, We first analyze the impact of the number of MCAB on network performance, and then form four variants by removing DA module accordingly. Moreover, in order to check the efficiency of our module, we replace the residual block in EDSR [3] with the proposed MCA module and build a model, named as MCASR.

**Table 1.** Quantitative results in terms of average PSNR and SSIM results on four datasets with scale factors of ×2, ×3 and ×4. Best results are **highlighted**.

| Methods | Scale | Params (K) | Set5 | | Set14 | | B100 | | Urban100 | |
|---|---|---|---|---|---|---|---|---|---|---|
| | | | PSRN | SSIM | PSRN | SSIM | PSRN | SSIM | PSRN | SSIM |
| Bicubic | ×2 | – | 33.66 | 0.9299 | 30.24 | 0.8688 | 29.56 | 0.8431 | 26.88 | 0.8403 |
| VDSR [2] | ×2 | 666 | 37.53 | 0.9590 | 33.05 | 0.9130 | 31.90 | 0.8960 | 30.76 | 0.9140 |
| DRCN [7] | ×2 | 1774 | 37.63 | 0.9588 | 33.04 | 0.9118 | 31.85 | 0.8942 | 30.75 | 0.9133 |
| DRRN [8] | ×2 | 298 | 37.74 | 0.9591 | 33.23 | 0.9136 | 32.05 | 0.8973 | 31.23 | 0.9188 |
| IDN [9] | ×2 | 553 | 37.83 | 0.9600 | 33.30 | 0.9148 | 32.08 | 0.8985 | 31.27 | 0.9196 |
| LESRCNN [12] | ×2 | 516 | 37.65 | 0.9586 | 33.32 | 0.9148 | 31.95 | 0.8964 | 31.45 | 0.9207 |
| CARN [10] | ×2 | 1592 | 37.76 | 0.9590 | 33.52 | 0.9166 | 32.09 | 0.8978 | 31.92 | 0.9256 |
| OISR-LF-s [11] | ×2 | 1370 | 38.02 | 0.9605 | 33.62 | 0.9178 | 32.20 | 0.9000 | 32.21 | 0.9290 |
| MCAN | ×2 | 939 | **38.06** | **0.9608** | **33.66** | **0.9181** | **33.22** | **0.9002** | **32.26** | **0.9296** |
| Bicubic | ×3 | – | 30.39 | 0.8682 | 27.55 | 0.7742 | 27.21 | 0.7385 | 24.46 | 0.7349 |
| VDSR [2] | ×3 | 666 | 33.66 | 0.9213 | 29.77 | 0.8314 | 28.82 | 0.7976 | 27.14 | 0.8279 |
| DRCN [7] | ×3 | 1774 | 33.82 | 0.9226 | 29.76 | 0.8311 | 28.80 | 0.7963 | 27.15 | 0.8276 |
| DRRN [8] | ×3 | 298 | 34.03 | 0.9244 | 29.96 | 0.8349 | 28.95 | 0.8004 | 27.53 | 0.8378 |
| IDN [9] | ×3 | 553 | 34.11 | 0.9253 | 29.99 | 0.8354 | 28.95 | 0.8013 | 27.42 | 0.8359 |
| LESRCNN [12] | ×3 | 516 | 33.93 | 0.9231 | 30.12 | 0.8380 | 28.91 | 0.8005 | 27.76 | 0.8424 |
| CARN [10] | ×3 | 1592 | 34.29 | 0.9255 | 30.29 | 0.8407 | 29.06 | 0.8034 | 28.06 | 0.8493 |
| OISR-LF-s [11] | ×3 | 1550 | 34.39 | 0.9272 | 30.35 | 0.8426 | 29.11 | 0.8058 | 28.24 | 0.8544 |
| MCAN | ×3 | 1124 | **34.43** | **0.9275** | **30.41** | **0.8430** | **29.12** | **0.8059** | **28.25** | **0.8546** |
| Bicubic | ×4 | – | 28.42 | 0.8104 | 26.00 | 0.7027 | 25.96 | 0.6675 | 23.14 | 0.6577 |
| VDSR [2] | ×4 | 666 | 31.35 | 0.8838 | 28.01 | 0.7674 | 27.29 | 0.7251 | 25.18 | 0.7524 |
| DRCN [7] | ×4 | 1774 | 31.53 | 0.8854 | 28.02 | 0.7670 | 27.23 | 0.7233 | 25.14 | 0.7510 |
| DRRN [8] | ×4 | 298 | 31.68 | 0.8888 | 28.21 | 0.7720 | 27.38 | 0.7284 | 25.44 | 0.7638 |
| IDN [9] | ×4 | 553 | 31.82 | 0.8903 | 28.25 | 0.7730 | 27.41 | 0.7297 | 25.41 | 0.7632 |
| LESRCNN [12] | ×4 | 516 | 31.88 | 0.8903 | 28.44 | 0.7772 | 27.45 | 0.7313 | 25.78 | 0.7739 |
| CARN [10] | ×4 | 1592 | 32.13 | 0.8937 | 28.60 | 0.7806 | 27.58 | 0.7349 | 26.07 | 0.7837 |
| OISR-LF-s [11] | ×4 | 1520 | 32.14 | 0.8947 | 28.63 | 0.7819 | 27.60 | 0.7369 | 26.17 | 0.7888 |
| MCAN | ×4 | 1087 | **32.29** | **0.8962** | **28.64** | **0.7820** | **27.61** | **0.7369** | **26.20** | **0.7891** |

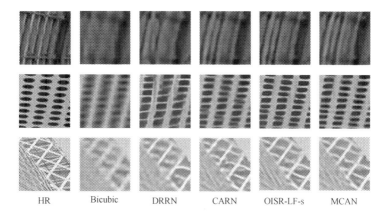

HR        Bicubic        DRRN        CARN        OISR-LF-s        MCAN

**Fig. 4.** Visual comparisons for 4× SR on "img002", "img04", "img039" from Urban100 dataset.

Table 2 shows the results of our first ablation study, in the experiment, we set the number of MCAB to 4, 6, 8, 10, respectively. With the increase of the number of blocks, the performance on Set5 dataset for ×2 SR is gradually improved, however, the number of parameters is also increasing. To achieve a good trade-off between effectiveness and efficiency, we adopt eight MCABs in our network. In addition, to investigate the effectiveness of our proposed DA module, we remove the module from the network for comparison.

**Table 2.** Ablation study on the effects of the DA module and the number of MCAB. "✓" means the corresponding module is used while "×" means not. PSRN and SSIM are calculated on Set5 (2×).

| Number of MCAB | Params (K) | DA | PSNR | SSIM |
|---|---|---|---|---|
| 4 | 473 | × | 37.82 | 0.9598 |
| 6 | 578 | × | 37.87 | 0.9600 |
| 8 | 684 | × | 37.91 | 0.9603 |
| 10 | 789 | × | 37.94 | 0.9604 |
| 4 | 600 | ✓ | 37.91 | 0.9602 |
| 6 | 770 | ✓ | 37.97 | 0.9604 |
| 8 | 939 | ✓ | 38.06 | 0.9608 |
| 10 | 1108 | ✓ | 38.10 | 0.9610 |

**Table 3.** Ablation study on the effectiveness of MCA module. MCASR is our proposed model by replacing residual block in [3] with MCA module. PSRN and SSIM are calculated on Set5 (2×).

| Model | Params (M) | PSNR | SSIM |
|---|---|---|---|
| EDSR [3] | 40.7 | 38.11 | 0.9602 |
| MCASR | 27.8 | 38.22 | 0.9614 |

As shown in Table 2, in general, the performance of PSNR can be increased by 0.1dB using the DA module, which indicates that the module is helpful to fuse multi-scale features. It is worth noting that the first variant with four MCA modules has fewer parameters while higher accuracy than LESRCNN [12], which demonstrates the effectiveness and efficiency of the MCA module.

The comparison between the MCASR and EDSR is shown in Table 3. According to the results, the proposed MCASR has nearly half size of parameters compared with EDSR, while the performance is 0.11dB and 0.0012 higher than EDSR in terms of PSNR and SSIM. Empirically, the decrease of parameters is due to channel split operation and the performance improvement is owing to multi-channel aggregation operation.

## 4 Conclusion

In this paper, we propose a light-weight yet effective MCAN for single image super-resolution, Specifically, the network consists of multiple MCABs, each of which is the combination of a MCA module and a DA module. The MCA module is good at extracting multi-scale features via multi-channel interaction and achieves light-weight with channel split and concatenation operation. Besides, in order to improve model representation capability and increase the receptive field, we adopt the DA module for the further fusion of multi-scale features. Extensive experiments on four benchmark datasets demonstrate that our network outperforms other state-of-the-art light-weight networks in terms of accuracy and visual results.

## References

1. Dong, C., Loy, C.C., He, K., Tang, X.: Learning a deep convolutional network for image super-resolution. In: Fleet, D., Pajdla, T., Schiele, B., Tuytelaars, T. (eds.) ECCV 2014. LNCS, vol. 8692, pp. 184–199. Springer, Cham (2014). https://doi.org/10.1007/978-3-319-10593-2_13
2. Kim, J., Lee, J. K., Lee, K. M.: Accurate image super-resolution using very deep convolutional networks. In: The IEEE Conference on Computer Vision and Pattern Recognition (CVPR), pp. 1646–1654 (2016)
3. Lim, B., Son, S., Kim, H., Nah, S., Lee, K. M.: Enhanced deep residual networks for single image superresolution. In: The IEEE Conference on Computer Vision and Pattern Recognition Workshops (CVPRW), pp. 1132–1140 (2017)
4. Zhang, Y., Li, K., Li, K., Wang, L., Zhong, B., Fu, Y.: Image super-resolution using very deep residual channel attention networks. In: Ferrari, V., Hebert, M., Sminchisescu, C., Weiss, Y. (eds.) ECCV 2018. LNCS, vol. 11211, pp. 294–310. Springer, Cham (2018). https://doi.org/10.1007/978-3-030-01234-2_18
5. Dai, T., Cai, J., Zhang, Y., Xia, S., Zhang, L.: Second-order attention network for single image superresolution. In: The IEEE Conference on Computer Vision and Pattern Recognition (CVPR), pp. 11057–11066 (2019)
6. Liu, J., Zhang, W., Tang, Y., Tang, J., Wu, G.: Residual feature aggregation network for image superresolution. In: The IEEE Conference on Computer Vision and Pattern Recognition (CVPR), pp. 2356–2365 (2020)
7. Kim, J., Lee, J.K., Lee, K. M.: Deeply-recursive convolutional network for image super-resolution. In: The IEEE Conference on Computer Vision and Pattern Recognition (CVPR), pp. 1637–1645 (2016)
8. Tai, Y., Yang, J., Liu, X.: Image super-resolution via deep recursive residual network. In: The IEEE Conference on Computer Vision and Pattern Recognition (CVPR), pp. 2790–2798 (2017)
9. Hui, Z., Wang, X., Gao, X.: Fast and accurate single image super-resolution via information distillation network. In: The IEEE Conference on Computer Vision and Pattern Recognition (CVPR), pp. 723–731 (2018)
10. Ahn, N., Kang, B., Sohn, K.-A.: Fast, accurate, and lightweight super-resolution with cascading residual network. In: Ferrari, V., Hebert, M., Sminchisescu, C., Weiss, Y. (eds.) ECCV 2018. LNCS, vol. 11214, pp. 256–272. Springer, Cham (2018). https://doi.org/10.1007/978-3-030-01249-6_16

11. He, X., Mo, Z., Wang, P., Liu, Y., Yang, M., Cheng, J.: Ode-inspired network design for single image superresolution. In: Proceedings of the IEEE Conference on Computer Vision and Pattern Recognition (CVPR), pp. 1732–1741 (2019)

12. Tian, C., Zhuge, R., Wu, Z., Xu, Y., Zuo, W., Chen, C., Lin, C.: Lightweight image super-resolution with enhanced CNN. Knowl.-Based Syst. **205**, 106235 (2020)

13. Yuan, P., Lin, S., Cui, C., Du, Y., Guo, R., He D., Ding, E., Han, S.: HS-ResNet: hierarchical-split block on convolutional neural network. arXiv preprint arXiv:2010.07621 (2020)

14. Krizhevsky, A., Sutskever, I., et al.: ImageNet classification with deep convolutional neural networks. In: Advances in Neural Information Processing Systems, pp. 1097–1105 (2012)

15. Ren, S., He, K., Girshick, R., Sun, J.: Faster R-CNN: towards real-time object detection with region proposal networks. In: Advances in Neural Information Processing Systems, pp. 91–99 (2015)

16. Shi, W., et al.: Real-time single image and video super-resolution using an efficient subpixel convolutional neural network. In: The IEEE Conference on Computer Vision and Pattern Recognition (CVPR), pp. 1874–1883 (2016)

17. Timofte, R., Agustsson, E., Van Gool, L., Yang, M.H., Zhang, L.: NTIRE 2017 challenge on single image super-resolution: methods and results. In: The IEEE Conference on Computer Vision and Pattern Recognition Workshops (CVPRW), pp. 1110–1121 (2017)

18. Bevilacqua, M., Roumy, A., Guillemot, C., Alberi-Morel, M.L.: Low-Complexity Single-image Super-Resolution Based on Nonnegative Neighbor Embedding. BMVA Press (2012)

19. Zeyde, R., Elad, M., Protter, M.: On single image scale-up using sparse-representations. In: Boissonnat, J.-D., et al. (eds.) Curves and Surfaces 2010. LNCS, vol. 6920, pp. 711–730. Springer, Heidelberg (2012). https://doi.org/10.1007/978-3-642-27413-8_47

20. Martin, D., Fowlkes, C., Tal, D., Malik, J., et al.: A database of human segmented natural images and its application to evaluating segmentation algorithms and measuring ecological statistics. In: ICCV, Vancouver (2001)

21. Huang, J.B., Singh, A., Ahuja, N.: Single image super-resolution from transformed self-exemplars. In: Proceedings of the IEEE Conference on Computer Vision and Pattern Recognition (CVPR), pp. 5197–5206 (2015)

22. Wang, Z., Bovik, A.C., Sheikh, H.R., Simoncelli, E.P.: Image quality assessment: from error visibility to structural similarity. IEEE Trans. Image Process. **13**(4), 600–612 (2004)

# Slow Video Detection Based on Spatial-Temporal Feature Representation

Jianyu Ma[1,2], Haichao Yao[1,2], Rongrong Ni[1,2(✉)], and Yao Zhao[1,2]

[1] Institute of Information Science, Beijing Jiaotong University, Beijing 100044, China
`rrni@bjtu.edu.cn`
[2] Beijing Key Laboratory of Advanced Information Science and Network Technology,
Beijing 100044, China

**Abstract.** As the carrier of information, digital video plays an important role in daily life. With the development of video editing tools, the authenticity of video is facing enormous challenges. As an inter-frame forgery, video speed manipulation may lead to the complete change of the video semantics. In this paper, in order to achieve effective detection for both frame sampling and frame mixing in video slow speed forgery, we proposed a spatial-temporal feature for classification. First, the periodic traces of frame difference are extracted through autocorrelation analysis, and the corresponding coefficients are used as the temporal feature. Secondly, aiming at making full use of the artifacts left in the spatial domain, and overcoming the issue of the temporal feature when the periodic traces are weak, we employ the Markov feature of the frame difference to reveal spatial traces of the forgery and utilize minimum fusion strategy to obtain the video-level spatial feature. Finally, a specific joint spatial-temporal feature is used to detect the slow speed videos through Ensemble classifier. A large number of experiments have proved the superiority of our proposed feature compared with the state-of-the-art method under two kinds of slow speed forgeries.

**Keywords:** Video forensics · Slow speed forgery · Spatial-temporal feature · Ensemble classifier

## 1 Introduction

With the advancement of editing tools, it has become easier for people to maliciously forge a video, which makes it difficult to distinguish from authentic video. Once these videos are uploaded to a public network, they will have a great impact on society. Therefore, it is necessary to find fast and effective video authenticity identification methods.

This work was supported in part by the National Key Research and Development of China (2018YFC0807306), National NSF of China (U1936212), Beijing Fund-Municipal Education Commission Joint Project (KZ202010015023).

H. Ma et al. (Eds.): PRCV 2021, LNCS 13021, pp. 298–309, 2021.
https://doi.org/10.1007/978-3-030-88010-1_25

**Fig. 1.** News of video speed manipulation

Digital video forgery includes two categories: intra-frame forgery and inter-frame forgery. Intra-frame forgery implies tampering on the spatial domain. Inter-frame forgery aims to destroy the original temporal information of video, such as frame deletion, insertion, duplication, interpolation. Compared with the intra-frame forgery, the inter-frame forgery is usually simple and difficult to distinguish by the human visual system. In the condition of the invariant frame rate, if the video is inserted with some frames evenly, the speed of the video will be slowed down. Once the speed of the video changes, the semantics of the video can be misinterpreted or completely opposed. For example, as shown in Fig. 1, the distorted video of Pelosi who is the House Speaker, altered to make her sound as if she has drunkenly slurring her words. This video was spreaded rapidly across the social media in 2019. If similar news is used maliciously, it will misunderstand the public and bring serious social problems. So in this paper, we discusses the forgery of video speed.

In the literature, there are many works focusing on inter-frame forensics [2–7], but not much work for speed forgery forensics. Frame rate is an important property of video, which indicates the number of frames played per second. Speed forgery is divided into two cases, the case of constant frame rate and the case of changing frame rate. For the case of frame rate increase, Ding *et al.* [15] designed spatial-temporal Markov statistical features to capture the difference in the residual signal. They also proposed a combination feature of pixel domain and optical domain to detect frame rate increase in [16]. For the case of invariant frame rate, Hosier *et al.* [1] used the number of bytes encoded in each P-frame as the basis for detecting inserted frames. The advantage of the way is timesaving, but it is only for a speed tampering method. In summary, there are few works have the ability to defeat the two slow speed forgery methods under the condition of the invariant frame rate. Therefore, our work focuses on the case of invariant frame rate.

In this paper, we propose a joint spatial-temporal feature based on AutoCorrelation Coefficients and Markov feature (ACCM) to detect slow videos, which obtained by combining spatial information on the basis of time traces. It can detect the slow videos faked by different operation methods. The experimental results show that the accuracy of the detection results of the proposed method can reach 99%.

Our contributions are summarized as follows:

- To improve the accuracy of detection towards different forgery methods, we designed a spatial-temporal feature representation based on based on theoretical analysis.
- We have developed algorithms to detect slow speed videos that have been manipulated in two methods, it improves the detection accuracy when forgery traces are weak especially.

The rest of the paper is organized as follows. After discussing the background related work in Sect. 2, we introduce the proposed method in Sect. 3. We present the experimental results in Sect. 4 and conclude this paper in Sect. 5.

## 2   Background and Related Work

For slow video forgery, while maintaining the invariant frame rate, it is necessary to evenly insert the frames to the video in order to make the video speed slower and smoother. It can be easily implemented through software such as Adobe Premiere etc. without professional knowledge.

Based on the Adobe Premiere operating technical documentation [17], there are three optional methods of video interpolation, namely frame sampling, frame mixing, and optical-flow based method. As shown in Fig. 2(a), the frame sampling generates interpolated frames by copying the previous frame. Besides, frame mixing is to merge the two frames before and after the interpolated position to generate a new frame. For example, as shown in Fig. 2(b), averaging the pixels of the two frames before and after as a new frame is the most common case. $t$ is defined as the multiple of original duration. For example, when $t = 2$ as shown in Fig. 2, the number of video frames is twice as many as before, and the video speed becomes half of the original video. Optical-flow based method means that the software needs to compensate motion information into the interpolated frames by inferring the track of the pixel movement based on the before and after frames. However, this method takes a long time to generate a new frame and consumes a lot of resources. Therefore, in this paper, we consider two simpler and more common interpolation methods between frames, namely frame sampling and frame mixing.

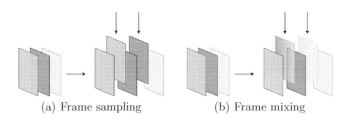

(a) Frame sampling          (b) Frame mixing

**Fig. 2.** Methods of video speed manipulation

We found that the video generated by ffmpeg [13] can simulate frame sampling. Figure 3(a) is used as an example to demonstrate. As shown in Fig. 3(b), it is the sequence diagram of the average value of the frame difference under the frame sampling method when $t = 2$. The frame difference is obtained by subtracting the previous frame from the next frame. We can see that the correlation between the two frames before and after is very high and the difference is small. Therefore, frame sampling slow video can be generated using ffmpeg, as follows:

$$ffmpeg \quad -i \quad Original\,Video \quad -filter:v \quad "setpts = rate*PTS" \quad newvideo \tag{1}$$

(a) A video example

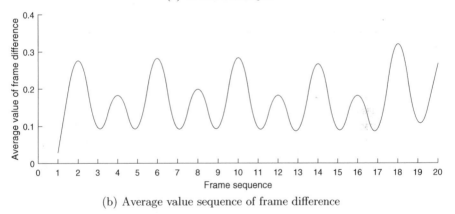

(b) Average value sequence of frame difference

**Fig. 3.** The average value of the frame difference under the frame sampling method

Besides, the matlab tools are used for simulating frame mixing. We first calculate the position that need to be inserted, then select the before and after frames to calculate the average frame.

Next, the related works are introduced. There have been many methods for inter-frame forgery forensics. From the perspective of correlation, Wang *et al.* [2] capture the correlation change between P-frames according to the video GOP structure to detect the peak caused by the sudden change of the signal, thereby judging the fake videos. Both of these methods are designed for MPEG-1 and

MPEG-2 encoded video, which is not common today. Frame tampering will destroy the consistency of the optical flow and the similarity of the characteristics of the frames. They also proposed a method of extracting discontinuous points using optical flow change sequence to detect anomalies and identify forgery based on inter-frame in [3]. Due to optical flow estimation, their method requires a lot of calculation time. Kingra *et al.* [4] proposed a hybrid model by using the optical flow gradient and predicting the residual error of the P-frame. The technology also performs well in complex scenes. However, for high-illuminance videos, the performance of this technology will decrease. Kobla *et al.* [5] proposed a method to detect slow motion playback in motion videos through macroblock types and motion vectors. Zhao *et al.* [6] proposed a static background video frame deletion detection based on multi-scale mutual information. Normalized mutual information is used to measure the similarity of adjacent frames. The toampering position can be located by performing a modified generalized extreme studentized deviate(ESD) test. Deep learning can also be used to detect inter-frame forgery. Sondos *et al.* [7] proposed 2D-CNN features of the average images of a video frame sequence for classification. There are few research solutions for video speed manipulation detection. Hosier *et al.* [1] track the number of bytes in P-frames and capture the traces of the speed manipulation according to the encoding laws. Such traces are extracted from the video faster than the video decoding, which allows a large amount of video to be processed in a relatively short time. But only one type of speed tampering is targeted, i.e. frame sampling. In this paper, we consider both sampling and mixing interpolation methods and the detection accuracy is improved comprehensively.

## 3    Proposed Method

In this section, we will discuss the method of detecting slow video forgrey in detail. Our proposed method needs to satisfy the detection effect for both forgery methods, frame sampling and frame mixing. According to the principle of interpolated frame generation we first explore the tampering traces left on the time domain and find that the signal has periodicity. Therefore, the feature based in the autocorrelation of the frame difference is proposed. Secondly we explore the traces of the feature representation in the spatial domain, and we find that there are statistical differences within the frames between the forged video and the naive video, so the Markov features of frame difference are utilized to reveal forgery. The framework of the method is shown in Fig. 4.

### 3.1    Temporal Feature Representation

For the slow video forgery, whether it is frame sampling or frame mixing, it will increase the correlation between the interpolated frame and its adjacent frames. Besides in order to make the video smoother without leaving obvious traces visually, the interpolated frames will be evenly inserted in the entire video sequence, which will cause the periodicity of inter-frame correlation.

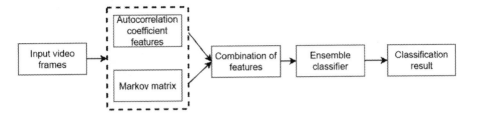

**Fig. 4.** The framework of the proposed method.

According to the slow video generation principle in Sect. 2, the method of frame sampling is to copy the previous frame to get the interpolated frame. The similarity of the two frames before and after is extremely high. The frame difference $D_1^m$ obtained by subtracting the two frames will show a periodicity as shown in Fig. 3(b). For frame mixing, considering the periodicity, $D_2^m$ is used as the capture signal. Therefore, we propose the $D_1^m, D_2^m$ frame difference to capture the difference between the original video and the slow video. We suppose the video $F$ has n frames, $D_1^m$ and $D_2^m$ are defined as:

$$
\begin{aligned}
D_1^m &= F^{m+1} - F^m \\
D_2^m &= 2 \times F^m - F^{m+1} - F^{m-1}
\end{aligned}
\tag{2}
$$

$D^m$ is defined as a fusion of $D_1^m$ and $D_2^m$. We adoped maximum fusion strategy as shown in (3), where $max\{.\}$ denotes the maximum value of the two matrices at the corresponding position.

$$
D^m = max\{D_1^m, D_2^m\}, \ m \in (1, n-2)
\tag{3}
$$

The two frame differences are calculated according to the interpolation principle of the slow video in Sect. 2. $D^m$ is considered as the object of feature extraction. Then we take the sum $S^m$ of the pixels of $D^m$ as the target signal.

$$
S^m = \sum_{i=0}^{w} \sum_{j=0}^{h} D^m(i, j)
\tag{4}
$$

where $i, j$ denote the index of the pixel, $w, h$ denote the resolution of the image.

We use $S_{ori}^m$ and $S_{slow}^m$ to represent the target signal of the original video and slow video respectively. As shown in Fig. 5, it can be found that the contrast between $S_{ori}^m$ and $S_{slow}^m$ is obvious. $S_{slow}^m$ has periodicity and $S_{ori}^m$ changes depending on the content of the video. We convert this periodic difference into a feature representation. Compared with the byte of the P-frame used in [1] as the research object, in this work, we directly perform periodic analysis on the sum of the frame difference pixels. The following is the generation process of auto-regressive(AR) parameters.

In order to create a low-dimensional feature set to capture important information about the existence and properties of the signal, we established an $N^{th}$

AR model of the residual sequence. According to our experience, we use a $21^{st}$ AR model for the test of our experiments.

$$S^m = \sum_{k=1}^{m} a_k S^{m-k} + \xi(m) \tag{5}$$

where $a_1, a_2, ..., a_N$ are the AR model coefficients and $\xi(m)$ is the white noise. Then, we combine the AR model parameters to form a feature vector $\varphi_{AC}$ of a video, defined as

$$\varphi_{AC} = [a_1, a_2, ..., a_N]^T \tag{6}$$

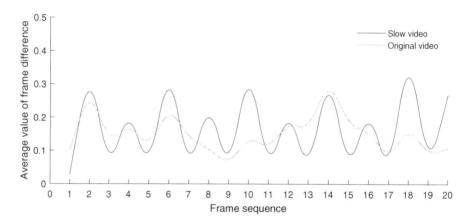

**Fig. 5.** The average value of frame difference from $30^{th}$ to $50^{th}$ frame at $t = 1.5$

## 3.2 Spatial Feature Representation

Slow video forgery not only produce periodic artifacts in the time domain, but also the intra-frame correlation of the video will be affected. The original intra-frame correlation is related to movement of the video content, but the interpolation frame will cause abnormalities. The probability distribution of the video frame difference pixels is shown in Fig. 6. As one can see, the probability of pixel value in slow video frame difference is more concentrated at 0, which confirms the above description. In other words, frame sampling can make the correlation between two frames so strong that the $S^m$ is almost zero; frame mixing will lead to a linear relationship between the interpolated frame and the adjacent frames, both of them may lead to changes of the statistical properties in spatial domain. Markov statistics has been proven to be simple and effective in characterizing the correlation between adjacent pixels [7–11], therefore, we choose Markov features to represent spatial differences. The process of Markov feature extraction is described in detail below.

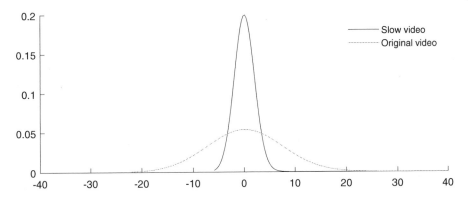

**Fig. 6.** The probability distribution of the video frame difference pixels at $t = 1.5$

According to the generation principle of slow video, it can be seen that the video frame difference is more beneficial for feature extraction. Therefore, we extract the Markov feature of video frame difference. In this paper, we use a second-order Markov chain to model the difference between adjacent pixels, and use a subset of the transition probabilities as the frame difference feature. The next step is the specific modeling process.

We calculate the difference between two adjacent pixels on the basis of the difference frame image and find the rules to construct image features, i.e. Markov feature. And each pixel has 8 adjacent directions, which are:

$$\{\leftarrow, \rightarrow, \downarrow, \uparrow, \nwarrow, \searrow, \nearrow, \swarrow\} \tag{7}$$

So there will be 8 difference values. Now let's explain in one of the directions, assume that the neighboring pixels on the right are discussed. Each pixel subtracts the pixel to its right to get a value. And the entire image matrix is subtracted like this to get a difference matrix:

$$D_{\overrightarrow{i,j}} = I_{i,j} - I_{i,j+1} \tag{8}$$

And the state transition probability matrix corresponding to the following:

$$M_{u,v,w} = Pr(D_{\overrightarrow{i,j+2}} = u | D_{\overrightarrow{i,j+1}} = v, D_{\overrightarrow{i,j}} = w), \ where \ u, v, w \in \{-T, ..., T\} \tag{9}$$

The value of $T$ is 3, and we focus on a small range of conditional probabilities for the value of $D$. The purpose of doing so is to reduce the dimensionality. The result obtained by (9) is a transition probability matrix $M$ in the right direction. The final features are represented by two $f$-matrices, which are the mean value of the 4 transition probability matrices in the positive direction, where $k$ denotes the $k^{th}$ video frame. After obtaining a series of frame-level $f$-feature, the minimum fusion strategy is used to obtain video-level feature $\varphi_{MAR}$ as shown in (11), where $min\{.\}$ denotes the minimum value of each matrices at the corresponding position. The experiments show that the accuracy is higher when the minimum strategy is used.

$$f^k = \{\frac{1}{4}[\overrightarrow{M} + \overleftarrow{M} + \overset{\downarrow}{M} + \overset{\uparrow}{M}], \frac{1}{4}[\overset{\searrow}{M} + \overset{\nearrow}{M} + \overset{\swarrow}{M} + \overset{\nearrow}{M}]\} \tag{10}$$

$$\varphi_{MAR} = min\{f^1, f^2, ..., f^k\} \tag{11}$$

### 3.3   Detecting Slow Videos

In order to obtain the detection results, we treat the speed forgery detection as a binary classification. The naive videos with unmanipulated speed are treated as negative samples, and the forged videos are treated as positive samples. We use the Ensemble classifier [12], which is not a separate machine learning algorithm, but is constructed and combined with multiple machine learning machines to complete the classification task. The classifier is trained through the joint feature $\varphi_{ACCM}$ defined in (12).

$$\varphi_{ACCM} = \{\varphi_{AC}, \varphi_{MAR}\} \tag{12}$$

## 4   Experiments

### 4.1   Dataset

To compare with the previous methods, 414 videos used in [1] are picked out from the Deepfake Detection Challenge dataset [14]. The dataset we produced contains two types of slow speed videos generated by two methods, namely frame sampling and frame mixing. All videos maintain the original bit rate by default, H.264/AVC and Mp4 file format are used for compression.

### 4.2   Experimental Results

In the experiments, we investigate the performance of the proposed method when the slow videos are manipulated with different speeds. The speed control parameter $t$ is set between 1.1 and 1.5 in steps of 0.1. For each speed, a training set is created for classifier and a test set for evaluating the performances. Detection accuracy $Acc$ is used as the metric in the experiments:

$$Acc = \frac{1}{2}(\frac{TN}{N} + \frac{TP}{P}) \times 100\% \tag{13}$$

where $P$ and $N$ donate the number of positive and negative samples respectively. $TP$ and $TN$ represent the amount of positive and negative samples detected correctly. We use the 10-fold cross-validation and 90/10 training/test splitting.

As shown in Table 1 and Table 2, the proposed $\varphi_{AC}$ and the SOTA method [1] have similar performances, this is because both features are based on periodic artifacts left by inter-frame forgery. Compared with [1], our $\varphi_{AC}$ utilize the sum of frame differences in pixel domain which reveals the inter-frame interpolation more directly than P frames byte used in [1]. However, when $t$ is relatively small, such as $t = 1.1$ and 1.2, the detection accuracy decreases. This is reasonable because when $t$ is very small, the number of inserted frames is small and the periodicity is weak in the sequence.

**Table 1.** Classification accuracy of different methods for frame sampling forgery method

| Video time | 1.1 | 1.2 | 1.3 | 1.4 | 1.5 |
|---|---|---|---|---|---|
| $\varphi_{AC}$ | 92.44% | 91.83% | 97.56% | 99.15% | 99.76% |
| Hosier | 92.44% | 90.61% | 97.56% | 98.78% | 97.56% |

**Table 2.** Classification accuracy of different methods for frame mixing forgery method

| Video time | 1.1 | 1.2 | 1.3 | 1.4 | 1.5 |
|---|---|---|---|---|---|
| $\varphi_{AC}$ | 92.07% | 95.49% | 98.05% | 96.95% | 100% |
| Hosier | 95.49% | 97.56% | 98.66% | 100% | 100% |

**Table 3.** Average classification accuracy of Markov features with different fusion strategies on two forgery methods

| Video time | 1.1 | 1.2 | 1.3 | 1.4 | 1.5 |
|---|---|---|---|---|---|
| Max | 78.97% | 92.20% | 91.83% | 80.25% | 86.22% |
| Min | 90.06% | 88.48% | 90.67% | 93.66% | 93.78% |
| Mid | 80.37% | 84.39% | 89.39% | 87.20% | 87.26% |
| Mean | 77.38% | 84.21% | 97.93% | 85.00% | 87.74% |

In order to solve the problem of $\varphi_{AC}$, we introduce intra-frame feature to improve the detection accuracy. Therefore, the performance of Markov features is further explored in the following. We adopted a fusion strategy to convert the image-level features obtained by Markov model to video-level. Four fusion strategies (maximum, minimum, average and median strategies) are considered in our experiments, and the average accuracy of them in both frame sampling and frame mixing forgery is calculated as shown in Table 3. The experimental results show that the lowest error rate is achieved when using the minimum strategy. We combined $\varphi_{AC}$ features with Markov features $\varphi_{MAR}$ to obtain the

**Table 4.** Classification accuracy of ACCM method for frame sampling forgery method

| Video time | 1.1 | 1.2 | 1.3 | 1.4 | 1.5 |
|---|---|---|---|---|---|
| $\varphi_{ACCM}$ | 95.97% | 99.02% | 97.44% | 98.78% | 99.39% |
| Hosier | 92.44% | 90.61% | 97.56% | 98.7% | 97.56% |

**Table 5.** Classification accuracy of ACCM method for frame mixing forgery method

| Video time | 1.1 | 1.2 | 1.3 | 1.4 | 1.5 |
|---|---|---|---|---|---|
| $\varphi_{ACCM}$ | 100% | 99.88% | 99.27% | 100% | 99.02% |
| Hosier | 95.49% | 97.56% | 98.66% | 100% | 100% |

joint feature $\varphi_{ACCM}$. The experimental results are shown in Table 4 and Table 5. The results show that the joint feature performs well in both forgery methods compared to [1]. This proves that we improve the detection accuracy in all the conditions by using our proposed method especially when $t$ is smaller.

## 5   Conclusion

In this paper, we focus on the slow video detection. Aiming at defeating two kinds of manipulations for slowing speed used by video editing tools, a spatial-temporal feature is proposed. Based on the observation that the generation process of slow video will introduce periodic artifacts in the time domain and destroy the inter-frame correlation of the original video, we first extract the autocorrelation coefficients of frame differences as a temporal feature, and then combine a spatial transition probability matrix feature to obtain a joint spatial-temporal feature in order to improve the detection accuracy when the forgery traces are relatively weak. The experimental results show that our proposed method outperforms the state-of-the-art method under different slow video forgeries.

## References

1. Hosier, B.C., Stamm, M.C.: Detecting video speed manipulation. In: 2020 IEEE/CVF Conference on Computer Vision and Pattern Recognition Workshops (CVPRW), pp. 2860–2869 (2020)
2. Wang, W., Farid, H.: Exposing digital forgeries in video by detecting double mpeg compression. In: Proceedings of the 8th Workshop on Multimedia and Security, MM&Sec 2006, pp. 37–47. Association for Computing Machinery, New York (2006)
3. Wang, W., Jiang, X., Wang, S., Wan, M., Sun, T.: Identifying video forgery process using optical flow. In: Shi, Y.Q., Kim, H.-J., Pérez-González, F. (eds.) IWDW 2013. LNCS, vol. 8389, pp. 244–257. Springer, Heidelberg (2014). https://doi.org/10.1007/978-3-662-43886-2_18
4. Kingra, S., Aggarwal, N., Singh, R.D.: Inter-frame forgery detection in H. 264 videos using motion and brightness gradients. Multimed. Tools Appl. **76**(24), 25767–25786 (2017)

5. Kobla, V., DeMenthon, D., Doermann, D.: Detection of slow-motion replay sequences for identifying sports videos. In: 1999 IEEE Third Workshop on Multimedia Signal Processing (Cat. No.99TH8451), pp. 135–140 (1999)
6. Zhao, Y., Pang, T., Liang, X., Li, Z.: Frame-deletion detection for static-background video based on multi-scale mutual information. In: Sun, X., Chao, H.-C., You, X., Bertino, E. (eds.) ICCCS 2017. LNCS, vol. 10603, pp. 371–384. Springer, Cham (2017). https://doi.org/10.1007/978-3-319-68542-7_31
7. Fadl, S., Han, Q., Li, Q.: CNN spatiotemporal features and fusion for surveillance video forgery detection. Signal Process.: Image Commun. **90**, 116066 (2021)
8. Pevny, T., Bas, P., Fridrich, J.: Steganalysis by subtractive pixel adjacency matrix. IEEE Trans. Inf. Forensics Secur. **5**(2), 215–224 (2010)
9. He, Z., Lu, W., Sun, W., Huang, J.: Digital image splicing detection based on Markov features in DCT and dwt domain. Pattern Recogn. **45**(12), 4292–4299 (2012)
10. Zhao, X., Wang, S., Li, S., Li, J., Yuan, Q.: Image splicing detection based on noncausal Markov model. In: 2013 IEEE International Conference on Image Processing, pp. 4462–4466 (2013)
11. Ravi, H., Subramanyam, A.V., Emmanuel, S.: Forensic analysis of linear and non-linear image filtering using quantization noise. ACM Trans. Multimed. Comput. **12**(3), 39–62 (2016)
12. Kodovsky, J., Fridrich, J., Holub, V.: Ensemble classifiers for steganalysis of digital media. IEEE Trans. Inf. Forensics Secur. **7**(2), 432–444 (2012)
13. FFmpeg Developers. Ffmpeg. http://ffmpeg.org/
14. The deepfake detection challenge (DFDC), 5 (2019)
15. Ding, X., Yang, G., Li, R., Zhang, L., Li, Y., Sun, X.: Identification of motion-compensated frame rate up-conversion based on residual signals. IEEE Trans. Circ. Syst. Video Technol. **28**(7), 1497–1512 (2018)
16. Ding, X., Huang, Y., Li, Y., He, J.: Forgery detection of motion compensation interpolated frames based on discontinuity of optical flow. Multim. Tools Appl. **79**(39–40), 28729–28754 (2020)
17. Premiere Pro User Guide. https://helpx.adobe.com/cn/premiere-pro/using/duration-speed.html

# Biomedical Image Processing
# and Analysis

# The NL-SC Net for Skin Lesion Segmentation

Ziming Chen[1] and Shengsheng Wang[2](✉)

[1] College of Computer Science and Technology, Jilin University, Changchun 130012, China
chenzm2118@mails.jlu.edu.cn
[2] Key Laboratory of Symbolic Computation and Knowledge Engineering of Ministry of Education, Jilin University, Changchun 130012, China
wss@jlu.edu.cn

**Abstract.** The problem of skin lesion segmentation remains to be a challenging task due to the low contrast of lesions, occlusions and varied sizes of foreground. The existing methods are unable to perform well on complex scenarios. In this paper, an accurate skin lesion segmentation method with Res-SC block and Res-NL block is proposed, which successfully increases the field of view by enhancing the feature representation and aggregating global information. Moreover, a novel loss function is designed, which allows us to focus more on the hard examples and further improve the accuracy rate. On the ISIC 2017 dataset, our method achieves very top performance with (AC of 0.93, DI of 0.88 and JA of 0.80).

**Keywords:** Skin lesion segmentation · Dermoscopic image · Res-NL block

## 1 Introduction

According to a report published by the American Cancer Society, melanoma, as one of the most dangerous skin cancers, constitutes 75% of all skin cancer-related deaths. In 2020, 100350 new melanoma cases are expected to be diagnosed in the United States alone, of which 6850 deaths are expected [1]. In order to distinguish between melanoma and benign lesions, dermoscopy, a safe and non-invasive skin imaging technique, is widely used by dermatologists to make a diagnosis. However, the process of checking demoscopic images is often considered complex and tedious. Therefore, a method capable of segmenting lesions automatically is strongly required in the computer-aided diagnosis system, which is still challenging as a result of low contrast between the skin lesions and normal areas, not to mention various forms of melanoma resulting from different skin conditions. Some examples are shown in Fig. 1.

Like most tasks in computer visions, many CNN-based methods have been adopted to solve the skin lesion segmentation problem. Bi et al. [2] proposed a multistage full convolution network (mFCN) method to precisely segment skin lesions, merging the outputs of each stage through a parallel integration method. Tang et al. [3] presented a multi-stage U-Net (MS-UNet) by injecting more than one U-Nets into the model for segmenting skin lesions. Besides, FCNs and Jaccard distance were employed by Yuan et al. [4] to conduct the segmentation.

---

Z. Chen–Undergraduate student and first author.

© Springer Nature Switzerland AG 2021
H. Ma et al. (Eds.): PRCV 2021, LNCS 13021, pp. 313–324, 2021.
https://doi.org/10.1007/978-3-030-88010-1_26

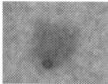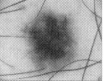

**Fig. 1.** Examples of skin lesions with occlusions, fuzzy boundaries, size variations and illumination changes.

However, the aforementioned CNN-based methods cannot make full use of global information of images. With the application of traditional convolutions, the field of view is also limited, resulting in misclassification where the foreground takes up most area of the image or there are occlusions in the images. Apart from that, the repetition of the sub-sampling structure in the encoder part of network increases the complexity by bringing in a great quantity of parameters to train, contributing to the inefficiency of the model. In addition, the imbalance ratio between hard examples and simple examples restricts further improvement of accuracy for traditional models.

In this paper, an efficient semantic skin lesion segmentation network named Non-Local Self-Calibrated Net (NL-SC Net), is presented. In the encoder part of the network, we introduce the Res-SC block with residual connection [5] and self-calibrated mechanism [6]. This block is capable of increasing the field of view by strengthening the convolution transformation of each layer. Meanwhile, based on the non-local aggregation block [7], the Res-NL Block is proposed to aggregate global information and decrease the loss of contextual information without traditional sub-sampling and deep decoder. Both the aforementioned blocks are efficient without introducing large amounts of parameters. A novel loss function with Tversky loss is also designed to solve the imbalance between background samples and foreground samples. Furthermore, with hard example mining, it may focus on optimizing the difficult cases. On ISIC 2017 dataset, our method can achieve very good result of AC 0.93, DI 0.88 and JA 0.80.

## 2    Related Works

### 2.1    Traditional Computer Vision Methods

These methods are often based on manually extracted features such as pixel values and colors. For instance, Fan et al. [8] employed a significance-based image enhancement method followed by Otsu threshold segmentation. An iterative random area merging method was employed by Wong et al. [9] to segment lesions from a macro image. Based on Gradient Vector Flow (GVF), [10] presented an active contour extraction method. However, not only do these methods rely heavily on manual parameter adjustment, but also, they are not capable of capturing advanced semantic information as the features are extracted by hand.

### 2.2    CNN-Based Methods

**Semantic Segmentation.** The goal of semantic segmentation is to assign semantic labels to every pixel in an image. One of the main problems is the contradiction between global segmentation performance and local location classification. To solve the issue, many deep learning methods with CNNs are proposed. Fully convolutional network (FCN) [11] removes the fully connected layers to compute low-resolution representations. After estimating segmentation maps from coarse segmentation confidence maps, it further combines the fine segmentation confidence maps attained by estimating intermediate representations. Though the up-sampling operation compensates the loss of resolution caused by pooling, it results in fuzzy segmentation results. U-Net [12] is composed of a down-sampling encoder and an up-sampling decoder. The encoder gradually reduces the spatial dimension through pooling layer, while the correspondingly decoder recovers contextual information and spatial dimension incrementally, between them the skip connection is added to assist decoder gaining more details about images from encoder. Many methods based on U-Net have been proposed. For instance, [7] proposed global aggregation blocks based on U-Nets to make use of long-range information. With the development of CNNs, more effective segmentation networks are also presented. A residual block is introduced in ResNets [5] to simplify deep training. The dense convolution network (DenseNet) with the dense block is introduced to reduce parameters successfully, which finally achieves excellent performance by constructing dense connections between former layers and latter layers.

**Skin-Lesion Segmentation.** Nowadays, CNNs are widely applied in the domain of skin lesion segmentation. Yuan [4] proposed a deep full convolution-deconvolution network in which the learning rate is adjusted according to the first and second moments of the gradient at each iteration. Al-masni et al. [13] presented a full resolution convolution network (FrCN). By removing all subsampling layers from the encoders, he decreased the loss of spatial information when obtaining full resolution from input images. However, the networks above are featured with many shortcomings. Most of them failed to exploit global information to segment images. Therefore, the performance is often poor under the circumstances of large foreground or occlusions.

## 3  The Proposed Method

In this section, more details about the NL-SC Net will be introduced. Firstly, the structure of the network, which achieves the segmentation of skin lesion through Res-SC blocks and Res-NL blocks, will be described. Next, more details about Res-SC blocks and Res-NL blocks will be explained. Apart from that, in the training section, the accuracy of skin lesion segmentation will be further enhanced by employing a new loss function.

### 3.1  Network Architecture

**Description of U-Net.** The U-Net is composed of two parts: the left contracting path and the right expanding path. The two parts connect together to form a U structure, which is shown in Fig. 2. In the beginning, the input feature map goes through an encoder input block that can extract low-level features. The input block is then followed by two subsampling blocks to reduce spatial sizes and attain high-level features. It is worth noted that the channels double every time the input map goes through the sub-sampling block. After subsampling process, the bottom block aggregates global information and produces

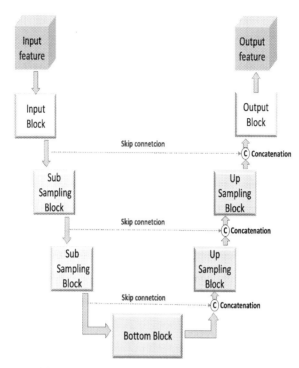

**Fig. 2.** The structure of the U-Net model is shown above. It is composed of the encoder part and decoder part; the channels double every time the input map goes through the sub-sampling block. Skip connection is operated through concatenation.

the output of encoders. Correspondingly, the decoder employs two up-sampling blocks to recover the spatial sizes of segmented output, and the number of channels halves every time after the up-sampling operation. During the decoder process, the feature maps are transferred from encoder blocks to decoder blocks through skip connections, which employs concatenation.

**The proposed NL-SC Net.** The NL-SC Net exploits the structure of an encoder and a decoder. Specifically, the NL-SC Net comprises a compression path with three Res-SC Blocks and an expansion path consisting of three Res-NL Blocks. An additional Res-NL Block is used as the bottom block in the middle. Here, the feature maps of decoders are combined with encoder feature maps copied by skip connections through summation instead of concatenation, which can both decrease the number of trainable parameters in the following layers and increase the efficiency for training part. The structure of the NL-SC Net is shown in Fig. 3.

For better feature extraction, the Res-SC block is proposed, the layout of the Res-SC block is shown in Fig. 4.

Res-SC block exploits self-calibrated convolution to generate richer features. Unlike traditional convolution, self-calibrated convolution [14] implements convolution transformation in two different scales of space: an original space and an after-down-sampling

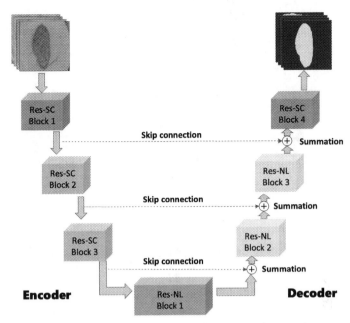

**Fig. 3.** The structure of NL-SC Net is shown above. It is made up of an encoder part and a decoder part. The encoder part is composed of three Res-SC Blocks and the decoder part consists of three Res-NL Blocks with an additional Res-NL Block in the middle. The skip connection is performed through summation.

space. The small one is used to guide the process of feature transformation in the original feature space, where specific layers of convolution filters are divided into uneven parts to adjust to each other, thereby increasing the perception area of space. At the same time, through residual connection, the original feature map is retained to a certain extent, which solves the problem of training in the network with deep layers. The settings for the Res-SC block are shown in Table 1.

The Res-NL block is introduced during the decoder phase, as shown in Fig. 5. In the residual path, deconvolution with corresponding scale is exploited, and we apply the SC-global aggregation block in the other path. A global aggregation block [7] can aggregate global information, where every location in the output feature map is determined by all the locations in the input feature map. In this case, connections between locations of the same channel can be built. So here comes the question, is it possible to build connections between locations in different channels? To solve this, we introduce the self-calibrated convolutions in the global aggregation block and attain the SC-global aggregation block. Unlike traditional convolution, self-calibrated convolution is capable of building connections between channels and enlarging the receptive field of convolutional layers in order to help CNNs produce more discriminative expression by merging richer information. The mechanism of SC-global aggregation block is shown below.

Let's use $X$ as the input of the SC-global aggregation block, and $Y$ as the output. $SC\_Conv\_1_N$ represents $1 \times 1$ self-calibrated convolution, the stride is set as 1, and $N$ means the number of output channels.

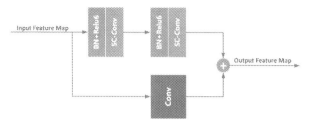

**Fig. 4.** The Res-SC Block is shown above. Instead of traditional convolution, self-calibrated convolution is employed. It also applies the mechanism of residual connection.

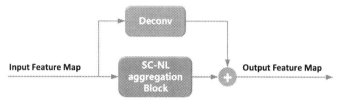

**Fig. 5.** The Res-NL Block is shown above. Deconvolution with corresponding scale is used in the residual path, and we apply the SC-global aggregation block in the other path.

**Table 1.** The Settings of Res-SC Blocks in the NL-SC Net.

| Res-SC Block | Residual Connection | SC-Convolution | |
|---|---|---|---|
| | | First | Second |
| 1 | Original map | $3 \times 3$, stride 1 | $3 \times 3$, stride 1 |
| 2 | $1 \times 1$, stride 2 | $3 \times 3$, stride 2 | $3 \times 3$, stride 1 |
| 3 | $1 \times 1$, stride 2 | $3 \times 3$, stride 2 | $3 \times 3$, stride 1 |
| 4 | Original map | $3 \times 3$, stride 1 | $3 \times 3$, stride 1 |

The first step is to produce matrices: $query(Q)$, $key(K)$ and $value(V)$

$$Q = Unfold\left(QueryTransform_{C_K}(X)\right), K = Unfold\left(SC\_Conv\_1_{C_K}(X)\right),$$
$$V = Unfold\left(SC\_Conv\_1_{C_K}(X)\right), \tag{1}$$

where the $Unfold(\cdot)$ operation expands a $H \times W \times C$ tensor into a matrix of $(H \times W) \times C$. $QueryTransform_{C_K}(\cdot)$ can be any operation that produces $C_K$ feature mapping. $C_K$, $C_v$ are hyper parameters representing the dimensions of key and value matrices.

In the second step, the attention mechanism is used:

$$A = Softmax\left(\frac{QK^T}{\sqrt{C_K}}\right), O = AV, \tag{2}$$

where the dimensions of the attention weight matrix is $(H_Q \times W_Q) \times (H \times W)$, and the dimension of the output $O$ matrix is $(H_Q \times W_Q) \times C_V$.

Finally, $Y$ is calculated as

$$Y = Conv_{1C_O}(Fold(O)), \tag{3}$$

where $fold(\cdot)$ is a verse operation of $Unfold(\cdot)$, $C_O$ is a hyperparameter that represents the output dimension. The dimension of $Y$ is $H_Q \times W_Q \times C_O$.

So far, we have obtained the SC-global aggregation block, and the up-sampling block is expanded from the SC-global aggregation block. See Table 2 for Res-NL block settings.

**Table 2.** Settings of the Res-NL Block

| Res-NL Block | Residual Connection | Other path |
|---|---|---|
| 1 | Original map | SC-NL aggregation Block |
| 2 | $3 \times 3$, stride 2 | Up-sampling SC-NL aggregation Block |
| 3 | $3 \times 3$, stride 2 | Up-sampling SC-NL aggregation Block |

### 3.2 Loss Function

To further improve the performance of our method, a novel loss function is proposed during the training part. For medical images, the lesion areas are usually much smaller than those of the unrelated background areas. As a result, the imbalance between background samples and foreground samples becomes a problem because only the cross-entropy function is used during training. Furthermore, the cross-entropy loss function does not pay special attention to hard examples, leading to their poor performance on images belong to hard examples. As a consequence, the focal loss function is employed as a replacement of the cross-entropy loss function to make it easier to learn hard examples. We further combine it with the Tversky loss function to adjust the weight between background samples and foreground samples.

Our loss function is shown below:

$$L_{sr}^* = \sum_{n}^{N_m} 1 - \lambda \frac{\sum_{i=1}^{N_{np}} m_{ni}g_{ni}}{\sum_{i=1}^{N_{np}} m_{ni}g_{ni} + \alpha \sum_{i=1}^{N_{np}} m_{ni}(1-g_{ni}) + \beta \sum_{i=1}^{N_{np}} (1-m_{ni})g_{ni} + \varepsilon} \tag{4}$$
$$-(1-\lambda)\frac{1}{N_{np}}\sum_{i=1}^{N_{np}} \kappa g_{ni}(1-m_{ni})^\gamma \log m_{ni} + (1-\kappa)(1-g_{ni})m_{ni}^\gamma \log(1-m_{ni})$$

$\alpha$ and $\beta$ are used to control the weight between background samples and foreground samples, and $\gamma$ is the parameter of the focal loss function.

## 4 Experimentation and Results

### 4.1 Experimentation Details

The experiments are performed on the ISIC 2017 Challenge dataset. Images of the dataset vary in size from $540 \times 722$ to $4499 \times 6478$, but their aspect ratios are all 4:3. Data argumentation like flipping the images randomly, zooming the images and changing the brightness of the images are also operated.

The metrices we employed include accuracy (AC), sensitivity (SE), specificity (SP), Jaccard index (JA) and the Dice coefficient (DI). The accuracy defines the proficiency of segmenting properly. Sensitivity and specificity represent the efficiency of skin lesion segmentation. JA indicates the similarity between segmented lesion and the ground truth. Their definitions are shown below.

$$AC = \frac{TP + TN}{TP + FP + TN + FN}, \tag{5}$$

$$SE = \frac{TP}{TP + FN}, \tag{6}$$

$$SP = \frac{TN}{TN + FP}, \tag{7}$$

$$JA = \frac{TP}{TP + FN + FP} \tag{8}$$

$$DI = \frac{2 \cdot TP}{2 \cdot TP + FN + FP} \tag{9}$$

An FCN with concatenate (CC) skip is used as the Baseline. We adopt the Adam optimizer with a batch size of 10 to train the NL-SC Network. The initial learning rate and the number of iterations is set at 0.0002 and 500 respectively. After every 25 epochs, the learning rate decreases with a decay rate of 0.5 until it reaches $1e \times 10^{-6}$. The architecture of our net is based on the pytorch, and 2 Nvidia 2080ti GPUs are used during training.

## 4.2  Ablation Analysis

To investigate how the innovative part of the proposed architecture affects the performance of segmentation, the controlled experiment with variable modules is conducted. We denote the architecture only with Baseline model as baseline 1. Baseline 2 is baseline 1 integrated with Res-SC block and Res-NL block. On the basis of baseline 2, the proposed loss function was inserted in to form our final method. We gradually add into components during the experiment as Table 3. The experimental results are listed in Table 4.

It can be seen that after Res-SC and Res-NL blocks being added, AC, SE, DI increase by 1.11%, 1.49%, 0.48% respectively. JA, as a metric which evaluates the similarity between ground truth and output, makes an obvious progress by increasing 4.5%, showing the validity of the proposed blocks. Figure 6 displays the comprehensive advantages of our proposed method.

In order to investigate the effectiveness of our loss function, we compare the results between baseline 2(without the proposed loss function) and ours (with the proposed loss function). The insertion of the loss function makes a remarkable improvement of AC, SE, JA and DI, as shown in Table 4. Especially for SE and DI, with the former increasing

**Table 3.** Ablation experimentation settings on ISIC2017 dataset.

| Model name | Baseline | Res-SC & Res-NL | Proposed loss function |
|---|---|---|---|
| Baseline 1 | Yes | No | No |
| Baseline 2 | Yes | Yes | No |
| Ours | Yes | Yes | Yes |

**Table 4.** The experimental results of Baseline 1, Baseline 2 and Ours.

| Modules | AC | SE | SP | DI | JA |
|---|---|---|---|---|---|
| Baseline 1 | 0.9163 | 0.8123 | **0.9653** | 0.8134 | 0.7586 |
| Baseline 2 | 0.9272 | 0.8272 | 0.9622 | 0.8594 | 0.7634 |
| Ours | **0.9317** | **0.9071** | 0.9592 | **0.8825** | **0.8023** |

by 7.99% and the latter increasing by 3.89%. The main reason is that our loss function not only adjusts the balance between foreground pixels and background pixels, but also focuses more on hard examples, which the traditional cross-entropy loss function cannot deal with. Generally, our proposed model enhanced the performance and achieved good effect in the aspect of skin segmentation.

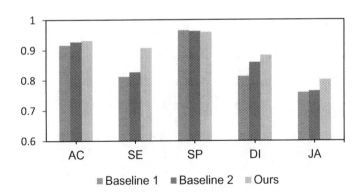

**Fig. 6.** The comparison of the five indexes between Baseline1, Baseline2 and ours.

## 4.3 Comparison with Other Methods

We make a comparison between other state-of-the-art methods on ISIC 2017 challenge (given in [13, 15, 16]) and our proposed architecture, which is shown in Table 5.

Our proposed NL-SC Net performs best in AC (0.9317), SE (0.9071) and JA (0.8023). Also, both SP (0.9592) and DI (0.8825) rank second among those methods with DI being

**Table 5.** Comparison between other state-of-the-art methods and our proposed architecture.

| Method | AC | SE | SP | DI | JA |
|---|---|---|---|---|---|
| FrCN | 0.9297 | 0.8350 | 0.9478 | **0.8834** | 0.6713 |
| FocusNet | 0.9266 | 0.7583 | 0.9386 | 0.8645 | 0.7866 |
| SU-SWA-SCB | 0.9267 | 0.8934 | **0.9672** | 0.8723 | 0.7974 |
| NL-SC Net | **0.9317** | **0.9071** | 0.9592 | 0.8825 | **0.8023** |

very close to the best results. Overall the NL-SC Net gains the state-of-art performance, outperforming the aforementioned three methods in ISIC 2017 challenge.

While low SE of the model means that image may be misclassified in the case of various changes of skin lesions, large foreground areas and low contrast, we achieved the highest SE (0.9071) mainly due to the proposed Res-SC blocks and Res-NL blocks, which can take advantage of global information to generate richer and more discriminative representations, thus increasing the field of view. Apart from that, we gain best result on JA (0.8023). As an important metric in melanoma diagnosis, it reveals that high precise shape of the skin lesion regions can be output by our network since our loss function can focus more on the hard examples and adjust the weight between foreground and background to obtain higher precision in pixel classification.

In Fig. 7, some examples of the ISIC 2017 challenge and the results of different methods are shown. FrCN is poor at the segmentation of low-contrast lesions. FocusNet and SU-SWA-SCB are better than the former one, but the image is incomplete when

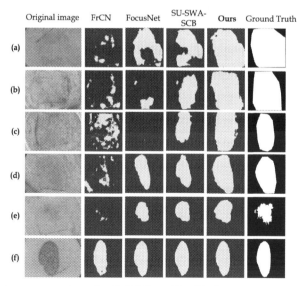

**Fig. 7.** Skin lesion segmentation using FrCN, FocusNet, SU-SWA-SCB and our method on ISIC 2017 challenge respectively. (a)-(f) list different challenges like low contrast, various sizes of lesions or occlusions.

faced with lesions with relatively large foreground but low contrast. For FocusNet, it can't even recognize lesion area and segments large area of foreground as background pixels in some cases. Problems listed above may affect the judgement of doctors during diagnosis and may result in serious consequences. But the NL-SC Net is capable of effectively exploiting the global information to produce rich features. Benefiting from that, the proposed method has a great advantage in images with large foreground but low-contrast images (Fig. 7 (a), (b)). At the same time, it also performs well on images with small foreground and low contrast (Fig. 7 (d), (e)), which further proves the robustness and effectiveness of the model. Our network can also segment images with hair occlusions and ink (Fig. 7 (b), (c)). The outputs show high similarity with Ground Truth overall.

## 5   Conclusion

In this paper, a non-local self-calibrated convolution network (NL-SC Net) for skin lesion segmentation is proposed. By using the Res-SC block and the NL-SC block, the network can mitigate the loss of information during down-sampling, reduce training parameters, and generate more differentiated features to enhance accuracy. Meanwhile, a new loss function is introduced, which enables the network to learn difficult samples and make a balance between foreground pixels and background pixels. The validity of NL-SC Net is further demonstrated by experiments on the ISIC 2017 dataset.

**Acknowledgment.** This work is supported by the National Key Research and Development Program of China (No. 2020YFA0714103), the Innovation Capacity Construction Project of Jilin Province Development and Reform Commission (2019C053-3) and the Science & Technology Development Project of Jilin Province, China (20190302117GX).

## References

1. American Cancer Society, Key statistics for melanoma skin cancer (2019). https://www.cancer.org/cancer/melanoma-skin-cancer/about/key-statistics.html. Accessed 10 May 2019
2. Bi, L., Kim, J., Ahn, E., Kumar, A., Fulham, M., Feng, D.: Dermoscopic image segmentation via multistage fully convolutional networks. IEEE Trans. Biomed. Eng. **64**(9), 2065–2074 (2017)
3. Tang, Y., Yang, F., Yuan, S.: A multi-stage framework with context information fusion structure for skin lesion segmentation. In: 2019 IEEE 16th International Symposium on Biomedical Imaging (ISBI 2019), pp. 1407–1410. IEEE, April 2019
4. Yuan, Y.: Automatic skin lesion segmentation with fully convolutional- deconvolutional networks (2017). arXiv:1703.05165
5. He, K., Zhang, X., Ren, S., Sun, J.: Deep residual learning for image recognition. In Proceedings IEEE Conference Computer Vision Pattern Recognition, pp. 770–778, June 2016
6. Liu, J.J., Hou, Q., Cheng, M.M., et al.: Improving convolutional networks with self-calibrated convolutions. In: Proceedings of the IEEE/CVF Conference on Computer Vision and Pattern Recognition, pp. 10096–10105 (2020)
7. Wang, Z., Zou, N., Shen, D., Ji, S.: Non-local U-nets for biomedical image segmentation. In: Proceedings of the AAAI Conference on Artificial Intelligence vol. 34, no. 4, pp. 6315–6322 (2020)

8. Fan, H., Xie, F., Li, Y., Jiang, Z., Liu, J.: Automatic segmentation of dermoscopy images using saliency combined with otsu threshold. Comput. Biol. Med. **85**, 75–85 (2017)

9. Wong, A., Scharcanski, J., Fieguth, P.: Automatic skin lesion segmentation via iterative stochastic region merging. IEEE Trans. Inf. Technol. Biomed. **15**(6), 929–936 (2011)

10. Erkol, B., Moss, R.H., Stanley, R.J., Stoecker, W.V., Hvatum, E.: 'Automatic lesion boundary detection in dermoscopy images using gradient vector flow snakes.' Skin Res. Technol. **11**(1), 17–26 (2005)

11. Long, J., Shelhamer, E., Darrell, T., et al.: Fully convolutional networks for semantic segmentation. Comput. Vis. Pattern Recogn. Boston **7–12**, 3431–3440 (2015)

12. Ronneberger, O., Fischer, P., Brox, T.: U-Net: convolutional networks for biomedical image segmentation. In: Navab, N., Hornegger, J., Wells, W.M., Frangi, A.F. (eds.) MICCAI 2015. LNCS, vol. 9351, pp. 234–241. Springer, Cham (2015). https://doi.org/10.1007/978-3-319-24574-4_28

13. Al-masni, M.A., Al-antari, M.A., Choi, M., Han, S., Kim, T.: Skin lesion segmentation in dermoscopy images via deep full resolution convolutional networks. Comput. Methods Programs Biomed. **162**, 221–231 (2018)

14. Liu, J.-J., Hou, Q., Cheng, M.-M., Wang, C., Feng, J.: Proceedings of the IEEE/CVF Conference on Computer Vision and Pattern Recognition (CVPR), pp. 10096–10105 (2020)

15. Kaul, C., Manandhar, S., Pears, N.: FocusNet: an attention-based fully convolutional network for medical image segmentation (2019)

16. Tang, P., Liang, Q., Yan, X., et al.: Efficient skin lesion segmentation using separable-Unet with stochastic weight averaging . Comput. Methods Programs Biomed. **178**, 289–301 (2019)

# Two-Stage COVID-19 Lung Segmentation from CT Images by Integrating Rib Outlining and Contour Refinement

Qianjing Wang[1], Changjian Wang[1], Kele Xu[1(✉)], and You-ming Zhang[2(✉)]

[1] School of Computer, National University of Defense Technology,
Changsha, Hunan, China
{wangqianjing,wangcj}@nudt.edu.cn
[2] Department of Radiology, Xiangya Hospital, Central South University,
Changsha, Hunan, China
zhangym0820@csu.edu.cn

**Abstract.** In the early 2020, the corona virus disease (COVID-19) has become a global epidemic, resulting in a profound impact on the lives of billions of people, from both of safety and economic perspective. Rapid screening is of great significance to control the spread of disease. In the clinic practice, computed tomography (CT) is widely utilized by the doctors to detect and evaluate novel coronavirus pneumonia and lung segmentation is a necessary initial step for lung image analysis. However, the segmentation task is still confronted with several challenges, such as high variations in intensity, indistinct edges and noise due to data acquisition process. To address aforementioned challenges, in this paper, we present a novel two-stage-based COVID-19 lung segmentation method. First, we design a coarse segmentation method combining threshold and rib outline, which can remove most background while retaining complete lung shapes. Then, a contour refinement algorithm was introduced to refine the coarse segmentation based on local information including intensity, shape and gradient. The proposed method was tested on 20 sets of COVID-19 CT cases. Quantitative evaluations are conducted with different methods (including the deep learning-based approach), and the results demonstrate that our method can provide superior performance with few-shot samples. Our method achieves an average symmetric surface distance (ASD) of $0.0101 \pm 0.0147$mm and dice similarity coefficient (DSC) of $99.22 \pm 0.99\%$ on lung CT image segmentation compared with ground truths. To better promote the research in this field, we have released our code to facilitate the research community(https://github.com/qianjingw/Two-Stage-COVID-19-Lung-Segmentation).

**Keywords:** Lung segmentation · COVID-19 · Contour refinement

Qianjing Wang is a graduate student.

H. Ma et al. (Eds.): PRCV 2021, LNCS 13021, pp. 325–336, 2021.
https://doi.org/10.1007/978-3-030-88010-1_27

# 1   Introduction

There have been a global outbreak and rapid spread of coronavirus disease (COVID-19) since the beginning of 2020. Due to the high false-negative rates of reverse transcription-polymerase chain reaction (RT-PCR) test [1], the chest computed tomography (CT) scan has been widely applied for early screening of the disease and assessment of disease progression [3]. As an important prepro-cessing step in automatically analyzing lung, automatic lung segmentation has received considerable attention from the researchers [9,16].

Accurate lung segmentation can save physicians' efforts to annotate lung anatomy since it is tedious and time-consuming to label each voxel in huge amount of slices. However, it is a challenging task to accurately and automati-cally segment lungs in CT images, especially in the COVID-19 CT images [2]. Firstly, large pathological lesions lead to large difference in image intensity val-ues and indistinct edges. Secondly, the CT used for detecting novel coronavirus pneumonia is often low-dose CT with low image quality. The movement arti-facts produced by breaths are obvious in 3D low-dose CT images. Thirdly, the anatomy of lungs varies largely from different individuals, both in shape and size. Lastly, many fully supervised learning-based approaches (such as the deep learning) require large scale labeled datasets, which is not easily to be obtained in practical settings.

Existing methods addressing lung segmentation can be roughly categorized into following four groups: (1) **Threshold-based methods**, [14,17] segment the lung by integrating threshold and postprocessing techniques. In the case of large lesions existing in COVID-19 CT images, no matter how skillful these post-processing techniques can not make up for the missing area caused by threshold segmentation. (2) **Texture-based methods**, [5,8] distinguish lung areas in CT image from its texture reflected by the gray distribution of pixels and their surrounding space. However, this kind of method will fail when the lung con-solidation appears at the edge of the lung because the lung consolidation and the surrounding thoracic tissue have similar texture features. (3) **Edge-based methods**, [6,18] applied the improved active contour method to lung segmen-tation. Such methods are sensitive to initialization and have a high computation cost. What's more, traditional external energy may not provide enough guid-ance for the curve to evolve to the correct boundary rather than the lesion edge. (4) **Deep learning-based methods** have shown great potential in med-ical image segmentation[15], including lung segmentation[4,12]. However, deep learning model training needs a large number of labeled data. There are not enough samples in the early stage of disease outbreak, and the cost of labeled data is very high.

Considering the aforementioned problems for lung segmentation methods, we propose a coarse-to-fine COVID-19 lung segmentation algorithm. Unlike tradi-tional threshold-based work, we fix the missing area caused by threshold segmen-tation with the shape of ribs, rather than convex hull or morphological operation. Further more, we utilize the local information of the coarse segmentation contour to refine the segmentation. In brief, our contributions are follows:

– A two-stage based segmentation framework is proposed, which combines the rib outline detection and contour refinement. Specifically, a coarse lung segmentation approach is developed to remove unrelated background while retaining lung shapes based on threshold and anatomy. Moreover, a new contour refinement algorithm is presented, leveraging the local information including intensity, shape and gradient to refine the primary segmentation results.
– Extensive experiments are conducted using different approaches, and the results suggest that our method can provide superior performance using few-shot samples. Compared to the deep learning-based approaches (UNet), our method does not require large-scale labeled dataset which is difficult to be obtained in practical settings.

The following of this paper is organized as follows: Sect. 2 presents the details of our methodology. In Sect. 3, we describe our experimental results and the conclusion is drawn in the last part.

## 2   Methodology

To segment the lung region from COVID-19 lung CTs accurately, we propose a two-stage lung segmentation method. Firstly, Otsu method is employed to extract the basic lung regions from the original CTs. Inspired by the work of Prasad [13] and Sun [18], we observed that the ribs were naturally close to the lung surface. Based on this anatomical feature, we fix the basic lung region with the rib outline. Then, the coarse segmentation results can be refined by a contour refinement algorithm. The overall steps of the algorithm are shown in Fig. 1.

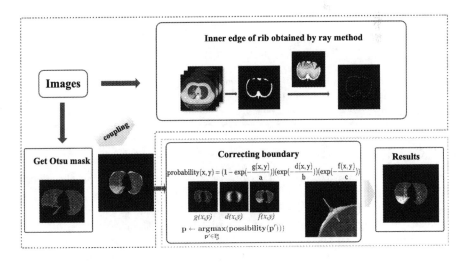

**Fig. 1.** The flow chart of the proposed method.

## 2.1    Rib Outline Detection

The CT intensity value of bone ranges from 150 to 1000 $HU$ (Hounsfield Unit), which is significantly higher than that of other surrounding tissues. The ribs can be extracted by three-dimensional region growing method. However, due to the gap between the ribs, there are not enough ribs on some slices to provide complete radian. To solve this problem, we stack adjacent layers to ensure that each slice has enough ribs to provide appropriate shape information.

Instead of centerline detection, we detect the inner edge of ribs so that the outline of ribs is better fit to lung surface. The whole process is shown in Algorithm 1. First, two center points are selected according to the transverse width of the rib cage(at 1/4 and 3/4 of the diameter). Then, a ray is emitted from a center point and the first rib pixel touched by the ray is recorded. The ray is rotated one circle at an interval of 1° and the recorded rib pixels are connected in turn to form a closed curve. Finally, the union formed by the two closed curves is filled and smoothed by open operation, so that we can get a close and smooth rib outline.

---

**Algorithm 1:** Approach for obtaining rib outline

---

**Input**: rib mask $M(x, y)$
**Output**: rib outline $O(x, y)$;
1  find the leftmost point$L$ and the rightmost point$R$;
2  get two center points $c_1, c_2$ at 1/4 and 3/4 of the line$LR$;
3  **for** $c \in (c_1, c_2))$ **do**
4      $center = c$;
5      **for** $\alpha \in [0, 360]$ **do**
6          compute the ray $l_\alpha$;
7          recorde the first rib pixel $p_\alpha$;
8          connecte $p_\alpha$ and $p_{\alpha-1}$;
9      **end**
10     get mask $mask_{center}$ by filling the closed curve;
11 **end**
12 smooth the union of $mask_{c_1}$ and $mask_{c_2}$ with open operation;
13 get the contour $O(x, y)$ of the union;
14 **return** $O(x, y)$

---

## 2.2    Coupling the Rib Outline and the Otsu Mask

It is worthwhile to notice that: if there is a large area of lesions near the pleura, the Otsu mask loses a large section of the lung contour. The existing contour repairing methods such as rolling ball and convex hull can not restore the correct shape of the lung. Considering that the ribs are tightly wrapped around the lung, the problem can be solved by coupling the rib outline with the Otsu mask. We connect the contour points of the Otsu mask with the rib outline points in a certain distance according to the principle of proximity. Then, the coarse segmentation mask can be obtained by filling and morphological operations. Figure 2 shows the process of forming the coarse segmentation mask.

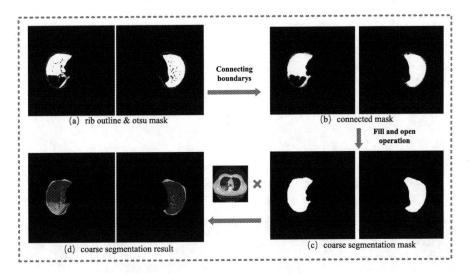

**Fig. 2.** Coupling the rib outline and the Otsu mask

## 2.3   Contour Refinement

The coarse segmentation results need to be refined due to the gap between the ribs and the lung surface. This is of great challenge as the intensity distribution of severe pathological areas is highly similar to that of surrounding thoracic tissues. Many methods only leverage the intensity or gradient, such as region growing [10,11] or active contour [7,18], which may fail to adjust the contour to the real boundary. The coarse segmentation results based on rib outlines can provide useful shape information. Here, we introduce a novel contour refinement method, which adjusts the contour points along the normal direction to the point with the highest probability of real boundary. The point with the highest probability of real boundary represents a good trade-off between intensity, gradient and shape. In order to define the boundary probability, two variables are defined to measure the gradient and shape: local maximum unidirectional gradient(LMUG) and distance.

**Local Maximum Unidirectional Gradient(LMUG):** We define an image of size $W \times H$ as $I = f(x,y), 0 \leq x \leq W, 0 \leq y \leq H, f(x,y)$ presents value on position $(x,y)$. The LMUG map at the $\delta$ scale is defined as $G = g(x,y)$ and $g(x,y)$ is defined as follow:

$$g(x,y) = \max_{-\delta \leq i \leq \delta, -\delta \leq j \leq \delta} f(x+i, y+j) - f(x,y) \tag{1}$$

In this way, only the lung points near the boundary with low intensity have larger gradients, while the points with high intensity or inside the lung have smaller gradients. The LMUG map is shown in Fig. 3(b).

**Distance.** Binary image corresponding to $I$ is defined as $M = m(x,y), 0 \leq x \leq W, 0 \leq y \leq H, m(x,y) \in \{0,1\}$ and its contour is defined in Eq.(2)

$$B = \{(x,y)|m(x,y) = 1, \exists m(x \pm 1, y \pm 1) = 0\} \tag{2}$$

The distance map $D = d(x,y)$ is defined in Eq.(3)

$$d(x,y) = \min_{(x',y') \in B} (|x - x'|^2 + |y - y'|^2)^{1/2} \tag{3}$$

$d(x,y)$ present the shortest Euclidean distance between the point at position $(x,y)$ and the contour. The distance map is shown in Fig. 3(c).

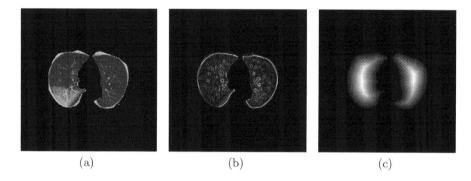

|(a)|(b)|(c)|

**Fig. 3.** (a) Coarse Segmentation Result; (b) LMUG Map; (c) Distance Map.

**Boundary Probability.** The real lung boundary should have all or part of the following characteristics: 1) Low intensity. The lungs usually have low CT intensity value because they are full of gas. 2) Large LMUG. Generally, the gray level of boundary changes strongly. 3) Short distance. In order to prevent local depression, the real boundary should not be too far from the rib outline. Therefore, we define a boundary probability function based on the above information:

$$probability(x,y) = (1 - exp(-\frac{g(x,y)}{a}))(exp(-\frac{d(x,y)}{b}))(exp(-\frac{f(x,y)}{c})) \tag{4}$$

where $a, b, c$ are the factors which control the sensitivity of the boundary probability function to LMUG, distance, intensity.In this work, $a, b, c$ were fixed to 0.25, 1 and 0.75.

The adjustment process of coarse contour points can be described by the following formula:

$$p \rightarrow p^*, p^* = \underset{p' \in l_p^k}{argmax}(possibility(p'))) \tag{5}$$

where $p^*$ is the most likely real boundary point corresponding to coarse segmentation contour point $p$. $l_p^k$ is a normal of lenght $k$ centered on $p$. The length $k$ is determined by the gap between the rib outline and the lung surface, which was 10 in this paper.

The coarse segmentation contour may appear discontinuity and local depression after refinement. To overcome this problem, we add Otsu mask contour as a supplement. Finally, the accurate segmentation mask is obtained by closing and filling the new contour. Algorithm 2 illustrates the process of contour refinement.

---

**Algorithm 2:** Approach for contour refinement

**Input**: Coarse segmentation result $I(x, y)$,
  Otsu segmentation result $I_{otsu}(x, y)$
**Output**: Refined segmentation result $O(x, y)$;

1  compute the gradient map $G(x, y)$ and distance map $D(x, y)$ of $I(x, y)$ ;
2  compute the contour $B(p_1, p_2, ..., p_n)$ of $I(x, y)$ and $B_{otsu}(q_1, q_2, ..., q_m)$ of $I_{otsu}(x, y)$ ;
3  **for** $i \in [1, n]$ **do**
4       compute the normal $l_{p_i}^k$ with length $k$ at point $p_i$;
5       calculate the possibility of each points in normal with $Eq.4$;
6       $p_i \leftarrow \underset{p' \in l_{p_i}^k}{argmax}(possibility(p'))$;
7  **end**
8  final boundary $B \leftarrow B + B_{otsu}$;
9  compute the binary mask $M$ with final boundary $B$;
10  $O(x, y) \leftarrow I * M$;
11  **return** $O(x, y)$

---

# 3 Results

## 3.1 Dataset

The datasets used in our study were obtained from the Xiangya Hospital Central South University in Changsha. The proposed method was evaluated on 20 sets of CT images. All original CT images are in DICOM format and have a size of $512 \times 512$ pixels.9 sets of them have a thickness of 5mm and each sets has 50 to 70 slices. The other sets have a thickness of 1mm and each set has more than 300 slices. Since there is little difference between adjacent layers of HRCT with the thickness of 1 mm, we extracted one every five for data analysis. Finally, a total of 1489 images were used for our study. In order to compare with the segmented results, the ground truth for lungs was manually labeled by an expert.

## 3.2  Metrics

To quantitatively assess the performance of our proposed method, we compared the segmentation results with the ground truth according to the following five volume and surface based metrics: average symmetric surface distance (ASD), maximum surface distance (MSD),dice similarity coefficient (DSC),true positive ratio(TPR) and false positive ratio (FPR).

ASD and MSD measure the differences between two contours. The smaller the value is, the smaller the difference is. Let $Aa_1, a_2, ..., a_p$ and $Bb_1, b_2, ..., b_q$ be the contour points of method segmented lung and ground truth, respectively, where $p$ and $q$ are the qualities of contour points, the ASD and the MSD can be calculated as follows,

$$ASD = \frac{1}{p} \sum_{a \in A} min_{b \in B} \|a - b\|, \ MSD = max_{a \in A} min_{b \in B} \|a - b\| \qquad (6)$$

DSC is the percent of dice similar coefficient, measures the degree of overlap between segmentation results and ground truth.$DSC = 100\%$ means the segmentation results are completely consistent with the ground truth. The DSC is defined as follow,

$$DSC = \frac{2 * (A \cap B)}{A + B} \qquad (7)$$

TPR represents the proportion of foreground pixels which are segmented correctly.FPR is the proportion of background pixels that are segmented as foreground. The closer TPR is to 1 and the closer FPR is to 0, the better the segmentation is. They are defined as follows,

$$TPR = \frac{A \cap B}{B}, FPR = \frac{A - A \cap B}{B} \qquad (8)$$

## 3.3  Comparison with Other Methods

To evaluate the performance of proposed method, the results are compared with the results of the ALTIS method [17], the method based on wavelet transform(WT) [8] and the manual segmentation results by expert. The segmentation results of three slices from typical COVID-19 CTs by three methods and expert are shown as Fig. 4. It can be observed from the figure that our proposed method obtains accurate lung segmentation results for the pathological lungs with different degrees of lesions. And the other two methods can identify the normal areas and slight lesions, but lose the lesion areas with high intensity near the lung boundary.

Table 1 shows the quantitatively comparative results by using three methods. All metrics show that our method achieves the best segmentation performance. In particular, ASD decreases significantly (0.0101 ± 0.0147mm), which is much lower than that of ALTIS (0.1236 ± 0.2335 mm) and WT (0.0552 ± 0.1014 mm). This indicates that our method provides a more accurate shape of lung surface. Besides, our method achieves higher TPR and lower FPR than ALTIS method and WT method. In summary, our method can not only obtain more accurate segmentation results, but also has more stable performance.

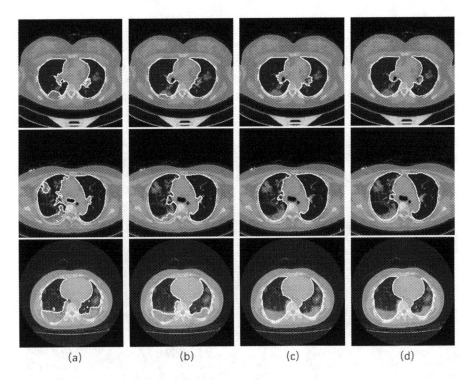

(a)                    (b)                    (c)                    (d)

**Fig. 4.** Results of lung segmentation with different methods. (a) Results of ALTIS method; (b) Results of WT method; (c) Results of the proposed method; (d) Ground Truth.

**Table 1.** Segmentation accuracy of ALTIS method, Wavelet Transform method (WT) and our proposed method for the Convid-19 lungs.

| Metrics | ASD(mm) | MSD(mm) | DSC(%) | TPR(%) | FPR(%) |
|---------|---------|---------|--------|--------|--------|
| ALTIS | $0.1236 \pm 0.2335$ | $31.71 \pm 10.62$ | $96.65 \pm 4.30$ | $95.09 \pm 7.34$ | $1.90 \pm 1.37$ |
| WT | $0.0552 \pm 0.1014$ | $19.76 \pm 35.60$ | $97.64 \pm 4.25$ | $96.51 \pm 3.50$ | $2.79 \pm 2.26$ |
| Our | $\mathbf{0.0101 \pm 0.0147}$ | $\mathbf{14.21 \pm 14.94}$ | $\mathbf{99.22 \pm 0.99}$ | $\mathbf{99.35 \pm 1.23}$ | $\mathbf{0.86 \pm 1.87}$ |

## 3.4 Comparison with Deep-Learning Method

In the early stage of disease outbreak, the number of samples is often insufficient and the labeled samples are scarce. It is well known that: when there are not enough samples, the performance of deep learning model will decline significantly. Our method will not be affected by the number of samples, so it can provide an effective tool for lung segmentation in the case of insufficient samples. In order to verify our claim, we trained the U-Net model with a small amount of data and tested its performance in the datasets mentioned above.

2001 training samples and 500 verification samples is collected from 40 cases of novel coronavirus pneumonia. We set the initial learning rate as 0.1 which gradually decreases when the network performance improves. RMSProp was selected as the optimization technique. The U-Net model is trained with a batch size of 1 for 10 epochs. The prediction results of the trained model on the above datasets are compared to the results of our method and the ground truth, as shown in Fig. 5. Table 2 shows the quantitative comparison of the U-Net and our method.

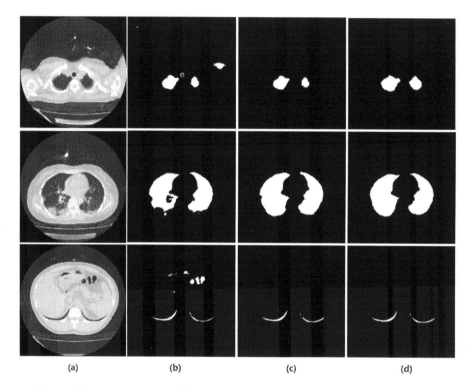

(a)          (b)          (c)          (d)

**Fig. 5.** (a) Original images (b) U-net masks; (c) Our masks; (d) Ground truth.

**Table 2.** Segmentation accuracy of U-Net and our proposed method for the Convid-19 lungs.

| Metrics | ASD(mm) | MSD(mm) | DSC(%) | TPR(%) | FPR(%) |
|---------|---------|---------|--------|--------|--------|
| U-Net | 1.2417 ± 8.0393 | 47.94 ± 51.14 | 79.13 ± 73.45 | 73.89 ± 70.97 | 1.88 ± 1.87 |
| Our | **0.0101 ± 0.0147** | **14.21 ± 14.94** | **99.22 ± 0.99** | **99.35 ± 1.23** | **0.86 ± 1.87** |

## 3.5   Running Time

The proposed algorithm is implemented in Python3.7 and test on a PC equipped with a 2.30 GHz i5 CPU processor and 16 GB RAM. The ALTIS method takes the shortest time to segment lungs (0.25 s per slice), which aims at implementing a fast automatic lung and trachea segmentation method while yielding poor segmentation results of pathological lungs. The average running time of the WT method is 2.37 s per slices. The average running time of our method is 2.19 s per slices.

## 4   Conclusion

In this paper, we propose a new two-stage approach to automatically segment pathological lungs from CT images. We first implement a coarse segmentation on original images by coupling Otsu-based results and rib outlines. This step can remove most background while retaining complete lung shape. Then an efficient contour refinement is introduced to refine coarse segmentation. To empirically investigate the effectiveness and robustness of our approach, we perform extensive experiments on the segmentation task. The experiment results show that our method has a good performance on COVID-19 lung datasets. The conclusion made in this work may allow us to reconsider the importance of traditional approaches, which can provide satisfying or superior performance with very limited labeled datasets. We believe that the simplicity and modularity of our method will enable us to scale to much larger datasets, without requiring the expensive labels. Our future work will explore combining our method with the deep learning-based method, such as formulating the prior information as a proper regularizer to improve the deep models.

## References

1. Ai, T., et al.: Correlation of chest CT and RT-PCR testing for coronavirus disease 2019 (COVID-19) in China: a report of 1014 cases. Radiology **296**(2), E32–E40 (2020)
2. Chung, M., et al.: CT imaging features of 2019 novel coronavirus (2019-nCoV). Radiology **295**(1), 202–207 (2020)
3. Deng, Y., Lei, L., Chen, Y., Zhang, W.: The potential added value of FDG PET/CT for COVID-19 pneumonia. Eur. J. Nucl. Med. Mol. Imaging 1–2 (2020)
4. Gerard, S.E., Herrmann, J., Kaczka, D.W., Musch, G., Fernandez-Bustamante, A., Reinhardt, J.M.: Multi-resolution convolutional neural networks for fully automated segmentation of acutely injured lungs in multiple species. Med. Image Anal. **60**, 101592 (2020)
5. Gill, G., Beichel, R.R.: Segmentation of lungs with interstitial lung disease in CT scans: a TV-L$^1$ based texture analysis approach. In: Bebis, G., et al. (eds.) ISVC 2014. LNCS, vol. 8887, pp. 511–520. Springer, Cham (2014). https://doi.org/10.1007/978-3-319-14249-4_48
6. Kiaei, A.A., Khotanlou, H.: Segmentation of medical images using mean value guided contour. Med. Image Anal. **40**, 111–132 (2017)

7. Li, Q., Deng, T., Xie, W.: Active contours driven by divergence of gradient vector flow. Sig. Process. **120**, 185–199 (2016)
8. Liu, C., Pang, M.: Automatic lung segmentation based on image decomposition and wavelet transform. Biomed. Signal Process. Control **61**, 102032 (2020)
9. Mansoor, A., et al.: Segmentation and image analysis of abnormal lungs at CT: current approaches, challenges, and future trends. Radiographics **35**(4), 1056–1076 (2015)
10. Mansoor, A., Bagci, U., Mollura, D.J.: Near-optimal keypoint sampling for fast pathological lung segmentation. In: 2014 36th Annual International Conference of the IEEE Engineering in Medicine and Biology Society, pp. 6032–6035. IEEE (2014)
11. Mesanovic, N., Grgic, M., Huseinagic, H., Males, M., Skejic, E., Smajlovic, M.: Automatic CT image segmentation of the lungs with region growing algorithm. In: 18th International Conference on Systems, Signals and Image Processing-IWSSIP, pp. 395–400 (2011)
12. Park, B., Park, H., Lee, S.M., Seo, J.B., Kim, N.: Lung segmentation on HRCT and volumetric CT for diffuse interstitial lung disease using deep convolutional neural networks. J. Digit. Imaging **32**(6), 1019–1026 (2019). https://doi.org/10.1007/s10278-019-00254-8
13. Prasad, M.N., et al.: Automatic segmentation of lung parenchyma in the presence of diseases based on curvature of ribs. Acad. Radiol. **15**(9), 1173–1180 (2008)
14. Pulagam, A.R., Kande, G.B., Ede, V.K.R., Inampudi, R.B.: Automated lung segmentation from HRCT scans with diffuse parenchymal lung diseases. J. Digit. Imaging **29**(4), 507–519 (2016)
15. Ronneberger, O., Fischer, P., Brox, T.: U-net: convolutional networks for biomedical image segmentation. In: Navab, N., Hornegger, J., Wells, W.M., Frangi, A.F. (eds.) MICCAI 2015. LNCS, vol. 9351, pp. 234–241. Springer, Cham (2015). https://doi.org/10.1007/978-3-319-24574-4_28
16. Shen, S., Bui, A.A., Cong, J., Hsu, W.: An automated lung segmentation approach using bidirectional chain codes to improve nodule detection accuracy. Comput. Biol. Med. **57**, 139–149 (2015)
17. Sousa, A.M., Martins, S.B., Falcao, A.X., Reis, F., Bagatin, E., Irion, K.: ALTIS: A fast and automatic lung and trachea CT-image segmentation method. Med. Phys. **46**(11), 4970–4982 (2019)
18. Sun, S., Bauer, C., Beichel, R.: Automated 3-D segmentation of lungs with lung cancer in CT data using a novel robust active shape model approach. IEEE Trans. Med. Imaging **31**(2), 449–460 (2011)

# Deep Semantic Edge for Cell Counting and Localization in Time-Lapse Microscopy Images

Tianwei Zhang and Kun Sun[✉]

Hubei Key Laboratory of Intelligent Geo-Information Processing, School of Computer
Sciences, China University of Geosciences, Wuhan 430074, China
sunkun@cug.edu.cn

**Abstract.** Cell counting and localization in microscopy images is one of
the most important steps in Assisted Reproduction Technology (ART).
This paper proposes a fully automatic method to achieve this goal,
which consists of three main parts. The first part is region of inter-
est(ROI) extracting and cell counting. These two tasks are transfered
to a multi-class target detection problem that can be jointly solved by
existing deep learning methods. To impose temporal consistency that
the number of cells should be non-decreasing in time, a simple yet effective post-processing strategy is adopted to smooth the result. Secondly,
an improved network with a new upsampling module and a new loss
function is proposed to predict crisp and complete contours of cells from
a higher semantic level. The edges are more robust to noise, blurring
and occlusion, which facilitates the following ellipse fitting a lot. Finally,
elliptical proposals are fitted on the extracted contours and correct ones
are selected in an effective way. Extensive experiments are carried out to
show the advantages of the proposed method.

**Keywords:** Semantic edge · Cell counting · Cell localization · Ellipse
fitting · Time-lapse microscopy images

## 1 Introduction

Cell counting and localization is an important way for evaluating the quality
of cell development in Assisted Reproduction Technology (ART). Experts traditionally observe the cells under a microscope manually. The most common
approach for imaging is Hoffman Modulation Contrast (HMC). It captures a
stack of 3D-like images, which are taken at different focal planes. However, taking the petri dish from the incubator frequently is not only burdensome, but also
may interfere the process of cell division. Hence, a non-invasive method that can
fulfill this task automatically with time-lapse microscopy images is preferable.

There are several challenges for cell microscopy image processing. The first is
deteriorated data quality. Due to limited imagery conditions, cell microscopy
images usually present low contrast, heavy noise and blurred cell contours.

© Springer Nature Switzerland AG 2021
H. Ma et al. (Eds.): PRCV 2021, LNCS 13021, pp. 337–349, 2021.
https://doi.org/10.1007/978-3-030-88010-1_28

Besides, the cytoplasm is nearly transparent. Different from some coloured corpuscle such as erythrocyte, it is hard to tell the difference between the interior and exterior of a cell from appearance only. In this case, many researches are based on finding boundaries of the cells. However, since the cells may divide in arbitrary direction, there is usually full or partial overlap between cells when viewing in the vertical direction after a period of time. Cells will occlude and shade each other, making contour extracting more difficult.

In this paper, an automatic cell counting and localization method which puts forward a series solutions to the above challenges is proposed. As the cells are not in a fixed position in the image, we first extract the region of interest (ROI) containing the cells and then predict the number of cells. These two tasks are jointly solved by a deep neural network by treating them as a multi-class target detection task. Removing irrelevant information facilitates the remaining steps such as edge extracting and ellipse fitting. To impose temporal consistency that the number of cells should be non-decreasing in time, a simple yet effective post-processing strategy is adopted to smooth the result. The second part of the proposed method performs semantic edge detection. As mentioned above, edges are important for locating cells. Traditional edge extractors are sensitive to blurred texture and noise in time-lapse microscopy images. They often produce small discontinued segments which covers part of the contour, or return thick edge maps that are not precise enough. To solve this problem, we introduce an improved network with a new loss function to predict crisp and complete contours from a higher semantic level. Finally, following existing methods performing cell localization, we fit elliptical proposals on the extracted contours. After removing obviously false candidates, we further propose a circle induced clustering module to compute the final correct cells.

In a nutshell, the contributions of this paper are three-fold. (1) A deep semantic edge detection network which provides a good initialization for ellipse fitting is proposed. (2) We jointly predict the ROI and number of cells via a single deep network. (3) A robust ellipse selection strategy is designed.

## 2    Related Work

The main studies in the literature can be divided into three categories: classification of cells at early stages of development based on quantitative analysis, segmentation of individual cells or the whole cell regions, and the localization of individual cell based on elliptical models.

**Classification Based Methods.** Methods in this category predict the number of cells by image classification. Wang et al. [30] used the adaboost model to predict the number of cells contained in each frame of a time-lapse microscopy video. They used 62 hand-labeled features and 200 automatically learned bag of features (BOF) to determine the stage of cell development. Tian et al. [28] proposed a circular detection method based on least square curve fitting (LSCF). The number of circles detected is deemed as the number of cells. Khan et al. [9] used the enhanced decision tree classifier to predict the number of cells in each time-lapse microscopy image. To impose smoothness consistency, they also optimized the sequence of predictions at different time by proposing a conditional random field model. Later, Khan et al. [11] proposed an end-to-end deep convolutional neural network framework to improve their previous work. Liu et al. [14] used dynamic programming in combination with a multi-task deep learning method to predict the number of cells in the video. Dynamic Programming was used to optimize the whole sequence of predictions to impose the smoothness constraint. Rad et al. [20] proposed an automatic framework based on deep learning to transform the cell counting task into an end-to-end regression problem. The method counts and localizes cells in 1–8 cell stages. Malmsten et al. [17] proposed a convolutional neural network based on Inception V3, which automatically classifies the number of mouse and human cells in 1–4 cell stages. However, most of methods in this category only predict the number of cells. The very useful accurate position of cells, e.g. centers or boundaries, are not available.

**Segmentation Based Methods.** Giusti et al. [7] proposed a graph segmentation based method. Horizontal image sets of individual cells at different focal planes were segmented. In addition, each cell was reconstructed to a 3D model. Cicconet et al. [4] developed a semi-automatic system to segment the contour of each cell by manually determining the cell center. In this way, they completed the precise localization of individual cells in the early stage. Khan et al. [12] calculated an average image of adjacent frames, and applied the graph segmentation method on the average image. Their method returned the contour of the whole cell region, rather than the contour of each individual cell. Grushnikov et al. [8] introduced a level-set algorithm to complete the segmentation of each individual cell by using active contour. Trivedi et al. [29] used threshold segmentation and the watershed algorithm to segment the HMC image stacks for the 2-cell stage. A 3D model of cells were reconstructed using MATLAB. Rad et al. [21] proposed a synthetic cell image scheme to augment the experimental data. Four new full convolution depth models are proposed based on the U-net. Each model adopts a multi-scale strategy to achieve semantic segmentation of the ectodermal layer in human cell images. However, segmentation becomes an increasingly difficult task if the cells are not stained or the cells divide into more and more cells. Fitting ellipse to a cell can also properly describe its location, pose and shape. If we can extract good edge map of the cell image, the ellipse fitting task could be tractable.

**Localization Based Methods.** Singh et al. [23] proposed an ellipse fitting algorithm for 1–4 cell stages. Firstly, the boundary of each cell were detected by the isoperimetric segmentation algorithm. Then ellipses were fitted by the least square method. Aprinaldi et al. [2] detected arcs and proposed an ellipse fitting algorithm (ARCPSO) based on particle swarm optimization. Syulistyo et al. [27] improved the ARCPSO algorithm by adding a line distance constraint, which effectively improved the accuracy of cell localization. Khan et al. [10] proposed a linear Markov model to evaluate the matching degree of each detected ellipse with the time-lapse image. The optimal results are selected according to this measurement. Syulistyo et al. [26] improved the EDCircles [1] ellipse fitting algorithm and optimized the results by combining RANSAC. Charalambos et al. [25] proposed a cell boundary segmentation method based on the Kohonnen Sofm neural network. They also fitted ellipses to the boundaries. Rad et al. [19] used a multi-scale capillary segmentation algorithm to detect cell edges. They proposed two measurement to select ellipses that best represented the cell distribution. However, the above methods still suffer from obtaining thick, inaccurate and incomplete cell contours. The quality of edge maps could be further improved.

## 3   The Proposed Method

In this paper, we use a HMC system to capture images every 15 min. In each shot, 7 images in a stack are obtained. Following [17] and [23], we only focus on early period of 1–4 cell stages. The proposed method consists of three main parts: ROI extraction and cell counting, semantic contour detection, and ellipse fitting based localization.

### 3.1   ROI Extracting and Cell Counting

Generally speaking, cells are not in a fixed position in the petri dish during the dynamic development procedure. A relatively wide field of view is set to make sure that the cells could be tracked. Consequently, the original image contains most of the background and the cells only take up a small portion of the pixels. Removing irrelevant regions will reduce computational overhead, as well as the interference of noise. We achieve this by cropping the image according to the rectangular region of interest (ROI), which can be solved by an object detection method. Cell counting is a regression problem, but it can be converted to a classification problem in our case because there are only four discrete values for it. By doing this, the above detection and classification problems can be jointly solved by a multi-class detection algorithm, $e.g.$ Faster R-CNN [22]. The class prediction of Faster R-CNN is treated as the number of cells and the detection result is treated as ROI.

To be specific, we manually label each image with a bounding box which contains all the cells and a category which is represented by an integer from 1 to 4. Then the pre-trained Faster R-CNN is fine-tuned on our data. During testing, we apply it to all the 7 images in a stack and use a voting-like strategy to get the final result of this stack. That is, we take the bounding box with the highest score and the class with the highest frequency among 7 images. In this way, we can get the number of cells at time $t$, denoted as $n_t$. However, sometimes we get inconsistent predictions, $i.e.$ $n_{t+1} < n_t$. To impose temporal consistency that the number of cells should be non-decreasing in time, a simple yet effective filtering strategy is adopted to smooth the result, which can be described as:

$$n_{t+1} = \epsilon(n_{t+1}, w), \quad if \quad n_{t+1} < n_t. \tag{1}$$

$\epsilon$ is a function that returns the most frequent elements in the 1D filter window, $n_{t+1}$ is the center of the filter and $w = 7$ is the half size of the window.

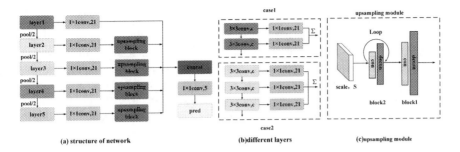

(a) structure of network
(a) structure of network    (b)different layers    (c)upsampling module

**Fig. 1.** (a) The overall structure of the proposed network. (b) Two kinds of structures for the layers in (a). Case 1 for the first two layers and case 2 for the last three layers. $c$ is the number of channels. (c) The upsampling module.

## 3.2 Semantic Edge Detection

Due to the challenges in microscopy images, traditional edge detection methods such as Canny [3] and Otsu [18] fail to properly capture cell contours. To solve this problem, we propose a deep learning based semantic edge detection method. It takes the outstanding RCF [13] network as backbone. According to [24], using networks to enlarge the resolution of the images shows several advantages. Hence, we also add a new upsampling module and a new term in the loss function. Figure 1 shows the structure of the network.

Figure 1(a) is the overall structure of the proposed network. The input image is passed through five consecutive layers. After each layer is a pooling operation, reducing the resolution of the feature map. Finally, the feature combining the side outputs of all the layers is used to predict if a pixel belongs to the edge. The structures of the layers are shown in Fig. 1(b). The first two layers use case 1 and the last three layers use case 2. $c$ is the number of channels, which takes the value of 64, 128, 256, 512 and 512 for each of the five layers. Different from original RCF [13] method, here we introduce a new upsampling module, which is shown in Fig. 1(c). It takes the down-sampled feature map at scale $S$ as input. Both block1 and block2 will enlarge the image size by 2*2 times. They have the same structure except for that the convolution kernel size is 1*1 for block1 while it is 16*16 for block2. The transpose convolution kernel size is $S$ for all the decon layers. Block2 is repeated several times until the image size reaches $\frac{1}{4}$ of the origin. Then block1 is used to scale the image to the same size of the original picture.

Training the above network is a typical unbalanced learning problem because most of the pixels belong to the non-edge category. To solve this problem, balanced cross-entropy loss function [31] is widely used. However, it still suffers from unclear and thick edges. In this paper, we introduce a dice loss [5] to the balanced cross-entropy loss. Dice loss has the following form:

$$L_D(MP, MG) = \sum_i^M Dist(MP_i, MG_i) = \sum_i^M \frac{\sum_i^N p_i^2 + \sum_i^N g_i^2}{2 \sum_i^N p_i g_i}, \quad (2)$$

where $p_i$ and $g_i$ are the value of the i-th pixel on the prediction map $P$ and ground truth $G$, respectively. $MP$ and $MG$ denote a mini-batch of predictions and their ground truth, respectively. $M$ is the total number of training samples in the mini-batch. Equation (2) is a measure of the similarity between two sets, rather than the similarity between individuals, which is quite different from the cross-entropy loss. The higher the similarity is, the greater the measurement is. It can be thought of a global, image-level constraint. Hence, we get the final loss function:

$$L_{final}(MP, MG) = \alpha L_C(MP, MG) + L_D(MP, MG) \qquad (3)$$

where $L_C(MP, MG)$ represents the balanced cross-entropy loss. $\alpha$ is the parameter that controls the trade-off between them. Empirically, we set $\alpha$=0.001.

### 3.3   Ellipse Fitting and Verification

Based on the estimated edge map, we apply an efficient ellipse fitting algorithm HQED [16] to generate cell proposals. These proposals could be quite noisy so we have to refine the results. First of all, we eliminate a large number of false ellipses according to the coverage of inlier points and angle defined in paper [16]. Inlier point coverage of an ellipse is the ratio of the arc length covered by inlier points to its circumference. In particular, when the minimum distance between an edge pixel and an ellipse is less than 2, it is deemed as an inlier of the ellipse. The angle coverage of an ellipse is the ratio of the arc angle covered by inlier points to 360. It is intuitive that an ellipse is more likely to be correct if it has higher coverage of inlier points and angle. Empirically, we delete the ellipses with inlier point coverage less than 0.1 and the angle coverage less than 1/3 for 1 cell stage and 1/6 for 2–4 cell stages. Secondly, we remove too large or too small ellipses by measuring their area ratio to the ROI, which is defined by $R$:

$$\begin{cases} \frac{1}{2} \leq R \leq \frac{3}{4}N & (N = 1) \\ \frac{1}{2N} \leq R \leq \frac{1}{N} & (N > 1), \end{cases} \qquad (4)$$

where $N$ is the number of cells. We also measure the ellipticity of each ellipse, which is denoted by $e$:

$$e = a/b, \qquad (5)$$

where $a$ and $b$ are the long and short semi-axes of the ellipse, respectively. Ellipses with $e \leq 1.7$ are removed empirically. Afterwards, for the proposals whose intersection over union (IoU) is larger than 0.55, non-maximum suppression (NMS) is carried to retain the one with the highest score, which is defined by the product of inlier point coverage and angle coverage.

The above steps filters most of the false positives, but some of them still survive. Thus we propose a circle induced clustering method to select the final correct ellipses. To be specific, we detect circles [15] on the images and encode them with a 3-dimensional vector (2-D position and radius). Here we use circles rather than ellipses because the same arc may have ambiguous ellipse fitting

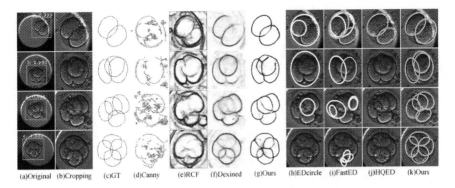

(a)Original  (b)Cropping   (c)GT   (d)Canny   (e)RCF   (f)Dexined   (g)Ours   (h)EDcircle   (i)FastED   (j)HQED   (k)Ours

**Fig. 2.** Visual results of different algorithms. (a) The results of ROI extraction and number of cells prediction. (b) Image after cropped. (c) The ground truth of edge. (d-g) Results of different edge detectors. (h-k) Results of different ellipse fitting methods. Wrong ellipses are in red. (Color figure online)

results, but circle-fitting is unique. The k-means algorithm is applied to get k centers in the circle feature space, where k is set to the number of cells. These centers are mapped to the 2D image coordinates. Finally, for each center the ellipse that is both the closest and has the highest score, which is defined by the product of inlier point coverage and angle coverage is selected.

## 4    Experiment

### 4.1    Dataset

The dataset to fine-tune the pretrained Faster R-CNN contains 368 stacks×7 images from 68 individuals. The percentage of 1 to 4 cell stages in the training set are 35.5%, 25.4%, 16.3% and 22.8%, respectively. It is not very common that two cells divide at obviously different times, so the number of images in the 3-cell stage is fewer than others. The test set contains images from 5 individuals of all 1–4 cell stages. Individual 1–5 contains 164, 140, 162, 229, 203 stacks×7 images, respectively. In the above data, the cell region is labeled as the smallest encasing rectangle box and the class is labeled by a number in 1–4. We annotate another 516 stacks×7 images from 97 different individuals for edge detection. The percentage of 1 to 4 cell stages are 28.7%, 25.2%, 19.1% and 27.0%, respectively. A line of one pixel width is used to mark the contour of each cell as ground truth. From the above data, we select 386 stacks×7 images and augment them to nearly 41000 samples to train our edge detection network. Another 15 stacks×7 images are used to test the performance. Meanwhile, another 115 stacks×7 images are used to test our ellipse fitting algorithm. An ellipse will be regarded as correct if its IoU with the ground truth is greater than a threshold of 0.7.

**Table 1.** The prediction results of our method.

| Individual | ROI | Number of Cells(before/after post-processing) |
|---|---|---|
| 1 | 100.00 | 96.95/**97.56**(+0.61) |
| 2 | 100.00 | 92.14/**100.00**(+7.86) |
| 3 | 100.00 | 96.30/**98.15**(+1.85) |
| 4 | 100.00 | 95.20/**99.56**(+4.36) |
| 5 | 100.00 | 96.55/**97.54**(+0.99) |
| Avg | 100.00 | 95.43/**98.56**(+3.13) |

**Table 2.** Results on different edge detectors.

| Method | Cell-stage | Precision | Recall | F-measure |
|---|---|---|---|---|
| Canny [3] | 1 | 0.0606 | 0.0606 | 0.0606 |
| | 2 | 0.4839 | 0.2586 | 0.3371 |
| | 3 | 0.4800 | 0.1875 | 0.2697 |
| | 4 | 0.7561 | 0.2500 | 0.3758 |
| Otsu [18] | 1 | 0.6667 | 0.6667 | 0.6667 |
| | 2 | 0.3878 | 0.3276 | 0.3551 |
| | 3 | 0.4528 | 0.3750 | 0.4103 |
| | 4 | 0.5568 | 0.3952 | 0.4623 |
| RCF [13] | 1 | 1.0000 | 1.0000 | 1.0000 |
| | 2 | 0.8475 | 0.8621 | 0.8547 |
| | 3 | 0.6515 | 0.6719 | 0.6615 |
| | 4 | 0.8537 | 0.8468 | 0.8502 |
| Dexined [24] | 1 | 0.9697 | 0.9697 | 0.9697 |
| | 2 | 0.9623 | 0.8793 | 0.9189 |
| | 3 | 0.8431 | 0.6719 | 0.7478 |
| | 4 | 0.9307 | 0.7581 | 0.8356 |
| Ours | 1 | **1.0000** | **1.0000** | **1.0000** |
| | 2 | **0.9831** | **1.0000** | **0.9915** |
| | 3 | **0.9091** | **0.9375** | **0.9231** |
| | 4 | **0.9756** | **0.9677** | **0.9717** |

## 4.2   Results on ROI Extracting and Cell Number Predicting

Faster R-CNN is trained using pytorch for 20 epochs, each with a maximum 4400 iterations. The network has 100% precision of ROI extraction on the test images. Examples are visualized in Fig. 2(a). We then test the precision of the predicted number of cells before and after post-processing. As shown in Table 1, our filtering strategy of imposing temporal consistency significantly improves the accuracy.

### 4.3 Comparison of Edge Detectors and Ellipse Fitting Methods

In this part, we present the results of different edge detectors as well as different ellipse fitting algorithms. The visualization results of different edge detectors are shown in Fig. 2(d-g), and the quantitative data is given in Table 2. In this case, the edge maps for different methods are directly sent to our ellipse fitting module. Due to the challenge of the microscopy images, traditional edge detectors such as canny fails to extract high quality edges. RCF [13] and Dexined [24] based on deep learning can effectively make up for the lack of accuracy, and then improve the performance of ellipse fitting. But their results are still not as good as ours, showing that our semantic edge is much better.

**Table 3.** Results on different ellipse fitting algorithms.

| Method | Cell-stage | Precision | Recall | F-measure |
|---|---|---|---|---|
| EDCircle [1] | 1 | 0.3834 | 0.4199 | 0.4008 |
| | 2 | 0.3026 | 0.1700 | 0.2177 |
| | 3 | 0.2733 | 0.1049 | 0.1516 |
| | 4 | 0.4091 | 0.1244 | 0.1908 |
| FastED [6] | 1 | 0.2644 | 0.3766 | 0.3107 |
| | 2 | 0.2500 | 0.2143 | 0.2308 |
| | 3 | 0.2602 | 0.1429 | 0.1844 |
| | 4 | 0.2861 | 0.1302 | 0.1789 |
| HQED [16] | 1 | 0.2469 | 0.2554 | 0.2511 |
| | 2 | 0.2212 | 0.1182 | 0.1541 |
| | 3 | 0.1274 | 0.0446 | 0.0661 |
| | 4 | 0.2522 | 0.0668 | 0.1056 |
| Ours | 1 | **1.0000** | **1.0000** | **1.0000** |
| | 2 | **0.9831** | **1.0000** | **0.9915** |
| | 3 | **0.9091** | **0.9375** | **0.9231** |
| | 4 | **0.9756** | **0.9677** | **0.9717** |

**Table 4.** Ablation study of the upsampling module and dice loss. Ours-w/o-FL refers to training with the balanced cross-entropy loss only, without using the dice loss. Ours-w/o-UP refers to using the bilinear interpolation for upsampling.

| Method | ODS | OIS |
|---|---|---|
| RCF [13] | 0.737 | 0.743 |
| Ours-w/o-FL | 0.765 | 0.777 |
| Ours-w/o-UP | 0.661 | 0.671 |
| Ours | **0.775** | **0.782** |

We also compare the proposed method with different ellipse fitting algorithms including EDCircles [1], FastED [6], as well as HQED [16]. In this case, the original images are feed to each pipeline. Among them, EDCircles is a real-time parameter-free circle detection algorithm, which can effectively detect circles and ellipses in cell images with the advantages of short running time and strong anti-noise performance. FastED is a fast ellipse fitting algorithm. HQED is the ellipse fitting method of the baseline adopted in this paper. All the above three methods are well known cell localization methods. Figure 2(h-k) shows visual results. It can be seen that our method performs better for cell localization both in accuracy and recall. The quantitative results are given in Table 3. The average performance of EDCircle, FastED and HQED on the test set are less than 50%, for which the reason might largely be the lack of reliable edge extractors. Since our method involves a better edge detector and a more reasonable ellipse selecting scheme, it outperforms the baseline HQED several times.

**Table 5.** Ablation study of our ellipse selecting strategy. Ours w/o DA refers to our method without Density Analysis using circle induced clustering.

| Method | Cell-stage | Precision | Recall | F-measure |
|---|---|---|---|---|
| Ours w/o DA | 1 | 0.9697 | 0.9697 | 0.9697 |
| | 2 | 0.8814 | 0.8966 | 0.8889 |
| | 3 | 0.7121 | 0.7344 | 0.7231 |
| | 4 | 0.8862 | 0.8790 | 0.8826 |
| Ours | 1 | **1.0000** | **1.0000** | **1.0000** |
| | 2 | **0.9831** | **1.0000** | **0.9915** |
| | 3 | **0.9091** | **0.9375** | **0.9231** |
| | 4 | **0.9756** | **0.9677** | **0.9717** |

### 4.4    Ablation Study

We conduct a series of ablation studies to evaluate the importance of each component in the proposed method. Our first experiment is to examine the effectiveness of the upsampling module and dice loss. The semantic edge detection algorithm is trained for 30 epoch, each with a maximum of 13333 iterations. The accuracy of the prediction is evaluated via two standard measures: fixed contour threshold (ODS) and per-image best threshold (OIS). RCF is the baseline network which is not equipped with the upsampling module and dice loss. Ours-w/o-FL refers to the proposed method trained by the balanced cross-entropy loss only, without using the dice loss. Ours-w/o-UP refers to the proposed method using the bilinear interpolation for upsampling. As is shown in Table 4, the upsampling module can improve the accuracy of RCF, but using dice loss will reduce its accuracy.

However, under the dual action of the upsampling module and the dice loss, our method achieves the best performance.

We also evaluated our clustering based ellipse selecting strategy. The final ellipse fitting results such as average precision, recall and F-measure are reported in Table 5. It shows that by performing circle induced clustering, our method works better in selecting correct proposals in multicellular images.

## 5   Conclusion

This paper proposes a fully automatic method for cell counting and localization in microscopy images. Our method differs from existing methods in the following aspects. First, we use CNN to extract ROI and predict the number of cells in a one-shot manner. Second, our edge maps are estimated from deep richer features, thus capturing more semantic property of the object. At last, a clustering based cell center rectification module is proposed to further increase the accuracy. One limitation of this work is that it is applied up to 4-cell stage. We plan to extend this work to 8-cell stage in the future.

**Acknowledgment.** This work is supported by the National Natural Science Foundation of China (61802356), by Open Research Project of The Hubei Key Laboratory of Intelligent Geo-Information Processing (KLIGIP-2019B03), also in part by National Natural Science Foundation of China (41925007,61806113). We would also like to thank Wuhan Huchuang Union Technology Co., Ltd. for data support.

## References

1. Akinlar, C., Topal, C.: Edcircles: a real-time circle detector with a false detection control. Pattern Recognit. **46**, 725–740 (2013)
2. Aprinaldi, Habibie, I., Rahmatullah, R., Kurniawan, A., Bowolaksono, A., Jatmiko, W., Wiweko, B.: Arcpso: ellipse detection method using particle swarm optimization and arc combination. In: International Conference on Advanced Computer Science and Information System, pp. 408–413 (2014)
3. Canny, J.F.: A computational approach to edge detection. IEEE Trans. Pattern Anal. Mach. Intell. **8**, 679–698 (1986)
4. Cicconet, M., Gutwein, M., Gunsalus, K.C., Geiger, D.: Label free cell-tracking and division detection based on 2d time-lapse images for lineage analysis of early embryo development. Comput. Biol. Med. **51**, 24–34 (2014)
5. Deng, R., Shen, C., Liu, S., Wang, H., Liu, X.: Learning to Predict Crisp Boundaries. In: Ferrari, V., Hebert, M., Sminchisescu, C., Weiss, Y. (eds.) ECCV 2018. LNCS, vol. 11210, pp. 570–586. Springer, Cham (2018). https://doi.org/10.1007/978-3-030-01231-1_35
6. Fornaciari, M., Prati, A., Cucchiara, R.: A fast and effective ellipse detector for embedded vision applications. Pattern Recogn. **47**, 3693–3708 (2014)
7. Giusti, A., Corani, G., Gambardella, L.M., Magli, C., Gianaroli, L.: Blastomere segmentation and 3d morphology measurements of early embryos from hoffman modulation contrast image stacks. In: International Symposium on Biomedical Imaging: From Nano to Macro, pp. 1261–1264. IEEE (2010)

8. Grushnikov, A., Niwayama, R., Kanade, T., Yagi, Y.: 3d level set method for blastomere segmentation of preimplantation embryos in fluorescence microscopy images. Mach. Vis. Appl. **29**(1), 125–134 (2018)
9. Khan, A., Gould, S., Salzmann, M.: Automated monitoring of human embryonic cells up to the 5-cell stage in time-lapse microscopy images. In: International Symposium on Biomedical Imaging, pp. 389–393. IEEE (2015)
10. Khan, A., Gould, S., Salzmann, M.: A linear chain markov model for detection and localization of cells in early stage embryo development. In: Winter Conference on Applications of Computer Vision, pp. 526–533. IEEE Computer Society (2015)
11. Khan, A., Gould, S., Salzmann, M.: Deep convolutional neural networks for human embryonic cell counting. In: Hua, G., Jégou, H. (eds.) ECCV 2016. LNCS, vol. 9913, pp. 339–348. Springer, Cham (2016). https://doi.org/10.1007/978-3-319-46604-0_25
12. Khan, A., Gould, S., Salzmann, M.: Segmentation of developing human embryo in time-lapse microscopy. In: International Symposium on Biomedical Imaging, pp. 930–934. IEEE (2016)
13. Liu, Y., Cheng, M., Hu, X., Wang, K., Bai, X.: Richer convolutional features for edge detection. In: Conference on Computer Vision and Pattern Recognition, pp. 5872–5881. IEEE Computer Society (2017)
14. Liu, Z., et al.: Multi-task deep learning with dynamic programming for embryo early development stage classification from time-lapse videos. IEEE Access **7**, 122153–122163 (2019)
15. Lu, C., Xia, S., Huang, W., Shao, M., Fu, Y.: Circle detection by arc-support line segments. In: International Conference on Image Processing, pp. 76–80. IEEE (2017)
16. Lu, C., Xia, S., Shao, M., Fu, Y.: Arc-support line segments revisited: an efficient high-quality ellipse detection. IEEE Trans. Image Process. **29**, 768–781 (2020)
17. Malmsten, J., Zaninovic, N., Zhan, Q., Rosenwaks, Z., Shan, J.: Automated cell stage predictions in early mouse and human embryos using convolutional neural networks. In: International Conference on Biomedical & Health Informatics, pp. 1–4. IEEE (2019)
18. Otsu, N.: A threshold selection method from gray-level histogram. Automatica **11**, 285–296 (1975)
19. Rad, R.M., Saeedi, P., Au, J., Havelock, J.: A hybrid approach for multiple blastomeres identification in early human embryo images. Comput. Biol. Med. **101**, 100–111 (2018)
20. Rad, R.M., Saeedi, P., Au, J., Havelock, J.: Cell-net: embryonic cell counting and centroid localization via residual incremental atrous pyramid and progressive upsampling convolution. IEEE Access **7**, 81945–81955 (2019)
21. Rad, R.M., Saeedi, P., Au, J., Havelock, J.: Trophectoderm segmentation in human embryo images via inceptioned u-net. Med. Image Anal. **62**, 101612 (2020)
22. Ren, S., He, K., Girshick, R.B., Sun, J.: Faster r-cnn: towards real-time object detection with region proposal networks. IEEE Trans. Pattern Anal. Mach. Intell. **39**, 1137–1149 (2017)
23. Singh, A., Buonassisi, J., Saeedi, P., Havelock, J.: Automatic blastomere detection in day 1 to day 2 human embryo images using partitioned graphs and ellipsoids. In: International Conference on Image Processing, pp. 917–921. IEEE (2014)
24. Soria, X., Riba, E., Sappa, Á.D.: Dense extreme inception network: Towards a robust CNN model for edge detection. In: Winter Conference on Applications of Computer Vision, pp. 1912–1921. IEEE (2020)

25. Strouthopoulos, C., Anifandis, G.: An automated blastomere identification method for the evaluation of day 2 embryos during IVF/ICSI treatments. Comput. Methods Programs Biomed. **156**, 53–59 (2018)

26. Syulistyo, A.R., Aprinaldi, Bowolaksono, A., Wiweko, B., Prati, A., Purnomo, D.M.J., Jatmiko, W.: Ellipse detection on embryo imaging using Random Sample Consensus (RANSAC) method based on arc segment. Int. J. Smart Sens. Intell. Syst. **9**(3), 1384–1409 (2016)

27. Syulistyo, A.R., Wisesa, H.A., Aprinaldi, Bowolaksono, A., Wiweko, B., Jatmiko, W.: Ellipse detection on embryo image using modification of arc particle swarm optimization (arcpso) based arc segment. In: International Symposium on Micro-Nano Mechatronics and Human Science, pp. 1–6. IEEE (2015)

28. Tian, Y., Yin, Y., Duan, F., Wang, W., Wang, W., Zhou, M.: Automatic blastomere recognition from a single embryo image. Comput. Math. Methods Med. **2014**, 628312:1–628312:7 (2014)

29. Trivedi, M.M., Mills, J.K.: Centroid calculation of the blastomere from 3d z-stack image data of a 2-cell mouse embryo. Biomed. Signal Process. Control. **57**, 101726 (2020)

30. Wang, Yu., Moussavi, F., Lorenzen, P.: Automated embryo stage classification in time-lapse microscopy video of early human embryo development. In: Mori, K., Sakuma, I., Sato, Y., Barillot, C., Navab, N. (eds.) MICCAI 2013. LNCS, vol. 8150, pp. 460–467. Springer, Heidelberg (2013). https://doi.org/10.1007/978-3-642-40763-5_57

31. Xie, S., Tu, Z.: Holistically-nested edge detection. In: International Conference on Computer Vision, pp. 1395–1403. IEEE Computer Society (2015)

# A Guided Attention 4D Convolutional Neural Network for Modeling Spatio-Temporal Patterns of Functional Brain Networks

Jiadong Yan[1], Yu Zhao[2], Mingxin Jiang[1], Shu Zhang[3], Tuo Zhang[4], Shimin Yang[1], Yuzhong Chen[1], Zhongbo Zhao[1], Zhibin He[4], Benjamin Becker[1], Tianming Liu[5], Keith Kendrick[1], and Xi Jiang[1]([✉])

[1] School of Life Science and Technology, MOE Key Lab for Neuroinformation, University of Electronic Science and Technology of China, Chengdu, China
xijiang@uestc.edu.cn
[2] Syngo Innovation, Siemens Healthineers, Malvern, USA
[3] Center for Brain and Brain-Inspired Computing Research, School of Computer Science, Northwestern Polytechnical University, Xi'an, China
[4] School of Automation, Northwestern Polytechnical University, Xi'an, China
[5] Computer Science Department, The University of Georgia, Athens, USA

**Abstract.** Since the complex brain functions are achieved by the interaction of functional brain networks with the specific spatial distributions and temporal dynamics, modeling the spatial and temporal patterns of functional brain networks based on 4D fMRI data offers a way to understand the brain functional mechanisms. Matrix decomposition methods and deep learning methods have been developed to provide solutions. However, the underlying nature of functional brain networks remains unclear due to underutilizing the spatio-temporal characteristics of 4D fMRI input in previous methods. To address this problem, we propose a novel Guided Attention 4D Convolutional Neural Network (GA-4DCNN) to model spatial and temporal patterns of functional brain networks simultaneously. GA-4DCNN consists of two subnetworks: the spatial 4DCNN and the temporal Guided Attention (GA) network. The 4DCNN firstly extracts spatio-temporal characteristics of fMRI input to model the spatial pattern, while the GA network further models the corresponding temporal pattern guided by the modeled spatial pattern. Based on two task fMRI datasets from the Human Connectome Project, experimental results show that the proposed GA-4DCNN has superior ability and generalizability in modeling spatial and temporal patterns compared to other state-of-the-art methods. This study provides a new useful tool for modeling and understanding brain function.

**Keywords:** Functional MRI · Functional brain network · Spatio-temporal pattern · Guided attention · 4D convolutional neural network

---

This is a student paper.

© Springer Nature Switzerland AG 2021
H. Ma et al. (Eds.): PRCV 2021, LNCS 13021, pp. 350–361, 2021.
https://doi.org/10.1007/978-3-030-88010-1_29

# 1  Introduction

Modeling the spatial and temporal patterns of functional brain networks through functional MRI (fMRI) plays an important role in understanding the brain functional mechanisms [1, 2]. Researchers have been continuously contributing to developing effective brain modeling methodologies [3–13]. Initial attempts re-order the fMRI data into the 2D matrix and then employ matrix decomposition methods such as principal component analysis (PCA) [3], independent component analysis (ICA) [4], and sparse representation (SR) [5–7]. However, these methods deal with the 2D matrix resulting in the underutilization of spatial features of fMRI data. With the recent development of deep learning methodologies, a variety of models have provided new solutions to model spatiotemporal functional brain networks [8–14]. For instance, researchers adopt recurrent neural network (RNN) [8] with recurrent connections to model the temporal patterns of functional brain networks. However, they obtain the spatial patterns by a correlation operation. Later on, convolutional auto-encoder (CAE) model [9] characterizes the temporal patterns first and then generates the corresponding spatial patterns through regression. In another recent research, restricted Boltzmann machine (RBM) model [10, 11] obtains the temporal patterns via probability analysis and then adopts Deep LASSO to model the corresponding spatial maps. Although promising results have been achieved, all these studies focus on merely the temporal brain network pattern and obtain spatial pattern by regression, also resulting in the underutilization of 4D fMRI input's spatio-temporal features.

To tackle the above problem, a recent Spatio-Temporal CNN (ST-CNN) [12, 13] models the spatial and temporal patterns of the targeted functional brain network simultaneously. This method models the spatial pattern from the whole brain fMRI signals using a 3D U-Net, and then obtains the corresponding temporal pattern using a 1D CAE. Though simultaneous modeling is an improvement that more spatio-temporal features are considered, researchers adopt merely the convolution of 4D fMRI data and the modeled spatial pattern as the inputs of 1D CAE, thus the spatial and temporal characteristics of fMRI are still not fully utilized during the temporal pattern modeling. In order to address the abovementioned limitations and better utilize the spatio-temporal characteristics of the 4D fMRI data, we propose a novel Guided Attention 4D Convolutional Neural Network (GA-4DCNN) to simultaneously model both spatial and temporal patterns of functional brain networks from whole-brain fMRI data. The GA-4DCNN model consists of two parts: spatial network and temporal network. In the spatial network, we adopt the novel 4D convolution to fully characterize the 4D nature of fMRI data and to model the spatial pattern of functional brain networks. For the temporal network, we design a novel Guided Attention network based on Non-local network [15] to model the corresponding temporal pattern guided by the modeled spatial pattern adopting 4D fMRI as input. We use the default mode network (DMN) as the example functional brain network to evaluate the proposed GA-4DCNN model. Based on the data from two task-based fMRI (t-fMRI, emotion, motor) of the same 200 subjects from the Human Connectome Project, GA-4DCNN has shown superior ability and generalizability of modeling spatio-temporal patterns of functional brain networks compared to other state-of-the-art (SOTA) models across different brains and t-fMRI datasets. Our work provides a useful tool to understand intrinsic functional brain architecture.

## 2    Methods

The whole framework of the proposed GA-4DCNN model is shown in Fig. 1. The 4D whole-brain fMRI data are the input, and both spatial and temporal patterns of the targeted functional brain network are the outputs. The model has two core parts: the spatial network (4D CNN) and the temporal network (Guided Attention Network). The spatial pattern output together with the 4D fMRI data are adopted as the inputs of temporal network for the guidance of temporal pattern modeling.

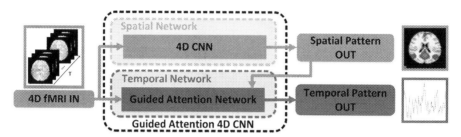

**Fig. 1.** An overview of the GA-4DCNN framework.

### 2.1    Data Acquisition, Preprocessing and Training Label Identification

We adopted the t-fMRI data of healthy adults (age range 22–35) from the publicly available Human Connectome Project (HCP) S900 release [16]. Detailed demographic information of all subjects is presented in [12]. The major acquisition parameters of t-fMRI are: TR $= 0.72$ s, TE $= 33.1$ ms, $90 \times 104$ matrix, 72 slices, FOV $= 220$ mm, and 2.0 mm isotropic voxels. In consideration of computational capacity, the same 200 subjects of emotion and motor t-fMRI data were randomly selected for the model training and testing. The t-fMRI data pre-processing included gradient distortion correction, motion correction, field map preprocessing, distortion correction, spline resampling to atlas space, intensity normalization, multiple regression with autocorrelation modeling, pre-whitening, and spatial smoothing. We adopted FSL and FreeSurfer [17–19] to preprocess t-fMRI data. The preprocessed fMRI data were normalized to 0–1 distribution. Moreover, given computational capacity, we down-sampled the 4D fMRI data to the spatial size of 48 * 56 * 48 and temporal size of 88 before feeding into the GA-4DCNN. Later on, the temporal size of output pattern was up-sampled to the original one for temporal pattern accuracy assessment, while the spatial size remained the down-sampled size. In this study, we randomly split the emotion t-fMRI data of 200 subjects into 160 for training and 40 for testing, while the motor t-fMRI data of 200 subjects were all used for testing.

The default mode network (DMN) [20–22] was used as the targeted functional network to evaluate the GA-4DCNN. To obtain the training labels of both spatial and temporal patterns of DMN in each individual's fMRI data via SR method [5], we first re-ordered the 4D input fMRI as a 2D matrix $X$ with the size of t * n (n is the number of whole-brain voxels and t is the length of the time points). $X$ was then decomposed as a dictionary matrix $D$ and a coefficient matrix $a$, w.r.t $X = D * a$ [5]. We finally identified the spatial and temporal patterns of DMN from $D$ and $a$ respectively as the training labels [12], which can represent the modeling ability of SR method for subsequent comparison. Note that the training labels obtained via SR were only utilized for the training of GA-4DCNN and evaluating the temporal modeling ability of other methods. We calculated the spatial similarity between the modeled spatial patterns and well-established DMN [20] to evaluate the spatial modeling ability of all brain function modeling methods.

## 2.2 Model Architecture of GA-4DCNN

The model architecture of GA-4DCNN is illustrated in Fig. 2. The spatial network (Fig. 2(a)) and the temporal network (Fig. 2(b)) are adopted to model the spatial and temporal patterns of the targeted functional brain network, respectively. Note that the spatial pattern out of spatial network together with 4D fMRI is adopted as the inputs of temporal network to model the spatial and temporal patterns simultaneously.

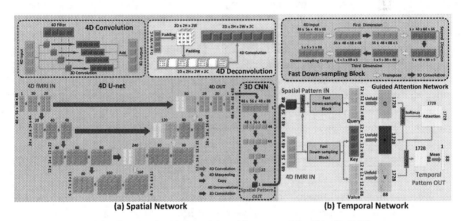

**Fig. 2.** The detailed model architecture of the GA-4DCNN.

**Spatial Part.** As illustrated in Fig. 2(a), the spatial network consists of two parts: 4D U-net and 3D CNN. We first adopted a 4D U-net with 21 layers to fully learn the spatio-temporal features of 4D fMRI, and then a 3D CNN with 5 layers reducing the output's temporal dimension to 1. The 4D U-net adopted '4D Maxpooling' for down-sampling and '4D Deconvolution' for up-sampling. There are two crucial operations including '4D Convolution' and '4D Deconvolution' in the 4D U-net. In '4D Convolution', the 4D filter was firstly decomposed into a series of 3D convolution filters along the temporal dimension. Next, series of 4D outputs were obtained by performing 3D convolution operations with the 4D input and above 3D filters, and further we added them together to obtain the output of '4D Convolution'. In summary, the '4D Convolution' models the spatial correlation among different voxels at different time points during the convolution, which is a significant improvement compared to previous studies which merely consider

3D [12, 13] or 2D information [3–11]. In '4D Deconvolution', the spatial block (with size D * H * W at each time point) in the 4D input data (with size D * H * W * C, C is the temporal dimension) was first taken out, and the same padding operation was performed as in the 3D deconvolution [12]. Then we padded a 3D all-zero block between every two deconvoluted 3D spatial blocks to obtain the new 4D data with size 2D * 2H * 2W * 2C. Finally, a '4D Convolution' operation was performed on the new 4D data to obtain the output of '4D Deconvolution'.

We fed 4D fMRI into the spatial network and the final output of the spatial network was the modeled spatial pattern of the targeted functional brain network. The size of all 4D filters was 3 * 3 * 3 * 3, and all 3D ones were 3 * 3 * 3. A batch norm layer was added after each convolution layer except for the last one. Each convolution layer was followed by a rectified linear unit (ReLU). The 'overlap rate' was adopted [12] to evaluate the spatial pattern accuracy between the modeled pattern and the training label:

$$overlap\ rate = \frac{sum(min(P_m, P_l))}{(sum(P_m) + sum(P_l))/2} \tag{1}$$

where $P_m$ and $P_l$ represent the modeled pattern and the training label pattern, respectively. The loss function of the spatial network was then set as the negative overlap rate.

**Temporal Part.** As illustrated in Fig. 2(b), the temporal network was called 'Guided Attention network', which was based on the widely adopted 'attention' mechanism [23]. We used $Q, K, V$, and $M$ to represent Query, Key, Value matrices, and the feature number of the Key, respectively. The attention output was obtained by multiplying the attention matrix $Softmax\left(\frac{QK^T}{\sqrt{M}}\right)$ and $V$ in (2):

$$attention\ output = Softmax\left(\frac{QK^T}{\sqrt{M}}\right) \times V \tag{2}$$

There is a 'Fast Down-sampling' block in the temporal network which helps quickly down-sample all of the three spatial dimensions to fit in the GPU memory and prevent model overfitting. For the 4D data with size D * H * W * C, each of the three spatial dimensions (D, H, W) was down-sampled as follows. For dimension D, we transposed it to the last dimension, i.e., H * W * C * D, and then performed a 3D convolution on the 4D data to reduce D to a smaller size S before being transposed back to the original dimension. The same down-sampling was adopted to H and W, respectively. The output 4D data was with size S * S * S * C (S was set to 12 in this study). All 3D filters' size was 3 * 3 * 3 and there was a batch norm layer and a ReLU following each convolution layer.

In the temporal network (Fig. 2(b)), we adopted 4D fMRI and modeled spatial pattern of the targeted functional network as inputs and obtained the corresponding temporal pattern as output. The proposed guided attention mechanism fixed the $Q$ in (2) with 4D fMRI and modeled spatial pattern in order to guide the temporal modeling with the corresponding spatial pattern. Specifically, we multiplied the 3D spatial block of each time point of the 4D fMRI data with the modeled spatial pattern to fix the query part and utilize the corresponding temporal characteristics of the 4D fMRI data, which is different from the conventional attention mechanism [23]. The modeled spatial pattern was with the size of 48 * 56 * 48, and 4D fMRI input was with the size of 48 * 56 * 48 * 88. Then the fixed query part was 48 * 56 * 48 * 88 after the multiply operation. As shown in Fig. 2(b), after operations of 'Fast Down-sampling' and matrix unfolding to obtain the $Q$, $K$, and $V$, the attention mechanism was performed to obtain the attention output with size P * C (P = S * S * S) using Eq. (2). Note that we did not divide $QK^T$ by the root of $M$. Besides, $K$ and $V$ were set to be the same to simplify the temporal network structure. Finally, after an average operation on the attention output, the temporal pattern of the targeted brain network with size 1 * C was obtained as the output. The temporal pattern accuracy was defined as Pearson correlation coefficient (PCC) between the modeled temporal pattern and the training label pattern. The loss function of the temporal network was defined as the negative PCC.

## 2.3   Model Training Scheme, Evaluation, and Validation

The entire GA-4DCNN model training process consists of two stages corresponding to the spatial and temporal networks, respectively. At the first stage, the learning rate was set to 0.00001. After 100 epochs, the spatial network loss converged and reached $-0.42$ (Fig. 3(a)). At the second stage, the learning rate was set to 0.0001. After 100 epochs, the temporal network loss converged and reached $-0.81$ (Fig. 3(b)). We used Adam [24] as the optimizer at both stages.

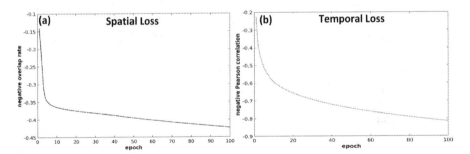

**Fig. 3.** Training loss curves of (a) the spatial network and (b) the temporal network.

To evaluate the performance of GA-4DCNN in the training process, we calculated both spatial pattern accuracy and temporal pattern accuracy (Sect. 2.2) of the modeled pattern with the training label. We also calculated the spatial pattern accuracy of the modeled spatial pattern with the DMN template [20] to measure the spatial modeling ability of different methods. Besides, the temporal modeling ability of different methods was evaluated by calculating the temporal pattern accuracy of the modeled temporal pattern with the training label obtained via SR. Moreover, since the SR is a well-performed matrix decomposition method [5–7] and ST-CNN [12] is the only deep learning method with simultaneous modeling, we compared the GA-4DCNN with these two SOTA models in modeling spatial and temporal patterns. We adopted the motor t-fMRI data of 200 subjects as well as emotion t-fMRI data of the 40 subjects which were not used for model training as independent testing data to validate the generalizability of the GA-4DCNN model.

## 3  Results

### 3.1  Spatio-Temporal Pattern Modeling of DMN via GA-4DCNN

The modeled spatial and temporal patterns of DMN in three randomly selected subjects of emotion t-fMRI testing data are shown in Fig. 4. The figure visualizes that both the spatial and temporal patterns of DMN via GA-4DCNN have reasonable similarity with the training labels, while the spatial pattern of DMN via GA-4DCNN has more clustered activation areas with fewer noise points. The spatial and temporal pattern accuracies of the three subjects are reported in Table 1. We further applied the trained model onto the motor t-fMRI data of 200 subjects to evaluate the generalizability of GA-4DCNN. Similarly, three subjects were randomly selected as examples and reported in Fig. 4 and Table 1. Again, we observed that both spatial and temporal patterns of DMN via GA-4DCNN also have satisfying similarity with the training labels, and more clustered activation areas with fewer noise points in the spatial pattern. Since the training labels were obtained via SR and could represent the modeling ability of SR, the results of spatial pattern accuracy with DMN template in Table 1 show that GA-4DCNN has a superior spatial modeling ability than SR.

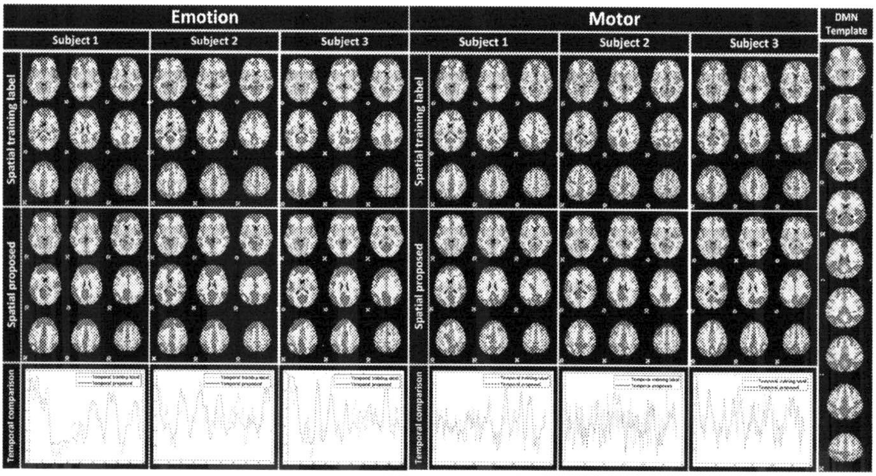

**Fig. 4.** Spatio-temporal pattern modeling of DMN via GA-4DCNN in three example subjects of emotion and motor t-fMRI data. The DMN spatial template is shown in the last column.

In conclusion, GA-4DCNN not only has superior or at least comparable performance compared to SR methods in modeling both spatial and temporal patterns of functional brain network, but also has reasonable modeling generalizability across different t-fMRI data.

**Table 1.** Spatio-temporal pattern accuracy of DMN in three example subjects.

| Datasets | Subject | Spatial pattern accuracy between GA-4DCNN and training label | Temporal pattern accuracy between GA-4DCNN and training label | Spatial pattern accuracy with DMN template | |
|---|---|---|---|---|---|
| | | | | **GA-4DCNN** | Training label |
| Emotion | #1 | 0.41 | 0.89 | **0.24** | 0.14 |
| | #2 | 0.42 | 0.73 | **0.25** | 0.23 |
| | #3 | 0.47 | 0.84 | **0.24** | 0.21 |
| Motor | #1 | 0.37 | 0.73 | **0.28** | 0.16 |
| | #2 | 0.47 | 0.30 | **0.27** | 0.26 |
| | #3 | 0.31 | 0.70 | **0.24** | 0.14 |

### 3.2 Group-Averaged Spatio-Temporal Pattern of DMN via GA-4DCNN

We calculated the group-averaged spatial pattern of DMN via GA-4DCNN across all testing subjects within each of the two t-fMRI datasets, and compared with those via ST-CNN and SR. Figure 5 shows that GA-4DCNN retains all key brain regions of DMN in both t-fMRI datasets, thus achieving satisfying spatial pattern modeling of DMN across all subjects. While SR and ST-CNN also have reasonable spatial pattern accuracy in the t-fMRI data, these two methods fail to determine a big cluster instead of scattered points in the frontal lobe (yellow circles in Fig. 5), which represents one of the key brain regions of the DMN. We then visualized the modeled temporal patterns of DMN in another five randomly selected subjects within each of the two t-fMRI datasets in Fig. 5. Note that we did not calculate the group-averaged temporal patterns of DMN across all testing subjects since the temporal patterns of the DMN exhibit considerable individual variability compared to the spatial patterns [12], which would be smoothed out by simply averaging across different subjects. We observed that the temporal patterns of DMN via GA-4DCNN (blue curves) have greater similarity with the training labels (SR, green curves) as compared to those generated via ST-CNN (red curves).

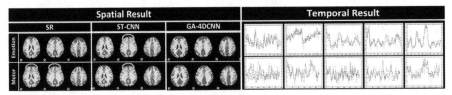

**Fig. 5.** Spatial result: the group-averaged spatial patterns of modeled DMNs across all subjects within each of the two t-fMRI datasets using three different methods (SR, ST-CNN, and GA-4DCNN). Temporal result: the temporal patterns of DMN in another five subjects within each of the two t-fMRI datasets. In each sub-figure, the temporal patterns of training label, identified one via ST-CNN and one via GA-4DCNN are colored in green, red and blue, respectively. (Color figure online)

We further calculated the averaged spatial and temporal pattern accuracies across all testing subjects within each of the t-fMRI datasets, and compared GA-4DCNN with ST-CNN (see Table 2). GA-4DCNN achieved both higher mean and lower standard deviation of spatial and temporal pattern accuracies with the training label compared to ST-CNN. In addition, GA-4DCNN achieved a higher mean and lower standard deviation of spatial pattern accuracy with the DMN template [20] compared to ST-CNN and SR. In conclusion, GA-4DCNN has a superior performance compared to other SOTA methods in modeling spatial and temporal patterns of the functional brain network.

**Table 2.** Averaged spatio-temporal pattern accuracy of DMN across all testing subjects.

| Datasets | Spatial pattern accuracy with training label | | Temporal pattern accuracy with training label | | Spatial pattern accuracy with DMN template | | |
|---|---|---|---|---|---|---|---|
| | ST-CNN | **GA-4DCNN** | ST-CNN | **GA-4DCNN** | SR | ST-CNN | **GA-4DCNN** |
| Emotion | $0.26 \pm 0.07$ | **$0.39 \pm 0.04$** | $0.52 \pm 0.18$ | **$0.68 \pm 0.16$** | $0.21 \pm 0.03$ | $0.25 \pm 0.02$ | **$0.25 \pm 0.01$** |
| Motor | $0.18 \pm 0.05$ | **$0.36 \pm 0.06$** | $0.44 \pm 0.18$ | **$0.57 \pm 0.19$** | $0.19 \pm 0.04$ | $0.23 \pm 0.03$ | **$0.25 \pm 0.02$** |

### 3.3    Evaluation of Different Model Structures and Parameters

We designed four different model structures to evaluate the superiority of the proposed model structure of GA-4DCNN. Firstly, we designed two different structures for the spatial network of GA-4DCNN. The first one (Network #1) remained the same structure with GA-4DCNN (Fig. 2(a)) but used mean squared error instead of negative overlap rate as the loss function. The second one (Network #2) reduced the number of 3D convolutional layers from 5 to 3. Table 3 shows that the proposed spatial network structure obtained the best spatial pattern accuracy compared to Networks #1 and #2 indicating that a more complex spatial network leads to a superior spatial modeling ability. Secondly, we designed two different structures for the temporal network of GA-4DCNN. The first one (Network #3) performed two 'Fast Down-sampling' blocks on 4D fMRI data to obtain different $K$ and $V$ values instead of being the same (Fig. 2(b)). The second one (Network #4) performed the division by the root of $M$ in Eq. (2) instead of skipping it. Table 3 shows that the proposed temporal network structure also obtained the best temporal pattern accuracy compared to Networks #3 and #4 indicating that a simpler temporal attention network leads to a superior temporal modeling ability.

We further compared four different parameters of the spatial size of the Query, Key, and Value matrices in the attention, which was a crucial parameter in the temporal network training (Fig. 2(b)). Besides 12 * 12 * 12 used in the proposed model, we also tried 3 * 3 * 3, 6 * 6 * 6, and 9 * 9 * 9 sizes. Table 4 shows that the adopted parameter (12 * 12 * 12) achieved the best temporal pattern accuracy. This result indicates that a larger spatial size of attention results in better temporal pattern accuracy, which further proves the effectiveness of guided attention mechanism.

**Table 3.** Comparisons of different model structures for spatio-temporal modeling.

| Spatial network structure | Testing spatial pattern accuracy | Temporal network structure | Testing temporal pattern accuracy |
|---|---|---|---|
| **Proposed** | **0.25 ± 0.01** | **Proposed** | **0.68 ± 0.16** |
| Network 1 | 0.24 ± 0.01 | Network 3 | 0.65 ± 0.15 |
| Network 2 | 0.23 ± 0.01 | Network 4 | 0.66 ± 0.17 |

**Table 4.** Comparisons of different parameters of attention size for spatio-temporal modeling.

| Spatial size after down-sampling block | Testing temporal pattern accuracy |
|---|---|
| 3 * 3 * 3 | 0.67 ± 0.17 |
| 6 * 6 * 6 | 0.67 ± 0.16 |
| 9 * 9 * 9 | 0.67 ± 0.14 |
| **12 * 12 * 12** (adopted in the study) | **0.68 ± 0.16** |

## 4 Conclusion

In this work, we propose a novel GA-4DCNN to model both spatial and temporal patterns of the targeted functional brain network. As far as we know, it is one of the first studies to incorporate both 3D spatial and 1D temporal features into the model training in order to better utilize the 4D nature of fMRI data. Experimental results based on two different t-fMRI datasets of the same 200 subjects demonstrate that the GA-4DCNN achieves a superior modeling ability of the targeted functional brain networks compared to other SOTA deep learning as well as matrix decomposition methods. Moreover, the GA-4DCNN has satisfying generalizability of modeling spatio-temporal patterns across different t-fMRI data. Considering the remarkable structural and functional variability across different individual brains, our work provides a new and powerful tool to model functional brain networks and to further understand brain functional mechanisms. In future work, we plan to use GA-4DCNN to model both task-evoked and intrinsic functional brain networks. We also plan to apply GA-4DCNN on clinical samples, such as individuals with autism spectrum disorder, to model potential functional network abnormalities in mental disorders.

**Acknowledgements.** This work was partly supported by the National Natural Science Foundation of China (61976045), Sichuan Science and Technology Program (2021YJ0247), Sichuan Science and Technology Program for Returned Overseas People (2021LXHGKJHD24), Key Scientific and Technological Projects of Guangdong Province Government (2018B030335001), National Natural Science Foundation of China (62006194), the Fundamental Research Funds for the Central Universities (3102019QD005), High-level researcher start-up projects (06100-20GH020161), and National Natural Science Foundation of China (31971288 and U1801265).

## References

1. Naselaris, T., Kay, K.N., Nishimoto, S., Gallant, J.L.: Encoding and decoding in fMRI. Neuroimage **56**(2), 400–410 (2011)
2. Logothetis, N.K.: What we can do and what we cannot do with fMRI. Nature **453**(7197), 869–878 (2008)
3. Andersen, A.H., Gash, D.M., Avison, M.J.: Principal component analysis of the dynamic response measured by fMRI: a generalized linear systems framework. Magn. Reson. Imaging **17**(6), 795–815 (1999)
4. McKeown, M.J., Hansen, L.K., Sejnowski, T.J.: Independent component analysis of functional MRI: what is signal and what is noise? Curr. Opin. Neurobiol. **13**(5), 620–629 (2003)
5. Lv, J.L., et al.: Sparse representation of whole-brain fMRI signals for identification of functional networks. Med. Image Anal. **20**(1), 112–134 (2015)
6. Jiang, X., et al.: Sparse representation of HCP grayordinate data reveals novel functional architecture of cerebral cortex. Hum. Brain Mapp. **36**(12), 5301–5319 (2015)
7. Zhang, W., et al.: Experimental comparisons of sparse dictionary learning and independent component analysis for brain network inference from fMRI data. IEEE Trans. Biomed. Eng. **66**(1), 289–299 (2019)
8. Hjelm, R.D., Plis, S.M., Calhoun, V.: Recurrent neural networks for spatiotemporal dynamics of intrinsic networks from fMRI data. NIPS Brains Bits (2016)
9. Huang, H., et al.: Modeling task fMRI data via deep convolutional autoencoder. IEEE Trans. Med. Imaging **37**(7), 1551–1561 (2018)
10. Zhang, W., et al.: Identify hierarchical structures from task-based fMRI data via hybrid spatiotemporal neural architecture search net. Med. Image Comput. Comput. Assist. Interv. **2019**, 745–753 (2019)
11. Zhang, W., et al.: Hierarchical organization of functional brain networks revealed by hybrid spatiotemporal deep learning. Brain Connect. **10**(2), 72–82 (2020)
12. Zhao, Y., et al.: Four-dimensional modeling of fMRI data via spatio-temporal convolutional neural networks (ST-CNNs). IEEE Trans. Cognit. Dev. Syst. **12**(3), 451–460 (2020)
13. Zhao, Y., et al.: Modeling 4D fMRI data via spatio-temporal convolutional neural networks (ST-CNNs). In: Medical Image Computing and Computer Assisted Intervention (2018)
14. Jiang, X., Zhang, T., Zhang, S., Kendrick, K.M., Liu, T.M.: Fundamental functional differences between gyri and sulci: implications for brain function, cognition, and behavior. Psychoradiology **1**(1), 23–41 (2021)
15. Wang, Z.Y., Zou, N., Shen, D.G., Ji, S.W.: Non-local U-nets for biomedical image segmentation. In: Proceedings of the AAAI Conference on Artificial Intelligence, vol. 34, no. 4, pp. 6315–6322 (2020)
16. Van Essen, D.C., Smith, S.M., Barch, D.M., Behrens, T.E.J., Yacoub, E., Ugurbil, K.: The WU-Minn human connectome project: an overview. NeuroImage **80**, 62–79 (2013)
17. Woolrich, M.W., Ripley, B.D., Brady, M., Smith, S.M.: Temporal autocorrelation in univariate linear modeling of fMRI data. Neuroimage **14**(6), 1370–1386 (2001)
18. Jenkinson, M., Beckmann, C.F., Behrens, T.E., Woolrich, W.M., Smith, SM.: FSL. Neuroimage **62**(2), 782–790 (2012)
19. Dale, A.M., Fischl, B., Sereno, M.I.: Cortical surface-based analysis. Neuroimage **9**(2), 179–194 (1999)
20. Smith, S.M., et al.: Correspondence of the brain's functional architecture during activation and rest. Proc. Natl. Acad. Sci. **106**(31), 13040–13045 (2009)
21. Raichle, M.E., MacLeod, A.M., Snyder, A.Z., Powers, W.J., Gusnard, D.A., Shulman, D.L.: A default mode of brain function. Proc. Natl. Acad. Sci. U.S.A. **98**(2), 676–682 (2001)

22. Greicius, M.D., Krasnow, B., Reiss, A.L., Menon, V.: Functional connectivity in the resting brain: a network analysis of the default mode hypothesis. Proc. Natl. Acad. Sci. U.S.A. **100**(1), 253–258 (2003)
23. Vaswani, A., et al.: Attention is all you need. In: 31st Annual Conference on Neural Information Processing Systems, pp. 6000–6010 (2017)
24. Kingma, D., Ba, J.: Adam: a method for stochastic optimization. In: International Conference on Learning Representations 2015 (2015)

# Tiny-FASNet: A Tiny Face Anti-spoofing Method Based on Tiny Module

Ce Li[1][(✉)], Enbing Chang[1], Fenghua Liu[1], Shuxing Xuan[1], Jie Zhang[1], and Tian Wang[2]

[1] College of Electrical and Information Engineering, Lanzhou University of Technology, Lanzhou 730050, China
[2] Institute of Artificial Intelligence, Beihang University, Beijing 100191, China

**Abstract.** Face Anti-spoofing (FAS) has arisen as one of the essential issues in face recognition systems. The existing deep learning FAS methods have achieved outstanding performance, but most of them are too complex to be deployed in embedded devices. Therefore, a tiny single modality FAS method (Tiny-FASNet) is proposed. First, to reduce the complexity, the tiny module is presented to simulate fully convolution operations. Specifically, some intrinsic features extracted by convolution are used to generate more features through cheap linear transformations. Besides, a simplified streaming module is proposed to keep more spatial structure information for FAS task. All models are trained and tested on depth images. The proposed model achieves **0.0034(ACER)**, **0.9990(TPR@FPR = 10E–2)**, and **0.9860(TPR@FPR = 10E–3)** on CASIA-SURF dataset only with **0.018M parameters** and **12.25M FLOPS**. Extensive evaluations in two publicly available datasets (CASIA-SURF and CASIA-SURF CeFA) demonstrate the effectiveness of the proposed approach.

**Keywords:** Face Anti-spoofing · Tiny models · Depth image

## 1 Introduction

As a convenient and fast way of identity verification, face recognition has been widely used in attendance, mobile payment, unlocking devices, etc. However, the current face recognition system is easy to be defrauded by presentation attacks, such as print, replay and 3D mask. Therefore, face anti-spoofing (FAS) has captured much public attention. Figure 1 shows some examples of common attacks.

Exciting FAS methods can be divided into hand-crafted features based and deep learning based. Hand-crafted features based methods mainly using binary classifier with different features between live and fake face, such as DoG [2], HOG [3], LBP [4], SIFT [5]. However, these methods are easily disturbed by lighting conditions and new attacks.

Depth images can indicate the distance between the object and the camera. 2D presentation attack commonly is a plane but real face is not, so using depth

© Springer Nature Switzerland AG 2021
H. Ma et al. (Eds.): PRCV 2021, LNCS 13021, pp. 362–373, 2021.
https://doi.org/10.1007/978-3-030-88010-1_30

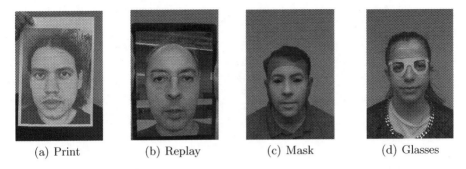

(a) Print          (b) Replay          (c) Mask          (d) Glasses

**Fig. 1.** Common presentation attacks. Image taken from [1].

images will be more distinguishable than RGB. Therefore, in this work we use depth images to train all models.

Over the years, deep learning based methods are more and more popular. These methods mainly using CNN to extract abstract semantic information. Although some works have achieved outstanding performance, it is too complex to deploy in embedded devices. How to reduce the parameters and computational cost become an important issue.

Han et al. [16] found that the feature maps extracted by CNN layers have much similarity, based on this, they employed some linear transformations to replace convolution and cut down computational complexity. As for FAS task, this idea can also work well. Figure 2 shows some output of the first residual group in ResNet-50. It can be seen that many features are similar. Therefore, we use several linear transformations to take the place of some convolution operations. In addition, to make the model more suitable for FAS task, we use a new operator called Central Difference Convolution (CDC) [14] as one of the linear transformations. CDC can extract rich high-level abstract semantic features, and keep a lot of detail gradient information which is vital for FAS task but easy to be lost by CNN.

Specifically, in this work we proposed a tiny FAS method (Tiny-FASNet) to detect presentation attacks. Firstly, we present a light module called Tiny module. It uses few convolution operations to get intrinsic features, and then more features are generated by intrinsic features though some cheap linear transformations. To make the model portable and adaptable, the Depthwise Convolution (DWConv) and CDC are chosen as two linear transformations. Furthermore, the streaming module is simplified and used to cope with the final features output by CNN system, which can replace global average pooling and fully connected layer and reduce over fitting. Besides, Representative Batch Normalization (RBN) [17] is utilized in our method. The experiment results show our method achieves 0.0034 (ACER), 0.9990 (TPR@FPR = 10E−2), and 0.9860 (TPR@FPR = 10E−3) on CASIA-SURF dataset only with 0.018M parameters and 12.25M FLOPS.

Broadly, the main contributions in this paper are listed below:

- We propose a portable module called Tiny module, which uses cheap linear transformations to simulate convolutions.
- A simplified streaming module is proposed to keep more spatial structure information.
- We propose Tiny-FASNet, an extremely light network which has less complexity and better performance.

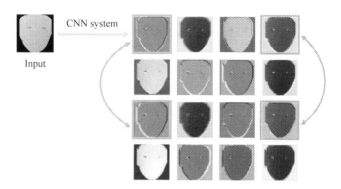

**Fig. 2.** Feature maps generated by the first residual group in ResNet-50. The input of CNN system is a depth image. The blue box and the red box mark two pairs of similar feature maps, respectively. (Color figure online)

## 2  Related Work

**Face Anti-spoofing.** The traditional FAS method mainly based on hand-crafted features. These features include: Difference of Gaussian (DoG) [2], Local Binary Patterns (LBP) [4], histogram of oriented gradients (HOG) [3], Scale Invariant Feature Transform (SIFT) [5]. CNN based methods have surpassed most of traditional methods. Patel et al. [6] proposed a method to learn generalized texture features from aligned and misaligned face images. Li et al. [7] fine tuned VGG-face model to extract deep features for classification. Liu et al. [13] proposed a method to estimate single frame depth map and the frequency domain distribution of multi-frame rPPG signals. Yang et al. [9] proposed a data collection scheme and data synthesis approach to reduce the gap between data and real scene. Shen et al. [10] proposed a multi-modality fusion method (FaceBagNet), which takes randomly cropped local images as input and uses RGB, depth and infrared data. Li et al. [12] employed generation adversarial network (GAN) with hypercomplex wavelet transform. Wang et al. [8] estimated the depth of face images by multi-frame images with video data, and extracted the depth information of space and time. However, most of these need GPUs with high computing power.

**Efficient Network.** With the popularity of mobile devices, the tiny and efficient networks are paid on much attention currently. Many efficient networks are presented such as MobileNets [18], MobileNetV2 [19], shuffleNetV2 [20], and Ghostnet [16]. Based on MobileNetV2 and MobilefaceNet [23]. Zhang et al. [15] proposed FeatherNets for FAS task, which have better performance and smaller structure. However, the usage of $1 \times 1$ convolution still causes a certain amount of computational cost.

Therefore, in order to further reduce model complexity, we proposed a lighter network based on Tiny module and simplified streaming module.

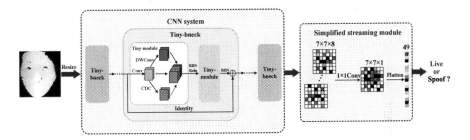

**Fig. 3.** Overview of the Tiny-FASNet. The model is composed of a CNN system and a simple streaming module. The CNN system is based on several cascade Tiny bottlenecks, which is built on Tiny modules. More features are generated by two cheap linear transformations, DWConv and CDC, which can replace parts of convolution operations.

## 3   Approach

In this section, we will firstly introduce the architecture, then introduce details of the Tiny-FASNet, which include CDC, Tiny module and simplified streaming module.

### 3.1   Architecture

The architecture of the Tiny-FASNet is shown in the Fig. 3 and Table 1. The $224 \times 224 \times 3$ image is input into CNN system which is built on cascade two types of Tiny bottlenecks (Stride = 1, 2), while the output are sent to simplified streaming module, finally the Softmax function is considered to get the predicted value.

### 3.2   Central Difference Convolution

CNN can extract abstract high-level semantic feature information through cascaded convolutions and complete tasks such as image classification and face

**Table 1.** Overall architecture of the Tiny-FASNet. All spatial convolutions use $3 \times 3$ kernels. $t$ is the expansion factor of input size, and $c$ denotes number of channel.

| Input | Module | $t$ | $c$ | Stride |
|---|---|---|---|---|
| $224^2 \times 3$ | Conv2d $3 \times 3$ | / | 32 | 2 |
| $112^2 \times 32$ | T-bneck | 6 | 16 | 2 |
| $56^2 \times 32$ | T-bneck | 6 | 32 | 2 |
| $28^2 \times 16$ | T-bneck | 6 | 32 | 1 |
| $28^2 \times 32$ | T-bneck | 6 | 48 | 2 |
| $14^2 \times 32$ | T-bneck | 6 | 48 | 1 |
| $14^2 \times 48$ | T-bneck | 6 | 48 | 1 |
| $14^2 \times 48$ | T-bneck | 6 | 48 | 1 |
| $14^2 \times 48$ | T-bneck | 6 | 48 | 1 |
| $14^2 \times 48$ | T-bneck | 6 | 48 | 1 |
| $14^2 \times 48$ | T-bneck | 6 | 64 | 2 |
| $7^2 \times 64$ | T-bneck | 6 | 64 | 1 |
| $7^2 \times 64$ | Conv2d $1 \times 1$ | / | 8 | 1 |

recognition. However, for FAS task, the gradient detailed information is as important as the high-level semantic information. It can indicate the difference in texture and space between the real face image and the attacking face image, enabling model capture the essential characteristics of attacks. In order to solve this problem, Yu et al. [14] proposed CDC, which alleviates the loss of gradient detailed information.

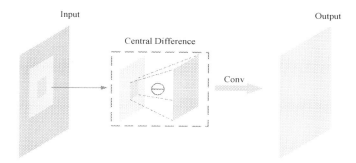

**Fig. 4.** Central Difference Convolution. Green : receptive field; bule: pixel of the center of the field. (Color figure online)

CDC combines the advantages of LBP and convolution operators, and can extract rich gradient detailed information. The usage of CDC will not increase the parameters. As shown in Fig. 4, the CDC has two steps: 1) making the central pixel value of the convolution kernel as the base value to subtract with other pixels; 2) using convolution to extract information from the result after subtraction. The process is formulated as (1)

$$y(p_0) = \theta \cdot \sum_{p_n \in R} w(p_n) \cdot (x(p_0 + p_n) - x(p_0)) + (1 - \theta) \cdot \sum_{p_n \in R} w(p_n) \cdot x(p_0 + p_n) \quad (1)$$

where, the $\theta \in [0, 1]$ is used to balance the amount of the gradient detailed information and high-level semantic information. The first term of this expression is central differential convolution, and the second term is ordinary convolution.

## 3.3  Simplified Streaming Module

Chen et al. [23] found that employing global average pooling (GAP) in the face tasks will lose the spatial structured information and drop the performance. In order to alleviate this problem, Zhang et al. [15] proposed the Streaming module to replace the GAP and Fully Connected (FC) Layer, which not only maintains structured feature information, decreases the amount of parameters and overfitting, but also obtains better performance. However, the down-sampling step of the streaming module will still lose much spatial structure information. Therefore, we cancel the down-sampling step, compress the feature map extracted by the CNN into a single channel, and then flatten it into a one-dimensional feature vector.

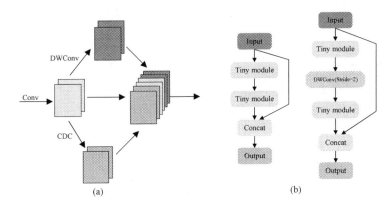

**Fig. 5.** Ghost module and bottlenecks present in this paper: (a) Ghost module; (b) Ghost bottlenecks (Stride = 1, 2).

## 3.4  Tiny Module and Tiny Bottlenecks

Inspired by the Ghost module [16], we propose the Tiny module for FAS task. As demonstrated in the Fig. 5(a), the Tiny module uses a few of convolution operations to generate some features, then performs linear transformations on the features, and at last concatenate feature maps generated by all operations. To make the Tiny module more adaptive for FAS task, we use DWConv and CDC as linear transformations, which can be formulated as

$$Y = \Phi(F(X)) + F(X) \tag{2}$$

where, $X$ and $Y$ denote the input and output, respectively. $\Phi$ denotes linear transformations, while $F$ is convolution operation.

In addition, following the structure of the Ghost bottleneck [16], we develop two kind of Tiny bottleneck. The two bottlenecks only have different stride, 1 and 2. If stride $= 1$, the width and height of input will not change, while stride $= 2$, a down sampling process will be implemented.

# 4   Experiments

To ensure the fairness of the experimental results, we first introduce the datasets and evaluation method, then compare and analyze the two public datasets with various methods, at last perform an ablation experiment to verify the effectiveness of the proposed method.

All experiments in this article use the PyTorch 1.4.0 deep learning framework, Intel(R) Core(TM) i7-9700K CPU, and GeForce RTX 2080 (8G) GPU. In the training process, the learning rate is 10E–2, and the decaying is 0.001 after every 60 epochs. As optimization, the Stochastic Gradient Descent (SGD) optimizer is used with 0.9 momentum. Focal Loss are employed with $\alpha = 1$ and $\gamma = 3$. The $\theta$ of CDC setting to 1.

## 4.1   Dataset

We mainly employ depth images from two publicly datasets, CASIA-SURF and CASIA-SURF CeFA.

**CASIA-SURF Dataset.** The CASIA-SURF dataset is a face anti-spoofing dataset proposed by Zhang et al. [21] in 2019. This dataset contains 1000 acquisition objects, 21000 videos, and each sample has 3 modal data (RGB, depth and infrared). Each image is preprocessed through four steps: 1) align the face area and remove the background; 2) reconstruct the face; 3) establish the mask of the face area; 4) based on mask, the pixels of the face area are retained the background area are set to zero.

**CASIA-SURF CeFA Dataset.** The CASIA-SURF CeFA dataset is a cross-ethnic dataset proposed by et al. [22] in 2020. The dataset contains 3 types of ethnicities (East Asia, Central Asia, and Africa), 3 modal data (RGB, depth, and infrared), 1607 objects, covering 2D and 3D attacks (print attack, replay attack, 3D print, and silica gel attacks) and a variety of light conditions. Four protocols are provided, the most difficult protocol 4 is performed here. As shown in the Table 2, the protocol 4 has 3 sub-protocols (4_1, 4_2, 4_3), which denote different cross-ethnicity & PAI protocols.

**Table 2.** Definition of Protocol 4 in CeFA. Protocol 4 has 3 sub-protocols (4_1, 4_2, and 4_3). The 3D attacks subset are included in each testing protocol (not shown in the table). & means merging; R: RGB, D: Depth, I: IR.

| Protocol | Subset | Ethnicity | | | PAIs | Modalities | | |
|---|---|---|---|---|---|---|---|---|
| 4 | | 4_1 | 4_2 | 4_3 | | | | |
| | Train | A | C | E | Replay | R | D | I |
| | Test | C& E | A& E | A& C | Print | R | D | I |

### 4.2   Metrics

To accurately evaluate the model, this article uses a variety of metrics. ACER is the average classification error rate, which is the average value attack presentation classification error rate (APCER) and normal presentation classification error rate (NPCER). APCER means that the attacked sample is incorrectly identified as a real sample. NPCER means that the real sample is incorrectly identified as an attack sample. The definition formulas of ACER is formulated in Eq. (3). Besides, we also use TPR@FPR = 10E–2, 10E–3 [21].

$$ACER = \frac{APCER + NPCER}{2} \tag{3}$$

**Table 3.** Performance in CASIA-SURF validation dataset.Baseline is a method which fusing three modalities data (Infrared, RGB, and Depth). Other models are trained on depth data. The proposed approach has achieved better performance with very few parameters and computing resources.

| Model | TPR@FPR $=10^{-2}$ | TPR@FPR $=10^{-3}$ | ACER | Params | FLOPS |
|---|---|---|---|---|---|
| ResNet-18 [21] | 0.8830 | 0.2720 | 0.0500 | 11.18M | 1800M |
| Baseline [21] | 0.9796 | 0.9469 | 0.0213 | / | / |
| MobileNetV2 [19] | 0.9626 | 0.8904 | 0.0214 | 2.23M | 306.10M |
| ShuffleNetV2 [20] | 0.9606 | 0.9036 | 0.0243 | 1.28M | 151.00M |
| FeatherNetA [15] | 0.9916 | 0.9562 | 0.0088 | 0.35M | 79.99M |
| FeatherNetB [15] | 0.9926 | 0.9676 | 0.0102 | 0.35M | 83.05M |
| GhostNet [16] | 0.9605 | 0.8901 | 0.0228 | 3.9M | 145.86M |
| Tiny-FASNet(ours) | 0.9990 | 0.9860 | 0.0034 | 0.018M | 12.25M |

### 4.3   Result Analysis

**Results on CASIA-SURF.** As illustrated in Table 3, our proposed model is better than other efficient networks MobileNetV2 [19], ShuffleNetV2 [20] Ghost-Net [16], FeatherNetA [15] and FeatherNetB [15]. All models are trained on the CASIA-SURF training set and tested on the validation set. Compared with the second-performing model, our model reduces parameters and FLOPS by nearly 20 times and 8 times, respectively.

**Table 4.** Performance on the three sub-protocols in Protocol 4 of CASIA-SURF CeFA dataset, where A_B represents sub-protocol B from Protocol A, and Avg±Std indicates the mean and variance operation.

| Method | Protocol | APCER(%) | BPCER(%) | ACER(%) |
|---|---|---|---|---|
| PSMM-Net [22] | 4_1 | 33.3 | 15.8 | 24.5 |
| | 4_2 | 78.2 | 8.3 | 43.2 |
| | 4_3 | **50.0** | 5.5 | **27.7** |
| | Avg ± Std | 53.8 ± 22.7 | 9.9 ± 5.3 | 31.8 ± 10.0 |
| MobileNetV2 [19] | 4_1 | 34.97 | 5.70 | 20.34 |
| | 4_2 | 73.43 | 0.97 | 37.20 |
| | 4_3 | 53.27 | 17.01 | 35.14 |
| | Avg ± Std | 53.89 ± 19.24 | 7.89 ± 8.24 | 30.89 ± 9.20 |
| ShuffleNetV2 [20] | 4_1 | 54.10 | 0.91 | 27.51 |
| | 4_2 | 60.30 | 1.99 | 31.15 |
| | 4_3 | 67.7 | 4.19 | 35.96 |
| | Avg ± Std | 60.70 ± 6.81 | 2.36 ± 1.67 | 31.54 ± 4.24 |
| FeatherNetA [15] | 4_1 | 52.68 | **0.76** | 26.72 |
| | 4_2 | 66.46 | 3.04 | 34.75 |
| | 4_3 | 59.92 | 5.67 | 32.80 |
| | Avg ± Std | 59.69 ± 6.89 | 3.16 ± 2.46 | 31.42 ± 4.19 |
| FeatherNetB [15] | 4_1 | 52.07 | 1.15 | 26.61 |
| | 4_2 | 66.67 | 4.59 | 35.63 |
| | 4_3 | 68.91 | 3.61 | 36.26 |
| | Avg ± Std | 62.55 ± 9.14 | 3.12 ± 1.77 | 32.83 ± 5.40 |
| GhostNet [16] | 4_1 | 39.48 | 0.91 | 20.20 |
| | 4_2 | 57.83 | **0.34** | 29.09 |
| | 4_3 | 62.39 | **1.83** | 33.61 |
| | Avg ± Std | 53.23 ± 12.13 | **1.03 ± 0.75** | 27.63 ± 6.82 |
| Tiny-FASNet(**ours**) | 4_1 | **27.46** | 1.03 | **14.24** |
| | 4_2 | **15.97** | 22.99 | **19.48** |
| | 4_3 | 55.23 | 7.32 | 31.28 |
| | Avg ± Std | **32.89 ± 20.18** | 10.44 ± 11.31 | **21.67 ± 8.73** |

**Results on CASIA-SURF CeFA.** Table 4 compares the performance of our method and five efficient networks, MobileNetV2 [19], ShuffleNetV2 [20] Ghost-Net [16], FeatherNetA [15] and FeatherNetB [15]. PSMM-Net is a baseline proposed in [22], which is a multi-modality method using three modalities image (RGB, Depth, and Infrared). It can be seen that our method ranks or close to first on 3 sub-protocols, which verifies the efficiency of proposed method. However, the performance of all efficient networks are weak. The main reason is 3D attack contains rich spatial depth information, which is similar to the bonafide presentation. It manifests that depth image is more suitable for detecting 2D attacks than 3D attacks.

### 4.4 Ablation Experiment

Table 5 compares the results of the ablation experiment on CASIA SURF dataset. Model 1 and model 2 demonstrate simplified streaming module is more effective. Model 2 and model 3 indicate CDC and DWConv is useful for detecting attacks, and CDC is better than DWConv. Model 4 is the best model with 0.34% ACER, which simultaneously deploy CDC, DWConv, and simplified streaming module.

**Table 5.** Ablation experiments.

| Model | DWConv | Streaming module [15] | Simplified streaming module | CDC | ACER(%) |
|---|---|---|---|---|---|
| 1 | ✓ | ✓ | ✗ | ✗ | 1.59 |
| 2 | ✓ | ✗ | ✓ | ✗ | 0.65 |
| 3 | ✗ | ✗ | ✓ | ✓ | 0.47 |
| 4 | ✓ | ✗ | ✓ | ✓ | **0.34** |

## 5 Conclusion

In this paper, we propose a novel tiny network for FAS task. Two linear transformations, Depthwise Convolution (DWConv) and Central Differential Convolution (CDC) are added in the Tiny module, and the simplified streaming module is presented. Extensive experiments are performed to show our method is useful. We trained and tested on RGB and infrared images in two datasets (CASIA SURF and CeFA) and found that all models are difficult to detect attacks, which indicates the depth image is suitable for detecting 2D attacks, but weak for 3D attacks. As future work, the multi modalities network will be proposed to improve the model generalization for 2D and 3D attacks.

**Acknowledgments.** The work was supported in part by the National Natural Science Foundation of China (61866022, 61972016, 62032016), and the Beijing Natural Science Foundation (L191007).

# References

1. Heusch, G., George, A., Geissbuhler, D., Mostaani, Z., Marcel, S.: Deep models and shortwave infrared information to detect face presentation attacks. IEEE Trans. Biometrics Behav. Identity Sci. **2**(4), 399–409 (2020)
2. Peixotom, B., Michelassi, C., Rocha, A.: Face liveness detection under bad illumination conditions. In: IEEE International Conference on Image Processing, pp. 3557–3560 (2011)
3. Komulainen, J., Hadid, A., Pietikainen, M.: Context based face anti-spoofing International. In: International Conference on Biometrics: Theory, Applications and Systems, pp. 1–8 (2013)
4. Boulkenafet, Z., Komulainen, J., Hadid, A.: Face anti-spoofing based on color texture analysis. In: IEEE International Conference on Image Processing, pp. 2636–2640 (2015)
5. Patel, K., Han, H., Jain, A.: Secure face unlock: spoof detection on smartphones. IEEE Trans. Inf. Forensics Secur. **11**(10), 2268–2283 (2016)
6. Patel, K., Han, H., Jain, A.: Cross-database face anti-spoofing with robust feature representation. In: Chinese Conference on Biometric Recognition, pp. 611–619, (2016)
7. Li, L., Feng, X.Y., Boulkenafet, Z., Xia, Z.Q., Li, M.M., Hadid, A.: An original face anti-spoofing approach using partial convolutional neural network. In: International Conference on Image Processing Theory, tools and Applications, pp. 1–6 (2016)
8. Wang, Z.Z., et al.: Exploiting temporal and depth information for multi-frame face anti-spoofing (2019). arXiv: 1811.05118
9. Yang, X., et al.: Face anti-spoofing: model matters, so does data. In: IEEE Conference on Computer Vision and Pattern Recognition, pp. 3502–3511 (2019)
10. Shen, T., Huang, Y.Y., Tong, Z.J.: FaceBagNet: bag-of-local-features model for multi-modal face anti-spoofing. In: IEEE Conference on Computer Vision and Pattern Recognition, pp. 1611–1616 (2019)
11. Yu, Z.T., et al.: Searching central difference convolutional networks for face anti-spoofing. In: IEEE Conference on Computer Vision and Pattern Recognition, pp. 5294–5304 (2020)
12. Li, C., Li, L., Xuan, S.X., Yang, J., Du, S.Y.: Face anti-spoofing algorithm using generative adversarial networks with hypercomplex wavelet. J. Xi'an Jiaotong Univ. (2014). http://kns.cnki.net/kcms/detail/61.1069.T.20201215.0923.002.html
13. Liu, Y.J., Jourabloo, A., Liu, X.M.: Learning deep models for face anti-spoofing: binary or auxiliary supervision. In: IEEE Conference on Computer Vision and Pattern Recognition, pp. 389–398 (2018)
14. Yu, Z.T., et al.: Searching central difference convolutional networks for face anti-spoofing. In: IEEE International Conference on Computer Vision, pp. 5294–5304 (2020)
15. Zhang, P., et al.: FeatherNets: convolutional neural networks as light as feather for face anti-spoofing. In: European Conference on Computer Vision, pp. 1574–1583 (2019)
16. Han, K., et al.: GhostNet: more features from cheap operations. In: IEEE Conference on Computer Vision and Pattern Recognition, pp. 1577–1586 (2020)
17. Gao, S.H., Han, Q., Li, D., Cheng, M.M., Peng, P.: Representative batch normalization with feature calibration. In: IEEE Conference on Computer Vision and Pattern Recognition, pp. 1–11 (2021)

18. Howard, A., et al.: MobileNet: efficient convolutional neural networks for mobile vision applications. In: IEEE Conference on Computer Vision and Pattern Recognition, pp. 1–9 (2017)
19. Sandler, M., Howard, A., Zhu, M.L., Zhmoginov, A., Chen, L.: MobileNetV2: inverted residuals and linear bottlenecks. In: IEEE Conference on Computer Vision and Pattern Recognition, pp. 4510–4520 (2018)
20. Ma, N.N., Zhang, X.Y., Zheng, H., Sun, J.: ShuffleNet V2: practical guidelines for efficient CNN architecture design. In: European Conference on Computer Vision, pp. 1–16 (2018)
21. Zhang, S., et al.: A dataset and benchmark for large-scale multi-modal face anti-spoofing. In: IEEE Conference on Computer Vision and Pattern Recognition, pp. 919–928 (2019)
22. Liu, A., et al.: CASIA-SURF CeFA: a benchmark for multi-modal cross-ethnicity face anti-spoofing (2020). arXiv: 2003.05136v1
23. Chen, S., Liu, Y., Gao, X., Han, Z.: MobileFaceNets: efficient CNNs for accurate real-time face verification on mobile devices. In: Chinese Conference On Biometric Recognition, pp. 428–438 (2018)

# Attention-Based Node-Edge Graph Convolutional Networks for Identification of Autism Spectrum Disorder Using Multi-Modal MRI Data

Yuzhong Chen[1], Jiadong Yan[1], Mingxin Jiang[1], Zhongbo Zhao[1], Weihua Zhao[1], Rong Zhang[2,3], Keith M. Kendrick[1], and Xi Jiang[1(✉)]

[1] School of Life Science and Technology, University of Electronic Science and Technology of China, Chengdu 610083, China
xijiang@uestc.edu.cn
[2] Neuroscience Research Institute, Key Laboratory for Neuroscience, Ministry of Education of China, Key Laboratory for Neuroscience, National Committee of Health and Family Planning of China, Peking University, Beijing 100083, China
[3] Department of Neurobiology, School of Basic Medical Sciences, Peking University, Beijing 100083, China

**Abstract.** Autism Spectrum Disorder (ASD) is a widely prevalent neurodevelopmental disorder with symptoms of social interaction and communication problems and restrictive and repetitive behavior. In recent years, there has been increasing interest in identifying individuals with ASD patients from typical developing (TD) ones based on brain imaging data such as MRI. Although both traditional machine learning and recent deep learning methodologies have achieved promising performance, the classification accuracy is still far from satisfying due to large individual differences and/or heterogeneity among data from different sites. To help resolve the problem, we proposed a novel Attention-based Node-Edge Graph Convolutional Network (ANEGCN) to identify ASD from TD individuals. Specifically, it simultaneously models the features of nodes and edges in the graphs and combines multi-modal MRI data including structural MRI and resting state functional fMRI in order to utilize both structural and functional information for feature extraction and classification. Moreover, an adversarial learning strategy was used to enhance the model generalizability. A gradient-based model interpretability method was also applied to identify those brain regions and connections contributing to the classification. Using the worldwide Autism Brain Imaging Data Exchange I (ABIDE I) dataset with 1007 subjects from 17 sites, the proposed ANEGCN achieved superior classification accuracy (72.7%) and generalizability than other state-of-the-art models. This study provided a powerful tool for ASD identification.

**Keywords:** Autism spectrum disorder · Graph convolutional network · Multi-modal MRI · Adversarial learning · Gradient-based model interpretability

---

This is a student paper.

© Springer Nature Switzerland AG 2021
H. Ma et al. (Eds.): PRCV 2021, LNCS 13021, pp. 374–385, 2021.
https://doi.org/10.1007/978-3-030-88010-1_31

# 1  Introduction

Autism spectrum disorder (ASD) is a widely prevalent neurodevelopmental disorder associated with persistent impairment in reciprocal social communication and interaction, and restricted and repetitive patterns of behavior, interests, or activities [1]. Although ASD can generally be identified with extant diagnostic protocols from the age of three years onwards [2], it is still challenging for accurate ASD diagnosis since it is primarily based on behavioral criteria rather than reliable pathophysiological markers [3]. Recently, there has been increasing interest in identifying ASD from typical developing (TD) individuals based on non-invasive in vivo brain imaging data such as Magnetic Resonance Imaging (MRI), since ASD is associated with structural and functional abnormalities in the brain.

Both traditional machine learning and recent deep learning methods have been widely used for ASD classification based on MRI, such as support vector machine (SVM) [4], deep neural network [5], autoencoder [6], etc., and achieved promising classification accuracy. Specifically, graph convolutional network (GCN), a deep learning based method, has received growing interest recently. Compared to the conventional Convolutional Neural Network, GCN is not only able to model the non-Euclidean structured data such as graphs, but also facilitates the graph embedding which represents graph nodes, edges or subgraphs in low-dimensional vectors [7]. Moreover, it can learn the topological structure information of graphs [8], which is an important characteristic for brain network studies [9]. There have been studies using GCN for ASD classification based on two categories of graph definition [10–12]. The first one is to establish edges between individuals through phenotype information together with the imaging-based features for nodes. For example, Parisot et al. [10] used acquisition site, sex and age as the three phenotypic measures to define edges and adopted functional connectivity derived from resting state functional MRI (rsfMRI) as feature vectors for nodes, turning the classification of ASD into node classification. Anirudh et al. [11] used gender and site information as edges between individuals to construct a population graph and defined node features the same as in [10]. However, this category is simply a node classification task, and might be largely affected by the definition of edges as well as establishment of node features. Moreover, there are no universal criteria to classify the subjects into different groups. The second category is graph classification, in which each individual is a graph. For instance, Yao et al. [12] proposed a k-nearest neighbor graph from the group-level function connectivity network to capture the node-centralized local topology, and used the so-called Triplet GCN for classification. Although promising results have been achieved, the existing graph classification methods merely established the adjacency between brain regions through a pre-defined functional connectivity matrix, leading to a risk of losing functional connection information for classification. Moreover, the previous studies merely adopted a single-modal MRI (e.g., fMRI) for classification, while ignoring multi-modal data which provided complementary information for classification. In conclusion, the existing methods are still far from satisfying in dealing with the ASD identification problem of limited data samples, large individual differences, and/or huge heterogeneity among the data from different sites.

In order to address the problem, and to make full use of both graph edge and node information as well as multi-modal MRI data, we proposed a novel Attention-based

Node-Edge Graph Convolution Network (ANEGCN) to classify ASD from TD based on functional and structural MRI data. Instead of a pre-defined adjacency matrix, we used the edge features to determine the adjacency and to further update the weights through an attention-based adjacency matrix, which could preserve the edge feature information for classification. Using the world-wide Autism Brain Imaging Data Exchange I (ABIDE I) dataset with 1007 subjects from 17 sites, we hypothesized that integrating both node and edge features as well as using multi-modal MRI data could improve the ASD classification accuracy than state-of-the-art (SOTA) methods.

The main contributions of this paper are summarized as follows: (1) We integrated both node and edge features to perform the graph classification through an attention-based adjacency matrix; (2) we used multi-modal MRI data in order to utilize both structural and functional information for feature extraction and classification; (3) we used an adversarial learning strategy to enhance the model generalizability; (4) we used a gradient-based model interpretability method to identify those brain regions and connections contributing to the classification in order to identify a potential biomarker for ASD.

## 2    Materials and Methods

### 2.1    Data Acquisition and Preprocessing

The present study adopted both rsfMRI and T1 structural (sMRI) data from the publicly available Autism Brain Imaging Data Exchange I (ABIDE I) dataset. ABIDE I is one of the largest ASD and TD datasets involving 17 international sites with 1112 subjects. In order to have a fair comparison of our method to other methods, we used the rsfMRI data from the public Preprocessed Connectomes Project (PCP) which were preprocessed using the Configurable Pipeline for the Analysis of Connectomes (C-PAC). The major preprocessing steps included slice timing correction, motion correction, voxel intensity normalization. Nuisance signal removal was performed using 24 motion parameters, CompCor with 5 components, low-frequency drifts, and global signal as repressor. The rsfMRI data was also band-pass filtered (0.01–0.1 Hz) and spatially registered to the MNI152 template space. The T1-weighted sMRI data were preprocessed using the Computational Anatomy Toolbox (CAT) under the default setting. 481 ASD and 526 TD subjects were finally included in this study after excluding those subjects with missing multi-modal MRI data.

### 2.2    Construction of Node and Edge Feature Maps

In this study, we adopted the widely used Automated Anatomical Labeling (AAL) [13] atlas to divide the whole-brain into 116 regions of interest (ROIs). In this way, each ROI was viewed as a graph node. We then defined the feature map of each node using three measures: the mean amplitude of low-frequency fluctuations (ALFF) in two different frequency bands (Slow-5: 0.01–0.027 Hz, Slow-4: 0.027–0.073 Hz) based on rsfMRI, and the mean T1-weighted intensity based on sMRI. ALFF has been shown to exhibit differences between ASD and TD subjects in certain brain regions in previous studies

[14]. The T1-weight intensity also reflected certain physiological significance [15] as well as aberrations in certain diseases [16]. For the feature map of each edge between two nodes, we adopted the resting state functional connectivity since it could reflect the intrinsic synchronous activity among distant brain regions [17]. The functional connectivity has also been shown to be both increased and decreased in ASD compared to TD [9]. Actually, we can also select some other features as in [18] to construct the node features, but in this paper we mainly focused on the superiority of model, and therefore we just used several simple features.

The constructed feature maps of input nodes and edges are shown in Fig. 1(a), which are represented as $\mathbf{X} = (X_1, X_2, \cdots X_N) \in \mathbb{R}^{N*M}$ and $\mathbf{Z} = (Z_1, Z_2, \cdots, Z_N) \in \mathbb{R}^{N*N}$ respectively, where $N = 116$ and $M = 3$ denoting the number of nodes and node features. $X_n = (x_1, \cdots x_M) \in \mathbb{R}^M$ $(n = 1, \cdots, N)$ is the M-dimensional feature of the n-th ROI, and $Z_n = (z_1, z_2 \cdots, z_N) \in \mathbb{R}^N$ $(n = 1, \cdots, N)$ is the Pearson's correlation coefficient between n-th ROI with each of the other N-1 ROIs. Each feature in the node feature map was normalized to 0–1.

## 2.3  Model Architecture of ANEGCN

Figure 1(b) illustrates the model architecture of the proposed ANEGCN. This model was designed to address the two main limitations of traditional GCN. The first limitation was that since the graph convolution operation required a pre-defined neighborhood of the nodes, traditional approaches merely determined the neighborhood by setting an arbitrary threshold for the functional connectivity values [12], which led to the loss of feature information of edges. The second limitation was that GCN assigned the same weight to its neighborhood nodes similar to a low-pass filter [19], which led to an over smoothing problem when the number of model layers was too deep. As a consequence, the node features tended to be the same and resulted in reduced model fitting ability. Although GAT (graph attention networks) [20] was proposed to alleviate the second limitation by assigning weights to different neighborhood nodes based on their similarity, the first limitation was still not addressed. In this proposed model, inspired by the 'attention' mechanism, we designed a novel attention-based adjacency matrix (Fig. 1(d)) to preserve the feature information of edges by giving larger weights to those connections with similar node features as well as to those with larger eigenvalues of edges. Moreover, we performed graph convolution on both node and edge feature maps in each layer of the graph convolution operation (Fig. 1(c)), extracted the hidden feature maps through a feed forward network and aggregated them to form the final feature maps for classification. Finally, we used a multi-layer perception (MLP) to perform classification of the concatenated feature maps. We explained the core parts of model in detail as follows:

**Node-Edge Graph Convolution (NE-GC) Block.** As shown in Fig. 1(c), the NE-GC block first calculated the adjacency matrix according to the input feature maps in Fig. 1(a), and then applied the graph convolution operation to both node and edge feature maps. Since the residual connection was widely used in various models, especially for those with deep layers, we used it to increase the depth of the model and to improve the model representation power (Fig. 1(c)). Equation (1) shows the propagation rules for the edge graph:

$$\mathbf{Z}_{l+1} = \sigma \left( A_l Z_l W_l^Z \right) + \mathbf{Z}_l \tag{1}$$

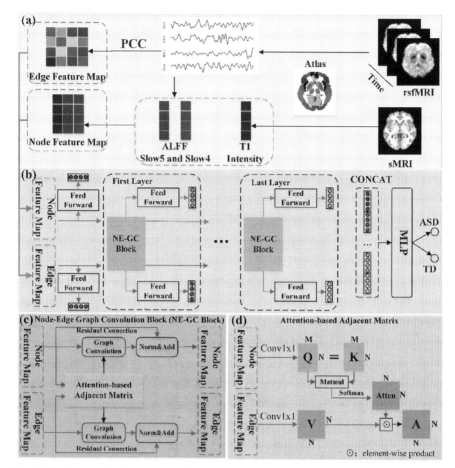

**Fig. 1.** The framework of our proposed Attention-based Node-Edge Graph Convolution Network (ANEGCN) model. (a) Generation of input feature maps based on multi-modal MRI data. (PCC: Pearson Correlation Coefficient). (b) The model architecture of the proposed model. (c) Detailed illustration of the Node-Edge Graph Convolution (NE-GC) Block in (b). (d) Detailed illustration of the attention-based adjacent matrix in (c).

where $\mathbf{Z}_l$, $\mathbf{Z}_{l+1}$ and $W_l^Z \in \mathbb{R}^{N*N}$ are the input, output edge graphs and learning parameters of the l-th layer, respectively. $\mathbf{A}_l$ denotes l-th layer of adjacency matrix, and $\sigma$ is the activation function. In this model, we used BatchNorm and ReLU as the activation function. Moreover, the propagation rule for node graph is shown in Eq. (2):

$$\mathbf{X}_{l+1} = \sigma\left(\mathbf{A}_l X_l W_l^X\right) + X_l \tag{2}$$

where $\mathbf{X}_l$, $\mathbf{X}_{l+1}$ and $W_l^X \in \mathbb{R}^{M*M}$ are the input, output node graphs and the learning parameter of l-th layer, respectively.

**Attention-Based Adjacent Matrix.** As shown in Fig. 1(d), the attention-based adjacent matrix took both node and edge feature maps of each layer as inputs and then generated the corresponding adjacency matrix to participate in the graph convolution operation of this layer. The self-attention technique was first proposed for natural language processing (NLP) and the core idea was to calculate the similarity between different features [21]. The proposed attention-based adjacent matrix model allowed the nodes with both higher edge feature value (i.e., functional connectivity in the first layer) and larger feature similarity to be connected with each other. Specifically, we first used the matrix product of the node feature maps as the attention matrix, and then performed a dot product of the attention matrix with the edge feature map to obtain the adjacency matrix of this layer as detailed in Eqs. (3–4):

$$\mathbf{Q} = \mathbf{K} = \text{Conv}(\mathbf{X_l}), \quad V = Conv(\mathbf{Z}_l) \tag{3}$$

$$\mathbf{A} = \text{Softmax}(\mathbf{Q}\mathbf{K}^{\mathrm{T}}) \odot \mathbf{V} \tag{4}$$

where $\mathbf{Q}$ and $\mathbf{V}$ are the queries and values matrices, respectively. The keys matrix $\mathbf{K}$ is the same as $\mathbf{Q}$. $\mathbf{X_l}$ and $\mathbf{Z_l}$ are the l-th layer's node and edge feature maps, respectively.

**Feed Forward Network.** The feed forward network has shown powerful learning capability in other models [21]. In this study, we used it to perform dimension reduction of each layer's output feature map after the NE-GC block (Fig. 1(b)) as detailed in Eq. (5):

$$Y = \text{BatchNorm}(\text{ReLU}(WX + b)) \tag{5}$$

where X is the reshaped one-dimensional vector of the feature map matrix, W and b are the learning parameters. The dimension of Y was 128 and 128 * 3 for the node and edge feature maps, respectively.

**Multi-layer Perception (MLP).** As shown in Fig. 1(b), a MLP model was adopted to perform the final classification based on the concatenated feature maps. The MLP model contained 2 linear layers, with the first layer followed by ReLU and dropout functions to enhance the robustness of the model. The dimensionality of the concatenated feature maps was determined by the number of layers. In this study, we used 5-layer and the size of the feature map was 512 * (5 + 1) = 3072. The dimensionality of the feature map was reduced to 1024 after passing the first layer and to 2 after the second layer to complete the final classification.

## 2.4  Model Training

We used 10-fold cross-validation to evaluate the model capability. Adaptive moment estimation was used as the optimizer for this model. Learning rate was set to 0.0001. Batch size, epoch, and dropout rate were set to 64, 100 and 0.2, respectively. To avoid overfitting, L2 regularization was used for all the weights of full connection layers, including those in the feed forward network and MLP classification layers. The weight delay was set to 0.0001. We also performed label smoothing to avoid model overfitting [22] as illustrated in Eq. (6):

$$y_{\mathrm{k}}^{LS} = y_k(1 - \alpha) + \alpha/K \tag{6}$$

where K is class number, $y_k \in \{0, 1\}$ is the true label and $y_k^{LS}$ is the label after smoothing. In our model, we set $\alpha$ to 0.1. The whole loss function of model training was described in Eq. (7):

$$\text{Loss (y, p)} = \beta \|W\|_2 + \sum_{k=1}^{K} -y_k^{LS} \log(p_k) \qquad (7)$$

where $W$ is the weight of full connection linear layers in MLP and feed forward network, $p_k$ is the predicted probability of class k and $\beta$ is the weight delay.

### 2.5   Model Generalizability and Interpretability

Due to different scanning parameters, scanning machines, and/or subject demographics in different sites, it is challenging to achieve satisfying generalization ability of the classification model when applying it to a new dataset from different sites [5, 9]. Therefore, besides the normal trained model which used the loss function in Eq. (7), we further adopted the adversarial learning approach of a fast gradient sign method (FGSM) to enhance the robustness of the model [24]. By overlaying small perturbations in the negative gradient direction on the input samples, the FGSM model is able to learn those more important features similar to the $L_1$ regulation. The loss function of FGSM training model was in Eq. (8):

$$\tilde{L}(\theta, x, y) = \gamma L(\theta, x, y) + (1 - \gamma)L(\theta, x + \epsilon sign(\nabla_x L(\theta, x, y))) \qquad (8)$$

where x, y and $\theta$ are the input data, label and model parameters. $L(*)$ is the loss function in Eq. (7). We set $\gamma$ to 0.5 and $\epsilon$ to 0.05 in this study.

The model interpretability was crucial to identify those important features of graph nodes (brain regions) and edges (connections) contributing to the classification, which might serve as potential biomarkers for ASD. Therefore, we further used gradient-based visualization techniques [23], in which the saliency map was computed based on the gradient of the class score with respect to each subject. This interpretability technique could be applied to either the normal trained model or the FGSM trained model. Since the FGSM trained model was more robust and might improve the interpretability of the gradient-based approach [24], we used the FGSM trained model to interpret those important brain regions and connections.

## 3   Results

### 3.1   Classification Accuracy Between ASD and TD

We first combined all 1007 subjects across 17 sites together and performed classification using 10-fold cross-validation. As reported in Table 1, our model outperformed other SOTA models using the same ABIDE I dataset. Specifically, our model with normal training and with FGSM training achieved the classification accuracy of 72.7% and 71.6%, respectively, and both outperformed other SOTA methods (the highest is 70.9%).

We further evaluated model's generalizability across different sites. Specifically, the leave-one-site-out approach was adopted in which the dataset from a single site was

**Table 1.** Classification accuracy based on all sites using 10-fold cross-validation.

| Method | Count | Accuracy | Sensitivity | Specificity |
|---|---|---|---|---|
| ASD-DiagNet [6] | 1035 | 70.1 | 67.8 | 72.8 |
| DNN [5] | 1035 | 70 | 74 | 63 |
| TGCN [12] | 1029 | 67.3 | 70.4 | 64.2 |
| GCN [10] | 871 | 70.4 | – | – |
| G-CNN [11] | 872 | 70.9 | – | – |
| InceptionGCN [25] | 871 | 70.3 | – | – |
| **Ours (normal trained)** | 1007 | **72.7** | 67.8 | 76.6 |
| **Ours (FGSM trained)** | 1007 | **71.6** | 68.6 | 74.3 |

**Table 2.** Averaged classification accuracy of leave-one-site-out across all 17 sites. The averaged accuracy was weighted by the subject count of each site.

| Site | Count (ASD/TD) | Norm trained | FGSM trained | Heinsfeld's result [5] |
|---|---|---|---|---|
| CALTECH | 9/10 | 78.95 | 78.95 | 68.0 |
| CMU | 5/8 | 76.92 | 76.92 | 66.0 |
| KKI | 20/31 | 56.86 | 66.67 | 67.0 |
| LEUVEN | 29/33 | 70.97 | 70.97 | 65.0 |
| MAXMUN | 24/31 | 61.82 | 61.82 | 68.0 |
| NYU | 78/103 | 69.61 | 71.27 | 66.0 |
| OHSU | 13/15 | 64.29 | 67.86 | 64.0 |
| OLIN | 20/16 | 58.33 | 69.44 | 64.0 |
| PITT | 21/19 | 70.00 | 72.50 | 66.0 |
| SBL | 3/6 | 88.89 | 77.78 | 66.0 |
| SDSU | 9/18 | 70.37 | 66.67 | 63.0 |
| STANFORD | 20/20 | 60.00 | 62.50 | 66.0 |
| TRINITY | 24/24 | 75.00 | 70.83 | 65.0 |
| UCLA | 54/45 | 72.73 | 72.73 | 66.0 |
| UM | 67/77 | 69.44 | 71.53 | 64.0 |
| USM | 57/43 | 75.00 | 78.00 | 64.0 |
| YALE | 28/27 | 74.55 | 76.36 | 64.0 |
| **AVERAGE** | 481/526 | **69.42** | **71.30** | 65.0 |

used as the testing dataset and the data from all the other sites were used as the training dataset each time. As reported in Table 2, our model with normal training and with

FGSM training achieved an averaged classification accuracy of 69.42% and 71.30% across different sites, respectively, and both outperformed the SOTA method (65% in [5]). In conclusion, our model with FGSM training achieved satisfying classification accuracy both based on all sites and across different sites, and outperformed other SOTA methods.

### 3.2   Superiority of Using Multi-modal Data for Classification

We further evaluated the superiority of adopting multi-modal MRI data compared to a single-mode one for classification. Note that we only compared the classification accuracy of 'rsfMRI + sMRI' to rsfMRI not sMRI, since the rsfMRI data was adopted for constructing both node and edge features while the sMRI was only used for node features (Sect. 2.2). As illustrated in Fig. 2, the classification accuracy based on single-modal data (rsfMRI) decreased from 72.7% to 70.8%, and from 71.6% to 70.1% using normal and FGSM training, respectively, indicating the superiority of using multi-modal MRI data which provided complementary structural and functional information for ASD classification.

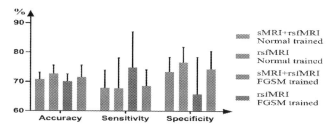

**Fig. 2.** The classification accuracy between using multi-modal and single-mode data based on 10-fold cross-validation.

### 3.3   Node and Edge Features Contributing to ASD/TD Classification

We further identified those important features of graph nodes (brain regions) and edges (connection) contributing to the ASD/TD classification using gradient-based visualization techniques (Sect. 2.5) in order to obtain potential biomarkers for ASD. The individual saliency maps in ASD were first normalized and averaged to obtain the group-wise saliency map. Those important features of nodes and edges were then identified as the top N% ones with total energy (sum of squares) of the ASD saliency map. To facilitate interpreting those features from a neuroscience perspective, we divided all 116 ROIs into 17 categories including frontal, temporal, parietal, occipital, limbic, central region, insula, sub cortical gray nuclei in both left and right hemispheres, as well as cerebellum according to the AAL atlas [13].

For the node features (Fig. 3), we found that: (1) There were increased but no decreased T1-weighted intensities in the regions associated with default mode, reward, memory, and motor functions (Fig. 3(a)); (2) There were increased but no decreased

ALFF Slow-5 in the regions associated with reward, language, emotion, face recognition, visual, and motor functions (Fig. 3(b)); (3) There were increased but no decreased ALFF Slow-4 in the regions associated with cognition, reward, memory, and motor functions (Fig. 3(c)). These functional deficits in ASD have been reported in the existing literature. Note that we tested the node features from top 30% (22 nodes) to 50% (49 nodes) and obtained consistent findings. As an example, Fig. 3 shows those top 30% features with 22 nodes.

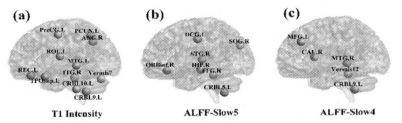

**Fig. 3.** The identified important node features in ASD. (a) T1-weighted intensity feature. (b) ALFF Slow-5 feature. (c) ALFF Slow-4 feature.

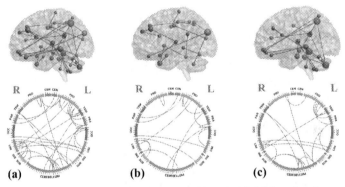

**Fig. 4.** The identified important edge features in ASD. (a) All 35 functional connections. (b) increased and (c) decreased ones.

For the edge features (Fig. 4), we found that: (1) The cerebellum showed both increased (Fig. 4(b)) and decreased (Fig. 4(c)) functional connectivity with other brain regions; (2) There were more dominant between-network connections (32 out of 35) than within-network ones (Fig. 4(a)); (3) There were decreased homotopic interhemispheric connections in limbic regions (Fig. 4(c)). Note that we tested the edge features from the top 2% (22 edges) to 7% (102 edges) and obtained consistent findings. As an example, Fig. 4(a) shows those top 3% features with 35 edges. Figures 4(b–c) show the increased and decreased connections, respectively.

## 4  Conclusion

In this paper, we proposed a novel Attention-based Node-Edge Graph Convolutional Network (ANEGCN) to identify ASD from TD using both functional and structural MRI data. Adversarial training of FGSM was also used to improve the model generalizability. Results showed that the proposed model achieved satisfying classification accuracy and generalizability compared to other SOTA methods in 1007 subjects from 17 sites of the ABIDE I dataset. This study provided a powerful tool for ASD classification and identification based on promising neuroimaging markers. In the future, we plan to apply the proposed model on more ASD datasets such as ABIDE II to verify the robustness of our model.

**Acknowledgements.** This work was partly supported by the Sichuan Science and Technology Program (2021YJ0247), National Natural Science Foundation of China (61976045), Sichuan Science and Technology Program for Returned Overseas People (2021LXHGKJHD24), Key Scientific and Technological Projects of Guangdong Province Government (2018B030335001), and Beijing Municipal Science & Technology Commission (Z181100001518005).

## References

1. American Psychiatric Association. Diagnostic and statistical manual of mental disorders (DSM-5®). American Psychiatric Pub. (2013)
2. Landa, R.J.: Diagnosis of autism spectrum disorders in the first 3 years of life. Nat. Clin. Pract. Neurol. **4**(3), 138–147 (2008)
3. Yazdani, S., Capuano, A., Ghaziuddin, M., Colombi, C.: Exclusion criteria used in early behavioral intervention studies for young children with autism spectrum disorder. Brain Sci. **10**(2), 99–121 (2020)
4. Liu, Y., Xu, L., Li, J., Yu, J., Yu, X.: Attentional connectivity-based prediction of autism using heterogeneous rs-fMRI Data from CC200 Atlas. Exp. Neurobiol. **29**(1), 27–37 (2020)
5. Heinsfeld, A.S., Franco, A.R., Craddock, R.C., Buchweitz, A., Meneguzzi, F.: Identification of autism spectrum disorder using deep learning and the ABIDE dataset. NeuroImage Clin. **17**, 16–23 (2018)
6. Eslami, T., Mirjalili, V., Fong, A.: ASD-DiagNet: a hybrid learning approach for detection of autism spectrum disorder using fMRI data. Front. Neuroinform. **13**, 70–78 (2019)
7. Zhou, J., et al.: Graph neural networks: a review of methods and applications. AI Open **1**, 57–81 (2020)
8. Dehmamy, N., Barabási, A.L., Yu, R.: Understanding the representation power of graph neural networks in learning graph topology. In: Advances in Neural Information Processing Systems, pp. 15413–15423 (2019)
9. Hull, J.V., Dokovna, L.B., Jacokes, Z.J., Torgerson, C.M., Irimia, A., VanHorn, J.D.: Resting-state functional connectivity in autism spectrum disorders: a review. Front. Psychiatry **7**(205) (2017)
10. Parisot, S., et al.: Disease prediction using graph convolutional networks: application to autism spectrum disorder and Alzheimer's disease. Med. Image Anal. **48**, 117–130 (2018)
11. Anirudh, R., Thiagarajan, J.J.: Bootstrapping graph convolutional neural networks for autism spectrum disorder classification. In: 2019 IEEE International Conference on Acoustics, Speech and Signal Processing (ICASSP), pp. 3197–3201 (2019)

12. Yao, D., et al.: A mutual multi-scale triplet graph convolutional network for classification of brain disorders using functional or structural connectivity. IEEE Trans. Med. Imaging **40**(4), 1279–1289 (2021)

13. Tzourio-Mazoyer, N., et al.: Automated anatomical labeling of activations in SPM using a macroscopic anatomical parcellation of the MNI MRI single-subject brain. Neuroimage **15**(1), 273–289 (2002)

14. Raichle, M.E., MacLeod, A.M., Snyder, A.Z., Powers, W.J., Gusnard, D.A., Shulman, G.L.: A default mode of brain function. Proc. Natl. Acad. Sci. **98**(2), 676–682 (2001)

15. Guo, X., Chen, H., Long, Z., Duan, X., Zhang, Y., Chen, H.: Atypical developmental trajectory of local spontaneous brain activity in autism spectrum disorder. Sci. Rep. **7**(1), 1–10 (2017)

16. Glasser, M.F., VabEssen, D.C.: Mapping human cortical areas in vivo based on myelin content as revealed by T1- and T2-weighted MRI. J. Neurosci. **31**(32), 11597–11616 (2011)

17. Ginat, D.T., Meyers, S.P.: Intracranial lesions with high signal intensity on T1-weighted MR images: differential diagnosis. Radiographics **32**(2), 499–516 (2012)

18. Jiang, X., Zhang, T., Zhang, S., Kendrick, K.M., Liu, T.: Fundamental functional differences between gyri and sulci: implications for brain function, cognition, and behavior. Psychoradiology **1**(1), 23–41 (2021)

19. Nt, H., Maehara, T.: Revisiting graph neural networks: all we have is low-pass filters. arXiv preprint arXiv:1905.09550 (2019)

20. Veličković, P., Cucurull, G., Casanova, A., Romero, A., Lio, P., Bengio, Y.: Graph attention networks. arXiv preprint arXiv:1710.10903 (2017)

21. Vaswani, A., et al.: Attention is all you need. arXiv preprint arXiv:1706.03762 (2017)

22. Müller, R., Kornblith, S., Hinton, G.: When does label smoothing help. In: Advances in Neural Information Processing Systems, pp. 4694–4703 (2019)

23. Simonyan, K., Vedaldi, A., Zisserman, A.: Deep inside convolutional networks: visualising image classification models and saliency maps. arXiv preprint arXiv:1312.6034 (2013)

24. Goodfellow, IJ., Shlens, J., Szegedy, C.: Explaining and harnessing adversarial examples. arXiv preprint arXiv:1412.6572 (2015)

25. Kazi, A., et al.: InceptionGCN: receptive field aware graph convolutional network for disease prediction. In: Chung, A., Gee, J., Yushkevich, P., Bao, S. (eds.) IPMI 2019. LNCS, vol. 11492, pp. 73–85. Springer, Cham (2019). https://doi.org/10.1007/978-3-030-20351-1_6

# Segmentation of Intracellular Structures in Fluorescence Microscopy Images by Fusing Low-Level Features

Yuanhao Guo[1,2], Jiaxing Huang[1,2], Yanfeng Zhou[1,2], Yaoru Luo[1,2], Wenjing Li[1,2], and Ge Yang[1,2(✉)]

[1] National Laboratory of Pattern Recognition, Institute of Automation, Chinese Academy of Sciences, Beijing, China
ge.yang@ia.ac.cn
[2] School of Artificial Intelligence, University of Chinese Academy of Sciences, Beijing, China

**Abstract.** Intracellular organelles such as the endoplasmic reticulum, mitochondria, and the cell nucleus exhibit complex structures and diverse morphologies. These intracellular structures (ICSs) play important roles in serving essential physiological functions of cells. Their accurate segmentation is crucial to many important life sciences and clinical applications. When using deep learning-based segmentation models to extract ICSs in fluorescence microscopy images (FLMIs), we find that U-Net provides superior performance, while other well-designed models such as DeepLabv3+ and SegNet perform poorly. By investigating the relative importance of the features learned by U-Net, we find that low-level features play a dominant role. Therefore, we develop a simple strategy that modifies general-purpose segmentation models by fusing low-level features via a decoder architecture to improve their performance in segmenting ICSs from FLMIs. For a given segmentation model, we first use a group of convolutions at the original image scale as the input layer to obtain low-level features. We then use a decoder to fuse the multi-scale features, which directly passes information of low-level features to the prediction layer. Experimental results on two custom datasets, ER and MITO, and a public dataset NUCLEUS, show that the strategy substantially improves the performance of all the general-purpose models tested in segmentation of ICSs from FLMIs. Data and code of this study are available at https://github.com/cbmi-group/icss-segmentation.

## 1 Introduction

Intracellular structures (ICSs) such as the endoplasmic reticulum (ER), mitochondria (MITO), and the cell nucleus serve many essential physiological functions and have been studied extensively [1–3]. In practice, a wide range of imaging modalities have been used for acquiring images of these ICSs, such as widefield and confocal fluorescence

---

Y. Guo and J. Huang—Equal contributors.

---

**Electronic supplementary material** The online version of this chapter (https://doi.org/10.1007/978-3-030-88010-1_32) contains supplementary material, which is available to authorized users.

© Springer Nature Switzerland AG 2021
H. Ma et al. (Eds.): PRCV 2021, LNCS 13021, pp. 386–397, 2021.
https://doi.org/10.1007/978-3-030-88010-1_32

microscopy [4]. Accurate segmentation of these structures in fluorescence microscopy images (FLMIs) is required by many important biomedical applications, such as shape analysis of the ER network for plant biology [5] and shape analysis of the dynamic mitochondrial network for cell biology [6, 7].

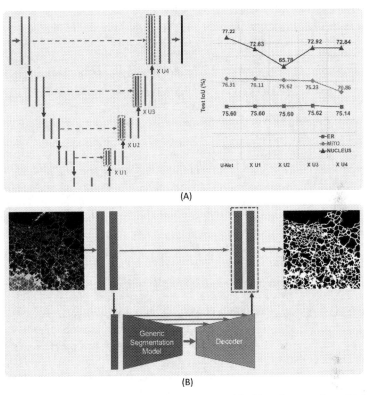

**Fig. 1. Architecture of the proposed method.** (A) By blocking features from high to low-level ($\times$U1 – $\times$ U4), performance of U-Net does not deteriorate substantially on ER, MITO, and NUCLEUS datasets. This indicates that the low-level features contribute prominently in segmentation of ICSs from FLMIs. (B) To improve performance of segmentation of ICSs from FLMIs, we propose a simple strategy to modify general-purpose segmentation models by fusing low-level features with the decoded high-level features, which specifically takes the form of concatenation. An ER image as well as its ground-truth mask are shown as an example.

Overall, segmentation of the ICSs must accurately recover their morphology from images so that key properties of these structures, e.g., their intensity, surface area, tortuosity, connectivity as well as their dynamic behavior can be accurately characterized. However, due to the limited depth-of-field inherent to high-resolution imaging, FLMIs show distinct properties compared to natural images. First, FLMIs contain continuous regions of background noise generated by optics of the imaging modality; Second, FLMIs often contain single-class targets, which define the segmentation of this type of images as a binary-classification task; Third, objects in FLMIs present diverse morphologies, e.g., the ER in complex network shapes, the MITO in diverse ribbon shapes, and the nucleus in irregular ellipsoidal shapes. Examples of these ICSs are shown in Fig. 1 and 2.

When applying general-purpose segmentation models that provide excellent performance in segmenting natural scene images [8, 9], their performance often degrades substantially in segmentation of ICSs from FLMIs. In comparison, segmentation models such as U-Net [10] and its variants [11, 12] achieve much better performance. We reason that U-Net may learn more representative features of the ICSs in FLMIs. Considering the encoder-decoder architecture of U-Net, we reason that features at different levels may contribute differently to the segmentation of ICSs from FLMIs. We are thus motivated to devise a feature blocking method to study the significance of the features learned by the U-Net. As shown in Fig. 1(A), for a converged U-Net, we gradually block its decoded features from high to low level, while keeping the remaining features constant and then re-evaluate the performance of the U-Net. From the results, we see that performance of the U-Net does not deteriorate much when blocking the middle and high-level features.

We therefore conclude that low-level features are playing more important roles in segmentation of ICSs from FLMIs. As for general-purpose segmentation models such as DeepLabv3+ [13], SegNet [14] and FCNs [15], they are developed to differentiate high-level semantics of different classes. Most of these methods employ downsampling operation for efficient learning of large-scale features, and their predictions are often performed using such features as input. In some cases, global contexts are more advantageous in semantic segmentation [16]. However, ignoring low-level features in these segmentation models leads to failure in fully capturing local shape and texture patterns in FLMIs, which partially explains their poor performance in the segmentation of ICSs from FLMIs.

To fill the performance gap between the general-purpose segmentation models and U-Net, we devise a simple strategy to modify these general-purpose segmentation models based on our findings from the feature blocking study. In Fig. 1(B), we show the architecture of our method. Specifically, for a segmentation model such as DeepLabv3+ [13] and FCNs [15], we design the input layer using a group of convolutions, for example, a cascaded two-layer convolutions with small kernel size ($3 \times 3$) and small stride ($s = 1$), before the original downsampling layer. This operation is performed on the original dimension of the input image to preserve low-level features in the network. To directly use these features to produce the final segmentation maps, we use a similar design as developed in U-Net that concatenates these low-level features into the features decoded from high-level using a decoder architecture. To preserve generalization capability of the segmentation models, we do not remove high-level features entirely.

In our work, we select a few representative general-purpose segmentation models to evaluate the performance of our method, which can be categorized into three groups. (1) Encoder type models: FCNs [15] and DeepLabV3+ [13]; (2) Encoder-decoder type models without decoding low-level features: SegNet [14] and HRNet [17]; (3) Standard encoder-decoder type models as baseline methods: U-Net [10], U-Net++ [12] and AGNet [11]. We choose to use these methods because of their excellent performance and generalization capability in both biomedical and natural scene image segmentation.

Regarding feature fusion in segmentation models, there are quite a few possible solutions. PSPNet [18] proposes a pyramid pooling module that aggregates contextual information from different locations in images to improve the capability of capturing global information. ExFuse [19] devises a novel architecture which combines the high-level with low-level features by element-wise multiplication to leverage the semantic information in low-level features and spatial information in high-level features. DFANet [20] introduces a segmentation network that consists of multiple interconnected encoding streams to incorporate high-level features into decoded features. PANet [21] improves the performance of instance segmentation, which strengthens the feature pyramid by improving the path of information transmission from low-level to high-level and fuses multi-scale features through an adaptive feature pooling. It should be noted that none of these works consider the segmentation problem of FLMIs. Instead of developing intricate architectures to improve the segmentation performance, we aim at a deep understanding of the behaviors of current segmentation models in segmenting ICSs from FLMIs and explore a general solution to improve their performance.

## 2    Methodology

We first describe our feature blocking method to analyze the significance of the features learned by the U-Net. We then detail our method that fuses low-level features in selected general-purpose segmentation models, including FCN, DeepLabv3+, SegNet and HRNet.

### 2.1   Feature Blocking

According to our initial study, U-Net has shown its priority in segmenting the ICSs from FLMIs. Compared to U-Net, a well-designed model for segmenting natural scene images performs much worse. Considering differences between their backbone networks, we note that the encoder-decoder architecture and the skip connections in the U-Net may be key to its excellent performance in our task. Our assumption is that features learned by U-Net may better represent the ICSs in FLMIs. So, we devise the feature blocking method to study how the U-Net behaves in segmenting the FLMIs.

We first formulate the mathematical representation of the U-Net. As shown in Fig. 1(A), we use "U" to denote the upsampling operation in the decoder of the U-Net. We use $F_{dl}$ to denote the features from the decoder at level $l$. These features are obtained by applying convolutions on the concatenation of the features upsampled from the higher level $U_{(l-1)}[F_{d(l-1)}]$ with the features copied from the encoder at the same scale $F_{e(l)}$, which is formally defined in Eq. (1).

$$F_{dl} = Conv\left(cat\left(U_{(l-1)}\left[F_{d(l-1)}\right], F_{e(l)}\right)\right) = W_{dl} \cdot cat\left(U_{(l-1)}\left[F_{d(l-1)}\right], F_{e(l)}\right) \quad (1)$$

Specifically, our feature blocking method removes the features of the U-Net from high to low-level and re-evaluates segmentation performance, aiming to show the importance of the features at different levels. Because of the skip connection architecture of the U-Net, the feature blocking can be implemented by setting the model weights for the features upsampled from higher level as zeros, such that all the messages passing from higher levels will be blocked, as is defined in Eqs. (2) and (3).

$$W_{dl}' \leftarrow W_{dl}\left[0 : D_{W_{dl}}/2\right] = 0 \quad (2)$$

$$F'_{dl} = W'_{dl} \cdot cat\big(U_{(l-1)}\big[F_{d(l-1)}\big], F_{e(l)}\big) \tag{3}$$

As shown in the right panel of Fig. 1 (A), we can see that by removing the high-level features of the U-Net, its performance on all the three datasets does not decrease too much, especially for the ER and MITO datasets (Details of the datasets will be given in Sect. 3). So, we can draw an important conclusion that the low-level features are playing key roles in segmenting the ICSs from FLMIs. Because these low-level features are ignored in general-purpose segmentation models, their performance is hardly comparable to the U-Net.

## 2.2   Low-Level Feature Fusion

Motivated by the above findings, one may ask if it is possible to devise a general-purpose solution to improve the performance of general-purpose models in segmenting ICSs from FLMIs. Therefore, we propose a simple strategy to modify the chosen models, *i.e.*, FCNs, DeepLabv3+, SegNet, and HRNet, by fusing the low-level features in their networks via a decoder architecture.

Our method consists of three main steps. (1) For the input layer of the model, we add a group of convolutions with stride 1 to remain the low-level features of the input images. (2) Similar to the U-Net, we upsample the high-level features using a decoder architecture which can be implemented by transposed convolution. (3) We concatenate these upsampled features to the low-level features with the same feature size. Instead of applying extra convolutions as used in the U-Net, we directly decode the concatenated features to obtain the features at the next level. In this way, the low-level features will be directly used for the prediction of the segmentation.

Because our chosen models differ from each other, we specify how we modify a particular network. The FCNs is the first deep learning-based segmentation method which uses the standard convolutional neural networks as the backbone and combines the predictions at middle and high feature level. Based on the same backbone network, the DeepLabv3+ uses dilated convolution and spatial pyramid pooling to better capture the contexts at different scales. Our method can be directly applied to modify these two types of models.

As for SegNet, it has included the low-level features in the network, which is however not used for the predictions. So, we perform steps (2) and (3) of our method to modify the SegNet. The HRNet connects the feature maps with different resolutions in parallel to maintain the high-resolution representation and obtains abundant high-resolution feature maps by performing multi-scale fusion repeatedly across the parallel convolutions. However, the HRNet uses two downsampling layers to reduce the size of feature map to 1/4 of the original image size, which improves its computation efficiency on natural scene images but deteriorates its performance in FLMIs. To modify the HRNet, we first remove the two downsampling layers, and then perform step (1) of our method. In Fig. S1–S4 of supplementary material, we provide detailed graphical representations of the modified models.

## 2.3  Loss Function

Intersection over union (IoU) is a commonly used metric for evaluation of segmentation accuracy. In our segmentation task, we must deal with the foreground-background imbalance challenge, so in this work we use the IoU to formulate the loss function which is robust against the data imbalance problem. A differentiable version of the IoU loss is defined as following.

$$\mathcal{L}_{iou} = 1 - \frac{\sum_{i=1}^{N} y_i \hat{y}_i}{\sum_{i=1}^{N} (y_i + \hat{y}_i - y_i \hat{y}_i) + \eta} \tag{4}$$

where $\eta$ is a smoothing coefficient for numerical stability of the loss function; $N$ is the number of total pixels in an image; $y_i$ is the ground-truth value of a pixel which takes 1 for foreground and 0 for background; $\hat{y}_i$ is the prediction score of the network which ranges between [0, 1]. To integrate all the images, we take the average of their total loss:

$$\mathcal{L} = \frac{1}{M} \sum_{j=1}^{M} \mathcal{L}_{IoU}^{j} \tag{5}$$

where $M$ is the total number of training images.

## 3  Experiments

Here we perform experiments to evaluate the performance of our method, using several standard FLMIs segmentation datasets of ICSs with quite different morphologies. We then perform an ablation study to verify the efficacy of each module of our method. We present representative segmentation results to visualize the effects of each method.

### 3.1  Experimental Setup

**Datasets:** We have developed two specialized datasets of fluorescence images, ER for the endoplasmic reticulum and MITO for mitochondria. In addition, we use a public dataset NUCLEUS [22]. The three datasets cover diverse morphologies of the ICSs, specifically, the ER in network shapes, the MITO in ribbon shapes and the NUCLREUS in ellipsoid shapes. All images are cropped into $256 \times 256$ patches. All the images are split into a training and a test set separately for the three datasets. We use data augmentation to increase the size of training data. Horizontal and vertical flipping as well as $90°/180°/270°$ rotation are used. This eventually generates 1232, 1320 and 6360 training/validation images, and 38, 18 and 143 test images for the ER, MITO, and NUCLEUS datasets, respectively.

**Training Configuration:** We implement all the models using PyTorch [23] and perform all the experiments using 4 NVIDIA 2080Ti GPU cards. During training, we use the following configurations for all the models. We use standard SGD optimizer and we set the initial learning rate as 0.05. We divide the learning rate by 10 for every 5 epochs and use 30 epochs in total. The batch size is 16. The regularization weight is 0.0005.

**Metrics:** The following metrics are used to measure the performance of all methods: IoU (intersection-over-union), F1 (F1 score), AUC (area under ROC curve), ACC (accuracy).

**Table 1.** Performance comparison of various segmentation models (%)

| Dataset | Model | F1 | AUC | IoU | ACC |
|---|---|---|---|---|---|
| ER | U-Net | 85.99 | 97.28 | 75.60 | 91.59 |
| | U-Net++ | 85.64 | 97.15 | 75.04 | 91.63 |
| | AGNet | 85.04 | 97.04 | 74.11 | 90.88 |
| | FCN-32s | 62.91 | 78.45 | 46.16 | 68.49 |
| | FCN-32s* | 85.92 | 97.15 | 75.46 | 91.40 |
| | DeepLabv3+ | 77.65 | 92.80 | 63.65 | 84.84 |
| | DeepLabv3+* | **86.31** | **97.46** | **76.08** | *91.78* |
| | SegNet | 83.83 | 95.91 | 72.39 | 90.36 |
| | SegNet* | 85.76 | 97.17 | 75.21 | 91.53 |
| | HR-Net | 83.23 | 95.87 | 71.50 | 90.18 |
| | HR-Net* | *86.07* | *97.43* | *75.71* | **91.80** |
| MITO | U-Net | *86.45* | 99.43 | 76.31 | *97.60* |
| | U-Net++ | 86.45 | **99.49** | 76.22 | 97.55 |
| | AGNet | 85.39 | 99.34 | 74.69 | 97.30 |
| | FCN-32s | 61.62 | 94.71 | 44.69 | 91.76 |
| | FCN-32s* | 85.92 | 98.76 | 73.21 | 97.13 |
| | DeepLabv3+ | 83.51 | 98.98 | 71.85 | 97.13 |
| | DeepLabv3+* | 86.51 | 99.41 | *76.38* | 97.52 |
| | SegNet | 78.88 | 98.13 | 65.44 | 96.47 |
| | SegNet* | 86.17 | 99.44 | 75.78 | 97.53 |
| | HR-Net | 85.64 | 99.40 | 74.97 | 97.43 |
| | HR-Net* | **86.71** | *99.45* | **76.64** | **97.67** |
| NUCLEUS | U-Net | 86.40 | 99.68 | 77.22 | 98.44 |
| | U-Net++ | 85.88 | 99.67 | 76.54 | 98.39 |
| | AGNet | 85.90 | 99.67 | 76.42 | 98.34 |
| | FCN-32s | 80.58 | 99.63 | 68.65 | 97.67 |
| | FCN-32s* | **86.96** | **99.69** | **77.97** | **98.53** |
| | DeepLabv3+ | 83.54 | 99.63 | 73.36 | 98.13 |
| | DeepLabv3+* | 85.80 | 99.67 | 76.27 | 98.39 |
| | SegNet | 85.10 | 99.64 | 75.23 | 98.24 |
| | SegNet* | 86.04 | 99.65 | 76.83 | 98.40 |
| | HR-Net | 85.80 | 99.67 | 76.21 | 98.27 |
| | HR-Net* | *86.64* | *99.69* | *77.63* | *98.50* |

## 3.2  Performance Evaluation

Table 1 summarizes evaluation results of different segmentation methods. We use the symbol of "*" to represent the model that is reformed using our proposed method. Specifically, FCN-32s*, DeepLabv3+*, SegNet* and HR-Net* represent modified FCN-32s, DeepLabv3+, SegNet and HR-Net respectively. We use the results from standard encoder-decoder based models, *i.e.* the U-Net, U-Net++ and AGNet, as strong baselines in the segmentation of ICSs from FLMIs. These results are shown in the top panel of Table 1, and the best baseline performance is shown with underlines. Among the results of all the models, the best performance for each metric is indicated in **bold**, and the second best in *italic*.

From the results we can draw the following important conclusions.

(1) All the models that are modified by our proposed method have obtained a large-margin performance improvement compared to their original architectures on all the three datasets. This confirms that fusing low-level features in general-purpose segmentation models is playing a key role in improving their performance in segmenting the ICSs from FLMIs.

(2) Overall, our method shows better performance compared to the baseline methods, *i.e.*, the standard encoder-decoder networks. This means that a simple strategy to modify current general-purpose models is preferred in improving the segmentation of ICSs from FLMIs. In other words, the merits of currently popular segmentation models should not be abandoned when applied in the task of ICSs segmentation from FLMIs. Relatively poor performance has been achieved though. A proper low-level feature fusion strategy should be paid sufficient attention. We note that the performance of the SegNet* is lower than the U-Net. In fact, the former has more convolution layers than the latter, which shows that the performance improvement of the segmentation models modified by our method is gained from their intrinsic properties, rather than extra trainable parameters. In Table S1 from supplementary material, we present the number of parameters and computation efficiency (FLOPS and inference time).

(3) The segmentation performance of our method remains consistent on different datasets which include various ICSs with quite different morphologies. *This indicates that low-level features are generally important in FLMIs, which is independent to the specific type and morphology of the objects in images.*

(4) Finally, the HRNet* shows a balanced performance in all the datasets. Specifically, the DeepLabv3+* and FCN-32s* have achieved the best performance on the ER and NUCLEUS datasets, respectively. For a new segmentation task of FLMIs, we thus recommend initially applying these well-performed models. In Fig. 2, we visualize the segmentation results of these models and the corresponding results from their original architectures as well as the U-Net for comparison.

## 3.3  Ablation Study

In this experiment, we perform an ablation study to check the effectiveness of the low-level features and the method of fusion. We use DeepLabv3+ as an example.

**Table 2.** Ablation study on DeepLabv3+ (%)

| Dataset | Feature level | F1 | AUC | IoU | ACC |
|---------|---------------|------|-------|-------|-------|
| ER | L4 | 70.33 | 88.39 | 54.66 | 79.25 |
| | L4+L3 | 77.65 | 92.80 | 63.65 | 84.87 |
| | L4+L3+L2 | 84.07 | 96.57 | 72.75 | 90.39 |
| | L4+L3+L2+L1 | **86.31** | **97.46** | **76.08** | **91.78** |
| | ADD | 84.92 | 96.95 | 73.99 | 90.81 |
| MITO | L4 | 71.49 | 96.97 | 57.31 | 93.67 |
| | L4+L3 | 83.51 | 98.98 | 71.85 | 97.13 |
| | L4+L3+L2 | 83.82 | 98.98 | 72.47 | 96.86 |
| | L4+L3+L2+L1 | **86.51** | **99.41** | **76.38** | **97.52** |
| | ADD | 85.50 | 99.36 | 74.77 | 97.36 |
| NULEUS | L4 | 81.69 | 99.28 | 72.66 | 98.29 |
| | L4+L3 | 83.54 | 99.63 | 73.36 | 98.13 |
| | L4+L3+L2 | 85.16 | 99.66 | 75.50 | 98.36 |
| | L4+L3+L2+L1 | **85.80** | **99.67** | **76.27** | **98.39** |
| | ADD | 83.54 | 99.61 | 73.24 | 98.15 |

Table 2 summarizes the experimental results. We use L1 to L4 to denote the features from high to low-level. "ADD" means that we add the low-level features to these decoded from high-level features, which serves as the feature fusion operator and is defined in Eq. (6).

$$F_{dl} = Conv\left(U_{(l-1)}\left[F_{d(l-1)}\right] + F_{e(l)}\right) \tag{6}$$

From the results, a clear trend can be seen that when fusing low-level features, the segmentation performance for ICSs from FLMIs improves significantly, especially for the ER and MITO datasets, which include the organelles with more elaborate morphologies. As for the fusion operator, concatenation performs much better than addition. The former may explicitly preserve more structural information from the low-level features.

## 4  Conclusions

In this study, through a feature blocking analysis, we have found that low-level features are essential in segmentation of intracellular structures (ICSs) from the fluorescence microscopy images (FLMIs). General-purpose segmentation models that do not consider fusing these low-level features generally perform worse than U-Net and its variants, the standard encoder-decoder models that integrate low-level features. To keep advantages of the general-purpose segmentation models and further improve their performance in the segmentation of ICSs from FLMIs, we propose a simple strategy that modifies these

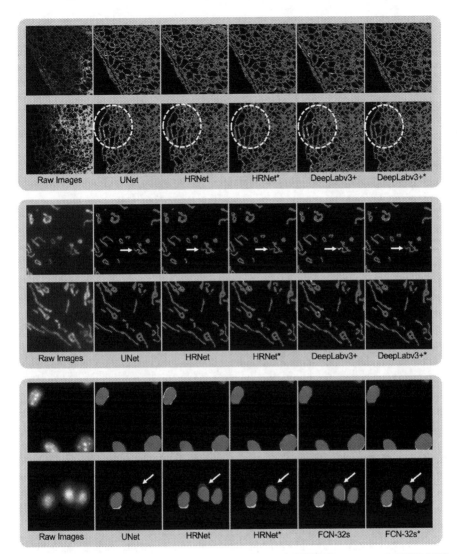

**Fig. 2. Segmentation results.** Top panel: ER; Middle panel: MITO; Bottom panel: NUCLEUS. Red: True positive; Green: False negative; Blue: False positive. Results of U-Net are shown as baselines. For each dataset, results of the top two performing models and their original networks are shown. For the ER and MITO images, performance improvement using our method is clearly visible. For the NUCLEUS images, our method reduces false positives, i.e. blue regions are substantially decreased. We use white circles and arrows to indicate these regions.

models by fusing low-level features with features decoded from high-level semantics. Experimental results show that our proposed method substantially enhances performance of all of the selected segmentation models compared to their original architectures. More importantly, models modified using our method outperform the U-Net and its variants across all the datasets, regardless of the types of image objects. This shows that local textural patterns encoded in the low-level features of a deep neural network are more informative to represent the ICSs from FLMIs. Therefore, for the segmentation of these structures, it is important to integrate low-level features. We note that a balance between low-level primitive features and high-level semantics at different scales are easier to achieve for the models modified using our strategy. This balanced strategy maintains original strengths of these models, *i.e.*, utilization of multi-scale contextual information, which results in their better performance in segmentation of ICSs from FLMIs.

**Acknowledgements.** This study was supported in part by NSFC grant 91954201 and grant 31971289, the Strategic Priority Research Program of the Chinese Academy of Sciences grant XDB37040402, the Chinese Academy of Sciences grant 292019000056, the University of Chinese Academy of Sciences grant 115200M001, and the Beijing Municipal Science & Technology Commission grant 5202022.

# References

1. Moen, E., Bannon, D., Kudo, T., et al.: Deep learning for cellular image analysis. Nat. Methods **16**(12), 1233–1246 (2019)
2. Nixon-Abell, J., Obara, C.J., Weigel, A.V., et al.: Increased spatiotemporal resolution reveals highly dynamic dense tubular matrices in the peripheral ER. Science **354**(6311), aaf3928 (2016)
3. Mootha, V.K., Bunkenborg, J., Olsen, J.V., et al.: Integrated analysis of protein composition, tissue diversity, and gene regulation in mouse mitochondria. Cell **115**(5), 629–640 (2003)
4. Diaspro, A.: Confocal and Two-Photon Microscopy: Foundations, Applications, and Advances. Wiley-Liss. Hoboken (2002)
5. Pain, C., Kriechbaumer, V., Kittelmann, M., et al.: Quantitative analysis of plant ER architecture and dynamics. Nat. Commun. **10**(1), 1–15 (2019)
6. Mitra, K., Lippincott-Schwartz, J.: Analysis of mitochondrial dynamics and functions using imaging approaches. Curr. Protoc. Cell Biol. **46**(1), 4.25. 1–4.25. 21 (2010)
7. Yaffe, M.P.: Dynamic mitochondria. Nat. Cell Biol. **1**(6), E149–E150 (1999)
8. Lin, T.Y., et al.: Microsoft COCO: common objects in context. In: Fleet, D., Pajdla, T., Schiele, B., Tuytelaars, T. (eds.) ECCV 2014. LNCS, vol. 8693, pp. 740–755. Springer, Cham (2014). https://doi.org/10.1007/978-3-319-10602-1_48
9. Everingham, M., Van Gool, L., Williams, C.K., et al.: The pascal visual object classes (VOC) challenge. Int. J. Comput. Vis. **88**(2), 303–338 (2010)
10. Ronneberger, O., Fischer, P., Brox, T.: U-net: convolutional networks for biomedical image segmentation. In: Navab, N., Hornegger, J., Wells, W., Frangi, A. (eds.) MICCAI 2015. LNCS, vol. 9351, pp. 234–241. Springer, Cham (2015). https://doi.org/10.1007/978-3-319-24574-4_28
11. Hu, X., Yu, L., Chen, H., Qin, J., Heng, P.A.: AGNet: attention-guided network for surgical tool presence detection. In: Cardoso, M., et al. (eds.) DLMIA 2017, ML-CDS 2017. LNCS, vol. 10553, pp. 186–194. Springer, Cham (2017). https://doi.org/10.1007/978-3-319-67558-9_22
12. Zhou, Z., Siddiquee, M.M.R., Tajbakhsh, N., et al.: UNet++: redesigning skip connections to exploit multiscale features in image segmentation. IEEE Trans. Med. Imaging **39**(6), 1856–1867 (2019)

13. Chen, L.C., Zhu, Y., Papandreou, G., Schroff, F., Adam, H.: Encoder-decoder with atrous separable convolution for semantic image segmentation. In: Ferrari, V., Hebert, M., Sminchisescu, C., Weiss, Y. (eds.) ECCV 2018. LNCS, vol. 11211, pp. 833–851 Springer, Cham (2018). https://doi.org/10.1007/978-3-030-01234-2_49

14. Badrinarayanan, V., Kendall, A., Cipolla, R.: SegNet: a deep convolutional encoder-decoder architecture for image segmentation. IEEE Trans. Pattern Anal. Mach. Intell. **39**(12), 2481–2495 (2017)

15. Long, J., Shelhamer, E., and Darrell, T.: Fully convolutional networks for semantic segmentation. In: Proceedings of the IEEE Conference on Computer Vision and Pattern Recognition, pp. 3431–3440. IEEE (2015)

16. Peng, C., Zhang, X., Yu, G., et al.: Large kernel matters–improve semantic segmentation by global convolutional network. In: Proceedings of the IEEE Conference on Computer Vision and Pattern Recognition, pp. 4353–4361. IEEE (2017)

17. Wang, J., Sun, K., Cheng, T., et al.: Deep high-resolution representation learning for visual recognition. IEEE Trans. Pattern Anal. Mach. Intell. (2020)

18. Zhao, H., Shi, J., Qi, X., et al.: Pyramid scene parsing network. In: Proceedings of the IEEE Conference on Computer Vision and Pattern Recognition, pp. 2881–2890. IEEE (2017)

19. Zhang Z., Zhang X., Peng C., Xue X., Sun J.: ExFuse: enhancing feature fusion for semantic segmentation. In: Ferrari, V., Hebert, M., Sminchisescu, C., Weiss, Y. (eds.) ECCV 2018. LNCS, vol. 11214, pp. 273–288. Springer, Cham (2018). https://doi.org/10.1007/978-3-030-01249-6_17

20. Li, H., Xiong, P., Fan, H., et al.: DFANet: deep feature aggregation for real-time semantic segmentation. In: Proceedings of the IEEE Conference on Computer Vision and Pattern Recognition, pp. 9522–9531. IEEE (2019)

21. Liu, S., Qi, L., Qin, H., et al.: Path aggregation network for instance segmentation. In: Proceedings of the IEEE Conference on Computer Vision and Pattern Recognition, pp. 8759–8768. IEEE (2018)

22. Caicedo, J.C., Goodman, A., Karhohs, K.W., et al.: Nucleus segmentation across imaging experiments: the 2018 Data Science Bowl. Nat. Methods **16**(12), 1247–1253 (2019)

23. Paszke, A., Gross, S., Massa, F., et al.: Pytorch: an imperative style, high-performance deep learning library. In: Advances in Neural Information Processing Systems, pp. 8026–8037 (2019)

# Interactive Attention Sampling Network for Clinical Skin Disease Image Classification

Xulin Chen[1], Dong Li[1(✉)], Yun Zhang[1], and Muwei Jian[2,3]

[1] School of Automation, Guangdong University of Technology, Guangzhou, China
dong.li@gdut.edu.cn
[2] School of Information Science and Engineering, Linyi University, Linyi, China
[3] School of Computer Science and Technology, Shandong University of Finance and Economics, Jinan, China

**Abstract.** Skin disease is one of the global burdens of disease, and affects around 30% to 70% individuals worldwide. Effective automatic diagnosis is indispensable for doctors and patients. Compared with dermoscopic imaging, using clinical images captured by a portable electronic device (e.g. a mobile phone) is more available and low-cost. However, the existing large clinical skin-disease image datasets do not have the spatial annotation information, thus posing challenges for localizing the skin-disease regions and learning detailed features. To address the problem, we propose the Interactive Attention Sampling Network (IASN) which automatically localizes the target skin-disease regions and highlight the regions into high resolution. Specifically, the top-$K$ local peaks of the class activation maps are collected, which indicate the key clues of skin-disease images. Then the features of the local peaks are interacted with the features of the surrounding context. With the guidance of the interactive attention maps, the non-uniform sampled images are generated, which facilitate the model to learn more discriminative features. Experimental results demonstrate that the proposed IASN outperforms the state-of-the-art methods on the SD-198 benchmark dataset.

**Keywords:** Clinical skin disease images classification · Class activation maps · Interactive attention · Non-uniform sampling · Interactive Attention Sampling Network (IASN)

## 1 Introduction

Skin disease, with detrimental effects on health, ranging from physical incapacity to death, is one of the global burdens of disease [1]. Effective automatic diagnosis

This work was supported by the Guangdong Basic and Applied Basic Research Foundation No. 2021A1515011867, the Taishan Young Scholars Program of Shandong Province, the Key Development Program for Basic Research of Shandong Province No. ZR2020ZD44, and the National Natural Science Foundation of China No. 61503084 and No. 61976123.

H. Ma et al. (Eds.): PRCV 2021, LNCS 13021, pp. 398–410, 2021.
https://doi.org/10.1007/978-3-030-88010-1_33

is beneficial for both doctors and patients. Compared with dermoscopic images, using clinical images captured by a portable electronic device (e.g. a mobile phone) is more available and low-cost. Accordingly, developing a skin-disease recognition system based on clinical images could provide easy access for more people.

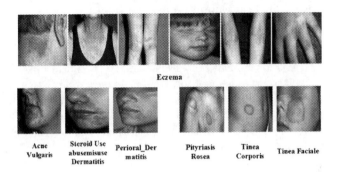

**Fig. 1.** Illustration of the characteristics of clinical skin-disease images. Images are from the SD-198 dataset [2].

However, recognizing skin diseases from clinical images is difficult. Clinical images present more variations due to a number of factors, including shooting distance, viewing angle, background, and illumination [3], as shown in Fig. 1. Because of the above-mentioned characteristics, it is crucial to capture skin-disease regions in clinical images. However, since the existing large datasets of clinical images do not provide the annotation information, it is hard for the annotation-based methods to learn localizing the relevant regions.

In this paper, we address the problem of localizing the target regions for clinical skin-disease image classification by proposing the Interactive Attention Sampling Network (IASN). IASN learns to localize the skin-disease regions in a weakly-supervised manner, and highlights the target regions with high resolution. Specifically, the top-$K$ local peaks of the class activation maps are collected, which indicate the key clues of skin-disease images. Then the features of the local peaks are interacted with the features of the global context, which adaptively capture the regions semantically similar to the local peaks. Meanwhile, the local interactive attention is also obtained by computing the interaction between the local peaks and the local context, which represents the attention for the local regions around the peaks. With the guidance of the final aggregated interactive attention, the non-uniform sampled images are generated, which highlight the attended regions and facilitate the model to learn more discriminative features.

By taking the advantage of the feature maps learned by convolutional neural network (CNN), our model can accurately localize diverse and informative visual patterns of skin-disease images, without additional spatial annotation. Moreover, compared with the cropped skin-disease regions which lose the information of context, our re-sampled images highlight the skin-disease regions while preserving the surrounding information, i.e., the body parts shown in skin-disease images. This facilitates the classification of skin diseases, because each skin-disease category may affect some specific body parts. Furthermore, the performance of the backbone network can be improved significantly by sharing the feature extractor among the re-sampled images. Therefore, IASN can achieve evident gain with a single stream in the testing stage.

Our main contributions are summarized as follows.

- We propose the novel interactive attention which adaptively localizes the important regions for clinical skin-disease image classification.
- The interactive attention is incorporated in the backbone CNN to sample the attended regions into high resolution and extract discriminative features.
- Experimental results on the SD-198 dataset [2] demonstrate that the proposed IASN achieves the new state-of-the-art performance concerning classification accuracy and other evaluation metrics of imbalance.

## 2   Related Work

In this section, we review the previous works of skin-disease recognition and visual attention.

### 2.1   Skin-Disease Recognition

Recently, several works have been developed for the recognition of clinical images, focusing on most of common skin diseases. Among the CNN-based methods, Yang et al. [4] crawled additional 80 thousand web images for clinical image classification, and the performance of CNN was improved by the filtered web data. Yang et al. [5] addressed the class imbalance issue in clinical skin-disease images. They trained the CNN model by the balanced self-paced curriculum. As far as we know, there are no previous works that research on capturing the discriminative regions for clinical skin-disease image classification.

### 2.2   Visual Attention

The visual attention model was inspired by human perception, which did not process the entire scene instantly, but instead selectively paid attention to parts of the visual space to acquire the information required [6]. Mnih et al. [7] employed a recurrent neural network to localize a set of attention regions. They used policy gradient in reinforcement learning to learn task-specific policies. NTS [8] generated the region proposals, and designed the ranking loss to obtain the most relevant regions for classification.

Different from cropping the attention regions used in the above methods, SSN [9] first proposed the non-uniformed sampling under the guidance of saliency maps. S3Ns [10] further generated a set of sparse attention for the object parts.

Our method also conducts non-uniformed sampling guided by the attention maps. In S3Ns [10], they employed Gaussian function to compute the attention for the local peak. Different from [10], our method computes interactive attention for the local peak, in which the attention weights of other positions are determined by their relationship with the local peak.

# 3    Methodology

In this section, we introduce the proposed IASN. The overview structure is shown in Fig. 2. IASN learns the interaction between the key points and the contextual information for localizing the informative regions. Then the interactive attention is used to sample the attended regions into high resolution. The backbone network of the framework, e.g., ResNet50, is reused for the attention-based resampled images.

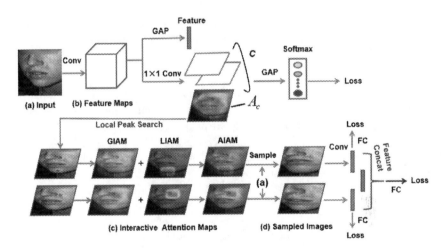

**Fig. 2.** The architecture of the proposed IASN. FC denotes the fully connected network.

## 3.1    Class Activation Map Revisit

The class activation maps indicate the locations of discriminative regions for each category, and have been studied in some tasks [11]. Specifically, the last convolutional layer outputs the feature maps which are denoted as $F \in \mathbb{R}^{N \times H \times W}$, where $H \times W$ is the resolution of the feature maps and $N$ is the number of channels. Then a $1 \times 1$ convolutional layer with the channel size of $C$, the stride of 1 is employed to the feature maps $F$, where $C$ is the number of skin-disease classes. The class activation maps $A_c$, $c = 0, 1, ..., C-1$ are then fed to a Global Average Pooling (GAP) layer followed by a softmax operation to produce the probability of each class, $P \in \mathbb{R}^C$.

### 3.2   Local Peaks Search

In the training and testing stages, the class activation map $A_c$ of the class which predicts the highest probability is selected. The local peaks of $A_c$ is obtained by non-maximum suppression (NMS). In particular, the elements of $A_c$ is sorted in descending order. The location $(x_1, y_1)$ of the first element $A_c(1)$ in sorted list is recorded. Given the threshold $t$, a $(2t + 1) \times (2t + 1)$ region centered around $A_c(1)$ is located at the class activation map $A_c$. The elements inside the region are removed from the sorted list. Then the location $(x_{P_2}, y_{P_2})$ of the next first element $A_c(P_2)$ in sorted list is recorded. The above operation is repeated until the location $(x_{P_K}, y_{P_K})$ of the $K$-th local peak is recorded. The collected local peaks can represent the important visual patterns of clinical skin-disease images. In our experiments, the threshold $t$ is set to 2.

### 3.3   Learning Interactive Attention

We introduce our interactive attention module for modeling the relationship between the local peaks and their context, which effectively localizes the important skin-disease regions.

**Global Interactive Attention.** We first learn the interaction between the local peaks and the global context to obtain the global interactive attention map (GIAM). Specifically, given the local peak $P_k$, $k = 0, 1, ..., K - 1$, and the feature maps $F \in \mathbb{R}^{N \times H \times W}$, we reshape $F$ to $\mathbb{R}^{N \times HW}$. Let $F_{P_k} \in \mathbb{R}^{N \times 1}$ denote the feature vector of local peak $P_k$ at the feature maps $F$. Then the global interactive attention is formulated as:

$$I_k^{glo} = F_{P_k}^T F \quad (k = 0, 1, ..., K - 1),  \tag{1}$$

where $I_k^{glo} \in \mathbb{R}^{1 \times HW}$. Then $I_k^{glo}$ is normalized by conducting $I_k^{glo} = \frac{I_k^{glo} - min(I_k^{glo})}{max(I_k^{glo}) - min(I_k^{glo})}$. We reshape $I_k^{glo} \in \mathbb{R}^{1 \times HW}$ into the shape of $1 \times H \times W$, where $I_k^{glo}(0, i, j)$ represents the relationship between the local peak $P_k$ and the position $(0, i, j)$. The greater value in $I_k^{glo}$ indicates the more similar features between the local peak and the other position. Since the collected local peaks indicate the key visual clues of skin-disease images, the global interactive attention can precisely localize the important regions which are related to the local peaks.

**Local Interactive Attention.** The global interactive attention captures the relevant regions in the global context, and may pay attention to the global structure. We also learn the interactive attention in the local context, which enables the model to learn more details from the local regions. In particular, given the radius $r$ of the local context and the location $(x_{P_K}, y_{P_K})$, we use the mask $M_k \in \mathbb{R}^{1 \times H \times W}$ to denote the range of the local context:

$$M_k(x,y) = \begin{cases} 1, & |x - x_{P_K}| \le r \quad and \quad |y - y_{P_K}| \le r \\ 0, & otherwise \end{cases} \tag{2}$$

Then the local interactive attention map (LIAM) is formulated as:

$$I_k^{loc} = M_k \odot I_k^{glo} \quad (k = 0, 1, ..., K - 1), \tag{3}$$

where $\odot$ denotes element-wise multiplication. The LIAM $I_k^{loc}$ represents the attention distribution around the local peak, which can guide the network to learn more fine-grained skin-disease contents.

**Aggregated Interactive Attention.** We further aggregate the GIAM and the LIAM to form the aggregated interactive attention map (AIAM):

$$I_k^{agg} = I_k^{loc} + I_k^{glo} \quad (k = 0, 1, ..., K - 1). \tag{4}$$

The AIAM can not only pay attention to the regions associated with the local peaks, but also highlight the local regions.

### 3.4   Attention-Based Sampling

Given the input image $X$ and the AIAM $I_k^{agg}$, the re-sampled images $R_k$ are generated, such that the areas in $I_k^{agg}$ with larger attention weights have more chances to be sampled. Let the mapping functions between the coordinate of the re-sampled image $R_k$ and that of the input image $X$ be $h(u,v)$ and $z(u,v)$, such that $R_k(u,v) = X(h(u,v), z(u,v))$. The AIAM $I_k^{agg}$ is used to compute the mapping functions. Following the solution in [9], the mapping functions are calculated as

$$h(u,v) = \frac{\sum_{u',v'} I_k^{agg}(u',v')k((u,v),(u',v'))u'}{\sum_{u',v'} I_k^{agg}(u',v')k((u,v),(u',v'))}, \tag{5}$$

$$z(u,v) = \frac{\sum_{u',v'} I_k^{agg}(u',v')k((u,v),(u',v'))v'}{\sum_{u',v'} I_k^{agg}(u',v')k((u,v),(u',v'))}, \tag{6}$$

where $I_k^{agg}$ is the $k$-th AIAM, $k((u,v),(u',v'))$ is a Gaussian kernel to avoid the case in which all the pixels are calculated to the same value. We obtain $K$ re-sampled images.

### 3.5   Network Optimization

We make the final classification results by combining the re-sampled images $R$ with the input image $X$. The feature vectors of the re-sampled images and that of the input image are concatenated, and fed into a fully connected layer followed by a softmax function. We employ function $B$ to denote these transformations. The total classification losses are defined as

$$L_{cls} = -\sum_{i=1}^{K} logG(R_i) - logU(X) - logB(X, R_1, \cdots, R_K), \qquad (7)$$

where $G$ is the function mapping the re-sampled image $R_i$ to the probability being ground-truth class $y$. It should be noted that our interactive attention modules do not increase any parameters yet capture the important regions effectively.

## 4   Experiments

### 4.1   Dataset

The IASN is evaluated on the SD-198 clinical skin-disease image categorization dataset [2]. It is the largest publicly available dataset acquired by digital cameras or mobile phones, containing 198 different diseases and 6,584 clinical images. The number of samples for each class is between 10 and 60. There are no bounding boxes for targets provided with the dataset, and only the class labels for images are available. There are 3,292 training and 3,292 testing images.

### 4.2   Experimental Settings

**Implementation Details.** We adopt ResNet50 [12] as the backbone of the CNN. The input images are resized to $336 \times 336$. The $K$ is set to 2, which means two re-sampled images are input to train the parameters of the backbone. We use the Stochastic Gradient Descent (SGD) optimizer, with the momentum of 0.9, the weight decay of 1e−4, and the batch size of 16 on a NVIDIA GeForce RTX 2080Ti GPU. The initial learning rate is set to 0.001, and decays by 0.1 after 60 epochs. We implement our algorithm using software package PyTorch.

**Evaluation Metrics.** The classification accuracy (Acc) is used to evaluate the performance of all the methods. Since the number of samples of different classes is imbalanced (i.e., 10 to 60), we also consider both the precision and the recall by using the metrics $F$-measure and $M_{\text{AUC}}$. The recall $R_i$ and the precision $P_i$ of class $c_i$ are defined as $R_i = \frac{(TP)_i}{(TP)_i + (FN)_i}$ and $P_i = \frac{(TP)_i}{(TP)_i + (FP)_i}$. The average recall and precision are calculated as Recall $= \frac{1}{C}\sum_{i=1}^{C} R_i$ and Precision $= \frac{1}{C}\sum_{i=1}^{C} P_i$, where $C$ denotes the number of classes. The $F$-measure integrates the precision and the recall, which can effectively reflect the performance of the classifier

$$F-\text{measure} = \frac{1}{C}\sum_{i=1}^{C} \frac{(1 + \beta^2)P_i R_i}{\beta^2 P_i + R_i}. \qquad (8)$$

The factor $\beta$ is set to 1 (F1) in our experiments.

Similar to the formulation of $F$-measure, $M_{\mathrm{AUC}}$ combines the microaverage precision $M_{\mathrm{P}}$ and the recall $M_{\mathrm{R}}$

$$M_{\mathrm{AUC}} = \frac{2M_{\mathrm{P}}M_{\mathrm{R}}}{M_{\mathrm{P}} + M_{\mathrm{R}}} \qquad (9)$$

where the $M_{\mathrm{P}}$ and the $M_{\mathrm{R}}$ are defined as $M_{\mathrm{P}} = \frac{\sum_{i=1}^{C}(TP)_i}{\sum_{i=1}^{C}((TP)_i+(FP)_i)}$ and $M_{\mathrm{R}} = \frac{\sum_{i=1}^{C}(TP)_i}{\sum_{i=1}^{C}((TP)_i+(FN)_i)}$.

### 4.3   Ablation Study

**Different Interactive Attention Modules.** We conduct experiments with different interactive attention modules to verify the performance of our interactive attention.

**Table 1.** Ablation experiments on the SD-198 dataset based on different interactive attention modules of IASN.

| Method | Precision | Recall | F1 | $M_{\mathrm{AUC}}$ | Acc |
|---|---|---|---|---|---|
| ResNet50 [12] | 63.6 | 61.4 | 60.9 | 62.3 | 62.8 |
| IASN without LIAM | 70.9 | 69.6 | 68.9 | 70.3 | 70.6 |
| IASN without GIAM | 71.5 | 69.7 | 69.4 | 70.5 | 71.3 |
| IASN | 72.8 | 71.1 | 71.0 | 71.9 | 71.9 |

As shown in Table 1, all the three types of interactive attention modules can help the IASN improve the performance significantly over the ResNet50 baseline. It demonstrates the effectiveness of the interactive attention for modeling the distribution of the skin-disease regions. Furthermore, the final IASN which is based on AIAM achieves the best performance, indicating that the aggregated interactive attention includes more effective information for skin-disease image classification.

**Table 2.** Classification accuracy (Acc) on the SD-198 dataset for the input image $X$, the re-sampled image $R_1$, the re-sampled image $R_2$, and the combination of them for the IASN with $K = 2$.

| Method | $X$ | $R_1$ | $R_2$ | Total |
|---|---|---|---|---|
| IASN | 69.2 | 70.2 | 70.3 | 71.9 |

**Different Branches of IASN.** We also report the classification accuracy (Acc) for the input image $X$, the re-sampled image $R_1$, the re-sampled image $R_2$, and the combination of them for the IASN. As shown in Table 2, each branch of the IASN can have a significant improvement over the ResNet50 baseline (62.8). It indicates that the performance of the backbone network is improved by the attention-based re-sampled images in the training stage. Moreover, the combination of different branches achieves the best performance (71.9), showing that the features learned from the different branches are complementary.

## 4.4    Quantitative Results

**Comparison to Sampling-Based Methods with or Without Attention.** The IASN is compared with three types of sampling-based methods: 1) extracting multi-resolution patches of the input image by center cropping, 2) attention-based uniformed sampling (i.e., cropping the attended regions), 3) attention-based non-uniformed sampling.

**Table 3.** Comparison to the sampling-based methods with or without attention on the SD-198 dataset under different evaluation metrics. The number in () denotes the number of backbones used in the testing stage.

| Method | Precision | Recall | F1 | $M_{\mathrm{AUC}}$ | Acc |
|---|---|---|---|---|---|
| ResNet50 [12] (1) | 63.6 | 61.4 | 60.9 | 62.3 | 62.8 |
| Center Cropping (3) | 69.1 | 62.9 | 63.8 | 65.3 | 65.6 |
| RAM [13] (3) | 69.4 | 63.8 | 65.0 | 67.3 | 67.5 |
| CAM [11] (2) | 68.5 | 65.1 | 65.3 | 67.1 | 66.2 |
| NTS [8] (3) | 70.3 | 68.1 | 68.2 | 68.9 | 69.4 |
| STN [14] (1) | 68.1 | 64.1 | 64.1 | 65.9 | 64.8 |
| SSN [9] (2) | 68.4 | 64.8 | 65.1 | 67.0 | 65.9 |
| CAM+SSN (2) | 69.4 | 66.5 | 66.3 | 67.8 | 68.0 |
| S3Ns [10] (3) | 70.8 | 68.5 | 68.4 | 69.3 | 70.0 |
| IASN (Ours) (3) | **72.8** | **71.1** | **71.0** | **71.9** | **71.9** |

As shown in Table 3, with the same or even less backbone numbers, the attention-based methods outperform the method without attention (i.e., center cropping). It demonstrates that paying attention to the discriminative regions automatically is beneficial for skin-disease image classification. Among the attention-based uniformed sampling methods, NTS [8] achieves the best performance. However, the NTS [8] can't outperform the state-of-the-art non-uniformed sampling methods. This may be because the cropping operation in NTS usually neglects the body parts of skin-disease images, which limits the performance of it.

Among the attention-based non-uniformed sampling methods, the CAM+SSN has an improvement over the SSN [9], indicating that the class activation based attention is more effective than the class-agnostic attention used in SSN [9]. Compared with the class activation map, the sparse attention introduced in S3Ns [10] has a better performance, because the sparse attention pays more attention to the object parts. Our IASN can further have an evident improvement over the S3Ns [10]. Compared with the Gaussian function used in S3Ns [10] to estimate the attention distribution, our IASN models the attention by computing the interaction between the local peak and its context, which is more flexible and more related to the skin-disease regions.

**Table 4.** Comparison to the skin-disease classification approaches on the SD-198 dataset in terms of classification accuracy. "J-Doctor" is the recognition accuracy of junior dermatologists.

| Method | SIFT [2] | CN [2] | VGG+ft [2] | J-Doctor [3] | TCA [3] | HLPI [15] | RFWD [4] | Ours |
|--------|----------|--------|------------|--------------|---------|-----------|----------|------|
| Acc | 25.9 | 20.2 | 50.3 | 52.0 | 56.5 | 59.5 | 70.5 | **71.9** |

**Table 5.** Comparison to the SPBL algorithm on the SD-198 dataset. It conducted experiments in a different training/testing set partition, which is 8:2.

| Method | Precision | Recall | F1 | $M_{AUC}$ | Acc |
|--------|-----------|--------|----|-----------|-----|
| SPBL [5] | $71.4 \pm 1.7$ | $65.7 \pm 1.6$ | $66.2 \pm 1.6$ | $68.5 \pm 1.6$ | $67.8 \pm 1.8$ |
| Ours | $\mathbf{71.9 \pm 0.8}$ | $\mathbf{70.0 \pm 0.9}$ | $\mathbf{68.6 \pm 0.7}$ | $\mathbf{71.5 \pm 0.7}$ | $\mathbf{70.7 \pm 0.8}$ |

**Comparison to Skin-Disease Classification Methods.** The IASN is also compared with the state-of-the-art skin-disease classification approaches on the SD-198 dataset, and the comparison results are tabulated in Table 4 and Table 5. The RFWD [4] crawled 80 thousand web images for the SD-198 training set, and employed a progressive method for filtering the noisy data. Our IASN outperforms the RFWD [4] by 1.4%. It indicates that our networks can learn representative features from the attention-based re-sampled images.

The SPBL algorithm proposed by [5], addressed the class imbalance problem in clinical skin-disease images. The SPBL conducted experiments in a training/testing set partition of 8:2, which is different from the standard split of 1:1 provided by the SD-198. For a fair comparison, we also implement five cross-validation experiments with a training/testing split of 8:2. The results of the mean and the variance are reported in Table 5. Our IASN has a considerable gain against the SPBL [5] in terms of all evaluation metrics, which demonstrates the effectiveness of our method.

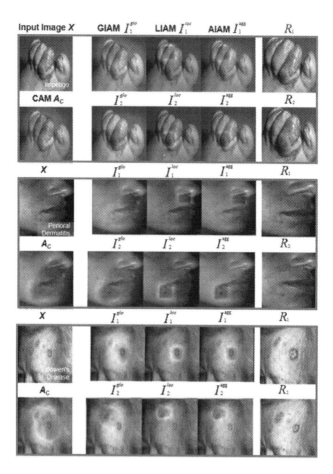

**Fig. 3.** Visualization results on the SD-198 dataset.

## 4.5 Qualitative Results

In Fig. 3, for each example, we show the three kinds of interactive attention maps for the top-2 local peaks $P_1$ and $P_2$ in rows 1 and 2, respectively. It can be observed that the collected local peaks represent different visual clues, and the global interactive attention can selectively localize the regions with similar semantics to the local peaks. Meanwhile, the local interactive attention can adaptively model the attention for the local region around the peak. Furthermore, the aggregated interactive attention provides more information, and is used for non-uniform sampling.

## 5    Conclusion

This paper proposes a Interactive Attention Sampling Network (IASN) for addressing the challenge of clinical skin-disease image classification. The IASN learns interactive attention, which can effectively localize the important regions for skin-disease classification. The attended regions are sampled into high resolution, which provides more details of the skin diseases, and helps the model learn representative features. The experimental results show that the proposed IASN is effective and outperforms other state-of-the-art methods on clinical skin-disease image classification.

# References

1. Lim, H.W., et al.: The burden of skin disease in the united states. J. Am. Acad. Dermatol. **76**(5), 958–972 (2017)
2. Sun, X., Yang, J., Sun, M., Wang, K.: A benchmark for automatic visual classification of clinical skin disease images. In: Leibe, B., Matas, J., Sebe, N., Welling, M. (eds.) ECCV 2016. LNCS, vol. 9910, pp. 206–222. Springer, Cham (2016). https://doi.org/10.1007/978-3-319-46466-4_13
3. Yang, J., Sun, X., Liang, J., Rosin, P.L.: Clinical skin lesion diagnosis using representations inspired by dermatologist criteria. In: 2018 IEEE/CVF Conference on Computer Vision and Pattern Recognition, June 2018, pp. 1258–1266 (2018)
4. Yang, J., Sun, X., Lai, Y., Zheng, L., Cheng, M.: Recognition from web data: a progressive filtering approach. IEEE Trans. Image Process. **27**(11), 5303–5315 (2018)
5. Yang, J., et al.: Self-paced balance learning for clinical skin disease recognition. IEEE Trans. Neural Netw. Learn. Syst. **31**, 2832–2846 (2019)
6. Rensink, R.A.: The dynamic representation of scenes. Vis. Cogn. **7**(1–3), 17–42 (2000)
7. Mnih, V., Heess, N., Graves, A., Kavukcuoglu, K.: Recurrent models of visual attention. In: Proceedings of the 27th International Conference on Neural Information Processing Systems - Volume 2, ser, NIPS 2014, pp. 2204–2212. MIT Press, Cambridge (2014). http://dl.acm.org/citation.cfm?id=2969033.2969073
8. Yang, Z., Luo, T., Wang, D., Hu, Z., Gao, J., Wang, L.: Learning to navigate for fine-grained classification. In: Ferrari, V., Hebert, M., Sminchisescu, C., Weiss, Y. (eds.) Computer Vision – ECCV 2018. LNCS, vol. 11218, pp. 438–454. Springer, Cham (2018). https://doi.org/10.1007/978-3-030-01264-9_26
9. Recasens, A., Kellnhofer, P., Stent, S., Matusik, W., Torralba, A.: Learning to zoom: a saliency-based sampling layer for neural networks. In: Ferrari, V., Hebert, M., Sminchisescu, C., Weiss, Y. (eds.) ECCV 2018. LNCS, vol. 11213, pp. 52–67. Springer, Cham (2018). https://doi.org/10.1007/978-3-030-01240-3_4
10. Ding, Y., Zhou, Y., Zhu, Y., Ye, Q., Jiao, J.: Selective sparse sampling for fine-grained image recognition. In: 2019 IEEE/CVF International Conference on Computer Vision (ICCV), pp. 6598–6607 (2019)
11. Zhou, B., Khosla, A., Lapedriza, A., Oliva, A., Torralba, A.: Learning deep features for discriminative localization. In: 2016 IEEE Conference on Computer Vision and Pattern Recognition (CVPR), pp. 2921–2929 (2016)
12. He, K., Zhang, X., Ren, S., Sun, J.: Deep residual learning for image recognition. In: 2016 IEEE Conference on Computer Vision and Pattern Recognition (CVPR), June 2016, pp. 770–778 (2016)
13. Sermanet, P., Frome, A., Real, E.: Attention for fine-grained categorization. In: International Conference on Learning Representations (2015)

14. Jaderberg, M., Simonyan, K., Zisserman, A., Kavukcuoglu, K.: Spatial transformer networks. CoRR, vol. abs/1506.02025 (2015). http://arxiv.org/abs/1506.02025
15. Lin, J., Guo, Z., Li, D., Hu, X., Zhang, Y.: Automatic classification of clinical skin disease images with additional high-level position information. In: 2019 Chinese Control Conference (CCC), pp. 8606–8610 (2019)

# Cross-modality Attention Method for Medical Image Enhancement

Zebin Hu[1], Hao Liu[1,2(✉)], Zhendong Li[1,2], and Zekuan Yu[3]

[1] School of Information Engineering, Ningxia University, Yinchuan 750021, China
liuhao@nxu.edu.cn, lizhendong13@mails.ucas.ac.cn
[2] Collaborative Innovation Center for Ningxia Big Data and Artificial Intelligence
Co-founded by Ningxia Municipality and Ministry of Education,
Yinchuan 750021, China
[3] Academy for Engineering and Technology, Fudan University,
Shanghai 200433, China
yzk@fudan.edu.cn

**Abstract.** In this paper, we propose a cross-modality attention method (CMAM) for medical image enhancement especially in magnetic resonance imaging, which typically addresses the issue of exploiting the clean feature by generative model. To realize this goal, we distill the complementary information directly from different modalities of raw input images for reliable image generation. More specifically, our method integrates local features with exploiting the semantic high-order dependencies and thus explores attentional fields for robust feature representation learning. To evaluate the effectiveness of our CMAM, we conduct folds of experiments on the standard benchmark Brats 2019 dataset and experimental results demonstrate the effectiveness of CMAM.

**Keywords:** Cross-modality learning · Generative adversarial model · Self-attention · Medical imaging

## 1 Introduction

With the number of patients with brain tumors increasing rapidly in recent years, GLIOMAS has the highest mortality rate and prevalence in kinds of brain tumors [2]. The treatment of GLIOMAS includes surgery, chemotherapy, radiotherapy, or a combination of them [27]. Magnetic resonance imaging (MRI) is useful to assess GLIOMAS in clinical practice, since it shows the focus of soft tissue clearly [8,26]. Different MR modalities, such as T1, T2, T1 with contrast enhanced (T1ce) and Fluid Attenuation Inversion Recover (FLAIR) emphasize different types of biological information and tissue properties [1]. Specifically, T2 and FLAIR MRI indicate differences in tissue water relaxational properties, where T1ce MRI shows pathological through using contrast agents in tumor area [21]. They are always used simultaneously to diagnose brain tumors. Presently, the

This is a student paper.

© Springer Nature Switzerland AG 2021
H. Ma et al. (Eds.): PRCV 2021, LNCS 13021, pp. 411–423, 2021.
https://doi.org/10.1007/978-3-030-88010-1_34

absence of modality is an impending instance that undergoes the difficulty of the tumor diagnosing. However, it's hard to obtain T2-MRI which is crucial to the diagnosing of brain tumors. Therefore, cross modality synthesis of medical images is an emerging topic.

In these years, deep learning has been applied in many fields which is benefited from datasets and high computing power [16]. However, it is very difficult to collect large scale training samples in medical image, which leads to the performance bottleneck of deep learning methods in [19,20,22,23,25,30]. To solve this problem, Ian Goodfellow *et al.* [10] carefully designed generative adversarial networks (GANs) which synthesizes images from noise and then uses it for training to improve the performance by deep learning. Besides, most methods used CycleGAN to generate images from one modality to another one by learning the one-to-one mapping of pictures, which achieves promising performance [9,18,34]. However, in the context of image generation, features of the tumor area are usually distorted inevitably and undergo ambiguity, which likely causes the low quality of the synthetic images. In this work, the core problem is to improve the quality of the synthetic images and the diagnosis effectiveness.

To address the aforementioned issues, we introduce the attention mechanism to select important features, which is also effective in improving the quality of the synthetic images. The attention mechanism enforces the model to focus on important features and meanwhile ignore irrelevant details by learning the weight distribution based on feature maps. Nowadays, the attention mechanism shows superior performance in many different research fields [7,11,13], which has also been adopted in medical image analysis. Nevertheless, utilizing the simple attention technique can hardly model the nonlinear and high-order dependency between medical image regions. For example, Zhao *et al.* [34] used a self-attention to enhance the feature of tumor and improve the performance of tumor detection. Lei *et al.* [17] proposed a deep attention fully convolution network to pay more attention to prostate boundary for improving segmentation result of segmentation of the prostate on computed tomography(CT). In general, the distortion of the high-level feature can teach deep attention networks to focus on mistaken areas without supervisions. To solve this problem, Zhao *et al.* [34] introduced a tumor detection in the entire architecture and Lei *et al.* [17] combined a tumor segmentation to supervise the entire network. While encouraging performance has been obtained, these methods require a large number of additional labels. Meanwhile, these methods focus on the attention of single modality which ignore the correlation of two modalities, thus it cannot restrain noises in produced images without auxiliary labels.

In this paper, we propose a cross-modality attention method to fully exploit the correlation of two modalities. Due to the presence of noise in the synthesized image, we calculate the attention map of the original modality by introducing the attention mechanism mentioned above and perform a dot multiplication with the target modality. By doing this, we enhance the region of tumor and inhibit noises in synthetic images by utilizing the self-similarity of the source images. More specifically, we present an image-to-image cross-modality attention method which captures the most important region of the source images. Then we transform the attention map to the synthetic image. Finally, we evaluate the method in the standard benchmark database Brats 2019, which is typically used for brain tumor segmentation. Benefitting from the cross-modality attention map, our model enhances the important details of the tumor area and reduces artifacts in other areas.

## 2 Related Work

**Medical Image Generation.** Recently, medical image generation has become a popular issue due to the high costs of obtaining medical images that shows anatomically important features such as tumor areas. Earlier studies put forward a patch-based non-linear regression using random forests [14] and location-sensitive neural networks [28], which achieves the mapping from source to target. However, patch-based methods are unable to resolve the inconsistency between patches since they cannot take full advantage of the dependencies between patches. The generative adversarial network has demonstrated great performance in medical image generation since it was proposed by Goodfellow *et al.* [10]. After that, GAN-based models have been successfully applied to kinds of tasks including data augmentation [4–6] and image synthesis [3,12,33]. Nevertheless, as the traditional GAN has failed to meet the gradually higher application requirements, CycleGAN has recently begun to attract the attention of researchers.In 2019, Welander *et al.* [31] developed a CycleGAN-based method to synthesis T1 MRI and T2 MRI. However, the results of CycleGAN undergo noise because features will produce spatial deformation when learning the mapping between two sources of data. Different from that, our proposed method fuses the CycleGAN with cross-modality attention to relieve unexpected noise.

**Attention-Based Models.** Since Vaswani *et al.* [29] proposed to use the self-attention mechanism to draw global dependencies of inputs in machine translation, the attention mechanism has been widely used in various deep learning-based tasks. For example, Zhao *et al.* [34] used self-attention in generator to capture the relationships between the tumor area and other tissues with auxiliary labels, Yu *et al.* [32] developed an edge detector in GAN dubbed Ea-GANs to exploit contextual information constraint high-level feature learning. However, these methods need a large number of auxiliary labels or an additional algorithm to constraint high-level feature learning, which cannot explicitly model the spatial consistency in paired medical images. To fully exploit the dependencies between different modalities in the medical image, we propose an image-to-image cross-modality attention method. Besides, our proposed model is readily plugged into the attention-based models to solve the problem of noise in medical image generation.

## 3    Method

The overview of network framework is illustrated in Fig. 1. Our model consists of two stages: In the first stage, we use paired T1ce MRI and T2 MRI as input images. CycleGAN uses these images as groundtruth in the training stage which could intuitively generate better synthetic images, since the model then has more information about how the generated image should appear. In the second stage, we fixed the weights of CycleGAN, then used it to generate synthetic T2 MRI from T1ce MRI. Then, input synthetic T2 MRI in the cross-modality attention method to realize image enhancement, as detailed in Fig. 2.

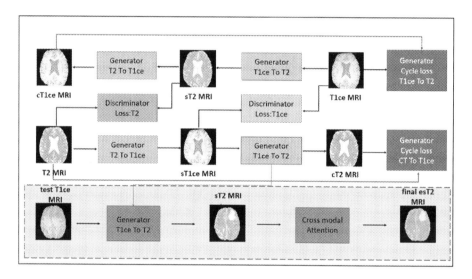

**Fig. 1.** Schematic flow chart of the proposed algorithm for t1ce-MRI-based synthetic enhanced T2 MRI which consists of CycleGAN (the upper method) and Cross-modality Attention method (the following method).

### 3.1    The Architecture of CycleGAN

The proposed CycleGAN model consists of a training stage and a synthesizing stage. For a given pair of T1ce MRI and T2 MRI, the T2 MRI is used as a deep learning based target of the T1ce MRI. In the training stage, a 2D image is cropped to the same size $(160 * 160 * 1)$ for removing the excess black background. Then, the cropped images are fed into the generator (T1ce MRI to T2 MRI) to get equal-sized synthetic T2 MRI, which is called sT2 MRI. The sT2 MRI is then fed into another generator (T2 MRI to T1ce MRI), creating a synthetic T1ce MRI which termed as the reconstructed T1ce MRI. Similarly, in order to enforce forward-backward consistency, the cropped T2 MR images are fed into the two generators in the opposite order first to create a synthetic T1ce

MRI and reconstruct T2 MRI. Then two discriminators are used to judge the authenticity of synthetic and cycle images.

Typically, the mean absolute error (MAE) is used as generator loss function between the original images and the synthetic images. The discriminator loss is computed by MAE between the discriminator results of input synthetic and real images. To update all the hidden layers parameters, the Adam gradient descent method was applied to minimize both generator loss and discriminator loss. In synthesizing stage, cropped T1ce MRI are fed into the T1ce MRI to T2 MRI generator which weights are fixed after training to obtain the sT2 MRI.

### 3.2   Cross-modality Attention Method (CMAM)

As introduced earlier, synthetic images generated by CycleGAN would damage the information of the source image. This limits the performance of downstream tasks like segmentation and classification. Thus, we propose a cross-modality attention method which consists of position attention method (PAM) and channel attention method (CAM) to relive this problem. Figure 2 depicts all details about these methods.

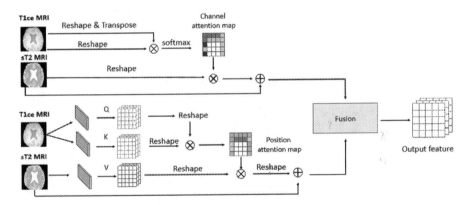

**Fig. 2.** The detail of Cross-modality Attention method. Upper method depicts the architecture of Channel attention method (CAM), the following method depicts the architecture of Position attention method (PAM).

**Position Attention Method (PAM):** The detail of PAM is depicted at the nether of Fig. 2. We denote an input feature map of T1ce MRI as $F^{p_1} \in R^{C \times W \times H}$ to the position attention method, where $C, W, H$ represent the channel, width and height dimensions respectively. In the first branch, $F$ is passed through a convolutional block, resulting in a feature map $F^{p_1 q} \in R^{C_1 \times W \times H}$ called query of $F^{p_1}$, where $C_1$ denotes $C/8$. Then, In the second branch, $F^{p_1 q}$ is reshaped to a feature map of shape $W \times H \times C_1$. In the second branch, $F$ is passed through an uniform convolutional block and then transpose as $F^{p_1 k} \in R^{C_1 \times W \times H}$ called key of $F^{P_1}$. Both maps are multiplied and softmax is applied on the resulted matrix to generate the position attention map $A^{P_1} \in R^{(W \times H) \times (W \times H)}$:

$$A_{i,j}^{P_1} = \frac{\exp\left(F_i^{p_1 q} \cdot F_j^{p_1 k}\right)}{\sum_{i=1}^{W \times H} \exp\left(F_i^{p_1 q} \cdot F_j^{p_1 k}\right)} \tag{1}$$

where $A_{i,j}^{P}$ denote the impact of the $i^{th}$ position to the $j^{th}$ position. The input $F^{p_2}$ denotes feature map of sT2 MRI, in the third branch, $F^{p_2}$ is fed into a different convolutional, resulting in $F^{p_2} \in R^{C \times W \times H}$, which has the same shape as $F^{p_1}$. Then it is multiplied by a permuted version of the spatial attention map S, whose output is reshaped to a $R^{C \times W \times H}$. The attention feature map corresponding to the position attention method called $F_{PAM}$, which can be formulated as follows:

$$F_{PAM,j} = \alpha_p \sum_{i=1}^{W \times H} A_{i,j}^{P_1} F_j^{p_2} + F^{p_2} \tag{2}$$

where $\alpha_p$ is initialized to 0 and it is gradually learned to give more importance to the position attention map. The final $F_{PAM}$ at each position is a weighted sum of the features at all positions and the original feature $F^{p_2}$. Therefore, it has a global contextual view and selectively aggregates contexts according to the global attention map.

**Channel Attention Method (CAM):** The detail of CAM is depicted at the upper of Fig. 2. We denote an input feature map of T1ce MRI as $F^{c_1} \in R^{C \times W \times H}$ to the channel attention method. Firstly, $F^{c_1}$ is reshaped in the first two branch which produces the query ($F^{c_1 q} \in R^{W \times H \times C}$) and the key ($F^{c_1 k} \in R^{C \times W \times H}$) of $F^{c_1}$. Secondly, we perform a matrix multiplication between $F^{c_1 q}$ and $F^{c_1 k}$ to obtain the channel attention map $A^{c_1} \in R^{C \times C}$ as:

$$A_{i,j}^{C_1} = \frac{\exp\left(F_i^{c_1 q} \cdot F_j^{c_1 k}\right)}{\sum_{i=1}^{C} \exp\left(F_i^{c_1 q} \cdot F_j^{c_1 k}\right)} \tag{3}$$

where $A_{i,j}^{C_1}$ measures the impact of $i^{th}$ channel on $j^{th}$ channel. Thirdly, we denote the input sT2 MRI as $F^{c_2} \in R^{C \times W \times H}$ and then perform a matrix multiplication between the transpose of $A_{i,j}^{C_1}$ and $F^{c_2}$. By the way, the result is reshaped to $R^{C \times W \times H}$. Lastly, we multiply the result by a scale parameter $\alpha_c$ and use an execution element summation operation to get the final output $F_{CAM}$:

$$F_{CAM,j} = \alpha_c \sum_{i=1}^{C} A_{i,j}^{C_1} F_j^{c_2} + F^{c_2} \tag{4}$$

where $\alpha_c$ is initialized as 0 and gradually increase weight through learning. The $F_{CAM}$ shows the final feature of each channel is a weighted sum of the features of all channels and original features, it boosts feature discriminability.

**Fusion**: Similarly, we apply the sequential convolutional block of PAM and CAM, which specifically emphasizes the information of some important regions in both channel and position. Meanwhile, this method will mask out irrelevant noise. In this way, we could repair the destruction of synthetic image in Cycle-GAN. We denote the final fusion feature map as $F_{fusion}$:

$$F_{fusion} = conv_1(F_{PAM} + F_{CAM}) \times conv_2(F^{c_2}) \tag{5}$$

**Loss Function:** Similar to traditional methods of image generation and image restoration, we adopt the pixel-wise loss in this paper. A universal loss to guide the method to generate synthetic T2 MRI as close to T2 MRI is the pixel-wise mean absolute error (MAE). Recently, more and more studies suggest that incorporation of a perceptual loss during network training can yield visually more realistic results in computer vision tasks. Unlike loss functions based on pixel-wise differences, perceptual loss relies on differences in higher feature representations that are often extracted from networks pre-trained for more generic tasks [15]. A commonly used network is VGG-net which trained on the ImageNet [24] dataset for object classification. Here, following [15], we extracted feature maps right before the second max-pooling operation of VGG16 pre-trained on ImageNet. The aggregate loss function can be written as:

$$L_{aggregate} = E_{F_{T2}, F_{output}} \left[ \|F_{T2} - F_{output}\|_1 + \|V(F_{T2}) - F_{output}\|_1 \right] \tag{6}$$

where $F_{output}$ denote synthetic T2 MRI which produce by image-to-image cross attention modality method. $F_{T2}$ denote T2 MRI groundtruth, $V$ is the set of feature maps extracted from VGG16.

The primary advantages of the image-to-image cross modality method are three-fold: 1) PAM and CAM methods enhance the ability to extract features by modeling the interdependencies between channels and encoding global contextual information into local features. 2) The ideology of image-to-image cross modality increases the weight of feature of T1ce MRI which is most important. Then multiply the feature map of synthetic T2 MRI by the attention map of T1ce MRI, in this way, some feature noise in synthetic T2 MRI will be relived. 3) After the training stage of CycleGAN and image-to-image cross attention modality method, only need to input the T1ce MRI the network that generate synthetic T2 MRI without damaging feature.

## 4 Experiments and Results

### 4.1 Evaluation Dataset and Implementation Details

The dataset used in the evaluation is provided by the Brats 2019. The experimental dataset we used totaling 1368 subjects, and each subject has corresponding T1ce MRI and T2 MRI. In particular, the error of the magnetic resonance sequence is tiny which can be ignored. The data were split into a training set of

1079 images in each domain. The remaining 289 images, in each domain, were used for testing. All images are resized as 160 * 160 before training.

CycleGAN is implemented in Tensorflow[1] with Adam optimizer, image-to-image cross attention modality method is implemented in Pytorch with Adam optimizer. All methods were trained and tested on 1 NVIDIA Tesla V100 with 32 GB of memory for each GPU. In the stage of training CycleGAN method, we set the epoch as 196, batch size as 1 which causes the training time increase to 10 h. In this way, the CycleGAN method could generate the synthetic T2 MRI from T1ce MRI better. In the stage of training cross modality attention method, we set the epoch as 200, batch size as 1, and the training time is about 2 h.

## 4.2   Results and Analysis

To validate the individual contribution of different components to the performance of enhancement, we perform an ablation experiment under different settings. We test the CycleGAN method without CMAM and CycleGAN+CMAM in 5 patients which consist of 289 images. Besides, We test the pix-to-pix Cycle-GAN in our dataset [35]. We employ two measurements to evaluate the synthesis performance of the proposed CycleGAN and CMAM in comparison: the mean absolute error (MAE) and peak-signal-to-noise ratio (PSNR) to compare the output images of CylceGAN with the output images of CMAM. The result of the MAE comparison is depicted in Fig. 3. The result of the PSNR comparison is depicted in Fig. 4.

**Table 1.** Comparisons between our proposed method with different approaches of MAE and PSNR (Data in the table denotes the average value and standard deviation of the test dataset.)

| Method | MAE | PSNR |
|---|---|---|
| pix2pix | $47.47 \pm 7.09$ | $34.50 \pm 1.03$ |
| CycleGAN | $41.79 \pm 6.24$ | $35.20 \pm 0.58$ |
| CycleGAN+CMAM | $\mathbf{39.40 \pm 5.45}$ | $\mathbf{34.68 \pm 1.06}$ |

As the figure shows, MAE is boosted clearly after the synthetic T2 MRI through the CMAM. Meanwhile, the value of PSNR is reduce by the operation of CMAM, we conclude that some feature which is not important like tiny streaks of soft tissue is restrained after analyzing this situation. However, this instance also proves that CMAM could enhance important features while suppressing unimportant features.

In the total test dataset, we employ an ablation experiment in each method, the measurable indicators is the mean absolute error (MAE) and peak-signal-to-noise ratio (PSNR), complete detail show in Table 1. To demonstrate the

---

[1] https://github.com/tensorflow/tensorflow.

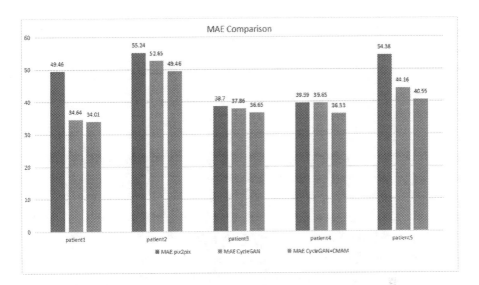

**Fig. 3.** The column map depicts the MAE comparison of only CycleGAN and Cycle-GAN+cross modality attention method. Blue denotes generate sT2 MRI by pix-to-pix CycleGAN, orange denotes generate sT2 MRI by only CycleGAN, orange column denotes generate sT2 MRI by CycleGAN+CMAM. MAE is reduced after adding CMAM. (Color figure online)

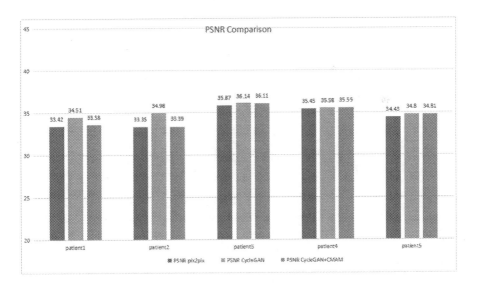

**Fig. 4.** The column map depicts the PSNR comparison of only CycleGAN and Cycle-GAN+cross modality attention method. Blue column denotes generate sT2 MRI by pix-to-pix CycleGAN, orange column denotes generate sT2 MRI by only CycleGAN, gray column denotes generate sT2 MRI by CycleGAN+CMAM. As CMAM restrains the features of tiny streaks of soft tissue, PSNR drops a bit. (Color figure online)

effectiveness of our image-to-image cross-modality attention method with regard to subjective quality, a demonstrated example is shown in Fig. 5. As Fig. 5 shows, the synthetic T2 MRI (sT2 MRI) from CycleGAN has some noise in white which may result in clinical diagnosis errors. To solve this problem, the CMAM method restrains noise generation by enhancing the feature in the region of focus and restraining the feature in an unimportant region like tiny streaks of soft tissue, the result of CMAM is shown as enhancement sT2 MRI (esT2 MRI).

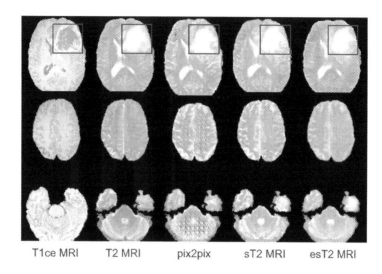

**Fig. 5.** The example of different modalities from a single case. From left to right input T1ce MRI, T2 MRI, synthetic T2 MRI from pix-to-pixCycleGAN, synthetic T2 MRI from CycleGAN and enhanced synthetic T2 MRI from CycleGAN+CMAM. (Zoomed in for better visualization).

## 5    Conclusion

In this paper, we have proposed an image-to-image cross-modality attention method. By taking both nonlinear correlation and high-order dependencies into consideration, our method has explicitly exploit inherent spatial information between paired multimodal medical images, which addresses the problem that synthetic images from CycleGAN would generate noise. With our model, the feature of tumor reinforces the diagnosis of brain tumors. Experimental results have demonstrated the effectiveness of the proposed method. In the future, we will focus on the medical image generation method which integrated multi-view and multi-modal information, which solves the problem 2D medical image generation cannot exploit 3D information and 3D medical image generation need high computing power.

**Acknowledgement.** This work was supported in part by the National Science Foundation of China under Grant 61806104 and 62076142, in part by the West Light Talent Program of the Chinese Academy of Sciences under Grant XAB2018AW05, and in part by the Youth Science and Technology Talents Enrollment Projects of Ningxia under Grant TJGC2018028.

# References

1. Aisen, A.M., Martel, W., Braunstein, E.M., McMillin, K.I., Phillips, W.A., Kling, T.: MRI and CT evaluation of primary bone and soft-tissue tumors. Am. J. Roentgenol. **146**(4), 749–756 (1986)
2. Bauer, S., Wiest, R., Nolte, L.P., Reyes, M.: A survey of MRI-based medical image analysis for brain tumor studies. Phys. Med. Biol. **58**(13), R97 (2013)
3. Beers, A., et al.: High-resolution medical image synthesis using progressively grown generative adversarial networks. arXiv preprint arXiv:1805.03144 (2018)
4. Bermudez, C., Plassard, A.J., Davis, L.T., Newton, A.T., Resnick, S.M., Landman, B.A.: Learning implicit brain MRI manifolds with deep learning. In: Medical Imaging: Image Processing, vol. 10574, p. 105741L (2018)
5. Bowles, C., et al.: GAN augmentation: augmenting training data using generative adversarial networks. arXiv preprint arXiv:1810.10863 (2018)
6. Calimeri, F., Marzullo, A., Stamile, C., Terracina, G.: Biomedical data augmentation using generative adversarial neural networks. In: Lintas, A., Rovetta, S., Verschure, P.F.M.J., Villa, A.E.P. (eds.) ICANN 2017. LNCS, vol. 10614, pp. 626–634. Springer, Cham (2017). https://doi.org/10.1007/978-3-319-68612-7_71
7. Chen, S., Tan, X., Wang, B., Hu, X.: Reverse attention for salient object detection. In: Ferrari, V., Hebert, M., Sminchisescu, C., Weiss, Y. (eds.) ECCV 2018. LNCS, vol. 11213, pp. 236–252. Springer, Cham (2018). https://doi.org/10.1007/978-3-030-01240-3_15
8. Devic, S.: MRI simulation for radiotherapy treatment planning. Med. Phys. **39**(11), 6701–6711 (2012)
9. Dong, X., et al.: Synthetic MRI-aided multi-organ segmentation on male pelvic CT using cycle consistent deep attention network. Radiother. Oncol. **141**, 192–199 (2019)
10. Goodfellow, I.J., et al.: Generative adversarial nets. In: Neural Information Processing Systems (2014)
11. Gupta, A., Agrawal, D., Chauhan, H., Dolz, J., Pedersoli, M.: An attention model for group-level emotion recognition. In: ACM International Conference on Multimodal Interaction, pp. 611–615 (2018)
12. Han, Z., Wei, B., Mercado, A., Leung, S., Li, S.: Spine-GAN: semantic segmentation of multiple spinal structures. Med. Image Anal. **50**, 23–35 (2018)
13. Huang, Z., Zhong, Z., Sun, L., Huo, Q.: Mask R-CNN with pyramid attention network for scene text detection. In: IEEE Winter Conference on Applications of Computer Vision, pp. 764–772 (2019)
14. Jog, A., Carass, A., Roy, S., Pham, D.L., Prince, J.L.: MR image synthesis by contrast learning on neighborhood ensembles. Med. Image Anal. **24**(1), 63–76 (2015)

15. Johnson, J., Alahi, A., Fei-Fei, L.: Perceptual losses for real-time style transfer and super-resolution. In: Leibe, B., Matas, J., Sebe, N., Welling, M. (eds.) ECCV 2016. LNCS, vol. 9906, pp. 694–711. Springer, Cham (2016). https://doi.org/10.1007/978-3-319-46475-6_43

16. LeCun, Y., Bengio, Y., Hinton, G.: Deep learning. Nature **521**(7553), 436–444 (2015)

17. Lei, Y., et al.: CT prostate segmentation based on synthetic MRI-aided deep attention fully convolution network. Med. Phys. **47**(2), 530–540 (2020)

18. Lei, Y., et al.: MRI-only based synthetic CT generation using dense cycle consistent generative adversarial networks. Med. Phys. **46**(8), 3565–3581 (2019)

19. Li, C., et al.: Attention based hierarchical aggregation network for 3D left atrial segmentation. In: Pop, M., et al. (eds.) STACOM 2018. LNCS, vol. 11395, pp. 255–264. Springer, Cham (2019). https://doi.org/10.1007/978-3-030-12029-0_28

20. Litjens, G., et al.: A survey on deep learning in medical image analysis. Med. Image Anal. **42**, 60–88 (2017)

21. Menze, B.H., et al.: The multimodal brain tumor image segmentation benchmark (BRATS). IEEE Trans. Med. Imaging **34**(10), 1993–2024 (2014)

22. Nie, D., Gao, Y., Wang, L., Shen, D.: ASDNet: attention based semi-supervised deep networks for medical image segmentation. In: Frangi, A.F., Schnabel, J.A., Davatzikos, C., Alberola-López, C., Fichtinger, G. (eds.) MICCAI 2018. LNCS, vol. 11073, pp. 370–378. Springer, Cham (2018). https://doi.org/10.1007/978-3-030-00937-3_43

23. Roy, A.G., Navab, N., Wachinger, C.: Concurrent spatial and channel 'squeeze & excitation' in fully convolutional networks. In: Frangi, A.F., Schnabel, J.A., Davatzikos, C., Alberola-López, C., Fichtinger, G. (eds.) MICCAI 2018. LNCS, vol. 11070, pp. 421–429. Springer, Cham (2018). https://doi.org/10.1007/978-3-030-00928-1_48

24. Russakovsky, O., et al.: ImageNet large scale visual recognition challenge. Int. J. Comput. Vision **115**(3), 211–252 (2015)

25. Schlemper, J., et al.: Attention gated networks: learning to leverage salient regions in medical images. Med. Image Anal. **53**, 197–207 (2019)

26. Schmidt, M.A., Payne, G.S.: Radiotherapy planning using MRI. Phys. Med. Biol. **60**(22), R323 (2015)

27. Tabatabai, G., et al.: Molecular diagnostics of gliomas: the clinical perspective. Acta Neuropathol. **120**(5), 585–592 (2010)

28. Van Nguyen, H., Zhou, K., Vemulapalli, R.: Cross-domain synthesis of medical images using efficient location-sensitive deep network. In: Navab, N., Hornegger, J., Wells, W.M., Frangi, A.F. (eds.) MICCAI 2015. LNCS, vol. 9349, pp. 677–684. Springer, Cham (2015). https://doi.org/10.1007/978-3-319-24553-9_83

29. Vaswani, A., et al.: Attention is all you need. In: Neural Information Processing Systems (2017)

30. Wang, Y., et al.: Deep attentional features for prostate segmentation in ultrasound. In: Frangi, A.F., Schnabel, J.A., Davatzikos, C., Alberola-López, C., Fichtinger, G. (eds.) MICCAI 2018. LNCS, vol. 11073, pp. 523–530. Springer, Cham (2018). https://doi.org/10.1007/978-3-030-00937-3_60

31. Welander, P., Karlsson, S., Eklund, A.: Generative adversarial networks for image-to-image translation on multi-contrast MR images-a comparison of CycleGAN and UNIT. arXiv preprint arXiv:1806.07777 (2018)

32. Yu, B., Zhou, L., Wang, L., Shi, Y., Fripp, J., Bourgeat, P.: Ea-GANs: edge-aware generative adversarial networks for cross-modality MR image synthesis. IEEE Trans. Med. Imaging **38**(7), 1750–1762 (2019)

33. Zhao, H., Li, H., Maurer-Stroh, S., Cheng, L.: Synthesizing retinal and neuronal images with generative adversarial nets. Med. Image Anal. **49**, 14–26 (2018)
34. Zhao, J., et al.: Tripartite-GAN: synthesizing liver contrast-enhanced MRI to improve tumor detection. Med. Image Anal. **63**, 101667 (2020)
35. Zhu, J.Y., Park, T., Isola, P., Efros, A.A.: Unpaired image-to-image translation using cycle-consistent adversarial networks. In: The IEEE International Conference on Computer Vision, pp. 2223–2232 (2017)

# Multi-modal Face Anti-spoofing Based on a Single Image

Quan Zhang[1,3], Zexiang Liao[1], Yuezhen Huang[2]([✉]), and Jianhuang Lai[1,3,4]

[1] The School of Computer Science and Engineering, Sun Yat-Sen University,
Guangzhou 510006, China
{zhangq48,liaozx5}@mail2.sysu.edu.cn, stsljh@mail.sysu.edu.cn
[2] Guangzhou Radio Group Co., Ltd., Guangzhou, China
huangyz@grg.net.cn
[3] The Guangdong Key Laboratory of Information Security Technology,
Guangzhou 510006, China
[4] The Key Laboratory of Machine Intelligence and Advanced Computing,
Ministry of Education China, Guangzhou, China

**Abstract.** Using multi-modal data, such as VIS, IR and Depth, for face anti-spoofing (FAS) is a robust and effective method, because complementary information between different modalities can better against various attacks. However, multi-modal data is difficult to obtain in application scenarios due to high costs, which makes the model trained with multi-modal data unavailable in the testing stage. We define this phenomenon as train-test inconsistency problem, which is ignored by most existing methods. To this end, we propose a novel multi-modal face anti-spoofing framework (GFF), which adopt multi-modal data during training, and only use a single modality during testing to simulate multi-modal input. Specifically, GFF is a two-step framework. In the step I, we adopt the GAN model to fit the face images distribution of different modalities, and learn the transform strategies between different distributions, so as to realize the generation from a single real modality image to other modalities. In the step II, we select the real face images in one modality and the generated images in the other modalities according to actual needs to construct a simulation dataset, which is used for training face anti-spoofing model. The advantage of GFF is that it has achieved a good trade-off between data capture cost and model performance in the real application scenarios. The experimental results show that the method proposed in this paper can effectively overcome the train-test inconsistency problem. On the CASIA-SRUF CeFA dataset, the performance of GFF surpasses the existing single-modality-based methods, and surprisingly surpasses some multi-modality-based methods.

**Keywords:** Multi-modal face anti-spoofing · Train-test inconsistency

This is a student paper.
This project is supported by the NSFC (62076258).

H. Ma et al. (Eds.): PRCV 2021, LNCS 13021, pp. 424–435, 2021.
https://doi.org/10.1007/978-3-030-88010-1_35

# 1   Introduction

Face Anti-Spoofing (FAS) is a very important part of the face recognition task, which ensures the reliability of face recognition in some key commercial or security scenarios, such as face-scanning payment and face-scanning unlocking. Since the types of attacks on face recognition increase rapidly, researchers believe that single-modal FAS is weak against attacks. Fortunately, multi-modal face images can provide additional and complementary information, which can greatly increase the robustness of FAS. Specifically, printing-based 2D attacks are very easy to distinguish in the depth modality, but it is difficult to distinguish in the VIS modality. Therefore, using multi-modal face images is one of the effective strategies for FAS. Commonly used modalities mainly include visible light (VIS), infrared light (IR) and depth (D).

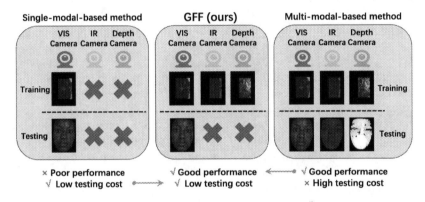

**Fig. 1.** The novelty of the proposed GFF. "×" means the faces of current modality are unavailable. The testing cost means the camera number of testing stage. The proposed GFF combines the advantages of the single-modal-based and multi-modal-based methods.

However, as shown in Fig. 1, multi-modal faces have the following limitations that make it unavailable to be widely used in some application scenes. 1) Multi-modal face images are difficult to obtain. Each modality needs a corresponding sensor to capture. The high cost of IR and D sensors makes it very difficult to obtain the IR and D modal data. 2) Multi-modal sensors are difficult to integrate and are widely deployed on mobile terminals. For example, it is usually impossible to integrate multiple sensors into the front camera of the mobile phones due to size and cost constraints. The FaceID of Apple's mobile phone tries to alleviate this problem, but the high cost makes it difficult to generalize. Due to the above limitations, the multi-modal FAS model trained through the public multi-modal face datasets cannot be used in real scenes. We define this gap between training and testing data as the train-test inconsistency problem. The existing single-modal and multi-modal FAS methods cannot solve this problem very well. The methods based on single modality cannot use the data of other modalities in the training phase, which leads to the discarding of complementary information among modalities, and further leads to the weak performance. The methods based on multi-modality are totally unavailable under this problem, because there are no multi-modal face images during the testing phase, which is unsuitable.

In this paper, we propose a novel FAS framework, GFF, to solve the train-test inconsistency problem, which is ignored by most existing works. The key idea of GFF is to construct a robust generative adversarial network in the training set, so that it can fit the distribution of face images in different modalities and learn the transformation relationships between different distributions. Specifically, the proposed GFF is a two-stage framework. In the step I, we train only one generator to achieve the generation of multiple modal images. In the step II, we select the corresponding modality as the real modality in the training set according to the modal availability during the test, and then use the GAN model obtained in the first stage to generate the corresponding image for other unselected modalities. After that, we use all the images in the real and the generated modalities to construct a new dataset instead of the original dataset, and apply this new synthetic dataset to train the face anti-spoofing model. In the test phase, the single-modal test image is first expanded into a multi-modal face image through the GAN model, and then sent to the FAS model for discrimination, which is consistent with the training phase.

The proposed GFF in this paper has the following benefits. 1) The GFF is **flexible**. The number of generators in our GAN model is independent with the number of modality classes. We only use one generator to realize the face generation between multiple modalities, regardless of how many modalities exist in the real scenes, which makes the network structure and the parameter amount does not need a lot of modification in applications. 2) The GFF is **generalizable**. From the description of GFF, it can be seen that the GAN model in this framework and the face anti-spoofing model are independent of each other. This shows that the GAN model in this paper can be compatible with any FAS model without any modification of the FAS model itself. 3) The GFF is **powerful**. The setting of GFF is to use multi-modal face images in the training phase and single-modal face images in the test phase. GFF has achieved the best performance under this setting, and has achieved a good trade-off between these two kind methods. We have conducted experiments on the current largest multi-modal face anti-spoofing dataset, CASIA-SURF CeFA, and the experimental result proves the effectiveness of our method.

Finally, the contributions of this paper can be summarized as follows:

1. We propose train-test inconsistency problem which is widespread in real-world scenarios and ignored by existing methods. We give an analysis that the existing methods cannot solve this problem well.
2. We propose the GFF framework specifically to solve the train-test inconsistency problem. GFF is a two-stage framework, mainly composed of a generative adversarial network and a face anti-spoofing model. The advantages of

GFF are flexibility and generalization. GFF does not require a lot of modification when deployed in a variety of real scenarios.

3. GFF has achieved the powerful performance on the CASIA-SURF CeFA dataset, 4.14% ACER, 6.78% APCER and 1.50% BPCER, which is 2.69%, 4.39% and 1.00% better than the-state-of-the-art model CDCN.

# 2 Related Work

## 2.1 Face Anti-spoofing

Face anti-spoofing [9] is a very critical step in face recognition. In early research, traditional hand-crafted descriptors [1,8,14], such as LBP and HOG, were used to extract texture features on face images. Traditional methods have limited feature representations and were extremely sensitive to environmental noise, so the performances were unsatisfactory. Recently, methods based on deep learning [13,16,18,19,21] have greatly improved the robustness of feature expression, and its performance far exceeds that of methods based on manual features. CDCN [21] combined the LBP operation in the traditional method with the convolution operation in the convolution layer, and brought more discriminative differential features on the basis of the original depth features, which greatly improves the performance of the model. However, these methods belonged to single-modal (visible light) face anti-spoofing methods. In the face of diversified types of attacks, multi-modal face anti-spoofing methods [2,6,7,17,20,22] are more effective, which are also the current mainstream researches. The advantage of the multi-modal methods is better accuracy, but more hardware devices and higher costs cannot be ignored.

However, the existing works ignored the train-test inconsistency problem in real-world scenarios. The multi-modal methods are not available because extra modal faces are not available in a real-world test scenarios. The performances of single-modal methods are unsatisfactory because extra modal training faces are discarded. The proposed GFF focuses about this phenomenon and is specifically designed for this issue.

## 2.2 Generative Adversarial Network

Generative adversarial network (GAN) has been widely used in face recognition tasks [3–5,11,15]. GAN achieves image transformation between multiple domains through alternating learning between the generator (G) and discriminator (D). STD-GAN [3] learned the decoupling relationship between facial features and pose features to obtain robust facial features. PFA-GAN [5] adopted adversarial learning to generate face images of the same ID at different ages. FA-GAN [11] used GAN to correct the face images in the training set to obtain high-quality faces.

However, the above GANs are not suitable for our task. So, we introduced the generative adversarial strategy to the face anti-spoofing task, on the one hand because of little attention, on the other hand of the challenge of train-test inconsistency problem. Our strategy is to design only one generator to achieve face transformation among multiple modalities. The advantage is that the structure and parameter amounts of G do not change significantly as the modality class increases, and deployment in real-world scenarios is very flexible.

## 3    The Proposed Method

### 3.1    Modeling

Given a dataset $\mathcal{X} = \mathcal{X}_{Tr} \cup \mathcal{X}_{Te}$ in a real-world scenario, its training set $\mathcal{X}_{Tr}$ and testing set $\mathcal{X}_{Te}$ contain inconsistent modality faces as following shown.

$$\begin{cases} \mathcal{X}_{Tr} = \left\{ \left( s_{VIS}^{i,j}, s_{IR}^{i,j}, s_{D}^{i,j}, y^i \right) \right\}^{N_{Tr}} \\ \mathcal{X}_{Te} = \left\{ \left( t_{VIS}^{i,j}, y^i \right) \right\}^{N_{Te}} \end{cases}, \tag{1}$$

where $s_{VIS}^{i,j}$ ($t_{VIS}^{i,j}$) denotes the $j$-th VIS modality face of $i$-th person in $\mathcal{X}_{Tr}$ ($\mathcal{X}_{Te}$), $y^i \in \{0, 1\}$ denotes the current face $x$ as a living face (0) or attack face (1), $j = 0, 1, \cdots, N_i - 1$, $N_i$ denotes the face number of $i$-th ID. $N_{Tr}$ and $N_{Te}$ denote the number of face IDs in training and testing set. Due to the train-test inconsistency problem of training and testing, the goal of this paper is to design a model $\mathcal{M}$ to achieve the following mapping.

$$\mathcal{M} : \left( \left( t_{VIS}^{i,j} \right) ; \left( s_{VIS}^{i,j}, s_{IR}^{i,j}, s_{D}^{i,j} \right) \xrightarrow{train} y^i \right) \xrightarrow{test} y^i \tag{2}$$

The mismatched input is difficult to solve by existing methods. Therefore, we propose a new two-stage framework GFF, which can be modeled as follows:

$$\mathcal{M} \triangleq (\mathcal{G}, \mathcal{M}_0), \tag{3}$$

where $\mathcal{G} : t_{VIS}^{i,j} \rightarrow \left( \hat{t}_{IR}^{i,j}, \hat{t}_{D}^{i,j} \right)$ is a generator learned from the GAN to achieve image generation among modalities, $\mathcal{M}_0 : \left( s_{VIS}^{i,j}, s_{IR}^{i,j}, s_{D}^{i,j} \right) \rightarrow y^i$ is a face anti-spoofing model that only accepts multi-modal input and produces corresponding predictions. The GFF can satisfy Eq. 2, which can be proofed as follows:

$$\mathcal{M} : \left( \left( t_{VIS}^{i,j} \right) ; \left( s_{VIS}^{i,j}, s_{IR}^{i,j}, s_{D}^{i,j} \right) \xrightarrow{train} y^i \right) \xrightarrow{test} y^i$$
$$\Longleftrightarrow (\mathcal{G}, \mathcal{M}_0) : \left( \left( t_{VIS}^{i,j}, \mathcal{G} \left( t_{VIS}^{i,j} \right) \right) ; \left( s_{VIS}^{i,j}, s_{IR}^{i,j}, s_{D}^{i,j} \right) \xrightarrow{\mathcal{M}_0} y^i \right) \xrightarrow{\mathcal{M}_0} y^i \tag{4}$$
$$\Longleftrightarrow (\mathcal{G}, \mathcal{M}_0) : \left( \left( t_{VIS}^{i,j}, \hat{t}_{IR}^{i,j}, \hat{t}_{D}^{i,j} \right) ; \left( s_{VIS}^{i,j}, s_{IR}^{i,j}, s_{D}^{i,j} \right) \xrightarrow{\mathcal{M}_0} y^i \right) \xrightarrow{\mathcal{M}_0} y^i$$

It can be seen from the Eq. 4 that in GFF, we first reconstruct the unavailable modal faces $(\hat{t}_{IR}^{i,j}, \hat{t}_{D}^{i,j})$ through the known modality $t_{VIS}^{i,j}$ and the $\mathcal{G}$, and then turn a single-modal testing to a multi-modal testing which is the same as the training process. On this basis, we can use a unified multi-modal face anti-spoofing model $\mathcal{M}_0$ to discriminate the multi-modal face images.

## 3.2   Framework

A detailed description of the proposed GFF is shown in Fig. 2, where Fig. 2(a) and 2(b) describe the two steps in training stage and Fig. 2(c) describes the testing stage. In the training step I, we mainly adopt a $\mathcal{G}$ and a $\mathcal{D}$ to achieve face generation between multiple modalities, which are trained alternately. When $\mathcal{G}$ is learnable and $\mathcal{D}$ is fixed, the $\mathcal{G}$ is used to transform a face from the source modality to the target modality. In order to ensure that the identity of the face has not changed, we reconstruct the face in the source modality from the generated face through $\mathcal{G}$ again. The reconstruction loss is used to constrain the reconstructed face to be sufficiently similar to the original face. In addition, we use the $\mathcal{D}$ to determine which modality the generated face belongs to and whether the generated face is real enough. When $\mathcal{G}$ is fixed and $\mathcal{D}$ is learnable, we send the original and the generated faces to the $\mathcal{D}$ for classification. On the one hand, the $\mathcal{D}$ is expected to correctly classify these two kinds of faces, and on the other hand, $\mathcal{D}$ needs to correctly classify the modality of the original faces to ensure the multi-modal generation.

We only focus on the results of the $\mathcal{G}$ and fix its parameters in the training step II (Fig. 2(b)). Given a face in the current modality, such as VIS, we first use $\mathcal{G}$ to generate faces in all other modalities (IR+D). The face images in three modalities are sent to a multi-modal-like face anti-spoofing model.[1] This face anti-spoofing model is composed of three branches, each of which focus on extracting the features of a certain modality face. The structure among these three branches is exactly the same, but the parameters are not shared with each other. In the process of extracting features, we consider that the differences in details and textures between the living face and the prosthetic face are more obvious, so we adopt the combination [20,21] of the traditional Laplacian operator and deep learning convolution kernels to replace the convolution kernels, which can be described as follows:

$$f_{out} = \theta \cdot (f_{in} \circledast w_l) \circledast w_c + (1 - \theta) \cdot (f_{in} \circledast w_c), \tag{5}$$

where $w_l = [1,1,1;1,-8,1;1,1,1]$ is the Laplacian operator, $w_c$ is the learnable convolution kernel of the current layer, $f_{in}/f_{out}$ is the input/output feature, $\theta$ is the hyper-parameter used to control the ratio of traditional convolution and deep convolution, $\circledast$ is the convolution operation. After that, we use the concat operation to splice the features under the three branches according to the channels, and then merge the features obtained from the three channels through a shared network structure, and finally obtain a complete feature representation of the current face for classification.

In the testing phase (Fig. 2(c)), we fix all model parameters in GFF. Given an input face, the GFF will give a probability that it belongs to a living face, and then GFF determines whether it is a living or a spoofing face by comparing the probability with a given threshold.

---

[1] Due to some of our input are generated rather than real, our model is a multi-modal-like model.

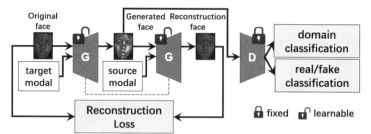

(a) Training step I of GFF (only shows learnable $\mathcal{G}$ and fixed $\mathcal{D}$). The
parameters of $\mathcal{G}$ and $\mathcal{D}$ in the step I are alternate learning. The $\mathcal{G}$
accepts a modality label to generate the corresponding modal face.
The blue dotted line indicates that the two generators are the same.

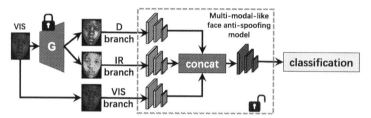

(b) Training step II of GFF. In the training step II, the $\mathcal{G}$ is fixed and
the multi-modal-like face anti-spoofing model is learnable. Different
colors (orange/yellow/green) indicate      he structures among d
rent modal branch    re the same but the p      ers are unsh

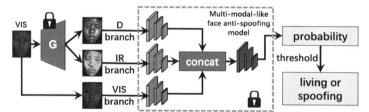

(c) Testing stage of GFF. All parameters are fixed.

**Fig. 2.** Illustration for the proposed GFF framework. The subfigure (a) and (b) describe
the training stage and the subfigure (c) describes the testing stage. (Color figure online)

### 3.3   Optimization

In this subsection, the loss functions we used are mainly introduced. In the training process of the $\mathcal{G}$ and the $\mathcal{D}$, we mainly adopt the adversarial loss function,
which can be described as follows:

$$L_a = \frac{1}{n} \sum_x [\log \mathcal{D}(x) + \log(1 - \mathcal{D}(\mathcal{G}(x, m_t)))], \tag{6}$$

where $x$ is the original face, $n$ is the batchsize and $m_t$ is the target modality
label. When $\mathcal{G}$ is learnable, we first use reconstruction loss to constrain the

reconstruction face to be same as the original face, which can be described as follows:

$$L_r = \frac{1}{n} \sum_x \|x - G\left(G\left(x, m_t\right), m_s\right)\|_1, \tag{7}$$

where $m_s$ is the original modality label of $x$. Then, the fixed $\mathcal{D}$ should classify the generated face to the target modality class, which can be described as follows:

$$L_{gc} = \frac{1}{n} \sum_x \left[-\log D\left(m_t|G\left(x, m_t\right)\right)\right]. \tag{8}$$

When $\mathcal{D}$ is learnable, the $\mathcal{D}$ also needs to correctly classify the modal class of the original faces in addition to the adversarial loss, which can be described as follows:

$$L_{rc} = \frac{1}{n} \sum_x \left[-\log D\left(m_s|x\right)\right]. \tag{9}$$

In summary, the complete loss functions of the $\mathcal{G}$ and $\mathcal{D}$ are described as follows:

$$\begin{cases} L_{\mathcal{G}} = L_a + \lambda_{gc}L_{gc} + \lambda_r L_r \\ L_{\mathcal{D}} = -L_a + \lambda_{rc}L_{rc} \end{cases} \tag{10}$$

When it comes to the loss functions of the face anti-spoofing model, on the one hand, we use the mean square error loss $L_{mse}$ to make the features more similar to the label; on the other hand, we use contrastive depth loss (CDL) $L_{cdl}$ to enable the network to capture more face details and textures [20, 21]. So the loss functions can be described as follows:

$$L_{FAS} = L_{mse} + L_{cdl}. \tag{11}$$

## 4  Experiments

### 4.1  Datasets and Settings

We have conducted experiments on the largest available multi-modal face anti-spoofing dataset, CASIA-SURF CeFA [22]. CASIA-SURF CeFA is the current largest available face anti-spoofing dataset, which covers three ethnicities (African, East Asian and Central Asian), three modalities (VIS, IR, Depth), 2D and 3D attack types, which is the benchmark of ChaLearn Face Anti-spoofing Attack Detection Challenge@CVPR2020 [9]. There are four protocols in CASIA-SURF CeFA. In this paper, our experiments are all conducted on the protocol 4, which are same as the Challenge@CVPR2020 for the fair comparison.

There are three metrics to evaluate the face anti-spoofing model, including Attack Presentation Classification Error Rate (APCER), Bona Fide Presentation Classification Error Rate (BPCER), and Average Classification Error Rate (ACER), which can be described as follows:

$$\begin{cases} APCER = FP/(TN + FP) \\ BPCER = FN/(FN + TP) \\ ACER = (APCER + BPCER)/2 \end{cases} \tag{12}$$

where $FP$, $FN$, $TN$ and $TP$ denote the false positive, false negative, true negative and true positive sample numbers. The ACER is more important than APCER and BPCER.

## 4.2    Implementation Details

We achieve the image generation among three modalities faces (VIS, IR and Depth) based on the generator and discriminator in StarGAN [4]. We only use the training data in CASIA-SURF CeFA for GAN's training. We resize the face to $256 \times 256$ as the input of the $\mathcal{G}$ and $\mathcal{D}$. We set batchsize to 16. The learning rate of $\mathcal{G}$ and $\mathcal{D}$ is $1e$–5. $\mathcal{D}$ will updated once until $\mathcal{G}$ is updated 5 times. We train $\mathcal{D}$ a total of 200,000 iterations. We set the $\lambda_r = 10$ and $\lambda_{gc} = \lambda_{rc} = 1$. The multi-modal-like face anti-spoofing model is based on the multi-modal CDCN [20]. We resize the input face to $256 \times 256$. We use random erasing ($p = 0.5$), random horizontal flip ($p = 0.5$) as data augmentation. The learning rate and weight decay are $1e-4$ and $5e-5$, respectively. The $\theta$ is 0.3. The threshold in the test phase is obtained from the data statistics in the verification set. We train models with 50 epochs. The batchsize is 8. The GFF is designed on PyTorch [12] Framework with totally 4 GPUs.

## 4.3    Performance

We select two methods, CDCN [20] and PSMM [10], to compare with the proposed GFF. We divide these methods into single-modality-based methods and multi-modality-based methods according to the available modalities in the training and testing phases. We regard the CDCN [20] as the state-of-the-art model for single-modal-based face anti-spoofing methods, and PSMM [10] as the current mainstream performance of the multi-modal-based face anti-spoofing methods. The CDCN can be compatible with different settings due to the flexibility of the network structure. Since the proposed GFF is based on CDCN, we consider that the performance of CDCN under the two settings is the lower and upper bounds of the performance of GFF.

The performances are shown in the Table 1. Three conclusions can be drawn as follows: 1) The proposed GFF is a hybrid method, which aims to achieve a better balance between the single-modality-based and multi-modality-based methods. Compared with the single-modal method, we have achieved better performance; compared with the multi-modal method, we have reduced the hardware cost in actual scenarios. To our best knowledge, we are the first to present training-testing inconsistent setting in FAS which is ignored by existing methods. 2) The proposed GFF achieves 4.14% ACER, 6.78% APCER and 1.50% BPCER, which is 2.69%, 4.39% and 1.00% better than the CDCN (lower bound). This shows that under the same network structure and testing modality, the GFF can obtain stable performance gains in actual applications. 3)The GFF has a very large performance advantage compared to other multi-modal methods, although the GFF is somewhat incomparable with the ideal upper bound. Compared with PSMM, the GFF is 20.36%, 26.52% and 14.30% better

**Table 1.** The performance comparison of existing methods on CASIA-SURF CeFA Protocol 4@1. The APCER, BPCER and ACER are reported (%). "LB/UB" means lower/upper bound.

| Method | Training | Testing | APCER ↓ | BPCER ↓ | ACER ↓ |
|---|---|---|---|---|---|
| CDCN [20] (LB) | VIS | VIS | 11.17 | 2.50 | 6.83 |
| PSMM [10] | VIS+IR+D | VIS+IR+D | 33.30 | 15.80 | 24.50 |
| CDCN [20] (UB) | VIS+IR+D | VIS+IR+D | 0.33 | 0.50 | 0.42 |
| **GFF** | VIS+IR+D | VIS | **6.78** | **1.50** | **4.14** |

than PSMM on ACER, APCER and BPCER. This shows that compared with some existing multi-modal methods, the GFF not only achieves performance improvement, but also achieves a lower cost.

### 4.4 Visualization

We demonstrate the performance of the generator $\mathcal{G}$ by visualizing some of the generated results from the original VIS faces. The visualization is shown in Fig. 3. Column 2 and 3 is the generated IR and Depth faces according to the original VIS face. Row 1, 2 and 3 are living faces and Row 4, 5 are spoofing faces.

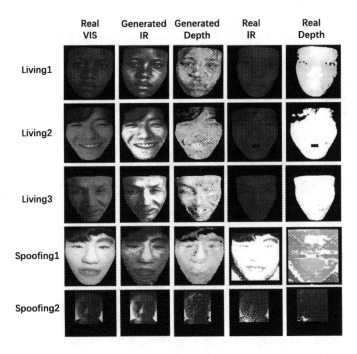

**Fig. 3.** Some generated results by generator $\mathcal{G}$.

It can be seen from the Fig. 3 that whether it is a living or a spoofing face, the $\mathcal{G}$ can simulate and generate the faces in the other two modalities, and the generated result also captures the information in the actual picture, which is supported by the performance results in Table 1.

## 5    Conclusion

In this paper, we first analyze the shortcomings of existing methods in real applications and present the training-testing inconsistency problem. Second, we proposed GFF framework specially designed for the inconsistency problem. The GFF is a two-step framework which is composed of GAN and face anti-spoofing model. Finally, we conduct some experiments to shown better performance and lower cost of the proposed method. In future research, we will continue to use GFF as the basis to achieve better performance closer to the ideal upper bound of this model.

## References

1. Chen, S., Li, W., Yang, H., Huang, D., Wang, Y.: 3D face mask anti-spoofing via deep fusion of dynamic texture and shape clues. In: FG, pp. 314–321 (2020)
2. Chen, X., Xu, S., Ji, Q., Cao, S.: A dataset and benchmark towards multi-modal face anti-spoofing under surveillance scenarios. IEEE Access **9**, 28140–28155 (2021)
3. Chikontwe, P., Gao, Y., Lee, H.J.: Transformation guided representation GAN for pose invariant face recognition. Multidimension. Syst. Signal Process. **32**(2), 633–649 (2021)
4. Choi, Y., Uh, Y., Yoo, J., Ha, J.: StarGAN v2: diverse image synthesis for multiple domains. In: CVPR, pp. 8185–8194 (2020)
5. Huang, Z., Chen, S., Zhang, J., Shan, H.: PFA-GAN: progressive face aging with generative adversarial network. IEEE Trans. Inf. Forensics Secur. **16**, 2031–2045 (2021)
6. Jiang, F., Liu, P., Shao, X., Zhou, X.: Face anti-spoofing with generated near-infrared images. Multimedia Tools Appl. **79**(29–30), 21299–21323 (2020)
7. Jiang, F., Liu, P., Zhou, X.: Multilevel fusing paired visible light and near-infrared spectral images for face anti-spoofing. Pattern Recogn. Lett. **128**, 30–37 (2019)
8. Kavitha, P., Vijaya, K.: Fuzzy local ternary pattern and skin texture properties based countermeasure against face spoofing in biometric systems. Comput. Intell. **37**(1), 559–577 (2021)
9. Liu, A., et al.: Cross-ethnicity face anti-spoofing recognition challenge: a review. CoRR (2020)
10. Liu, A., et al.: CASIA-SURF CeFA: a benchmark for multi-modal cross-ethnicity face anti-spoofing. CoRR abs/2003.05136 (2020)
11. Luo, M., Cao, J., Ma, X., Zhang, X., He, R.: FA-GAN: face augmentation GAN for deformation-invariant face recognition. IEEE Trans. Inf. Forensics Secur. **16**, 2341–2355 (2021)
12. Paszke, A., et al.: PyTorch: an imperative style, high-performance deep learning library. In: Wallach, H.M., Larochelle, H., Beygelzimer, A., d'Alché-Buc, F., Fox, E.B., Garnett, R. (eds.) NeurIPS, pp. 8024–8035 (2019)

13. Qin, Y., et al.: Learning meta model for zero-and few-shot face anti-spoofing. In: AAAI (2020)
14. Shu, X., Tang, H., Huang, S.: Face spoofing detection based on chromatic ED-LBP texture feature. Multimedia Syst. **27**(2), 161–176 (2021)
15. Wang, Q., Fan, H., Sun, G., Ren, W., Tang, Y.: Recurrent generative adversarial network for face completion. IEEE Trans. Multimedia **23**, 429–442 (2021)
16. Wang, Z., et al.: Deep spatial gradient and temporal depth learning for face anti-spoofing. In: CVPR, pp. 5041–5050 (2020)
17. Yang, Q., Zhu, X., Fwu, J., Ye, Y., You, G., Zhu, Y.: PipeNet: selective modal pipeline of fusion network for multi-modal face anti-spoofing. In: CVPR Workshops, pp. 2739–2747. IEEE (2020)
18. Yu, Z., Wan, J., Qin, Y., Li, X., Li, S.Z., Zhao, G.: NAS-FAS: static-dynamic central difference network search for face anti-spoofing. IEEE Trans. Pattern Anal. Mach. Intell. **43**(9), 3005–3023 (2021). https://doi.org/10.1109/TPAMI.2020.3036338
19. Yu, Z., Li, X., Niu, X., Shi, J., Zhao, G.: Face anti-spoofing with human material perception. In: Vedaldi, A., Bischof, H., Brox, T., Frahm, J.-M. (eds.) ECCV 2020. LNCS, vol. 12352, pp. 557–575. Springer, Cham (2020). https://doi.org/10.1007/978-3-030-58571-6_33
20. Yu, Z., et al.: Multi-modal face anti-spoofing based on central difference networks. In: CVPR Workshops, pp. 2766–2774. IEEE (2020)
21. Yu, Z., et al.: Searching central difference convolutional networks for face anti-spoofing. In: CVPR (2020)
22. Zhang, S., et al.: CASIA-SURF: a large-scale multi-modal benchmark for face anti-spoofing. IEEE Trans. Biometrics Behav. Identity Sci. **2**(2), 182–193 (2020)

# Non-significant Information Enhancement Based Attention Network for Face Anti-spoofing

Yangwei Dong, Jianjun Qian[✉], and Jian Yang

PCA Lab, Key Lab of Intelligent Perception and Systems for High-Dimensional Information of Ministry of Education, Nanjing University of Science and Technology, Nanjing, China
{dongyangwei,csjqian,csjyang}@njust.edu.cn

**Abstract.** Face anti-spoofing is an essential step in ensuring the safety of face recognition systems. Recently, some deep convolutional neural networks (CNNs) based methods have been developed to improve the performance of face anti-spoofing. These methods mainly employ the attention information of the facial images to learn the embedding feature. However, the previous work ignores the potential benefits of non-significant information. To overcome this issue, this paper presents a novel Non-Significant information Enhancement based Attention module (NSEA). NSEA not only focuses on the significant region for feature learning but also preserves the non-significant region to enhance feature representation. Additionally, we also introduce the Multi-Scale Refinement Strategy (MSRS) to capture the fine-grained information and refine the coarse binary mask at different scales. A network build with NESA and MSRS, called the Non-Significant information Enhancement based Attention Network (NSEAN). Experiments are conducted on five benchmark databases, including OULU-NPU, SiW, CASIA-MSFD, MSU-MFSD, and Replay-attack. The quantitative results demonstrate the advantages of the proposed method over state-of-the-art methods.

**Keywords:** Face anti-spoofing · Non-significant information · Attention · Multi-scale refinement strategy

## 1 Introduction

With the widespread application of face recognition technology in multiple fields of equipment and system, people have also asked a great deal for the security of this technology. Although the existing face recognition systems have high accuracy, they still can be easily deceived by presentation attacks (PAs), such as print photo, video replay and 3D masks. Face anti-spoofing (FAS) is actually an indispensable step to ensure the safety of face recognition system.

To address this problem, massive attempts have been made in the past few years, ranging from the traditional methods [3,4,18] to deep convolutional neural network based methods [11,12,15,20,24,34]. Traditional methods extracted

H. Ma et al. (Eds.): PRCV 2021, LNCS 13021, pp. 436–448, 2021.
https://doi.org/10.1007/978-3-030-88010-1_36

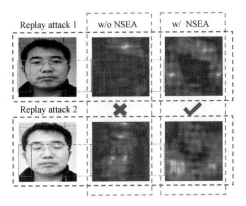

**Fig. 1.** Feature response of without and with Non-Significant information Enhancement based Attention module (NSEA) for spoofing faces under previously unseen environmental conditions (e.g., illumination varies). Notice that w/o NSEA fails to capture the spoofing pattern in some areas while w/NESA is able to extract the invariant detailed spoofing features.

manual design features, such as color [4], texture [18], motion [3], and other clues, to reflect the characteristic relations between the part and the neighborhood of the face. The CNN based methods learn characteristic relations from parts to a whole and finds the difference between the living and spoofing images. Most of these methods [12,20] use a binary classification to judge whether it is a real person (e.g., '0' for spoofing face and '1' for living face). However, the arbitrary cues (such as screen bezel) are easier to be learned than the faithful spoof patterns by these approaches, which severely limits the generalization ability of the model. In order to improve the model generalization and explainable, the researchers use auxiliary signals (i.e., depth [22,34], rPPG [15]) as supervisions. For example, Liu et al. [15] combine the Remote Phothplethysmography (rPPG) signal with CNN to distinguish live and 3D mask attacks well. Although auxiliary supervision perform better than traditional binary supervision, it still has the following two problems: 1) These auxiliary information requires additional generation or collection, which increases time overhead; 2) Auxiliary information has certain limitations. For example, rPPG signal captured from human face is little weak and it is sensitive to complex environment. Compared with auxiliary information, binary mask label is easier to generate and more suitable for all PAs.

The above CNN-based FAS methods just employ the embedding feature to complete the FAS task. In fact, the feature maps from different levels also contain rich information. Based on this, there are some methods that employ the multiscale strategy to enhance feature representation. They are connected online [34] or employed by multi-scale supervised methods [33], but the feature map of each level is still not fully and effectively utilized in their methods. Hence, exploring the feature fusion and binary mask supervision between different levels for FAS tasks is still a worthy study.

In addition, most of the FAS methods did not pay more attention to significant regions. Subsequently, the attention mechanisms are introduced to improve the feature discriminability [30,34]). However, these methods almost discard the non-significant information. In our opinion, the non-significant information is beneficial to improve the performance of FAS task. From Fig. 1, we can see that NSEA focuses on learning the significant region, and also retain the feature of non-significant region. The Multi-Scale Refinement Strategy (MSRS) integrates the relations between different scales and enhances the feature representation. To sum up, the main contributions of our work are summarized as follows:

– We propose a novel Non-Significant information Enhancement based Attention module (NSEA) to capture more discriminative features by preserving the feature of non-significant region.
– We employ the Multi-Scale Refinement Strategy (MSRS), which can both catch richer fine-grained information and refine the coarse binary mask between multiple scales to improve the robustness of the model.
– Experimental results demonstrate the advantages of the proposed method over the state-of-the-art face anti-spoofing methods.

## 2     Related Work

**Face Anti-spoofing Methods.** In the preliminary work, many researchers introduced various handcrafted features in conjunction with SVM to solve the face anti-spoofing task. Additionally, consecutive frames are used to characterize dynamic features, such as eye blinking [19], motion [3], etc.. None the less, these methods are very vulnerable to replay attacks.

In recent years, some deep learning-based methods have been developed for face anti-spoofing. Some researchers employ the pre-trained CNN model in conjunction with Softmax classifier to improve the performance of FAS [9,12,20]. Subsequently, many methods are proposed to utilize additional auxiliary information as supervision, such as depth [2], rPPG [15], 3D point cloud map [13]. Atoum et al. [2] regard the depth map as a supervisory signal and propose a two stream CNN based method to achieve the local features and holistic depth maps. In another work, Yu et al. [32] propose a face anti-spoofing method to capture intrinsic material-based patterns by using three different auxiliary supervisions (depth, binary mask and reflection supervision). However, it is time consuming to generate additional auxiliary information. To overcome this problem, George and Marcel [9] introduce deep pixel-wise binary supervision (PixBis) which predicts the confidence map to help in the final binary classification. To further exploit multi-scale spatial information, Yu et al. [33] unitize pyramid binary mask to constraint the CNN for learning discriminative feature. Comparing with binary supervision, the network can capture the detailed texture information since the pixel-wise supervision performs separate supervision on each pixel of feature map.

**Attention for Face Anti-spoofing.** The attention mechanisms of deep learning imitates that of human vision and have demonstrated their practicability in

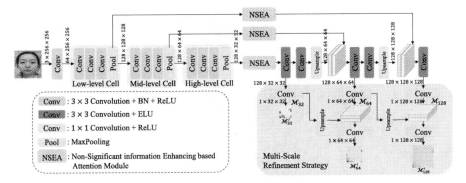

**Fig. 2.** The architecture of NSEAN. It consists of the NSEA and MSRS.

many areas, including image restoration, text classification, and video classification. For example, Hu et al. [10] propose the squeeze and excitation networks (SE-Net) to compresses global spatial information into a channel descriptor for achieving the channel dependency. Woo et al. [28] introduce a compact module to exploit both spatial and channel-wise attention in two branches. They mainly focus on the important features and ignore the unimportant ones. In the field of face anti-spoofing, Yang et al. [30] propose a spatio-temporal attention mechanism to fuse globally temporal and locally spatial information. Additionally, Yu et al. [34] introduce spatial attention that integrates multi-scale features so as to improve the role of important areas. The above attention based methods are sensitive to face anti-spoofing task when facing different attack modes.

## 3  Methodology

### 3.1  Non-significant Information Enhancement Based Attention Module

Our Non-Significant information Enhancement based Attention module (NSEA) consists of two components: Non-Significant Spatial information Enhancement based Attention branch (NSSEA) and Non-Significant Channel information Enhancement based Attention branch (NSCEA). The two branches work together to achieve global and fine-grained features and enable the network to preserve the efficient non-significant information. Therefore, our network can obtain a better feature representation for FAS tasks. As shown in Fig. 3, given an input feature $X \in \mathbb{R}^{C \times H \times W}$, $C$ is channel number and the feature map size is $H \times W$, then we apply one convolutional layer to get an initialize weight $F \in \mathbb{R}^{C \times H \times W}$, $F = \mathrm{Conv}(X)$, where Conv denotes one convolutional layer.

**Non-significant Spatial information Enhancement Based Attention Branch (NSSEA).** As shown in Fig. 3, after getting the initial weight $F$, we apply channel average pooling layer CAP to squeeze channel-wise features:

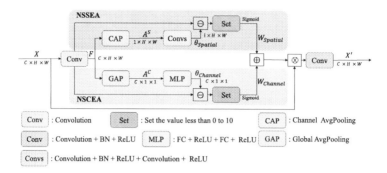

**Fig. 3.** The overview of the Non-Significant information Enhancement based Attention module.

$A^S \in \mathbb{R}^{1 \times H \times W}$. Subsequently, two convolutional layers are applied to get the threshold $\theta_{Spatial} \in \mathbb{R}^{1 \times H \times W}$ for dividing semantic information:

$$\theta_{Spatial} = \text{Convs}(\text{CAP}(F)) = \delta(Conv_1(\delta(\mathcal{B}(Conv_2(\text{CAP}(F)))))), \qquad (1)$$

where $\text{CAP}(F) = \frac{1}{C} \sum_{i=1}^{C} F_{[i,:,:]}$ is the channel average pooling layer. $\delta$ denotes the Rectified Linear Unit (ReLU). $\mathcal{B}$ denotes the Batch Normalization (BN). The kernel sizes of $Conv_1$ and $Conv_2$ are both $1 \times 1 \times 3 \times 3$. We use a bottleneck instead of only one convolutional layer because it can better fit the complex spatial correlation.

Afterwards, we subtract the initial weight $F$ from $\theta_{Spatial}$ to get the divided weights. The weights are greater than 0 represent the significant information region, and the weights are less than 0 represent the non-significant information region. Following this, setting the value less than 0 as 10, the value will become 1 after the Sigmoid function is applied. Finally, the Sigmoid function is used to obtain the final non-significant spatial information enhancement weight $W_{spatial} \in \mathbb{R}^{C \times H \times W}$:

$$W_{spatial} = \sigma\left(\text{Set}\left(F - \theta_{Spatial}\right)\right), \qquad (2)$$

where $\sigma$ is the Sigmoid function. $\text{Set}(\cdot)$ is the function that sets 0 to 10.

**Non-significant Channel Information Enhancement Based Attention Branch (NSCEA).** Similar to NSEEA, we apply global average pooling layer GAP to squeeze spatial features: $A^C \in \mathbb{R}^{C \times 1 \times 1}$. Subsequently, two fully connected (FC) layers are applied to get the threshold $\theta_{channel} \in \mathbb{R}^{C \times 1 \times 1}$ for dividing semantic information:

$$\theta_{Channel} = \text{MLP}(\text{GAP}(F)) = \delta(W_2 \delta(W_1(\text{GAP}(F))), \qquad (3)$$

where $\text{GAP}(F) = \frac{1}{H \times W} \sum_{i=1}^{H} \sum_{j=1}^{W} F_{[:,i,j]}$ is the global average pooling layer. Similar to SE-Net [10], here $W_1 \in \mathbb{R}^{\frac{C}{r} \times C}$ and $W_2 \in \mathbb{R}^{C \times \frac{C}{r}}$, $r$ is the channel reduction ratio.

Subsequently, we compute the $W_{Channel}$ by using the same way as $W_{Spatial}$:

$$W_{Channel} = \sigma(\text{Set}\,(F - \theta_{channel}))\,. \tag{4}$$

**Fusion.** In order to integrate spatial and semantic information effectively, we add $W_{Channel}$ and $W_{spatial}$ to get the final weight, then multiply the final weight with the input feature $X$. At last, we employ one convolutional layer to get the final output feature $X'$. Our NSEA can be formulated as:

$$X' = \text{Conv}\,((W_{Channel} + W_{spatial})\,X)\,. \tag{5}$$

### 3.2   Multi-scale Refinement Strategy

In [14], they introduce the multi-scale loss to improve the performance. Inspired by above work, we try to retain the multi-scale feature for FAS task. In this subsection, we conduct information refinement between binary masks of different scales to play a key constraint role.

In Fig. 2, the predicted binary mask of the current level $\mathcal{M}_i$ is connected with that of the previous level $\mathcal{M}_{i/2}$ that has been up-sampled, and then we feed it into one $3 \times 3$ convolutional layer to obtain the final output $\mathcal{M}_i'$:

$$\mathcal{M}_i' = \begin{cases} \text{Conv}\,([\mathcal{M}_i; Upsampling\,(\mathcal{M}_{i/2})]), & i = \{128, 64\} \\ \mathcal{M}_{32}, & i = \{32\} \end{cases} \tag{6}$$

where $\mathcal{M}_i \in \mathbb{R}^{1 \times i \times i}$, $\mathcal{M}_i' \in \mathbb{R}^{1 \times i \times i}$, $\mathcal{M}_{i/2} \in \mathbb{R}^{1 \times \frac{i}{2} \times \frac{i}{2}}$.

### 3.3   Loss Function

Given an input image, the network outputs the predicted binary mask $\mathcal{M}_i'$ of different scale. The loss function can be formulated as:

$$\mathcal{L} = \sum_i (\mathcal{L}_{MSE}(\mathcal{M}_i',\ Y_i) + \mathcal{L}_{CDL}(\mathcal{M}_i',\ Y_i)), \tag{7}$$

where $Y_i$ means the binary mask label with scale $i$, $\mathcal{L}_{MSE}$ and $\mathcal{L}_{CDL}$ denote mean square error loss and contrastive depth loss [25], respectively.

## 4   Experiments

### 4.1   Databases and Metrics

**Databases.** Five databases - OULU-NPU [6], SiW [15], CASIA-MFSD [35], Replay-Attack [7], and MSU-MFSD [27] are used in our experiments. OULU-NPU and SiW, high-resolution databases, consisting of four and three protocols, are used for intra-testing performance. CASIA-MFSD, Replay-Attack and MSU-MFSD, low-resolution databases, are used for cross testing.

**Performance Metrics.** To compare with previous works, we follow the original protocols and metrics [23]: Attack Presentation Classification Error Rate ($APCER$), Bona Fide Presentation Classification Error Rate ($BPCER$), $ACER = (APCER + BPCER)/2$. In the cross testing between CASIA-MFSD and Replay-Attack, we adopt Half Total Error Rate ($HTER$). we adopt Area Under Curve (AUC) for intra-database cross-type test on CASIA-MFSD, Replay-Attack and MSU-MFSD.

## 4.2   Implementation Details

To distinguish living from spoofing faces, during training, the binary mask labels are generated simply by filling each position with the corresponding binary label, and then down-sampled into multiple resolutions ($128 \times 128$, $64 \times 64$, $32 \times 32$), which is similar to [33]. In the training stage, the Adam optimizer is employed to optimize the training model. The initial learning rate (lr) and weight decay (wd) are 1e−4 and 5e−5, respectively. The maximum epochs of our model is 2000 and lr halves every 500 epochs. The batch size is 10 on 2080Ti GPU. In the testing stage, we calculate the mean value of the three predicted masks as the final score. In each NSEA module, we set the bottleneck ratio $r = 16$.

## 4.3   Ablation Study

In this subsection, to study the effects of our proposed NSEA and MSRS, we conduct ablation experiments on OULU-NPU protocol 1 to evaluate the proposed NSEA and MSRS.

**Table 1.** Comparison various attention on OULU-NPU Protocol 1.

| Method | ACER(%) |
|---|---|
| w/ SE attention [10] | 13.19 |
| w/ Spatial attention [34] | 0.78 |
| w/ NSCEA | 0.24 |
| w/ NSSEA | 0.52 |
| w/ NSEA | 0.00 |

**Table 2.** The results of ablation study on OULU-NPU Protocol 1.

| Module | 32 | 64 | 128 | FP | MSRS | NSEA | ACER(%) |
|---|---|---|---|---|---|---|---|
| Model 1 | ✓ | | | | | | 1.64 |
| Model 2 | | ✓ | | | | | 1.25 |
| Model 3 | | | ✓ | | | | 0.92 |
| Model 4 | | | | ✓ | | | 1.21 |
| Model 5 | | | | | ✓ | | 0.83 |
| Model 6 | ✓ | | | | | ✓ | 0.78 |
| Model 7 | | ✓ | | | | ✓ | 0.73 |
| Model 8 | | | ✓ | | | ✓ | 0.40 |
| Model 9 | | | | ✓ | | ✓ | 0.68 |
| Model 10 | | | | | ✓ | ✓ | 0.00 |

**NSEA Attention vs. Other Attention.** As illustrated in Table 1, we can see that both NSCEA and NSSEA achieve the better results than SE attention an Spatial attention. Our NSEA gives the best results among all the methods. The possible reason is that the non-significant can well capture the discriminative characteristics of the deception for the FAS task in different environments. It is worth raising that the ACER on the SE attention surpasses the value on the spatial attention by far, while the value of NSCEA is lower than NSSEA.

**Effectiveness of Scale and Multi-scale Refinement Strategy.** In order to evaluate the effectiveness of MSRS, we conduct experiments with or without attention on different scales and feature pyramid (FP). As shown in the Table 2, we can see clearly that the larger scale and the rich fine-grained information can achieve better performance. Compared with single scale $32 \times 32$ and $64 \times 64$, the FP obtains better results, while the larger scale $128 \times 128$ performs better than the FP. The ACER of MSRS is further improved by using attention scheme.

### 4.4  Intra Testing

We compare the performances of intra-database testing on OULU-NPU, and SiW datasets. For OULU-NPU and SiW, we strictly follow the standard protocol and then report their APCER, BPCER and ACER. To compare fairly, all compared methods are trained without extra datasets.

**Table 3.** The results of intra testing on four protocols of OULU-NPU [6]. For a fair comparison, we report the STASN [30] results without additional datasets training.

| Method | Prot.1 APCER (%) | BPCER (%) | ACER (%) | Prot.2 APCER (%) | BPCER (%) | ACER (%) | Prot.3 APCER (%) | BPCER (%) | ACER (%) | Prot.4 APCER (%) | BPCER (%) | ACER (%) |
|---|---|---|---|---|---|---|---|---|---|---|---|---|
| Auxiliary [15] | 1.6 | 1.6 | 1.6 | 2.7 | 2.7 | 2.7 | 2.7 ± 1.3 | 3.1 ± 1.7 | 2.9 ± 1.5 | 9.3 ± 5.6 | 10.4 ± 6.0 | 9.5 ± 6.0 |
| FaceDs [12] | 1.2 | 1.7 | 1.5 | 4.2 | 4.4 | 4.3 | 4.0 ± 1.8 | 3.8 ± 1.2 | 3.6 ± 1.6 | 1.2 ± 6.3 | 6.1 ± 5.1 | 5.6 ± 5.7 |
| FAS-TD [26] | 2.5 | 0.0 | 1.3 | 1.7 | 2.0 | 1.9 | 5.9 ± 1.9 | 5.9 ± 3.0 | 5.9 ± 1.0 | 14.2 ± 8.7 | 4.2 ± 3.8 | 9.2 ± 3.4 |
| STASN [30] | 1.2 | 2.5 | 1.9 | 4.2 | 0.3 | 2.2 | 4.7 ± 3.9 | 0.9 ± 1.2 | 2.8 ± 1.6 | 6.7 ± 10.6 | 8.3 ± 8.4 | 7.5 ± 4.7 |
| DeepPexBis [9] | 0.8 | 0.0 | 0.4 | 11.4 | 0.6 | 6.0 | 11.7 ± 19.6 | 10.6 ± 14.1 | 11.1 ± 9.4 | 36.7 ± 29.7 | 13.3 ± 14.1 | 25.0 ± 12.7 |
| CDCN++ [34] | 0.4 | 0.0 | 0.2 | 1.8 | 0.8 | 1.3 | 1.7 ± 1.5 | 2.0 ± 1.2 | 1.8 ± 0.7 | 4.2 ± 3.4 | 5.8 ± 4.9 | 5.0 ± 2.9 |
| NAS-FAS [31] | 0.4 | 0.0 | 0.2 | 1.5 | 0.8 | 1.2 | 2.1 ± 1.3 | 1.4 ± 1.1 | 1.7 ± 0.6 | 4.2 ± 5.3 | 1.7 ± 2.6 | 2.9 ± 2.8 |
| **NSEAN (Ours)** | 0.0 | 0.0 | **0.0** | 1.0 | 1.1 | 1.1 | 0.1 ± 0.2 | 0.6 ± 0.9 | **0.4 ± 0.7** | 0.8 ± 2.0 | 0.8 ± 2.0 | **0.8 ± 2.0** |

**Results on OULU-NPU.** Table 3 shows that the proposed NSEAN gives the leading results among all methods under 4 different protocols (0.0%, 1.1%, 0.4% and 0.8% ACER, respectively), which shows the proposed method functions well in three respects: the generalization of the external environment, attack mediums and input camera variation. Especially, our method significantly outperforms the competed methods in protocols 3 and 4.

**Results on SiW.** We compare our method with five state-of-the-art methods NAS-FAS [31], CDCN++ [34], Auxiliary [15], STASN [30] and FAS-TD [26] on SiW dataset as shown in Table 4. From Table 4, we can see that our method NSEAN performs great advantages on the generalization of (1) variations of face pose and expression, (2) cross spoof medium of replay attack, (3) cross presentation attack.

**Table 4.** The results of intra testing on three protocols of SiW [15].

| Method | Prot.1 | | | Prot.2 | | | Prot.3 | | |
|---|---|---|---|---|---|---|---|---|---|
| | APCER(%) | BPCER(%) | ACER(%) | APCER(%) | BPCER(%) | ACER(%) | APCER(%) | BPCER(%) | ACER(%) |
| Auxiliary [15] | 3.58 | 3.58 | 3.58 | 0.57 ± 0.69 | 0.57 ± 0.69 | 0.57 ± 0.69 | 8.31 ± 3.81 | 8.31 ± 3.81 | 8.31 ± 3.81 |
| STASN [30] | | | 1.00 | | | 0.28 ± 0.05 | | | 12.10 ± 1.50 |
| FAS-TD [26] | 0.96 | 0.50 | 0.73 | 0.08 ± 0.14 | 0.21 ± 0.14 | 0.15 ± 0.14 | 3.10 ± 0.81 | 3.09 ± 0.81 | 3.10 ± 0.81 |
| CDCN++ [34] | 0.07 | 0.17 | 0.12 | 0.00 ± 0.00 | 0.09 ± 0.10 | 0.04 ± 0.05 | 1.97 ± 0.33 | 1.77 ± 0.10 | 1.90 ± 0.15 |
| NAS-FAS [31] | 0.07 | 0.17 | 0.12 | 0.00 ± 0.00 | 0.09 ± 0.10 | 0.04 ± 0.05 | 1.58 ± 0.23 | 1.46 ± 0.08 | 1.52 ± 0.13 |
| **NSEAN (Ours)** | 0.00 | 0.00 | **0.00** | 0.00 ± 0.00 | 0.00 ± 0.00 | **0.00 ± 0.00** | 1.22 ± 0.69 | 1.25 ± 0.75 | **1.25 ± 0.74** |

**Table 5.** The results of cross-dataset testing between CASIA-MFSD [35] and Replay-Attack [7]. The evaluation metric is HTER(%). The multiple-frame based methods are shown in the upper half part while single-frame based methods in bottom half part.

| Method | Train | Test | Train | Test |
|---|---|---|---|---|
| | CASIA-MFSD | Replay-attack | Replay-attack | CASIA-MFSD |
| Motion-Mag [3] | 50.1 | | 47.0 | |
| LBP-TOP [8] | 49.7 | | 60.6 | |
| STASN [30] | 31.5 | | 30.9 | |
| Auxiliary [15] | 27.6 | | 28.4 | |
| FAS-TD [26] | **17.5** | | **24.0** | |
| LBP [4] | 47.0 | | 39.6 | |
| Spectral cubes [21] | 34.4 | | 50.0 | |
| Color texture [5] | 30.3 | | 37.7 | |
| FaceDs [12] | 28.5 | | 41.1 | |
| **NSEAN (Ours)** | 20.2 | | 26.7 | |

**Table 6.** AUC (%) of the model cross-type testing on CASIA-MFSD, Replay-Attack, and MSU-MFSD.

| Method | CASIA-MFSD [35] | | | Replay-Attack [7] | | | MSU-MFSD [27] | | | Overall |
|---|---|---|---|---|---|---|---|---|---|---|
| | Video | Cut photo | Wrapped phono | Video | Digital photo | Printed photo | Printed photo | HR video | Mobile video | |
| OC-SVM+BSIF [8] | 70.74 | 60.73 | 95.90 | 84.03 | 88.14 | 73.66 | 64.81 | 87.44 | 74.69 | 78.68 ± 11.74 |
| SVM+LBP [6] | 91.94 | 91.70 | 84.47 | 99.08 | 98.17 | 87.28 | 47.68 | 99.50 | 97.61 | 88.55 ± 16.25 |
| NN+LBP [29] | 94.16 | 88.39 | 79.85 | 99.75 | 95.17 | 78.86 | 50.57 | 99.93 | 93.54 | 86.69 ± 16.25 |
| DTN [16] | 90.0 | 97.3 | 97.5 | 99.9 | 99.9 | 99.6 | 81.6 | 99.9 | 97.5 | 95.9 ± 6.2 |
| CDCN++ [34] | 98.07 | 99.90 | 99.60 | 99.98 | 99.89 | **99.98** | 72.29 | 100.00 | 99.98 | 96.63 ± 9.15 |
| HMP [32] | **99.62** | 100.00 | 100.00 | 99.99 | 99.74 | 99.91 | 71.64 | 100.00 | 99.99 | 96.77 ± 9.99 |
| NAS-FAS [31] | **99.62** | 100.00 | 100.00 | 99.99 | 99.89 | **99.98** | 74.62 | 100.00 | 99.98 | 97.12 ± 8.94 |
| **NSEAN (Ours)** | 99.49 | 100.00 | 100.00 | 100.00 | 99.92 | 99.97 | 83.28 | 100.00 | 100.00 | **98.07 ± 5.23** |

## 4.5 Inter Testing

We evaluate the generalization ability in unknown presentation attacks and unseen environment via cross-type and cross-dataset testing, respectively.

**Cross-Type Testing.** We use CASIA-MFSD [35], Replay-Attack [7] and MSU-MFSD [27] to conduct intra-dataset cross-type testing between replay and print attacks based on the protocol proposed in [1]. As shown in Table 6, our proposed method's performance ranks first (98.07% AUC) among state-of-the-art methods, This verify that our method have good generalization ability in unknown attacks.

**Cross-Dataset Testing.** Here, we conduct experiments on CASIA-MFSD and Replay-attack database in HTER(%). For protocol CR, the CASIA-MFSD is used for training and the Replay-attack for testing. On the contrary, protocol RC employs Replay-attack as training set and CASIA-MFSD for testing. From Table 5, we can see that our method NSEAN achieves the lowest HTER on protocol CR (20.2%) and RC (26.7%) compared with the state-of-the-art methods. The improvement of performance showing that we always have good generalization ability under previously unseen environmental conditions.

### 4.6 Analysis and Visualization.

**Results Visualization.** The predicted binary mask (128 × 128) of samples on OULU-NPU under protocol 1 are shown in Fig. 4. It can be seen that our MSRS can reveal differences between the living and spoofing faces, which is more conducive to enhance the discriminability.

**Features Visualization.** Distribution of feature for the testing videos on Protocol-1 OULU-NPU is shown in Fig. 5 via t-SNE [17]. It is clear that the

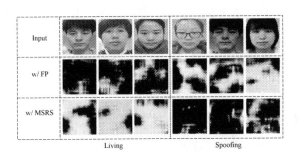

**Fig. 4.** The size of 128×128 predicted results of samples in OULU-NPU. The predicted binary mask from Feature Pyramid (FP) and Multi-Scale Refinement Strategy (MSRS) in the second and third row, respectively.

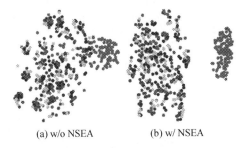

(a) w/o NSEA          (b) w/ NSEA

**Fig. 5.** Feature distribution visualization in 2D. Left: features w/o NSEA, Right: features W/ NSEA. Color code used: *red* = live, *green* = printer1, *blu* = printer2, *purple* = replay1, *cyan* = replay2. (Color figure online)

features with NSEA module (right image) performs better than that without NSEA (left image), which demonstrates the discrimination ability of NSEA to distinguish the living faces from spoofing faces.

## 5    Conclusion

In this paper, We propose a novel Non-Significant information Enhancement based Attention (NSEA) module for face anti-spoofing task. In order to capture more fine-grained information and refine the coarse binary mask at different scales, we employ the Multi-Scale Refinement Strategy (MSRS). Extensive experiments results demonstrate the advantages of the proposed method.

## References

1. Arashloo, S.R., Kittler, J., Christmas, W.: An anomaly detection approach to face spoofing detection: A new formulation and evaluation protocol. IEEE Access **5**, 13868–13882 (2017)
2. Atoum, Y., Liu, Y., Jourabloo, A., Liu, X.: Face anti-spoofing using patch and depth-based CNNs. In: 2017 IEEE International Joint Conference on Biometrics (IJCB), pp. 319–328. IEEE (2017)
3. Bharadwaj, S., Dhamecha, T.I., Vatsa, M., Singh, R.: Computationally efficient face spoofing detection with motion magnification. In: Proceedings of the IEEE Conference on Computer Vision and Pattern Recognition Workshops, pp. 105–110 (2013)
4. Boulkenafet, Z., Komulainen, J., Hadid, A.: Face anti-spoofing based on color texture analysis. In: 2015 IEEE International Conference on Image Processing (ICIP), pp. 2636–2640. IEEE (2015)
5. Boulkenafet, Z., Komulainen, J., Hadid, A.: Face spoofing detection using colour texture analysis. IEEE Trans. Inf. Forensics Secur. **11**(8), 1818–1830 (2016)
6. Boulkenafet, Z., Komulainen, J., Li, L., Feng, X., Hadid, A.: OULU-NPU: a mobile face presentation attack database with real-world variations. In: 2017 12th IEEE International Conference on Automatic Face & Gesture Recognition (FG 2017), pp. 612–618. IEEE (2017)
7. Chingovska, I., Anjos, A., Marcel, S.: On the effectiveness of local binary patterns in face anti-spoofing. In: 2012 BIOSIG-Proceedings of the International Conference of Biometrics Special Interest Group (BIOSIG), pp. 1–7. IEEE (2012)
8. de Freitas Pereira, T., Anjos, A., De Martino, J.M., Marcel, S.: Can face anti-spoofing countermeasures work in a real world scenario? In: 2013 International Conference on Biometrics (ICB), pp. 1–8. IEEE (2013)
9. George, A., Marcel, S.: Deep pixel-wise binary supervision for face presentation attack detection. In: 2019 International Conference on Biometrics (ICB), pp. 1–8. IEEE (2019)
10. Hu, J., Shen, L., Sun, G.: Squeeze-and-excitation networks. In: Proceedings of the IEEE Conference on Computer Vision and Pattern Recognition, pp. 7132–7141 (2018)
11. Jia, Y., Zhang, J., Shan, S., Chen, X.: Single-side domain generalization for face anti-spoofing. In: Proceedings of the IEEE/CVF Conference on Computer Vision and Pattern Recognition, pp. 8484–8493 (2020)

12. Jourabloo, A., Liu, Y., Liu, X.: Face de-spoofing: anti-spoofing via noise modeling. In: Proceedings of the European Conference on Computer Vision (ECCV), pp. 290–306 (2018)
13. Li, X., Wan, J., Jin, Y., Liu, A., Guo, G., Li, S.Z.: 3DPC-Net: 3D point cloud network for face anti-spoofing. In: 2020 IEEE International Joint Conference on Biometrics (IJCB), pp. 1–8. IEEE
14. Lin, T.Y., Dollár, P., Girshick, R., He, K., Hariharan, B., Belongie, S.: Feature pyramid networks for object detection. In: Proceedings of the IEEE Conference on Computer Vision and Pattern Recognition, pp. 2117–2125 (2017)
15. Liu, Y., Jourabloo, A., Liu, X.: Learning deep models for face anti-spoofing: binary or auxiliary supervision. In: Proceedings of the IEEE Conference on Computer Vision and Pattern Recognition, pp. 389–398 (2018)
16. Liu, Y., Stehouwer, J., Jourabloo, A., Liu, X.: Deep tree learning for zero-shot face anti-spoofing. In: Proceedings of the IEEE/CVF Conference on Computer Vision and Pattern Recognition, pp. 4680–4689 (2019)
17. Van der Maaten, L., Hinton, G.: Visualizing data using t-SNE. J. Mach. Learn. Res. 9(11) (2008)
18. Määttä, J., Hadid, A., Pietikäinen, M.: Face spoofing detection from single images using micro-texture analysis. In: 2011 International Joint Conference on Biometrics (IJCB), pp. 1–7. IEEE (2011)
19. Pan, G., Sun, L., Wu, Z., Lao, S.: Eyeblink-based anti-spoofing in face recognition from a generic webcamera. In: 2007 IEEE 11th International Conference on Computer Vision, pp. 1–8. IEEE (2007)
20. Patel, K., Han, H., Jain, A.K.: Cross-database face antispoofing with robust feature representation. In: You, Z., et al. (eds.) CCBR 2016. LNCS, vol. 9967, pp. 611–619. Springer, Cham (2016). https://doi.org/10.1007/978-3-319-46654-5_67
21. Pinto, A., Pedrini, H., Schwartz, W.R., Rocha, A.: Face spoofing detection through visual codebooks of spectral temporal cubes. IEEE Trans. Image Process. 24(12), 4726–4740 (2015)
22. Shao, R., Lan, X., Yuen, P.C.: Regularized fine-grained meta face anti-spoofing. In: Proceedings of the AAAI Conference on Artificial Intelligence, vol. 34, pp. 11974–11981 (2020)
23. international organization for standardization: Iso/iec jtc 1/sc 37 biometrics: Information technology biometric presentation attack detection part 1: Framework. In https://www.iso.org/obp/ui/iso (2016)
24. Wang, G., Han, H., Shan, S., Chen, X.: Cross-domain face presentation attack detection via multi-domain disentangled representation learning. In: Proceedings of the IEEE/CVF Conference on Computer Vision and Pattern Recognition, pp. 6678–6687 (2020)
25. Wang, Z., et al.: Deep spatial gradient and temporal depth learning for face anti-spoofing. In: Proceedings of the IEEE/CVF Conference on Computer Vision and Pattern Recognition, pp. 5042–5051 (2020)
26. Wang, Z., et al.: Exploiting temporal and depth information for multi-frame face anti-spoofing. arXiv preprint arXiv:1811.05118 (2018)
27. Wen, D., Han, H., Jain, A.K.: Face spoof detection with image distortion analysis. IEEE Trans. Inf. Forensics Secur. 10(4), 746–761 (2015)
28. Woo, S., Park, J., Lee, J.Y., Kweon, I.S.: CBAM: convolutional block attention module. In: Proceedings of the European Conference on Computer Vision (ECCV), pp. 3–19 (2018)

29. Xiong, F., AbdAlmageed, W.: Unknown presentation attack detection with face RGB images. In: 2018 IEEE 9th International Conference on Biometrics Theory, Applications and Systems (BTAS), pp. 1–9. IEEE (2018)
30. Yang, X., et al.: Face anti-spoofing: model matters, so does data. In: Proceedings of the IEEE/CVF Conference on Computer Vision and Pattern Recognition, pp. 3507–3516 (2019)
31. Yu, Z., Wan, J., Qin, Y., Li, X., Li, S.Z., Zhao, G.: NAS-FAS: static-dynamic central difference network search for face anti-spoofing. IEEE TPAMI, pp. 1 (2020). https://doi.org/10.1109/TPAMI.2020.3036338
32. Yu, Z., Li, X., Niu, X., Shi, J., Zhao, G.: Face anti-spoofing with human material perception. In: Vedaldi, A., Bischof, H., Brox, T., Frahm, J.-M. (eds.) ECCV 2020. LNCS, vol. 12352, pp. 557–575. Springer, Cham (2020). https://doi.org/10.1007/978-3-030-58571-6_33
33. Yu, Z., Li, X., Shi, J., Xia, Z., Zhao, G.: Revisiting pixel-wise supervision for face anti-spoofing. arXiv preprint arXiv:2011.12032 (2020)
34. Yu, Z., et al.: Searching central difference convolutional networks for face anti-spoofing. In: Proceedings of the IEEE/CVF Conference on Computer Vision and Pattern Recognition, pp. 5295–5305 (2020)
35. Zhang, Z., Yan, J., Liu, S., Lei, Z., Yi, D., Li, S.Z.: A face antispoofing database with diverse attacks. In: 2012 5th IAPR International Conference on Biometrics (ICB), pp. 26–31. IEEE (2012)

# Early Diagnosis of Alzheimer's Disease Using 3D Residual Attention Network Based on Hippocampal Multi-indices Feature Fusion

Yiyu Zhang[1], Qiang Zheng[1(✉)], Kun Zhao[2], Honglun Li[3], Chaoqing Ma[1], Shuanhu Wu[1], and Xiangrong Tong[1]

[1] School of Computer and Control Engineering, Yantai University, Yantai 264205, China
zhengqiang@ytu.edu.cn
[2] Beijing Advanced Innovation Centre for Biomedical Engineering, School of Biological Science and Medical Engineering, Beihang University, Beijing, China
[3] Departments of Medical Oncology and Radiology, Affiliated Yantai Yuhuangding Hospital of Qingdao University Medical College, Yantai 264000, China

**Abstract.** Alzheimer's disease (AD) is one of the most common causes of dementia in older individuals. Convergence evidence has confirmed that hippocampal atrophy is one of the most robust neuroimaging biomarkers of AD. However, most previous studies only independently consider the hippocampal volume or other morphological indicators, which cannot reflect the abnormal pattern of the hippocampus comprehensively and objectively. The primary aim of this study is to develop a classification model of AD based on a hippocampal multi-indices features fusion framework. The multi-indices features included 1) hippocampal gray volume block; 2) probability matrix obtained from the hippocampal segmentation; 3) hippocampal radiomics features. The 3D convolutional neural network based on the multi-indices feature fusion framework showed an ACC = 90.3% (AUC = 0.93) in classifying AD (N = 282) from NC (N = 603). The results suggested that the hippocampal multi-indices features are robust neuroimaging biomarkers in the early diagnosis of AD.

**Keywords:** Alzheimer's disease · Hippocampus · Multi-indices · Convolutional neural network · Classification

## 1 Introduction

Alzheimer's disease (AD), one of the most common causes of dementia in older individuals, is a fatal neurodegenerative disease that is characterized by progressive impairment of cognition, functional capacity, and memory loss [1]. Till now, the etiology and pathogenesis of AD have not been fully elucidated, and there are no effective drugs or clinical treatment methods to reverse the progression of AD. Besides, biomarkers for early diagnosis of the validated, stable, and effective disease still not exist yet [2, 3].

MRI studies showed that the structure of the hippocampus, parahippocampal gyrus, medial temporal lobe, and entorhinal cortex were significantly altered in AD [4], and

© Springer Nature Switzerland AG 2021
H. Ma et al. (Eds.): PRCV 2021, LNCS 13021, pp. 449–457, 2021.
https://doi.org/10.1007/978-3-030-88010-1_37

the hippocampal atrophy is the most robust [5–7]. However, it is difficult to obtain sufficiently sensitive information about hippocampal lesions due to the poor sensitivity of volume. Thus, the high-order features of the hippocampus were also involved in the previous study [8–10]. The previous study has confirmed that the hippocampal radiomics feature is a robust biomarker of AD [10]. Briefly, radiomics is a texture analysis method, which can quantitatively describe the subtle changes of the brain regions [11]. However, hippocampal single-indice features cannot reflect the abnormal pattern of the hippocampus comprehensively and objectively. Thus, we hypothesize that the multi-indices information of the hippocampus would obtain ideal performance in the classification of AD and NC.

Deep learning methods, especially convolutional neural networks (CNN), can automatically learn the most representative features of the data [12, 13], which have been used successfully in classifying AD from NC based on gray matter volume of the whole brain [14–16]. The primary aim of this paper is to develop a classification model of AD combined with 3D CNN and hippocampal multi-indices feature fusion strategy. Firstly, multi-indices features of the hippocampus are extracted from the T1-weighted MRI, including hippocampal gray volume block, probability matrix of the hippocampus and hippocampal radiomics features. At last, the classification model was created by combining a 3D residual attention network and a multi-indices features fusion strategy.

## 2    Methods

### 2.1    Multi-indices Feature Fusion Framework.

In this study, it was assumed that the diagnostic performance of AD with the multi-indices feature fusion is better than that with a single-indice feature. For each subject, the multi-indices features of the hippocampus were extracted from MRI. A 3D residual attention network was used to extract the hippocampal features based on the gray matter hippocampal block and the probability matrix. At last, a fully connected layer was used to generate the individual prediction by combining the output of the 3D residual attention network and hippocampal radiomics features (Fig. 1).

### 2.2    3D Residual Attention Network

We propose a 3D residual attention network (3DRAN) based on a previous study [17] (Fig. 2A), which includes four modules.

The max-pooling was used to retain the salient features and reduce the dimension of feature maps. The attention module can capture the significance of various voxels for classification during end-to-end training, which is instructive to explore potential imaging markers [18] (Fig. 2B). Besides, the residual block was also used for down-sampling to improve the capacity of representation (Fig. 2C), and the global average pooling (GAP) was used to compress all voxels of single-channel feature map into one value to reduce the computational complexity so as to prevent over-fitting. At last, the output of the 3DRAN is a vector with 128 dimensions.

The attention module including a trunk branch and a soft mask branch, which was used to capture more discriminative information of the hippocampus. Additionally, the

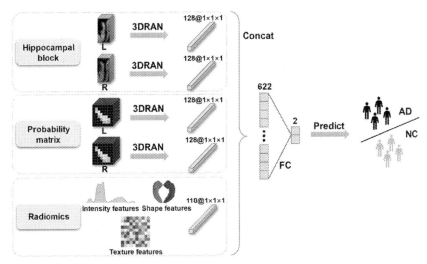

**Fig. 1.** The framework of multi-indices feature fusion. Abbreviations: 3DRAN = 3D residual attention network; Concat = concatenate; FC = fully con-nected layer; AD = Alzheimer's disease; NC = normal control.

max-pooling, up-sampling and the time of cross-layer connection in the soft mask branch will be reduced as the feature map shrinks. A novel residual module consisting of a trunk branch and a regulation branch was used in this study to preserve more valuable information [19, 20].

## 2.3 Data Preprocessing and Feature Extraction

The MRI images were registered to the Montreal Neurological Institute (MNI) 152 space $(1 \times 1 \times 1 \text{ mm}^3)$ after N4 bias field correction [21]. Firstly, the probability matrix of the bilateral hippocampus was obtained using the label fusion algorithm [22]. Secondly, the hippocampal radiomics features were computed based on a previous study [10], including intensity features (N = 14), shape features (N = 8) and textural features (N = 33). Detailed definition of the radiomics features can be found in previous studies [10, 11]. Thirdly, the gray matter volume of the subject was obtained by the SPM12 toolkit (www.fil.ion.ucl.ac.uk/spm/). Furthermore, to reduce the influence of other tissues and time complexity, the bilateral hippocampal block with the size of $62 \times 26 \times 38$ was segmented from the whole-brain image (Fig. 3).

## 2.4 Implementation

The proposed classification model was implemented on Pytorch 1.7.1 using the optimizer Adam with initial learning rate of $3 \times 10^{-4}$, weight decay rate of $1 \times 10^{-4}$ and batch size of 8. Besides, the Cross Entropy loss function was used in this study and the training time was set to 70 epochs.

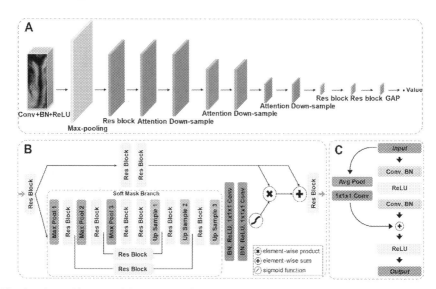

**Fig. 2.** The architecture of the network. (**A**) 3D residual attention network. (**B**) attention module. (**C**) residual block. Abbreviations: Conv = convolutional layer; BN = batch normalization; ReLU = rectified linear unit; Res Block = residual block; Attention = attention module; GAP = global average pooling.

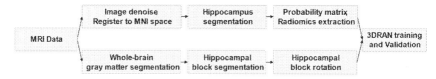

**Fig. 3.** The sketch pipeline for the data processing.

## 3  Results

### 3.1  Demographic Characteristics and Neuropsychological Assessment of the Groups

A total of 885 MRI images (603 NCs and 282 AD patients) were obtained from the ADNI (www.adni.loni.usc.edu), which included baseline T1-weighted MRI scans from the ADNI-1 and ADNI-GO&2 phases. The age was significantly different between the NC and AD groups, and the gender ratio was not significantly different between the NC and AD groups. As expected, the Mini-mental State Examination (MMSE) score and Clinical Dementia Rating (CDR) score were significantly different between the NC and AD groups (Table 1).

**Table 1.** Demographic information.

|  | NC (n = 603) | AD (n = 282) | p value |
|---|---|---|---|
| Age (Year) | 73.46 ± 6.16 | 74.91 ± 7.69 | 0.003 |
| Gender (M/F) | 277/326 | 151/131 | 0.847 |
| MMSE | 29.08 ± 1.1 | 23.18 ± 2.13 | <0.001 |
| CDR | 0.03 ± 0.13 | 4.38 ± 1.69 | <0.001 |

Abbreviations: NC = normal control; AD = Alzheimer's disease; MMSE = mini mental state exami-nation; CDR = clinical dementia rating.

### 3.2  The Performance of the Classification Model with Different Hippocampal Features

The classification model showed an ACC = 0.90 (AUC = 0.93, SEN = 0.84, SPE = 0.93) based on the multi-indices feature fusion algorithm with 10-fold cross-validation. These indicators are defined as follows:

$$ACC = \frac{TP + TN}{TP + TN + FP + FN} \tag{1}$$

$$SEN = \frac{TP}{TP + FN} \tag{2}$$

$$SPE = \frac{TN}{TN + FP} \tag{3}$$

where TP (true positive, the number of AD correctly identified as AD), TN (true negative, the number of NC patients correctly identified as NC), FN (false negative, the number of AD patients incorrectly identified as NC), and FP (false positive, the number of NC incorrectly identified as AD). The AUC is the area under the curve of receiver operating characteristic, which can accurately evaluate the performance of the classifier. Besides, the balanced accuracy of this study is 88.5%, which is defined as the (SEN + SPE)/2 due to the unbalanced data (the number of NC = 603 and the number of AD = 282) was involved in this study.

To compare the performance of the classification AD and NC with the different hippocampal features, we also computed the accuracy of the classification model with hippocampal block, probability matrix and radiomics features respectively. The result showed an ACC = 0.88 (AUC = 0.92, SEN = 0.80, SPE = 0.92) with the hippocampal block, an ACC = 0.87 (AUC = 0.92, SEN = 0.74, SPE = 0.93) with the probability matrix and an ACC = 0.88 (AUC = 0.91, SEN = 0.76, SPE = 0.93) with the radiomics features (Fig. 4 and Table 2). The experimental results demonstrate that the classification performance using multi-indices feature fusion of AD and NC is significantly higher than that with single-indice features.

**Table 2.** Comparison of the classification model with different hippocampal features.

| Feature | ACC (%) | SEN (%) | SPE (%) | AUC |
|---|---|---|---|---|
| Hippocampal block | 88.3 | 80.0 | 92.1 | 0.921 |
| Probability matrix | 87.1 | 73.6 | 93.3 | 0.918 |
| Radiomics | 87.5 | 76.4 | 92.6 | 0.905 |
| **Combination** | **90.3** | **83.6** | **93.4** | **0.930** |

Abbreviations: ACC = accuracy; SEN = sensitivity; SPE = specificity; AUC = area under curve.

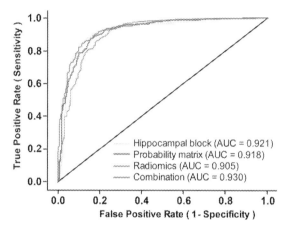

**Fig.4.** ROC curves of the classification model with different hippocampal features.

### 3.3   Comparison of Different Methods

The deep learning model has been used successfully in the classification of AD and NC. We also summarize the typical studies published in recent years [8, 9, 14, 23, 24]. For those studies based on the ADNI dataset, the ACC was ranged from 79.9% to 92.1% (Proposed method = 90.3%), and the AUC was ranged from 0.86 to 0.94 (Proposed method = 0.93). More importantly, the accuracy of this study is nearly or higher than that in previous studies (Table 3).

## 4   Discussion

In this study, we determined that the proposed method based on multi-indices hippocampal feature fusion can be used to classify AD and NC with an AUC = 0.93.

The best model is the hippocampal gray matter block-based in those only based on a single-indice hippocampal feature, which suggests that the surrounding area of the hippocampus can also provide essential information in AD analysis (Fig. 1). As

**Table 3.** Comparison of different methods.

| Method | Subjects | ACC (%) | SEN (%) | SPE (%) | AUC |
|---|---|---|---|---|---|
| Zhang et al. [23] | 51AD + 52NC | 83.1 | 80.5 | 85.1 | - |
| Cao et al. [24] | 192AD + 229NC | 88.6 | 85.7 | 90.4 | 0.90 |
| Lin et al. [8] | 188AD + 229NC | 79.9 | 84.0 | 74.8 | 0.86 |
| Liu et al. [9] | 97AD + 119NC | 88.9 | 86.6 | 90.8 | 0.93 |
| Jin et al. [14] | 227AD + 305NC | 92.1 | 89.0 | 94.4 | 0.94 |
| **Proposed method** | **282AD + 603NC** | **90.3** | **83.6** | **93.4** | **0.93** |

Abbreviations: AD = Alzheimer's disease; NC = normal control; ACC = accuracy; SEN = sensitivi-ty; SPE = specificity; AUC = area under curve.

expected, the multi-indices feature-based model was significantly higher than that based on a single-indice feature-based model. The three indices of the hippocampus can reflect different information of the hippocampus with different views. For example, the hippocampal block can reflect the gray matter volume of the hippocampus [18]. Similar to the hippocampal block, the probability matrix of the hippocampus reflected the possibility of belonging to the hippocampus for each voxel [22]. The radiomics features mainly reflected the distribution pattern of gray values (such as run-length nonuniformity and gray-length nonuniformity) and the shape of the hippocampus [10]. Thus, the more comprehensive information about the hippocampus can be reflected on multi-indices rather than single-indice.

The proposed method was compared with other traditional machine learning methods and deep learning methods. The proposed result was higher than the previous studies [8, 9, 23, 24] excluded Jin et al. [14]. One reason is that only the hippocampal features were involved in this study rather than the whole brain [14]. However, the computational complexity of classification was reduced significantly only based on hippocampal features. Another reason is that the performance of this classification model is limited by the unbalanced data (NC = 603, AD = 282). Thus we will add the OASIS (The Open Access Series of Imaging Studies, www.oasis-brains.org), EDSD (The European DTI Study on Dementia, www.neugrid4you.eu) and AIBL (Australian Imaging Biomarkers and Lifestyle Study of Aging, www.aibl.csiro.au) databases to validate the robustness of the proposed model in the future study.

## 5  Conclusion

This study proposed a 3D residual attention network based on the hippocampal multi-indices features fusion for individualized diagnosis of AD. The results suggest that promising classification performance could be achieved by the 3DRAN built on a combination of the hippocampal block, probability matrix and radiomics with reasonable accuracy (90.3%). The promising classification performance also indicates that hippocampal multi-indices features can be powerful neuroimaging biomarkers for AD.

**Acknowledgments.** This work was supported by National Natural Science Foundation of China (61802330, 61802331, 61801415), Natural Science Foundation of Shandong Province (ZR2018BF008).

# References

1. Querfurth, H.W., et al.: Alzheimer's disease. New England J. Med. **362**(4), 329 (2010)
2. Nakamura, A., et al.: High performance plasma amyloid-β biomarkers for Alzheimer's disease. Nature **554**(7691), 249–254 (2018)
3. Rathore, S., et al.: A review on neuroimaging-based classification studies and associated feature extraction methods for Alzheimer's disease and its prodromal stages. Neuroimage **155**, 530–548 (2017)
4. Karas, G., et al.: Precuneus atrophy in early-onset Alzheimer's disease: a morphometric structural MRI study. Neuroradiology **49**(12), 967–976 (2007)
5. Braak, H., et al.: Staging of Alzheimer's disease-related neurofibrillary changes. Neurobiol. Aging **16**(3), 271–278 (1995)
6. Ezzati, A., et al.: Differential association of left and right hippocampal volumes with verbal episodic and spatial memory in older adults. Neuropsychologia **93**, 380–385 (2016)
7. Pasquini, L., et al.: Link between hippocampus' raised local and eased global intrinsic connectivity in AD. Alzheimer's Dement. **11**(5), 475–484 (2015)
8. Lin, W., et al.: Convolutional neural networks-based MRI image analysis for the Alzheimer's disease prediction from mild cognitive impairment. Front. Neurosci. **12**, 777 (2018)
9. Liu, M., et al.: A multi-model deep convolutional neural network for automatic hippocampus segmentation and classification in Alzheimer's disease. NeuroImage **208**, 116459 (2020)
10. Zhao, K., et al.: Independent and reproducible hippocampal radiomic biomarkers for multisite Alzheimer's disease: diagnosis, longitudinal progress and biological basis. Sci. Bull. **65**(13), 1103–1113 (2020)
11. Aerts, H.J.W.L., et al.: Decoding tumour phenotype by noninvasive imaging using a quantitative radiomics approach. Nat. Commun. **5**, 4006 (2014)
12. Woo, S., Park, J., Lee, J.-Y., Kweon, I.S.: CBAM: Convolutional Block Attention Module. In: Ferrari, V., Hebert, M., Sminchisescu, C., Weiss, Y. (eds.) ECCV 2018. LNCS, vol. 11211, pp. 3–19. Springer, Cham (2018). https://doi.org/10.1007/978-3-030-01234-2_1
13. Vaswani, A., et al.: Attention is all you need. In: Advances in Neural Information Processing Systems, pp. 5998–6008 (2017)
14. Jin, D., et al.: Generalizable, reproducible, and neuroscientifically interpretable imaging biomarkers for Alzheimer's disease. Adv. Sci. **7**(14), 2000675 (2020)
15. Wu, C., et al.: Discrimination and conversion prediction of mild cognitive impairment using convolutional neural networks. Quant. Imaging Med. Surg. **8**(10), 992–1003 (2018)
16. Pan, D., et al.: Early detection of Alzheimer's Disease using magnetic resonance imaging: a novel approach combining convolutional neural networks and ensemble learning. Front. Neurosci. **14** (2020)
17. Wang, F., et al.: Residual attention network for image classification. In: Proceedings of the IEEE conference on computer vision and pattern recognition. pp. 3156–3164.(2017).
18. Jin, D., et al.: Attention-based 3D Convolutional Network for Alzheimer's Disease Diagnosis and Biomarkers Exploration. In: IEEE International Symposium on Biomedical Imaging.(2019).
19. He, K., et al.: Deep residual learning for image recognition. In: Proceedings of the IEEE conference on computer vision and pattern recognition. pp. 770–778.(2016).

20. He, T., et al.: Bag of tricks for image classification with convolutional neural networks. In: Proceedings of the IEEE/CVF Conference on Computer Vision and Pattern Recognition. pp. 558–567.(2019).
21. Avants, B.B., et al.: A reproducible evaluation of ANTs similarity metric performance in brain image registration. Neuroimage **54**(3), 2033–2044 (2011)
22. Zheng, Q., et al.: Integrating semi-supervised and supervised learning methods for label fusion in multi-atlas based image segmentation. Front. Neuroinform. **12**, 69 (2018)
23. Zhang, J., et al.: Detecting anatomical landmarks for fast Alzheimer's disease diagnosis. IEEE Trans. Med. Imaging **35**(12), 2524–2533 (2016)
24. Cao, P., et al.: Nonlinearity-aware based dimensionality reduction and over-sampling for AD/MCI classification from MRI measures. Comput. Biol. Med. **91**, 21–37 (2017)

# HPCReg-Net: Unsupervised U-Net Integrating Dilated Convolution and Residual Attention for Hippocampus Registration

Hu Yu[1], Qiang Zheng[1(⊠)], Kun Zhao[2], Honglun Li[3], Chaoqing Ma[1], Shuanhu Wu[1], and Xiangrong Tong[1]

[1] School of Computer and Control Engineering, Yantai University, Yantai 264205, China
zhengqiang@ytu.edu.cn
[2] Beijing Advanced Innovation Centre for Biomedical Engineering, School of Biological Science and Medical Engineering, Beihang University, Beijing, China
[3] Departments of Medical Oncology and Radiology, Affiliated Yantai Yuhuangding Hospital of Qingdao University Medical College, Yantai 264000, China

**Abstract.** The hippocampus plays a critical role in the human brain, which is mainly responsible for memory and other functions. Accurate and effective hippocampal registration significantly impacts all kinds of hippocampus-related analysis, particularly in the widely-used multi-atlas hippocampus segmentation and the associated clinical decision. However, the existing registration methods suffer from high computational cost and insufficient registration performance. A 3D unsupervised U-Net registration model HPCReg-Net was proposed under a coarse-fine registration strategy in this study, which combined dilated convolution and residual attention module. Specifically, in the coarse registration stage, a new gap-filling mechanism was designed to solve the semantic gap problem in U-Net, and a novel residual attention module was devised to characterize hippocampal deformation. In the fine registration stage, a cascaded dilated convolution module was adopted to capture the considerable deformation and position information of voxels from each pair of images. The experimental results based on ADNI data sets show that our method can improve hippocampal registration greatly in both computational efficiency and registration precision.

**Keywords:** Hippocampus · Image registration · U-Net · Dilated convolution · Gap-filling · Residual attention module

## 1 Introduction

The hippocampus plays a critical role in the human brain, which is mainly responsible for memory and other functions. Accurate and effective hippocampal registration has a significant impact on all kinds of hippocampus-related analysis, particularly in the widely-used multi-atlas hippocampus segmentation (MAHS) [1, 2] and the associated clinical decision such as Alzheimer's disease (AD). Specifically, hippocampus registration is an essential step in the preprocessing steps of MAHS, which affected the

H. Ma et al. (Eds.): PRCV 2021, LNCS 13021, pp. 458–466, 2021.
https://doi.org/10.1007/978-3-030-88010-1_38

segmentation significantly in the aspects of accuracy and efficiency, and further determines the subsequent feature extraction from hippocampus for medical image analysis [3]. Thus, improving the accuracy of hippocampus registration is of great significance for the research of hippocampus-related analysis.

Medical image registration methods are mainly divided into traditional and deep learning-based registration methods. The traditional registration method needs to be iteratively optimized for each pair of images [4] which suffers from large amounts of computation and instability. Recent studies have leveraged deep learning techniques to improve the medical image registration in computational efficiency and accuracy. A typical unsupervised registration model VoxelMorph [5] and its associated modifications [6, 7] were proposed to solve the time-consuming problem in medical image registration. However, most of them can not accurately capture the fine deformation and position information of voxels in each pair of images. Thus, more powerful techniques such as dilated convolution [8] and residual attention module [9] are expected to be adopted and improve the registration performance.

For this purpose, we designed a novel HPCReg-Net for hippocampus (HPC) registration (Reg), which was an unsupervised registration model integrating dilated convolution and residual attention for fast and high-precision hippocampal non-rigid registration. Our main contributions are:

(1) A cascaded dilated convolution and residual attention module was designed for gap-filling and to help characterize the coarse voxel deformation in hippocampal registration.
(2) A cascaded dilated convolution module was devised to further capture the fine deformation and position information of voxels.
(3) A residual attention module was introduced to preserve more valuable information in the down-sampling pathway.

The rest of this paper is as follows. In Sect. 2, we introduced the proposed HPCReg-Net model. In Sect. 3, the performance of HPCReg-Net registration was evaluated and compared with other methods. Sections 4 were the discussion and conclusion of our study.

## 2    Method

### 2.1    The Proposed HPCReg-Net for Hippocampus Registration

The proposed HPCReg-Net was established under an unsupervised registration framework (Fig. 1), followed by spatial transformation [10] to deform the moving image to fixed image space. HPCReg-Net is trained by maximizing the similarity between moved and fixed image, and smoothing constraints are imposed on deformation field (DF).

Specifically, a coarse-fine strategy was adopted in the proposed HPCReg-Net (Fig. 2(a)), where the U-Net [11] framework was for coarse registration of big deformations in each pair of hippocampus images, followed by a cascaded dilated convolution module (CDC-module) devised to further capture the fine deformation and position information of voxels.

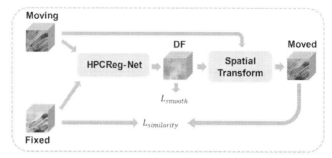

**Fig. 1.** The overall process of unsupervised registration. $L_{similarity}$ is the similarity loss function and $L_{smooth}$ is the smoothing constraint loss function.

In the coarse registration stage, a residual attention module (RA-module) and a cascaded dilated convolution and residual attention module (DCRA-module) were adopted to improve the performance of U-Net framework. Specifically, the RA-module was added in the contracting pathway of the U-Net to preserve more valuable information in the down-sampling process. The DCRA-module was to fill the semantic gap [12, 13] between contracting and expansive pathways in the U-Net framework, where the dilated convolution was to increase the receptive field while keeping the spatial resolution unchanged, and the followed residual attention module was to accurately extract the deformation characteristics of hippocampal voxels in each pair of images [14]. Of note, the residual attention module was divided into the trunk branch and the soft mask branch in our study, in which, the trunk branch learned the original features of the hippocampus, while the soft mask branch enhanced the features of the hippocampus.

In the fine registration stage, we cascaded four layers of dilated convolutions with different dilated rate to enhance the representation ability of the model and capture the slight deformation and position information of voxels. Additionally, considering that down-sampling too much in the contracting pathway of U-Net will cause the loss of hippocampus features due to the small volume comparing with the whole brain, the CDC-module can increase the receptive field while keeping the spatial resolution.

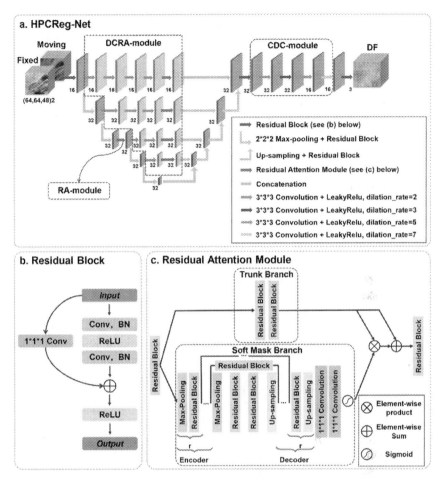

**Fig. 2.** Overview of HPCReg-Net framework. (a) HPCReg-Net network architecture. DCRA-module = cascaded dilated convolution and residual attention module, RA-module = residual attention module, CDC-module = cascaded dilated convolution module. (b) Residual Block. Conv = convolutional layer; BN = batch normalization; ReLU = rectified linear unit. (c) Residual attention module. The residual attention module includes a trunk branch and a soft mask branch. The trunk branch consists of two Residual Block. The soft mask branch is similar to a small U-Net with r being the depth of the cross-layer connection. The parameter r was set to 0,1,2,3 based on the depth of the cross-layer connection in HPCReg-Net.

## 2.2 Loss Functions

The loss function used in the HPCReg-Net was defined as follows:

$$Loss = L_{similarity} + \lambda \|\nabla \Phi\|^2 \tag{1}$$

where $L_{similarity}$ is the similarity loss function to optimize HPCReg-Net by calculating the similarity between the fixed image and the warped image. The second terms is the smoothness regularization loss function of the deformation field $\Phi$. Parameter $\lambda$ is used to balance the similarity loss and regularization loss.

We use local normalized cross-correlation (NCC) as our similarity loss function, as shown in [5]. The proposed similarity loss is then formulated as:

$$L_{similarity} = -NCC(F, M(\Phi)) \tag{2}$$

Where $F$ represents a fixed image and $M(\Phi)$ represents a warped image, $NCC$ represents the local normalized cross-correlation.

## 3  Experiments

### 3.1  Data and Pre-processing

In this study, 133 T1 images with hippocampus segmentation labels were obtained from the Alzheimer's Disease Neuroimaging Program (ADNI) database (www.adni. loni.usc.edu) [15], including 43 normal control (NC), 46 mild cognitive impairment (MCI) patients, and 44 AD patients.

The MRI images were registered to the Montreal Neurological Institute (MNI) 152 space ($1 \times 1 \times 1$ mm$^3$) after N4 bias field correction [16]. To reduce the computational cost, we use the same strategy proposed by Hao et al. [17] to cut all brain MRI to $60 \times 60 \times 48$ while preserving the hippocampus.

In the present study, two strategies were adopted for data augmentation: 1) The right hippocampus was flipped into left to double the data. The dataset was then divided into training (N = 160), validation (N = 52) and test (N = 54) sets in our study. 2) For each dataset of training, validation, or test, two images were randomly selected as fixed and moving images by an (n*(n–1)) strategy given N images in each set, generating 25440 pairs, 2652 pairs, and 2862 pairs for training, validation and test set used to train and assess the hippocampus registration in our study.

In order to quantitatively evaluate the registration performance, the Dice Similarity Coefficient (DSC) was used as the evaluation index. Higher DSC indicates better registration performance.

### 3.2  Baseline Methods

In this study, VoxelMorph [5] and symmetric normalized (SyN) [18] were compared with the proposed HPCReg-Net. Implementation of the SyN was obtained from (www.git hub.com/ANTsX/ANTsPy). For VoxelMorph, the code provided on the official website (www.github.com/voxelmorph/voxelmorph) was used in this study.

Pytorch [19] was used to implement HPCReg-Net and VoxelMorph with the Adam optimizer (learning rate = $1 \times 10^{-4}$). All the parameters are adjusted by grid searching algorithm, and the optimal result was obtained when $\lambda = 1$. The training, validation and testing experiments were completed on a single NVIDIA Geforce RTX 2080 Ti GPU.

**Table 1.** Average DSC score of different methods. The standard deviation is shown in parentheses.

|  | SyN | VoxelMorph | HPCReg-Net |
|---|---|---|---|
| Avg. DSC (%) | 71.86(7.4) | 73.37(5.7) | 78.05(4.7) |

### 3.3 Results

On the test data, the average DSC of SyN, VoxelMorph and HPCReg-Net was compared in Table 1. The results demonstrated the best performance of the proposed HPCReg-Net comparing with SyN and VoxelMorph.

A randomly selected subject with sagittal view of hippocampus was shown for further comparison of registration performance. Figure 3 showed the moving hippocampus image, the warped images obtained by SyN, VoxelMorph, and HPCReg-Net, as well as the fixed image, and the red part is the corresponding hippocampal label. A good registration will cause structures in warped image to look similar to structures in fixed image. The red hippocampal label on Fig. 3 demonstrated a better registration by the proposed HPCReg-Net comparing with the others.

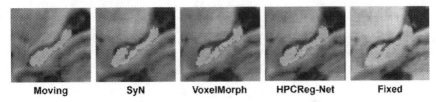

Moving          SyN          VoxelMorph     HPCReg-Net     Fixed

**Fig. 3.** Sagittal view of the hippocampus for registration comparison. The red hippocampal label demonstrated a better registration by the proposed HPCReg-Net. (Color figure online)

Additionally, the 2D and 3D visualization of the aligned masks between fixed image and the warped images by different registration methods were also presented in Fig. 4 and Fig. 5. In both 2D and 3D views, the red area is the overlap of the manual segmentation label and the aligned label by SyN, VoxelMorph, and the proposed HPCReg-Net, the blue area is the manual segmentation label, and the green area is the aligned label. The more red areas, the better the registration performance. The results demonstrated that HPCReg-Net can achieve better registration than others under comparison.

The average registration time of SyN, VoxelMorph and HPCReg-Net was also compared and the computational cost was summarized in Table 2. The results demonstrated that HPCReg-Net can complete registration in less than one second. In addition, the registration speed is hundreds of times higher than that of the traditional registration method.

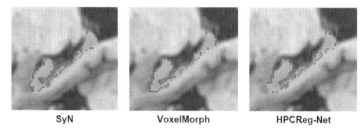

SyN                    VoxelMorph              HPCReg-Net

**Fig. 4.** The sagittal slice from 2D visualization of hippocampus registration. (Red: overlap of manual segmentation and aligned label by different registration methods; Blue: manual segmentation label; Green: aligned label by different registration methods) (Color figure online)

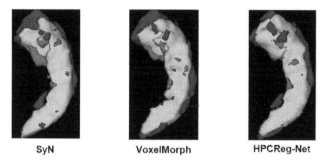

SyN                    VoxelMorph              HPCReg-Net

**Fig. 5.** The result of 3D visualization of registration by SyN, VoxelMorph and HPCReg-Net. (Red: overlap of manual segmentation and aligned label by different registration methods; Blue: manual segmentation label; Green: aligned label by different registration methods) (Color figure online)

**Table 2.** Comparison of the average time of hippocampal registration by different methods in seconds.

|              | SyN     | VoxelMorph | HPCReg-Net |
| ------------ | ------- | ---------- | ---------- |
| Avg. Time (s) | 54.8291 | 0.2232     | 0.266      |

## 4   Discussion and Conclusion

In this paper, a non-rigid registration model HPCReg-Net was proposed for hippocampus registration, which integrated dilated convolution module and residual attention module to represent the complex deformation of voxels. The experimental results demonstrated that the proposed HPCReg-Net was better than the traditional method and deep learning method under comparison. Besides the HPCReg-Net is much faster than the traditional method in hundreds of times.

In the registration task, too many down-samplings will make the model unable to capture the fine deformation and position information of voxels. The dilated convolution

[8] adopted in our study can increase the receptive field while keeping the spatial resolution unchanged. Besides, we found that dilated convolution has stronger representation ability to capture voxel deformation and position information, indicating that dilated convolution has great application potential in medical image registration. In the future research goal, we will further explore a new model that only uses dilated convolution to achieve non-rigid registration of medical images. Additionally, the residual attention module [9, 14] adopted in our study can help reduce the effect of voxel features around hippocampus, thus generating a high-precision registration of hippocampus.

In conclusion, compared with the traditional methods and deep learning methods under comparison, the HPCReg-Net proposed in this paper has a great improvement in registration performance and computational efficiency. In the future, we will further research the performance of HPCReg-Net to hippocampal multi-atlas segmentation [20–22].

**Acknowledgements.** This work was supported by National Natural Science Foundation of China (61802330, 61802331, 61801415), Natural Science Foundation of Shandong Province (ZR2018BF008).

# References

1. Zheng, Q., et al.: Integrating semi-supervised label propagation and random forests for multi-atlas based hippocampus segmentation. In: 2018 IEEE 15th International Symposium on Biomedical Imaging (ISBI 2018), pp. 154–157. IEEE.(2018)
2. Zheng, Q., et al.: Integrating semi-supervised and supervised learning methods for label fusion in multi-atlas based image segmentation. Front. Neuroinf. **12**, 69 (2018)
3. Aljabar, P., et al.: Multi-atlas based segmentation of brain images: atlas selection and its effect on accuracy. Neuroimage **46**(3), 726–738 (2009)
4. Holden, M.: A review of geometric transformations for nonrigid body registration. IEEE Trans. Med. Imaging **27**(1), 111–128 (2007)
5. Balakrishnan, G., et al.: VoxelMorph: a learning framework for deformable medical image registration. IEEE Trans. Med. Imaging **38**(8), 1788–1800 (2019)
6. Li, B., et al.: Longitudinal diffusion MRI analysis using Segis-Net: a single-step deep-learning framework for simultaneous segmentation and registration. NeuroImage **235**, 118004 (2021)
7. Zhang, L., et al.: Non-rigid joint registration for multi-contrast MR of infant brain based on the unsupervised deep regression network. In: 2019 12th International Congress on Image and Signal Processing, BioMedical Engineering and Informatics (CISP-BMEI), pp. 1–5. IEEE.(2019)
8. Chen, L.-C., Zhu, Y., Papandreou, G., Schroff, F., Adam, H.: Encoder-Decoder with Atrous Separable Convolution for Semantic Image Segmentation. In: Ferrari, V., Hebert, M., Sminchisescu, C., Weiss, Y. (eds.) ECCV 2018. LNCS, vol. 11211, pp. 833–851. Springer, Cham (2018). https://doi.org/10.1007/978-3-030-01234-2_49
9. Wang, F., et al.: Residual attention network for image classification. In: Proceedings of the IEEE Conference on Computer Vision and Pattern Recognition, pp. 3156–3164 (2017)
10. Jaderberg, M., et al.: Spatial transformer networks. Adv. Neural. Inf. Process. Syst. **28**, 2017–2025 (2015)
11. Ronneberger, O., et al.: U-net: convolutional networks for biomedical image segmentation. In: International Conference on Medical image computing and computer-assisted intervention, pp. 234–241. Springer (2015)

466    H. Yu et al.

12. Fan, J., et al.: BIRNet: brain image registration using dual-supervised fully convolutional networks. Med. Image Anal. **54**, 193–206 (2019)
13. Ibtehaz, N., et al.: MultiResUNet: rethinking the U-Net architecture for multimodal biomedical image segmentation. Neural Netw. **121**, 74–87 (2020)
14. Jin, Q., et al.: RA-UNet: a hybrid deep attention-aware network to extract liver and tumor in CT scans. Front. Bioeng. Biotechnol. **8**, 1471 (2020)
15. Boccardi, M., et al.: Training labels for hippocampal segmentation based on the EADC-ADNI harmonized hippocampal protocol. Alzheimer's Dement. **11**(2), 175–183 (2015)
16. Avants, B.B., et al.: A reproducible evaluation of ANTs similarity metric performance in brain image registration. Neuroimage **54**(3), 2033–2044 (2011)
17. Hao, Y., et al.: Local label learning (LLL) for subcortical structure segmentation: application to hippocampus segmentation. Hum. Brain Mapp. **35**(6), 2674–2697 (2014)
18. Avants, B.B., et al.: Symmetric diffeomorphic image registration with cross-correlation: evaluating automated labeling of elderly and neurodegenerative brain. Med. Image Anal. **12**(1), 26–41 (2008)
19. Paszke, A., et al.: Automatic differentiation in pytorch (2017)
20. Coupé, P., et al.: Patch-based segmentation using expert priors: Application to hippocampus and ventricle segmentation. Neuroimage **54**(2), 940–954 (2011)
21. Hao, Y., et al.: Local label learning (L3) for multi-atlas based segmentation. In: Medical Imaging 2012: Image Processing. pp. 83142E. International Society for Optics and Photonics (2012)
22. Rohlfing, T., et al.: Evaluation of atlas selection strategies for atlas-based image segmentation with application to confocal microscopy images of bee brains. Neuroimage **21**(4), 1428–1442 (2004)

# Characterization Multimodal Connectivity of Brain Network by Hypergraph GAN for Alzheimer's Disease Analysis

Junren Pan[1], Baiying Lei[2], Yanyan Shen[1], Yong Liu[3], Zhiguang Feng[4], and Shuqiang Wang[1(✉)]

[1] Shenzhen Institutes of Advanced Technology, Chinese Academy of Sciences, Shenzhen 518000, China
{jr.pan,yy.shen,sq.wang}@siat.ac.cn
[2] Shenzhen University, Shenzhen 518000, China
leiby@szu.edu.cn
[3] Renmin University of China, Beijing 100000, China
liuyonggsai@ruc.edu.cn
[4] Harbin Engineering University, Haerbin 150000, China
fengzhiguang@hrbeu.edu.cn

**Abstract.** Using multimodal neuroimaging data to characterize brain network is currently an advanced technique for Alzheimer's disease(AD) Analysis. Over recent years the neuroimaging community has made tremendous progress in the study of resting-state functional magnetic resonance imaging (rs-fMRI) derived from blood-oxygen-level-dependent (BOLD) signals and Diffusion Tensor Imaging (DTI) derived from white matter fiber tractography. However, Due to the heterogeneity and complexity between BOLD signals and fiber tractography, Most existing multimodal data fusion algorithms can not sufficiently take advantage of the complementary information between rs-fMRI and DTI. To overcome this problem, a novel Hypergraph Generative Adversarial Networks (HGGAN) is proposed in this paper, which utilizes Interactive Hyperedge Neurons module (IHEN) and Optimal Hypergraph Homomorphism algorithm (OHGH) to generate multimodal connectivity of Brain Network from rs-fMRI combination with DTI. To evaluate the performance of this model, We use publicly available data from the ADNI database to demonstrate that the proposed model not only can identify discriminative brain regions of AD but also can effectively improve classification performance.

**Keywords:** Hypergraph · Generative Adversarial Networks · Multimodal neuroimaging data · Brain network

## 1 Introduction

Alzheimer's disease (AD) is an irreversible, chronic neurodegenerative disease, and is the main reason for dementia among aged people [1]. Those people who

© Springer Nature Switzerland AG 2021
H. Ma et al. (Eds.): PRCV 2021, LNCS 13021, pp. 467–478, 2021.
https://doi.org/10.1007/978-3-030-88010-1_39

suffered from AD will gradually lose cognitive function such as remembering or thinking, and eventually lose the ability to perform daily activates [2,3]. During the past few decades, there are two methods that are widely applied to diagnose AD or other neurodegenerative diseases. One is resting-state functional magnetic resonance imaging (rs-fMRI) [4], which is based on blood-oxygen-level-dependent (BOLD)signals; the other is Diffusion Tensor Imaging(DTI) [5], which uses the white matter fiber tractography. But unfortunately, the cause and mechanism of AD are still not entirely clear. To overcome such barriers, new tools should be implemented. One of the modern approaches is the analysis of the brain network. Brain network is a representation of connectivity maps between brain regions (defined in an anatomical parcellation, or brain atlas), which can give essential insights in studying brain science. Specifically, Brain network provides enormous information about global and local features of neuronal network architecture, which can evaluate the disease status, identify crucial brain regions of AD, and reveal the mechanism of AD. In terms of mathematics, a brain network is equivalent to a weighted undirected graph, where each node in the graph corresponds to a brain region, and the value of edge between two different nodes represents the strength of connectivity of the corresponding brain regions. As the development of deep learning technology for neuroimaging data provides powerful tools to compute and analyze the brain network, many studies [6–16] have exploited deep learning models to obtain AD-related features from brain network. Recent studies [17–23] have shown that the combination of multimodal neuroimging data can discover complementary information of brain network, which is beneficial to improve the deep feature representation. Therefore, designing an effective multimodal fusion model for computing brain network has become a hot topic. However, most existing multimodal fusion models directly use neural fiber tractography (i.e., structural connectivity, short for SC) to determine the edges between brain regions and use the signal of brain activities (i.e., BOLD) to characterize the nodes feature. Due to the heterogeneity and complexity between BOLD signals and fiber tractography, such methods can not sufficiently take advantage of the complementary information. Moreover, the previous studies have demonstrated that brain cognitive mechanisms involve multiple co-activated brain regions (i.e., neural circuit) interactions rather than single pairwise interactions [24,25]. To overcome the above problem, some researchers began to use hypergraph to characterize brain network [26]. Hypergraphs are a generalization of graphs, which are increasingly important in data science thanks to the development of combinatorial mathematics and computer science. The most significant difference between hypergraphs and graphs is that each hyperedge in a hypergraph can contain multiple nodes. This feature of hypergraphs is a natural superiority to analyze the neural circuit in brain network. On the other hand, Generative Adversarial Network (GAN) [27–32] is nowadays the dominant method for processing multimodal medical images. GAN has a strong ability to deal with unsupervised learning tasks. Motivated by this advantage, we devise a hypergraph Generative Adversarial Networks (HGGAN) to characterize the multimodal connectivity of brain network based on the hypergraph theory for AD analysis.

In this paper, we propose a HGGAN to generate multimodal connectivity from rs-fMRI and DTI. We design the generator of HGGAN using the Interactive Hyperedge Neurons(IHEN) module, which is an improvement of recent work HNHN [33]. Compared with classical CNN-based GAN that can only operate on Euclidean data, our proposed model can learn intrinsic relationships and complementary information based on hypergraph structure multimodal imaging data.

## 2    Method

Figure 1 shows the proposed framework for multimodal connectivity generation. Specifically, we first extract the BOLD time series of each brain region (90 regions in total) from rs-fMRI data by using AAL atlas [34]. We constructed SC from DTI data by using PANDA [35]. We use BOLD to: (i) represent the features of nodes and (ii) calculate the incidence matrix of the hypergraph through the OHGH algorithm. And we use SC to calculate the features of hyperedges. In this way the features of nodes, the incidence matrix, and the features of hyperedges were fed into the generator to generate the multimodal connectivity. Simultaneously, we utilize GRETNA [36] to obtain functional connectivity (FC), and FC is used as real samples to train the discriminator.

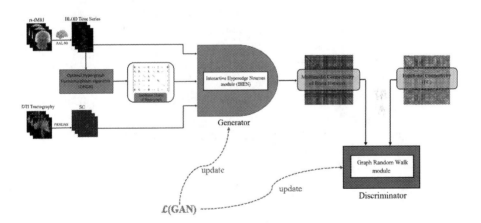

**Fig. 1.** The framework of the proposed HGGAN model.

### 2.1    Data and Pre-processing

We select a total of 219 subjects from the ADNI database. The composition of our dataset is given as follows: Our dataset includes 18 AD female patients and 32 AD male patients; 13 late mild cognitive impairment (LMCI) female patients and 12 LMCI male patients; 24 early MCI (EMCI) female patients and 45 EMCI male patients; 43 normal control (NC) female and 32 male NC. The average age of AD LMCI, EMCI and NC is 75.3, 74.9, 75.8 and 74.0, respectively.

Preprocessing of rs-fMRI data uses the DPARSF [37] toolbox and the GRETNA toolbox based on the data analysis software *statistical parameter mapping (SPM12)* [38]. First we use DPARSF to preprocess the initial DICOM format of rs-fMRI data into NIFTI format data. We apply the standard steps for rs-fMRI data preprocessing, including the discarding of the first 20 volumes, head motion correction, spatial normalization, and Gaussian smoothing in this stage. Then we use the AAL atlas to divide brain space into 90 brain regions-of-interest (ROIs). Finally, we send these NIFTI format data into the brain network analysis toolbox GRETNA to extract the BOLD time series corresponding to ROIs. We utilized DPARSF to obtain BOLD time series and we utilized GRETNA to obtain FC matrix. Also by using the AAL atlas, Preprocessing of DTI data uses the PANDA toolbox so that the number of white matter fiber tractography can be regarded as strength of physical connections in the $90 \times 90$ SC matrix.

## 2.2 Hypergraph and Optimal Hypergraph Homomorphism Algorithm

We first introduce the basic concepts and notations of hypergraphs. We define a hypergraph $H = (V, E)$ to consist of a set $V$ of nodes and set $E$ of hyperedges, where each hyperedge itself is a set of nodes. Let $n = |V|$ and $m = |E|$. We label the nodes as $v_i$ for $i \in \{1, \cdots, n\}$, and the hyperedges as $e_j$ for $j \in \{1, \cdots, m\}$. The incidence matrix $A \in \mathbb{R}^{n \times m}$ of hypergraph $H$ is denoted by

$$A(i, j) = \begin{cases} 1 & v_i \in e_j \\ 0 & v_i \notin e_j \end{cases}$$

In this paper, we regard each ROI as a node. We apply the Dynamic Hypergraph Construction algorithm (DHC) [39] to calculate the initial hypergraphs $\{H'_k\}_{k=1}^{219}$ for every subject. However, each initial hypergraph $H'_k$ only focuses on representing multiple co-activated ROIs information for the corresponding subject. Therefore, if we directly send initial hypergraphs $\{H'_k\}$ to the generator to obtain multimodal connectivity, the robustness of the generation result cannot be ensured. To overcome this shortage, we proposed a novel Optimal Hypergraph Homomorphism algorithm(OHGH). OHGH can calculate the hypergraph $H$ which have optimal homomorphism with respect to the initial hypergraphs $\{H'_k\}$. Before introducing OHGH, we first define the similarity on hypergraphs. Given two hypergraphs $H = (V, E)$ and $H' = (V, E')$ with the same nodes and $|E| = |E'|$, the similarity between $H, H'$ is defined by (Fig. 2)

$$\mathrm{Sim}(H, H') := \sup_{\substack{f : E \to E' \\ f \text{ is surjective}}} \frac{1}{|E|} \sum_{e \in E} s(e, f(e))$$

where

$$s(e, e') = \frac{|\mathcal{V}_H(e) \cap \mathcal{V}_{H'}(e')|}{|\mathcal{V}_H(e) \cup \mathcal{V}_{H'}(e')|},$$

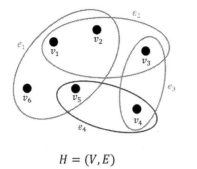

| | $e_1$ | $e_2$ | $e_3$ | $e_4$ |
|---|---|---|---|---|
| $v_1$ | 1 | 1 | 0 | 0 |
| $v_2$ | 1 | 1 | 0 | 0 |
| $v_3$ | 0 | 1 | 1 | 0 |
| $v_4$ | 0 | 0 | 1 | 1 |
| $v_5$ | 1 | 0 | 0 | 1 |
| $v_6$ | 1 | 0 | 0 | 0 |

$H = (V, E)$                                   $A$

**Fig. 2.** Left: a hypergraph with $V = (v_1, v_2, v_3, v_4, v_5.v_6)$ and $E = e_1, e_2, e_3, e_4$, where $e_1 = \{v_1, v_2, v_5, v_6\}$, $e_2 = \{v_1, v_2, v_3\}$, $e_3 = \{v_3, v_4\}$, $e_3 = \{v_4, v_5\}$. Right: its incidence matrix.

$$\mathcal{V}_H(e) = \{v|v \in e\}, \quad \mathcal{V}_{H'}(e') = \{v|v \in e'\}.$$

Now we can give OHGH as follows

$$H = \operatorname*{argmax}_H \sum_k \operatorname{Sim}(H, H'_k)$$

With the optimal homomorphism hypergraph $H$, we construct the hypergraphs $\{H_k\}$ for every subject by concatenating $H$ and $H'_k$ (i.e., $H_k = H \| H'_k$). Furthermore, we obtain the incidence matrices $\{A_k\}$ based on $\{H_k\}$.

### 2.3 Generator and Interactive Hyperedge Neurons Module

For each subject, say for the $k$-th subject, we use the BOLD time series $B_k \in \mathbb{R}^{90 \times d}$ of the $k$-th subject to represent the nodes features and we rewrite it as $X_{k,V}^{(0)}$ (where 90 is the number of nodes, $d$ is the length of the BOLD time series). Meanwhile, we calculate the hyperedges features $X_{k,E}^{(0)}$ by using the SC matrix $S_k \in \mathbb{R}^{90 \times 90}$ and the incidence matrix $A_k \in \mathbb{R}^{90 \times m}$ of the $k$-th subject (where $m$ is the number of hyperedges). Specifically, it is computed in the following way

$$X_{k,E}^{(0)} = A_k^T S_k$$

The proposed generator $G$ is composed of $L$ multi-layer Interactive Hyperedge Neurons modules (IHEN). The definition of IHEN is given as follows

$$X_{k,V}^{(l+1)} = \sigma(A_k X_{k,E}^{(l)} W_E^{(l)} + \lambda X_{k,V}^{(l)} W_V^{(l)}),$$

$$X_{k,E}^{(l+1)} = \sigma(A_k^T X_{k,V}^{(l)} W_V^{(l)} + \lambda X_{k,E}^{(l)} W_E^{(l)}),$$

where $X_{k,V}^{(l)}$ and $X_{k,E}^{(l)}$ are the $l$-th layer features of nodes and hyperedges, $W_V^{(l)}$ and $W_E^{(l)}$ are the $l$-th layer weight matrices of nodes and hyperedges, $\lambda$ is hyperparameters, $l = 0, 2, \cdots, L - 1$.

We compute the hyperedges weights and the hyperedge-independent nodes weights by using $X_{k,V}^{(L)}$ and $X_{k,E}^{(L)}$ as follows:

$$\gamma_{k,e_j}(v_i) = A_k(i,j)\langle X_{k,V}^{(L)}(i,\cdot), X_{k,E}^{(L)}(j,\cdot)\rangle$$

$$w_k(e_j) = \|X_{k,E}^{(L)}(j,\cdot)\|_2$$

where $\gamma_{k,e_j}(v_i)$ is the weight of the $i$-th node with respect to the $j$-th hyperedge for the $k$-th subject and $w_k(e_j)$ is the weight of the the $j$-th hyperedge for the $k$-th subject. From this, we obtain the multimodal connectivity matrix $M_k$ for the $k$-th subject by the formulas

$$M_k(i_1, i_2) = \sum_{j=1}^{m} \gamma_{k,e_j}(v_{i_1}) w_k(e_j) \gamma_{k,e_j}(v_{i_2}) \tag{1}$$

Combining the multimodal connectivity matrix $M_k$ with the nodes features $X_{k,V}^{(L)}$ , we give the nodes correlation coefficients as follows:

$$\mathrm{Co}_k(v_i) = \frac{1}{90} \sum_{j=1}^{90} M_k(i,j)\langle X_{k,V}^{(L)}(i,\cdot), X_{k,V}^{(L)}(j,\cdot)\rangle. \tag{2}$$

## 2.4   Discriminator and Loss Function

The discriminator $D$ is a normal MLP architecture, which can compare the difference of distributions between the FC matrix and the multimodal connectivity matrix by using random walk. Fixing an arbitrary node $v_{r_0}$, we take $v_{r_0}$ as the starting point for the random walk. The termination condition of the random walk is that the point comes back to the position of the previous step at some step of random walk. For example, a random walk having $T$-steps and eventually stopping at the $v_{r_T}$ means that the path $[v_{r_0}, v_{r_1}, \cdots, v_{r_{T-1}}, v_{r_T}, v_{r_{T+1}}]$ satisfies $v_{r_{T-1}} = v_{r_{T+1}}$, and we say the $v_{r_T}$ is the endpoint of the path. For the FC matrix of the $k$-th subject, the probability of walking through the path $[v_{r_0}, v_{r_1}, \cdots, v_{r_{T-1}}, v_{r_T}, v_{r_{T+1}}]$ is given as follows:

$$p_{real,k}([v_{r_0}, v_{r_1}, \cdots, v_{r_{T-1}}, v_{r_T}, v_{r_{T+1}}]) = \left(\prod_{t=1}^{T} \frac{\mathrm{FC}_k(r_{t-1}, r_t)}{\|\mathrm{FC}_k(r_{t-1}, \cdot)\|_1}\right) \cdot \frac{\mathrm{FC}_k(r_T, r_{T-1})}{\|\mathrm{FC}_k(r_T, \cdot)\|_1}.$$

Let $\mathrm{Path}(v_{r_0}, v)$ be the set of paths with the starting point at $v_{r_0}$ and the endpoint at $v$, then the conditional probability about $v_{r_0}$ is given as follows

$$p_{real,k}(v|v_{r_0}) = \sum_{\mathrm{path} \in \mathrm{Path}(v_{r_0}, v)} p_{real,k}(\mathrm{path})$$

Similarly, for the multimodal connectivity matrix of the $k$-th subject, the probability of walking through the path $[v_{r_0}, v_{r_1}, \cdots, v_{r_{T-1}}, v_{r_T}, v_{r_{T+1}}]$ is given by

$$p_{G,k}([v_{r_0}, v_{r_1}, \cdots, v_{r_{T-1}}, v_{r_T}, v_{r_{T+1}}]) = \left(\prod_{t=1}^{T} \frac{M_k(r_{t-1}, r_t)}{\|M_k(r_{t-1}, \cdot)\|_1}\right) \cdot \frac{M_k(r_T, r_{T-1})}{\|M_k(r_T, \cdot)\|_1}$$

and conditional probability about $v_{r_0}$ is that

$$p_{G,k}(v|v_{r_0}) = \sum_{\text{path}\in\text{Path}(v_{r_0},v)} p_{G,k}(\text{path})$$

The loss function of discriminator is formulated by

$$\max_{D} \sum_{k=1}^{K} \sum_{i=1}^{90} \mathbb{E}_{v\sim p_{real,k}(v|v_i)}[\log D(v,v_i)] + \mathbb{E}_{v\sim p_{G,k}(v|v_i)}[\log(1 - D(v,v_i))].$$

where $K$ represents the total number of subject in the training dataset.

The loss function of the generators depends on the feedback of discriminator, which is formulated by

$$\max_{G} \sum_{k=1}^{K} \sum_{i=1}^{90} \mathbb{E}_{v\sim p_{G,k}(v|v_i)}[\log D(v,v_i)].$$

## 3   Experiments

In order to evaluate the performance of the multimodal connectivity matrix(MC) generated by our proposed method, six binary classification experiments including AD vs. NC, AD vs. EMCI, AD vs. LMCI, EMCI vs. NC, LMCI vs. NC, and EMCI vs. LMCI are designed to validate the prediction performance. We use prediction accuracy (ACC), sensitivity (SEN), specificity (SPE) to measure the results of our experiments.

Table 1 and Table 2 summarize the prediction results in different classifiers by using structural connectivity matrix (SC), functional connectivity matrix (FC), and our proposed multimodal connectivity matrix (MC) in Eq. (1). Classifiers include Multiple Layer Perception (MLP) [40], Support Vector Machine (SVM) [41], Random Forest (RF) [42], and Graph Convolution Networks (GCN) [43]. In detail, the parameters of MLP set as follows: 3-layers with 16, 16, 2 neurons, ReLU activation, 0.001 learning rate. The parameters of SVM set as follows: Gaussian Kernel, 0.15 kernel coefficient. The parameters of RF set as follows: 400 trees, 3 maximum depth. The parameters of GCN parameters set as follows: 3 Chebyshev graph convolutional layers, 0.1 dropout rate, 0.0001 learning rate. The dataset is randomly split into 65% for training and 35% for testing. All the models are randomly initialized for 5 times. The result shows that the classification accuracy is significantly improved by using the proposed MC matrix, which means the complementary information of different modal is successfully extracted from the proposed method.

We compare the average correlation coefficient in Eq. (2) between each corresponding node of the AD group and the NC group. The result are shown in Fig. 3. We choose the top 7 nodes in Fig. 3(c), the IDs of these node are 37,38,39,41,83,84, and 87, which represent Hippocampus_L, Hippocampus_R, ParaHippocampal_L, Amygdala_L, Temporal_Pole_Sup_L, Temporal_Pole_Sup_R, and Temporal_Pole_ Mid_L. We can see that these brain regions

**Table 1.** Prediction performance in AD vs. NC, AD vs. EMCI and AD vs. LMCI.

| Classifier | Connectivity matrix | AD vs. NC | | | AD vs. EMCI | | | AD vs. LMCI | | |
|---|---|---|---|---|---|---|---|---|---|---|
| | | ACC | SEN | SPE | ACC | SEN | SPE | ACC | SEN | SPE |
| MLP | SC | 79.06 | 52.94 | **96.15** | 78.04 | **88.23** | 65.38 | 60.00 | **76.47** | 25.00 |
| | FC | 74.41 | 52.94 | 88.46 | 68.29 | 64.70 | 65.38 | 56.00 | 64.70 | 37.50 |
| | MC (Ours) | **81.39** | **64.70** | 92.30 | **80.48** | 76.47 | **76.92** | 64.00 | 58.82 | **75.00** |
| SVM | SC | 83.72 | 70.58 | **92.30** | 80.48 | 64.70 | **84.61** | 64.00 | 64.70 | 62.50 |
| | FC | 79.06 | 70.58 | 84.61 | 73.17 | 52.94 | 80.76 | 56.00 | 52.94 | 62.50 |
| | MC (Ours) | **86.04** | **82.35** | 88.46 | **82.92** | **76.47** | 80.76 | **68.00** | **70.58** | 62.50 |
| RF | SC | 81.39 | 70.58 | 88.46 | 78.04 | 64.70 | **80.76** | 60.00 | 70.58 | **37.50** |
| | FC | 76.74 | 70.58 | 80.76 | 73.17 | 58.82 | 76.92 | 60.00 | 70.58 | **37.50** |
| | MC (Ours) | **86.04** | **88.23** | 84.61 | **82.92** | **82.35** | 76.92 | **64.00** | **88.23** | 12.50 |
| GCN | SC | 86.04 | 94.11 | 80.76 | 85.36 | **94.11** | 73.07 | 68.00 | 76.47 | **50.00** |
| | FC | 83.72 | 94.11 | 76.92 | 80.48 | 70.58 | 80.76 | 64.00 | 76.47 | 37.50 |
| | MC (Ours) | **93.02** | 94.11 | **92.30** | **90.24** | 82.35 | **88.46** | **72.00** | **82.35** | **50.00** |

**Table 2.** Prediction performance in EMCI vs. NC, LMCI vs. NC and EMCI vs. LMCI.

| Classifier | Connectivity matrix | EMCI vs. NC | | | LMCI vs. NC | | | EMCI vs. LMCI | | |
|---|---|---|---|---|---|---|---|---|---|---|
| | | ACC | SEN | SPE | ACC | SEN | SPE | ACC | SEN | SPE |
| MLP | SC | 66.00 | 62.50 | **69.23** | 76.47 | 50.00 | **84.61** | 68.75 | **79.16** | 37.50 |
| | FC | 64.00 | 70.83 | 57.69 | 73.52 | 75.00 | 73.07 | 71.87 | 75.00 | **62.50** |
| | MC (Ours) | **70.00** | **75.00** | 65.38 | **79.41** | **87.50** | 76.92 | **75.00** | **79.16** | **62.50** |
| SVM | SC | 68.00 | 66.66 | **69.23** | 82.35 | 62.50 | **88.46** | 71.87 | 83.33 | 37.50 |
| | FC | 70.00 | 70.83 | **69.23** | 82.35 | 75.00 | 84.61 | 71.87 | **87.50** | 25.00 |
| | MC (Ours) | **72.00** | **83.33** | 61.53 | **85.29** | **87.50** | 84.61 | **78.12** | **87.50** | **50.00** |
| RF | SC | 68.00 | 58.33 | 76.92 | 76.47 | 62.50 | 80.76 | 71.87 | 75.00 | 62.50 |
| | FC | 68.00 | 62.50 | 73.07 | 79.41 | 62.50 | **84.61** | 75.00 | **83.33** | 50.00 |
| | MC (Ours) | **74.00** | **66.66** | **80.76** | **82.35** | **87.50** | 80.76 | **81.25** | 79.16 | **87.50** |
| GCN | SC | 72.00 | 70.83 | 73.07 | 85.29 | **87.50** | 84.61 | 78.12 | 83.33 | 62.50 |
| | FC | 74.00 | 75.00 | 73.07 | 79.41 | 75.00 | 80.76 | 81.25 | **91.66** | 50.00 |
| | MC (Ours) | **80.00** | **79.16** | **80.76** | **91.17** | **87.50** | **92.30** | **90.62** | **91.66** | **87.50** |

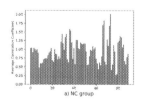
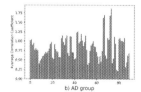
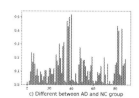

**Fig. 3.** In this figure, (a) and (b) shows the average correlation coefficient of each node of the NC group and AD group. (c) shows the different between the AD group and NC group.

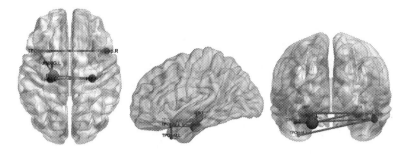

**Fig. 4.** The NC subject whose subject ID is 014_S_6148.

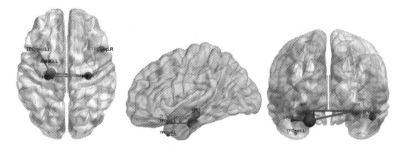

**Fig. 5.** The AD subject whose subject ID is 037_S_6216.

are mainly concentrated on the memory and reasoning areas, which are highly related to the AD according to the clinical studies [44]. Figure 4 and Fig. 5 show the connection relationship of these top 7 brain regions by using MC matrix. We display the connection relationship graph of brain regions from the perspective of the sagittal plane view, axial plane view, and coronal plane view.

## 4    Conclution

In this paper, we proposed a novel hypergraph generative adversarial network (HGGAN) to generate individual multimodal connectivity matrix by using corresponding rs-fMRI and DTI data. We designed the Interactive Hyperedge Neurons module such that the generators can efficiently capture the complex relationship between rs-fMRI and DTI. Moreover, we proposed the Optimal Hypergraph Homomorphism algorithm to construct hypergraph structure data, which significantly improved the robustness of the generation results. The analyses of the experimental results proved that the proposed method successfully extracted the interrelated hidden structures and complementary information from different modal data. Although this paper only focuses on AD, it is worth mention that the proposed model can be easily extended to other neurodegenerative disease.

**Acknowledgement.** This work was supported by the National Natural Science Foundations of China under Grant 61872351, the International Science and Technology

Cooperation Projects of Guangdong under Grant 2019A050510030, the Distinguished Young Scholars Fund of Guangdong under Grant 2021B1515020019, the Excellent Young Scholars of Shenzhen under Grant RCYX20200714114641211 and Shenzhen Key Basic Research Project under Grant JCYJ20200109115641762.

# References

1. Dadar, M., et al.: Validation of a regression technique for segmentation of white matter hyperintensities in Alzheimers disease. IEEE Trans. Med. Imaging **36**(8), 1758–1768 (2017)
2. Association, A., et al.: 2018 Alzheimer's disease facts and figures. Alzheimer's Dementia **14**(3), 367–429 (2018)
3. Wang, S., Wang, H., Shen, Y., Wang, X.: Automatic recognition of mild cognitive impairment and Alzheimers disease using ensemble based 3D densely connected convolutional networks. In: 2018 17th IEEE International Conference on Machine Learning and Applications (ICMLA), pp. 517–523. IEEE (2018)
4. Huettel, S., Song, A., McCarthy, G.: Functional magnetic resonance imaging. Sinauer associates. Inc, Sunderland, MA, pp. 162–170 (2004)
5. Westlye, L.T., et al.: Life-span changes of the human brain white matter: diffusion tensor imaging (DTI) and volumetry. Cereb. Cortex **20**(9), 2055–2068 (2010)
6. Wang, S., Hu, Y., Shen, Y., Li, H.: Classification of diffusion tensor metrics for the diagnosis of a myelopathic cord using machine learning. Int. J. Neural Syst. **28**(02), 1750036 (2018)
7. Wang, S., et al.: Skeletal maturity recognition using a fully automated system with convolutional neural networks. IEEE Access **6**, 29979–29993 (2018)
8. Wang, S., Shen, Y., Zeng, D., Hu, Y.: Bone age assessment using convolutional neural networks. In: 2018 International Conference on Artificial Intelligence and Big Data (ICAIBD), pp. 175–178. IEEE (2018)
9. Zeng, D., Wang, S., Shen, Y., Shi, C.: A GA-based feature selection and parameter optimization for support tucker machine. Procedia Comput. Sci. **111**, 17–23 (2017)
10. Jeon, E., Kang, E., Lee, J., Lee, J., Kam, T.-E., Suk, H.-I.: Enriched representation learning in resting-state fMRI for early MCI diagnosis. In: Martel, A.L., et al. (eds.) MICCAI 2020. LNCS, vol. 12267, pp. 397–406. Springer, Cham (2020). https://doi.org/10.1007/978-3-030-59728-3_39
11. Wang, S.Q., Li, X., Cui, J.L., Li, H.X., Luk, K.D., Hu, Y.: Prediction of myelopathic level in cervical spondylotic myelopathy using diffusion tensor imaging. J. Magn. Reson. Imaging **41**(6), 1682–1688 (2015)
12. Mo, L.F., Wang, S.Q.: A variational approach to nonlinear two-point boundary value problems. Nonlinear Anal. Theory Meth. Appl. **71**(12), e834–e838 (2009)
13. Wang, S.Q.: A variational approach to nonlinear two-point boundary value problems. Comput. Math. Appl. **58**(11–12), 2452–2455 (2009)
14. Wang, S.Q., He, J.H.: Variational iteration method for a nonlinear reaction-diffusion process. Int. J. Chemi. Reactor Eng. **6**(1) (2008)
15. Wang, S., et al.: An ensemble-based densely-connected deep learning system for assessment of skeletal maturity. IEEE Trans. Syst. Man Cybern. Syst. (2020)
16. Wu, K., Shen, Y., Wang, S.: 3D convolutional neural network for regional precipitation nowcasting. J. Image Signal Process. **7**(4), 200–212 (2018)
17. Zhang, D., Shen, D., Initiative, A.D.N., et al.: Multi-modal multi-task learning for joint prediction of multiple regression and classification variables in Alzheimer's disease. Neuroimage **59**(2), 895–907 (2012)

18. Wang, S., Shen, Y., Chen, W., Xiao, T., Hu, J.: Automatic recognition of mild cognitive impairment from MRI images using expedited convolutional neural networks. In: Lintas, A., Rovetta, S., Verschure, P.F.M.J., Villa, A.E.P. (eds.) ICANN 2017. LNCS, vol. 10613, pp. 373–380. Springer, Cham (2017). https://doi.org/10.1007/978-3-319-68600-4_43

19. Lei, B., et al.: Self-calibrated brain network estimation and joint non-convex multi-task learning for identification of early Alzheimer's disease. Med. Image Anal. **61**, 101652 (2020)

20. Lei, B., et al.: Deep and joint learning of longitudinal data for Alzheimer's disease prediction. Patt. Recogn. **102**, 107247 (2020)

21. Wang, S., Wang, H., Cheung, A.C., Shen, Y., Gan, M.: Ensemble of 3D densely connected convolutional network for diagnosis of mild cognitive impairment and. Deep Learn. Appl. **1098**, 53 (2020)

22. Hu, S., Yuan, J., Wang, S.: Cross-modality synthesis from MRI to pet using adversarial U-Net with different normalization. In: 2019 International Conference on Medical Imaging Physics and Engineering (ICMIPE), pp. 1–5. IEEE (2019)

23. Yu, S., et al.: Multi-scale enhanced graph convolutional network for early mild cognitive impairment detection. In: Martel, A.L., et al. (eds.) MICCAI 2020. LNCS, vol. 12267, pp. 228–237. Springer, Cham (2020). https://doi.org/10.1007/978-3-030-59728-3_23

24. Lee, M.H., Smyser, C.D., Shimony, J.S.: Resting-state fMRI: a review of methods and clinical applications. Am. J. Neuroradiol. **34**(10), 1866–1872 (2013)

25. Cao, P., et al.: Generalized fused group lasso regularized multi-task feature learning for predicting cognitive outcomes in Alzheimers disease. Comput. Methods Programs Biomed. **162**, 19–45 (2018)

26. Munsell, B.C., Wu, G., Gao, Y., Desisto, N., Styner, M.: Identifying relationships in functional and structural connectome data using a hypergraph learning method. In: Ourselin, S., Joskowicz, L., Sabuncu, M.R., Unal, G., Wells, W. (eds.) MICCAI 2016. LNCS, vol. 9901, pp. 9–17. Springer, Cham (2016). https://doi.org/10.1007/978-3-319-46723-8_2

27. Goodfellow, I., et al.: Generative adversarial nets. Adv. Neural Inf. Process. Syst. **27** (2014)

28. Wang, S., et al.: Diabetic retinopathy diagnosis using multichannel generative adversarial network with semisupervision. IEEE Trans. Autom. Sci. Eng. **18**(2), 574–585 (2020)

29. Yu, W., Lei, B., Ng, M.K., Cheung, A.C., Shen, Y., Wang, S.: Tensorizing GAN with high-order pooling for Alzheimer's disease assessment. IEEE Trans. Neural Networks Learn. Syst. (2021)

30. Hu, S., Shen, Y., Wang, S., Lei, B.: Brain MR to PET synthesis via bidirectional generative adversarial network. In: Martel, A.L., et al. (eds.) MICCAI 2020. LNCS, vol. 12262, pp. 698–707. Springer, Cham (2020). https://doi.org/10.1007/978-3-030-59713-9_67

31. Hu, S., Yu, W., Chen, Z., Wang, S.: Medical image reconstruction using generative adversarial network for Alzheimer disease assessment with class-imbalance problem. In: 2020 IEEE 6th International Conference on Computer and Communications (ICCC), pp. 1323–1327. IEEE (2020)

32. Lei, B., et al.: Skin lesion segmentation via generative adversarial networks with dual discriminators. Med. Image Anal. **64**, 101716 (2020)

33. Dong, Y., Sawin, W., Bengio, Y.: HNHN: hypergraph networks with hyperedge neurons. arXiv preprint arXiv:2006.12278 (2020)

34. Tzourio-Mazoyer, N., et al.: Automated anatomical labeling of activations in SPM using a macroscopic anatomical parcellation of the MNI MRI single-subject brain. Neuroimage **15**(1), 273–289 (2002)
35. Cui, Z., Zhong, S., Xu, P., Gong, G., He, Y.: Panda: a pipeline toolbox for analyzing brain diffusion images. Front. Hum. Neurosci. **7**, 42 (2013)
36. Wang, J., Wang, X., Xia, M., Liao, X., Evans, A., He, Y.: Gretna: a graph theoretical network analysis toolbox for imaging connectomics. Front. Hum. Neurosci. **9**, 386 (2015)
37. Yan, C., Zang, Y.: DPARSF: a MATLAB toolbox for "pipeline" data analysis of resting-state fMRI. Front. Syst. Neurosci. **4**, 13 (2010)
38. Ashburner, J., et al.: Spm12 manual. wellcome trust centre for neuroimaging. London, UK (2014)
39. Jiang, J., Wei, Y., Feng, Y., Cao, J., Gao, Y.: Dynamic hypergraph neural networks. In: IJCAI, pp. 2635–2641 (2019)
40. Golkov, V., et al.: Q-space deep learning: twelve-fold shorter and model-free diffusion MRI scans. IEEE Trans. Med. Imaging **35**(5), 1344–1351 (2016)
41. Suykens, J.A., Vandewalle, J.: Least squares support vector machine classifiers. Neural Process. Lett. **9**(3), 293–300 (1999)
42. Gray, K.R., Aljabar, P., Heckemann, R.A., Hammers, A., Rueckert, D., Initiative, A.D.N., et al.: Random forest-based similarity measures for multi-modal classification of Alzheimer's disease. Neuroimage **65**, 167–175 (2013)
43. Kipf, T.N., Welling, M.: Semi-supervised classification with graph convolutional networks. arXiv preprint arXiv:1609.02907 (2016)
44. Veitch, D.P., et al.: Understanding disease progression and improving Alzheimer's disease clinical trials: Recent highlights from the Alzheimer's disease neuroimaging initiative. Alzheimer's Dementia **15**(1), 106–152 (2019)

# Multimodal Representations Learning and Adversarial Hypergraph Fusion for Early Alzheimer's Disease Prediction

Qiankun Zuo[1], Baiying Lei[2], Yanyan Shen[1], Yong Liu[3], Zhiguang Feng[4], and Shuqiang Wang[1(✉)]

[1] Shenzhen Institutes of Advanced Technology, Chinese Academy of Sciences, Shenzhen 518000, China
{qk.zuo,yy.shen,sq.wang}@siat.ac.cn
[2] Shenzhen University, Shenzhen 518000, China
leiby@szu.edu.cn
[3] Renmin University of China, Beijing 100000, China
liuyonggsai@ruc.edu.cn
[4] Harbin Engineering University, Haerbin 150000, China
fengzhiguang@hrbeu.edu.cn

**Abstract.** Multimodal neuroimage can provide complementary information about the dementia, but small size of complete multimodal data limits the ability in representation learning. Moreover, the data distribution inconsistency from different modalities may lead to ineffective fusion, which fails to sufficiently explore the intra-modal and inter-modal interactions and compromises the disease diagnosis performance. To solve these problems, we proposed a novel multimodal representation learning and adversarial hypergraph fusion (MRL-AHF) framework for Alzheimer's disease diagnosis using complete trimodal images. First, adversarial strategy and pre-trained model are incorporated into the MRL to extract latent representations from multimodal data. Then two hypergraphs are constructed from the latent representations and the adversarial network based on graph convolution is employed to narrow the distribution difference of hyperedge features. Finally, the hyperedge-invariant features are fused for disease prediction by hyperedge convolution. Experiments on the public Alzheimer's Disease Neuroimaging Initiative(ADNI) database demonstrate that our model achieves superior performance on Alzheimer's disease detection compared with other related models and provides a possible way to understand the underlying mechanisms of disorder's progression by analyzing the abnormal brain connections.

**Keywords:** Multimodal representation · Adversarial hypergraph fusion · Alzheimer's disease · Graph convolutional networks

H. Ma et al. (Eds.): PRCV 2021, LNCS 13021, pp. 479–490, 2021.
https://doi.org/10.1007/978-3-030-88010-1_40

# 1    Introduction

Alzheimer's disease (AD) is a severe neurodegenerative diseases among the old people and the pathological changes are reflected on the symptoms including memory decline, aphasia and other decreased brain functions [1]. Since there is no effective medicine for AD, much attention has been attracted on its pro-dromal stage, that is, mild cognition impairment (MCI) [2], so that intervention can be implemented to slow down or stop the progression of the disease. With the success of deep learning on medical images analysis [3–7] and other fields [8,9], non-invasive magnetic imaging technology becomes an effective tool for detecting dementia at early disease stages, and different modalities carry complementary disease-related information. For example, abnormal functional and structural connectivity between brain regions has been discovered in the resting-state functional magnetic resonance imaging (fMRI) [10] and diffusion tensor imaging (DTI) [11] modality, respectively; and the T1-weighted magnetic resonance imaging (MRI) [12] data contains the information of volume changes in different brain regions. Many researchers [13–17] have achieved good performance in brain disease prediction by fusing either two of the above modalities. Therefore, we take all the three modalities as the input of our model to conduct representations learning and fusion for disease diagnosis.

Considering the number of subjects with complete three modalities is limit, it is necessary to make full use of the input data for learning latent representations. The input data can be used to estimate additional distribution, which is prior information for training a much more discriminative and robust model. To make use of additional distribution, the Generative Adversarial Networks (GAN) [18] provides an appropriate way for representation learning of the graph data by matching the distribution consistency in representation space. The basic principle is variational inference [19–21] which maximizes the entropy of the probability distribution. It has been applied successfully in medical image analysis [22–25] and citation network [26,27]. Besides, Convolution Neural Network (CNN) has great power in recognizing disease-related images [28–30,32,33], which can be utilized to extract features of MRI in data space by a model pre-trained from a great many of unimodal images [31,34]. Therefore, we designed a Distribution-based Graph GAN (D-GraphGAN) and a CNN-based Graph AutoEncoder (CNN-GraphAE) to extract latent representations from fMRI&DTI and MRI&DTI, respectively.

After the representations extraction, direct fusion of representations concatenation may lead to bad performance in exploring cross-modal interactions, since the data distributions in representation space may be heterogeneous [35]. Adversarial strategy is suitable for translating modality distribution [36]. As traditional graph with pairwise regions interaction is not sufficient to characterize the brain network connectivity and fail to encode high-order intra-modal correlations, a hypergraph [37] beyond pairwise connections is more suitable to describe the complex brain activities behind dementia. It is found that Hypergraph Neural Networks(HGNN) achieve better performance than Graph Convolutional Networks (GCN) in citation networks [38]. Motivated by this, we develop an adversarial hyperedge network to boost multimodal representation fusion performance for AD diagnosis.

In this paper, we propose a Multimodal Representation Learning and Adversarial Hypergraph Fusion (MRL-AHF) to make use of inter-modal complementary and intra-modal correlation information to improve the performance of Alzheimer's disease detection. The estimated additional distribution and pretrained model are incorporated to improve the ability of representation learning. A hypergraph fusion strategy is adopted to narrow distribution difference in hyperedge space for efficiently fusion by adversarial training. Our MRL-AHN approach is able to enhance the ability of representation learning and boost the multimodal fusing performance. Experiments on the Alzheimer's Disease Neuroimging Initiative (ADNI) database show that our approach achieves superior performance on MCI detection compared with other related works.

## 2  Method

An overview of MRL-AHF is given in Fig. 1. Our framework is comprised of two stages: a representation space learning stage and a adversarial hypergraph fusion stage. The first stage learns the latent representations from fMRI & DTI and MRI & DTI by distribution-based GraphGAN and CNN-based GraphAE, respectively. The second stage utilizes the representations output by encoders $G$ and $S$ to conduct hypergraph fusion via adversarial training. The symbol meanings are given below: $A$ and $A'$ represent the structural connection (SC) and reconstructed SC matrix, respectively. $X$ and $X'$ denote the functional time-series (FT) at each brain Region-of-Interest (ROI), the reconstructed FT feature, respectively. $V$ and $V'$ are the feature vector (FV) and reconstructed FV. $\hat{Z}$ and $R$ are features in representation space.

### 2.1  Distribution-Based GraphGAN

**Graph Construction.** Suppose an indirect graph $\mathcal{G}(\mathcal{V}, \mathcal{E})$ is formed with N brain Regions of Interest(ROIs) based on anatomical atlas, $\mathcal{V} = \{\nu_1, \nu_2, ..., \nu_N\}$ and $\mathcal{E} = \{\varepsilon_1, \varepsilon_2, ..., \varepsilon_N\}$ are a set of nodes and edges, respectively. Specifically, $X = \{x_1, x_2, ..., x_N\} \in \mathbb{R}^{N \times d}$ denotes the node feature matrix of brain functional activities derived from fMRI time series, and $A \in \mathbb{R}^{N \times N}$ represents the physical connections matrix reflecting the brain structural information. The element in adjacent matrix $A$ is represented with $A_{ij} = 1$ if there exists connection between $i$th and $j$th region, otherwise $A_{ij} = 0$.

**Additional Distribution Estimation.** Normal distribution $\mathbb{N}(0, 1)$ cannot represent the graph properly, and an appropriate $Pz$ can boost the ability in learning discriminative representations in adversarial network. In terms of no other known information except for the give graph data $A$ and $X$, we introduce a non-parametric estimation method, Kernel Density Estimation (KDE), to exstimate $Pz(Z|X)$ that approximates to $Pz(Z|X, A)$ by combining both

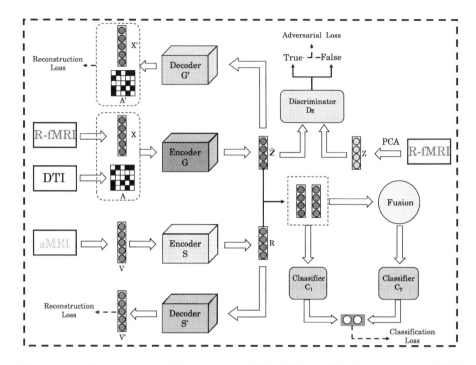

**Fig. 1.** Overall framework of the proposed MRL-AHF for AD diagnosis using fMRI, DTI and MRI data.

anatomical and nueroimaging information. Specifically, based on some certain disease-related ROIs, we can obtain a set of nodes $U \subseteq \mathcal{V}$ by applying Determinant Point Process (DPP) [39] method on matrix $A$, and the corresponding node features are selected to form features matrix $X_U \in \mathbb{R}^{m \times d}$ with $m = |U|$ nodes, followed with dimension reduction by Principal Component Analysis(PCA) to get $Z_U \in \mathbb{R}^{m \times q}$. $q$ is the dimension in latent representation space. Assuming $Z_i$ is a latent representation of each node, $Pz(Z)$ can be defined by

$$Pz(Z) \approx \frac{1}{mb} \sum_{i=1}^{m} K(\frac{Z - Z_i}{b}) \tag{1}$$

Where $K(\cdot)$ is a multi-dimensional Gaussian Kernel function, $b$ denotes the bandwidth that determines the smoothness of the distribution

**GraphGAN.** The encoder $G$ encodes $A$ and $X$ as latent representations $\widehat{Z}$, which are sent to the discriminator $D_Z$ as negative samples. The positive samples $Z$ are estimated from the additional distribution $Pz(Z|X, A)$. The adversarial loss function is defined as follows

$$\pounds_{D_Z} = -\mathbb{E}_{A \sim P_A, X \sim P_X}[D_Z(G(A, X))] + \mathbb{E}_{Z \sim P_Z}[D_Z(Z)] \tag{2}$$

$$\mathcal{L}_G = \mathbb{E}_{A \sim P_A, X \sim P_X}[D_Z(G(A, X))] \tag{3}$$

Besides, the reconstruction loss and the classification loss are given bellow:

$$\mathcal{L}_{Rec1} = \mathbb{E}_{A \sim P_A, X \sim P_X}[f(X, X')] + \mathbb{E}_{A \sim P_A, X \sim P_X}[f(A, A')] \tag{4}$$

$$\mathcal{L}_{Cls1} = \mathbb{E}_{A \sim P_A, X \sim P_X}[y \cdot log y'] \tag{5}$$

Where, $X' = G'(A, \hat{Z})$, $\hat{Z} = G(A, X)$ and $A' = \sigma(\hat{Z}\hat{Z}^T)$ are the reconstructed graph data, $f(a, b) = a \cdot log b + (1 - a) \cdot log(1 - b)$ is binary cross entropy function, $y' = C_1(\hat{Z})$ is the predicted labels. $C_1$ is a two-layer perception. $G$ and $G'$ are two-layer GCN, specifically.

## 2.2  CNN-Based GraphAE

A dense convolutional network with 4 blocks is trained on large number of labeled images and then used to extract a feature vector $V$ for each MRI using the last fully connected layer. In order to deploy CNN feature on the ROIs, we equally distribute the feature $V \in \mathbb{R}^{1 \times 128}$ on the ROIs, and the SC is used to guide the feature to flow between two connected nodes. The latent representations $R$ is obtained by a two-layer GCN Encoder $S$, followed with a decoder $S'$ to reconstruct features. The reconstruct loss and classification loss are defined as

$$\mathcal{L}_{Rec2} = \mathbb{E}_{V \sim P_V}[f(V, V')] \tag{6}$$

$$\mathcal{L}_{Cls2} = \mathbb{E}_{V \sim P_V}[y \cdot log y''] \tag{7}$$

Where, $V' = S'(R) = S'(S(V))$, $y$ is the truth one-hot label, $y'' = C_1(R) = C_1(S(V))$ is the predicted label.

## 2.3  Adversarial Hypergraph Fusion

**Hypergraph Construction.** By denoting a hyperedge $E$ connecting multiple nodes, we can construct a hyperedge for each node centered. Specifically, we use K-NearestNeighbor (KNN) method to select the nodes for each hyperedge based on the Euclidean distance. At last, we can get an incident matrix $H_1$ and $H_2$ from the learned representations $\hat{Z}$ and $R$, respectively. The formula is given as follows:

$$H(\mathcal{V}, E) = \begin{cases} 0, if & \nu \in E \\ 1, if & \nu \notin E \end{cases} \tag{8}$$

**Adversarial Hypergraph Learning.** In order to narrow the gap between the representations, we adopt the adversarial training strategy to make the distribution from different modalities the same. The hypergraph convolution is spitted into convex convolution and hyperedge convolution. The hyperedge feature of $\hat{Z}_H$ is computed by Vertex aggregation is sent to the discriminator $D_H$ as a positive sample, the negative sample $R_H$ is obtained by Vertex convolution of hypergraph $R$, the formula is illustrated as follows:

$$\hat{Z}_H = D_{1e}^{-1/2} H_1^T D_{1e}^{-1/2} \hat{Z} \tag{9}$$

$$R_H = D_{2e}^{-1/2} H_2^T D_{2e}^{-1/2} R\Theta \tag{10}$$

Where, $D_{1e}$ and $D_{2e}$ are the edge degree of $H_1$ and $H_2$, respectively; $\Theta$ is the weighting parameters. Both $\hat{Z}_H$ and $R_H$ are sent to the discrminator $D_H$ for adversarial training. Then, we fuse the hyperedge features by using edge aggregation to get vertex feature matrix $F$ as follows

$$F = D_{1v}^{-1/2} H_1 D_{1v}^{-1/2} \hat{Z}_H + D_{2v}^{-1/2} H_2 D_{2v}^{-1/2} R_H \tag{11}$$

Finally, the fused features is used to construct connectivity matrix by bilinear pooling and then sent to the classifier for task learning. The adversarial and classification loss are given below

$$\begin{aligned}
\mathcal{L}_{AHF} &= \mathcal{L}_{D_H} + 0.1\mathcal{L}_{Ver} + \mathcal{L}_{Cls3} \\
&= \mathbb{E}_{A \sim P_A, Z \sim P_Z}[D_H(\hat{Z}_H)] - 0.1 \cdot \mathbb{E}_{V \sim P_V}[D_H(R_H)] \\
&\quad + \mathbb{E}_{A \sim P_A, Z \sim P_Z, V \sim P_V}[y \cdot log y''']
\end{aligned} \tag{12}$$

Here, $D_{1v}$ and $D_{2v}$ are the node degree of $H_1$ and $H_2$, respectively; and $y''' = C_2(\sigma(FF^T))$ is the predicted label.

### 2.4   Training Strategy

In Conclusion, the total loss of the proposed frame is:

$$\mathcal{L}_{MRLAHF} = \mathcal{L}_G + 0.1\mathcal{L}_{D_Z} + \mathcal{L}_{Rec1} + \mathcal{L}_{Rec2} + \mathcal{L}_{Cls1} + \mathcal{L}_{Cls2} + \gamma\mathcal{L}_{AHF} \tag{13}$$

Where $\gamma$ is a hyper-parameter that determines the relative importance of feature fusion loss items.

During the training process, firstly, we update the generators, encoders and decoders with the loss backpropagation of $\mathcal{L}_{Rec1}$, $\mathcal{L}_{Rec2}$ and $\mathcal{L}_G$; next, we use the $\mathcal{L}_{D_Z}$ to update the discriminator to improve the discriminator ability of joint and marginal distribution; then, $\mathcal{L}_{Cls1}$ and $\mathcal{L}_{Cls2}$ are utilized to update encoders and classifier to boost the performance of task learning. After the discriminative representations have been extracted, $\mathcal{L}_{D_H}$ and $\mathcal{L}_{Ver}$ are performed to update the parameters in vertex convolution and discriminator $D_H$ alternatively; finally, $\mathcal{L}_{Cls3}$ updates the classifier $C_2$ to get a discrminative decision on the fused features.

## 3   Experiments

### 3.1   Data

A total of 300 subjects from ADNI database are used for this study with complete three modalities: fMRI, DTI and T1-weighted MRI, including 64 AD patients (39 male and 25 female, mean age 74.7, standard deviation 7.6), 76 late MCI patients (43 male and 33 female, mean age 75.8, standard deviation 6.4), 82 early MCI patients (40 male and 42 female, mean age 75.9, standard deviation 7.5), and 78 normal controls (39 male and 39 female, mean age 76.0, standard deviation 8.0).

For T1-weighted MRI data, we follow the standard proprocessing steps, including strip non-brain tissue of the whole head, image reorientation, resampling into a voxel size of 91 × 109 × 91 in Neuroimaging Informatics Technology Initiative (NIFTI) file format and extracting a 128-dimensional feature vector FV by a pre-trained densnet model. The fMRI data is preprocessed using GRETNA toolbox to obtain node features FT with a size of 90 × 187, the main steps include magnetization equilibrium, head-motion artifacts, spatial normalization, spatial filter with 0.01–0.08Hz, regression of local time-series, warping automated anatomical labeling (AAL90) atlas and removing the first 10 time-points. The DTI data preprocessing operation is performed using PANDA toolbox to get 90 × 90 matrix SC. The detailed procedures are skull stripping, resolution resampling, eddy currents correction, fiber tracking. The generated structural connectivity is input to our model as graph structure.

### 3.2   Experimental Settings

In this study, we use three kinds of binary classification task, i.e., (1) EMCI vs. NC; (2) LMCI vs. NC; (3) AD vs. NC. 10-fold cross validation is selected for task learning. In order to demonstrate the superiority of our proposed model compared with other models, we introduce previous methods for comparison. (1) Support Vector Machine (SVM) [40]; (2) two layers of the diffusion convolutional neural networks (DCNN) [41]; (3) our method with only fMRI and DTI; (4) our method with complete three modalities. For convenient viewing, the above methods using fMRI and DTI are denoted SVM (F-D), DCNN (F-D) and Ours (F-D).

In the experiments, we set the model parameters as follows:$N = 90$, $m = 10$, $q = 32$, $\gamma = 0.5$, tanh and sigmoid activation function for generators and decoders, respectively. The disease-related ROIs are selected according to previous studies [2,15,16]. $C_1$ is a two-layer perception with 16-neuron and 2-neuron in the hidden and output layers. $C_1$ is a two-layer perception with 90-neuron and 2-neuron in the hidden and output layers. $G$ and $G'$ are two-layer GCN, specifically, the hidden and output layers of $G$ is 64-neuron and 32-neuron, while the hidden and output layers of $G'$ is 64-neuron and 187-neuron. The hidden and output layers of $S$ is 64-neuron and 32-neuron, the hidden and output layers of $S'$ is 64-neuron and 128-neuron. For the discriminator $D_Z$, the hidden layer contains 1 filter with the size 32 × 1, the output layer contains 1 filters with the size 90 × 1. For the discriminator $D_H$, the filter size of hidden layer is 1 × 90, the filter size of output layer is 90 × 1. To balance the adversarial training, we choose 0.001 learning rate for the generators, encoders, decoders, and classifiers, 0.0001 learning rate for the discriminators. In the training process, 100 epochs are employed on representation learning, followed with 200 epochs for adversarial hypergraph fusion.

## 3.3  Results

Table 1 summarizes the results of different methods in three binary classification tasks using 10-fold cross validation. As can be seen that our proposed model has the best accuracy of 95.07%, 91.56%, and 87.50% in the tasks of AD vs. NC, LMCI vs. NC, EMCI vs. NC, respectively. Our method behaves better than other methods. It is found that introducing more modal images is beneficial to improve model detection performance. In addition, comparisons between ours(F-D) and DCNN(F-D) indicate that adding distribution-guided GraphGAN can improve detection accuracy. What's more, when compared with other related algorithms as illustrated in Table 2, the proposed method has achieved superior performance for MCI detection. It ourperforms the literature by 2.08%. Note that, methods using fMRI and DTI are denoted F-D, and Ours mean the proposed model using three complete modalities.

**Table 1.** Mean detection performance of the proposed and related methods.(%)

| Method | AD vs. NC | | | | LMCI vs. NC | | | | EMCI vs. NC | | | |
|---|---|---|---|---|---|---|---|---|---|---|---|---|
| | Acc | Sen | Spec | Auc | Acc | Sen | Spec | Auc | Acc | Sen | Spec | Auc |
| SVM (F-D) | 76.05 | 70.31 | 80.76 | 83.16 | 69.48 | 64.47 | 74.35 | 78.23 | 65.62 | 54.87 | 76.92 | 71.46 |
| DCNN (F-D) | 84.51 | 87.50 | 82.05 | 89.40 | 79.87 | 77.63 | 82.05 | 84.29 | 76.25 | 76.83 | 75.64 | 82.68 |
| Ours (F-D) | 88.73 | 84.37 | 92.31 | 97.48 | 84.42 | 84.21 | 84.62 | 94.01 | 82.50 | 82.93 | 82.05 | 91.65 |
| **Ours** | **95.07** | **93.75** | **96.15** | **98.20** | **91.56** | **94.74** | **88.89** | **94.64** | **87.50** | **86.59** | **88.46** | **93.05** |

**Table 2.** Algorithm comparison with the related works.(%)

| Method | Modality | Subject | MCI vs. NC | | | |
|---|---|---|---|---|---|---|
| | | | Acc | Sen | Spec | Auc |
| Xing et al. [14] | fMRI & MRI | 368 | 79.73 | 86.49 | 72.97 | – |
| Yu et al. [15] | fMRI & DTI | 184 | 85.42 | 86.57 | 84.42 | 89.98 |
| Zhu et al. [42] | MRI & PET & CSF | 152 | 83.54 | 95.00 | 62.86 | 78.15 |
| **Ours** | MRI & fMRI & DTI | 160 | **87.50** | 86.59 | **88.86** | **93.05** |

We further investigate the classification performance of our model by t-SNE analysis. Figure 2 shows the projection of features of three methods on the two dimensional plane in different task learning. Our model has slim and easily divisible plane compared with SVM and DCNN, indicating that the feature obtained from our method is more discriminative than that of SVM or DCNN. This investigation explains in detail why our model performs better than others in task learning.

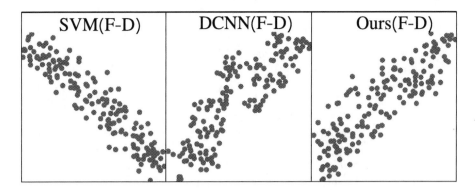

**Fig. 2.** Visualization of features of SVM, DCNN and our method using t-SNE tools for EMCI vs. NC. F-D means the three methods are input with fMRI and DTI.

Since the interactions among multiple regions are beneficial for characterizing disease-related brain activities, we construct connectivity matrix using the fused features by bilinear pooling. As is displayed in Fig. 3, we mean the connectivity matrices of each group for each binary classification task and then subtract patients connectivity matrix from NC connectivity matrix to obtain the change of brain network connections. It gives the following information: the connections gradually reduce as the disease worsens, while the increased connections rise up in early stages and drop to a low level when deteriorated to AD. This phenomenon may be explained by compensatory mechanism generation and weakening in the progression of MCI to AD [43–45].

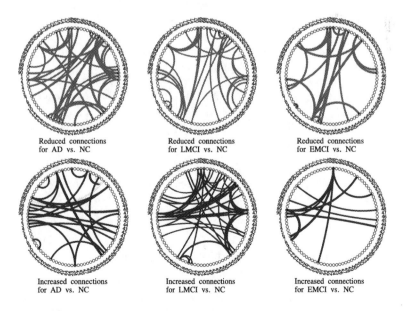

**Fig. 3.** Visualization of brain connection changes at different stages.

## 4   Conclusion

In this paper, we proposed a novel Multimodal-Representaion-Learning and Adversarial-Hypergraph-Fusion frame work for Alzheimer's disease diagnosis. Specifically, features in representations space are extracted by distribution-based GraphGAN and CNN-based GraphAE, respectively. And an adversarial strategy in modal fusion is utilized for AD detection. Results on ADNI dataset demonstrate that prior information can help to enhance discrimination of representation learning and adding more modalities can boost the detection performance. Furthermore, The study on multimodal fusion gives a possible way to understand the disorder's underlying mechanisms by analyzing the abnormal brain connections. In our future work, we will focus the abnormal connections among some certain ROIs and extend this work to multitask classification.

**Acknowledgment.** This work was supported by the National Natural Science Foundations of China under Grant 61872351, the International Science and Technology Cooperation Projects of Guangdong under Grant 2019A050510030, the Distinguished Young Scholars Fund of Guangdong under Grant 2021B1515020019, the Excellent Young Scholars of Shenzhen under Grant RCYX20200714114641211 and Shenzhen Key Basic Research Project under Grant JCYJ20200109115641762.

## References

1. Alzheimer's Association: 2019 Alzheimer's disease facts and figures. Alzheimer's Dementia. **15**(3), 321–387 (2019)
2. Li, Y., Liu, J., Tang, Z., et al.: Deep spatial-temporal feature fusion from adaptive dynamic functional connectivity for MCI identification. IEEE Trans. Med. Imaging **39**(9), 2818–2830 (2020)
3. Wang, S., Shen, Y., Shi, C., et al.: Skeletal maturity recognition using a fully automated system with convolutional neural networks. IEEE Access **6**, 29979–29993 (2018)
4. Wang, S., Shen, Y., Zeng, D., et al.: Bone age assessment using convolutional neural networks. In: 2018 International Conference on Artificial Intelligence and Big Data (ICAIBD), pp. 175–178 (2018)
5. Wang, S., Hu, Y., Shen, Y., et al.: Classification of diffusion tensor metrics for the diagnosis of a myelopathic cord using machine learning. Int. J. Neural Syst. **28**(02), 1750036 (2018)
6. Lei, B., Xia, Z., Jiang, F., et al.: Skin lesion segmentation via generative adversarial networks with dual discriminators. Med. Image Analy. **64**, 101716 (2020)
7. Wang, S., Wang, X., Shen, Y., et al.: An ensemble-based densely-connected deep learning system for assessment of skeletal maturity. IEEE Trans. Syst. Man Cybern. Syst. (2020)
8. Zeng, D., Wang, S., Shen, Y., et al.: A GA-based feature selection and parameter optimization for support tucker machine. Procedia Comput. Sci. **111**, 17–23 (2017)
9. Wu, K., Shen, Y., Wang, S.: 3D convolutional neural network for regional precipitation nowcasting. J. Image Signal Process. **7**(4), 200–212 (2018)
10. Franzmeier, N., Dyrba, M.: Functional brain network architecture may route progression of Alzheimer's disease pathology. Brain **140**(12), 3077–3080 (2017)

11. Pereira, J.B., Van Westen, D., Stomrud, E., et al.: Abnormal structural brain connectome in individuals with preclinical Alzheimer's disease. Cereb. Cortex **28**(10), 3638–3649 (2018)
12. Schuff, N., Woerner, N., Boreta, L., et al.: MRI of hippocampal volume loss in early Alzheimer's disease in relation to ApoE genotype and biomarkers. Brain **132**(4), 1067–1077 (2009)
13. Huang, J., Zhou, L., Wang, L., et al.: Attention-diffusion-bilinear neural network for brain network analysis. IEEE Trans. Med. Imaging **39**(7), 2541–2552 (2020)
14. Xing, X., Li, Q., Wei, H., et al.: Dynamic spectral graph convolution networks with assistant task training for early mci diagnosis. In: International Conference on Medical Image Computing and Computer-Assisted Intervention, pp. 639–646 (2019)
15. Yu, S., et al.: Multi-scale enhanced graph convolutional network for early mild cognitive impairment detection. In: Martel, A.L., et al. (eds.) MICCAI 2020. LNCS, vol. 12267, pp. 228–237. Springer, Cham (2020). https://doi.org/10.1007/978-3-030-59728-3_23
16. Li, Y., Liu, J., Tang, Z., et al.: Graph convolution network with similarity awareness and adaptive calibration for disease-induced deterioration prediction. Medical Image Analysis. **69**, 101947 (2021)
17. Yu, W., Lei, B., Michael, K., et al.: Tensorizing GAN with high-order pooling for Alzheimer's disease assessment. IEEE Trans. Neural Netw. Learn. Syst. (2021). https://doi.org/10.1109/TNNLS.2021.3063516
18. Goodfellow, I.J., Pouget-Abadie, J., Mirza, M., et al.: Generative adversarial nets. In: Proceedings of the 27th International Conference on Neural Information Processing Systems, pp. 2672–2680 (2014)
19. Mo, L.F., Wang, S.Q.: A variational approach to nonlinear two-point boundary value problems. Nonlinear Anal. Theory Methods Appl. **71**(12), e834–e838 (2009)
20. Wang, S.Q.: A variational approach to nonlinear two-point boundary value problems. Comput. Math. Appl. **58**(11–12), 2452–2455 (2009)
21. Wang, S.Q., He, J.H.: Variational iteration method for a nonlinear reaction-diffusion process. Int. J. Chem. Reactor Eng. **6**(1) (2008)
22. Wang S.Q., Wang X., Hu Y., et al.: Diabetic retinopathy diagnosis using multi-channel generative adversarial network with semisupervision. IEEE Trans. Autom. Sci. Eng. **18**, 574–585 (2020)
23. Hu, S., Shen, Y., Wang, S., Lei, B.: Brain MR to PET synthesis via bidirectional generative adversarial network. In: Martel, A.L., et al. (eds.) MICCAI 2020. LNCS, vol. 12262, pp. 698–707. Springer, Cham (2020). https://doi.org/10.1007/978-3-030-59713-9_67
24. Hu, S., Shen, Y., Wang, S., Lei, B.: Brain MR to PET synthesis via bidirectional generative adversarial network. In: MartelMartel, A.L., et al. (eds.) MICCAI 2020. LNCS, vol. 12262, pp. 698–707. Springer, Cham (2020). https://doi.org/10.1007/978-3-030-59713-9_67
25. Hu, S., Yu, W., Chen, Z., et al.: Medical image reconstruction using generative adversarial network for Alzheimer disease assessment with class-imbalance problem. In 2020 IEEE 6th International Conference on Computer and Communications (ICCC), pp. 1323–1327 (2020)
26. Dai, Q., Li, Q., Tang, J., et al.: Adversarial network embedding. In: Proceedings of the AAAI Conference on Artificial Intelligence, vol. 32(1) (2018)
27. Pan, S., Hu, R., Long, G., et al.: Adversarially regularized graph autoencoder for graph embedding. In: Proceedings of the 27th International Joint Conference on Artificial Intelligence, pp. 2609–2615 (2018)

28. Wen, J., Thibeau-Sutre, E., Diaz-Melo, M., et al.: Convolutional neural networks for classification of Alzheimer's disease: overview and reproducible evaluation. Med. Image Anal. **63**, 101694 (2020)
29. Wang, H., Shen, Y., Wang, S., et al.: Ensemble of 3D densely connected convolutional network for diagnosis of mild cognitive impairment and Alzheimer's disease. Neurocomputing **333**, 145–156 (2019)
30. Wang, S., Shen, Y., Chen, W., et al.: Automatic recognition of mild cognitive impairment from MRI images using expedited convolutional neural networks. In: International Conference on Artificial Neural Networks, pp. 373–380 (2017)
31. Wang, S., Wang, H., Shen, Y., et al.: Automatic recognition of mild cognitive impairment and Alzheimers disease using ensemble based 3D densely connected convolutional networks. In: 2018 17th IEEE International Conference on Machine Learning and Applications, pp. 517–523 (2018)
32. Hu, S., Yuan, J., Wang, S., et al.: Cross-modality synthesis from MRI to PET using adversarial U-net with different normalization. In 2019 International Conference on Medical Imaging Physics and Engineering (ICMIPE), pp. 1–5 (2019)
33. Lei, B., Yang, M., Yang, P., et al.: Deep and joint learning of longitudinal data for Alzheimer's disease prediction. Patt. Recogn. **102**, 107247 (2020)
34. Wang, S., Wang, H., Cheung, A.C., et al.: Ensemble of 3D densely connected convolutional network for diagnosis of mild cognitive impairment and Alzheimer's disease. Deep Learn. Appl. **1098**, 53 (2020)
35. Baltrušaitis, T., Ahuja, C., Morency, L.P.: Multimodal machine learning: a survey and taxonomy. IEEE Trans. Pattern Anal. Mach. Intell. **41**(2), 423–443 (2018)
36. Makhzani, A., Shlens, J., Jaitly, N., et al.: Adversarial autoencoders. arXiv preprint arXiv:1511.05644. (2015)
37. Li, Y., Liu, J., Gao, X., et al.: Multimodal hyper-connectivity of functional networks using functionally-weighted LASSO for MCI classification. Med. Image Anal. **52**, 80–96 (2019)
38. Feng, Y., You, H., Zhang, Z., et al.: Hypergraph neural networks. In: Proceedings of the AAAI Conference on Artificial Intelligence, pp. 3558–3565 (2019)
39. Kulesza, A., Taskar, B.: Fixed-size determinantal point processes. In: Proceedings of the 28th International Conference on Machine learning, pp. 1193–1200 (2011)
40. Suykens, J.A.K., Vandewalle, J.: Least squares support vector machine classifiers. Neural Process. Lett. **9**(3), 293–300 (1999)
41. Atwood, J., Towsley, D.: Diffusion-convolutional neural networks. In: Advances in Neural Information Processing Systems, pp. 1993–2001 (2016)
42. Zhu, Q., Yuan, N., Huang, J., et al.: Multi-modal AD classification via self-paced latent correlation analysis. Neurocomputing **255**, 143–154 (2019)
43. Montembeault, M., Rouleau, I., Provost, J.S., et al.: Altered gray matter structural covariance networks in early stages of Alzheimer's disease. Cereb. Cortex **26**(6), 2650–2662 (2016)
44. Sun, Y., Dai, Z., Li, Y., et al.: Subjective cognitive decline: mapping functional and structural brain changes–a combined resting-state functional and structural MR imaging study. Radiology **281**(1), 185–192 (2016)
45. Jin, D., Wang, P., Zalesky, A., et al.: Grab- AD: generalizability and reproducibility of altered brain activity and diagnostic classification in Alzheimer's Disease. Hum. Brain Mapp. **41**(12), 3379–3391 (2020)

# Model-Based Gait Recognition Using Graph Network with Pose Sequences

Zhihao Wang[1], Chaoying Tang[1(✉)], Han Su[2], and Xiaojie Li[3]

[1] College of Automation Engineering, Nanjing University of Aeronautics and Astronautics, Nanjing 211106, China
cytang@nuaa.edu.cn
[2] College of Computer Science, Sichuan Normal University, Chengdu 610066, China
[3] College of Information Science and Engineering, Shandong Normal University, Jinan 250014, China

**Abstract.** At present, the existing gait recognition systems are focusing on developing methods to extract robust gait feature from silhouette images and they indeed achieved great success. However, gait can be sensitive to appearance features such as clothing and carried items. Compared with appearance-based method, model-based gait recognition is promising due to the robustness against some variations, such as clothing and baggage carried. With the development of human pose estimation, the difficulty of model-based methods is mitigated in recent years. We leverage recent advances in action recognition to embed human pose sequence to a vector and introduce Spatial Temporal Graph Convolution Blocks (STGCB) which has been commonly used in action recognition for gait recognition. Furthermore, we build the velocity and bone's angle features to enrich the input of network. Experiments on the popular OUMVLP-Pose gait dataset show that our method archives state-of-the-art (SOTA) performance in model-based gait recognition.

**Keywords:** Gait recognition · Graph neural network · Skeleton · Spatial temporal

## 1  Introduction

Gait is one of the most popular behavioral biometrics in the world because it has unique advantages compared with face, iris, palm print, etc. Gait features can be captured at a long distance and are hard to disguise, and consequently, gait recognition technology has been added to the repertoire of tools available for crime prevention and forensic identification. Most of the current methods [1–3] usually take the silhouette sequence extracted from the video as the input. In general, there are three steps in appearance-based methods: silhouette extraction, feature learning and distance measurement. However, most of the studies do not include very specific approach of silhouette extraction. The existing silhouette extraction approaches such as background subtraction [4] fail to perform well in a cluttered and rapidly-changing scenarios. In addition, the silhouette contains not only gait information, but also other appearance cues such as body shape

© Springer Nature Switzerland AG 2021
H. Ma et al. (Eds.): PRCV 2021, LNCS 13021, pp. 491–501, 2021.
https://doi.org/10.1007/978-3-030-88010-1_41

and hairstyle. The complexity of information weakens its robustness especially when appearance changed. On the contrary, the model-based approach has achieved more attention since current pose estimation algorithms are robust against occlusion, cluttered and changing backgrounds, carried items, and clothing.

In this paper, we take the pose sequences from pose estimation and take the velocity and bone's angle features as the input. Furthermore, we adopt AGCN network which is commonly used in skeleton-based action recognition. Concretely, AGCN network is the stack of Spatial Temporal Graph Convolution Blocks (STGCB). Then, we use Euclidean distance of the corresponding feature vectors to measure the similarity between gallery and probe. Our experiments on the OUMVLP-Pose gait dataset have proved the effectiveness of the proposed method. More specifically, we achieved an average rank-1 recognition rates of 30.08% on the OpenPose part and 37.22% on the AlphaPose part which achieves the state-of-the-art performance. We also do experiment on CASIA-B dataset, a widely used gait dataset and still achieve competitive results against the appearance-based method.

Our contributions can be summarized as follows:

(1) We adapted the experience of action recognize and introduced graph neural network into gait recognition. And we build the velocity and bone's angle features to utilize the second-order information.
(2) Our empirical experiments show state-of-the-art results compared to the current model-based approaches.

## 2  Related Work

The current work of gait recognition can basically be categorized into two parts. One is the temporal modeling which can be further divided into single-image, sequence-based, and set-based approaches. Early single-image approaches proposed to encode a gait sequence into a single image, *i.e.*, Gait Energy Image (GEI) [5]. In sequence-based approaches each input is separately focused in modeling, and the temporal information such as 3D-CNNs [6, 7] or LSTMs [8, 9] is used. The set-based approach [2] models no temporal information, thus has less computational complexity, such as GaitNet.

The other part is based on spatial feature extraction, which have two common methods: appearance-based methods and model-based methods. Appearance-based methods rely on a binary human silhouette extracted from the original image [4] to encode the spatial and temporal information. Model-based methods extract features by fitting a human joint model to an image and extracting kinematic information (such as a sequence of joint positions or joint angles) [6, 10–13]. It is obvious that human model fitting is a key process for model-based methods, which is considered error-prone and computationally exhaustive. As a result, model-based methods have not gotten enough attention for more than a decade, although it can be robust against appearance changes due to clothing and carrying condition, since extracted joint positions/angles are less affected by them. Recently Liao et al. [8] used a pose estimation by deep learning to recover human skeleton models. They also converted 2D pose data to 3D for view invariant feature extraction [8]. The models obtained by deep learning are much better than those by traditional methods. We believe that model-based methods will be promoted greatly with the development of pose estimation.

## 3   Skeleton-Based Gait Recognition

In this section, we describe our method for learning discriminative information from a sequence of human poses.

### 3.1   Notation and Graph Convolutional Networks (GCNs)

A human skeleton graph is denoted as $\mathcal{G} = (\mathcal{V}, \mathcal{E})$, where $\mathcal{V} = \{v_1, \ldots, v_N\}$ is the set of $N$ nodes representing joints and $\mathcal{E}$ is the set of edges representing bones captured by an adjacency matrix $A \in \mathbb{R}^{N \times N}$. And $A_{n,m} = 1$ represents that an edge connects between joint $v_n$ and joint $v_m$.

Gait can be seen as a sequence of graphs. In our program, node feature set is represented by a feature tensor $X \in \mathbb{R}^{\wedge}(T \times N \times C)$, where $x_{t,n} \in X$ is the $C$ dimensional feature vector for node $v_n$ at time $t$ over total $T$ frames. In our paper, every node $v$ in feature tensor $X$ consists of 3 scales: the 2D coordinate, and its confidence. So, it is obvious that $C$ is 3.

The inputs to the network are feature $X$ and graph structure $A$. The graph structure $A$ is an adjacency matrix and $A$ representing the information of connections.

The layer-wise update rule of Graph Convolutional Networks (GCNs) can be applied to features at time $t$ as:

$$X_t^{l+1} = \sigma(\tilde{D}^{-\frac{1}{2}} \tilde{A} \tilde{D}^{-\frac{1}{2}} X_t^l W^l) \tag{1}$$

where $\tilde{A} = A + I$ is identity features, $I$ is an identity matrix, $\tilde{A}$ is the skeleton graph to keep identify features, $W^l \in \mathbb{R}^{C_l \times C_{l+1}}$ is a learnable weight matrix at layer $l$, $\tilde{D}$ is the diagonal degree matrix of $\tilde{A}$, and $\sigma$ is an activation function. The term $\tilde{D}^{-\frac{1}{2}} \tilde{A} \tilde{D}^{-\frac{1}{2}} X_t^l W^l$ can be considered as a spatial convolution to aggregate the information from the neighbors which is direct connected.

### 3.2   Network and Implementation Details

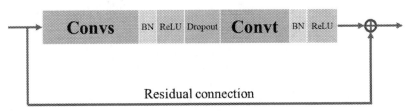

**Fig. 1.** Illustration of the adaptive graph convolutional block. Convs and Convt represent the spatial and temporal GCNs, respectively.

**ST-GCN Block [14].**  In general, it is composed of two major blocks: one for spatial convolution and the other for temporal convolution. As is shown in Fig. 1, there is a dropout layer between two convolution layers. Both convolution blocks include convolution, BatchNorm (BN) followed by ReLU as the activation function.

**AGCN.**  The network's main architecture adopts AGCN in [15] with adaptions to our use case. The network is composed of ST-GCN blocks, as is shown in Table 1.

**Table 1.**  Implementation details of the AGCN network.

| Layers | Input channels | Output channels | Strides | Activation function |
|---|---|---|---|---|
| Batch Norm | – | – | – | ReLU |
| ST-GCN.1 | 3 | 64 | 1 | ReLU |
| ST-GCN.2 | 64 | 64 | 1 | ReLU |
| ST-GCN.3 | 64 | 64 | 1 | ReLU |
| ST-GCN.4 | 64 | 128 | 2 | ReLU |
| ST-GCN.5 | 128 | 128 | 1 | ReLU |
| ST-GCN.6 | 128 | 128 | 1 | ReLU |
| ST-GCN.7 | 128 | 256 | 2 | ReLU |
| ST-GCN.8 | 256 | 256 | 1 | ReLU |
| GAP | The global average pooling layer | | | |
| FC | 256 | 256[a] | – | – |

[a]: the channels of FC depend on the shape of embeddings.

**Loss Function.**  For a graph embedding problem, normalized embeddings from the same class should be pulled closer together than embeddings from different classes. We take supervised contrastive (SupConLoss), a loss for supervised learning that builds on the contrastive self-supervised literature by leveraging label information [16], as the loss function. The loss takes features (L2 normalized) and labels as input and shows benefits for robustness to natural corruptions and is more stable to hyperparameter settings such as optimizers and data augmentations [16].

**Augmentation.** To enrich the features of data, we use multiple techniques to augment the skeleton graph. As is shown in Fig. 2, the feature $x_{t,n}$ is the feature of the $n_{th}$ node (or joint) at time $t$ and the velocity of $x_{t,n}$ is denoted as $V_{t,n}$. $V_{t,n} = x_{t,n} - x_{t-1,n}$ and the angle of bone which connects the $n_{th}$ and $m_{th}$ joints is $\theta_{t,n} = \arccos(\frac{x_{t,n}-x_{t,m}}{\|x_{t,n}-x_{t,m}\|})$. Following this way, we get more features of gait. The overall pipeline is illustrated in Fig. 3.

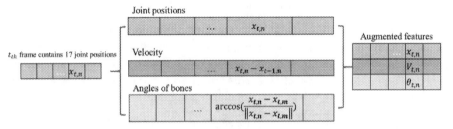

**Fig. 2.** Extract three different features from a frame

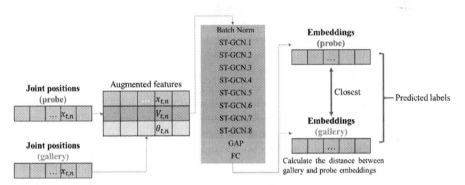

**Fig. 3.** Overview of the pipeline.

## 4    Experiments

In this part, firstly, we evaluated the recognition accuracy of our method using the rank-1 recognition rates on two datasets: OUMVLP-Pose and CASIA-B. Secondly, we do spatio-temporal study on OUMVLP-Pose to evaluate the ability of our method to model temporal features.

### 4.1    Dataset and Training Details

Most gait datasets do not provide pose sequence. However, last year, the OU-ISIR Gait Database [17] provided a Multi-View Large Population Database with Pose Sequence (OUMVLP-Pose) to aid research efforts in the general area of developing, testing and evaluating algorithms for model-based gait recognition.

**Dataset.** OUMVLP-Pose set was built upon OU-MVLP. It contains 10,307 subjects of round-trip walking sequences captured by seven network cameras at intervals of 15° (this sums to 14 views by considering the round trip on the same walking course) with an image size of 1,280 x 980 pixels and a frame-rate of 25 fps. Two data sets are provided for OUMVLP-Pose, which were obtained by the OpenPose and AlphaPose models, respectively. These two datasets contain the same number of subjects and the same parameters. Each of the data set is divided into two disjoint subsets, *i.e.*, training and testing sets with almost the same number of samples [17].

**Protocol.** For a fair comparison, this paper follows the protocol by OUMVLP-Pose dataset [17]. We divided 10,307 subjects into two sets. The first one with 5,153 subjects is the training set, and the second with the remaining 5,154 subjects is the test set. The test set is separated into a gallery set and a probe set. In our training phase, we set the training batch as 512.

**Train Details.** We use OneCycle [18] scheduler to dynamically adjust the learning rate and we set the initial learning rate as 0.001.

**Metric.** The rank-1 recognition rate was employed to evaluate the recognition accuracies.

## 4.2   Performance of Networks

First, we evaluated the recognition accuracy of our method with the rank-1 recognition rates on OpenPose and AlphaPose datasets. The results of the 0–270° gallery *vs.* the 0–270° probe are shown in Table 2 and Table 3. It should be mentioned that the horizontal axis represents gallery angle while the vertical axis represents probe angle. The models of both were trained for 1000 epochs. We find that the recognition rate will be relatively high when the probe angle is the same as the gallery angle. So, we take probe = 0 as an example. As is shown in Fig. 4, view variation can greatly reduce the recognition rate.

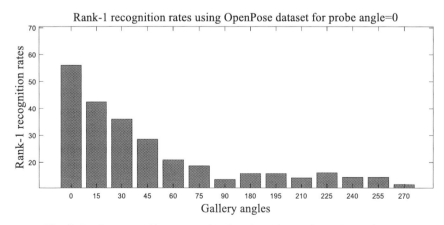

**Fig. 4.** Rank-1 recognition rates using OpenPose dataset for probe angle = 0.

The average rate of AGCN on OpenPose is 30.08% and better than the result 14.76% of CNN-Pose from [17]. In Table 3, the average rate of AlphaPose (37.22%) is also greater than the result (20.42%) from [17].

**Table 2.** Rank-1 recognition rates by AGCN network using OpenPose dataset for all combinations of views.

| Probe\Gallery | 0 | 15 | 30 | 45 | 60 | 75 | 90 | 180 | 195 | 210 | 225 | 240 | 255 | 270 | Mean |
|---|---|---|---|---|---|---|---|---|---|---|---|---|---|---|---|
| 0 | 56.1 | 32.2 | 27.4 | 22.8 | 18.4 | 14.7 | 9.7 | 12.1 | 14.1 | 11.9 | 15.1 | 15.0 | 12.4 | 10.8 | 19.5 |
| 15 | 42.5 | 71.3 | 52.0 | 45.6 | 36.6 | 28.3 | 18.2 | 14.7 | 22.3 | 16.6 | 22.1 | 21.4 | 19.1 | 16.3 | 30.5 |
| 30 | 36.0 | 55.6 | 73.6 | 66.3 | 47.7 | 39.5 | 25.4 | 16.6 | 21.7 | 20.5 | 26.6 | 25.8 | 23.3 | 20.5 | 35.7 |
| 45 | 28.6 | 49.4 | 64.5 | 79.0 | 65.2 | 50.7 | 32.2 | 16.5 | 22.2 | 20.5 | 31.6 | 30.1 | 27.1 | 24.1 | 38.7 |
| 60 | 20.9 | 34.9 | 42.0 | 57.4 | 76.8 | 53.6 | 31.4 | 13.9 | 19.7 | 16.4 | 26.3 | 33.5 | 26.0 | 22.5 | 34.0 |
| 75 | 18.7 | 31.0 | 38.3 | 52.3 | 60.9 | 74.7 | 51.8 | 15.6 | 21.2 | 19.3 | 29.4 | 31.1 | 33.9 | 30.2 | 36.3 |
| 90 | 13.7 | 20.9 | 26.6 | 33.3 | 36.0 | 52.3 | 63.6 | 13.5 | 16.8 | 17.5 | 25.2 | 26.4 | 30.7 | 32.9 | 29.2 |
| 180 | 15.9 | 15.6 | 16.6 | 17.4 | 16.5 | 16.4 | 13.7 | 58.7 | 39.8 | 27.7 | 28.0 | 21.0 | 16.8 | 13.3 | 22.7 |
| 195 | 15.9 | 20.4 | 19.4 | 20.0 | 18.4 | 18.5 | 14.2 | 35.6 | 70.9 | 43.6 | 44.3 | 32.6 | 25.0 | 17.1 | 28.3 |
| 210 | 14.3 | 16.0 | 19.3 | 19.6 | 16.7 | 17.2 | 14.7 | 26.4 | 46.4 | 57.0 | 51.6 | 34.6 | 26.6 | 19.2 | 27.1 |
| 225 | 16.2 | 19.6 | 22.2 | 26.4 | 23.6 | 23.8 | 20.2 | 23.8 | 44.7 | 50.8 | 75.8 | 56.0 | 40.4 | 26.8 | 33.6 |
| 240 | 14.5 | 18.2 | 19.3 | 22.8 | 29.4 | 24.2 | 19.1 | 17.0 | 29.7 | 29.5 | 51.2 | 70.3 | 42.4 | 27.4 | 29.6 |
| 255 | 14.5 | 17.2 | 19.9 | 24.2 | 24.2 | 28.3 | 25.7 | 14.7 | 24.5 | 25.0 | 41.3 | 50.2 | 65.9 | 46.2 | 30.1 |
| 270 | 11.8 | 14.7 | 17.2 | 21.4 | 21.7 | 25.7 | 28.2 | 10.4 | 18.0 | 18.4 | 26.9 | 31.2 | 45.7 | 57.1 | 24.9 |

**Table 3.** Rank-1 recognition rates by AGCN network using AlphaPose dataset for all combinations of views.

| Probe\Gallery | 0 | 15 | 30 | 45 | 60 | 75 | 90 | 180 | 195 | 210 | 225 | 240 | 255 | 270 | Mean |
|---|---|---|---|---|---|---|---|---|---|---|---|---|---|---|---|
| 0 | 70.3 | 47.9 | 38.5 | 32.5 | 26.7 | 22.2 | 16.5 | 15.9 | 18.6 | 13.8 | 20.8 | 20.2 | 19.8 | 17.8 | 27.3 |
| 15 | 60.6 | 79.5 | 66.1 | 55.1 | 45.7 | 36.7 | 26.4 | 19.8 | 27.9 | 21.2 | 28.6 | 27.6 | 26.6 | 24.6 | 39.0 |
| 30 | 52.3 | 71.0 | 84.5 | 75.6 | 59.8 | 48.7 | 34.9 | 21.6 | 28.4 | 26.2 | 34.9 | 32.8 | 32.7 | 30.4 | 45.3 |
| 45 | 43.8 | 60.2 | 73.8 | 84.6 | 71.1 | 58.9 | 42.8 | 20.1 | 25.8 | 24.4 | 38.2 | 35.0 | 36.6 | 35.0 | 46.4 |
| 60 | 31.0 | 42.3 | 51.4 | 62.6 | 81.3 | 60.8 | 44.1 | 17.9 | 23.7 | 21.1 | 33.0 | 42.3 | 33.5 | 31.5 | 41.2 |
| 75 | 29.7 | 40.2 | 48.8 | 61.0 | 69.9 | 83.0 | 68.3 | 20.0 | 26.0 | 24.3 | 38.7 | 40.6 | 47.6 | 45.2 | 46.0 |
| 90 | 22.4 | 29.3 | 35.2 | 43.9 | 50.5 | 67.2 | 78.3 | 18.4 | 22.0 | 20.8 | 35.0 | 37.7 | 48.6 | 49.3 | 39.9 |
| 180 | 20.4 | 21.2 | 22.3 | 20.6 | 19.7 | 19.9 | 18.3 | 59.8 | 42.4 | 28.1 | 29.8 | 23.5 | 21.3 | 17.5 | 26.1 |
| 195 | 18.8 | 24.8 | 25.1 | 23.0 | 22.2 | 21.4 | 18.7 | 39.3 | 70.7 | 44.9 | 42.7 | 32.3 | 26.5 | 19.8 | 30.7 |
| 210 | 17.7 | 21.8 | 25.0 | 23.1 | 22.1 | 22.3 | 19.2 | 28.1 | 48.0 | 57.1 | 52.7 | 37.5 | 30.2 | 22.8 | 30.5 |
| 225 | 22.1 | 26.1 | 30.6 | 33.4 | 31.6 | 32.3 | 30.1 | 26.4 | 43.0 | 50.0 | 79.9 | 62.5 | 48.9 | 35.8 | 39.5 |

*(continued)*

**Table 3.** (*continued*)

| Probe\Gallery | 0 | 15 | 30 | 45 | 60 | 75 | 90 | 180 | 195 | 210 | 225 | 240 | 255 | 270 | Mean |
|---|---|---|---|---|---|---|---|---|---|---|---|---|---|---|---|
| 240 | 18.9 | 22.6 | 25.0 | 26.9 | 37.1 | 31.3 | 29.5 | 19.4 | 30.2 | 31.1 | 55.6 | 76.9 | 52.1 | 37.4 | 35.3 |
| 255 | 21.9 | 24.5 | 29.2 | 32.7 | 34.0 | 40.5 | 41.3 | 18.2 | 27.5 | 27.4 | 51.0 | 61.5 | 77.3 | 62.6 | 39.2 |
| 270 | 21.1 | 22.1 | 25.4 | 29.5 | 31.6 | 39.0 | 42.5 | 14.9 | 22.2 | 22.1 | 38.3 | 43.4 | 62.3 | 71.6 | 34.7 |

### 4.3 Comparison with Other Model-Based Methods

Table 4 shows the rank-1 recognition rates of two other model-based methods on the OpenPose and AlphaPose datasets where the probe angle is the same as the gallery angle. One is a recent deep learning-based approach named pose-based temporal-spatial network (PTSN) [6], and the other is CNN-Pose method [17].

Take the pose sequences as input, CNN-Pose applies two-dimensional convolution layers, pooling layers, and a full connection layer. For feature extraction, cross-entropy loss based on softmax and a center loss are employed to optimize the network.

Table 5 shows the average rank-1 recognition rates on different probe angles with three different specific gallery angles. Our method has better performance than the PTSN and CNN-Pose methods [17].

**Table 4.** The rank-1 recognition rates of three model-based methods on the OpenPose and AlphaPose dataset where the probe angle is the same as the gallery angle.

| Methods | 0 | 30 | 60 | 90 | mean |
|---|---|---|---|---|---|
| PTSN [6] | 24.0 | 38.2 | 29.3 | 28.5 | 30.0 |
| CNN-Pose (OpenPose) [17] | 31.98 | 53.39 | 69.07 | 37.93 | 48.09 |
| Our method (OpenPose) | **56.43** | **73.32** | **77.21** | **63.53** | **67.62** |
| CNN-Pose (AlphaPose) [17] | 47.25 | 69.13 | 73.21 | 49.07 | 59.67 |
| Our method (AlphaPose) | **70.26** | **84.49** | **81.25** | **78.34** | **78.59** |

**Table 5.** The rates are the averages on different probe angles with a specific gallery angle 0°, 30°, 60° and 90° on the OpenPose and AlphaPose dataset.

| Methods | 0 | 30 | 60 | 90 | mean |
|---|---|---|---|---|---|
| CNN-Pose (OpenPose) [17] | 7.52 | 18.56 | 22.81 | 11.83 | 18.0 |
| Our method (OpenPose) | **22.81** | **29.78** | **32.74** | **36.32** | **29.23** |
| CNN-Pose (AlphaPose) [17] | 12.27 | 29.32 | 30.50 | 18.06 | 22.54 |
| Our method (AlphaPose) | **32.21** | **38.11** | **41.49** | **43.18** | **38.32** |

### 4.4 Result on CASIA-B Dataset and Comparison with Appearance-Based Method

CASIA-B [19] is a widely used gait dataset and composed of 124 subjects. For each subject the dataset contains 11 views ($0°$, $18°$,..., $180°$) and 3 waking conditions. The walking conditions are normal (NM), walking with a bag (BG), and wearing a coat or a jacket (CL). For getting pose sequences from the raw input images, we use OpenPose [20] as a 2D human pose estimator to obtain the human pose in each frame. Table 6 shows the comparison of our method with GaitNet [1], which is a typical appearance-based approach to gait recognition in recent years. Notably, with our lower dimension feature representation, we can still achieve competitive results against the appearance-based method.

**Table 6.** Rank-1 recognition rates by AGCN network using CASIA-B dataset with OpenPose for all combinations of views.

|          | 0    | 18   | 36   | 54   | 72   | 90   | 108  | 126  | 144  | 162  | 180  | Mean | GaitNet[1] |
|----------|------|------|------|------|------|------|------|------|------|------|------|------|------------|
| NM#5–6   | 72.4 | 81.2 | 85.6 | 80.4 | 79.4 | 85.0 | 81.0 | 77.6 | 82.5 | 79.1 | 80.2 | 80.4 | 91.6       |
| BG#1–2   | 62.5 | 68.7 | 69.4 | 64.8 | 62.8 | 67.2 | 68.3 | 65.7 | 60.7 | 64.1 | 60.3 | 65.0 | 85.7       |
| CL#1–2   | 57.8 | 63.2 | 68.3 | 64.1 | 66.0 | 64.8 | 67.7 | 60.2 | 66.0 | 68.3 | 60.3 | 64.2 | 58.9       |

### 4.5 Spatio-Temporal Study

Furthermore, our approach shows a high ability to model temporal features as shown in Table 7. When trained with sorted sequences and tested with shuffled sequences (row 3), the performance drops profoundly. These results support that our method rely on temporal features within pose sequences. Table 7 also illustrates the spatial modeling abilities in row 1. Despite the missing temporal and appearance information, the network is still able to learn spatial features of gait.

**Table 7.** Control Condition: sort/shuffle the input sequence at train/test phase. Results are rank-1 accuracies averaged on 14 views.

|   | Train   | Test    | OpenPose | AlphaPose |
|---|---------|---------|----------|-----------|
| 1 | Shuffle | Sort    | 11.16    | 21.74     |
| 2 | Sort    | Sort    | 30.08    | 37.22     |
| 3 | Sort    | Shuffle | 6.03     | 11.10     |

## 5 Conclusion

In this work, we introduce AGCN network into model-based gait recognition. It parameterizes the graph structure of the skeleton sequences. Furthermore, we embed the graph structure into the network. This model-based approach increases the flexibility of the graph convolutional network and is more robust to the gait recognition task in real world. Furthermore, we build the velocity and bone's angle features to enrich the input of network. The traditional methods always ignore or underestimate the importance of the skeleton information because it used to be hard to fit human model (or estimate human pose). The model is evaluated on a large population database with multi-view pose sequences, OUMVLP-Pose, and it achieves the new state-of-the-art performance.

**Acknowledgement.** This work was supported by the Key Research & Development Programs of Jiangsu Province (BE2018720) and the Open project of Engineering Center of Ministry of Education (NJ2020004).

# References

1. Song, C., Huang, Y., Huang, Y., Jia, N., Wang, L.: GaitNet: an end-to-end network for gait based human identification. Pattern Recognit. **96**, 106988 (2019)
2. Chao, H., He, Y., Zhang, J., Feng, J.: Gaitset: regarding gait as a set for cross-view gait recognition. In: Proceedings of the AAAI Conference on Artificial Intelligence, pp. 8126–8133 (2019)
3. Fan, C., et al.: Gaitpart: temporal part-based model for gait recognition. In: Proceedings of the IEEE/CVF Conference on Computer Vision and Pattern Recognition, pp. 14225–14233 IEEE (2020)
4. Wang, L., Tan, T., Ning, H., Hu, W.: Silhouette analysis-based gait recognition for human identification. IEEE Trans. Pattern Anal. Mach. Intell. **25**(12), 1505–1518 (2003)
5. Han, J., Bhanu, B.: Individual recognition using gait energy image. IEEE Trans. Pattern Anal. Mach. Intell. **28**(2), 316–322 (2005)
6. Liao, R., Cao, C., Garcia, E.B., Yu, S., Huang, Y.: Pose-based temporal-spatial network (PTSN) for gait recognition with carrying and clothing variations. In: Chinese Conference on Biometric Recognition, pp. 474–483. Springer, Cham (2017)
7. Wolf, T., Babaee, M., Rigoll, G.: Multi-view gait recognition using 3D convolutional neural networks. In: 2016 IEEE International Conference on Image Processing (ICIP), pp. 4165–4169. IEEE (2016)
8. Liao, R., Yu, S., An, W., Huang, Y.: A model-based gait recognition method with body pose and human prior knowledge. Pattern Recognit. **98**, 107069 (2020)
9. Sokolova, A., Konushin, A.: Pose-based deep gait recognition. IET. Biometrics **8**(2), 134–143 (2019)
10. Cunado, D., Nixon, M.S., Carter, J.N.: Using gait as a biometric, via phase-weighted magnitude spectra. In: Bigün, J., Chollet, G., Borgefors, G. (eds.) AVBPA 1997. LNCS, vol. 1206, pp. 93–102. Springer, Heidelberg (1997). https://doi.org/10.1007/BFb0015984
11. Wang, L., Ning, H., Tan, T., Hu, W.: Fusion of static and dynamic body biometrics for gait recognition. IEEE Trans. Circ. Syst. Video Technol. **14**(2), 149–158 (2004)
12. Yam, C., Nixon, M.S., Carter, J.N.: Automated person recognition by walking and running via model-based approaches. Pattern Recognit. **37**(5), 1057–1072 (2004)
13. Urtasun, R., Fua, P.: 3D tracking for gait characterization and recognition. In: Sixth IEEE International Conference on Automatic Face and Gesture Recognition, 2004. Proceedings, pp. 17–22. IEEE (2004)
14. Yan, S., Xiong, Y., Lin, D.: Spatial temporal graph convolutional networks for skeleton-based action recognition. In: Thirty-second AAAI Conference on Artificial Intelligence (2018)

15. Shi, L., Zhang, Y., Cheng, J., Lu, H.: Two-stream adaptive graph convolutional networks for skeleton-based action recognition. In: Proceedings of the IEEE/CVF Conference on Computer Vision and Pattern Recognition, pp. 12026–12035 (2019)
16. Khosla, P., et al.: Supervised contrastive learning. arXiv preprint arXiv:2004.11362. (2020)
17. An, W., et al.: Performance evaluation of model-based gait on multi-view very large population database with pose sequences. IEEE Trans. Biometr. Behav. Identity Sci. **2**(4), 421–430 (2020)
18. Smith, L.N., Topin, N.: Super-convergence: very fast training of neural networks using large learning rates. In: Artificial Intelligence and Machine Learning for Multi-Domain Operations Applications. International Society for Optics and Photonics (2019)
19. Yu, S., Tan, D., Tan, T.: A framework for evaluating the effect of view angle, clothing and carrying condition on gait recognition. In: 18th International Conference on Pattern Recognition (ICPR 2006), vol. 4, pp. 441–444. IEEE (2006)
20. Cao, Z., Hidalgo, G., Simon, T., Wei, S.E., Sheikh, Y.: OpenPose: realtime multi-person 2D pose estimation using Part Affinity Fields. IEEE Trans. Pattern Anal. Mach. Intell. **43**(1), 172–186 (2019)

# Multi-directional Attention Network for Segmentation of Pediatric Echocardiographic

Zhuo Xiang, Cheng Zhao, Libao Guo, Yali Qiu, Yun Zhu, Peng Yang, Wei Xiong, Mingzhu Li, Minsi Chen, Tianfu Wang[✉], and Baiying Lei[✉]

School of Biomedical Engineering, Shenzhen University, Shenzhen 518060, China
{tfwang,leiby}@szu.edu.cn

**Abstract.** Accurate segmentation of key anatomical structures in pediatric echocardiography is essential for the diagnosis and treatment of congenital heart disease. However, most of the existing segmentation methods for echocardiography have the problem of loss of detailed information, which has a certain impact on the accuracy of segmentation. Based on this, we propose a multi-directional attention (MDA) network for echocardiographic segmentation. This method uses U-Net as the backbone network to extract the initial features of different layers, and then sends the initial features to our proposed MDA module for feature enhancement. Among them, MDA includes two parts: First, considering the different contribution rates of spatial information in different directions to features, we construct a multi-directional spatial attention (MDSA) module to extract spatial information in different directions. Then to avoid the loss of channel information, we construct a channel weight constraint module (CWC) to constrain the weight of the spatial features extracted by MDSA. Finally, the group fusion feature output by MDA is used as the input of the decoder, and the final segmentation prediction result is obtained by setting the layered feature fusion (LFF) module. We conduct an extensive evaluation of 4,485 two-dimensional (2D) pediatric echocardiograms from 127 echocardiographic videos. Experiments show that the proposed algorithm can achieve the results of pediatric echocardiographic anatomical structures (left ventricle (LV), left atrium (LA)) with the average dice, precision, and recall were 0.9346, 0.9370, and 0.9406.

**Keywords:** Pediatric echocardiography segmentation · Multi-directional attention · Weight constraint module · Layered feature fusion module

## 1 Introduction

Congenital heart disease is one of the important causes of death in pediatric [1]. Because ultrasound has the advantages of no damage, no radiation, real-time, dynamic observation of heart structure and blood flow, echocardiography has become the most common method for diagnosing congenital heart disease. In clinical practice, we need to segment the key anatomical structures of echocardiography to measure clinical parameters

© Springer Nature Switzerland AG 2021
H. Ma et al. (Eds.): PRCV 2021, LNCS 13021, pp. 502–512, 2021.
https://doi.org/10.1007/978-3-030-88010-1_42

for further diagnosis. Currently, manual annotations are usually performed by experienced doctors, which is time-consuming and laborious and highly dependent on doctors. Therefore, an automatic and efficient segmentation method is needed to assist doctors to improve diagnosis efficiency.

However, due to the inherent limitations of low contrast and noise, the automatic segmentation of echocardiography faces a huge challenge. Because the boundary information of pediatric echocardiography is blurred and the structure and shape change drastically (Fig. 1 (a–c)), it is difficult to accurately determine the contours of the left ventricle (LV) and left atrium (LA). Secondly, lower contrast and artifacts will affect the accuracy of the segmentation algorithm (Fig. 1 (d–f)).

In recent years, more and more scholars have applied segmentation algorithms based on deep learning to medical image segmentation [2–7]. Among them, segmentation methods based on U-Net [7] and its variants are common segmentation networks [7, 8]. However, some algorithms simply consider spatial information globally and ignore some details in the spatial information. In addition, the attention mechanism has aroused the interest of many scholars [9–13]. It can emphasize the features that provide useful information while suppressing those less useful features. Such as SE [10] uses two full connection layers to explore the relationship between channels. CBAM [9] combine spatial attention with channel attention.

Therefore, we propose a multi-directional attention network for automatic segmentation of echocardiography. This network uses U-Net as the basic architecture and inputs the initial feature groups into the multi-directional spatial attention module to enhance the spatial information of the target. Finally, the enhanced features are sent to the U-Net decoder, merged with the bottom-up features of each layer to obtain the hierarchical

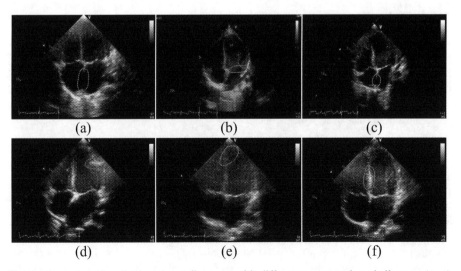

**Fig. 1.** Examples of pediatric echocardiograms with different segmentation challenges. (a–c) The green area depicts fuzzy boundary information of LV and LA. (d–f) Depicts artifacts and low contrast. (Color figure online)

features, and the hierarchical features are added and sent to softmax function to obtain the final prediction result.

## 2    Methodology

### 2.1    Overview

Figure 2 shows the overall structure of the segmentation network used for pediatric cardiograms. We use the U-Net network as the backbone network. On this basis, to be able to capture more semantic information, we set the U-Net networked encoder part of 6 layers. In the encoder part, MDA extracts useful spatial information from the basic features extracted by the encoder. Then, the obtained spatial information is used to enhance the basic features. The enhanced features are used as the input of the decoder, combined with the up-sampling features of each layer full of semantic information to obtain the output of each layer, and finally, the output of each layer is added together as the final prediction result.

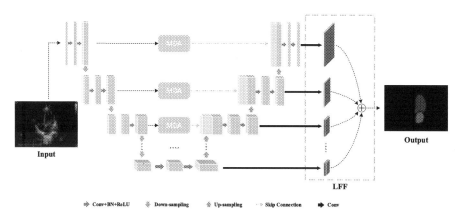

**Fig. 2.** The proposed segmentation network architecture. MDA can enhance the spatial information in the encoder features. LFF obtains the segmentation results of LV and LA by combining the predictions of each layer of the decoder.

### 2.2    Multi-direction Attention Module

In the segmentation of the LV and the LA in pediatric ultrasound images, the edge information is very important, and the difficulty of segmentation is mostly the prediction of the edge. To get better segmentation results, we add an MDA module to the encoder to enhance the edge information in the basic features. Since the information in different directions has different effects on spatial pixels, we enhance the spatial representation ability of features by considering the information in the four directions of horizontal, vertical, positive diagonal, and negative diagonal. At the same time, a weight constraint module is constructed to calculate the correlation between channels. As shown in Fig. 3, the MDA module includes two parts: MDSA and CWC.

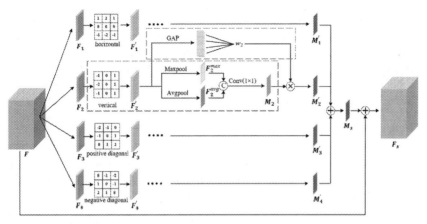

**Fig. 3.** The proposed MDA module. We mainly describe the feature extraction path in the vertical direction. The red line represents the MDSA. The green line represents the CWC. (Color figure online)

**Multi-directional Spatial Attention Module.** As shown in Fig. 3, given a basic feature map $F \in \mathbb{R}^{C \times H \times W}$ extracted by an encoder, $C$, $H$ and $W$ are the number of channels, the height and width of the feature map, respectively. To better extract the edge information in the feature, we choose to extract the edge information separately from the four directions of horizontal, vertical, positive diagonal, and negative diagonal. At the same time, to improve the computational efficiency of the network, we use group segmentation to divide the basic feature $F$ into four groups of features in the channel dimension: $F_i \in \mathbb{R}^{\frac{C}{4} \times H \times W}$, $i = 1, 2, 3, 4$. For each set of features $F_i$, we first use the Sobel filter of the corresponding direction to obtain the directional feature map $F'_i$ of the corresponding direction through the convolution operation. This process can be summarized as:

$$F'_i = \text{Sobel}(F_i), i = 1, 2, 3, 4 \tag{1}$$

where Sobel() represents the use of Sobel filter for convolution operation.

Then, we integrate the spatial information about each set of directional features. For the obtained directional feature map $F'_i$, we first perform average pooling and maximum pooling operations along the channel dimension to extract the spatial information and obtain two different spatial information feature maps: maximum pooling feature $F_i^{avg} \in \mathbb{R}^{1 \times H \times W}$ and average pooling feature $F_i^{max} \in \mathbb{R}^{1 \times H \times W}$. Then the maximum pooling feature and the average pooling feature are connected along the channel to obtain an effective spatial information descriptor, and then the spatial attention map $F_s$ corresponding to each set of directional features is obtained through $1 \times 1$ convolution, which is full of the current direction edge information. This process can be expressed as:

$$M_i = g([F_i^{avg}, F_i^{max}]) = g\left(\left[\text{AvgPool}(F'_i); \text{MaxPool}(F'_i)\right]\right), \tag{2}$$

where g() represents a convolution operation with the filter size of $1 \times 1$.

**Channel Weight Constraint Module.** After fully considering the extraction of spatial information, how to use the characteristics of each direction becomes the next task. In feature processing, in addition to considering the spatial information in the features, the channel information between the features is also important. Therefore, from the perspective of channel correlation, we design a channel weight constraint module to realize the effective use of directional features. The global average pooling operation can make full use of the global information of each channel feature to extract the channel information between features. Therefore, as shown in Fig. 3, for each directional feature map $F'_i$, we first obtain the channel information of the directional feature $F'_i$ through global average pooling, and then we send the extracted channel information to a multi-layer perceptron (MLP) containing two hidden layers, the importance weight $w_i$ of the direction feature calculated from the channel information is obtained.

$$w_i = \mathrm{MLP}\Big(\mathrm{GAP}\big(F'_i\big)\Big) \tag{3}$$

where MLP() stands for multi-layer perceptron.

Then, for each group of direction features $M_i$, we use the corresponding weight $w_i$ containing channel information to multiply the spatial attention map $M_i$ to obtain the weighted attention map $M'_i$ for each directional feature. Finally, add up each direction feature attention map $M'_i$ to get the final feature attention map: $M_s$:

$$M_s = \sum_{i=1}^{4} w_i * M_i. \tag{4}$$

After obtaining the feature attention map $M_s \in \mathbb{R}^{1 \times H \times W}$ containing the edge information of each direction, we choose to use the addition method to enhance the basic features extracted by the encoder. That is, using the broadcast mechanism in the tensor matrix operation, the feature attention map and each channel feature of the basic feature is added element by element to obtain the enhanced basic feature $F_s$:

$$F_s = \mathrm{ADD}(M_s, F), \tag{5}$$

where ADD() stands for matrix addition using broadcast mechanism.

### 2.3   Layered Feature Fusion Model

To obtain more semantic information to assist segmentation, we perform bottom-up up-sampling process in the decoder part. Also, we directly obtain a prediction result of the current layer through the features of each layer of the decoder, and then add the prediction results of each layer through linear interpolation to obtain the segmentation prediction result. The supervision of the final segmentation prediction result adopts the standard cross-entropy loss function. Since the network output is directly connected to each layer of the decoder, the efficiency of the gradient backpropagation is improved, and the deep semantic information is also considered.

## 3   Experiments

### 3.1   Experimental Setup

The data used in this paper is a four-chamber (4CH) video of 2D pediatric echocardiography of children aged 0–10 collected by Shenzhen Children's Hospital. These data are in line with the US echocardiographic standards, a total of 127 cases. To verify the effectiveness of our proposed algorithm, we randomly select 100 videos and extract 3654 4CH images frame by frame for training. 831 4CH images obtained by decimating the remaining 27 videos frame by frame were used as test data. All labels of the data are completed by two sonographers and confirmed by another senior sonographer.

We train and optimize the network through the stochastic gradient descent method, and the momentum is set to 0.99. The initial learning rate in the training phase is set to $10^{-3}$, and it is dynamically adjusted with the number of learning steps. We choose Dice index, Jaccard similarity coefficient, recall (sensitivity), precision and accuracy as evaluation indicators to evaluate our method. At the same time, we set up ablation experiments with different modules and comparison experiments with common computer vision methods to verify the effectiveness of our proposed method.

### 3.2   Results and Analysis

**Ablation Study.** To test the effect of each module, we conduct ablation experiments on each module. We show the impact of each module on the network in Table 1 and Table 2. Table 1 is the evaluation of the segmentation results of LV, and Table 2 is the evaluation of the segmentation performance of LA. Among them, (A) means that only the MDSA is used in the MDA module, and CWC are not used for feature fusion, but the feature attention maps of various directions are directly integrated by element addition; (B) represents the use of the CWC to fuse the feature attention map of each direction; (C) represents the use of the LFF to obtain the final prediction result. It can be seen from the results that after using edge features in different directions to enhance the network features, the segmentation performance of the network has been greatly improved, which fully illustrates the importance of edge information in each direction.

**Table 1.** The LV segmentation results of different modules in 4CH view.

| A | B | C | Accuracy | Jaccard | Dice | Recall | Precision |
|---|---|---|---|---|---|---|---|
|  |  |  | 0.9878 | 0.8595 | 0.8948 | 0.9526 | 0.9274 |
| √ |  |  | 0.9900 | 0.8953 | 0.9426 | 0.9443 | 0.9441 |
| √ | √ |  | 0.9905 | 0.9010 | 0.9487 | 0.9476 | 0.9466 |
| √ | √ | √ | **0.9914** | **0.9127** | **0.9551** | **0.9565** | **0.9532** |

**Table 2.** The LA segmentation results of different modules in 4CH view.

| A | B | C | Accuracy | Jaccard | Dice | Recall | Precision |
|---|---|---|---|---|---|---|---|
|  |  |  | 0.9878 | 0.7993 | 0.8741 | 0.8964 | 0.8805 |
| √ |  |  | 0.9906 | 0.8345 | 0.9039 | 0.9121 | 0.9083 |
| √ | √ |  | 0.9910 | 0.8445 | 0.9111 | 0.9171 | 0.9137 |
| √ | √ | √ | **0.9914** | **0.8523** | **0.9189** | **0.9247** | **0.9161** |

**Comparison with Common Methods.** To better evaluate the performance of the network, we have compared with some common methods in computer vision. These networks all perform well in image segmentation and are also widely used in the field of medical images. Table 3 and Table 4 show the segmentation results of each method LV and LA. It can be seen that, except for the Recall metric in the LA segmentation of the 4CH image, which is slightly worse than DANet [13], our algorithm has achieved the best results in all other metric. Overall, the segmentation results of LA are worse than those of LV. This is because in 4CH images, the edge information of LA is usually lost more seriously especially at the boundary between LA and the right atrium. The

**Table 3.** The LV segmentation results of common methods in 4CH view.

| Network | Accuracy | Jaccard | Dice | Recall | Precision |
|---|---|---|---|---|---|
| Bisenet [14] | 0.9890 | 0.8923 | 0.9411 | 0.9460 | 0.9447 |
| DANet [13] | 0.8997 | 0.8893 | 0.9393 | 0.9516 | 0.9378 |
| DeepLab_V3 [15] | 0.9901 | 0.9013 | 0.9462 | 0.9516 | 0.9418 |
| PSPNet [16] | 0.9887 | 0.8796 | 0.9347 | 0.9364 | 0.9394 |
| Segnet [17] | 0.9856 | 0.8654 | 0.9220 | 0.9285 | 0.9316 |
| U-Net [7] | 0.9878 | 0.8595 | 0.9274 | 0.9526 | 0.8948 |
| U-Net + ASPP [18] | 0.9862 | 0.8489 | 0.9135 | 0.9472 | 0.8903 |
| FCN [19] | 0.9873 | 0.8530 | 0.9140 | 0.9415 | 0.9230 |
| OURS | **0.9914** | **0.9127** | **0.9532** | **0.9565** | **0.9551** |

boundary information is shown in Fig. 1(a), which is partially missing. Therefore, we can extract edge information more carefully to improve the segmentation performance of the network.

Figure 4 shows the visualization results of different methods. It can be found that each method has different degrees of segmentation error. Due to the influence of blurred boundary information, artifacts, and low image contrast of LV and LA, the network has made errors in the boundary judgment of LV and LA. Therefore, each method can predict the approximate contours of LV and LA, but the prediction at the edge has a certain error compared with the label. Our proposed method emphasizes more on the edge information. Therefore, the prediction result of our proposed method is closer to the ground truth, and the prediction of the boundary is more similar to the label.

**Table 4.** The LA segmentation results of common methods in 4CH view.

| Network | Accuracy | Jaccard | Dice | Recall | Precision |
|---|---|---|---|---|---|
| BiseNet [14] | 0.9890 | 0.8388 | 0.9099 | 0.9192 | 0.9086 |
| DANet [13] | 0.8997 | 0.8250 | 0.8972 | **0.9267** | 0.8831 |
| DeepLab_V3 [15] | 0.9901 | 0.8179 | 0.8956 | 0.9124 | 0.8931 |
| PSPNet [16] | 0.9887 | 0.8075 | 0.8888 | 0.9278 | 0.8659 |
| Segnet [17] | 0.9856 | 0.7980 | 0.8808 | 0.9001 | 0.8793 |
| U-Net [7] | 0.9878 | 0.7993 | 0.8805 | 0.8964 | 0.8741 |
| U-Net + ASPP [18] | 0.9862 | 0.8081 | 0.8610 | 0.8827 | 0.8651 |
| FCN [19] | 0.9873 | 0.8064 | 0.8871 | 0.9107 | 0.8849 |
| OURS | **0.9914** | **0.8523** | **0.9161** | 0.9247 | **0.9189** |

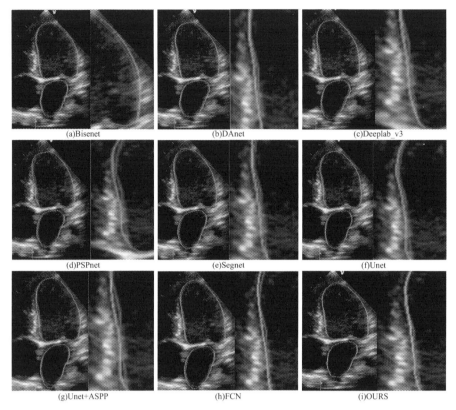

(a)Bisenet          (b)DAnet          (c)Deeplab_v3

(d)PSPnet          (e)Segnet          (f)Unet

(g)Unet+ASPP          (h)FCN          (i)OURS

**Fig. 4.** The Visualization of segmentation results. The red curve represents the outline drawn manually by the doctor, and the green curve represents the prediction result of the network. (Color figure online)

## 4    Conclusion

This paper proposes a MDA network to segment echocardiography. The MDA module is used to enhance the edge information in the feature to improve the network performance to complete the segmentation of LV and LA in 4CH. In the encoder part, MDA extracts the edge information in four directions: horizontal, vertical, positive diagonal, and negative diagonal through MDSA. After the edge information is further extracted, the importance of edge information in each direction is measured by CWC, and further weighted constraint fusion is carried out. Finally, the fused edge information is used to enhance the basic features and send them to the decoder, and then the prediction results are obtained by LFF. The experimental results show that the proposed method achieves better segmentation results in the segmentation of pediatric echocardiographic than the selected method.

# References

1. Zimmerman, M.S., Smith, A.G.C., Sable, C.A., et al.: Global, regional, and national burden of congenital heart disease, 1990–2017: a systematic analysis for the global burden of disease study 2017. Lancet Child Adolesc. Health **4**, 185–200 (2020)
2. Guo, L., Lei, B., Chen, W., et al.: Dual attention enhancement feature fusion network for segmentation and quantitative analysis of paediatric echocardiography. Med. Image Anal. **71**,102042 (2021)
3. Liu, F., Wang, K., Liu, D., et al.: Deep pyramid local attention neural network for cardiac structure segmentation in two-dimensional echocardiography. Med. Image Anal. **67**,101873 (2021)
4. Hu, Y., Xia, B., Mao, M., et al.: AIDAN: an attention-guided dual-path network for pediatric echocardiography segmentation. IEEE Access **8**, 29176–29187 (2020)
5. Li, K., Wang, S., Yu, L., et al.: Dual-teacher++: exploiting intra-domain and inter-domain knowledge with reliable transfer for cardiac segmentation. IEEE Trans. Med. Imaging (2020)
6. Xu, L., Liu, M., Zhang, J., et al.: Convolutional-neural-network-based approach for segmentation of apical four-chamber view from fetal echocardiography. IEEE Access **8**, 80437–80446 (2020)
7. Ronneberger, O., Fischer, P., Brox, T.: U-net: convolutional networks for biomedical image segmentation. In: Navab, N., Hornegger, J., Wells, W., Frangi, A., (eds.) International Conference on Medical image computing and computer-assisted intervention. Lecture Notes in Computer Science, vol. 9351, pp. 234–241. Springer, Cham (2015). https://doi.org/10.1007/978-3-319-24574-4_28
8. Leclerc, S., Smistad, E., Østvik, A., et al.: LU-Net: a multistage attention network to improve the robustness of segmentation of left ventricular structures in 2-D echocardiography. IEEE Trans. Ultrason. Ferroelectr. Freq. Control **67**, 2519–2530 (2020)
9. Woo, S., Park, J., Lee, J.-Y., Kweon, I.S.: CBAM: convolutional block attention module. In: Ferrari, V., Hebert, M., Sminchisescu, C., Weiss, Y. (eds.) ECCV 2018. LNCS, vol. 11211, pp. 3–19. Springer, Cham (2018). https://doi.org/10.1007/978-3-030-01234-2_1
10. Hu, J., Shen, L., Sun, G.: Squeeze-and-excitation networks. In: Proceedings of the IEEE Conference on Computer Vision and Pattern Recognition, pp. 7132–7141 (2018)
11. Qilong, W., Banggu, W., Pengfei, Z., et al.: ECA-Net: Efficient Channel Attention for Deep Convolutional Neural Networks (2020)
12. Zhang, Y., Li, K., Li, K., Wang, L., Zhong, B., Fu, Y.: Image super-resolution using very deep residual channel attention networks. In: Ferrari, V., Hebert, M., Sminchisescu, C., Weiss, Y. (eds.) ECCV 2018. LNCS, vol. 11211, pp. 294–310. Springer, Cham (2018). https://doi.org/10.1007/978-3-030-01234-2_18
13. Fu, J., Liu, J., Tian, H., et al.: Dual attention network for scene segmentation. In: Proceedings of the IEEE/CVF Conference on Computer Vision and Pattern Recognition, pp. 3146–3154 (2019)
14. Yu, C., Wang, J., Peng, C., Gao, C., Yu, G., Sang, N.: BiSeNet: bilateral segmentation network for real-time semantic segmentation. In: Ferrari, V., Hebert, M., Sminchisescu, C., Weiss, Y. (eds.) ECCV 2018. LNCS, vol. 11217, pp. 334–349. Springer, Cham (2018). https://doi.org/10.1007/978-3-030-01261-8_20
15. Chen, L.-C., Papandreou, G., Schroff, F., et al.: Rethinking atrous convolution for se-mantic image segmentation. arXiv preprint arXiv:1706.05587 (2017)
16. Zhao, H., Shi, J., Qi, X., et al.: Pyramid scene parsing network. In: Proceedings of the IEEE Conference on Computer Vision and Pattern Recognition, pp. 2881–2890 (2017)
17. Badrinarayanan, V., Kendall, A., Cipolla, R.: Segnet: a deep convolutional encoder-decoder architecture for image segmentation. IEEE Trans. Pattern Anal. Mach. Intell. **39**, 2481–2495 (2017)

18. Weng, Y., Zhou, T., Li, Y., et al.: NAS-Unet: neural architecture search for medical image segmentation. IEEE Access **7**, 44247–44257 (2019)
19. Long, J., Shelhamer, E., Darrell, T.: Fully convolutional networks for semantic segmentation. In: Proceedings of the IEEE Conference on Computer Vision and Pattern Recognition, pp. 3431–3440 (2015)

# Deep-Based Super-Angular Resolution for Diffusion Imaging

Zan Chen[1], Chenxu Peng[1], Hao Zhang[2], Qingrun Zeng[1], and Yuanjing Feng[1(✉)]

[1] College of Information Engineering, Zhejiang University of Technology, Hangzhou 310023, China
fyjing@zjut.edu.cn
[2] China Mobile Communications Corporation, Hangzhou 310000, China

**Abstract.** High angular resolution diffusion imaging (HARDI) allows for more detailed fiber structures to be obtained by scanning in more directions than conventional diffusion MRI. However, the scanning time of HARDI increases linearly with the number of directions, which limits its use in clinical practice. And directly reducing the directions of HARDI to shorten the scan time would lead to a non-accurate reconstruction of microstructural tissues, such as complex white matter fibers. In this work, we propose a deep-based super-angular resolution scheme to reduce scanning orientations while maintaining reconstruction accuracy, in which an end-to-end neural network is proposed to map low-angular resolution diffusion imaging (LARDI) data to HARDI data. Specifically, our deep network is designed for a tailored farthest point sampling in q-space, which can maximize the separation angles between nearest gradients. For implementation, we transform the sampled 4-D diffusion data into six 3-D data and feed them respectively into six 3-D sub-networks to extract features in the spatial and angular domains. Experimental results show that our scheme can yield an accurate prediction of HARDI from LARDI on the human connectome program (HCP) dataset.

**Keywords:** HARDI · Super-angular resolution · Deep network.

## 1 Introduction

Diffusion magnetic resonance imaging (dMRI) is a non-invasive imaging technology, which can obtain microscopic information in the brain [1]. In dMRI, the diffusion signal is measured in the q-space, which reflects the motion trend of water molecules in magnetic field gradient orientations [2]. However, some fiber crossings, scallops, bottleneck structures may not be obtained properly from traditional dMRI such as diffusion-weighted imaging (DWI) and diffusion tensor imaging (DTI) [3]. High-angular resolution diffusion imaging (HARDI) can compensate for such shortcomings by scanning more directions [4,5]. Nevertheless, the total scanning time of HARDI increases linearly with the number of directions, limiting the usage of HARDI-based analysis in clinical practice [6]. On the

© Springer Nature Switzerland AG 2021
H. Ma et al. (Eds.): PRCV 2021, LNCS 13021, pp. 513–523, 2021.
https://doi.org/10.1007/978-3-030-88010-1_43

other hand, low-angular resolution diffusion imaging (LARDI) data, obtained by reducing directions of HARDI, can not guarantee the precision of the reconstructed fibers. As illustrated in Fig. 1, halving the directions of HARDI will lead to the serious distortion of the reconstructed fibers.

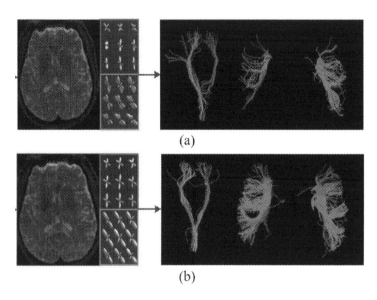

**Fig. 1.** Illustration of fiber orientation distribution function (fODF) in 32 directions (a) and 64 dircetions (b) and corresponding generated fiber images.

Many methods have been proposed to estimate brain fiber microstructure from low-angular resolution data. For instance, authors in [6,7] use compressive sampling with spherical ridgelet dictionary to reduce the number of diffusion orientations without compromising the informational content of HARDI data. [8] exploits the separable spatial-angular structure of diffusion data to build a globally sparse HARDI base. Some deep-based methods have also been designed. For example, [9] utilizes two convolutional layers and three fully connected layers to map LARDI data from spherical harmonics to fODF. Based on efficient subpixel-shifted convolutional network (ESPCN) [10], authors in [11] exploit a two-stage deep network (SR-q-DL) with a patch-based strategy for super-resolved tissue microstructure estimation. However, all these methods do not consider the effect of the q-space sampling method on the obtained LARDI data, nor do they exploit the relevance between different dimensions of the 4-D diffusion data.

In this work, we present a deep-based super-angular resolution for diffusion MRI, which utilizes the farthest point sampling and relevance of different dimensions for the diffusion image. For farthest point sampling, we follow the principle of maximizing the angular resolution of the sampled orientations in q-space, which can ensure the distribution of sampled orientations to be uniform.

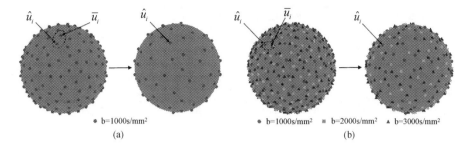

**Fig. 2.** Visualization of single-shell (a) and multi-shell sampling (b) in q-space, where different colors represent samples on different spherical shells. $\hat{u}_i$ and $\bar{u}_i$ denote the cartesian coordinate of the sampling point and the remaining un-sampled point in q-space respectively.

To mine the dimension relevance of diffusion image, we transfer the original 4-D diffusion data into 6 3-D data, and we integrate six sub-networks to extract features from the transferred 3-D data, respectively. Experimental results show that our scheme can yield an accurate prediction of HARDI from LARDI on the human connectome program (HCP) dataset.

## 2   Methods

Denoting $S \in R^{W \times H \times S \times O}$ as the original HARDI data, where $W$, $H$, $S$, and $O$ refer to the width, height, slice, and orientation size of the diffusion data. Our method can estimate $S$ from its q-space sampling data $\hat{S} \in R^{W \times H \times S \times M}$, $M < O$. This section describes the tailored q-space sampling process and designed network architecture.

### 2.1   Q-Space Sampling

The principle of q-space sampling design is to distribute the sampling points evenly, thus reducing the correlation of sampling points and retaining more spatial information. Let $\hat{S} = S(\{\hat{u}_i\}_{i=1}^{N})$ be the $N$ sampling points from $S$, in which $u_i = [x_i, y_i, z_i]^{\mathrm{T}}$ denotes the cartesian coordinate of the $i$-th point in q-space.

Considering that all points are on one unit sphere as shown in Fig. 2, we utilize angular distance to measure the difference between two points in q-space. For each point in q-space, we firstly find one point that differs least from it,

$$d(\{u_i\}_{i=1}^{N}) = \min_{i \neq j} \arccos |u_i^T u_j|. \tag{1}$$

Then, we realize uniformly sampling by maximizing the minimal angular difference (i.e., covering radius) [12],

$$\underset{\{u_i\}_{i=1}^{N}}{\arg \max} \, d(\{u_i\}_{i=1}^{N}). \tag{2}$$

---

**Algorithm 1.** Framework of farthest point sampling.

---

**Input:**
    The set of orientations in q-space, $\{\mathbf{u}_i\}_{i=1}^{N}$;
    Number of selected orientations, $K$;
    Initial covering radius, $\theta \leftarrow 0$;
**Output:**
    The set of selected points in q-space, $\{\mathbf{u}_j\}_{j=1}^{K}$;
1: **for** $m \leftarrow 1$ *to* $N$ **do**
2:     $A \leftarrow \emptyset,\ A \leftarrow A \cup \{\mathbf{u}_m\},\ k \leftarrow 1$;
3:     $C_A(\mathbf{u}_m) \leftarrow \min \arccos |\mathbf{u}_m^T \mathbf{u}_n|,\ \mathbf{u}_n \in \{\mathbf{u}_i\}_{i=m}^{N}$;
4:     **while** $k < K$ **do**
5:         $\mathbf{u}_{max} \leftarrow \arg\max C_A(\mathbf{u}_m)$;
6:         $D_A(\mathbf{u}_{max}) \leftarrow \min \arccos |\mathbf{u}_{max}^T \mathbf{u}_n|, \mathbf{u}_n \in \{\mathbf{u}_i\}_{i=1}^{N,/k}$;
7:         $A \leftarrow A \cup \{\mathbf{u}_{max}\},\ k \leftarrow k + 1$;
8:         **if** $D_A(\mathbf{u}_{max}) < C_A(\mathbf{u}_m)$ **then**
9:             $C_A(\mathbf{u}_m) \leftarrow D_A(\mathbf{u}_{max})$;
10:       **end if**
11:    **end while**
12:    **if** $D_A(\mathbf{u}_{max}) > \theta$ **then**
13:       $\theta \leftarrow D_A(\mathbf{u}_{max}),\ \{\mathbf{u}_j\}_{j=1}^{K} \leftarrow A$;
14:    **end if**
15: **end for**

---

In specific, we apply farthest point sampling (FPS) to solve Eq. 2. FPS is a global point searching algorithm, which has been widely used in the field of 3-D applications, such as 3-D point cloud recognition and human pose estimation [13]. Such farthest point sampling can also be extended to multi-shell HARDI data by revising Eq. 2 as follows,

$$\max_{\{\mathbf{u}_{q,i}\}} \frac{w}{n_q} \sum_{q=1}^{n_q} d(\{\mathbf{u}_{q,i}\}_{i=1}^{N_q}) + (1-w)d(\{\mathbf{u}_{q,i}\}_{q=1,i=1}^{n_q,N_q}), \qquad (3)$$

where $n_q$ is the number of shells, $N_q$ is the number of orientations on the $q$-th shell, and $w$ denotes a weighting factor. We set $w$ to 0.5 to ensure that the sampling points within the different shells are staggered [12]. The pseudocode for embedding FPS in HARDI data is given in Algorithm 1. The main difference between single- and multi-shell farthest point sampling is on the distance function $D_A(\cdot)$ in Algorithm 1, i.e. Eq. 2 and Eq. 3 for single- and multi-shell, respectively.

## 2.2 Mapping Network of Architecture

In this subsection, we give components of the network structure in detail. For $\hat{S}$ bing the LARDI data from farthest point sampling, the remaining un-sampled points $\bar{S} = S(\{\bar{u}_i\}_{i=1}^{(O-N)})$ form the complement of $\hat{S}$ with respect to $S$. By training the designed network with the loss

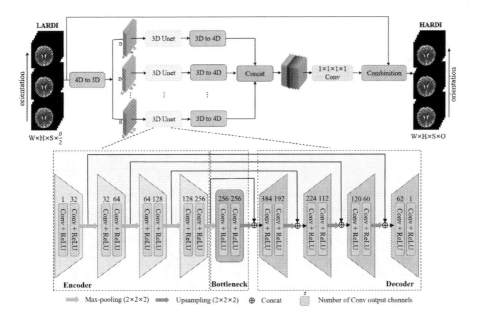

**Fig. 3.** Proposed super-angular resolution mapping.

$$\underset{\theta}{\arg\min}\ \|\mathcal{F}(\hat{S}) - \bar{S}\|, \tag{4}$$

the mapping network $\mathcal{F}$ can realize the super-angular resolution.

As shown in Fig. 3, the designed mapping network mainly consists of three modules, i.e. the feature transformation module, the feature extraction module, and the feature fusion module. By merging any two dimensions of $\hat{S}$, the 4-D to 3-D feature transformation module can transform the original diffusion data of the size $[W, H, S, D]$ into 6 3-D data of the sizes $[WH, S, D]$, $[WS, H, D]$, $[WD, H, S]$, $[HS, W, D]$, $[HD, W, S]$, and $[SD, W, H]$, respectively. And the 3-D to 4-D feature transformation module works inversely. We denote the $k$-th forward and inverse transformation as $R_k$ and $R_k^{-1}$.

The feature extraction module is the core part of the designed network, where six branched networks are used to deal with the transformed 3-D data. In specific, each branch further consists of the encoder, bottleneck, and decoder. Both encoder and decoder consist of four convolutional blocks, and the bottleneck consists of a convolutional block, of which one convolutional block consists of two $3 \times 3 \times 3$ Conv+Relu layers [15]. We also include some short and long skip connections to improve the feature expression ability of the network [14,16].

After feature extraction, we do the inverse transformation of the features of six branched networks, and further fuse the channel-concatenation feature. The overall network can be formulated as

$$\bar{S} = \mathcal{F}(\hat{S}) = f_2(\text{Concate}(\{R_i^{-1} \circ f_1^i \circ R_i(\hat{S})\}_{i=1}^6)), \tag{5}$$

where $f_1^k$ and $f_2$ denote the $k$-th feature extraction branch and feature fusion model, respectively. Finally, we can reconstruct an approximate HARDI data by combining $\hat{S}$ and $\bar{S}$ in angular dimension.

## 3   Experiments

### 3.1   Dataset Description and Implementation Details

We validate our method using the human connectome project (HCP) young adult dataset[1], which has $145 \times 174 \times 145 \times 288$ size. The diffusion data are acquired with b-values 0, 1000, 2000, and $3000\,\mathrm{s/mm^2}$, which contain 18, 90, 90, and 90 orientations, respectively. Routine preprocessing operations such as distortion correction, motion correction, registration to MNI space have been completed in advance [15]. We randomly select 80 subject datasets, splitting them into 56 subjects for training and 24 subjects for testing. We test 0.5 sampling ratio (i.e. N = O/2) using three q-space sampling methods: random sampling (RS), FPS, and mixed-integer linear programming (MILP) [12].

Training convolutional neural networks with 4-D medical images usually requires a large amount of GPU memory. To alleviate this problem, we utilize the advantage of the shift-invariance property of convolutional neural networks to train our models in small patched data. Each subject is partitioned into 150 $(32 \times 32 \times 32 \times 90)$ patches for training [11,16]. In our experiment, we set half sampling, resulting in $32 \times 32 \times 32 \times 45$ spatial dimensions for the input volume. For the training process, we use adam optimizer with an initial learning rate $10^{-4}$ and decrease the learning rate with a 0.5 ratio every 20 epochs.

### 3.2   Effect of Sampling Scheme

FPS, MILP, and RS are performed to sample directions from single- and multi-shell respectively. MILP can also be used to sample in a discrete set of spherical samples. The main idea of MILP is to set the initial covering radius for each shell and use the branch and bound method to update the extend of the covering radius. Figure 4 gives the covering radius obtained by different methods in single-shell and multi-shell, respectively. The larger the covering radius, the more evenly the orientations are distributed in the q-space. From Fig. 4, we can see that the covering radius of MILP outperforms FPS at a small number of sampling points, and they are almost consistent at a high sampling number.

---

[1] https://www.humanconnectome.org/study/hcp-young-adult.

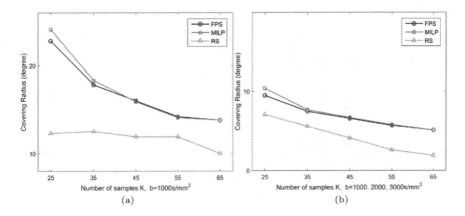

**Fig. 4.** Quantitative comparison between different sampling schemes on single-shell (a) and multi-shell (b). The horizontal axis is the number of sampling points and the longitudinal axis is covering radius.

**Table 1.** Quantitative metrics of estimated HARDI using different methods.

| Methods | Shell 1 | Shell 2 | Shell 3 | Multi-shell |
|---|---|---|---|---|
| | PSNR | PSNR | PSNR | PSNR |
| RS + Our Net | 33.81 | 28.84 | 29.39 | 30.56 |
| FPS + Our Net | 36.55 | **33.28** | **32.23** | 32.47 |
| MILP + Our Net | **36.62** | 33.20 | 32.16 | **32.52** |

### 3.3 Performance on HARDI Data

Table 1 presents average peak signal-to-noise ratio (PSNR) results of HARDI data on the predicted directions, of which shell 1, shell 2, and shell 3 refer to spherical shells with b-values of 1000, 2000, and 3000 s/mm$^2$, respectively. From Table 1, we can see that using FPS or MILP with the proposed network can predict more accurate HARDI data from LARDI data.

Figure 5 further shows the predicted HARDI data and the corresponding error maps using different methods, from which we can see that FPS or MILP with our net can achieve smaller error than FPS with Unet. Figure 5 also shows that FPS with the proposed network has comparable performance with MILP with the proposed network, and adding a deep network after q-space sampling yields better reconstructed PSNR.

### 3.4 Performance on Fiber Reconstruction from HARDI Data

We further utilize the constrained spherical deconvolutional (CSD) with 642 vertices to reconstructed fODF from the predicted HARDI data and test three metrics, including normalized sum-of-squares error (NSSE), average angular error (AAE), and rate of false peak (RFP) [17]. Table 2 presents the metrics for the reconstructed fODF using different q-space sampling, from which we can see

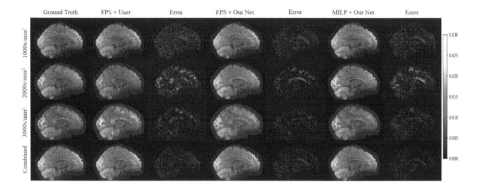

**Fig. 5.** Visualization of estimated HARDI and error maps. Estimated HARDI map refers to the mean signal values in all orientations on the same subject.

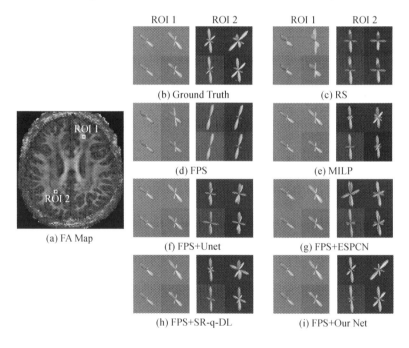

**Fig. 6.** Comparison of the fODF on the fractional anisotropy (FA) map (b = 1000, 2000, 3000 s/mm²) using different methods.

that FPS and MILP have a significant improvement on NSSE, AAE, and RFP for both the single-shell and multi-shell diffusion data. Besides, our network outperforms Unet, ESPN and SR-q-DL in super-angular resolution reconstructions, with decreases of 0.04, 0.76 and 0.03 in the NSSE, AAE and RFP metrics, respectively, compared to SR-q-DL for single-shell data, and 0.03, 0.59 and 0.02 for multi-shell data.

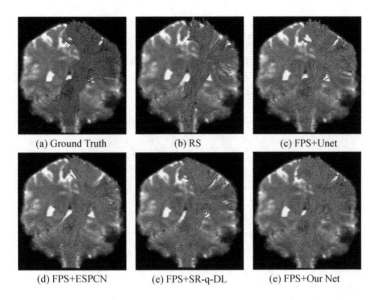

(a) Ground Truth　　　　　(b) RS　　　　　(c) FPS+Unet

(d) FPS+ESPCN　　　(e) FPS+SR-q-DL　　(e) FPS+Our Net

**Fig. 7.** Comparison of the CST (b = 1000, 2000, 3000 s/mm$^2$) using different methods.

**Table 2.** Quantitative metrics of fODF using different methods. Single-shell indicates HARDI data with a b-values 1000 s/mm$^2$.

| Methods | Single-shell | | | Multi-shell | | |
|---|---|---|---|---|---|---|
| | NSSE | AAE | RFP | NSSE | AAE | RFP |
| RS | 0.53 | 15.73 | 0.25 | 0.61 | 16.36 | 0.32 |
| FPS | 0.40 | 8.65 | 0.12 | 0.43 | 9.09 | 0.15 |
| MILP | 0.39 | 8.61 | 0.13 | 0.43 | 8.97 | 0.16 |
| FPS + Unet | 0.36 | 8.07 | 0.10 | 0.39 | 8.52 | 0.13 |
| FPS + ESPCN | 0.33 | 7.58 | 0.08 | 0.36 | 8.03 | 0.10 |
| FPS + SR-q-DL | 0.32 | 6.95 | 0.07 | 0.33 | 7.64 | 0.09 |
| FPS + Our Net | **0.28** | **6.19** | **0.04** | **0.30** | **7.05** | **0.07** |

We also present the corresponding reconstructed fODF maps and corticospinal tract (CST) fiber bundles in Fig. 6 and Fig. 7. We obtain the CST fibers by isolating them from the generated whole-brain bundles in Fig. 7. From Fig. 6 and Fig. 7, we can also see that the reconstructed fiber from sampling points without network (RS, FPS, and MILP) would lose some detailed structure, while the proposed net can improve the accuracy of the reconstructed fibers.

## 4    Conclusion

In this work, we have developed a deep-based super-angular resolution scheme for diffusion imaging, which can reduce the scanning time while maintaining the accuracy of the reconstructed brain fibers. We propose a six-branch deep network to extract features from different dimensions, meanwhile embedding farthest point sampling into the designed network to reduce the redundancy among neighbor sampling points. Experimental results show that the proposed scheme can accurately predict high angular resolution diffusion imaging data from low angular resolution diffusion imaging data, and can reconstruct more detailed structures of brain fibers.

**Acknowledgments.** This research was sponsored in part by the National Natural Science Foundation of China (Grant Nos. 62002327, 61976190), and Natural Science Foundation of Zhejiang Province (Grant No. LQ21F020017).

## References

1. Shrot, S., Salhov, M., Dvorski, N., Konen, E., Averbuch, A., Hoffmann, C.: Application of MR morphologic, diffusion tensor, and perfusion imaging in the classification of brain tumors using machine learning scheme. Neuroradiology **61**(7), 757–765 (2019). https://doi.org/10.1007/s00234-019-02195-z
2. Koay, C.G., Özarslan, E.: Conceptual foundations of diffusion in magnetic resonance. Concepts Magn. Reson. Part A Bridg. Educ. Res. **42**(4), 116–129 (2013)
3. Tuch, D.S., Reese, T.G., Wiegell, M.R., Makris, N., Belliveau, J.W., Wedeen, V.J.: High angular resolution diffusion imaging reveals intravoxel white matter fiber heterogeneity. Magn. Reson. Med. **48**(4), 577–582 (2002)
4. Tournier, J.D., Calamante, F., Connelly, A.: Robust determination of the fibre orientation distribution in diffusion MRI: non-negativity constrained super-resolved spherical deconvolution. Neuroimage **35**(4), 1459–1472 (2007)
5. Cheng, J., Deriche, R., Jiang, T., Shen, D., Yap, P.T.: Non-negative spherical deconvolution (NNSD) for estimation of fiber orientation distribution function in single-/multi-shell diffusion MRI. Neuroimage **101**, 750–764 (2014)
6. Michailovich, O., Rathi, Y.: Fast and accurate reconstruction of HARDI data using compressed sensing. Med Image Comput. Comput. Assist. Interv. **13**(1), 607–614 (2010)
7. Michailovich, O., Rathi, Y.: On approximation of orientation distributions by means of spherical ridgelets. IEEE Trans. Image Process **19**(2), 461–477 (2009)
8. Schwab, E., Vidal, R., Charon, N.: Spatial-angular sparse coding for HARDI. In: Ourselin, S., Joskowicz, L., Sabuncu, M.R., Unal, G., Wells, W. (eds.) MICCAI 2016. LNCS, vol. 9902, pp. 475–483. Springer, Cham (2016). https://doi.org/10.1007/978-3-319-46726-9_55
9. Lin, Z., et al.: Fast learning of fiber orientation distribution function for MR tractography using convolutional neural network. Med Phys **46**(7), 3101–3116 (2019)
10. Shi, W., et al.: Real-time single image and video super-resolution using an efficient sub-pixel convolutional neural network. In: CVPR, pp. 1874–1883 (2016)
11. Qin, Y., Liu, Z., Liu, C., Li, Y., Zeng, X., Ye, C.: Super-Resolved q-Space deep learning with uncertainty quantification. Med. Image Anal. **67**, 101885 (2020)

12. Cheng, J., Shen, D., Yap, P.T., Basser, P.J.: Single- and multiple-shell uniform sampling schemes for diffusion MRI using spherical codes. IEEE Trans. Med. Imaging **37**(1), 185–199 (2018)
13. Qi, C.R., Yi, L., Su, H., Guibas, L.J.: PointNet++: deep hierarchical feature learning on point sets in a metric space. arXiv preprint arXiv:1706.02413 (2017)
14. Koay, C.G., Chang, L.C., Carew, J.D., Pierpaoli, C., Basser, P.J.: A unifying theoretical and algorithmic framework for least squares methods of estimation in diffusion tensor imaging. J. Magn. Reson. **182**(1), 115–125 (2006)
15. Wasserthal, J., Neher, P., Maier-Hein, K.H.: TractSeg-Fast and accurate white matter tract segmentation. Neuroimage **183**, 239–253 (2018)
16. Jung, W., et al.: Exploring linearity of deep neural network trained QSM: QSM-net+. NeuroImage **211**, 116619 (2020)
17. Mani, M., Jacob, M., Guidon, A., Magnotta, V., Zhong, J.: Acceleration of high angular and spatial resolution diffusion imaging using compressed sensing with multichannel spiral data. Magn. Reson. Med. **73**(1), 126–138 (2015)

# A Multiple Encoders Network for Stroke Lesion Segmentation

Xiangchen Zhang[1], Huan Xu[1(✉)], Yujun Liu[1], Jiajia Liao[1], Guorong Cai[1], Jinhe Su[1], and Yehua Song[2(✉)]

[1] Computer Engineering College, Jimei University, 180 Yinjiang Road, Jimei District, Xiamen 361021, China
xuhuan@jmu.edu.cn
[2] Department of Neurology, The Second Affiliated Hospital of Xiamen Medical College, Xiamen City 361021, Fujian, China
songyehua@sina.com

**Abstract.** Medical image segmentation plays a vital role in clinical application of auxiliary diagnosis. Having said that, it is still a challenging task to accurately segment lesion areas from case images, because lesions are always different in size and shape, and the boundaries of lesion area is usually too rough, which greatly limits the accuracy of the current mainstream automatic segmentation algorithms. The lesions in stroke data are mostly small targets, and the boundary area are very tortuous, which greatly increases the difficulty of segmentation. Therefore, there is still a lot of space for segmentation of stroke data sets. In this paper, we propose a novel multiple encoders network for stroke lesion segmentation, called ME-Net, which is mainly composed of the atrous spatial pyramid pooling (ASPP) module and residual encoder. Particularly, ASPP uses a parallel structure of porous convolutions with different sampling rates to obtain context information for multi-scale features. The residual encoding can obtain high-level semantic features at high resolution. In addition, ME-Net adopts an encoding and decoding framework. We divided the pathological images into three levels according to the number of pixels in the masked area and evaluated our proposed method on an open dataset Anatomical Tracings of Lesions After Stroke (ATLAS) with encouraging performance achieved compared to other state-of-the-art approaches.

**Keywords:** MRI · Stroke segmentation · ATLAS · Multiple encoders

## 1 Introduction

Medical image segmentation is the foundation of various applications of medical image. Medical image segmentation technology is showing more and more important clinical value in clinical diagnosis, image-guided surgery and radiotherapy. Medical image segmentation in clinical medicine can help doctors focus on specific disease areas and extract detailed information for clinicians to refer to. It can effectively improve the

---

X. Zhang---Student.

The original version of this chapter was revised: the funding acknowledgement has been added. The correction to this chapter is available at https://doi.org/10.1007/978-3-030-88010-1_53

© Springer Nature Switzerland AG 2021, corrected publication 2022
H. Ma et al. (Eds.): PRCV 2021, LNCS 13021, pp. 524–535, 2021.
https://doi.org/10.1007/978-3-030-88010-1_44

accuracy of diagnosis, and make up for the misjudgment and misjudgment caused by the inexperience and limited knowledge of the diagnosticians.

Stroke is an acute cerebrovascular disease [1]. It refers to a disease caused by sudden rupture of blood vessels or blockage of blood vessels, and is the second largest cause of death in the world. At present, the main diagnosis and treatment scheme is manual segmentation of MRI images layer by layer by professional radiologist. Because of the large number of images, this work is time-consuming and laborious, and because of human error, this work is not accurate. Therefore, in clinical practice, it is necessary to use the method of computer automatic segmentation to extract the focal area of stroke. It is still challenging. Firstly, the shape, size and position of the lesions are different, which greatly limits the accuracy of the current mainstream automatic segmentation algorithms. Secondly, the boundaries of the lesion area is often too rough, which makes it the biggest challenge to restore the boundary of the lesion area accurately.

Since 2015, the algorithms from FCN to U-Net [2, 3], Double-UNet [4], D-UNet [5] and X-Net [6] have been referenced and improved many times, making great contributions in the field of medical image segmentation. However, the current algorithm do not perform well in the boundary segmentation of multi-scale targets, especially large targets and small targets. In order to solve this problem, we design a new network called ME-Net based on the existing algorithms. In this new model, different sizes of information can be analyzed effectively. This improvement enabled us to show excellent results in the repair of damaged edges. First, in order to fully capture the semantic information of the upper layer and the lower layer, an ASPP module is added behind the network encoder to conduct multi-scale sampling on the features extracted by the encoder to extract more abundant semantic information. Secondly, the residual sub-encoder module is added to extract the deeper image feature information. At last, the method is tested on the ATLAS data set [7], and compared with the latest method on three different scales, which proves the superiority of the method.

## 2  Related Work

In recent years, automatic segmentation algorithm based on deep learning has been paid more and more attention. It solves the limitations of traditional machine learning methods that require engineers to design manually. This chapter summarizes the methods based on deep learning.

Since 2015, the FCN proposed by Long J et al. [2] It is the pioneering work of deep learning in the field of image segmentation. Before this, deep learning was often used to classify and detect problems. The advantage of FCN is to achieve end-to-end segmentation. The input is the original data, and the output is pixel-by-pixel classification on the upsampled feature map. The semantic image segmentation problem is solved. The disadvantage is that the details of the segmentation result are not good enough. Zhao H et al. [8] Proposed a Pyramid Scene Analysis Network (PSPNet) based on the FCN-based pixel prediction framework. The pyramid pool module and the pyramid scene analysis network are used to aggregate context information according to different regions, and provide a better framework for pixel-level prediction. The V-net proposed by Milletari F et al. [9] A new objective function is introduced, which is optimized based on Dice coefficient in the training process, thus solving the serious imbalance between foreground and background voxels. SegNet is proposed by Kendall A et al. [10] It uses de-pooling in the decoder to up-sample the feature map and maintain the integrity of high-frequency details during segmentation. Oskar Maier et al. Proposed a public evaluation benchmark for the segmentation of ischemic stroke lesions based on multispectral MRI, and the U-net network and training strategy proposed by Ronneberger et al. [3], which can perform end-to-end with a small amount of data. End of training surpassed the best method at that time (sliding window convolution network). In the field of biomedical image segmentation, U-Net has been widely used and cited more than 4,000 times. However, this network has two obvious disadvantages: (1) the network speed is very slow. For each neighborhood, the network must run once, and for the overlapping part of the neighborhood, the network will repeatedly perform operations. (2) the network needs to strike a balance between accurate location and obtaining context information. A larger patch need more maximum pool layers, which will reduce the accuracy of location, while smaller neighbors will make the network get less context information. 3 D CNN proposed by Kamnitsas, K et al. [11], there is great potential for analysis based on 3 DMRI data. The method combines context information effectively. By using the improved dense network tight connection structure, it can enhance the back propagation of image information and gradients, and thus make the network deeper. Since 2D CNN ignores the 3d information of medical images, 3D CNN needs a lot of computing resources [12].

Zhou, y et al. [5] Proposed a new architecture D-UNet. The architecture innovatively combines 2d and 3d convolution in the encoding stage. Compared with 2d network, the proposed architecture has better segmentation performance, at the same time, it needs less computation time than 3d networks [11]. Li X et al. [13] Proposed a novel end-to-end system called Hybrid Dense Connected UNet (H-DenseUNet), in which one-chip features and 3d context are effectively detected and jointly optimized to accurately perform liver and Lesion segmentation. Chen LC et al. A Deeplab series has been proposed. Deeplabv1 is modified on the basis of VGG 16, converting the fully connected layer of VGG 16 to convolution; The last two pooling layers are removed, and then hole convolution is used. Deeplabv2 adopts multi-scale to get better segmentation results (using ASPP), and the basic layer is transformed from VGG 16 to ResNet, using different learning strategies; Deeplabv1 and v2 use dense DCNN with hollow convolution, which is faster and more accurate than the fully connection layer. The main innovation of Deeplabv3 is to improve the ASPP module [14–17], using spatial pyramid pooling to capture multiple levels of context. Deep lab v3 + is composed of Spatial Pyramid Pool Module (SPP) and coding and decoding structure, which is a deep network for semantic segmentation. Constructions. SPP processes and mines multi-scale contextual content information by using multiple ratios and multiple effective receptive fields with different resolution features, and the encode structure reconstructs spatial information step by step to better capture the object boundaries. Zhang Z et al. [18] Combined U-Net residual to design a network structure, Deep residual U-Net. Residual units can simplify the training of deep networks. Jha, D, etc. [4] stacked two U-Net architectures on each other to form a novel architecture called Double U-Net. This method can capture more semantic information effectively and generate more accurate segmentation masks.

## 3  Proposed Method

The framework of the proposed ME-Net is illustrated in Fig. 1. Regarding many current mainstream methods, we apply to the structure of encoder-decoder and skip connection as our basic structure. Firstly, the high-dimensional features are extracted by adding a deep residual encoder network. Secondly, the semantic information of different scales is effectively fused by using the atrous Spatial Pyramid Pool (ASPP) module. However, after the addition of decoding, the current mainstream encoder networks often do not use enough depth to obtain the deeper semantic information of objects in the image, which may lead to the failure of small object detection and inaccurate object boundaries. Considering these two factors, we designed a residual coding network for our proposed model, and inserted the ASPP module.

Specifically, we use a residual encoder with enough depth to extract the deeper semantic information of the image. The residual encoder will generate four feature maps of a specific size. The feature maps from different layers are combined by the skip connection and merged these features through concatenated operation, and then fed into the decoder for up-sampling. Finally, more semantic information is collected for object segmentation, thus improving the detection accuracy of lesions.

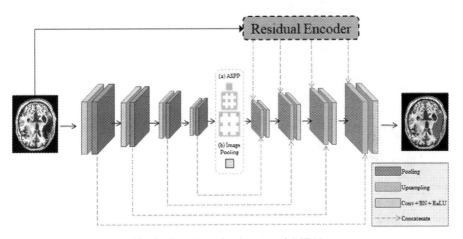

**Fig. 1.** Structure of main network ME-Net

**Residual Encoder.** The residual encoder uses the structure of more convolutional layers to encode the image. Compared with the shallow encoder, the deep encoder adopts a combination of continuous small filters (3 × 3) convolution layers, which can increase the depth of the network and preserve the low-level features existing in the shallow layer, which is helpful to better maintain the image attributes, and thus restore the boundary information of the large object more accurately. Residual encoder is designed to extract image features using residual blocks [20]. The biggest advantage of using residual is that it can construct a deep enough structure with less parameters, which greatly improves the feature extraction of image depth semantic information by the encoder. In addition, because the residual encoder uses multiple $3 \times 3$ convolution kernels to construct a segmented convolutional network, and at the same time through the max-pooling transition to make the network deeper and wider, and obtains a large receptive field. Therefore, this kind of network structure makes it a very good feature extractor, which can extract feature representations from input images and feature maps (Fig. 2).

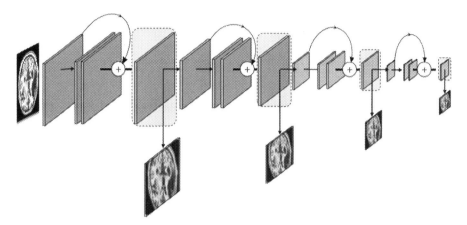

**Fig. 2.** Architectural details of the residual encoder.

## 4   Experiments

### 4.1   Experimental Setup

In our experiments, we use the Anatomical Tracings of Lesions-After-Stroke (ATLAS) dataset as the training set, test set and validation set [7]. The dataset has a total of 229 cases of chronic stroke with MRI T1 sequence scans, and the size of each case is $233 \times 197 \times 189$. We divided the training set, validation set and test set according to the ratio of 8:1:1, and randomly selected 183 cases as training set, 23 cases as the validation set, 23 cases as the test set. In order to verify the effectiveness of the proposed algorithm, we selected mainstream methods as the baseline, including X-Net, Double-UNet, D-UNet, etc. In addition, we divide the mask region into three levels based on the number of pixels. 1–100 pixels is the level 1, and the task level is the small target. 100–1000 pixels is the level 2, and the task level is the medium target. More than 1000 pixels is the large target, the task level is the third level.

The performance of the model was evaluated by Dice Similarity Coefficient (DSC), Precision and Recall. DSC is an important indicator to evaluate the overall difference between prediction and ground truth. Recall usually reflects the degree of recall in the lesion area, which is an important reference in clinical practice.

## 4.2 Mixing Loss Function

In 3d medical data, the volume occupied by the stroke is usually very small throughout the whole scan interval. In the training process, a large number of background regions may dominate the loss function, which leads to the learning process easily falling into a local optimum. Therefore, we propose a new loss function, which refers to the method addressing the foreground-background voxel imbalance in, and combines two traditional loss functions in a concise manner.

### 4.2.1 Binary Cross Entropy Loss

The loss function of cross entropy mainly describes the distance between the actual output and the expected output, that is, the smaller the value of cross entropy, the closer the distribution of the two probability. Assuming that the probability distribution y is the expected output, the probability distribution $\hat{y}$ is the actual output, and $L_{BCE}(y, \hat{y})$ is the cross entropy, then:

$$L_{BCE}(y, \hat{y}) = -\sum_{i=1}^{N} y_i \ln \hat{y}_i + (1 - y_i) \ln(1 - \hat{y}_i) \tag{1}$$

As shown in the above formula, y represents the distribution of real marks, and a is the predicted mark distribution of the trained model. Binary cross entropy (BCE) function can measure the similarity between y and $\hat{y}$. Another advantage of binary cross entropy (BCE) as a loss function is that the use of sigmoid functions avoids the problem that the learning rate of mean square error loss function decreases when the gradient decreases, because the learning rate can be controlled by the output error.

### 4.2.2 Dice Coefficient Loss

The dice coefficient loss (DL) is used when the samples are extremely unbalanced, which makes it achieve good performance in medical segmentation.

$$L_{Dice}(y, \hat{y}) = 1 - \frac{2\sum_{i=1}^{N} y_i \hat{y}_i + \delta}{\sum_{i=1}^{N} y_i^2 + \sum_{i=1}^{N} \hat{y}_i^2 + \delta} \tag{2}$$

Among them, [0, 1] is an adjustable parameter, which is used to prevent the error of division by zero and make negative samples have a gradient propagation.

### 4.2.3 Proposed Mixing Loss

Based on the above two kinds of losses, we propose a mixing loss (ML) to improve the convergence speed. We use the L2 norm of two kinds of losses as the new loss value, thus enhancing the gradient obtained by each iteration. We hope that the function with larger loss value of BCE loss and Dice loss can play a leading role in the training process. The formula of ML is as follows:

$$ML(y, \hat{y}) = \sqrt{L_{BCE}(y, \hat{y})^2 + L_{Dice}(y, \hat{y})^2} \tag{3}$$

**Table 1.** Comparison of brain stroke segmentation results on ATLAS dataset. ME-Net-lite indicates not used residual encoder.

| Method | DSC | Recall | Precision | Total parameters |
|---|---|---|---|---|
| SegNet [10] | 0.2767 | 0.2532 | 0.3938 | 29.5M |
| PSPNet [8] | 0.3571 | 0.3335 | 0.4769 | 48.1M |
| U-Net [3] | 0.4606 | 0.4449 | 0.5994 | 15.1M |
| Deeplab v3 + [17] | 0.4609 | 0.4491 | 0.5831 | 41.3M |
| ResUNet [18] | 0.4702 | 0.4537 | 0.5941 | 33.2M |
| 2D Dense-UNet [13] | 0.4741 | 0.5613 | 0.4875 | 50.0M |
| X-Net [6] | 0.4867 | 0.4752 | 0.6000 | 15.1M |
| Double-UNet [4] | 0.5853 | 0.5878 | 0.6345 | 29.2M |
| D-UNet [5] | 0.5892 | 0.5796 | 0.6352 | 8.6M |
| ME-Net (ours) | **0.6627** | **0.6640** | **0.6942** | 9.9M |
| ME-Net-lite (ours) | **0.6353** | **0.6372** | **0.6677** | 3.8M |

## 4.3   Overall Accuracy Evaluation

As shown in Table 1, we have compared our proposed model with other models. It can be seen that the proposed ME-Net achieved the best performance, considering the value DSC and Precision. The main reason is that atrous convolutions with different sampling rates is used to get the context information on multi-scale features. In addition, the residual encoder obtains high-level semantic features and plays an important role in the pipelines. Regarding the DSC score, our method ranks first with a score of 0.6355, which is at least 4% higher than state-of-the-art methods.

## 4.4   The Performance on Different Levels

Firstly, we analyzed the results on level 1. As shown in Table 2, the performance of ME-Net is obviously superior to the existing detection methods. The first-level targets is relatively small, so it is difficult to find it with naked eyes. Figure 3 shows the typical case results obtained from four methods. As shown in Fig. 3, ME-Net can effectively detect the presence of the lesion area. The residual encoder plays a key role in the detection of small targets. The traditional medical segmentation model does not provide enough depth network structure and does not use the residual module. Therefore, for most tiny target areas, the traditional medical segmentation model are more prone to missing detection.

**Table 2.** Quantitatively compare the proposed method to the current best results on small targets, scoring based on the mean ± standard deviation calculated in each case.

Level 1: small target

| Method | DSC | mIOU | Recall | Precision |
|---|---|---|---|---|
| Double-UNet [4] | 0.2084 ± 0.3185 | 0.1626 ± 0.2618 | 0.2118 ± 0.3386 | 0.2756 ± 0.3923 |
| D-UNet [5] | 0.3473 ± 0.3798 | 0.2842 ± 0.3244 | 0.3448 ± 0.3940 | 0.3956 ± 0.4255 |
| X-Net [6] | 0.4358 ± 0.3814 | 0.3581 ± 0.3283 | 0.4297 ± 0.3955 | 0.3960 ± 0.3329 |
| ME-Net (ours) | **0.4469 ± 0.3879** | **0.3714 ± 0.3373** | **0.4579 ± 0.4136** | **0.4909 ± 0.4132** |

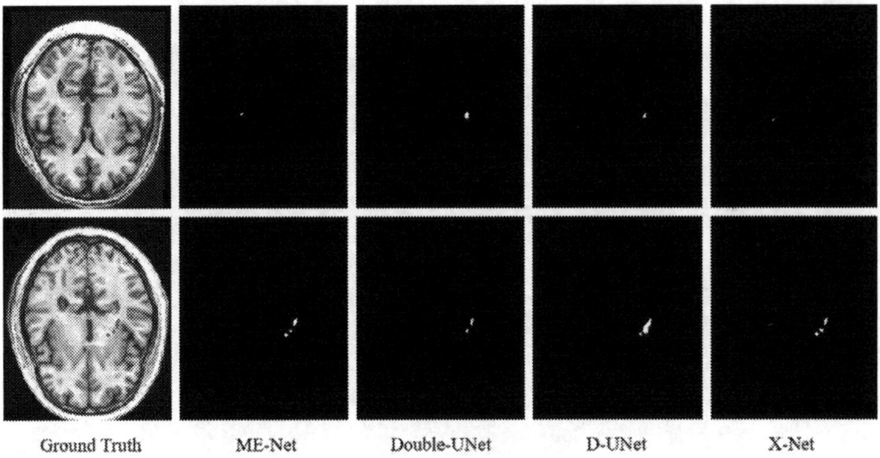

Ground Truth          ME-Net          Double-UNet          D-UNet          X-Net

**Fig. 3.** Qualitative result on small target from Lesion Boundary segmentation challenge.

The second experiment was conducted on Level 2. Table 3 shows the DSC of each algorithm on Level 2. Intuitively, our algorithm is significantly better than other algorithms. As shown in the Fig. 4, it is very challenging to extract the lesion area, since the lesion texture is very similar to its adjacent area. In this situation, X-unet and Double-unet failed to extract the complete lesion area. Fortunately, ME-Net concate the context information with different sampling rates, which successfully detects the lesion area. Furthermore, Residual encoder provides a wider field of vision for the network, which makes our method more accurate to restore the contour information of the lesion area without missing the surrounding small lesions.

The third experiment was conducted on Level 3. As shown in Table 4, ME-Net significantly outperforms the rest methods. The biggest challenge for Level 3 targets is to balance the restoration of large target boundaries and the detection of discrete small targets around them. Figure 5 shows the results of each algorithm on large target. It is worth

532     X. Zhang et al.

**Table 3.** Quantitatively compare the proposed method to the current best results on medium targets, scoring based on the mean ± standard deviation calculated in each case.

| Level 2: medium target | | | | |
|---|---|---|---|---|
| Method | DSC | mIOU | Recall | Precision |
| Double-UNet [4] | 0.6185 ± 0.3337 | 0.5199 ± 0.3022 | 0.6209 ± 0.3592 | 0.6842 ± 0.3334 |
| D-UNet [5] | 0.7094 ± 0.2785 | 0.6056 ± 0.2636 | 0.6922 ± 0.3014 | 0.7722 ± 0.2764 |
| X-Net [6] | 0.7384 ± 0.2385 | 0.6276 ± 0.2274 | 0.7502 ± 0.2690 | 0.7760 ± 0.2228 |
| ME-Net (ours) | **0.7912 ± 0.2108** | **0.6904 ± 0.2096** | **0.7797 ± 0.2318** | **0.8318 ± 0.1968** |

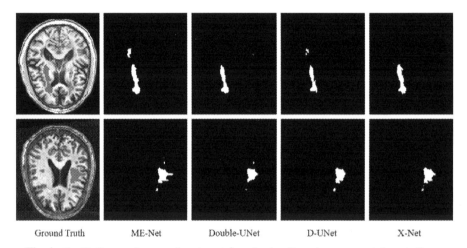

Ground Truth       ME-Net       Double-UNet       D-UNet       X-Net

**Fig. 4.** Qualitative result on medium target from Lesion Boundary segmentation challenge

noting that X-Net, D-UNet and Double-UNet perform poorly in this case. However, ME-Net also more accurate detected the lesion area. The reason is still that our proposed ME-Net adds a novel ASPP on the original basis to accurately segment multiple targets at different scales. The ASPP module uses multiple sampling rate filters to obtain the relevant information of the lesion area extracted at multiple scales (Table 5).

### 4.5  Loss Validity

To prove the effectiveness of the proposed loss function, we trained the proposed model and compared it with several common loss functions in segmentation tasks. As shown in the figure, we quantified these four kinds of losses. Our loss function is more advantageous because our proposed mixing loss (ML) uses a mixture of Binary cross entropy (BCE) and dice coefficient loss (DL). Therefore, compared with other three loss functions, the performance of mixing loss (ML) is competitive.

**Table 4.** Quantitatively compare the proposed method to the current best results on large targets, scoring based on the mean ± standard deviation calculated in each case.

| Level 3: large target | | | | |
|---|---|---|---|---|
| Method | DSC | mIOU | Recall | Precision |
| Double-UNet [4] | 0.8665 ± 0.1343 | 0.7814 ± 0.1476 | 0.8660 ± 0.1573 | 0.8818 ± 0.1218 |
| D-UNet [5] | 0.9102 ± 0.0403 | 0.8376 ± 0.0651 | 0.8983 ± 0.0658 | 0.9271 ± 0.0482 |
| X-Net [6] | 0.9019 ± 0.0472 | 0.8246 ± 0.0745 | 0.8879 ± 0.0801 | 0.9226 ± 0.0478 |
| ME-Net (ours) | **0.9273 ± 0.0317** | **0.8661 ± 0.0533** | **0.9291 ± 0.0497** | **0.9282 ± 0.0401** |

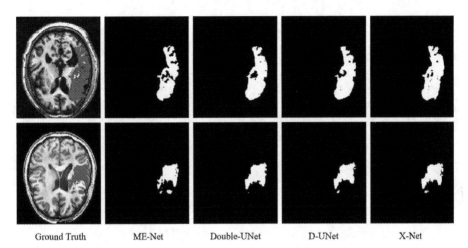

Ground Truth     ME-Net     Double-UNet     D-UNet     X-Net

**Fig. 5.** Qualitative result on large target from Lesion boundary segmentation challenge

**Table 5.** Quantitative analysis of the four loss functions.

| Method | DSC | Recall | Precision |
|---|---|---|---|
| Focal loss | 0.6460 ± 0.3373 | 0.5772 ± 0.3261 | **0.7818 ± 0.3639** |
| Binary cross entropy loss | 0.6412 ± 0.3590 | 0.6391 ± 0.3709 | 0.6782 ± 0.3683 |
| Dice coefficient loss | 0.6355 ± 0.3598 | 0.6302 ± 0.3710 | 0.6751 ± 0.3719 |
| Mixing loss (ours) | **0.6627 ± 0.3534** | **0.6640 ± 0.3653** | 0.6942 ± 0.3584 |

## 5  Conclusion

In this paper, we proposed a multiple encoders network for stroke lesion segmentation. On the basis of encoding-decoding framework, we conduct ASFF module and residual encoder to improve the efficiency of detecting process. Specifically, ASFF adopts atrous convolutions with different sampling rates to obtain the context information on multi-scale features. And residual encoder obtains the high-level semantic features. Experimental results on the ATLAS dataset demonstrated that the proposed ME-Net outperforms state-of-the-art methods, considering the DSC. We believe that these promising results pave the way to numerous extensions.

**Acknowledgments.** This work research was funded by the National Natural Science Foundation of China under grant no. 41971424 and no. 61701191; the key technical project of Xiamen Ocean Bureau under grant no.18CZB033HJ11; the key technical project of Xiamen Science and Technology Bureau under grant nos. 3502Z20194061, 3502Z20191018, 3502Z20201007, 3502Z20191022,3502Z20203057; the science and technology project of the Education Department of Fujian Province under grant nos. JAT190321, JAT190318, JAT190315.

# References

1. Ferlay, J., Shin, H.R., Bray, F., et al.: Estimates of worldwide burden of cancer in 2008: GLOBOCAN 2008. Int. J. Canc. **127**(12), 2893–2917 (2010)
2. Long, J., Shelhamer, E., Darrell, T.: Fully convolutional networks for semantic segmentation. In: Proceedings of the IEEE Conference on Computer Vision and Pattern Recognition, pp. 3431–3440 (2015)
3. Ronneberger, O., Fischer, P., Brox, T.: U-net: Convolutional networks for biomedical image segmentation. In: Navab, N., Hornegger, J., Wells, W.M., Frangi, A.F. (eds.) MICCAI 2015. LNCS, vol. 9351, pp. 234–241. Springer, Cham (2015). https://doi.org/10.1007/978-3-319-24574-4_28
4. Jha, D., Riegler, M.A., Johansen, D., et al.: Doubleu-net: a deep convolutional neural network for medical image segmentation. In: 2020 IEEE 33rd International Symposium on Computer-Based Medical Systems (CBMS), pp. 558–564. IEEE (2020)
5. Zhou, Y., Huang, W., Dong, P., et al.: D-UNet: a dimension-fusion U shape network for chronic stroke lesion segmentation. IEEE/ACM Trans. Comput. Biol. Bioinform. (2019)
6. Qi, K., Yang, H., Li, C., et al.: X-net: Brain stroke lesion segmentation based on depthwise separable convolution and long-range dependencies. In: International Conference on Medical Image Computing and Computer-Assisted Intervention. Lecture Notes in Computer Science, vol. 11766. Springer, Cham, pp. 247–255 (2019). https://doi.org/10.1007/978-3-030-32248-9_28
7. Liew, S.L., Anglin, J.M., Banks, N.W., et al.: A large, open source dataset of stroke anatomical brain images and manual lesion segmentations. Sci. Data, **5**, 180011 (2018)
8. Zhao, H., Shi, J., Qi, X., et al.: Pyramid scene parsing network. In: Proceedings of the IEEE Conference on Computer Vision and Pattern Recognition, pp. 2881–2890 (2017)
9. Milletari, F., Navab, N., Ahmadi, S.A.: V-net: Fully convolutional neural networks for volumetric medical image segmentation. In: 2016 Fourth International Conference on 3D Vision (3DV), pp. 565–571. IEEE (2016)
10. Badrinarayanan, V., Kendall, A., Cipolla, R.: Segnet: a deep convolutional encoder-decoder architecture for image segmentation. IEEE Trans. Pattern Anal. Mach. Intell. **39**(12), 2481–2495 (2017)
11. Kamnitsas, K., Ledig, C., Newcombe, V.F.J., et al.: Efficient multi-scale 3D CNN with fully connected CRF for accurate brain lesion segmentation. Med. Image Anal. **36**, 61–78 (2017)
12. Ni, T., Xie, L., Zheng, H., et al.: Elastic boundary projection for 3D medical image segmentation. In: Proceedings of the IEEE/CVF Conference on Computer Vision and Pattern Recognition, pp. 2109–2118 (2019)

13. Li, X., Chen, H., Qi, X., et al.: H-DenseUNet: hybrid densely connected UNet for liver and tumor segmentation from CT volumes. IEEE Trans. Med. Imaging **37**(12), 2663–2674 (2018)
14. Chen, L.C., Papandreou, G., Kokkinos, I., et al.: Deeplab: semantic image segmentation with deep convolutional nets, atrous convolution, and fully connected crfs. IEEE Trans. Pattern Anal. Mach. Intell. **40**(4), 834–848 (2017)
15. Chen, L.C., Papandreou, G., Kokkinos, I., et al.: Semantic image segmentation with deep convolutional nets and fully connected crfs. arXiv preprint arXiv:1412.7062 (2014)
16. Chen, L.C., Papandreou, G., Schroff, F., et al.: Rethinking atrous convolution for semantic image segmentation. arXiv preprint arXiv:1706.05587 (2017)
17. Chen, L.-C., Zhu, Y., Papandreou, G., Schroff, F., Adam, H.: Encoder-decoder with atrous separable convolution for semantic image segmentation. In: Ferrari, V., Hebert, M., Sminchisescu, C., Weiss, Y. (eds.) ECCV 2018. LNCS, vol. 11211, pp. 833–851. Springer, Cham (2018). https://doi.org/10.1007/978-3-030-01234-2_49
18. Zhang, Z., Liu, Q., Wang, Y.: Road extraction by deep residual u-net. IEEE Geosci. Remote Sens. Lett. **15**(5), 749–753 (2018)
19. Simonyan, K., Zisserman, A.: Very deep convolutional networks for large-scale image recognition. arXiv preprint arXiv:1409.1556 (2014)
20. He, K., Zhang, X., Ren, S., et al.: Deep residual learning for image recognition. In: Proceedings of the IEEE Conference on Computer Vision and Pattern Recognition, pp. 770–778 (2016)

# Nodule Synthesis and Selection for Augmenting Chest X-ray Nodule Detection

Zhenrong Shen[1], Xi Ouyang[1,2], Zhuochen Wang[1], Yiqiang Zhan[2], Zhong Xue[2], Qian Wang[1(✉)], Jie-Zhi Cheng[2], and Dinggang Shen[2,3]

[1] School of Biomedical Engineering, Shanghai Jiao Tong University, Shanghai, China
`wang.qian@sjtu.edu.cn`
[2] Shanghai United Imaging Intelligence Co., Ltd., Shanghai, China
`jiezhi.zheng@united-imaging.com`
[3] School of Biomedical Engineering, Shanghai Tech University, Shanghai, China
`dgshen@shanghaitech.edu.cn`

**Abstract.** Nodule detection in chest X-ray (CXR) images is important for early screening of lung cancer. It typically requires a large number of well-annotated data to train an effective nodule detector. However, high-quality annotations are hard to obtain due to the difficulty of locating nodules in CXR images and high cost of recruiting experienced radiologists. To address this issue, we propose an inpainting-based data augmentation (DA) framework, which consists of *Nodule Synthesis* stage and *Nodule Selection* stage, to synthesize CXR images with plausible nodules for facilitating the subsequent task of nodule detection. A partial convolutional U-Net is applied in *Nodule Synthesis* stage, which can offer flexibility to generate nodules at various locations in lungs. Since not all the synthesized CXR images are effective for data augmentation, we introduce *Nodule Selection* stage to identify efficacious nodules from the synthesized CXR images, to effectively augment the variety of training data for nodule detection. Our experimental results show that our DA framework can produce synthesized CXR images with plausible nodules of high quality, whereas the data augmentation can significantly improve the nodule detection performance.

**Keywords:** Lung nodule detection · Data augmentation · Image inpainting · Nodule synthesis · Nodule Selection

## 1 Introduction

Lung cancer is the leading healthcare challenge, accounting for 18.4% of the total cancer deaths in both females and males [1]. While lung nodules are typical positive indicators of potential lung cancers, the chest X-ray (CXR) imaging is widely used for lung cancer screening due to its low cost. However, it is easy to miss nodules even for experienced radiologists, as the task of reading and diagnosing CXR images is highly difficult [2]. A recent study [3] shows that the average sensitivity of nodule detection in CXR images

---

† Z. Shen and X. Ouyang—Contributed equally to this work.

© Springer Nature Switzerland AG 2021
H. Ma et al. (Eds.): PRCV 2021, LNCS 13021, pp. 536–547, 2021.
https://doi.org/10.1007/978-3-030-88010-1_45

by radiologists is 65.1% with 95% confidence interval. Notably, the sensitivity of radiologists can be boosted to 70.3% by using a deep learning (DL) based nodule detection software to assist the diagnosing process. Accordingly, the DL techniques are getting attention in clinical CXR diagnosis scenarios.

Several previous studies explore the DL techniques for the task of lung nodule detection. Li et al. [4] proposed a multi-resolution convolutional neural network framework using hundreds of public and private CXR images to classify whether an image patch includes nodules or not. Two clinical studies [2, 5] adapted ResNet models with more than 40,000 and 19,000 CXR images, respectively, to illustrate improved nodule detection in the reading workflow of radiologists. In general, the promising performance of nodule detection in the DL paradigm commonly requires a large number of high-quality annotations.

Although the annotations can be in different forms (e.g., in detailed contouring of the nodules, or much simpler bounding-boxes), the efforts in collecting reliable annotations can hardly be negligible. A reason points to the fact that reading CXR images for nodules is intrinsically difficult and requires high expertise from experienced radiologists. To this end, several studies [6, 7] attempted to exploit the weakly-supervised learning framework, by leveraging the well-known NIH dataset of tens of thousands of CXR images in particular [8], to mitigate the insufficiency of the annotated data. However, while only fewer than 100 bounding-box annotations of nodules are provided in the NIH dataset, the reported performances of nodule detection are not satisfactory yet.

To improve the nodule detection performance, data augmentation (DA) techniques based on image synthesis are introduced to increase the number of the training data. The study in [9] was the first work that applied a generative adversarial network (GAN) to synthesize the whole CXR images with salient abnormalities, in order to tackle data imbalance problem in the image-level classification task. However, the whole image synthesis may not easily preserve local details and hence not be suitable for extremely small or subtle abnormalities like lung nodules.

In this paper, we propose an inpainting-based DA framework to synthesize visually plausible CXR images, which can assist to train the nodule detection model. The DA framework consists of two stages named *Nodule Synthesis* and *Nodule Selection*, respectively. In *Nodule Synthesis* stage, we adopt a partial convolutional U-Net for CXR image synthesis by considering the visual plausibility at the levels of nodules. Once a bounding-box is specified inside the CXR image, the inpainting scheme can automatically generate a nodule inside the bounding-box. Then, in *Nodule Selection* stage, we are inspired by the core concept of active learning and build up a nodule selector to predict the realistic probability of the synthesized nodules. In this way, we can select those hard training samples, which further boost nodule detection performance subsequently. To support the development and evaluation of our proposed method, we collect more than 10,000 CXR images from multiple collaborative medical centers. We further investigate the data augmentation efficacy in nodule detection, by adding different numbers and nodule probabilities of the synthesized CXR images to RetinaNet [10]. The experimental results show that the performance and generalization of the nodule detector can be effectively improved by incorporating the synthesized images into the training data.

## 2 Related Work

### 2.1 Nodule Detection

The lung nodule in CXR image is defined as "solitary white nodule-like blob" by radiologists [11]. Nodules usually appear in CXR images with small size, which cannot provide abundant 3D rendering. These issues thus make nodule detection in CXR images challenging. Early researches for nodule detection usually contain two steps: (1) feature extraction to detect some region-of-interest (ROI) candidates, and (2) classification to identify target nodules from all ROI candidates. Different features can be extracted to represent nodules, e.g., intensity and shape features [12, 13], gradient and texture features [14, 15]. These two steps can be optimized separately, which may reduce computation burden yet sacrifice the detection performance.

For the object detection task in natural images, DL based methods have achieved superior progress in last decade. Basically, DL based detection models can be divided into two categories: two-stage model [16] and one-stage model [10, 17]. In this paper, we employ a typical one-stage model of RetinaNet [10] as our basic detection network for evaluating nodule detection performance. It uses different scales of feature maps that help detect nodules of various sizes, and achieves both good detection precision and high speed.

Although DL based methods have achieved high performance in the detection task, large-scale and high-quality annotated data are still required for model training. However, high-quality annotations are hard to obtain and very expensive, especially for lung nodules in CXR images. To alleviate this problem, we will propose the inpainting-based DA framework for nodule synthesis and selection, to assist the nodule detection task.

### 2.2 Image Synthesis

With the development of generative models, image synthesis becomes a hot research topic recently and has various applications in many fields. It can be used to generate images from latent vectors for the data augmentation of classification tasks. For example, Zhu et al. proposed CycleGAN [18] to synthesize images from source domain to target domain. In [9], GAN was used to synthesize whole CXR images with salient abnormalities. Due to the GPU memory and the upper limit of network capacity, the synthesized whole CXR image may produce blurring artifacts and distorted anatomical structures. Moreover, when treating the image entirely, the locations of the synthesized nodules cannot be easily controlled. This limits the scenarios of data augmentation as the synthesized images can be only used for the classification task but not detection.

Image inpainting, which can fill holes in an image, is also a popular field of image synthesis. Inspired by [19], we adopt an inpainting scheme for CXR image synthesis in this work, by considering the visual plausibility at the level of nodules. We train a partial convolutional network [20] to inpaint normal CXR images with synthesized nodules. By controlling the locations of specified bounding boxes to fill, we can place synthesized nodules with clear shape and texture in high-resolution CXR images.

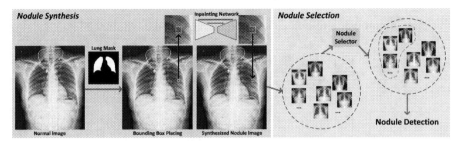

**Fig. 1.** Overview of the proposed data augmentation framework, which consists of the *Nodule Synthesis* stage and the *Nodule Selection* stage.

## 3   Method

As shown in Fig. 1, the proposed DA framework is comprised of two stages. First, in Nodule Synthesis stage, we apply a partial convolutional U-Net to generate visually plausible nodules at reasonable locations. In the subsequent Nodule Selection stage, we can select efficacious synthesized CXR images to augment the variety of training data with the assistance of a nodule selector.

### 3.1   Nodule Synthesis

In *Nodule Synthesis* stage (illustrated in the left part of Fig. 1), we develop an inpainting network to model high-quality nodule synthesis in normal CXR images. First, the lung segmentation using a pre-trained FCDenseNet [21] is carried out to obtain lung masks from the corresponding CXR images. Second, several bounding-boxes that tightly enclose the synthesized nodules are randomly placed within these lung masks. Third, $256 \times 256$ local image patches centered at each bounding-box are cropped from the original CXR images as the inputs to the inpainting network. Finally, the inpainted local image patches are pasted back to the original CXR images, to interleave toward the synthesized results. All the synthesized CXR images can be served as the candidates of augmented data for training the nodule detection model.

We use real nodule CXR images with bounding-box annotations to train the proposed inpainting network, which is illustrated in Fig. 2. Specifically, for each training image, we randomly crop a $256 \times 256$ image patch $I_{patch}$ centered at the annotated nodule. The bounding box is further masked out in $I_{patch}$. The masked image patch $I_{masked}$ and the paired binary mask of bounding-box are inputted to the inpainting network. The inpainting network is designed to be a U-Net [22] and is equipped with partial convolutional layers as well as mask-update mechanism [20] for promising inpainting effect. The partial convolution can learn surrounding context from the unmasked pixels and hence predicts plausible values to fill the masked region. The binary mask is used to indicate which region needs to be inpainted. The mask-update mechanism will automatically generate an updated mask for the next layer in each forward pass by a partial convolution operation and then gradually replace the masked holes with plausible inpainted values.

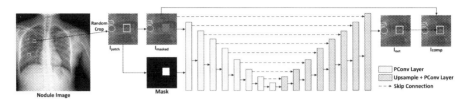

**Fig. 2.** Training details of the inpainting network in *Nodule Synthesis* stage.

As shown in Fig. 2, we use 8 partial convolutional layers in the encoder of the inpainting network and 8 symmetrical partial convolutional layers in the decoder. All the partial convolutional layers in the encoder have a kernel size of $3 \times 3$ except that the kernel sizes of the first three layers are $7 \times 7$, $5 \times 5$ and $5 \times 5$, respectively. Each layer in the decoder part is composed of a nearest-neighbor upsampling operation and a $3 \times 3$ partial convolution operation.

Similar to [20], the loss function for training the proposed inpainting network is comprised of pixel loss, content loss, texture loss and total variation loss to ensure pixel-wise reconstruction accuracy as well as synthesized nodule rationality. The losses are detailed in the next.

**Pixel Loss.** Pixel loss constrains the inpainted output patch $I_{out}$ to be close enough to the ground-truth patch $I_{gt}$ on the pixel intensity values. It computes the $L1$ distance between $I_{out}$ and $I_{patch}$ with different weights for the hole and the non-hole pixels:

$$L_{pixel} = \|\lambda_1 M \odot (I_{gt} - I_{out}) + \lambda_2 (1 - M) \odot (I_{gt} - I_{out})\|_1 \tag{1}$$

where $\odot$ denotes element-wise product operation. $M$ is the initial binary mask (0 for holes). $\mathbf{1}$ has the same shape with $M$ and filled with the value of 1. $\lambda_1$ and $\lambda_2$ are weighting factors for pixel losses outside and inside the masked region, respectively. $\lambda_1$ is set to 1 while $\lambda_2$ is set to 2 in our experiments.

**Content Loss.** Content loss is introduced to evaluate perceptual quality $I_{out}$. The $L1$ distance between high-level feature representations of $I_{out}$ and $I_{patch}$ computed to constrain their high-level contextual consistency:

$$L_{content} = \sum_{n=0}^{N-1} \|\Psi_n(I_{out}) - \Psi_n(I_{gt})\|_1 + \sum_{n=0}^{N-1} \|\Psi_n(I_{comp}) - \Psi_n(I_{gt})\|_1 \tag{2}$$

where $I_{comp}$ is the composited image which sets the pixels outside the masked region in $I_{out}$ directly to the ground truth $I_{gt}$. $\Psi_n$ is the activation map of the $n$ th selected layer, and we use layers *pool1*, *pool2* and *pool3* from pre-trained VGG-16 [23] on ImageNet [24] to project these images into high-level feature spaces.

**Texture Loss.** Image texture is regarded as the correlations between different feature channels and defined as the Gram matrix $G(A) = A^{\mathrm{T}}A$, $A \in R^{m \times n}$ [25], where $G(A)$ is the inner product between an $m \times n$ matrix $A$ and the transpose of itself. To produce

$I_{out}$ with anatomically authentic texture, texture loss is designed to measure the $L1$ distance between the Gram matrices of $I_{out}$ and $I_{gt}$ projected by feature map $\Psi_n$:

$$L_{texture} = \sum_{n=0}^{N-1} K_n \|G(\Psi_n(I_{out})) - G(\Psi_n(I_{gt}))\|_1 + \sum_{n=0}^{N-1} K_n \|G(\Psi_n(I_{comp})) - G(\Psi_n(I_{gt}))\|_1 \qquad (3)$$

where $I_{comp}$ is the composited image, and $K_n$ is the normalization factor $\frac{1}{C_n H_n W_n}$ ($C_n$, $H_n$ and $W_n$ are channels, height, and width of the feature map, respectively) for the same $n$ th selected layer used in the content loss.

**Total Variation Loss.** To ensure smoothness and suppress noise, the total variation loss serves a regularization term and is computed over the composited image $I_{comp}$ to make the neighboring pixels have similar values:

$$L_{tv} = \sum_{(i,j)\in P,(i,j+1)\in P} \|I_{comp}^{i,j+1} - I_{comp}^{i,j}\|_1 + \sum_{(i,j)\in P,(i+1,j)\in P} \|I_{comp}^{i+1,j} - I_{comp}^{i,j}\|_1 \qquad (4)$$

where $P$ is the masked region processed by 1-pixel dilation.

**Total Objective.** Combining all the aforementioned loss functions, the total objective function to train the proposed inpainting network can be expressed as:

$$L_{total} = L_{pixel} + \alpha L_{content} + \beta L_{texture} + \gamma L_{tv} \qquad (5)$$

where $\alpha$, $\beta$ and $\gamma$ are weighting factors for different loss terms and they are set to 0.05, 150, and 0.1 in our experiments, respectively.

### 3.2  Nodule Selection

In *Nodule Synthesis* stage, the proposed inpainting network can be easily applied in various normal CXR images and generate a plenty of synthesized nodule CXR images for the nodule detection task. However, data augmentation efficacy of the synthesized CXR images remains unknown. In order to boost nodule detection performance effectively, it is necessary to develop an algorithm to select efficacious augmented data.

Therefore, in *Nodule Selection* stage as shown in the right part of Fig. 1, we propose a nodule selector to efficiently select efficacious synthesized nodule CXR images for effective training of nodule detection model. This is inspired by the progress of active learning [26]. The core concept of active learning mainly relates to the idea that using a machine learning or DL method to choose a few hard training samples that can significantly improve the model's performance. Specifically, we employ a ResNet-50 [27] as the nodule selector for the training of 'normal/nodule' binary classification. The nodule selector takes the whole synthesized CXR image as the input, and predicts the probability that a synthesized CXR image contains lung nodules. Intuitively, lower predicted probability means this synthesized CXR image will be a harder case for nodule detector to identify the generated nodules. Thus, the predicted nodule probability can be used to indicate whether a synthesized nodule CXR image can be selected to augment the training data.

## 4  Experimental Results

### 4.1  Dataset and Experimental Setup

In this study, we involve 12,737 patients and their frontal-view CXR images. All the data are collected from our collaborative hospitals with the IRB approvals. Specifically, 3,024 images are diagnosed with nodules while the other 9,713 images are normal cases. All the nodules are well-annotated with bounding-boxes by an experienced radiologist and further quality check is performed by a second radiologist.

- We randomly select 2,420 nodule CXR images as the training set for the inpainting network. For the training of the inpainting network, Adam optimization is adopted and the momentum is set to 0.9. The learning rate is set to 0.0002 while the total training epochs and the batch size are set to 3,000 and 6, respectively.
- For the nodule selector, 9,327 normal CXR images together with the same 2,420 nodule cases are chosen for the training. Note that all images in training and inference for nodule selector are resized to $512 \times 512$ concerning the computation. We use Adam optimizer to train the selector for 50 epochs. The batch size is set to 54 and the initial learning rate is set to 0.00002.
- The training of RetinaNet, which is employed as the final nodule detector to assess data augmentation efficacy, are conducted on several combinations of 2,420 real nodule cases and the synthesized data of different numbers and nodule probabilities. For the training of RetinaNet with ResNet-101-FPN backbone, the batch size is set to 2 while the settings of [10] are adopted for the rest hyperparameters.

The rest 604 nodule cases and 386 normal cases are prepared as the testing set to evaluate the classification accuracy of the nodule selector as well as the detection performance of the nodule detector. For the evaluation of nodule detection performance, the average precisions (AP) at different intersection over union (IoU) thresholds are used as the metrics.

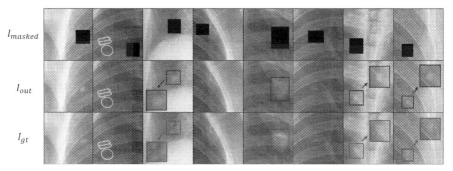

**Fig. 3.** Qualitative results of the proposed inpainting network for 8 examples (Columns): masked input $I_{masked}$ (Row 1); synthesized output $I_{out}$ by our method (Row 2); ground truth $I_{gt}$ (Row 3).

## 4.2  Nodule Synthesis Assessment

We compare several cases of the synthesized nodules $I_{out}$ with the original local patches $I_{gt}$ for qualitative illustration of nodule synthesis in Fig. 3. All the cases shown in Fig. 3 are from the testing dataset. It can be observed through visual comparison that the synthesized nodules appear anatomically plausible in context and pathologically authentic in different sizes. It can also be found in Fig. 3 that the nodule synthesis is contextually robust in regardless of the surrounding anatomical structures such as ribs (Column 5 and Column 8), diaphragm (Column 3), and spine (Column 7). The proposed inpainting network can thus generate plausible nodules with variety in size, appearance,

**Table 1.** The quantitative comparison between the baseline model trained with 2,420 real nodule CXR images and other nodule detectors trained with 2,420 real and 1,000 synthesized data. We show results in different nodule probability ranges.

| Metrics | 2420 real | 2420 real + 1000 synthesized | | | |
|---|---|---|---|---|---|
| | | Nodule probability range | | | |
| | | [0, 0.01) | [0.01, 0.5) | [0.5, 0.99) | [0.99, 1] |
| $AP_{0.3}$ | 0.778 | **0.790** | 0.783 | 0.782 | 0.773 |
| $AP_{0.5}$ | 0.768 | **0.778** | 0.774 | 0.771 | 0.765 |
| $AP_{0.7}$ | 0.620 | **0.662** | 0.653 | 0.643 | 0.588 |

density, and location within the lungs, and a proper number of various synthesized images may boost the generalization capability of the detection model.

## 4.3  Data Augmentation Efficacy Assessment

The proposed nodule selector achieves a classification accuracy of 0.919 on the testing set, which suggests that the synthesized CXR images with nodules can be well distinguished in *Nodule Selection* stage. To illustrate the data augmentation efficacy of the proposed DA framework, we conduct experiments on different combinations of real and synthesized data for the training of RetinaNet, which is used for subsequent nodule detection. Specifically, we consider a RetinaNet trained with 2,420 real nodule CXR images as the baseline model. Then we train the other nodule detectors of RetinaNet with 2,420 real nodule cases plus the synthesized data. In this way, we can compare with the baseline model and identify the contributions of the augmented data.

As illustrated in Table 1, the data augmentation using synthesized CXR nodule images is shown to be helpful for the improvement of nodule detection performance. To reveal the effect of different nodule probabilities on data augmentation efficacy, 9,327 synthesized nodule CXR images are generated in *Nodule Synthesis* stage and each 1,000 of them are selected for different predicted nodule probability ranges including [0, 0.01), [0.01, 0.5), [0.5, 0.99) and [0.99, 1] in *Nodule Selection* stage. It can be observed that the detection performance is increasingly boosted as the nodule probability range decreases.

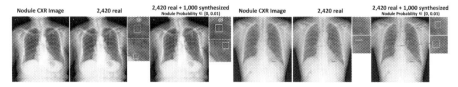

**Fig. 4.** Visualization of detection results. The ground-truth and the detected bounding-boxes are shown in red and green, respectively. It can be found that the baseline model trained with 2,420 real nodule CXR images identifies some false positives and false negatives, which is inferior to the nodule detector trained with the combination of 2,420 real images and 1,000 synthesized nodule cases in the nodule probability range of [0, 0.01).

**Table 2.** The quantitative comparison among the nodule detectors trained with 2,420 real nodule CXR images, 2,420 real and 1,000 synthesized data, and 2,420 real and 2,000 synthesized data, respectively. We show results in the nodule probability ranges of [0, 0.01) and [0.01, 0.5).

| Metrics | 2420 real | 2420 real + 1000 synthesized | | 2420 real + 2000 synthesized | |
|---|---|---|---|---|---|
| | | Nodule probability range | | Nodule probability range | |
| | | [0, 0.01) | [0.01, 0.5) | [0, 0.01) | [0.01, 0.5) |
| $AP_{0.3}$ | 0.778 | 0.790 | 0.783 | **0.804** | 0.771 |
| $AP_{0.5}$ | 0.768 | 0.778 | 0.774 | **0.790** | 0.759 |
| $AP_{0.7}$ | 0.620 | 0.662 | 0.653 | **0.673** | 0.629 |

The highest average precisions are achieved when using the nodule probability range of [0, 0.01) for augmentation. It is also worth noting that the detection performance in the nodule probability range of [0.99, 1] is even lower than the baseline, which suggests that adding a large number of easy training samples makes little and even no contribution. The corresponding visual comparison with the baseline is shown in Fig. 4. The experimental results above show that the data augmentation efficacy has an approximately negative correlation with the nodule probability of synthesized nodule CXR image, which fits the core idea of active learning that hard training samples, though synthesized, can better improve the performance of nodule detection.

To reveal the effect of different numbers of synthesized images on data augmentation efficacy, we generate and select 2,000 synthesized CXR images in the nodule probability ranges of [0, 0.01) and [0.01, 0.5), respectively. The experimental results are shown in Table 2. Compared with the training setting of using 2,420 real cases and 1,000 synthesized cases in the nodule probability range of [0, 0.01), the performance can be further improved when the number of synthesized images is added to 2000. However, all the average precisions decrease when adding 2000 synthesized images in the nodule probability range of [0.01, 0.5) compared with the training settings of adding 1,000 synthesized nodule cases. Especially the $AP_{0.3}$ and the $AP_{0.5}$ are even lower than the baseline. This indicates that randomly adding synthesized images may not boost the detection performance. Thus, we believe that increasing the number of augmented data works well, only when the synthesized nodule CXR images belonging to a relatively low nodule probability range are selected. That is, those selected nodule images can be deemed as hard training samples.

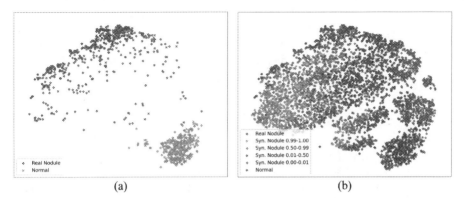

**Fig. 5.** Feature distributions of the real and synthesized data using t-SNE: (a) Visualization of real CXR images including both normal and nodule cases; (b) Visualization of normal cases, real nodule cases, and synthesized nodule cases in different nodule probability ranges.

To further analyze the effect of different nodule probabilities on data augmentation efficacy, we perform t-Distributed Stochastic Neighbor Embedding (t-SNE) [28] to visualize the high-dimension feature distributions of the training data as shown in Fig. 5. We pass the real data from our testing set and the synthesized data produced by our method through the nodule selector and take the feature representation before the last fully-connected layer for t-SNE visualization. It can be observed that the points of synthesized cases with different nodule probabilities fill in the feature space between the normal and real nodule cases. We believe that our DA framework extends the distribution of nodule CXR images by interpolating the latent feature representation between the normal cases and the real nodule cases. The distribution of the synthesized data in high nodule probability ranges occupies a space near to the real nodule cases with a large overlap. In contrast, the distribution of the synthesized data in the nodule probability range of [0, 0.01) is closer to the normal cases and is extended to the space where the original distribution of the real nodule cases hardly reaches, which can help to train a more robust nodule detector.

## 5   Conclusion and Discussion

In this paper, we present a novel inpainting-based DA framework to synthesize nodules in CXR images for data augmentation of nodule detection. The inpainting network in *Nodule Synthesis* stage can offer flexibility to generate anatomically plausible and pathologically authentic nodules in various sizes and appearance at reasonable locations within a CXR image. The idea of active learning is adopted in *Nodule Selection* stage that a classification-based nodule selector is employed to select efficacious synthesized images to effectively augment the variety of training data. Experiments conducted on different combinations of real and synthesized data have shown that our DA framework can significantly improve the performance and generalization of nodule detection.

Meanwhile, there exist several limitations in our study. First, we cannot control the detailed characteristics of the synthesized nodule, e.g., size, shape and density. We plan to design more powerful generative models to control more attributes for nodule synthesis. Second, in this paper, we select the synthesized cases for augmenting nodule detection according to the nodule probabilities. It is worth conducting more studies for the correlation between the real and the synthesized cases in feature space.

# References

1. Bray, F., Ferlay, J., Soerjomataram, I., Siegel, R.L., Torre, L.A., Jemal, A.: Global cancer statistics 2018: Globocan estimates of incidence and mortality worldwide for 36 cancers in 185 countries. CA: Canc. J. Clin. **68**(6), 394–424 (2018)
2. Shah, P.K., Austin, J.H., et al.: Missed non–small cell lung cancer: radiographic findings of potentially resectable lesions evident only in retrospect. Radiology **226**(1), 235–241 (2003)
3. Sim, Y., Chung, M.J., Kotter, E., et al.: Deep convolutional neural network-based software improves radiologist detection of malignant lung nodules on chest radiographs. Radiology **294**(1), 199–209 (2020)
4. Li, X., Shen, L., Xie, X., et. al.: Multi-resolution convolutional networks for chest x-ray radiograph based lung nodule detection. Artif. Intell. Med. **103**, 101744 (2019)
5. Nam, J.G., Park, S., Hwang, E.J., et al.: Development and validation of deep learning-based automatic detection algorithm for malignant pulmonary nodules on chest radiographs. Radiology **290**(1), 218–228 (2019)
6. Li, Z., Wang, C., Han, M., Xue, Y., Wei, W., Li, L.J., Fei-Fei, L.: Thoracic disease identification and localization with limited supervision. In: Proceedings of the IEEE Conference on Computer Vision and Pattern Recognition, pp. 8290–8299 (2018)
7. Liu, J., Zhao, G., Fei, Y., Zhang, M., Wang, Y., Yu, Y.: Align, attend and locate: Chest x-ray diagnosis via contrast induced attention network with limited supervision. In: Proceedings of the IEEE International Conference on Computer Vision, pp. 10632–10641 (2019)
8. Wang, X., Peng, Y., Lu, L., Lu, Z., Bagheri, M., Summers, R.M.: Chestx-ray8: Hospital-scale chest x-ray database and benchmarks on weakly-supervised classification and localization of common thorax diseases. In: Proceedings of the IEEE Conference on Computer Vision and Pattern Recognition, pp. 2097–2106 (2017)
9. Salehinejad, H., Colak, E., et. al.: Synthesizing chest x-ray pathology for training deep convolutional neural networks. IEEE Tran. Med. Imaging **38**(5), 1197–1206 (2018)
10. Lin, T.Y., Goyal, P., Girshick, R., et. al.: Focal loss for dense object detection. In: Proceedings of the IEEE International Conference on Computer Vision, pp. 2980–2988 (2017)
11. Austin, J.H., Romney, B.M., Goldsmith, L.S.: Missed bronchogenic carcinoma: radio-graphic findings in 27 patients with a potentially resectable lesion evident in retrospect. Radiology **182**(1), 115–122 (1992)
12. Giger, M.L.: Image feature analysis and computer-aided diagnosis in digital radiography. 3. Automated detection of nodules in peripheral lung fields. Med. Phys. **15**(2), 158–166 (1988)
13. Xu, X., Doi, K., Kobayashi, T., et. al.: Development of an improved cad scheme for automated detection of lung nodules in digital chest images. Med. Phys. **24**(9), 1395–1403 (1997)
14. Chen, S., Suzuki, K.: Computerized detection of lung nodules by means of virtual dual-energy radiography. IEEE Trans. Biomed. Eng. **60**(2), 369–378 (2013)
15. Li, X., Shen, L., Luo, S.: A solitary feature-based lung nodule detection approach for chest X-ray radiographs. IEEE J. Biomed. Health Inform. **22**(2), 516–524 (2017)

16. Ren, S., He, K., Girshick, R., Sun, J.: Faster R-CNN: towards real-time object detection with region proposal networks. IEEE Trans. Pattern Anal. Mach. Intell. **39**(6), 1137–1149 (2017)
17. Redmon, J., Divvala, S., Girshick, R., Farhadi, A.: You only look once: unified, real-time object detection. In: Proceedings of the IEEE Conference on Computer Vision and Pattern Recognition, pp. 779–788 (2016)
18. Zhu, J.-Y., Park, T.P., Isola, T., Efros, A.A.: Unpaired image-to-image translation using cycle-consistent adversarial networks. In: Proceedings of the IEEE International Conference on Computer Vision, pp. 2223–2232 (2017)
19. Gündel, S., Setio, A.A.A., Grbic, S., Maier, A., Comaniciu, D.: Extracting and leveraging nodule features with lung inpainting for local feature augmentation. In: Liu, M., Yan, P., Lian, C., Cao, X. (eds.) MLMI 2020. LNCS, vol. 12436, pp. 504–512. Springer, Cham (2020). https://doi.org/10.1007/978-3-030-59861-7_51
20. Liu, G., Reda, F.A., Shih, K.J., Wang, T.-C., Tao, A., Catanzaro, B.: Image inpainting for irregular holes using partial convolutions. In: Ferrari, V., Hebert, M., Sminchisescu, C., Weiss, Y. (eds.) ECCV 2018. LNCS, vol. 11215, pp. 89–105. Springer, Cham (2018). https://doi.org/10.1007/978-3-030-01252-6_6
21. J´egou, S., Drozdzal, M., Vazquez, D., Romero, A., Bengio, Y.: The one hundred layers tiramisu: fully convolutional densenets for semantic segmentation. In: Proceedings of the IEEE Conference on Computer Vision and Pattern Recognition Workshops, pp. 11–19 (2017)
22. Ronneberger, O., Fischer, P., Brox, T.: U-Net: convolutional networks for biomedical image segmentation. In: Navab, N., Hornegger, J., Wells, W.M., Frangi, A.F. (eds.) MICCAI 2015. LNCS, vol. 9351, pp. 234–241. Springer, Cham (2015). https://doi.org/10.1007/978-3-319-24574-4_28
23. Simonyan, K., Zisserman, A.: Very deep convolutional networks for large-scale image recognition. arXiv preprint arXiv:1409.1556 (2014)
24. Deng, J., Dong W, Socher R, et al: Imagenet: A large-scale hierarchical image database. IEEE Conference on Computer Vision and Pattern Recognition, pp. 248–255 (2009)
25. Gatys, L.A., Ecker, A.S., Bethge, M.: Image style transfer using convolutional neural networks. In: Proceedings of the IEEE Conference on Computer Vision and Pattern Recognition, pp. 2414–2423 (2016)
26. Settles, B.: Active learning literature survey. University of Wisconsin-Madison Department of Computer Sciences, Tech. Rep., Santa Cruz (2009)
27. He, K., Zhang, X., et. al.: Deep residual learning for image recognition. In: Proceedings of the IEEE Conference on Computer Vision and Pattern Recognition, pp. 770–778 (2016)
28. Laurens, V.D.M., Hinton, G.: Visualizing data using t-SNE. J. Mach. Learn. Res. **9**(2605), 2579–2605 (2008)

# Dual-Task Mutual Learning for Semi-supervised Medical Image Segmentation

Yichi Zhang[1] and Jicong Zhang[1,2,3,4]($\boxtimes$)

[1] School of Biological Science and Medical Engineering, Beihang University,
Beijing, China
jicongzhang@buaa.edu.cn
[2] Hefei Innovation Research Institute, Beihang University, Hefei, China
[3] Beijing Advanced Innovation Centre for Biomedical Engineering, Beijing, China
[4] Beijing Advanced Innovation Centre for Big Data-Based Precision Medicine,
Beijing, China

**Abstract.** The success of deep learning methods in medical image segmentation tasks usually requires a large amount of labeled data. However, obtaining reliable annotations is expensive and time-consuming. Semi-supervised learning has attracted much attention in medical image segmentation by taking the advantage of unlabeled data which is much easier to acquire. In this paper, we propose a novel dual-task mutual learning framework for semi-supervised medical image segmentation. Our framework can be formulated as an integration of two individual segmentation networks based on two tasks: learning region-based shape constraint and learning boundary-based surface mismatch. Different from the one-way transfer between teacher and student networks, an ensemble of dual-task students can learn collaboratively and implicitly explore useful knowledge from each other during the training process. By jointly learning the segmentation probability maps and signed distance maps of targets, our framework can enforce the geometric shape constraint and learn more reliable information. Experimental results demonstrate that our method achieves performance gains by leveraging unlabeled data and outperforms the state-of-the-art semi-supervised segmentation methods.

**Keywords:** Semi-supervised learning · Medical image segmentation · Mutual learning · Signed distance maps

## 1 Introduction

Medical image segmentation aims to understand images in pixel-level and label each pixel into a certain class, which is a fundamental step for many clinical

---

Our code is available at https://github.com/YichiZhang98/DTML.

© Springer Nature Switzerland AG 2021
H. Ma et al. (Eds.): PRCV 2021, LNCS 13021, pp. 548–559, 2021.
https://doi.org/10.1007/978-3-030-88010-1_46

applications [19,22]. Recently, deep learning techniques have showed significant improvements and achieved state-of-the-art performances in many medical image segmentation tasks [2,7,12]. However, training deep neural networks usually relies on massive labeled dataset, while it is extremely expensive and time-consuming to obtain large-amount of well-annotated data where only professional experts can provide reliable annotations for medical imaging. To reduce the labeling cost, many studies have focused on developing annotation-efficient medical image segmentation methods with scarce annotations or weak annotations [3,20,23,28]. For medical imaging, unlabeled data is much easier to acquire and can be used in conjunction with labeled data to train segmentation models. As a result, semi-supervised learning has been widely explored to learn from a limited amount of labeled data and an arbitrary amount of unlabeled data [9,17], which is a fundamental, challenging problem and has a high impact on real-world clinical applications.

In this paper, we propose a novel dual-task mutual learning framework for semi-supervised medical image segmentation. The framework can be formulated as an integration of two individual segmentation networks based on different tasks. The segmentation task aims at generating segmentation probabilistic maps while the regression task aims at regressing the signed distance maps. Since the output of different tasks can be mapped to the same predefined space, dual-task networks can learn different representations of segmentation targets from different perspectives. Following the mutual learning manner [29], we aim at encouraging dual-task networks to learn collaboratively and explore useful knowledge from each other during the training process. Each network is primarily directed by a conventional supervised learning loss for training. With supervised learning, both networks learn reliable representation of the segmentation task from different task-level condition, therefore estimate the probabilities of the most likely categories differently. Under the semi-supervised learning setting, we activate the unsupervised cross-task consistency loss to encourage consistent predictions of the same input in order to utilize the unlabeled data. By jointly learning the segmentation probability maps and signed distance maps, our framework can enforce the geometric shape constraint and collaboratively learn more reliable information for segmentation throughout the training procedure.

Our method is evaluated on the Atrial Segmentation Challenge dataset for left atrium (LA) segmentation [25] with extensive comparisons to existing methods. The experimental results demonstrate that our method achieves performance gains by leveraging unlabeled data and outperforms the state-of-the-art semi-supervised segmentation methods.

## 2  Related Work

### 2.1  Semi-supervised Medical Image Segmentation

To utilize unlabeled data for semi-supervised medical image segmentation, a simple and intuitive method is to assign pseudo annotations to unlabeled data and then train the segmentation model using both labeled and pseudo labeled data.

Pseudo annotations are commonly generated in an iterative approach wherein a model iteratively improves the quality of pseudo annotations by learning from its own predictions on unlabeled data [1]. Zhang *et al.* [30] introduced adversarial learning for biomedical image segmentation by encouraging the segmentation output of unlabeled data to be similar to annotations of labeled data. Although semi-supervised learning with pseudo annotations has shown promising performance, model-generated annotations can still be noisy and has detrimental effects to the subsequent segmentation model [14,16].

Recent efforts in semi-supervised segmentation have been focused on incorporating unlabeled data into the training procedure with an unsupervised loss function. Some of these methods enforce the consistency between model predictions on the original data and the perturbed data by adding small perturbations to the unlabeled data. For example, Li *et al.* [9] proposed to constrain the consistency under transformation like rotation to utilize unlabeled data. Yu *et al.* [27] extended the mean teacher paradigm [21] with the guidance of uncertainty map for semi-supervised learning. [6] proposed to utilize unlabeled data by minimizing the difference between soft masks generated by two decoders. Some other methods focus on enforcing the similar distribution of predictions using an adversarial loss [8,16].

## 2.2    Signed Distance Maps

Different from most existing segmentation methods that use binary or multi-label mask as ground truth, signed distance maps (SDM) can provide an alternative to classical ground truth by transforming binary masks to gray-level images where the intensities of pixels are changed according to the distance to the closest boundary [11], which has been applied for medical image segmentation tasks to obtain further improvements by offering an implicit representation of the ground truth [5,15]. A commonly used method is adding auxiliary regression head to the end of classic encoder-decoder network to generate signed distance maps. Specifically, the network can be divided into two branches to generate the segmentation probabilistic maps and regress the signed distance maps at the same time. Due to the task difference, these two branches can learn different representations of segmentation targets from different perspectives, so as to obtain further improvements. On the condition that the output of different tasks can be mapped to the same predefined space, instead of existing data-level regularization methods, we focus on building task-level regularization to utilize unlabeled data in our framework.

## 3    Method

In this section, we introduce details about our proposed dual-task mutual learning framework. As illustrated in Fig. 1, our framework can be formulated as an integration of two individual segmentation networks. These two networks share the same backbone structure and have specific segmentation and regression heads

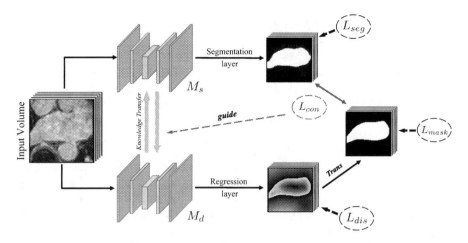

**Fig. 1.** The overview of our proposed dual-task mutual learning framework for semi-supervised medical image segmentation. The framework can be formulated as an integration of two individual segmentation networks, the upper one named $M_s$ for generating the segmentation probabilistic maps and the lower one named $M_d$ for regressing the signed distance maps. These two networks share the same backbone structure, and have task specific segmentation/regression output layers. During the training process, the networks are optimized with mutual learning manner to implicitly explore useful knowledge from each other.

for different tasks. The upper one $M_s$ aims at generating segmentation probabilistic maps while the lower one $M_d$ aims at regressing the signed distance maps. Since the output of different tasks can be mapped to the same predefined space, dual-task networks can learn different representations of segmentation targets from different perspectives. We focus on building task-level regularization to enable each network learn from peer network's guidance and introduce a cross-task consistency regularization to enforce the representation of predictions to be consistent. To fully utilize the spatial information, we task 3D volumes as the input for both networks.

### 3.1   Dual-Task Networks

Following the design of encoder-decoder architecture [4,13,18] to generate segmentation probabilistic maps, an auxiliary regression head is added to generate the signed distance maps composed by a 3D convolution block followed by the *tanh* activation. The signed distance maps of ground truth $G$ can be defined by

$$
G_{SDF} = \begin{cases} - \inf\limits_{y \in \partial G} \|x - y\|_2, & x \in G_{\text{in}} \\[2mm] 0, & x \in \partial G \\[2mm] + \inf\limits_{y \in \partial G} \|x - y\|_2, & x \in G_{\text{out}} \end{cases} \tag{1}
$$

where $\|x - y\|$ is the Euclidean distance between voxels $x$ and $y$, and $G_{in}$, $\partial G$, $G_{out}$ represents the inside, boundary and outside of the target object. In general, $G_{SDF}$ takes negative values inside the target and positive values outside the object, and the absolute value is defined by the distance to the closest boundary point. To transform the output of signed distance maps to segmentation output, we utilize a smooth approximation to the inverse transform as in [10], which can be defined by

$$G_{mask} = \frac{1}{1 + e^{-k \cdot z}}, z \in G_{SDF} \tag{2}$$

where $z$ is the value of signed distance maps at voxel $x$, and $k$ is a transform factor selected as large as possible to approximate the transform. Our dual-task networks share the same backbone structure and differ at the end of the network. Specifically, for $M_s$ only the segmentation head is activated, while for $M_d$ only the regression head is activated. Given an input image $X \in R^{H \times W \times D}$, dual-task networks $M_s$ and $M_d$ generate the confidence score map $\hat{Y}_{seg} \in [0,1]^{H \times W \times D}$ and signed distance map $\hat{Y}_{dis} \in \mathbf{R}^{H \times W \times D}$ as follows

$$\hat{Y}_{seg} = f_{seg}(X; \theta_{seg}), \quad \hat{Y}_{dis} = f_{dis}(X; \theta_{dis}) \tag{3}$$

where $\theta_{seg}$, $\theta_{dis}$ are corresponding parameters of segmentation network $M_s$ and regression network $M_d$, respectively.

## 3.2   Mutual Learning for Semi-supervised Segmentation

For semi-supervised segmentation of 3D medical images, where the training set $\mathcal{D}$ contains $M$ labeled cases and $N$ unlabeled cases, we denote the labeled set as $\mathcal{D}_L = \{X_i, Y_i\}_{i=1}^{M}$ and the unlabeled set as $\mathcal{D}_U = \{X_i\}_{i=1}^{N}$, where $X_i \in \mathbf{R}^{H \times W \times D}$ is the input volume and $Y_i \in \{0,1\}^{H \times W \times D}$ is the corresponding ground truth.

For labeled cases, each network is primarily directed by supervised loss to learn reliable representation of the segmentation task. We employ the combination of dice loss and cross-entropy loss as the supervised loss $\mathcal{L}_{seg}$ for the segmentation of $M_s$. While for $M_d$, two options of supervision can be applied for the training. The first choice is using $\mathcal{L}_2$ loss between the output signed distance maps and transformed distance maps of ground truth named $\mathcal{L}_{dis}$ as the supervision. Another choice is using dice loss between transformed segmentation mask and the ground truth named $\mathcal{L}_{mask}$. We empirically found that supervised directly on segmentation masks with $\mathcal{L}_{mask}$ can achieve better performance. Under the semi-supervised learning setting, to utilize unlabeled cases for training, we activate the unsupervised cross-task consistency loss to encourage consistent predictions of the same input in order to utilize the unlabeled data. By jointly learning the segmentation probability maps and signed distance maps, our framework can enforce the geometric shape constraint and collaboratively learn more reliable information for segmentation throughout the training procedure. To quantify the match of the two network's predictions, we focus on enforcing cross-task consistency between segmentation predictions and transformed regression predictions:

$$\mathcal{L}_{con} = \lambda_{con} \|f_{seg}(X; \theta_{seg}) - f_{mask}^{-1}(f_{dis}(X; \theta_{dis}))\|^2 \tag{4}$$

where $f_{mask}^{-1}$ is the transformation of signed distance maps to segmentation maps as described in (2), and $\lambda_{con}$ is the ramp-up weighting coefficient to control the trade-off between the segmentation loss and consistency loss. Following [27], we use a Gaussian ramp-up function $\lambda_{con}(t) = 0.1 * e^{-5(1-T/T_{max})}$ in all our experiments where t represents the number of iterations.

Therefore, the goal of our semi-supervised segmentation framework is to minimize the following combined functions.

$$\min_{\theta_{seg}} \sum_{i \in \mathcal{D}_L} \mathcal{L}_{seg}(f_{seg}(X_i; \theta_{seg}), Y_i) + \sum_{i \in \mathcal{D}} \mathcal{L}_{con}(f_{mask}^{-1}(f_{dis}(X_i; \theta_{dis})), f_{seg}(X_i; \theta_{seg}))$$

(5)

$$\min_{\theta_{dis}} \sum_{i \in \mathcal{D}_L} \mathcal{L}_{mask}(f_{mask}^{-1}(f_{dis}(X_i; \theta_{dis})), Y_i)$$
$$+ \sum_{i \in \mathcal{D}} \mathcal{L}_{con}(f_{mask}^{-1}(f_{dis}(X_i; \theta_{dis})), f_{seg}(X_i; \theta_{seg}))$$

(6)

## 4   Experiments

### 4.1   Dataset and Implementation Details

We evaluate our method on the Left Atrium (LA) dataset from Atrial Segmentation Challenge[1] [25]. The dataset contains 100 3D gadolinium-enhanced MR imaging scans (GE-MRIs) and corresponding LA segmentation mask for training and validation. These scans have an isotropic resolution of $0.625 \times 0.625 \times 0.625 \, mm^3$. Following the task setting in [27], we split the 100 scans into 80 scans for training and 20 scans for testing, and apply the same pre-processing methods. Out of the 80 training scans, we use the same 20%/16 scans as labeled data and the remaining 80%/64 scans as unlabeled data for semi-supervised segmentation task.

Our framework is implemented in PyTorch, using an NVIDIA Tesla V100 GPU. In this work, we use V-Net [13] as the backbone structure for all experiments to ensure a fair comparison. To incorporate signed distance maps for mutual learning, an auxiliary regression head is added at the end of the original V-Net. We use the Stochastic Gradient Descent (SGD) optimizer to update the network parameters for 6000 iterations, with an initial learning rate (lr) 0.01 decayed by 0.1 every 2500 iterations. The batch size is 4, consisting of 2 labeled images and 2 unlabeled images. We randomly crop $112 \times 112 \times 80$ sub-volumes as the network input and the final segmentation results are obtained using a sliding window strategy. We use the standard data augmentation techniques on-the-fly to avoid overfitting during the training procedure [26], including randomly flipping, and rotating with 90, 180 and $270°$ along the axial plane.

---

[1] http://atriaseg2018.cardiacatlas.org/data/.

**Table 1.** Comparison of different supervised loss functions for our dual-task mutual learning framework. All the models follow the same task setting with 16 labeled scans and 64 unlabeled scans for training.

| Supervised loss $M_s/M_d$ | Metrics | | | |
|---|---|---|---|---|
| | Dice [%] | Jaccard [%] | ASD [voxel] | 95HD [voxel] |
| DTML($\mathcal{L}_{seg}/\mathcal{L}_{dis}$) | 89.72 | 81.55 | 1.97 | 7.64 |
| DTML($\mathcal{L}_{seg}/\mathcal{L}_{mask}$) | 90.12 | 82.14 | 1.82 | 7.01 |
| DTML($\mathcal{L}_{seg}/\mathcal{L}_{dis} + \mathcal{L}_{mask}$) | 89.89 | 81.82 | 1.93 | 6.61 |

**Table 2.** Ablation analysis of our dual-task mutual learning framework.

| Method | Scans used | | Metrics | | | |
|---|---|---|---|---|---|---|
| | Labeled | Unlabeled | Dice [%] | Jaccard [%] | ASD [voxel] | 95HD [voxel] |
| $M_s$ only | 16 | 0 | 86.03 | 76.06 | 3.51 | 14.26 |
| $M_d$ only | 16 | 0 | 88.69 | 79.91 | 3.12 | 11.62 |
| DTML | 16 | 0 | 89.17 | 80.68 | 2.13 | 7.82 |

We use four complementary evaluation metrics to quantitatively evaluate the segmentation results. Dice similarity coefficient (Dice) and Jaccard Index (Jaccard), two region-based metrics, are used to measure the region mismatch. Average surface distance (ASD) and 95% Hausdorff Distance (95HD), two boundary-based metrics, are used to evaluate the boundary errors between the segmentation results and the ground truth.

## 4.2   Ablation Analysis

We conduct detailed experimental studies to examine the effectiveness of our proposed framework. For supervised loss of $M_d$, $L_2$ loss between the output signed distance maps and transformed distance maps of ground truth named $\mathcal{L}_{dis}$, and segmentation loss between transformed segmentation mask of output distance maps and binary ground truth mask named $\mathcal{L}_{mask}$, can both be employed for the training. We make an comparison between different settings for $M_d$. It can be observed from Table 1 that using $\mathcal{L}_{mask}$ for supervised loss can obtain higher performance compared with using $\mathcal{L}_{dis}$ or their sum. Experimental results demonstrate that direct supervision based on segmentation masks for both $M_s$ and $M_d$ is the best practice for our framework, since minor differences on signed distance maps may somehow mislead the training.

Besides, to analyze the effectiveness of our method, we conduct experiments to implement our method with only labeled cases and remove the cross-task consistency loss between dual-task networks for comparison. The first and second rows in Table 2 are segmentation results of $M_s$ and $M_d$ training independently. We can observe that our method significantly outperforms both tasks training independently on all metrics. Paired T-test shows that the improvements are statistically significant at $p < 0.05$ compared with both $M_s$ and $M_d$, validating the

**Table 3.** Quantitative comparison between our method and other semi-supervised methods. All the models use the same V-Net as the backbone. The first and second rows are upper-bound performance and fully supervised baseline. Experimental results demonstrate that our method outperforms the state-of-the-art results consistently.

| Method | Scans used | | Metrics | | | |
|---|---|---|---|---|---|---|
| | Labeled | Unlabeled | Dice [%] | Jaccard [%] | ASD [voxel] | 95HD [voxel] |
| V-Net (upper bound) | 80 | 0 | 91.14 | 83.82 | 1.52 | 5.75 |
| V-Net (lower bound) | 16 | 0 | 86.03 | 76.06 | 3.51 | 14.26 |
| ASDNet [16] | 16 | 64 | 87.90 | 78.85 | 2.08 | 9.24 |
| TCSE [9] | 16 | 64 | 88.15 | 79.20 | 2.44 | 9.57 |
| UA-MT [27] | 16 | 64 | 88.88 | 80.21 | 2.26 | 7.32 |
| DTC [10] | 16 | 64 | 89.42 | 80.89 | 2.10 | 7.32 |
| SASS [8] | 16 | 64 | 89.54 | 81.24 | 2.20 | 8.24 |
| DoubleUnc [24] | 16 | 64 | 89.65 | 81.35 | 2.03 | 7.04 |
| **DTML (ours)** | 16 | 64 | **90.12** | **82.14** | **1.82** | **7.01** |

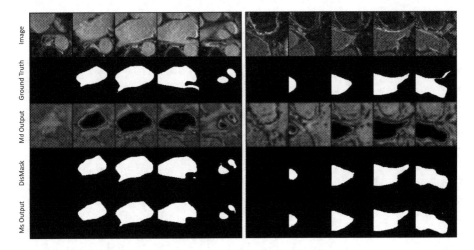

**Fig. 2.** Visual comparison of output signed distance maps ($M_d$ Output), transformed segmentation masks (DisMask) and output segmentation maps ($M_s$ Output) in our framework. The first two rows are corresponding image and ground truth.

effectiveness of our mutual learning framework. Figure 2 presents some examples of output from different network in our framework. It can be observed that both networks can achieve promising segmentation results. Besides, the transformed segmentation masks and output segmentation maps are slightly different due to the task difference, which enables the knowledge transfer between dual-task networks. In Fig. 3, we show some segmentation examples of supervised method and our proposed semi-supervised method for visual comparison. We can observe that our segmentation results have higher overlap ratio with the ground truth.

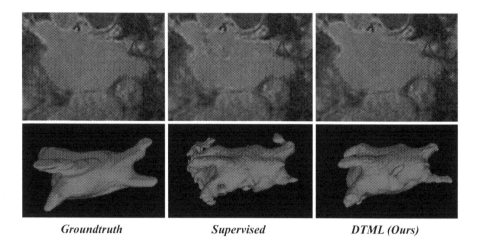

| *Groundtruth* | *Supervised* | *DTML (Ours)* |

**Fig. 3.** Examples of 2D and 3D visual comparison of different segmentation results.

### 4.3  Quantitative Evaluation and Comparison

To demonstrate the effectiveness of our method, a comprehensive comparison with existing methods is conducted. We evaluate our method in with comparisons to state-of-the-art semi-supervised segmentation methods, including ASDNet [16], TCSE [9], UA-MT [27], DTC [10], SASS [8] and Double-Uncertainty [24]. To ensure a fair comparison, we used the same V-Net backbone in these methods. As a contrast, we conduce experiments of V-Net under fully-supervised settings with 20% and all labeled data as the lower-bound and upper-bound performances for the task. Compared with semi-supervised learning settings, only labeled scans are used for the lower-bound subtask and both labeled and unlabeled scans with annotations are used for the upper-bound subtask. The results of comparison experiments are shown in Table 3. As can be observed, by exploiting unlabeled data for training, our proposed method can produce significant performance gains and obtain comparable results (90.12% vs. 91.14% of Dice) with the upper-bound performance. In addition, our method achieves better performance on all the evaluation metrics compared with state-of-the-art segmentation methods.

## 5   Conclusion

In this paper, we propose a novel dual-task mutual learning framework for semi-supervised medical image segmentation. Our method can effectively leverage abundant unlabeled data by encouraging the output consistency of two tasks: learning region-based shape constraint and learning boundary-based surface mismatch. By jointly learning the semantic segmentation and signed distance maps of targets and building task-level regularization, our framework can enforce the geometric shape constraint and collaboratively learn more reliable information from unlabeled images throughout the training procedure. Comprehensive experimental analysis demonstrates the effectiveness of our proposed method and significant improvement compared with state-of-the-art semi-supervised segmentation methods.

**Acknowledgments.** This work is supported by the National Key Research and Development Program of China (2016YFF0201002), the University Synergy Innovation Program of Anhui Province (GXXT-2019-044), and the National Natural Science Foundation of China (61301005).

# References

1. Bai, W., et al.: Semi-supervised learning for network-based cardiac MR image segmentation. In: Descoteaux, M., Maier-Hein, L., Franz, A., Jannin, P., Collins, D.L., Duchesne, S. (eds.) MICCAI 2017. LNCS, vol. 10434, pp. 253–260. Springer, Cham (2017). https://doi.org/10.1007/978-3-319-66185-8_29
2. Bernard, O., et al.: Deep learning techniques for automatic MRI cardiac multi-structures segmentation and diagnosis: is the problem solved? IEEE Trans. Med. Imaging **37**(11), 2514–2525 (2018)
3. Cheplygina, V., de Bruijne, M., Pluim, J.P.: Not-so-supervised: a survey of semi-supervised, multi-instance, and transfer learning in medical image analysis. Med. Image Anal. **54**, 280–296 (2019)
4. Çiçek, Ö., Abdulkadir, A., Lienkamp, S.S., Brox, T., Ronneberger, O.: 3D U-Net: learning dense volumetric segmentation from sparse annotation. In: Ourselin, S., Joskowicz, L., Sabuncu, M.R., Unal, G., Wells, W. (eds.) MICCAI 2016. LNCS, vol. 9901, pp. 424–432. Springer, Cham (2016). https://doi.org/10.1007/978-3-319-46723-8_49
5. Dangi, S., Linte, C.A., Yaniv, Z.: A distance map regularized CNN for cardiac cine MR image segmentation. Med. Phys. **46**(12), 5637–5651 (2019)
6. Fang, K., Li, W.-J.: DMNet: difference minimization network for semi-supervised segmentation in medical images. In: Martel, A.L., et al. (eds.) MICCAI 2020. LNCS, vol. 12261, pp. 532–541. Springer, Cham (2020). https://doi.org/10.1007/978-3-030-59710-8_52
7. Heller, N., et al.: The state of the art in kidney and kidney tumor segmentation in contrast-enhanced CT imaging: results of the KiTS19 challenge. Med. Image Anal. **67**, 101821 (2020)
8. Li, S., Zhang, C., He, X.: Shape-aware semi-supervised 3D semantic segmentation for medical images. In: Martel, A.L., et al. (eds.) MICCAI 2020. LNCS, vol. 12261, pp. 552–561. Springer, Cham (2020). https://doi.org/10.1007/978-3-030-59710-8_54
9. Li, X., Yu, L., Chen, H., Fu, C.W., Xing, L., Heng, P.A.: Transformation-consistent self-ensembling model for semisupervised medical image segmentation. IEEE Trans. Neural Netw. Learn. Syst. **32**, 523–534 (2020)
10. Luo, X., Chen, J., Song, T., Wang, G.: Semi-supervised medical image segmentation through dual-task consistency. In: Proceedings of the AAAI Conference on Artificial Intelligence. vol. 35, pp. 8801–8809 (2021)

11. Ma, J., et al.: How distance transform maps boost segmentation CNNs: an empirical study. In: Medical Imaging with Deep Learning, pp. 479–492. PMLR (2020)

12. Ma, J., et al.: AbdomenCT-1K: is abdominal organ segmentation a solved problem. IEEE Trans. Pattern Anal. Mach. Intell. (2021)

13. Milletari, F., Navab, N., Ahmadi, S.A.: V-Net: fully convolutional neural networks for volumetric medical image segmentation. In: 2016 4th International Conference on 3D Vision (3DV), pp. 565–571. IEEE (2016)

14. Min, S., Chen, X., Zha, Z.J., Wu, F., Zhang, Y.: A two-stream mutual attention network for semi-supervised biomedical segmentation with noisy labels. Proc. AAAI Conf. Artif. Intell. **33**, 4578–4585 (2019)

15. Navarro, F.: Shape-aware complementary-task learning for multi-organ segmentation. In: Suk, H.-I., Liu, M., Yan, P., Lian, C. (eds.) MLMI 2019. LNCS, vol. 11861, pp. 620–627. Springer, Cham (2019). https://doi.org/10.1007/978-3-030-32692-0_71

16. Nie, D., Gao, Y., Wang, L., Shen, D.: ASDNet: attention based semi-supervised deep networks for medical image segmentation. In: Frangi, A.F., Schnabel, J.A., Davatzikos, C., Alberola-López, C., Fichtinger, G. (eds.) MICCAI 2018. LNCS, vol. 11073, pp. 370–378. Springer, Cham (2018). https://doi.org/10.1007/978-3-030-00937-3_43

17. Qi, G.J., Luo, J.: Small data challenges in big data era: a survey of recent progress on unsupervised and semi-supervised methods. IEEE Trans. Pattern Anal. Mach. Intell. (2020)

18. Ronneberger, O., Fischer, P., Brox, T.: U-Net: convolutional networks for biomedical image segmentation. In: Navab, N., Hornegger, J., Wells, W.M., Frangi, A.F. (eds.) MICCAI 2015. LNCS, vol. 9351, pp. 234–241. Springer, Cham (2015). https://doi.org/10.1007/978-3-319-24574-4_28

19. Sykes, J.: Reflections on the current status of commercial automated segmentation systems in clinical practice. J. Med. Radiat. Sci. **61**(3), 131 (2014)

20. Tajbakhsh, N., Jeyaseelan, L., Li, Q., Chiang, J.N., Wu, Z., Ding, X.: Embracing imperfect datasets: a review of deep learning solutions for medical image segmentation. Med. Image Anal. **63**, 101693 (2020)

21. Tarvainen, A., Valpola, H.: Mean teachers are better role models: weight-averaged consistency targets improve semi-supervised deep learning results. In: Proceedings of the 31st International Conference on Neural Information Processing Systems, pp. 1195–1204 (2017)

22. Van Ginneken, B., Schaefer-Prokop, C.M., Prokop, M.: Computer-aided diagnosis: how to move from the laboratory to the clinic. Radiology **261**(3), 719–732 (2011)

23. Wang, L., Guo, D., Wang, G., Zhang, S.: Annotation-efficient learning for medical image segmentation based on noisy pseudo labels and adversarial learning. IEEE Trans. Med. Imaging (2020)

24. Wang, Y., et al.: Double-uncertainty weighted method for semi-supervised learning. In: Martel, A.L., et al. (eds.) MICCAI 2020. LNCS, vol. 12261, pp. 542–551. Springer, Cham (2020). https://doi.org/10.1007/978-3-030-59710-8_53

25. Xiong, Z., et al.: A global benchmark of algorithms for segmenting the left atrium from late gadolinium-enhanced cardiac magnetic resonance imaging. Med. Image Anal. **67**, 101832 (2021)

26. Yu, L., et al.: Automatic 3D cardiovascular MR segmentation with densely-connected volumetric ConvNets. In: Descoteaux, M., Maier-Hein, L., Franz, A., Jannin, P., Collins, D.L., Duchesne, S. (eds.) MICCAI 2017. LNCS, vol. 10434, pp. 287–295. Springer, Cham (2017). https://doi.org/10.1007/978-3-319-66185-8_33

27. Yu, L., Wang, S., Li, X., Fu, C.-W., Heng, P.-A.: Uncertainty-aware self-ensembling model for semi-supervised 3D left atrium segmentation. In: Shen, D., et al. (eds.) MICCAI 2019. LNCS, vol. 11765, pp. 605–613. Springer, Cham (2019). https://doi.org/10.1007/978-3-030-32245-8_67
28. Zhang, Y., Liao, Q., Yuan, L., Zhu, H., Xing, J., Zhang, J.: Exploiting shared knowledge from non-covid lesions for annotation-efficient covid-19 CT lung infection segmentation. IEEE J. Biomed. Health Inform. (2021)
29. Zhang, Y., Xiang, T., Hospedales, T.M., Lu, H.: Deep mutual learning. In: Proceedings of the IEEE Conference on Computer Vision and Pattern Recognition, pp. 4320–4328 (2018)
30. Zhang, Y., Yang, L., Chen, J., Fredericksen, M., Hughes, D.P., Chen, D.Z.: Deep adversarial networks for biomedical image segmentation utilizing unannotated images. In: Descoteaux, M., Maier-Hein, L., Franz, A., Jannin, P., Collins, D.L., Duchesne, S. (eds.) MICCAI 2017. LNCS, vol. 10435, pp. 408–416. Springer, Cham (2017). https://doi.org/10.1007/978-3-319-66179-7_47

# DPACN: Dual Prior-Guided Astrous Convolutional Network for Adhesive Pulmonary Nodules Segmentation on CT Sequence

Ning Xiao[1], Shichao Luo[1], Yan Qiang[1(✉)], Juanjuan Zhao[1], and Jianhong Lian[2]

[1] Taiyuan University of Technology, Taiyuan 030000, China
[2] Shanxi Province Cancer Hospital, Taiyuan 030000, China

**Abstract.** The segmentation of malignant nodules is crucial to pre-operative planning, while it adhere to lung tissue extremely, which leads to false positive too high. Considering inaccurate segmentation of adhesive pulmonary nodules, Dual prior-guided Astrous Convolutional Network (DPACN) is proposed to achieve coarse-to-fine nodules segmentation. In view of spatial continuity and visual similarity of pulmonary nodules in CT sequences, visual prior module is proposed to focus on the visual feature and location prior module is proposed to focus on the spatial feature. The result of dual prior concatenated into Astrous Convolutional Network to fine-tune previous result and obtain the more accurate nodules segmentation result of other slices. In order to verify the validity of our method, we conduct experiment on 1,200 adhesive pulmonary nodules. Our method yielded Dice coefficient of 87.57%, Volumetric Overlap Error of 4.86% and demonstrated that proposed method can distinguish pulmonary nodules and lung other tissue and segment adhesive nodules effectively.

**Keywords:** Adhesive pulmonary nodules · Sequence segmentation · Astrous convolution · Prior knowledge

## 1 Introduction

Precise segmentation of pulmonary nodules from Computed Tomography (CT) is significant for the clinical diagnosis, surgical planning and pathological research. 1) Segmentation is preparatory work of identification Region of Interest(RoI) for radiologists, such as to locate tumors, lesions and other abnormal tissues [9]. 2) For the evolution of chronic cancer, it is more beneficial to observe tumor growth and develop therapeutic strategies [1]. 3) The segmentation results can further help radiologists analyze pathological information and determine tumor characteristics.

Although segmentation of pulmonary nodule are widely studied, these methods are lack of explainable feature, diagnose objectivity and may bring about

© Springer Nature Switzerland AG 2021
H. Ma et al. (Eds.): PRCV 2021, LNCS 13021, pp. 560–569, 2021.
https://doi.org/10.1007/978-3-030-88010-1_47

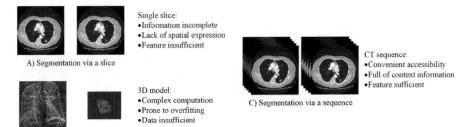

**Fig. 1.** Pulmonary nodule segmentation in different data dimensions. The advantages of using sequences lie on solving incomplete feature compare to single slice and reducing computation complexity compared to 3D modeling.

high false positive. 1) Radiologists just make annotations on key image instead of whole sequence, so most algorithm train models by treating each images as an independent sample [2] (as shown in Fig. 1). This approach misses explainable feature interaction among different images. 2) For some pulmonary nodules near the pleura and mediastinal, it required manual intervention by radiologists during segmentation, resulting in lacking of objectivity and consistency in the results [13]. 3) Pulmonary nodules are prone to adhere to lung tissue during the growth, the appearance of both on CT images is extremely analogous [4], which is likely to dis-segment lung tissues and cause high false positive.

Most of researchers proposed lots of automatic methods via Fully Convolutional Network (FCN), which can effectively improve consistency and reduce false positive. Despite the effective results achieved by these methods, the direct segmentation without fine-tuning has inferior accuracy in detail, which is lack of focus on nodules and makes it unconvincing clinically. 1) For pooling in FCN, while increasing the receptive field, it will also reduce the image size and lose some details [2]. 2) These end-to-end methods can achieve extending from image-level classification to pixel-level classification. For nodules segmentation, they focus on the whole images information instead of appearance and context information [17]. 3) A key to segmentation is distinguish the morphological feature from other tissue, which can generate more interpretable information which offer convincing evidence [7,11].

In this paper, we propose a Dual Prior-guided Astrous Convolutional Network (DPACN) for segmentation of adhesive pulmonary nodules and design a special loss function for the segmentation of tiny targets. Aiming at the characteristics of nodules, we employ ACN as main segmentation network (SegNet). To make better use of the spatial continuity of CT sequence, we utilize nodule sequence as input of network and design two types of prior module to capture rich contextual and visual representation [16,18], the spatial feature and visual feature of lesion extracted from continuous slices as prior guide to improve the segmentation result. The parameters composed of spatial feature and visual feature are used to control the behavior of the segmentation network.

Our main contributions can be summarized as follows:

(i) A coarse-to-fine segmentation network with dual prior was proposed to solve tiny target segmentation. The prior mechanism also can enhance the interpretability of feature representations of nodules segmentation.

(ii) Spatial prior module is designed to capture spatial feature, which build rich sequence context interdependencies. Visual prior module is proposed to learn the visual characteristic.

(iii) The loss function used in this paper takes into account the pixel imbalance between the tiny target and the background. It uses different weights to suppress network segmentation inefficiencies.

## 2    Dual Prior Astrous Convolutional Network

As show in Fig. 2, we propose the module-constrained-network, Dual prior-guided Astrous Convolutional Network which emphasizes the importance of morphological appearance and spatial location of pulmonary nodules on segmentation. We append two parallel prior modules on top of ACN. One is a visual prior module and the other is a location prior module. The dual prior module constrain segmentation results through feature weight allocation.

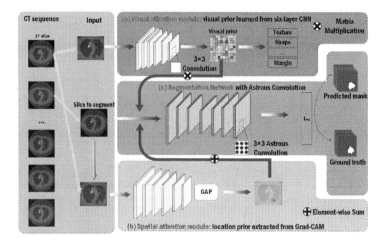

**Fig. 2.** A framework of proposed network algorithm. Given a nodule image, we propagate the image through different feature specific CNN and obtain spatial and visual feature. These representation is then feed to the segmentation network to constrain segmentation feature.

## 2.1  Segmentation Net

As well known, the basic structure in convolutional neural networks is convolution and pooling. The shallower the feature map in the network, the easier it is to represent tiny targets; however, the shallow feature cannot express semantic information sufficiently due to pooling operation. Therefore, in this paper, we use ACN as main segmentation network. The Astrous Convolution [8] is to increase the reception field via injecting holes into the standard convolutional map without pooling. Astrous convolution can achieve the pooling operation without losing the original information of the tiny targets. The design of each astrous convolutional block has a kernel size of $3 \times 3$ and each kernel has a dilation rate of 1.

## 2.2  Visual Prior Module

Previous work confirms that the representations in convolutional neural networks can capture richer semantic information [10,11]. Visual prior module using convolutional neural networks as the backbone is proposed to extract the visual characteristics of pulmonary nodules as the labels of lung nodules, such as shape, texture, speculation, lobulation and the contour information and extract the semantic feature of the nodule in the high-level original image through the visual prior module based on the six-layer convolutional neural network.

The visual prior module can learn various feature maps of pulmonary nodules. For the segmentation of pulmonary nodules, the visual prior module first learns the feature maps of the pulmonary nodules according to the visual characteristics of the pulmonary nodules. The result feature maps will be fed into the segmentation network as focus. The concatenate operation will be described in Sect. 2.4.

## 2.3  Location Prior Module

The spatial feature refers to the mutual spatial position or relative orientation relationship between objects with different semantics in the image. Compared to visual feature, the spatial feature of the image can reflect the characteristics of the targets contained in the image, especially when distinguishing some targets with similar visual characteristics.

As the nodules in CT sequence are often continuous in space and fixed in position, we introduce location prior module Class Activation Mapping (CAM) to extract the spatial features of nodules and feed results into the SegNet. Intuitively, CAM requires modifying the structure of the model with Global Average Pooling to replace the fully connected layer, the model needs to be retrained, so we employ Gradient-weighted CAM (Grad-CAMs) [12] to extract activation mapping of images.

## 2.4    Concatenate Strategy

After different feature maps are obtained through the visual prior module and the location prior module, we use the conditional batch normalization (CBN) [3,6] to add two feature maps to the input of the segmentation network. The CBN can be expressed by the following formula:

$$y = \gamma \otimes x \oplus \epsilon \tag{1}$$

where $x$ and $y$ are feature maps of input and output respectively, $\gamma$ and $\epsilon$ are visual prior mapping and location prior mapping produced by the prior module. $\otimes$ and $\oplus$ are matrix multiplication and element-wise sum. The CBN layer applies a scale-and-shift operation on the feature map. The visual characteristics of lung nodules often vary from those of other lung tissues, physicians often firstly observe the visual characteristics of the nodules, and the position of the same pulmonary nodule is relatively fixed. Therefore, the results produced by the visual prior module are used as the scaling parameters and location features is used as a shift parameter.

## 2.5    Loss Function

The loss function consists of three parts: segmentation loss $L_{seg}$, visual prior loss $L_{vis}$, location prior loss $L_{loc}$. Among them, the whole image is $C$, the predicted nodule area is represented by $A$ and the corresponding ground truth is represented by $B$ respectively. The optimized objective function is defined as follows:

$$L = L_{seg} + L_{vis} + L_{loc} \tag{2}$$

An improved segmentation loss function is as follows:

$$L_{seg} = C - \frac{A \bigcap B}{A \bigcap B + \alpha |A - B| + \beta |B - A|} - B(1 - A)^2 log A \tag{3}$$

At the same time, the losses of the dual prior modules respectively:

$$L_{vis} = -(ylog(p(y)) + (1 - y)log(1 - p(y))) \tag{4}$$

$$L_{loc} = -\frac{1}{|S_c|} log f_s(A) \tag{5}$$

For segmentation loss $L_{seg}$, the false positive and false negative can be adjusted via the magnitude of penalties $\alpha$ and $\beta$. $B(1 - A)^2 log A$ solve excessive regional difference between target and background. For visual prior loss $L_{vis}$, $y$ is the visual characteristics label, $p(y)$ is the predicted probability. For location prior loss $L_{loc}$, $S_c$ is region of nodule feature map generated by Grad-CAM, $f_s(A)$ represent probability that the predicted position output score for the network model belongs to the nodule.

# 3  Experiment and Results

To evaluate our proposed method, a series of experiments were performed on the data extracted from the National Lung Screening Trial (NLST) database. In the next section, we present our experimental results from implementation details, qualitative evaluation, quantitative comparison, and ablation study.

## 3.1  Dataset and Implementation

**Dataset.** The NLST dataset was initiated by the American College of Radiology Imaging Network. The experimental data were evaluated by a ten-fold cross-validation test. In this paper, 1,200 clinical cases of adhesive pulmonary nodules were selected as our experimental data, of which 1,080 cases were used as training data and 120 cases were used as test data. Specific lung nodule boundary were marked by experienced physicians from partner hospitals.

**Implementation.** For the input preprocessing of the visual prior module, we crop CT images into size of $64 \times 64$ as the input and characteristic features marked by the physician were extracted as labels. For the input preprocessing of the location prior module, we select same cropped images without augment and compute saliency map as spatial guide via Grad-CAMs. Figure 3 show some Grad-CAM results using the above method and the nodule region location is highlighted. When training SegNet, we use Adam optimizer to optimize it, the exponential decay rates $\beta_1$ and $\beta_2$ default to 0.9 and 0.999. The learning rate decreases according to the training round index which is $lr = 0.95^{epoch_{num}} * lr_0$. Initial learning rate $lr_0$ is set to 0.1 For loss function, the magnitude of false positive $\alpha$ set to 0.3 and magnitude of false negative $\beta$ set to 0.7 respectively according to multiple experiments. The experimental platform is based on Intel Xeon, the memory is 32 GB and the GPU is NVIDIA TITAN.

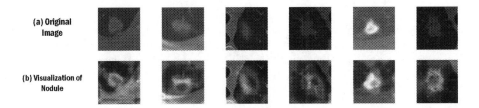

(a) Original Image

(b) Visualization of Nodule

**Fig. 3.** The Grad-CAM visualization of pulmonary nodules. Given the nodule images, we observe that the highlighted region vary across predicted images. Grad-CAM can find the spatial feature and highlight discriminative images regions used for nodules segmentation.

## 3.2    Qualitative Evaluation

In order to evaluate the overall performance of the proposed method for adhesive pulmonary nodule segmentation, we compare our method with particle swarm optimization-self-generating neural network (PSO-SGNN) [19], Central Focused Convolutional Neural Networks (CF-CNN) [14], 3D Conditional Generative Network (3DCGAN) [5], Deep Active Self-Paced Learning (DASPL) [15].

Figure 4 exhibits the segmentation results of different methods on our dataset. From the overall segmentation results, all segmentation results are still good. However, some methods often confuse the pleura, blood vessels with pulmonary nodules when segmenting, resulting in a segmentation result with high false positive. Compared them, our approach is more robust to nodule segmentation.

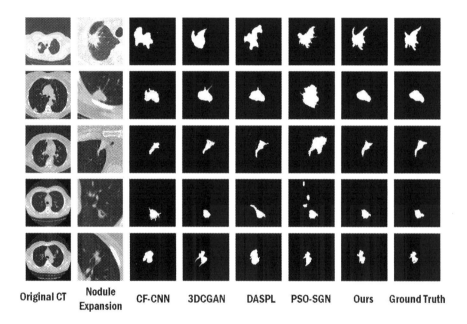

| Original CT | Nodule Expansion | CF-CNN | 3DCGAN | DASPL | PSO-SGN | Ours | Ground Truth |

**Fig. 4.** The qualitative results of our method compared with four other methods on dataset. From the overall segmentation results, all segmentation results are still good. However, some methods often confuse the pleura, blood vessels with pulmonary nodules when segmenting.

## 3.3    Quantitative Comparison

We performed comparative experiments on NLST and used a variety of evaluation indicators, Dice coefficients, Recall, Precision, Hausdorff distance, and VOE to quantitatively prove the effectiveness of our method as shown in Table 1.

From Table 1, we observed all our indicators are superior than other methods except Recall which is inferior that of PSO-SGN. After analyzing the experiment result, we found our method didn't segment some pleural nodule well due to its large margin adhere to lung.

**Table 1.** Comparisons of our method and four other methods on test dataset.Dice coefficient, Recall, Precision, Hausdorff distance and VOE are used to evaluate to the performance.

|  | Dice (%) | Recall (%) | Precision (%) | Hausdorff distance | VOE |
|---|---|---|---|---|---|
| CF-CNN | 84.53 | 89.35 | 83.85 | 6.3946 | 6.27 |
| 3DCGAN | 76.21 | 89.71 | 70.58 | 6.2105 | 24.45 |
| DASPL | 79.19 | 90.78 | 71.76 | 5.8042 | 26.33 |
| PSO-SGN | 68.78 | **94.60** | 57.81 | 14.7292 | 30.98 |
| OURS | **87.57** | 93.97 | **86.84** | **4.3829** | **4.89** |

## 3.4   Ablation Study

In order to verify the effectiveness of the prior model on the segmentation network, we also studied the segmentation results of different modules in the algorithm, and performed segmentation experiments without prior and using only single prior as shown in Table 2.

**Table 2.** Ablation experiment of our methods on test dataset.

|  | Dice | Recall | Precision | Hausdorff distance | VOE |
|---|---|---|---|---|---|
| SegNet | 68.62 | 60.89 | 52.24 | 11.5364 | 27.94 |
| SegNet with visual prior | 79.69 | 74.04 | 72.20 | 9.2724 | 8.25 |
| SegNet with location prior | 70.43 | 62.25 | 62.16 | 11.2352 | 14.71 |
| SegNet with dual prior | **87.57** | **93.97** | **86.84** | **4.3829** | **4.89** |

The experimental results show that the influence of the visual prior module on the segmentation network is higher than that of the location prior module. The location prior module has a small impact on the segmentation result of the segmentation network. The reason is that convolutional neural networks are mainly segmented according to the shape of the target in the CT sequence, and the spatial position of the target is only helpful in distinguishing objects that are adhere to the target.

## 4   Conclusion

The growth of pulmonary nodules is often accompanied by invasiveness and adhere to surrounding lung tissue structures. Aiming at the problems of conventional algorithms when segmenting adhesive lung nodules, which the segmentation results are poor and the boundary is uncertain, we proposed a DPACN that perform coarse-to-fine segmentation of pulmonary nodules. It employs conditional batch normalization to concatenate the visual prior feature map and location prior map of pulmonary nodules to the main segmentation network to accommodate the final segmentation result. For loss function, we used improved Diss loss to adapt to tiny target segmentation and reduce high false positive. In order to verify the capability of the proposed method, we performed comparative experiments and ablation experiments on 1,200 adhesive pulmonary nodules extracted from NLST. The results from different indicators show the strength of the proposed method in adhesive pulmonary nodule segmentation compared to four state-of-the-art methods.

## References

1. Chen, K., Li, B., Tian, L.-F., Zhu, W.-B., Bao, Y.-H.: Vessel attachment nodule segmentation using integrated active contour model based on fuzzy speed function and shape-intensity joint Bhattacharya distance. Sig. Process. **103**, 273–284 (2014)
2. Chen, L.C., Papandreou, G., Kokkinos, I., Murphy, K., Yuille, A.L.: DeepLab: semantic image segmentation with deep convolutional nets, atrous convolution, and fully connected CRFs. IEEE Trans. Pattern Anal. Mach. Intell. **40**(4), 834–848 (2016)
3. De Vries, H., Strub, F., Mary, J., Larochelle, H., Pietquin, O., Courville, A.C.: Modulating early visual processing by language. In: Advances in Neural Information Processing Systems, pp. 6594–6604 (2017)
4. Garzelli, L., et al.: Improving the prediction of lung adenocarcinoma invasive component on CT: value of a vessel removal algorithm during software segmentation of subsolid nodules. Eur. J. Radiol. **100**, 58–65 (2018)
5. Jin, D., Xu, Z., Tang, Y., Harrison, A.P., Mollura, D.J.: CT-realistic lung nodule simulation from 3D conditional generative adversarial networks for robust lung segmentation. In: Frangi, A.F., Schnabel, J.A., Davatzikos, C., Alberola-López, C., Fichtinger, G. (eds.) MICCAI 2018. LNCS, vol. 11071, pp. 732–740. Springer, Cham (2018). https://doi.org/10.1007/978-3-030-00934-2_81
6. Leopold, H.A., Orchard, J., Zelek, J.S., Lakshminarayanan, V.: PixelBNN: augmenting the PixelCNN with batch normalization and the presentation of a fast architecture for retinal vessel segmentation. J. Imaging **5**, 2 (2017)
7. Liu, D., et al.: Unsupervised instance segmentation in microscopy images via panoptic domain adaptation and task re-weighting. In: 2020 IEEE/CVF Conference on Computer Vision and Pattern Recognition (CVPR) (2020)
8. Liu, M., Zhang, C., Zhang, Z. Multi-scale deep convolutional nets with attention model and conditional random fields for semantic image segmentation. In: 2019 2nd International Conference on Signal Processing and Machine Learning, SPML 2019 (2019)
9. MacMahon, H., et al.: Guidelines for management of incidental pulmonary nodules detected on CT images: from the Fleischner society 2017. Radiology **284**(1), 228–243 (2017)
10. Meraj, T., Rauf, H.T., Zahoor, S., Hassan, A., Shoaib, U.: Lung nodules detection using semantic segmentation and classification with optimal features. Neural Comput. Appl. **33**, 10737–10750 (2020)
11. Munir, K., Elahi, H., Ayub, A., Frezza, F., Rizzi, A.: Cancer diagnosis using deep learning: a bibliographic review. Cancers **11**(9), 1235 (2019)

12. Selvaraju, R.R., Cogswell, M., Das, A., Vedantam, R., Parikh, D., Batra, D.: Grad-CAM: visual explanations from deep networks via gradient-based localization. In: Proceedings of the IEEE International Conference on Computer Vision, pp. 618–626 (2017)
13. Sun, Y., Wang, J. Automatic method for lung segmentation with juxta-pleural nodules from thoracic CT based on border separation and correction. In: 2016 9th International Congress on Image and Signal Processing, BioMedical Engineering and Informatics (CISP-BMEI), pp. 330–335. IEEE (2016)
14. Wang, S., et al.: Central focused convolutional neural networks: developing a data-driven model for lung nodule segmentation. Med. Image Anal. **40**, 172–183 (2017)
15. Wang, W., Lu, Y., Wu, B., Chen, T., Chen, D.Z., Wu, J.: Deep active self-paced learning for accurate pulmonary nodule segmentation. In: Frangi, A.F., Schnabel, J.A., Davatzikos, C., Alberola-López, C., Fichtinger, G. (eds.) MICCAI 2018. LNCS, vol. 11071, pp. 723–731. Springer, Cham (2018). https://doi.org/10.1007/978-3-030-00934-2_80
16. Wang, Z., Xu, J., Liu, L., Zhu, F., Shao, L.: RANet: ranking attention network for fast video object segmentation. In: Proceedings of the IEEE International Conference on Computer Vision, pp. 3978–3987 (2019)
17. Xu, H., Gao, Y., Yu, F., Darrell, T.: End-to-end learning of driving models from large-scale video datasets. In: Proceedings of the IEEE Conference on Computer Vision and Pattern Recognition, pp. 2174–2182 (2017)
18. Zhang, P., Li, J., Wang, Y., Pan, J.: Domain adaptation for medical image segmentation: a meta-learning method. J. Imaging **7**(2), 31 (2021)
19. Zhao, J.-J., Ji, G.-H., Xia, Y., Zhang, X.-L.: Cavitary nodule segmentation in computed tomography images based on self-generating neural networks and particle swarm optimisation. Int. J. Bio-Inspired Comput. **7**(1), 62–67 (2015)

# Face Anti-spoofing Based on Cooperative Pose Analysis

Poyu Lin[1,2], Xiaoyu Wang[1], Jiansheng Chen[1,2,3(✉)], Huimin Ma[2],
and Hongbing Ma[1]

[1] Department of Electronic Engineering, Tsinghua University, Beijing 100084, China
[2] School of Computer and Communication Engineering, University of Science
and Technology Beijing, Beijing 100083, China
jschen@ustb.edu.cn
[3] Beijing National Research Center for Information Science and Technology,
Tsinghua University, Beijing 100084, China

**Abstract.** Face anti-spoofing has been vital to preventing face recognition systems from fake faces. However, most state-of-the-art passive methods treat face anti-spoofing as a classification problem, relying on purposive databases and well-designed backend algorithms. In this paper, we propose a novel active face anti-spoofing framework named *Cooperative Pose Analysis* (CPA), in which a higher cooperation degree is required in the manner of head pose changes. And we propose a new pose representation named *Pose Aware Quadrilateral* (PAQ), which is sensitive to pose changes of living faces and easy to identify spoof faces such as printed and twisted photographs. The proposed PAQ is easily accessed by utilizing a lightweight projective Spatial Transformer Network [11]. The whole system does not require much computational or storage resources and is easy to deploy and use. Experiments on both datasets and human subjects are conducted and indicate the effectiveness of our work.

**Keywords:** Face anti-spoofing · Liveness detection · Spatial transformer network

## 1 Introduction

Face recognition has been an essential topic in computer vision research and applied to various scenarios due to its convenience and high accuracy. But spoof attacks may happen in practical application scene, which deceives the recognition systems and bring security risks. As a result, face anti-spoofing techniques are introduced to defend face spoofs.

Existing approaches could be divided into passive back-end methods that rely on algorithms and active ways that require the user's cooperation. There are lots of researches focusing on the former type. Methods based on hand-crafted features [4,8,9,13,23] and CNNs [1,10,14,16,22,29] have been proposed.

© Springer Nature Switzerland AG 2021
H. Ma et al. (Eds.): PRCV 2021, LNCS 13021, pp. 570–580, 2021.
https://doi.org/10.1007/978-3-030-88010-1_48

input images

pose
representations

**Fig. 1.** Differences in PAQ changes between real faces and printed faces. The real faces and the printed attack photos come from CASIA-Webface [30] and NUAA dataset [25].

In the meanwhile, datasets have been established for this task, including NUAA [25], CASIA-MFSD [27], Replay-Attack [7] and OULU-NPU [5], etc. Current passive methods are trained on the aforementioned datasets and tested on intra- or inter-datasets, but are not comprehensively judged in the real scenarios. In addition, complex network architectures and long-sequence inputs are essential commonly. On the contrary, active methods are frequently adopted in practice. The subjects are instructed to make several reactions to prove their liveness, e.g. open mouths or shake heads. The pre-set instructions are constant so that the reaction patterns could be easily obtained. Thus they are weak in detecting pre-recorded video attacks. Aiming to solve these existing flaws in current approaches and resolve the contradiction between research and applications, we propose an active face anti-spoofing method. The subject's more proactive cooperation is deterministic to the anti-spoofing process.

The direct motivation is that a living face has a faculty of cooperating with the face anti-spoofing system and changing its pose precisely as is required. For picking up the pose clues, We propose a face pose representation named Pose-Aware Quadrilateral(PAQ), which is only sensitive to 3D face pose changes rather than printed 2D planar or curved faces. The comparison is shown in Fig. 1. PAQ is generated by making use of the output transformation parameters of a projective Spatial Transformer Network (STN) [11]. When a living face changes its pose in the 3-dimensional space, its PAQ change differently from those of a planar or curved face. And this characteristic can help distinguish living faces from the spoof ones. We propose an active face anti-spoofing method called Cooperative Pose Analysis (CPA). In the proposed CPA framework, the subject is required to turn its head and make its real-time PAQ and a target PAQ as identical as possible. And in practice, to improve the robustness and ensure security, we set a series of target PAQs for the user to cooperate. The pre-set target PAQs are random and have a wide range of variation, so it is theoretically difficult to record a video beforehand and deceive the system. In order to detect multi-pose video attacks, we analyze the cooperation manner of living faces and set a cooperation coefficient to ensure the initiative of the cooperation.

In summary, our contributions include:

- We design a face anti-spoofing framework Cooperative Pose Analysis, which is safer than existing active methods, owing to the unpredictability of the target PAQs.
- We extract our face pose representation named Pose-Aware Quadrilateral from STN and examine that it can express the meaning of Euler angles. It serves as the target of the cooperation process, and the similarity of poses could be easily calculated.
- We compare the subject's PAQs with the target ones in real-time, using STN that requires no extra face anti-spoofing datasets and few computational resources.

## 2 Related Work

In this section, we review previous face anti-spoofing works, starting from the passive methods. Handcrafted descriptors have been adopted for the face anti-spoofing task, including LBP [8,9], HOG [4], SURF [13], SIFT [23], etc. Subsequently, CNN-based approaches have been developed [1,14,22]. For the sake of robustness to illumination and shadow variation, [2,3] convert input images into other color spaces such as HSV and YCbCr and trying to seek a solution.

There are researchers making use of temporal cues to detect spoof faces. Early attempts try to recognize a living face via detecting eye-blinking [21] and micro actions of mouth and lips [12,24]. In [10,29], multi-frame inputs are fed into 3D CNN and LSTM architectures to extract temporal features for face anti-spoofing. There are also methods adopting auxiliary supervisions, such as rPPG [15,16,19], depth [16,26] to make further improvement.

Although there are lesser research on active methods than passive ones, we review some active face anti-spoofing approaches. According to [18,20], the system asks the person in front of the camera to perform a few simple actions, including blinking, nodding, smiling, and head or facial movements.

## 3 Methodology

Detailed information will be given about our novel proposed Cooperative Pose Analysis (CPA) framework and its core detection method, Pose Aware Quadrilateral (PAQ).

### 3.1 System Design

During the face anti-spoofing process, the subject is required to turn its head and reach a series of target PAQs given by our instruction. And for CPA system, the process flow is as Fig. 2. Firstly the face region of the input frame (detected and cropped by FaceBoxes [31]) is fed into the STN model and the output is an 8-dimensional transformation vector, which turns into PAQ later. Then the

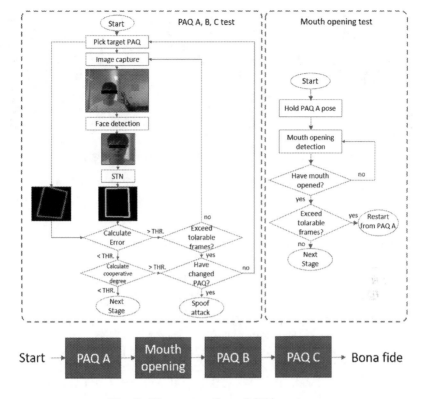

**Fig. 2.** The process flow of CPA system.

PAQ is compared with the target one. If the difference becomes less than the threshold, the cooperation degree estimation starts, or the subject fails after $c$ frames have been received (in our case, $c = 180$). The cooperation degree estimation is judged by whether the motion trajectory of the subject changes toward the target PAQ.

The process above can be looped arbitrarily to increase the reliability and the difficulty (we loop the process 3 times). Pre-collected PAQs were divided into 3 levels, A to C. Details are in Table 1. We use different levels of PAQs for each loop, respectively. Moreover, it is flexible to make changes for different application scenarios. For example, we insert a mouth test module to detect

**Table 1.** About how PAQs divided into 3 standard categories

| PAQ | Pitch | Yaw | Roll | Remarks |
|---|---|---|---|---|
| A | $(-20°, 20°)$ | $(-10°, 10°)$ | $(-10°, 10°)$ | – |
| B | $(-30°, 30°)$ | $(-25°, 25°)$ | $(-20°, 20°)$ | Not in A |
| C | $(-40°, 40°)$ | $(-45°, 45°)$ | $(-30°, 30°)$ | Not in A, B |

**Fig. 3.** STN image process. Row 1: input images, row 2: PAQ of each subject, row 3: STN output images

mouth open and close (a simple 3-layer CNN), maintaining the flexibility that still has room for preventing potential mask attack.

### 3.2 STN for Automatic Face Alignment

Spatial Transformer Network (STN) was proposed in [11] in 2014 to enhance the invariance to 2D spatial transforms robustness of CNNs. Tradition CNNs outputting different features after input image is transformed, while STN could automatically apply a transformation to the input image.

STN consists of a localization network, a grid generator and a sampler. Image or feature map $U$ is input into The localization network before transformation and the transformation parameters $\Theta$ is output. The grid generator creates a set of grids according to transformation parameters $\Theta$ of each source coordinates. The sampler samples pixels from the feature maps $U$ at the coordinates of the grids and produces the output image $V$.

The original paper [11] only analyzed and experimented on the affine transformation version of STN. For the projective transformation, the coordinate generating process can be expressed by Eq. 1. $(x_i^t, y_i^t, 1)$ represents the ith point of output image, while its corresponding point in input image is $(x_i^s, y_i^s, 1)$ $A$ to $H$ are eight transformation parameters $\Theta$ and $z_i^s = Gx_i^t + Hy_i^t + 1$.

$$\begin{pmatrix} x_i^s \\ y_i^s \\ 1 \end{pmatrix} = \frac{1}{z_i^s} \begin{pmatrix} A & B & C \\ D & E & F \\ G & H & 1 \end{pmatrix} \begin{pmatrix} x_i^t \\ y_i^t \\ 1 \end{pmatrix} \tag{1}$$

In [32], Zhong *et al.* integrates a projective STN with a recognition network and training the entire network end-to-end without extra supervisions except for the identification information. STN automatically transforms the input face image to the most conducive form for recognition, which can be considered a kind of alignment. The results after STN are shown in Fig. 3. The second row of the figure is the visualized result of the projective transformation matrix. We define it as a pose representation which can be applied to liveness detection, Pose Aware Quadrilateral (PAQ).

## 3.3 Pose Aware Quadrilateral

As mentioned above, it has been proved in [32] that a projective Spatial Transform Network could align the input face image automatically and we reshape the transformation parameter vector into a $3 \times 3$ projective transform matrix. And it could be visually illustrated by simply performing the transformation to a square. Then a quadrilateral is obtained as the pose representation, namely Pose-Aware Quadrilateral(PAQ).

More descriptions are given to PAQ about its capability to discriminate different face pose. Firstly, different poses, of which the porjective transformation parameters must be different, leads to differences in the shape of PAQ obtained. Here introduce Euler angles, $(pitch, yaw, roll)$, which is a set of three angles to describe the orientation of a rigid body with respect to a fixed coordinate system. Intuitively the ratio of the left edge to the right edge represents the yaw angle of the face. It rises as the face turns from left to right. Similarly the ratio of the top edge to the bottom represents the pitch angle. On the other hand, the change of roll angle reflects in the slopes of four edges. Besides, another important characteristic of this quadrilateral is that its shape is only sensitive to 3D face pose changes. It is shown in Fig. 1.

## 3.4 PAQ Similarity Measurement

In our system design, the subject needs to complete the active of the three target poses, that is, making their real-time PAQ close enough to the corresponding target PAQ. We propose two metrics to detect spoof attacks in our CPA system, for PAQs and cooperation time respectively.

For PAQs, we define the error in two ways. The first one is directly calculating the Euclidean distances between their corresponding vertices, that is:

$$E_1 = \sum_{i=0}^{3} \sqrt{(x_i^s - x_i^t)^2 + (y_i^s - y_i^t)^2} \tag{2}$$

Here $x$ and $y$ indicate coordinates and $s$ and $t$ represent the subject's real-time PAQ and target PAQ. This formula is simple and intuitive, but effective under most circumstances. Besides, We also introduced a couple of formula for estimating Euler angles to further improve fault tolerance.

$$E_2 = \| \sqrt{\frac{(x_0^t - x_2^t)^2 + (y_0^t - y_2^t)^2}{(x_1^t - x_3^t)^2 + (y_1^t - y_3^t)^2}} - \sqrt{\frac{(x_0^s - x_2^s)^2 + (y_0^s - y_2^s)^2}{(x_1^s - x_3^s)^2 + (y_1^s - y_3^s)^2}} \| \tag{3}$$

$$E_3 = \| \frac{(y_1^t + y_3^t) - (y_0^t + y_2^t)}{(x_1^t + x_3^t) - (x_0^t + x_2^t)} - \frac{(y_1^s + y_3^s) - (y_0^s + y_2^s)}{(x_1^s + x_3^s) - (x_0^s + x_2^s)} \| \tag{4}$$

As described in Sect. 3.3, the ratio of the left and the right edges' lengths shown in Eq. (3) indicates the yaw angle of the face. Similarly, Eq. (4) represents the pitch angle by calculating the slope of midpoints of the left and the right edges.

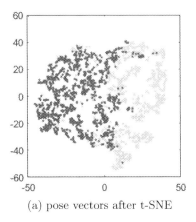
(a) pose vectors after t-SNE

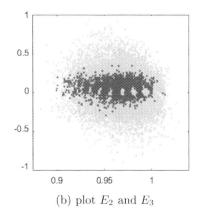
(b) plot $E_2$ and $E_3$

**Fig. 4.** Visualization of three error formula. Living faces and printed photos are represented respectively by yellow and purple dots. (Color figure online)

However, the change of the PAQ caused by pitch angle is not as obvious as the previous two, so we did not list another formula for the pitch angle. In practice, the total criterion is:

$$E_1 < THR_1 \vee (E_2 < THR_2 \wedge E_3 < THR_3) \tag{5}$$

## 4  Experiment

In this section we present experiment results of the CAP framework. It is worth noting that there exist no appropriate datasets and metrics to evaluate our method, because the subject shall pass the test only if it cooperates with the system actively. Under this circumstance we design methods to evaluate the proposed CPA framework, consisting of two parts: theoretical experiment and applied experiment.

### 4.1  PAQ Discriminability Test

Here we choose 1500 images randomly from CASIA-Webface dataset as the positive samples, and 1500 printed attack images from NUAA dataset to be the negative samples. We verify the ability of PAQ to distinguish between living and non-living from visualization and quantitative aspects. It is important to note that this part is only used to verify the discriminability, and the actual application framework is shown in Fig. 2. Discriminant Eq. (5) is combined by location condition Eq. (2) and Euler angles condition Eq. (3, 4). Figure 4(a) adopted t-SNE [17] dimension-reduction algorithm and visualized the distribution. And Fig. 4(b) presents the distribution on the yaw factor Eq. (3) and the roll factor Eq. (4). These results show that the distribution of printed photos is narrower than real image. Real human can cooperate with the instructions of the system

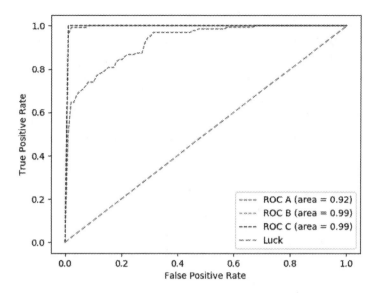

**Fig. 5.** The Receiver Operating Characteristic curves of the SVMs trained for binary classification between negative samples from NUAA and different positive sample sets.

to actively change its PAQ to reach a location that is difficult to reach by printed photo attack.

In order to simulate the CPA process, we take respectively the A, B and C target PAQs as positive samples, and select equal numbers of negative samples from the NUAA dataset. Then a Gauss kernel SVM is trained and adopted to classify them under the 5-fold cross validation setting. The classification accuracy goes from 0.876 (PAQ A), 0.982 (PAQ B), up to 0.995 (PAQ C). And ROC curves is shown in Fig. 5.

### 4.2  CPA System Test

In this test, the only positive samples are real subjects. Volunteers participate in the experiment after the fundamental use means of the CPA system are taught. 59 attempts were made in total. Negative samples include three categories: 1. Printed attack, of which we prepared three different postures, the front, the left and the right side face. We hold photos and try to pass the test by rotating, bending and change the orientation of the photos. 2. Natural state video attack. We adopted videos from the YouTube Face Database (YTF) [28] as the replay attack. Note that we did not use the video in the liveness detection datasets here. Because OULU-NPU [5], SiW [16] and other video attack datasets ensure that the positive and negative samples look as close as possible, the poses of faces do not change. 3. Multi-pose video attack. In view of the characteristics of the designed system, we recorded videos that combined opening mouth and continuously changing poses randomly.

Then we calculate the metrics, including Attack Presentation Classification Error Rate (APCER), Bona Fide Presentation Classification Error Rate (BPCER) and their average, Average Classification Error Rate (ACER) [6], and present them in Table 2. Besides, for the two types of video attack tests, we further counted the rejection reasons in Table 3 to analyze the role of each module of the system. $X1, X2, X3$ are used here to refer to PAQ $X(X = A, B, C)$: 1. matching timeout twice, 2. the cooperation degree fails twice, 3. matching timeout and the cooperation degree each once. $M$ refers mouth test fails twice (Table 3).

**Table 2.** results of the applied experiment.

|  | Attempts | Acceptd | APCER | BPCER |
|---|---|---|---|---|
| Living human | 59 | 59 | – | 0.00% |
| Printed photos | 15 | 0 | 0.00% | – |
| YTF videos | 3425 | 1 | 0.02% | – |
| Multi-pose | 1000 | 15 | 1.50% | – |

**Table 3.** Statistics on the rejection reasons

|  | A1 | A2 | A3 | M | B1 | B2 | B3 | C1 | C2 | C3 |
|---|---|---|---|---|---|---|---|---|---|---|
| YTF videos | 2038 | 19 | 72 | 1094 | 136 | 0 | 0 | 65 | 0 | 0 |
| Multi-pose | 0 | 577 | 0 | 214 | 0 | 26 | 158 | 2 | 0 | 8 |

**Table 4.** Estimation of the system complexity

|  | Faceboxes | STN | Mouth test module | Total |
|---|---|---|---|---|
| FLOPs | 0.277G | 0.119G | 0.021G | 0.417G |
| Params | 1.007M | 1.632M | 0.618M | 3.257M |
| AvgTime | 0.022 s | 0.003 s | 0.002 s | 0.077 s* |

* The total computing time, including PAQ A, B, C and mouth test.

## 5   Conclusion

We propose a novel Cooperative Pose Analysis framework for face anti-spoofing. It does not rely on specific datasets as much as existing methods traditional passive methods, and its required poses are not as predictable as existing active methods. And we utilize a projective STN model to calculate the pose representations, named Pose-Aware Quadrilaterals. The proposed CPA framework is flexible for different scenarios with little computational and resource cost. A series of experiments are conducted and indicate the effectiveness of our method. We have run the demo on Ubuntu and Android.

**Acknowledgement.** This work is supported by the National Natural Science Foundation of China (No. 61673234, No. U20B2062), and Beijing Science and Technology Planning Project (No. Z191100007419001).

# References

1. Atoum, Y., et al.: Face anti-spoofing using patch and depth-based CNNs. In: IJCB, pp. 319–328 (2017)
2. Boulkenafet, Z., et al.: Face spoofing detection using colour texture analysis. IEEE Trans. Inf. Forensics Secur. **11**(8), 1818–1830 (2016)
3. Boulkenafet, Z., et al.: Face anti-spoofing based on color texture analysis. In: ICIP, pp. 2636–2640 (2015)
4. Boulkenafet, Z., et al.: Face antispoofing using speeded-up robust features and fisher vector encoding. IEEE Signal Process. Lett. **24**(2), 141–145 (2016)
5. Boulkenafet, Z., et al.: OULU-NPU: a mobile face presentation attack database with real-world variations. In: FG, pp. 612–618 (2017)
6. Busch, C.: Standards for biometric presentation attack detection. In: Marcel, S., Nixon, M., Fierrez, J., Evans, N. (eds.) Handbook of Biometric Anti-Spoofing, pp. 503–514. Springer, Cham (2019). https://doi.org/10.1007/978-3-319-92627-8_22
7. Chingovska, I., et al.: On the effectiveness of local binary patterns in face anti-spoofing. In: BIOSIG, pp. 1–7 (2012)
8. de Freitas Pereira, T., Anjos, A., De Martino, J.M., Marcel, S.: *LBP – TOP* based countermeasure against face spoofing attacks. In: Park, J.-I., Kim, J. (eds.) ACCV 2012. LNCS, vol. 7728, pp. 121–132. Springer, Heidelberg (2013). https://doi.org/10.1007/978-3-642-37410-4_11
9. de Freitas Pereira, T., et al.: Can face anti-spoofing countermeasures work in a real world scenario? In: ICB, pp. 1–8 (2013)
10. Gan, J., et al.: 3D convolutional neural network based on face anti-spoofing. In: ICMIP, pp. 1–5 (2017)
11. Jaderberg, M., et al.: Spatial transformer networks. In: NIPS 28, pp. 2017–2025 (2015)
12. Kollreider, K., et al.: Real-time face detection and motion analysis with application in "liveness" assessment. IEEE Trans. Inf. Forensics Secur. **2**(3), 548–558 (2007)
13. Komulainen, J., et al.: Context based face anti-spoofing. In: BTAS, pp. 1–8 (2013)
14. Li, L., et al.: An original face anti-spoofing approach using partial convolutional neural network. In: IPTA, pp. 1–6 (2016)
15. Liu, S., Yuen, P.C., Zhang, S., Zhao, G.: 3D mask face anti-spoofing with remote photoplethysmography. In: Leibe, B., Matas, J., Sebe, N., Welling, M. (eds.) ECCV 2016. LNCS, vol. 9911, pp. 85–100. Springer, Cham (2016). https://doi.org/10.1007/978-3-319-46478-7_6
16. Liu, Y., et al.: Learning deep models for face anti-spoofing: binary or auxiliary supervision. In: CVPR, pp. 389–398 (2018)
17. Maaten, L.V.D., Hinton, G.: Visualizing data using t-SNE. J. Mach. Learn. Res. **9**, 2579–2605 (2008)
18. Maksymenko, S.: Anti-spoofing techniques for face recognition solutions. [EB/OL] (2020)
19. Nowara, E.M., et al.: PPGSecure: biometric presentation attack detection using photopletysmograms. In: FG, pp. 56–62 (2017)
20. Nyheter: Face anti-spoofing methods in face recognition systems. [EB/OL] (2019)

21. Pan, G., et al.: Eyeblink-based anti-spoofing in face recognition from a generic webcamera. In: ICCV, pp. 1–8 (2007)
22. Patel, K., Han, H., Jain, A.K.: Cross-database face antispoofing with robust feature representation. In: You, Z., Zhou, J., Wang, Y., Sun, Z., Shan, S., Zheng, W., Feng, J., Zhao, Q. (eds.) CCBR 2016. LNCS, vol. 9967, pp. 611–619. Springer, Cham (2016). https://doi.org/10.1007/978-3-319-46654-5_67
23. Patel, K., et al.: Secure face unlock: spoof detection on smartphones. IEEE Trans. Inf. Forensics Secur. **11**(10), 2268–2283 (2016)
24. Shao, R., et al.: Deep convolutional dynamic texture learning with adaptive channel-discriminability for 3d mask face anti-spoofing. In: IJCB, pp. 748–755 (2017)
25. Tan, X., Li, Y., Liu, J., Jiang, L.: Face liveness detection from a single image with sparse low rank bilinear discriminative model. In: Daniilidis, K., Maragos, P., Paragios, N. (eds.) ECCV 2010. LNCS, vol. 6316, pp. 504–517. Springer, Heidelberg (2010). https://doi.org/10.1007/978-3-642-15567-3_37
26. Wang, Z., et al.: Deep spatial gradient and temporal depth learning for face anti-spoofing. In: CVPR, pp. 5042–5051 (2020)
27. Wen, D., et al.: Face spoof detection with image distortion analysis. IEEE Trans. Inf. Forensics Secur. **10**(4), 746–761 (2015)
28. Wolf, L., et al.: Face recognition in unconstrained videos with matched background similarity. In: CVPR 2011, pp. 529–534 (2011)
29. Yang, X., et al.: Face anti-spoofing: model matters, so does data. In: CVPR, pp. 3507–3516 (2019)
30. Yi, D., et al.: Learning face representation from scratch. arXiv preprint arXiv:1411.7923 (2014)
31. Zhang, S., et al.: Faceboxes: a CPU real-time face detector with high accuracy. In: IJCB, pp. 1–9 (2017)
32. Zhong, Y., et al.: Toward end-to-end face recognition through alignment learning. IEEE Signal Process. Lett. **24**(8), 1213–1217 (2017)

# A Dark and Bright Channel Prior Guided Deep Network for Retinal Image Quality Assessment

Ziwen Xu, Beiji Zou, and Qing Liu[✉]

School of Computer Science and Engineering, Central South University,
Changsha 410083, China
{xuziwen,bjzou,qingliucs}@csu.edu.cn

**Abstract.** Retinal image quality assessment is an essential task in the diagnosis of retinal diseases. Recently, there are emerging deep models to grade quality of retinal images. Current state-of-the-arts either directly transfer classification networks originally designed for natural images to quality classification of retinal images or introduce extra image quality priors via multiple CNN branches or independent CNNs. This paper proposes a dark and bright channel prior guided deep network for retinal image quality assessment called GuidedNet. Specifically, the dark and bright channel priors are embedded into the start layer of network to improve the discriminate ability of deep features. Experimental results on the public retinal image quality dataset Eye-Quality demonstrate the effectiveness of the proposed GuidedNet.

**Keywords:** Retinal image quality assessment · Deep network · Dark channel prior · Bright channel prior

## 1 Introduction

High-quality retinal images are required for the diagnosis of diabetic retinopathy, glaucoma and other retinal disorders [1,2]. They facilitate ophthalmologists make correct clinical decisions efficiently. On the contrary, low-quality images may confuse ophthalmologists. What is worse, for computer-aided retinal image analysis systems which commonly are designed with high-quality retinal images, low quality retinal images would be a catastrophe. Thus it would be desired to automaticaly assess the retinal image quality and filter low-quality images before performing downstream tasks. Clinically, retinal image quality assessment (Retinal-IQA) is performed by a well trained optometrist manually, which heavily depends on operator's experience and is time-consuming. To improve the efficiency of retinal image acquisition, automated Retinal-IQA becomes necessary.

The goal of automated image quality assessment (IQA) is to grade images in terms of quality measures. According to type of image, IQA can be subdivided into natural image quality assessment (Natural-IQA) [3–5], Retinal-IQA [6,7],

© Springer Nature Switzerland AG 2021
H. Ma et al. (Eds.): PRCV 2021, LNCS 13021, pp. 581–592, 2021.
https://doi.org/10.1007/978-3-030-88010-1_49

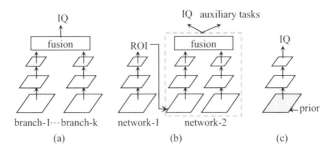

**Fig. 1.** Comparison of different CNN architectures combining priors for Retinal-IQA. (a) Combining priors via multiple branches. (b) Combining priors via multiple independent networks and branches. (c) Our proposed prior guided single branch network.

etc. Most IQA methods are designed for natural images, however, Natural-IQA methods may be not suitable for Retinal-IQA. The reason is that Natural-IQA methods usually rely on the assumption that high-quality natural images have certain statistics which can be damaged by low-quality factors. However, these statistics are not consistent with those of retinal images. Current state-of-the-art Retinal-IQA methods solve it with modern CNNs as they have achieved huge successes in the field of computer vision. Some works such as [6] and [7] directly fine-tune CNNs originally designed for natural scene image classification with retinal images to learn rich deep features for Retinal-IQA. To exploit more powerful representation for Retinal-IQA, complex frameworks involving multiple parallel CNN branches as shown in Fig. 1(a) or multiple independent CNN networks as shown in Fig. 1(b) to make use of priors about IQA are proposed. For example, Fu et al. claim that different colour spaces represent different characteristics and propose Multiple Colour-space Fusion Network (MCF-Net) [8]. MCF-Net unifies three parallel CNN branches into one framework to learn complementary informative contexts from RGB, HSV and Lab colour spaces for retinal-IQA. Muddamsetty et al. propose a combined model for Retinal-IQA [9], which ensembles deep features from a CNN branch and generic features from two texture branches. In [10], Shen et al. claim that auxiliary tasks contribute to IQA and propose a multi-task framework for Retinal-IQA, named MFIQA. MFIQA [10] consists of a ResNet-50 network [11] for detection of region of interest (ROI), a VGG-16 network [12] for refinement of ROI location, a network consisting of two encoders to encode the global retinal images and local ROI for Retinal-IQA and three auxiliary classification tasks, i.e., artifact, clarity and field definition. It is further improved by introducing domain invariance and interpretability in [13]. Comparing to framework consisting of single networks with single branch, those complex frameworks make use of extra priors about IQA and achieve superior performances. However, the parameters to be optimised rapidly multiply. Additionally, in [10,13], auxiliary task learning requires extra annotated data and the whole framework can not be trained end-to-end. These motivate us to develop a framework which can make priors incorporate in CNNs without increasing extra parameters and annotated data, as shown in Fig. 1(c).

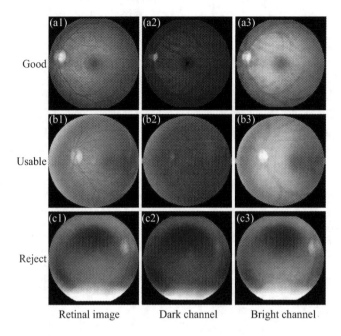

**Fig. 2.** Examples for dark and bright channel priors of different quality retinal images.

To this end, we go back to the basics and notice that, within the context of Retinal-IQA, a high-quality retinal image commonly captured under even illumination, in which salient structures such as optic disc and vessels etc. are clearly and definitely visible as shown in the first example in Fig. 2. Accordingly, we propose two novel priors. The first one is dark channel prior. It is based on the observation that, in retinal images captured with even illumination, most of local patches contain some pixels which have very low intensities in at least one channel. On the contrary, in retinal images captured with uneven illumination, pixels in regions with strong illumination have high intensities in all channels. It is exactly inline with the dark channel prior which is first proposed in [14]. Figure 2 shows the dark channels of three examples respectively graded as 'Good', 'Usable' and 'Reject'. Obviously, except for the bright structure region, i.e., optic disc region, the intensities of pixels in the dark channel map of image graded as 'Good' are always low. On the contrary, the intensities of pixels in the dark channel map of images graded as 'Usable' and 'Reject' are uneven. Particularly, pixels in regions with strong illumination have high intensities. The second prior is bright channel prior. It is based on the observation that most bright pixels have high intensities for retinal image captured with even illumination. On the contrary, for retinal image captured with uneven illumination, intensities of the bright pixels in regions with weak illumination are low. Bright channels of three examples graded as 'Good', 'Usable' and 'Reject' shown in the third column of Fig. 2 illustrate our observation. To make priors of dark channel and bright channel incorporate in CNNs, we develop a novel framework named GuidedNet. Particularly, in GuidedNet, convolution with fixed kernels is plugged in the first layer to estimate the priors of dark channel and bright channel and guide the network to pay attention to bright regions in dark channel prior map and dark regions in bright channel prior map.

The contributions of this paper can be summarized as follows.

1) We introduce dark channel prior and bright channel prior for Retinal-IQA and demonstrate their effectivenesss.
2) We propose a novel deep network named GuidedNet for Retinal-IQA. It is able to make priors of dark channel and bright channel incorporate in CNNs without increasing extra parameters and can be trained end-to-end.
3) We demonstrate the effectiveness of the proposed GuidedNet on Eye-Quality [8] and experimental results show that our GuidedNet achieves state-of-the-art performances.

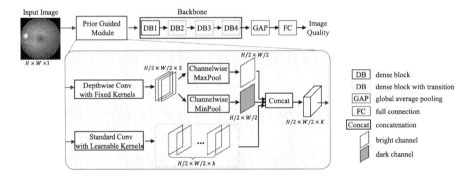

**Fig. 3.** Architecture of proposed dark and bright channel prior guided network (GuidedNet). Our proposed prior guided module takes the colour retinal image size of $H \times W \times 3$ as input and estimates the dark and bright channel priors via depthwise convolution with fixed Gaussian kernel and channel-wise pooling layer. It outputs a group of feature maps size of $\frac{H}{2} \times \frac{W}{2} \times K$, where $K$ is set to 64.

## 2   Proposed Method

In this section, we first present the dark and bright channel priors in retinal image. Then we detail the architecture of our proposed GuidedNet.

**Dark Channel Prior.** Dark channel prior is first proposed to haze removal in [14]. Thereafter it has been proved that the dark channel prior is a suitable image characteristic in distinguishing whether images are polluted by uneven illumination or not and widely applied to blind image deblurring [15] and dynamic scene deblurring [16]. The dark channel describes the minimum values in an image patch across all colour channels. Formally, according to [14], in a colour image $I$, the dark pixel at location $x$ is defined as:

$$D(I)(x) = \min_{y \in P(x)} \left( \min_{c \in \{r,g,b\}} I^c(y) \right) \qquad (1)$$

where $x$ and $y$ denote pixel locations, $P(x)$ is an image patch centred on $x$, and $I^c$ is intensity map in colour channel $c$. The Fig. 2 shows the dark channel prior maps of three retinal images graded as quality levels of 'Good', 'Usable' and 'Reject'. In good quality retinal image, most dark pixels except for optic disc area have low intensities as the image is captured with even illumination, as shown in Fig. 2(a2). For retinal images captured with slight uneven illumination as shown in Fig. 2(b1), dark channel prior map exhibits slight uneven intensities as shown in Fig. 2(b2). For image captured with serious uneven illumination as shown in Fig. 2(c1), dark pixels of retinal images affected by strong illumination are brighter than those exposed with week illumination, which results in an uneven dark channel prior map, as shown in Fig. 2(c2). This implies that dark channel prior map is an intuitive quality measure which indicates whether the image is captured with even illumination.

**Bright Channel Prior.** Bright channel prior describes the maximum values in an image patch across all channels. It is first explored for shadow estimation [17] and has been widely applied to correct under-exposed images [18,19] and image deblurring [15]. Here we propose to use bright channel prior to guide the CNN to pay attention to regions with week illumination. Formally, according to [17], for an image $I$, the bright pixel at location $x$ is defined as:

$$B(I)(x) = \max_{y \in P(x)} \left( \max_{c \in \{r,g,b\}} I^c(y) \right) \qquad (2)$$

where $x$ and $y$ denote pixel locations, $P(x)$ is an image patch centred on $x$, and $I^c$ is intensity map in colour channel $c$. Figure 2 shows that most pixels are bright in an retina image with good quality, except for some vascular pixels. However, bright pixels in the low-illumination area of retinal images are darker, and the bright channels present a cloud of dark region. These imply that the bright channel prior is a property to identify abnormal dark region from retinal images.

**Network Architecture.** The architecture of our GuidedNet is illustrated in Fig. 3. It updates from DenseNet-121 [20], which consists of four dense blocks followed by a global average pooling (GAP) layer and a full connection (FC) layer. The FC layer maps the deep features into an image quality level. Different from DenseNet-121 [20], our GuidedNet involves a prior guided module, which replaces the first layer of DenseNet-121 [20]. In practice, the dark channel prior is estimated by convolving each colour channel with a fixed Gaussian kernel followed a channel-wise minimisation pooling operator. The bright channel prior can be estimated in a same way by changing the channel-wise minimisation pooling layer to channel-wise maximisation pooling layer. To implement these, we propose to use a depthwise convolutional layer [21] with three fixed Gaussian kernels and stride step of 2, followed by a channel-wise MaxPool layer and MinPool layer, as shown in the blue box in Fig. 3. In this way, we obtain the bright channel prior map and dark channel prior map both of size $\frac{H}{2} \times \frac{W}{2}$. As the second convolution layer in DenseNet-121 requires input with $K = 64$ channels, we learn the rest 62 feature maps via the standard convolution with stride step of 2. Then we concatenate the bright channel prior map, dark channel prior map and learnable feature maps as the output of our prior guided module. We note that the dark and bright channel prior maps involve the forward propagation afterwords and guide the learning of all the parameters in network via back propagation. This enforces the network pay more attention to the informative regions in dark and bright channel prior maps and make correct decisions.

## 3    Experimental Results

In this section, we first describe dataset used in this paper, and then detail experimental setting, and subsquently present experimental results to demonstrate the effectiveness of the proposed GuidedNet, and finally analyze the contributions to the performance of the proposed two priors. Following [8], four metrics are employed for evaluation, including average accuracy, precision, recall and F-score.

### 3.1    Datasets

We validate the effectiveness of the proposed GuidedNet on the pucblic retinal image quality dataset Eye-Quality [8]. It contains 28792 retinal images including 12543 images for training and 16249 images for testing. The training dataset contains three-level images: 'Good' (8347 images), 'Usable' (1876 images) and 'Reject' (2320 images), and the testing dataset contains also three-level images: 'Good' (8470 images), 'Usable' (4559 images) and 'Reject' (3220 images). To the best of our knowledge, it is the largest public available dataset with manual quality annotations. The image size ranges from $211 \times 320$ to $3456 \times 5184$ pixels.

### 3.2    Experimental Setting

All the experiments are performed on one GTX1080 Ti GPU, and our GuidedNet is built on the top of implementation of DenseNet-121 [20] within the PyTorch framework. The parameters in backbone network are initialized with the pretrained model on ImageNet [22]. Parameters associated with full connection layers are initialized by Kaiming uniform initialization [23]. The model is trained by stochastic gradient descent for totally 15 epochs with batch size 8. The initial learning rate is set to 0.01, and then is changed to 0.001 after 10 epoches.

Following [8], we first crop the field of view (FoV) via Hough Circle Transform, and then pad the short side with zero to make the width and height of the cropped field of view regions be equal length. Finally, we rescale padded regions to 224 × 224 pixels. To enrich training data, images are augmented by random vertical and horizontal flipping and rotation.

### 3.3    Comparison with the State-of-the-arts

We compare our GuidedNet with eight methods: BRISQUE [3], NBIQA [4], TS-CNN [5], HVS-based algorithm [24], DenseNet121-RGB [8], DenseNet121-MCF [8], Multivariate-Regression CNN (MR-CNN) [25] and Combine model [9]. The first three methods are originally designed for Natural-IQA, in which BRISQUE [3] and NBIQA [4] use hand-crafted features and TS-CNN [5] utilizes deep features. Their results are obtained by adjusting authors' codes to Retinal-IQA task with Eye-Quality [8]. Considering that these three Natural-IQA methods aim to regress natural image quality scores while Retinal-IQA task prefers to classify retinal image into three quality grades, regression should be replaced by classification in the three Natural-IQA methods to make them adapt to Retinal-IQA. Specifically, in the implementation of BRISQUE [3] and NBIQA [4], we directly predict retinal image quality label rather than regressing quality score. They are conducted by Matlab2014A on the platform of a PC with an i5 CPU and 16 GB RAM. In the implementation of TS-CNN [5], we use a classification layer with three-dimensional outputs to replace the original regression layer with one-dimensional output, and adopt multi-class cross-entropy loss. The last five methods are specially designed for Retinal-IQA. The HVS-based algorithm [24] uses hand-crafted features and the DenseNet121-RGB [8], DenseNet121-MCF [8], MR-CNN [25] adopt deep features, and Combine model [9] ensembles hand-crafted and deep features. The results of HVS-based algorithm [24], DenseNet121-RGB [8] and DenseNet121-MCF [8] are taken from paper [8]. For fair comparison, the accuracy results of HVS-based algorithm [24], DenseNet121-RGB [8] and DenseNet121-MCF [8] are not presented in this paper because they do not report their corrected results. We also provide our reproductions of DenseNet121-RGB [8] and DenseNet121-MCF [8]. The results of MR-CNN [25] and Combine model [9] are directly taken from their original papers.

We report results in Table 1, where results marked with * are taken from the original papers or reproduced by others while those without any mark are our reproduction. The implementation of our methods and our reproduction of other methods are conducted three times, and the average results are reported. From Table 1, we have following observations. Comparing with methods using hand-crafted features, i.e. BRISQUE [3], NBIQA [4] and HVS-based algorithm [24], methods based on deep features have better performances on Retinal-IQA. For methods using deep features, Retinal-IQA methods significantly outperforms Natural-IQA methods, i.e. TS-CNN [5]. Compared with DenseNet121-RGB* [8], our GuidedNet has a remarkable improvement 6.51% in terms of F-score, achieving 88.03%. In terms of accuracy, our GuidedNet achieves 89.23% which is significantly 3.55% higher than DenseNet121-RGB [8]. As for DenseNet121-MCF*

**Table 1.** Comparison of the proposed method and state-of-the-arts on Eye-Quality [8]. * indicates that results are taken from the original papers or reproduced by others.

| Methods | Accuracy | Precision | Recall | F-score | Parameters |
|---|---|---|---|---|---|
| BRISQUE [3] | 76.92 | 76.08 | 70.95 | 71.12 | – |
| NBIQA [4] | 79.17 | 76.41 | 75.09 | 74.41 | – |
| TS-CNN [5] | 79.26 | 79.76 | 74.46 | 74.81 | 1.44M |
| HVS-based algorithm* [24] | – | 74.04 | 69.45 | 69.91 | – |
| DenseNet121-RGB* [8] | – | 81.94 | 81.14 | 81.52 | 6.96M |
| DenseNet121-RGB [8] | 85.68 | 84.81 | 82.39 | 83.15 | 6.96M |
| DenseNet121-MCF* [8] | – | 86.45 | 84.97 | 85.51 | 28.26M |
| DenseNet121-MCF [8] | 87.22 | 85.63 | 84.82 | 85.06 | 28.26M |
| MR-CNN* [25] | 88.43 | 86.97 | 87.00 | 86.94 | 101.80M |
| Combined model* [9] | – | 87.8 | 88.0 | 87.8 | ~29.3M |
| GuidedNet (ours) | 89.23 | 88.63 | 87.58 | 88.03 | 6.96M |

[8], the F-score of our GuidedNet outperforms it by 2.97% and the parameters of our GuidedNet are much lighter, approximately 1/4 of DenseNet121-MCF* [8]. Compared with MR-CNN [25], F-score and accuracy of our model are superior by 1.09% and 0.80%, respectively. Moreover, the parameters of MR-CNN [25] are approximately 15 times of our model. Compared with Combined model [9], our GuidedNet is slightly higher in F-score and our model has less parameters than it. In short, our model achieves superior performances to the state-of-the-arts, and is much lighter than other improved deep model.

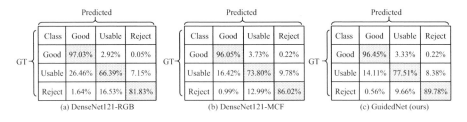

**Fig. 4.** Confusion matrices of DenseNet-121-RGB [8], DenseNet-121-MCF [8] and our GuidedNet on Eye-Quality [8].

Furthermore, the confusion matrices of DenseNet121-RGB [8], DenseNet121-MCF [8] and our GuidedNet are shown in Fig. 4, respectively. From Fig. 4, we can observe that the accuracy of our model for recognizing retinal images graded as 'Good' has achieved 96.45%, which is slightly inferior to DenseNet121-RGB [8] by 0.58% and superior to DenseNet121-MCF [8] by 0.40%. However, compared with these models, our model obviously performs better in classification on retinal images graded as 'Usable' and 'Reject' achieving 77.51% and 89.78% in accuracy respectively, which is more important than recognizing retinal images graded as 'Good'.

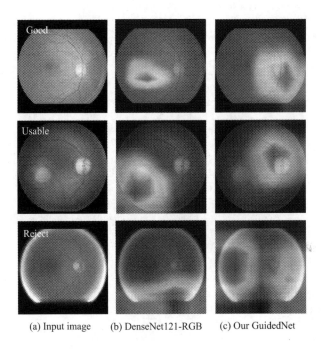

(a) Input image        (b) DenseNet121-RGB        (c) Our GuidedNet

**Fig. 5.** Examples of Grad-cams of different models generated according to [26]. These images are wrongly predicted by DenseNet121-RGB [8], but correctly identificated by our GuidedNet. Obviously, incorporating dark and bright channel prior, the model prefers to learn discriminate information from informative regions highlighted by prior.

We further present three examples of gradient-weighted class activation maps (Grad-cams) [26] of DenseNet121-RGB [8] and our GuidedNet in Fig. 5. These three examples, labeled as 'Good', 'Usable' and 'Reject' from top to bottom in Fig. 5, are wrongly graded as 'Usable', 'Reject' and 'Usable' by DenseNet121-RGB [8] but correctly classified by our GuidedNet. As shown in the second column in Fig. 5, DenseNet121-RGB [8] fails to capture the most informative information for quality prediction. However, our GuidedNet tends to learn more discriminate information from regions highlighted by prior. As shown in the third column in Fig. 5, our GuidedNet focuses on the distorted regions with strong and weak illumination for the classification of 'Reject' images, while it prefers to learn information from optic disc for the classification of 'Good' and 'Usable' images.

### 3.4   Ablation Study

**Effectiveness of Dark and Bright Channel Prior.** To validate the effects of dark and bright channel prior, we perform ablation study on Eye-Quality

[8]. The average results are reported in Table 2, where the method marked with * is trained following settings of [8] while methods without any marks follow settings of this paper. In addition, the baseline in Table 2 refers to DenseNet121 [20]. From Table 2, we can see that (1) the result of baseline using our settings are superior than that using settings of [8]. The possible reason is that random drifting in [8] may cause label noise, because distortions in retinal images are uneven. (2) Our GuidedNet achieves best overall evaluation value F-score while incorporating both dark and bright prior into network. (3) Embedding either dark or bright prior can also contribute to improve the performance of Retinal-IQA.

**Table 2.** Effectiveness of dark and bright channel prior on Eye-Quality [8]. Baseline*: DenseNet121-RGB [8]. Baseline: DenseNet121 [20]. D: Dark channel prior. B: Bright channel prior. DB: Dark and bright channel prior.

| Methods | Accuracy | Precision | Recall | F-score |
|---|---|---|---|---|
| Baseline* | 85.68 ± 0.69 | 84.81 ± 0.47 | 82.39 ± 1.23 | 83.15 ± 0.85 |
| Baseline | 88.95 ± 0.17 | 87.73 ± 0.11 | 87.00 ± 0.40 | 87.07 ± 0.23 |
| Baseline+D | 89.16 ± 0.30 | 87.95 ± 0.10 | 87.23 ± 0.57 | 87.40 ± 0.37 |
| Baseline+B | 89.36 ± 0.16 | 88.27 ± 0.30 | 87.38 ± 0.58 | 87.67 ± 0.21 |
| Baseline+DB | 89.23 ± 0.82 | **88.63 ± 0.16** | **87.58 ± 0.31** | **88.03 ± 0.18** |

**Table 3.** Performance comparisons of different settings for batch size and learning rate on Eye-Quality [8].

| Parameters | Network | Accuracy | Precision | Recall | F-score |
|---|---|---|---|---|---|
| b4-lr0.01 | DenseNet121 [20] | 88.25 | 87.06 | 86.08 | 86.38 |
| | GuidedNet | 88.83 | 87.15 | 87.47 | 87.23 |
| b4-lr0.01 (0.001 after 10 epoches) | DenseNet121 [20] | 88.34 | 87.11 | 86.24 | 86.41 |
| | GuidedNet | 88.88 | 87.51 | 87.10 | 87.12 |
| b8-lr0.01 | DenseNet121 [20] | 88.74 | 87.99 | 86.21 | 86.94 |
| | GuidedNet | 88.95 | 88.31 | 86.22 | 87.16 |
| b8-lr0.01 (0.001 after 10 epoches) | DenseNet121 [20] | 88.95 | 87.73 | 87.00 | 87.07 |
| | GuidedNet | **89.23** | **88.63** | **87.58** | **88.03** |

**Parameter Settings.** We look into the influences of different settings, i.e. batch size and learning rate. Table 3 reports the performances of four settings of two networks including DenseNet121 [20] and our GuidedNet. In Table 3, four settings are seperately defined as: (1) b4-lr0.01, means that models are trained 20 epoches with bacth size 4 and learning rate 0.01. (2) b4-lr0.01 (0.001 after 10 epoches), means that models are first trained 10 epoches with bacth size 4 and learning rate 0.01 and then trained another 10 epoches with decreased learning rate 0.001. (3) b8-lr0.01, means that models are optimized for 15 epoches with batch size 8 and learning rate 0.01. (4) b8-lr0.01 (0.001 after 10 epoches), means that models are trained totally 15 epoches and the initial learning rate is set to 0.01, and the learning rate is decreased to 0.001 after 10 epoches. From Table 3, we can observe that (1) our GuidedNet has achieved the best performance when parameters are set as b8-lr0.01 (0.001 after 10 epoches). (2) with the same setting, our GuidedNet incorporating dark and bright channel prior is superior to DenseNet121 [20].

## 4  Conclusion

This paper presents a simple framework named GuideNet for retina image quality assessment. It introduces dark and bright channel priors to predict image quality. The proposed GuidedNet builds a dark and bright channel prior guided layer to highlight image quality prior and does not increase much model burden. Our model does not require auxiliary landmark detection module and can be trained end-to-end. Validation on Eye-Quality [8] shows the superior performances of our GuidedNet and the effectiveness of dark and bright channel priors in retinal image quality assessment.

**Acknowledgment.** This research is supported by the National Key R&D Program of China (NO. 2018AAA0102100).

## References

1. Diaz-Pinto, A., Colomer, A., Naranjo, V., Morales, S., Xu, Y., Frangi, A.F.: Retinal image synthesis and semi-supervised learning for glaucoma assessment. IEEE Trans. Med. Imaging **38**(9), 2211–2218 (2019)
2. Quellec, G., Lamard, M., Conze, P.-H., Massin, P., Cochener, B.: Automatic detection of rare pathologies in fundus photographs using few-shot learning. Med. Image Anal. **61**, 101660 (2020)
3. Mittal, A., Moorthy, A.K., Bovik, A.C.: No-reference image quality assessment in the spatial domain. IEEE TIP **21**, 4695–4708 (2012)
4. Ou, F.-Z., Wang, Y.-G., Zhu, G.: A novel blind image quality assessment method based on refined natural scene statistics. In: 2019 IEEE International Conference on Image Processing (ICIP), pp. 1004–1008. IEEE (2019)
5. Yan, Q., Gong, D., Zhang, Y.: Two-stream convolutional networks for blind image quality assessment. IEEE Trans. Image Process. **28**(5), 2200–2211 (2018)
6. Zago, G.T., Andreão, R.V., Dorizzi, B., Salles, E.O.T.: Retinal image quality assessment using deep learning. Comput. Biol. Med. **103**, 64–70 (2018)
7. Yu, F., Sun, J., Li, A., Cheng, J., Wan, C., Liu, J.: Image quality classification for DR screening using deep learning. In: EMBC 2017 (2017)

8. Fu, H., et al.: Evaluation of retinal image quality assessment networks in different color-spaces. In: Shen, D., et al. (eds.) MICCAI 2019. LNCS, vol. 11764, pp. 48–56. Springer, Cham (2019). https://doi.org/10.1007/978-3-030-32239-7_6

9. Muddamsetty, S.M., Moeslund, T.B.: Multi-level quality assessment of retinal fundus images using deep convolution neural networks. In: VISAPP 2021 (2021)

10. Shen, Y., et al.: Multi-task fundus image quality assessment via transfer learning and landmarks detection. In: Shi, Y., Suk, H.-I., Liu, M. (eds.) MLMI 2018. LNCS, vol. 11046, pp. 28–36. Springer, Cham (2018). https://doi.org/10.1007/978-3-030-00919-9_4

11. He, K., Zhang, X., Ren, S., Sun, J.: Deep residual learning for image recognition. In: CVPR, pp. 770–778 (2016)

12. Simonyan, K., Zisserman, A.: Very deep convolutional networks for large-scale image recognition. In: ICLR (2015)

13. Shen, Y., et al.: Domain-invariant interpretable fundus image quality assessment. Med. Image Anal. **61**, 101654 (2020)

14. He, K., Sun, J., Tang, X.: Single image haze removal using dark channel prior. IEEE TPAMI **33**(12), 2341–2353 (2010)

15. Pan, J., Sun, D., Pfister, H., Yang, M.-H.: Blind image deblurring using dark channel prior. In: CVPR (2016)

16. Cai, J., Zuo, W., Zhang, L.: Dark and bright channel prior embedded network for dynamic scene deblurring. IEEE TIP **29**, 6885–6897 (2020)

17. Panagopoulos, A., Wang, C., Samaras, D., Paragios, N.: Estimating shadows with the bright channel cue. In: Kutulakos, K.N. (ed.) ECCV 2010. LNCS, vol. 6554, pp. 1–12. Springer, Heidelberg (2012). https://doi.org/10.1007/978-3-642-35740-4_1

18. Wang, Y., Zhuo, S., Tao, D., Jiajun, B., Li, N.: Automatic local exposure correction using bright channel prior for under-exposed images. Signal Process. **93**(11), 3227–3238 (2013)

19. Tao, L., Zhu, C., Song, J., Lu, T., Jia, H., Xie, X.: Low-light image enhancement using CNN and bright channel prior. In: ICIP 2017 (2017)

20. Huang, G., Liu, Z., Van Der Maaten, L., Weinberger, K.Q.: Densely connected convolutional networks. In: CVPR, pp. 4700–4708 (2017)

21. Howard, A.G., et al.: MobileNets: efficient convolutional neural networks for mobile vision applications. arXiv (2017)

22. Deng, J., Dong, W., Socher, R., Li, L.-J., Li, K., Fei-Fei, L.: ImageNet: a large-scale hierarchical image database. In: CVPR, pp. 248–255. IEEE (2009)

23. He, K., et al.: Delving deep into rectifiers: surpassing human-level performance on ImageNet classification. In: ICCV (2015)

24. Wang, S., Jin, K., Haitong, L., Cheng, C., Ye, J., Qian, D.: Human visual system-based fundus image quality assessment of portable fundus camera photographs. IEEE Trans. Med. Imaging **35**(4), 1046–1055 (2015)

25. Raj, A., Shah, N.A., Tiwari, A.K., Martini, M.G.: Multivariate regression-based convolutional neural network model for fundus image quality assessment. IEEE Access **8**, 57810–57821 (2020)

26. Selvaraju, R.R., Cogswell, M., Das, A., Vedantam, R., Parikh, D., Batra, D.: Grad-CAM: visual explanations from deep networks via gradient-based localization. In: ICCV, pp. 618–626 (2017)

# Continual Representation Learning via Auto-Weighted Latent Embeddings on Person ReID

Tianjun Huang, Weiwei Qu, and Jianguo Zhang[✉]

Department of Computer Science and Engineering, Southern University of Science and Technology, Shenzhen 518055, China
{huangtj,zhangjg}@sustech.edu.cn, 11930667@mail.sustech.edu.cn

**Abstract.** Popular deep neural network models in artificial intelligence systems are found having catastrophic forgetting problem: when learning on a sequence of tasks, deep networks tend to only achieve high performance on the current task, while losing performance on previously learned tasks. This issue is often addressed by continual learning or lifelong learning. The majority of existing continual learning approaches adopt class incremental strategy, which will continuously expand the network structure. Representation learning, which only leverages the feature vector before classification layer, is able to maintain the model capacity in continual learning. However, recent continual representation learning methods are not well evaluated on unseen classes. In this paper, we pay attention to the performance of continual representation learning on unseen classes, and propose a novel auto-weighted latent embeddings method. For each task, autoencoders are developed to reconstruct feature maps from different levels in the neural network. The embeddings generated by these autoencoders on the manifolds are constrained when learning a new task so as to preserve the knowledge in previous tasks. An adapted auto-weighted approach is developed in this paper to assign different levels of importance to the embeddings based on reconstruction errors. Our experiments on three widely used Person Re-identification datasets expose the existence of catastrophic forgetting problem for representation learning on unseen classes, and demonstrate that our proposed method outperforms other related methods in continual representation learning setup.

**Keywords:** Continual learning · Representation learning · Person Re-Identification

## 1 Introduction

Our human has the ability to continually learn new knowledge without dramatically forgetting previously studied knowledge. However, current popular deep neural network model in machine learning has been found tending to catastrophically lose performance on its previously learned tasks after training on a new

© Springer Nature Switzerland AG 2021
H. Ma et al. (Eds.): PRCV 2021, LNCS 13021, pp. 593–605, 2021.
https://doi.org/10.1007/978-3-030-88010-1_50

task [7]. Methods which attempt to alleviate the catastrophic forgetting issue of models are often referred to as continual learning [9].

Recent continual learning approaches often incrementally fuse the classes of new tasks into the classification layer of the deep network to solve conventional classification problem [15,22]. The model capacity of the network will continually increase due to the expansion of classification layer. Representation learning, whose aim is to match images based on their representations, is able to ease the requirement of model capacity in continual learning since the classification layer is not required after the training of representation learning. Current continual representation learning methods [17,20] usually represent classes with a prototype and then classify inputs by applying nearest-class-mean approach. Since the generated prototypes are only for the classes in training set, these methods cannot address the situation when testing set contains unseen classes, such as in Person Re-identification.

In this paper, we explore the performance of continual representation learning on unseen classes and propose a novel auto-weighted latent embedding method. Data in previous tasks are not required in the setting to avoid the issue of data privacy (e.g., medical image data). Specifically, we train autoencoders to capture latent embeddings on the manifolds from multiple layers as the compressed knowledge for previous tasks. Furthermore, an adapted auto-weighted approach is developed in this work to measure the level of importance for each feature map in the embeddings. Restricting the feature maps with high level importance can further improve the performance of continual representation learning. It should be noted that, in the testing phase of our method, the size of the deep network remains the same after learning new tasks.

We conduct the experiments on three popular Person Re-identification (ReID) datasets for simulating continual representation learning on unseen classes. ReID is a fundamental research problem for intelligent video surveillance systems. Especially in nowadays, the requirement of public safety and the increasing number of surveillance cameras have greatly promoted the development of ReID technology. The aim of ReID is to spot a specific person across different cameras. Person IDs in testing set are different from IDs in training set so that representations rather than classifiers are often learned to match image pairs. Previous continual learning methods always assume that labels in testing set are the same with labels in training set, which makes them hard to be implemented in ReID scenario due to the increasing number of unseen people in real time. In consideration of data privacy issue, we compare related continual learning methods without preserving exemplars in previous tasks and evaluate them on ReID scenario. The results consistently illustrate that our proposed method achieves the best performance compared to other related continual learning methods on representation learning for unseen classes.

In summary, the contributions of our work are as follows:

- We evaluate the performance of continual representation learning on unseen classes and propose a novel approach without storing previous data or expanding network structure. It utilizes autoencoders from multiple layer outputs to extract latent embeddings on the manifolds. We only constrain these low-dimensional embeddings to retain knowledge in previous tasks so that enhancing the flexibility of the network to learn new knowledge.

– Based on reconstruction errors, an adapted auto-weighted mechanism is developed to assign different weights to feature maps of the embeddings for continual learning. This helps network pay more attention to the features with great influence on the memory of previous tasks.

– The experiments on three popular ReID datasets demonstrate the catastrophic forgetting problem in this area and show that our proposed method achieves the best performance compared with other related continual learning methods on representation learning for unseen classes.

## 2 Related Work

### 2.1 Continual Learning

A common solution in continual learning methods for alleviating catastrophic forgetting is to maintain a small number of data from previous tasks and then replay them when training the network on a new task [2,17]. However, the previous data, such as medical images, may not be accessible due to privacy issue. The majority of recent continual learning methods gradually enlarge the classification layer of the network by adding classes of new tasks [15,22]. Although many of them do not require previously stored data, the increasing model capacity may restrict their applications.

Our proposed method is more related with *regularization-based* methods which often consider an additional regularization loss in continual learning. Learning without forgetting [13] adopted knowledge distillation concept [6] to retain the performance in previous tasks. However, this method is found having error build-up issue when facing a sequence situation [17]. Another straightforward idea is to constrain weights of a network [8,12], which means that parameters of the network after training on a new task are required to be similar with the original parameters. However, regulating weights is a strong constraint when training the network on a different task. It may tremendously affect the ability of this network to learn new knowledge. DELTA [11] shows that "behavior" regularization is possibly a better solution compared with weight regularization. The "behavior" regularization restricts output feature maps of multiple layers and hence can be considered as attempting to ensure the flexibility of the network when learning on a new task. In our work, the motivation is that, instead of restricting the entire output feature maps from different layers in the network, we utilize autoencoders to capture low-dimensional embeddings of old tasks on the manifolds as the compressed memories. The flexibility of the network when learning on a new task can be enhanced by only constraining the compressed memories. Autoencoder is able to learn the structure of the manifold and can represent the essential variations for reconstructing input samples [3]. The Encoder Based Lifelong Learning approach [16] also investigated the effectiveness of autoencoder, but they have only conducted a preliminary exploration by inserting an autoencoder between the feature extractor and classifier of the neural network. We utilize autoencoders trained on multiple layer outputs of the neural network to extract different levels of embeddings on the manifolds. Furthermore, an adapted auto-weighted approach is proposed in our work to impel the network to pay more attention to the most important features in the embeddings for previous tasks.

In this work, we concentrate on the performance of continual learning on representation learning, which does not increase model capacity after learning new tasks. Most current continual representation learning methods need to generate prototypes for each class and then classify inputs into the nearest prototype based on their representations [17, 20]. The labels in testing set and training set must be the same for these methods, which is not suitable for addressing unseen classes matching in testing set. Representation matching of unseen classes is a more robust way to evaluate the quality of learned representations, such as in the famous ReID application scenario.

## 2.2  Person Re-Identification

ReID is a popular application case for representation learning. Person IDs in testing set are different with IDs in training set. Most existing ReID methods focus on transfer learning problem without considering the catastrophic forgetting on previous tasks [14, 19]. Recently, [18] explored the forgetting issue on ReID by simply applying Learning without Forgetting algorithm [13]. [21] proposed an flexible knowledge distillation method for continual learning on ReID, which was also developed based on [13]. However, recently published related continual learning methods were not evaluated in their experiments. Meanwhile, the mixing and fixed ReID testing set in [21] may not be easy to show catastrophic forgetting on ReID datasets. In our work, we follow the conventional strategy of continual learning to sequentially learn three widely used ReID datasets. The comparison experiment with recently related continual learning algorithms exhibits the superiority of our proposed method on continual representation learning for unseen classes.

## 3  Methodology

Figure 1 shows the overview of our proposed method for continual learning on two tasks. After fine-tuning the network on the old task, autoencoders are trained on the outputs of multiple layers. The data of new task is sent to the network of old task to obtain the embeddings from trained autoencoders as the compressed memory of the old task. Reconstruction errors on these autoencoders are utilized to learn the levels of importance of feature maps in the embeddings. The network of old task is used as the starting point for the training of new task. The classification loss learns the new knowledge, while the stability loss represents

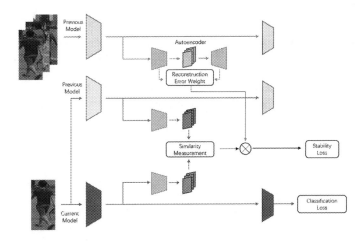

**Fig. 1.** Overview of the system.

the difference between embeddings obtained from the new network and old network using the same autoencoders for preserving old knowledge. Optimizing the classification loss and stability loss can achieve the trade-off between plasticity and stability. When the number of tasks increases, additional stability losses are gradually assembled in the total loss, which can easily handle a sequence of tasks in continual learning. The obtained feature vector before classification layer is extracted as the representation of the input image.

### 3.1 Latent Embeddings with Autoencoders

Autoencoders are used in this work to extract latent embeddings from outputs of multiple layers as the distinctive features. Autoencoder utilizes the opinion that input data is distributed on a low-dimensional manifold and it is able to capture the structure of the manifold [3]. Only the essential changes which are useful to reconstruct input data are represented in the embeddings. The mapping from input data to the embeddings in latent space concentrates on the variations along the manifold directions rather than orthogonal directions of manifold. Figure 2 shows the structure of our autoencoder. It is an undercomplete autoencoder with two convolution layers in encoder and two transposed convolution layers in decoder. Each convolutional layer is followed by a batch normalization layer and a leaky ReLU layer. Let $F_{ij}$ denote output feature maps from layer $j$ given the $i$-th input sample. $e_j()$ and $d_j()$ are the encoder and decoder functions, respectively. $N$ is the total number of input samples. The learning problem in our autoencoder is then can be defined as follows:

$$\min_{\mathbf{w}} \frac{1}{N} \sum_{i=1}^{N} \|F_{ij} - d_j(e_j(F_{ij}))\|_2^2 \tag{1}$$

where $\mathbf{w}$ is parameters of weights in the autoencoder.

There is no fully connected layers in our autoencoder model. Assuming $C$ is the number of channels of a layer output and the size of convolution filter is $3 \times 3$, the number of parameters $N_p$ for training an autoencoder on this output will be $N_p = 2 \times (C \times 3 \times 3 \times 0.5 \times C + 0.5 \times C \times 3 \times 3 \times 0.25 \times C)$. After the training of the new network is completed, autoencoders will be trained on outputs of multiple layers in this network and then preserved for learning the next task.

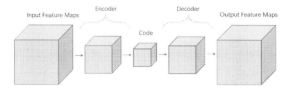

**Fig. 2.** The structure of our autoencoder.

### 3.2   Stability and Plasticity

Plasticity represents the ability to learn new knowledge, while stability refers to the memory of previously learned knowledge [4]. Assuming the network has already sequentially learned $T$ tasks from task 1 to task $T$, a new task $T+1$ with data $X^{t+1}$ and labels $Y^{t+1}$ is the problem to be solved at present. The plasticity ability is maintained by calculating the traditional cross-entropy loss:

$$p_i^{t+1} = f_{t+1}(X_i^{t+1}) \tag{2}$$

$$L_p = -\frac{1}{N} \sum_{i=1}^{N} \sum_{c=1}^{C} y_{ic}^{t+1} log(p_{ic}^{t+1}) \tag{3}$$

where $f_{t+1}$ is the network which uses the pre-trained model on task $t$ as the starting point, $C$ is the number of classes and $y_{ic}^{t+1}$ is equal to 1 only when $c = Y_i^{t+1}$.

We now consider the stability. It is measured by computing the similarities between the embeddings in previous networks and the embeddings in task $t+1$. Let $e_j^t$ denote the encoder on $j$-th layer output in task $t$, and $d_j^t$ is the corresponding decoder. $F_{ij}^*$ is the output feature maps of the $j$-th layer for the $i$-th input sample in task $t+1$, and $F_{ij}^t$ is the output feature maps in task $t$. We can then formulate the loss for stability as follows:

$$L_s = \frac{1}{N} \sum_{i=1}^{N} \sum_{t=1}^{T} \sum_{j=1}^{J} \|e_j^t(F_{ij}^*) - e_j^t(F_{ij}^t)\|_2^2 \tag{4}$$

In this stability loss, each sample in the new task $t+1$ is sent into network $f_{t+1}()$ and all previous networks. Output feature maps $F_{ij}^t$ in previous networks will go through their corresponding autoencoders to capture the impression (i.e., embeddings) for the input samples of task $t + 1$. Then, output feature maps $F_{ij}^*$ in task $t + 1$ are sent into the same autoencoders to generate latent embeddings. Embeddings of task $t + 1$ are constrained with previous network embeddings by using squared Euclidean distance during training. The total loss which is required to be minimized in our proposed method is:

$$L = L_p + \lambda L_s \tag{5}$$

where $\lambda$ is a hyper-parameter that controls the strength of stability.

### 3.3   Auto-Weighted Embedding

Equation (4) has proposed a strategy to preserve compressed memories for previous tasks. However, this loss function treats each feature map in the embedding equally. Intuitively, our humans can recognize an object by concentrating on some distinctive features. These distinctive features are often not on the same level of importance in the cognitive system. For instance, "color" may be a more distinctive feature to separate apples and oranges compared with "shape". Motivated by this idea, we propose an auto-weighted method adapted from the idea [11] to compute the weights for each feature map of the embedding by utilizing the reconstruction errors in the autoencoder.

Specifically, given output feature maps $F_{ij}^t$, the embedding is obtained by $M = e_j^t(F_{ij}^t)$, where $M = \{m_1, m_2, ..., m_k\}$ is the set of feature maps in the embedding. Let $R_0$ denote the original mean-squared reconstruction error between input data and output data from the decoder. The weight of feature map $m_k$ is computed by the change of the reconstruction error when disabling this feature map (i.e., set its values to zero) in the autoencoder. If the new mean-squared reconstruction error $R_k$ varies greatly compared with $R_0$, it means that this feature map is a critical characteristic for the autoencoder and hence should be assigned with a high weight. The equation for calculating the weight of $m_k$ is described as follows:

$$W_k = \frac{|R_k - R_0|}{\sum_{i=1}^K |R_i - R_0|} \tag{6}$$

where $K$ is the number of feature maps in the embedding.

We use Eq. (6) to compute the weights of embedding in each autoencoder for previous tasks and the final weights of each embedding are averaged through all input samples of task $t + 1$. These weights are multiplied by the differences of embeddings in Eq. (4) to build a new loss:

$$L_s = \frac{1}{N} \sum_{i=1}^N \sum_{t=1}^T \sum_{j=1}^J \sum_{k=1}^K W_{ijk}^t \|m_{ijk}^* - m_{ijk}^t\|_2^2 \tag{7}$$

where $W_{ijk}^t$ is the feature map weight computed by Eq. (6). When the input is the $i$-th sample of task $t+1$, $m_{ijk}^*$ refers to the $k$-th feature map of the embedding from the $j$-th layer of task $t + 1$.

The new stability loss replaces the original $L_s$ in Eq. (5) to produce our final loss function.

### 3.4   Matching Representation

After training the network, the feature vector which is followed by the classification layer is utilized as the representation of the input image. We use cosine distance to compute the difference between two image representations and then rank the matching.

## 4   Experiments

### 4.1   Datasets

We conduct our experiments on three widely used ReID datasets: **Market-1501** [23], **DukeMTMC-reID** [24] and **CUHK03** [10]. Person IDs in testing sets are unseen in training sets in all the datasets. For **CUHK03** dataset, instead of following the original separation of training and testing sets in the dataset, we apply the new protocol proposed in [25]. For each of the three datasets, the first image of each person in the training set is chosen to compose the validation set.

### 4.2   Implementation Details

We randomly decide the order of learning the three datasets. Market-1501, DukeMTMC-reID and CUHK03 are learned sequentially, corresponding to Task 1, Task 2 and Task 3, respectively. ResNet-50 [5] implemented in Pytorch is leveraged as the base model. For the first task, the ResNet-50 pre-trained on ImageNet dataset is used as the parameter initialization.

For the training of ResNet-50 network, the size of input image is 256*128 and batch size is set to 32. SGD with momentum of 0.9 is used for optimization. The initial learning rate for transferred parameters is 0.005 and is 0.05 for the rest parameters. Each ResNet-50 network is trained for 60 epochs with learning rate divided by 10 after each 20 epochs. The hyper-parameter $\lambda$ is set by using grid search.

The autoencoders are built on the outputs of four layers of ResNet-50 network implemented in Pytorch. Each layer has several bottlenecks. The initial learning rate is 0.05 for all the autoencoders. Each autoencoder network is trained for 60 epochs with learning rate divided by 10 after each 25 epochs. The training time of our system is around five hours using a single NVIDIA TITAN V GPU with 12G memory.

**Table 1.** Performance of continual learning on two tasks. Fine-tuning is the baseline approach that sequentially fine-tuned network on two tasks. The network trained on Task 2 is tested on both Task 1 and Task 2. Mean values of Rank-1 and mAP are used to evaluate the overall performance.

| Method | Task 1 | | Task 2 | | Mean | |
|---|---|---|---|---|---|---|
| | Rank-1 | mAP | Rank-1 | mAP | Rank-1 | mAP |
| No Forgetting | 0.872 | 0.702 | 0.792 | 0.632 | 0.832 | 0.667 |
| Fine-tuning | 0.439 | 0.182 | 0.792 | 0.632 | 0.616 | 0.399 |
| LwF [13] | 0.508 | 0.242 | 0.780 | 0.610 | 0.644 | 0.426 |
| EWC [8] | 0.564 | 0.282 | 0.781 | 0.602 | 0.673 | 0.442 |
| Encoder Lifelong [16] | 0.534 | 0.264 | 0.782 | 0.606 | 0.658 | 0.435 |
| MAS [1] | 0.599 | 0.319 | 0.781 | 0.602 | 0.690 | 0.461 |
| $L_2$-$SP$ [12] | 0.533 | 0.249 | 0.785 | 0.608 | 0.659 | 0.429 |
| DELTA (without ATT) [11] | 0.604 | 0.313 | 0.782 | 0.610 | 0.693 | 0.462 |
| E-EWC [20] | 0.695 | 0.424 | 0.585 | 0.395 | 0.640 | 0.410 |
| **EC (Ours)** | 0.617 | 0.332 | 0.780 | 0.606 | **0.699** | **0.469** |
| **Auto-Weighted EC (Ours)** | 0.627 | 0.341 | 0.778 | 0.607 | **0.703** | **0.474** |

**Table 2.** Performance of continual learning on three tasks. Fine-tuning sequentially fine-tuned network on three tasks. The network trained on Task 3 is tested on Task 1, Task 2 and Tasks 3. Mean values of Rank-1 and mAP are used to evaluate the overall performance.

| Method | Task 1 | | Task 2 | | Task 3 | | Mean | |
|---|---|---|---|---|---|---|---|---|
| | Rank-1 | mAP | Rank-1 | mAP | Rank-1 | mAP | Rank-1 | mAP |
| No Forgetting | 0.872 | 0.702 | 0.792 | 0.632 | 0.504 | 0.466 | 0.723 | 0.600 |
| Fine-tuning | 0.444 | 0.210 | 0.438 | 0.252 | 0.504 | 0.466 | 0.462 | 0.309 |
| LwF [13] | 0.488 | 0.245 | 0.468 | 0.278 | 0.503 | 0.463 | 0.486 | 0.329 |
| EWC [8] | 0.578 | 0.324 | 0.433 | 0.247 | 0.494 | 0.461 | 0.502 | 0.344 |
| Encoder Lifelong [16] | 0.516 | 0.267 | 0.485 | 0.291 | 0.502 | 0.463 | 0.501 | 0.340 |
| MAS [1] | 0.574 | 0.313 | 0.456 | 0.273 | 0.494 | 0.458 | 0.508 | 0.348 |
| $L_2$-$SP$ [12] | 0.576 | 0.310 | 0.428 | 0.252 | 0.494 | 0.461 | 0.499 | 0.341 |
| DELTA (without ATT) [11] | 0.573 | 0.310 | 0.437 | 0.248 | 0.495 | 0.463 | 0.502 | 0.340 |
| E-EWC [20] | 0.644 | 0.392 | 0.430 | 0.241 | 0.361 | 0.325 | 0.478 | 0.319 |
| **EC (Ours)** | 0.579 | 0.317 | 0.467 | 0.279 | 0.509 | 0.466 | **0.518** | **0.354** |
| **Auto-Weighted EC(Ours)** | 0.590 | 0.323 | 0.478 | 0.280 | 0.503 | 0.465 | **0.524** | **0.356** |

## 4.3   Results and Comparisons

Since existing continual learning methods are rarely designed for representation learning, we reimplement the related continual learning methods to compare their performance to ours on ReID datasets. Ablation study is then followed to evaluate the impact of embedding constraint from different levels in the network.

We use Rank-1 and mean Average Precision (mAP) which are commonly adopted in ReID as the measurements of performance. Rank-1 represents the accuracy when the highest ranking image in gallery set matches the query image correctly and mAP is the standard used in information retrieval.

For continual learning, average accuracy and average forgetting of all tasks are commonly used as the criteria to evaluate the performance of algorithms, regardless of the importance of the performance on the current task. In this paper, we emphasize that the performance on the current task should be ensured in the first place in continual learning. That is, the performance on the current task should be similar with the upper bound (e.g., fine-tuning), and then apply average measurements for all the tasks. We think this strategy is more consistent with the purpose of continual learning in applications.

**Comparison Methods.** To make a fair comparison, in Table 1 and Table 2, we only compare the proposed method with continual learning approaches that do not need samples in previous tasks, including LwF [13], EWC [8], Encoder Lifelong [16], MAS [1] and E-EWC [20]. L2SP [12] and DELTA [11] are also regularization-based methods by restricting the parameters of the network and the feature maps of the network, respectively. We only compare to the DELTA without attention algorithm, since the DELTA attention strategy is used for transfer learning on the target task rather than the catastrophic forgetting on previous tasks. Since the labels in testing sets are unseen in training sets, we compare with E-EWC without semantic drift compensation proposed in [20]. "No Forgetting" shows the fine-tuning results on each task, which can be treated as the upper bound of the performance. The Fine-tuning method indicates the catastrophic forgetting issue of continually fine-tuning the network on a sequence of tasks. EC represents our proposed embedding constraint method. Auto-Weighted EC adds our proposed auto-weighted strategy on EC.

The experiments on two tasks and three tasks continual learning for representation learning demonstrate that our proposed method consistently outperforms other related methods. We think the main reason is that the embeddings captured by autoencoders on the manifolds compress the knowledge of previous tasks. Restricting these embeddings allows the network to filter out irrelevant information and provides more flexibility for the network to learn new knowledge. The proposed auto-weighted mechanism further discovers the levels of importance in these features to assign large weights on the most important ones.

**Ablation Study.** The EC and Auto-Weight EC methods proposed in this paper leverage the embeddings of autoencoders trained on multiple layer outputs. In order to explore the influence of embedding constraint in different levels, we conduct the ablation study by restricting embeddings of each individual network

layer output. For simplicity, we only show the mean Rank-1 and mAP values on
two tasks continual learning.

From low level to high level, Layer-1, Layer-2, Layer-3 and Layer-4 are corresponding to the four layers of ResNet-50 network implemented by Pytorch. As it
can be seen in Fig. 3, the embedding constraint of high level feature maps obtains
better result than low level feature maps. This is probably due to the fact that
embedding constraint is able to affect the network parameters in its previous
layers. Therefore, the high level constraint can adjust more network parameters
than low level constraint to achieve a better performance. The combination of
embedding constraints of different layer outputs, i.e., the proposed Auto-Weight
EC method, obtains the best performance. This phenomenon reveals the contextual information from low level to high level layer outputs are helpful to guide
the continual representation learning of the network.

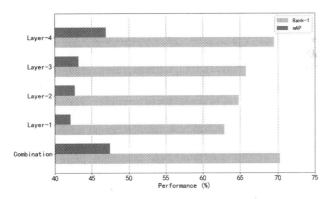

**Fig. 3.** Mean Rank-1 and mAP values for embedding constraints of different levels.

## 5    Conclusions

Continual learning is still an open research question, considering its complexity when learning different tasks. In this paper, we evaluate the performance
of continual representation learning for unseen classes on ReID, and propose a
novel auto-weighted latent embedding method. A single network is trained in a
sequential manner without accessing the samples in previous tasks or increasing
the model capacity in our proposed method. Multiple autoencoders are used to
compress previous knowledge into latent embeddings as the memory of previous
tasks. Meanwhile, an adapted auto-weighted mechanism is proposed to assign
different levels of importance to the feature maps in the embeddings. Experiments on ReID datasets show that our method achieves the state-of-the-art
performance compared to other related continual learning methods on representation learning for unseen classes. In the ablation study, we discovered the

influence of restricting embeddings on different levels of the network. Embedding constraint at higher level obtains better performance. Meanwhile, the combination of embedding constraints of different levels has the best performance. The shortcoming of our method is that we need additional storage to maintain autoencoders trained on previous tasks, which can be improved in the future.

# References

1. Aljundi, R., Babiloni, F., Elhoseiny, M., Rohrbach, M., Tuytelaars, T.: Memory aware synapses: learning what (not) to forget. In: ECCV (2018)
2. Chaudhry, A., Ranzato, M., Rohrbach, M., Elhoseiny, M.: Efficient lifelong learning with a-gem. In: ICLR (2019)
3. Goodfellow, I., Bengio, Y., Courville, A.: Deep Learning. MIT Press, Cambridge (2016). http://www.deeplearningbook.org
4. Grossberg, S.T.: Studies of Mind and Brain: Neural Principles of Learning, Perception, Development, Cognition, and Motor Control. Springer, Heidelberg (1982)
5. He, K., Zhang, X., Ren, S., Sun, J.: Deep residual learning for image recognition. In: CVPR (2016)
6. Hinton, G.E., Vinyals, O., Dean, J.: Distilling the knowledge in a neural network. In: NIPS Deep Learning Workshop (2014)
7. Kemker, R., McClure, M., Abitino, A., Hayes, T., Kanan, C.: Measuring catastrophic forgetting in neural networks. In: AAAI (2018)
8. Kirkpatrick, J., et al.: Overcoming catastrophic forgetting in neural networks. In: Proceedings of National Academy of Sciences (2017)
9. Lange, M.D., et al.: Continual learning: A comparative study on how to defy forgetting in classification tasks. In: arXiv:1909.08383 (2019)
10. Li, W., Zhao, R., Xiao, T., Wang, X.: Deepreid: Deep filter pairing neural network for person re-identification. In: CVPR (2014)
11. Li, X., et al.: Delta: deep learning transfer using feature map with attention for convolutional networks. In: ICLR (2019)
12. Li, X., Grandvalet, Y., Davoine, F.: Explicit inductive bias for transfer learning with convolutional networks. In: ICML (2018)
13. Li, Z., Hoiem, D.: Learning without forgetting. In: ECCV (2016)
14. Liu, J., Zha, Z.J., Chen, D., Hong, R., Wang, M.: Adaptive transfer network for cross-domain person re-identificaiton. In: CVPR (2019)
15. Liu, X., et al.: Generative feature replay for class-incremental learning. In: CVPR Workshop (2020)
16. Rannen, A., Aljundi, R., Blaschko, M.B., Tuytelaars, T.: Encoder based lifelong learning. In: ICCV (2017)
17. Rebuffi, S.A., Kolesnikov, A., Sperl, G., Lampert, C.H.: iCaRl: incremental classifier and representation learning. In: CVPR (2017)
18. Sugianto, N., Tjondronegoro, D., Sorwar, G., Chakraborty, P., Yuwono, E.I.: Continuous learning without forgetting for person re-identification. In: International Conference on Advanced Video and Signal Based Surveillance (AVSS) (2019)
19. Ye, M., Shen, J., Lin, G., Xiang, T., Shao, L., Hoi, S.C.H.: Deep learning for person re-identification: A survey and outlook. In: arXiv:2001.04193 (2020)
20. Yu, L., et al.: Semantic drift compensation for class-incremental learning. In: CVPR (2020)

21. Zhao, B., Tang, S., Chen, D., Bilen, H., Zhao, R.: Continual representation learning for biometric identification. In: WACV (2021)
22. Zhao, B., Xiao, X., Gan, G., Zhang, B., Xia, S.: Maintaining discrimination and fairness in class incremental learning. In: CVPR (2020)
23. Zheng, L., Shen, L., Tian, L., Wang, S., Wang, J., Tian, Q.: Scalable person re-identification: a benchmark. In: ICCV (2015)
24. Zheng, Z., Zheng, L., Yang, Y.: Unlabeled samples generated by gan improve the person re-identification baseline in vitro. In: ICCV (2017)
25. Zhong, Z., Zheng, L., Cao, D., Li, S.: Re-ranking person re-identification with k-reciprocal encoding. In: CVPR (2017)

# Intracranial Hematoma Classification Based on the Pyramid Hierarchical Bilinear Pooling

Haifeng Zhao[1], Xiaoping Wu[1], Dejun Bao[2], and Shaojie Zhang[1(✉)]

[1] Anhui Provincial Key Laboratory of Multimodal Cognitive Computation,
School of Computer Science and Technology, Anhui University, Hefei 230601, China
zhangshaojie@ahu.edu.cn
[2] Neurosurgery Department, The First Affiliated Hospital of USTC
(Anhui Provincial Hospital), Hefei, Anhui 230036, China

**Abstract.** Intracranial hematoma is a common and serious secondary lesion in craniocerebral injury, using computer aided diagnosis (CAD) system to assist clinicians to complete various tasks can greatly improve the accuracy and efficiency of hospital diagnosis. The traditional method require manual annotations of a large number of pathological feature data to train a voxel-level classifier. However, intracranial hematoma may occur in different parts of the brain and vary in severity. At the same time, there is great differences between the same subcategories and certain similarities between different subcategories of intracranial hematoma. Traditional methods require professionals to spend a lot of time to complete the part annotation and the annotation process is difficult. In order to reduce the cost of annotation and to get accurate results only by image level annotation, we propose a new intracranial hematoma classification network model (PHBP) based on the hierarchical bilinear pooling method. This model only uses the dataset of image level annotation to realize the cross-layer bilinear pooling communication of feature maps at different scales, and has better interpretability and sensitivity to the lesion area. In addition, to investigate the effectiveness of our approach, we establish a dataset of three types of hematoma (epidural hematoma, subdural hematoma and intracerebral hematoma) combined with physician's diagnostic reports. In the experimental part, we compare our method with several state-of-the-art classification methods and the results show that our method has better performance.

**Keywords:** Intracranial hematoma · Pyramid hierarchical bilinear pooling · Fine-grained classification · Computer aided diagnosis

## 1 Introduction

Intracranial hematoma is a common and serious secondary lesion in craniocerebral injury, and its incidence is about 10% of closed craniocerebral injury and

© Springer Nature Switzerland AG 2021
H. Ma et al. (Eds.): PRCV 2021, LNCS 13021, pp. 606–617, 2021.
https://doi.org/10.1007/978-3-030-88010-1_51

40% to 50% of severe craniocerebral injury. According to the source and location of hematoma, intracranial hematoma can be divided into epidural hematoma, subdural hematoma and intracerebral hematoma [1]. Intracranial hematoma is very harmful to the health of patients. Early detection, diagnosis and treatment can achieve the best curative effect for patients. Nowadays, modern high-definition imaging equipment such as digital radiography (DR), computerized tomography (CT), magnetic resonance imaging (MRI) and positron emission tomography (PET) are widely used, and with the rapid development of computer technology, medical imaging based CAD [2,3] technology can make the quantitative analysis of the clinical imaging features of pathological changes and make a judgment to avoid doctors' subjective judgment of the objective condition and improve the diagnosis accuracy and efficiency. Therefore, CAD is widely used in clinical diagnosis. Recent CAD systems exploit various modalities of neuroimaging data, such as MRI and PET. A frequently applied approach in the existing CAD systems assumes extracting voxel-level descriptors and feeding them to a classification algorithm that would learn how to separate the suspicious voxels from the healthy ones. However, such approaches are hard to exploit when the number of pathological cases in the training set is not sufficient to account for the complexity of the task. In particular, it is very difficult to obtain a well-annotated dataset of intracranial hematoma due to the great differences between the same subcategories and certain similarities between different subcategories of medical images.

Therefore, we adopt the fine-grained classification method in deep learning, and only image-level data annotation is needed to complete the learning of local features of lesions. Fine-grained classification methods based on target blocks make use of available border or partial labeling methods to locate foreground objects or object parts [4–7]. And then, extract discriminant features for further classification. Such methods take CNN as component detector and have achieved great improvement in fine-grained recognition. Some studies introduce the bilinear pool framework to model the local part of the object, capturing the pairwise correlation between the feature channels by calculating the translational invariant cross product of different spatial locations, and calculating the average convergence of different spatial locations to obtain the bilinear features, implementing the end-to-end optimization [8–11]. And comparing with the methods based on target blocks, it obtaines a quite or even higher performance. However, most of the models based on bilinear pools fuse the final results of the two feature extractors and ignore the discriminant information of important fine-grained categories in the middle convolutional layer. HBP [12] proposed a cross-layer bilinear pooling network to simulate a more interpretable human visual perception from coarse to fine. They consider convolution activations as responses to different components, and cross-layer interactions with local features are captured by cross-layer bilinear pools. It is noted that the HBP network utilizes the last three convolution layers of the same size of the VGG16 [13], while the previous feature maps containing more semantic and detailed information are still not fully utilized. In view of the large difference in the proportion of intracranial hematoma in the brain that we need to deal with it which is of great significance to use the feature map of different size to obtain the feature extraction of different size lesion area [14, 15].

In this article, we put forward a new kind of network to overcome the challenge. In the process of feature extraction by convolutional neural network, the size of feature maps change from large to small. The characteristics of different size of the figure adaptive resolution mean that the feature maps located in the bottom has more space characteristic information while the small feature maps located in the top contain more semantic information. On the basis of HBP, we change the selection of feature layers for fusion, so that the grasping ability of the model for the position, contour, shape, color and other information of fine-grained features is effectively improved. However, the problem of size mismatch exists when the feature maps are fused with the underlying feature maps with large size. If the size of the underlying feature maps are changed, the information will be lost, which can not achieve good classification effect. If the size of the underlying feature maps are changed, the parameters will become too large and the training time of the model will be too long. Therefore, we adopt the idea of feature fusion in pyramid network, and propose a new fine-grained classification network, Pyramid Hierarchical Bilinear Pooling (PHBP), on the promise of not losing the information of each fusion feature layers and reducing model training time.

However, there is a fundamental problem in fine-grained classification of craniocerebral injury using convolutional neural network, that is, a large number of data is needed in the training process of the model [16, 17]. The existing datasets of brain injury are small, especially for intracranial hematoma with high incidence, there is no specialized unified standard large-scale image database. In this work, we collect the CT images of 104 patients with craniocerebral hematoma from cooperative hospital, classify and process the CT images under the professional guidance of doctors, and obtain a small-scale data set of intracranial hematoma. It includes 136 epidural hematoma CT images, 136 subdural hematoma CT images and 136 intracerebral hematoma CT images. In addition, we hide patients' personal information from the CT images to protect personal privacy.

Our contributions are summarized as follows:

1. We improve the selection of fusion feature maps in HBP to make the classification results of fine-grained images of the model more accurate.
2. Feature pyramid is adopted to solve the problem of feature map size mismatch during feature fusion.
3. Intracranial hematoma dataset with image-level labels is produced in this work.

## 2    Methods

In order to solve the existing problems mentioned above, a pyramid hierarchical bilinear pooling model is presented in this part. Before this, we introduce the model structure of cross-layer bilinear pooling in Sect. 2.1. And then, we propose an improved network, pyramid hierarchical bilinear pooling, in order to solve the problem of HBP which realizes the multi-scale fusion of fine-grained feature maps in Sect. 2.2.

## 2.1   Hierarchical Bilinear Pooling

HBP uses the last three convolutional layers of the same size of the basic network as the feature fusion layers, capturing the discriminative part properties between fine-grained subcategories.

Suppose image is fed into the CNN network and the last three output feature maps are respectively with same height $h$, width $w$ and channels $c$. And Eq. 1 represents information exchange between layers.

$$z_i = x^T W_i y, \tag{1}$$

where $W_i \in R^{c \times c}$ is the projection matrix, $x$ and $y$ represent local descriptors from different convolution layers at the same spatial location and $z_i$ is the output of the bilinear model. We need to learn $W = [W_1, W_2, \cdots, W_o] \in R^{c \times c \times o}$ to get the output $z$ of $o$ dimension. According to matrix factorization in [13], the projection matrix in Eq. 1 can be factorized into two one-rank vectors.

$$z_i = x^T W_i y = x^T U_i V_i^T y = U_i^T x \circ V_i^T y, \tag{2}$$

where $U_i \in R_c$ and $V_i \in R_c$. Fine-grained classification results are obtained by HBP.

$$
\begin{aligned}
z_{HBP} &= HBP(x, y, z, ...) \\
&= P^T z_i \\
&= P^T concat\left(U^T x \circ V^T y, U^T x \circ S^T z, V^T y \circ S^T z, ...\right),
\end{aligned}
\tag{3}
$$

where $U \in R_{c \times d}$, $V \in R_{c \times d}$, $S \in R_{c \times d}$,... are the projection matrices of convolution layer features $x$, $y$, $z$,... respectively, $P \in R_{d \times o}$ is the classification matrix, $\circ$ is the Hadamard product and $d$ is a hyperparameter deciding the dimension of joint embeddings.

## 2.2   Pyramid Hierarchical Bilinear Model

The subcategories of fine-grained images are remarkably similar in appearance, and are judged essentially on the basis of differences in their local appearance such as contour, edge, color, texture and shape characteristics of the three types of intracranial hematoma. Hierarchical bilinear pooling is an improvement on the traditional bilinear pool fine-grained identification technique, which only focuses on learning pairs of feature relationships from the single convolutional layer. HBP uses multiple convolution layers to carry out information exchange, so that the fused feature map has more complete attributes that can distinguish subclass objects. However, the implementation of HBP network is to fuse the last three feature maps of the same size in the basic network, ignoring the fact that there may be large differences in size and shape among the same subcategories. For example, there are large differences in the size, number and shape of lesions in different medical images of intracerebral hematoma.

Therefore, for fine-grained images with large feature differences between the same subclasses, we adopt multi-scale feature fusion to solve the above mentioned problems, which is mainly divided into feature layer selection and multi-scale feature fusion method.

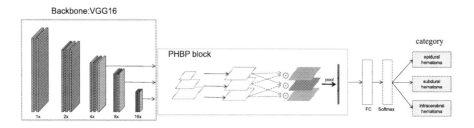

**Fig. 1.** Overall network framework.

**Feature Layer Selection.** The order of primates' visual perception of different objects is from global features to local detailed features. For example, from V1 to V4, the cortical layers encode the global facial features before encode more detailed information such as expressions [18]. In the convolutional neural network, the lower level feature maps can better describe the overall spatial feature information of the target object while the feature maps near the top level contain more semantic information. Therefore, we select the appropriate feature maps from the bottom to the top level to simulate the visual perception process of primates.

In general, the relationship between parameters near the top layer of the convolutional network and the specific image dataset is not very large, while parameters closer to the bottom layer of the network are closely related to the selected dataset and its task objectives [19], which has a great impact on the differentiation of different objects in the process of feature extraction for different objects. Therefore, we selected three feature layers of different scales in the basic network, which have distinguishing value and can well simulate the visual perception process, as the feature layers to be fused in the pyramid hierarchical bilinear pooling as shown in Fig. 1.

**Pyramid Hierarchical Bilinear Pooling.** The fusion of feature maps by bilinear pooling is to unify the dimension of feature maps with size matching and extend them into higher dimensional space through the cross product with translation invariance, so as to fuse the features at corresponding positions.

The realization of this process requires us to change the scale and dimension of the selected multi-scale feature maps with more interactive information. We are inspired by the pyramid network [20], where multi-scale feature maps are unified to the same size and dimension. As shown in Fig. 2, in order to make full use of the spatial information of the bottom feature maps and the rich semantic information of the top feature maps we enlarge the size of the smaller feature maps to the same size of the larger feature maps. We unify the dimensions of the selected feature maps to the minimum dimension feature maps, which reduce the increase in the number of parameters caused by enlarging the size of the feature maps.

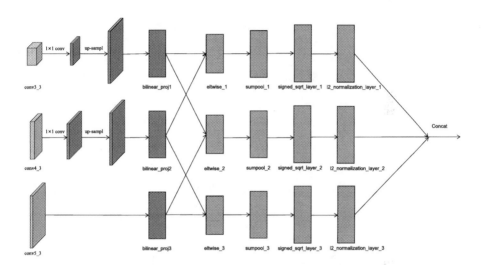

**Fig. 2.** The details of PHBP block. The left part represents the feature layers of three scales selected in the VGG16 network. firstly, their scale and dimension are the same through upsampling and dimension reduction. Secondly, the features of different layers are extended to higher dimensional space through independent linear mapping, and the attributes of different objects are obtained. Then, the corresponding position elements integrated by element-wise multiplication so that the interaction between the attribute layers of parts is established. Sum pooling is carried out for the obtained matrices, and the high-dimensional features generated are compressed into compact features. Finally, moment normalization and L2 normalization are conducted to obtain the fused features.

Since our network selects three feature layers of different sizes for fusion, the classification results obtained by PHBP can be written as

$$
\begin{aligned}
z_{PHBP} &= PHBP(x, y, z) \\
&= P^T z_i \\
&= P^T concat \left( U^T x \circ V^T y_{up\&re}, U^T x \circ S^T z_{up\&re}, V^T y_{up\&re} \circ S^T z_{up\&re} \right),
\end{aligned}
\tag{4}
$$

where $x$ is the feature map layers of the maximum size selected, $y_{up\&re}$ and $z_{up\&re}$ are the upsampling and dimension reduction of $y$ and $z$ to obtain the same scale as $x$.

## 3   Experiments

In this part, we will verify the performance of PHBP model in realizing fine-grained classification on intracranial hematoma dataset. The dataset's information and preprocessing process are introduced in Sect. 3.1. We compare the effects of the fusion of different feature layers on the experimental results in Sect. 3.2. Then, experimental comparison with other advanced networks on intracranial hematomas proves the accuracy and high efficiency of our method in the fine-grained classification in Sect. 3.3. Finally, we visualized the training process in Sect. 3.4.

### 3.1   Dataset and Implementation Details

**Dataset.** With the consent of the patients and their families, we collect CT images of 104 patients with intracranial hematoma from the cooperative hospital. Each patient's CT images contain 30 sections which size is $512 \times 512$. We obtain data of epidural hematoma, subdural hematoma and intracerebral hematoma under the guidance of the physician, which have a high probability of appearing in clinical practice and are of great harm. And this dataset shows obvious fine-grained image features in CT images as shown in Fig. 3. Because there were many images without lesions in the original data set, we eliminate useless images. We manually cut the retained CT images for hiding the patient's personal information and normalize them to $224 \times 224$ pixels. At last, we obtain 408 images with only category labels, among which 136 images are for each of the three categories.

**Implementation Detail.** In order to verify the effectiveness of our network in the classification of intracranial hematoma dataset and to make a fair comparison with other networks, we use the VGG16 baseline model pretrained on ImageNet [21] classification dataset as the backbone of PHBP network. In addition, the fully-connected layers of VGG16 network are removed and our proposed PHBP module is inserted. Like most blocks, our PHBP can also be incorporated into other basic networks with multi-scale feature maps. We use the intracranial hematoma dataset as the dataset to compare the performance of various networks. Due to the small amount of data, we enhance the data by flipping the images horizontally and finally obtained 816 pictures in order to avoid over-fitting. 70% of the dataset are used as the training set and 30% as the testing set.

We initially train the whole network by using stochastic gradient descent and cross entropy loss function with a batch size of 4, momentum of 0.9, weight decay of $10^{-4}$ and a learning rate of $10^{-3}$. All experiments implement with the pytorch and perform on a server with Titan Xp GPUs.

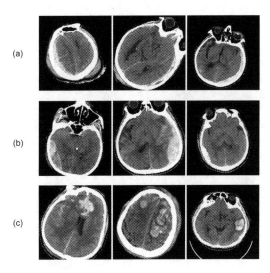

**Fig. 3.** Samples from intracranial hematoma dataset. (a): Subdural hematoma. (b): Extradural hematoma. (c): Intracerebral hematoma.

## 3.2    Ablation Experiments

PHBP network integrates multi-scale feature maps for information interaction, and obtains better classification of target objects of different size. We conduct comparative experiments on three combinations of selected multi-scale feature maps at different levels on the intracranial hematoma dataset to evaluate the influence of different combinations on the experimental results. As can be seen from Table 1, PHBP-3 achieve the best performance in the fine-grained classification of intracranial hematomas, which is consistent with the understanding that the last layer of the network has more complex semantic information [22]. Therefore, in the following experiments, We use relu3_3, relu4_3 and relu5_3 of the basic network for experiments in Sect. 3.3.

**Table 1.** Classification results (%) of PHBP using different fusion layers on intracranial hematoma dataset.

| Methods | PHBP-1[a] | PHBP-2[b] | PHBP-3[c] |
|---------|-----------|-----------|-----------|
| Accuracy | 98.2 | 98.67 | **98.88** |

[a]$relu3\_1 \times relu4\_1 + relu3\_1 \times relu5\_1 + relu4\_1 \times relu5\_1$.
[b]$relu3\_2 \times relu4\_2 + relu3\_2 \times relu5\_2 + relu4\_2 \times relu5\_2$.
[c]$relu3\_3 \times relu4\_3 + relu3\_3 \times relu5\_3 + relu4\_3 \times relu5\_3$.

**Table 2.** Comparison results(%) of different models on the intracranial hematoma dataset.

| Methods | No Transfer Learning | | | | Transfer Learning | | | |
|---|---|---|---|---|---|---|---|---|
| | Accuracy | Precision | Recall | F1-score | Accuracy | Precision | Recall | F1-score |
| VGG16 | 89.22 | 89.13 | 89.15 | 89.15 | 96.44 | 96.45 | 96.43 | 96.44 |
| LRBP | 89.35 | 89.37 | 89.33 | 89.37 | 96.54 | 96.57 | 96.56 | 96.59 |
| MoNet-2 [23] | 89.53 | 89.54 | 89.53 | 89.53 | 96.93 | 96.95 | 96.91 | 96.91 |
| FCBN [24] | 89.47 | 89.48 | 89.45 | 89.46 | 96.89 | 96.85 | 96.88 | 96.89 |
| HBP | 89.95 | 89.98 | 89.95 | 89.93 | 97.26 | 97.29 | 97.16 | 97.19 |
| iSQRT [25] | 90.27 | 90.28 | 90.25 | 90.23 | 97.67 | 97.69 | 97.66 | 97.69 |
| PHBP-nearest | 90.32 | 90.30 | 90.32 | 90.31 | 97.91 | 97.86 | 97.85 | 97.85 |
| PHBP-linear | 90.65 | 90.57 | 90.61 | 90.67 | **98.88** | **98.76** | **98.77** | **98.79** |

### 3.3 Comparison with Other Network

In order to avoid the influence of different upsampling methods on classification results, we consider using different upsampling method, PHBP-nearest and PHBP-linear, indicate that PHBP uses linear interpolation [26] and nearest neighbor interpolation [27] for upsampling respectively. Table 2 shows the results of different models on the intracranial hematoma dataset from different perspectives. Among them, pre-training parameters are obtained by VGG16 on ImageNet dataset. The following conclusions can be drawn from the Table 2.

- Since the linear upsampling method makes the feature maps more prominent after amplification of the lesion region, the PHBP using linear upsampling method has better performance than the PHBP using nearest neighbor upsampling method.
- Because PHBP fuses the semantic information of feature maps at multiple scales, our method achieves better results (accuracy, accuracy, recall rate, F1-score) than ohter methods, regardless of whether we use transfer learning or not.
- PHBP with linear upsampling method can achieve 98.88% accuracy after transfer Learning, which is 1.62% higher than that of HBP with the same transfer Learning method.

### 3.4 Visualization of Training Process

We believe that a good model should not only have high accuracy, but also have fast convergence speed. Figure 4 shows the training details of HBP and PHBP (with linear interpolation) on the intracranial hematoma dataset. From the figure, we can see that PHBP has a steeper convergence slope than HBP, and it is close to convergence at the 85 epoch. Therefore, we believe that PHBP training costs less and converges faster than HBP.

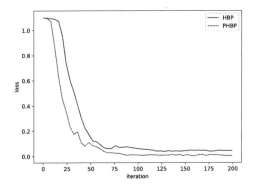

**Fig. 4.** Comparison of training details between PHBP and HBP

## 4 Conclusions

In this paper, we provide a new intracranial hematoma CT image dataset and use deep learning method to assist doctors to make more accurate judgment and treatment of three types of hematoma. We observed the presence of fine-grained features among intracranial hematoma CT images, and propose a pyramid hierarchical bilinear pooling method to integrate multi-scale cross-layer features for fine-grained recognition, so that feature layers with different attributes can realize information interaction and enhancement, and achieve fine-grained recognition.

In the future, we will add more data and make more detailed classification. In addition, we will continue to explore deep learning recognition methods suitable for intracranial hematoma and other craniocerebral injuries, so as to provide more help for doctors and patients.

**Acknowledgment.** This work was supported in part by the National Natural Science Foundation of China (No.61876002, 62076005).

## References

1. Tian, J., Zhang, C., Wang, Q.: Analysis of craniocerebral injury in facial collision accidents. PLoS ONE **15**(10), e0240359 (2020)
2. Liu, N., Zhao, H.: A non-parametric approach to population structure inference using multilocus genotypes. Hum. Genomics **2**(6), 353–364 (2006)
3. Wagner, J., Weber, B., Urbach, H., Elger, C.E., Huppertz, H.J.: Morphometric MRI analysis improves detection of focal cortical dysplasia type ii. Brain A J. Neurol. **134**(10), 2844–54 (2011)
4. Beaumont, J., Mudge, T.: Fine-grained management of thread blocks for irregular applications. In: 2019 IEEE 37th International Conference on Computer Design (ICCD) (2020)
5. Bouaziz, K., Obeid, A.M., Chtourou, S.: A review on embedded field programmable gate array architectures and configuration tools. Turk. J. Electr. Eng. Comput. Sci. **28**(1), 17–33 (2020)

6. Ju, J., Qian, C.: A fine-grained analysis and asip design strategy for specific algorithm. Int. J. Inf. **15**(7), 3031–3038 (2012)
7. Waidyasooriya, H.M., Chong, W., Hariyama, M., Kameyama, M.: Multi-context fpga using fine-grained interconnection blocks and its cad environment. Ieice Trans. Electron. **91-C**(4), 517–525 (2008)
8. Kong, S., Fowlkes, C.: Low-rank bilinear pooling for fine-grained classification. In: IEEE Conference on Computer Vision & Pattern Recognition, pp. 7025–7034 (2017)
9. Li, M., Lei, L., Sun, H., Li, X., Kuang, G.: Fine-grained visual classification via multilayer bilinear pooling with object localization. Vis. Comput. (10), 1–10 (2021)
10. Liao, Q., Wang, D., Holewa, H., Xu, M.: Squeezed bilinear pooling for fine-grained visual categorization. In: 2019 IEEE/CVF International Conference on Computer Vision Workshop (ICCVW) (2020)
11. Sánchez, D., Arrieta, A.G., Corchado, J.M.: Compact bilinear pooling via kernelized random projection for fine-grained image categorization on low computational power devices. Neurocomputing **398**, 411–421 (2019)
12. Tan, M., Wang, G., Zhou, J., Peng, Z., Zheng, M.: Fine-grained classification via hierarchical bilinear pooling with aggregated slack mask. IEEE Access **7**, 117944–117953 (2019)
13. Liu, B., Zhang, X., Gao, Z., Li, C.: Weld defect images classification with vgg16-based neural network. In: International Forum on Digital TV and Wireless Multimedia Communications (2017)
14. Redmon, J., Farhadi, A.: Yolo9000: better, faster, stronger. IEEE Conference on Computer Vision & Pattern Recognition, pp. 6517–6525 (2017)
15. Redmon, J., Farhadi, A.: Yolov3: An incremental improvement. arXiv e-prints (2018)
16. Liu, Y., Lasang, P., Pranata, S., Shen, S., Zhang, W.: Driver pose estimation using recurrent lightweight network and virtual data augmented transfer learning. IEEE Trans. Intell. Transp. Syst. **20**(10), 3818–3831 (2019)
17. Werder, K., Seidel, S., Recker, J., Berente, N., Benzeghadi, Y.: Data-driven, data-informed, data-augmented: how ubisoft's ghost recon wildlands live unit uses data for continuous product innovation. Calif. Manage. Rev. **62**(3), 86–102 (2020)
18. Ferro, D., Kempen, J.V., Boyd, M., Panzeri, S., Thiele, A.: Directed information exchange between cortical layers in macaque v1 and v4 and its modulation by selective attention (2020)
19. Yosinski, J., Clune, J., Bengio, Y., Lipson, H.: How transferable are features in deep neural networks? Adv. Neural Inf. Process. Syst. **27**, 3320–3328 (2014)
20. Guo, C., Cui, H., Yu, K.: Fine-grained image classification of red tide algae based on feature pyramid networks and computer aided technique. J. Phys. Conf. Ser. **1578**, 012020 (2020)
21. Jia, D., Wei, D., Socher, R., Li, L.J., Kai, L., Li, F.F.: Imagenet: a large-scale hierarchical image database. In: Proceedings of the IEEE Computer Vision & Pattern Recognition, pp. 248–255 (2009)
22. Sutskever, I., Hinton, G.E.: Deep, narrow sigmoid belief networks are universal approximators. Neural Comput. **20**(11), 2629–2636 (2014)
23. Gou, M., Xiong, F., Camps, O., Sznaier, M.: Monet: Moments embedding network. In: IEEE/CVF Conference on Computer Vision and Pattern Recognition, pp. 3175–3183 (2018)
24. Yu, T., Li, X., Li, P.: Fast and compact bilinear pooling by shifted random Maclaurin. In: Proceedings of the AAAI Conference on Artificial Intelligence, vol. 35, pp. 3243–3251 (2021)

25. Li, P., Xie, J., Wang, Q., Gao, Z.: Towards faster training of global covariance pooling networks by iterative matrix square root normalization. In: 2018 IEEE/CVF Conference on Computer Vision and Pattern Recognition (2018)
26. Blu, T., Thévenaz, P., Unser, M.: Linear interpolation revitalized. IEEE Trans. Image Process. **13**(5), 710 (2004)
27. Nan, J., Jian, W., Yue, M.: Quantum image scaling up based on nearest-neighbor interpolation with integer scaling ratio. Quantum Inf. Process. **14**(11), 4001–4026 (2015)

# Multi-branch Multi-task 3D-CNN for Alzheimer's Disease Detection

Junhu Li, Beiji Zou, Ziwen Xu, and Qing Liu[✉]

School of Computer Science and Engineering, Central South University,
Changsha 410083, China
{lijunhu,bjzou,xuziwen,qingliucs}@csu.edu.cn

**Abstract.** Mini-Mental State Examination (MMSE) and Magnetic Resonance Imaging (MRI) have been widely used for the diagnosis of Alzheimer's disease (AD) in clinical. The former provides a brief way to assess the severity of cognitive impairment while the latter provides a noninvasive way to enable doctors look inside the brain tissues e.g. cerebrospinal fluid (CSF), gray matter (GM), and white matter (WM) and rule out the possible causes of AD. Different brain tissues response for different cognitive functions, thus the abnormal of brain tissues and MMSE scores are usually highly related. To make full use of different brain tissues and the relationship between state of brain tissues and MMSE scores, this paper proposes a multi-branch multi-task learning framework for AD detection. In detail, three parallel 3D-CNN branches are used to learn deep features from individual brain tissues of CSF, GM and WM segmented from 3D MRI brain scans. Then the tissue-specific features are concatenated and used for AD prediction and MMSE score regression. To boost the feature learning, auxiliary predictions are attached on the top of tissue-specific features and auxiliary supervision are performed. We demonstrate our method on ADNI datasets which includes 415 subjects and conduct 10 repeated experiments to avoid the bias caused by data division. Experimental results show that our method without auxiliary predictions achieves the average accuracy of 89.63% and method with auxiliary predictions achieves average of accuracy of 91%. Both of them outperform the state-of-the-art AD detection methods.

**Keywords:** Alzheimer's disease detection · MRI images ·
Convolutional neural network · Multi-branch multi-task network

## 1 Introduction

Alzheimer's disease (AD) is an irreversible and progressive brain disease, which is the common cause of dementia. It is characterised by cognitive impairment, particularly mild loss of memory in early stage and loss of ability to response to environment. It seriously interferes with the patients's daily life and their health of patients. Early diagnosis and timely intervention are crucial to slow the progress of AD. In clinical, one of extensively used ways to measure the

© Springer Nature Switzerland AG 2021
H. Ma et al. (Eds.): PRCV 2021, LNCS 13021, pp. 618–629, 2021.
https://doi.org/10.1007/978-3-030-88010-1_52

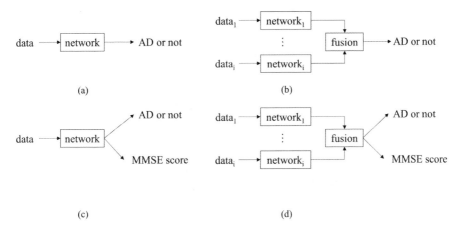

**Fig. 1.** Comparison of different architectures for AD diagnosis. (a) single-branch classification network (SBCN). (b) multi-branch classification network (MBCN). (c) single-branch multi-task learning network (SBMT). (d) multi-branch multi-task learning network (MBMT).

cognitive impairment is Mini-Mental State Examination (MMSE) [18]. MMSE is easy to measure but cannot rule out possible causes for symptoms. To look inside the brain tissues, as a non-invasive imaging technology, Magnetic Resonance Imaging (MRI) is widely adopted to scan the brain and vividly display the tissues. Thereafter, doctors analyse the MRI images manually. However, manual analysis is tedious and time consuming. Thus, automated MRI analysis becomes urgent.

Currently, the state-of-the-art AD detection methods are dominated by deep convolutional neural networks (CNN). Usually, it is formulated as a two-class classification task and many deep classification networks were developed. Generally, those methods utilise a single branch of CNN to learn abstract features from 3D MRI data for AD detection, as shown in Fig. 1(a). For example, Hosseini-Asl et al. [8] utilize a stack of unsupervised convolutional auto-encoder with locally connected nodes and shared convolutional weights to extract local features from 3D MRI for AD classification. To capture multi-scale information for AD detection, a 3D multi-scale CNN architecture is developed in [4]. To make use of the pre-trained models on Imagenet, Hon et al. [7] directly fine-tune VGGNet [21] and InceptionNet [24] for AD detection. Lian et al. [15] propose H-FCN, which first automatically and hierarchically identifies discriminative local patches and regions in whole brain MRI, then jointly learns multi-scale feature representations and fuses them to construct hierarchical classification models for AD diagnosis.

To make full use of the image data, multi-branch CNN networks are developed to learn powerful representations from either multiple individual brain tissues or multi-view data, as illustrated in Fig. 1(b). In clinical, the damages of tissues in brain such as cerebrospinal fluid (CSF), gray matter (GM), and white matter (WM) have been demonstrated to be important clinical manifestations of AD. Thus, Ge et al. [3] propose a multi-branch networks for AD detection, in which three sub-networks are used to learn powerful features from individual brain tissues of CSF, GM and WM separately, then tissue-specific features are fused and boosted by XGboost for final classification. Instead, Cheng et al. [1] and Liu et al. [16] utilise multimodal data for AD detection. In detail, Cheng et al. [1] develop two parallel 3D CNN to learn features from 3D MRI data and 3D Positron Emission Tomography data, then a 2D CNN is attached to fuse the features for AD detection. Liu et al. [16] notice the difference of number of brain regions in different atlases and features of the same brain region in different views and present a multi-atlas multi-view hybrid graph convolutional network to detect the early state of AD. More recently, noticing that the cognitive impairment is mainly caused by the abnormal of brain tissues and MMSE scores are closely relative to the state of brain tissues, researchers claim that learning to regress MMSE simultaneously from MRI data contributes to AD detection and propose a multi-task learning framework [14], as shown in Fig. 1(c). Particularly, in [14], the AD detection task is treated as the primary task and MMSE regression is treated as the auxiliary task to improve the AD detection performance and they are jointly learned via a single branch of 3D-CNN equipped with atrous convolution. However, although this approach using auxiliary labels improves the accuracy of detection to a certain extent, it does not fully utilize the feature information of MRI.

Motivate by the above, considering the feature extraction from multiple tissues and the use of auxiliary label to improve the detection accuracy, we propose a multi-branch multi-task learning network as shown in Fig. 1(d). The contributions of this paper can be summarized as follows: (1) We propose two different architectures of multi-branch multi-task 3D-CNN to detect AD; (2) We rationalize the use of different tissue features of MRI and use auxiliary labeling to supervise model learning; (3) We demonstrate the effectiveness of proposed architectures and experimental results show that our model achieves state of the art performances.

## 2   Materials and Methods

### 2.1   Materials and Preprocessing

The data used in this work were obtained from the Alzheimer's Disease Neuroimaging Initiative (ADNI) [10]. For more details with ADNI, please visit the website: http://adni.loni.usc.edu/. It is worth noting that in order to make a fair comparison with existing methods, we used the same subjects as in [14]. The subjects were selected from the baseline ADNI-1, which contains 187 AD and 228 NC 1.5T T1-weighted structural MRI data, in order to avoid different MRIs of the same subject interfering with each other, one subject corresponds to one MRI. Details of demographic and clinical information can be found in [14].

MRI usually contains some non-brain tissues such as skin, fat, muscle, neck and eye, and the presence of these non-brain tissues is considered to be a major

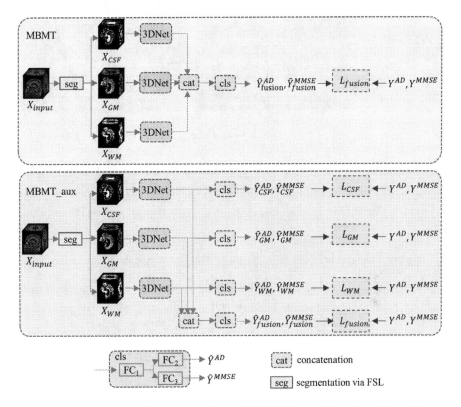

**Fig. 2.** The architecture of the proposed model. MBMT: multi-branch multi-task learning network. MBMT_aux: multi-branch multi-task learning network with auxiliary losses.

obstacle for automatic brain image segmentation and analysis techniques. Therefore, quantitative morphometric studies of MR brain images usually require preliminary processing to separate the brain from extracranial or non-brain tissues, which denote as skull stripping [12]. In this paper, we use the BET tool [22] in FSL package [23] to perform the skull stripping work. It is worth noting that in order to reduce the individual variability of different MRIs, we also used the FLIRT tool [11] available in the FSL package for registration beforehand.

## 2.2 Method Overview

Some studies [17,20,25,26] have demonstrated that the selection of appropriate biomarkers is very helpful for the detection of AD, among which the common biomarkers are CSF, GM and WM, so this paper designs a network to extract the features of three different tissues for better AD detection. Therefore, in the network proposed in this paper, these three different tissues are used as inputs to the network, as shown in Fig. 2. We denote the preprocessed MRI as $X_{input}$ and the three different tissues obtained by segmentation as $X_{CSF}$, $X_{GM}$, and

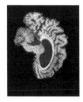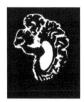

**Fig. 3.** Preprocess result of one sample sagittal MRI. From left to right: origin MRI, brain region, cerebrospinal fluid (CSF), gray matter (GM), white matter (WM)

$X_{WM}$, respectively. It is worth noting that this paper uses the FAST tool [27] in FSL for the segmentation task. Figure 3 shows the preprocessing results of sagittal MRI.

In order to combine the features of three different tissues, we propose multi-branch multi-task learning network, i.e., MBMT in Fig. 2, which extracts the features of different parts through three parallel networks and then combines them with auxiliary labels for AD detection. In addition, considering the existence of certain relationships between different branch networks, we propose multi-branch multi-task learning network with auxiliary losses, i.e., MBMT_aux in Fig. 2, which provides more complete supervision information. It is worth mentioning that the auxiliary label used in this paper is the corresponding subject's demographic information MMSE.

### 2.3   Multi-branch Multi-task Learning Network

In order to comprehensively consider the structural information of different tissues extracted from the raw MRI, we propose a multi-branch multi-task learning network (MBMT) for AD detection, as shown in Fig. 2 MBMT. Specifically, we designed three parallel branches to extract features through convolutional blocks, where the convolutional blocks consist of several convolutional and pooling layers of different sizes, i.e. the 3DNet module in Fig. 2, the 3DNet module consisted of four convolutional layers, while we add Batch Normalization [9] and Leaky Rectified Linear Unit(Leaky ReLU) [6] after each max pooling layer for faster convergence and better model fitting.

After the convolutional block operation, we can get three different characteristic tissue features of CSF, GM, and WM respectively, which are denoted as $\mathcal{F}_{CSF}$, $\mathcal{F}_{GM}$, $\mathcal{F}_{WM}$. By fusing these three different features, we can obtain a more informative feature representation, denoted as $\mathcal{F}_{fusion}$. Here, we take a simpler concatenation operation to reduce the complexity of the operation by fusing the features.

Subsequently, the obtained hybrid features are fed into the classification module, which can be seen from the cls module in Fig. 2. The features first pass through a fully-connected layer to reassemble the local features learned from the convolutional block into a complete feature vector through the weight matrix, and then pass through two different fully-connected layers to represent the classification prediction labels and the auxiliary prediction labels, i.e., $\hat{Y}^{AD}$ and $\hat{Y}^{MMSE}$ in Fig. 2. Here, we use $\hat{Y}^{AD}_{fusion}$ and $\hat{Y}^{MMSE}_{fusion}$ to represent the predicted values obtained from the hybrid features.

Considering that the categorical label is a binary classification label and the auxiliary label is a regression label, here we use the same loss function as in [14] to calculate the loss values of the two different labels separately, i.e., for the categorical label we use cross-entropy loss [2] and for the auxiliary label we use Smooth L1 loss [5], and the formula is shown below:

$$L^{AD} = \frac{1}{N}\sum_{n=1}^{N} -[\hat{Y}_n^{AD}\log(Y_n^{AD}) + (1 - \hat{Y}_n^{AD})\log(1 - Y_n^{AD})], \quad (1)$$

$$L^{MMSE} = \frac{1}{N}\sum_{n=1}^{N} Z_n, \quad (2)$$

$$Z_n = \begin{cases} 0.5(\hat{Y}_n^{MMSE} - Y_n^{MMSE})^2 & if \quad \left|\hat{Y}_n^{MMSE} - Y_n^{MMSE}\right| < 1 \\ \left|\hat{Y}_n^{MMSE} - Y_n^{MMSE}\right| - 0.5 & others \end{cases} \quad (3)$$

where $N$ denotes the number of subjects, $\hat{Y}_n^{AD}$ denotes the predicted value of the classification label for the $n$-th subject, $Y_n^{AD}$ denotes the true value of the classification label for the $n$-th subject. $\hat{Y}_n^{MMSE}$ denotes the predicted value of the auxiliary label for the $n$-th subject, $Y_n^{MMSE}$ denotes the true value of auxiliary label for the $n$-th subject.

After obtaining the loss function values of the classification labels and the auxiliary labels, we achieve our goal of improving the detection accuracy by minimizing the joint loss value of both, here, we use the following formula for the joint:

$$L = \alpha L^{AD} + (1 - \alpha)L^{MMSE}, \quad (4)$$

where $\alpha$ is a weighting factor to balance classification label loss and auxiliary label loss. Here we use $L_{fusion}$ to represent the joint loss of hybrid features.

## 2.4  Multi-branch Multi-task Learning Network with Auxiliary Losses

Although the performance of detecting AD can be improved by convolution extraction of different tissues and then fusion, the influence of individual tissues on the final result is ignored at this time, so we propose a multi-branch multi-task learning network with auxiliary losses (MBMT_aux) to integrate the individual tissue features and fusion features, i.e. MBMT_aux in Fig. 2. Specifically, after using the 3DNet module to extract features for different tissues, in addition to using the same hybrid features as MBMT, we also combine the feature of individual tissues with the hybrid features, which has the advantage of using the feature of individual tissues for supervised learning of the hybrid features and can better improve the AD detection accuracy. According to Eq. 1–4, the values of the loss functions of the three tissues, denoted as $L_{CSF}$, $L_{GM}$, $L_{WM}$, can be calculated. A formulation to improve detection accuracy by using multiple branches for mutual supervision is described as follows:

$$L_{total} = \omega_{CSF} L_{CSF} + \omega_{GM} L_{GM} + \omega_{WM} L_{WM} + \omega_{fusion} L_{fusion}, \qquad (5)$$

where $L_{total}$ denotes the summed value of many different loss functions, $\omega_{CSF}$, $\omega_{GM}$, $\omega_{WM}$ and $\omega_{fusion}$ denote the weighting factors by $L_{CSF}$, $L_{GM}$, $L_{WM}$ and $L_{fusion}$, respectively.

## 3    Experiments and Results

### 3.1    Experimental Setting

To avoid data leakage during the training process, we did not adopt data augmentation, we divided the whole dataset into training, validation and test sets at the beginning, and used random seeds for 10 replicate trials to evaluate the stability of the proposed method, and it is worth noting that the ratio of each of the three datasets is 3:1:1. We use Pytorch [19] for our experiments on a single GPU (i.e. NVIDIA GeForce GTX 1080Ti 12 GB). We use Adam [13] as our parameter optimizer, and the output of the three fully connected layers is 30, 2, 1. It is worth noting that to avoid overfitting, we use dropout before the fully connected layers. To make the model simpler, we set the loss weights of different branches to all 0.25, i.e., $\omega_{CSF} = \omega_{GM} = \omega_{WM} = \omega_{fusion} = 0.25$. Other hyperparameters include learning rate(0.0001), batch size(2), $\alpha$(0.7) and iteration epoch(300).

In order to make a fair comparison with other methods, we have used four general evaluation metrics: accuracy (ACC), sensitivity (SEN), specificity (SPE), and area under the receiver operating characteristic(ROC) curve(AUC) value. These evaluation indicators are defined as follows:

$$ACC = \frac{TP + TN}{TP + TN + FP + FN}, \qquad (6)$$

$$SEN = \frac{TP}{TP + FN}, \qquad (7)$$

$$SPE = \frac{TN}{TN + FP}, \qquad (8)$$

where TP, FP, TN and FN are true positive, false positive, true negative and false negative, respectively.

**Table 1.** Diagnosis results compare with other methods. Values are reported as mean ± stand deviation. * indicates that the result comes from [14].

| Method | ACC (%) | SEN (%) | SPE (%) | AUC |
|---|---|---|---|---|
| *RF** | 73.4 ± 4.6 | 68.7 ± 7.5 | 77.8 ± 3.3 | 0.783 ± 0.032 |
| *AlexNet** | 71.9 ± 4.6 | 63.7 ± 10.6 | 78.2 ± 10.7 | 0.757 ± 0.050 |
| *VGGNet** | 77.9 ± 2.5 | 65.4 ± 8.9 | 87.7 ± 5.6 | 0.864 ± 0.018 |
| JLMSR [14] | 86.75 ± 2.51 | 85.14 ± 2.80 | 88.00 ± 4.68 | 0.945 ± 0.017 |
| MBMT | 89.63 ± 2.44 | 84.86 ± 6.77 | 93.33 ± 4.33 | 0.959 ± 0.014 |
| MBMT_aux | **91.00 ± 1.84** | **87.14 ± 2.30** | **94.00 ± 2.64** | **0.959 ± 0.008** |

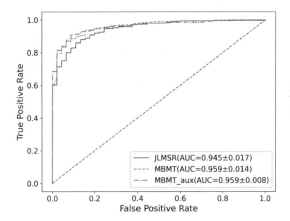

**Fig. 4.** ROC curves for AD diagnosis compare with other methods.

### 3.2 Comparison with the Other Methods

To demonstrate the validity of our proposed network, we compared it with three classical network structures i.e., random forest (RF), AlexNet and VGGNet and one recent method JLMSR [14]. Results of the first three methods are taken from [14], and the result of [14] is our reproduction. For fair comparison, we follow the same evaluation metrics in [14], and we conduct ten times trials and report the average results in Table 1.

As can be seen from Table 1, compared to three classical network structures, both the proposed MBMT and MBMT_aux have a significant improvement in four metrics. Especially, compared to VGGNet, achieving the best performance among these three methods, our MBMT_aux has improved 13.1% in accuracy, 21.7% in sensitivity, 6.3% in specificity and 9.5% in AUC value, and our MBMT have improved 11.73% in accuracy, 19.46% in sensitivity, 5.63% in specificity and 9.5% in AUC value.

Compared to the recent method JLMSR [14], our two models are able to make better use of the mutual information and are superior to it in accuracy. In addition, we also present the ROC curves of JLMSR [14] and our proposed two

**Table 2.** Diagnosis results of AD and NC with different components. Values are reported as mean ± stand deviation.

| Method | ACC (%) | SEN (%) | SPE (%) | AUC |
|---|---|---|---|---|
| SBMT_raw | 86.38 ± 3.13 | 85.43 ± 5.18 | 87.11 ± 6.87 | 0.927 ± 0.009 |
| SBMT_CSF | 88.38 ± 1.38 | 82.86 ± 5.99 | 92.67 ± 4.97 | 0.946 ± 0.007 |
| SBMT_GM | 87.75 ± 1.56 | 85.43 ± 5.02 | 89.56 ± 5.45 | 0.960 ± 0.012 |
| SBMT_WM | 79.38 ± 3.22 | 76.86 ± 7.50 | 81.33 ± 10.2 | 0.885 ± 0.212 |
| MBMT | 89.63 ± 2.44 | 84.86 ± 6.77 | 93.33 ± 4.33 | 0.959 ± 0.014 |
| MBMT_aux | **91.00 ± 1.84** | **87.14 ± 2.30** | **94.00 ± 2.64** | **0.959 ± 0.008** |

models in Fig. 4. From Fig. 4, our two models are better than JLMSR [14]. The possible reason may be that (1) compared with the original MRI image in [14], extracted tissues as the input of our model have finer features, and (2) auxiliary labels and branches can make better use of the available information for AD diagnosis.

### 3.3   Ablation Study

To more intuitively illustrate that the effectiveness of the different extracted tissues for AD detection, we perform ablation study on the single-branch multi-task learning network(SBMT), i.e. using raw MRI or individual tissues as input and MMSE as auxiliary labels. We use the origin MRI image and three extracted tissues, i.e., CSF, GM and WM, as the input of SBMT respectively, building four different models named SBMT_raw, SBMT_CSF, SBMT_GM, and SBMT_WM. Results are reported in Table 2 and Fig. 5 (a). As we can see that both SBMT_CSF and SBMT_GM are superior to SBMT_raw in accuracy and auc. Although SBMS_WM is inferior to SBMT_raw, our proposed multi-branch multi-task model combined CSF, GM and WM meanwhile has the best performance.

In addition, to verify the effectiveness of the multi-branch multi-task learning network, we perform comparison with single-branch classification network(SBCN), multi-branch classification network(MBCN) and single-branch multi-task learning network(SBMT). For building SBCN, MBCN and SBMT, we modify our proposed model respectively, making SBMT only allow raw MRI image as the input and MBCN supervised only by the classification label. And SBCN takes the raw MRI image as the input and meanwhile only uses the classification label for supervising. Results are reported in Table 3 and Fig. 5(b).

From Table 3 and Fig. 5(b), both of our proposed multi-branch multi-task learning networks MBMT and MBMT_aux have a large improvement compared to other networks. For MBMT, we achieve 89.63% in ACC, which is 4.75%, 1.38% and 3.25% higher than SBCN, MBCN, SBMT. For MBMT_aux, we achieve 91% in ACC, which is 6.12%, 2.75%, and 4.62% superior to SBCN, MBCN, SBMT.

**Table 3.** Diagnosis results of different network structures. Values are reported as mean ± stand deviation.

| Method | ACC (%) | SEN (%) | SPE (%) | AUC |
|---|---|---|---|---|
| SBCN_raw | 84.88 ± 1.72 | 85.14 ± 4.20 | 84.67 ± 3.91 | 0.914 ± 0.013 |
| MBCN | 88.25 ± 1.79 | 85.14 ± 4.57 | 90.67 ± 3.56 | 0.946 ± 0.019 |
| SBMT_raw | 86.38 ± 3.13 | 85.43 ± 5.18 | 87.11 ± 6.87 | 0.927 ± 0.009 |
| MBMT | 89.63 ± 2.44 | 84.86 ± 6.77 | 93.33 ± 4.33 | 0.959 ± 0.014 |
| MBMT_aux | **91.00 ± 1.84** | **87.14 ± 2.30** | **94.00 ± 2.64** | **0.959 ± 0.008** |

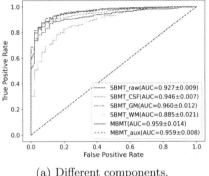

(a) Different components.

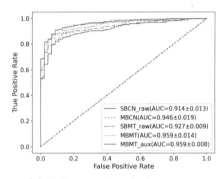

(b) Different network structures.

**Fig. 5.** ROC curves for AD diagnosis in Ablation Study.

MBMT and MBMT_aux have similar value in AUC, which all performs better than SBCN, MBCN and SBMT.

## 4  Conclusion

In this paper, we analyze and classify the existing methods, and propose a multi-branch multi-task learning network and a multi-branch multi-task learning network with auxiliary losses. The former uses three kinds of tissues obtained from the original MRI segmentation as the input, and uses MMSE as the auxiliary label supervision network training. The latter uses mutual supervision among different tissues to improve the detection accuracy on the basis of the former, The proposed method is tested on public data sets and compared with state of the art method, which proves the effectiveness of the proposed method. In general, the proposed method can make up for the vacancy of the existing methods, and has a certain guiding role for the diagnosis of AD.

**Acknowledgment.** This work is partially supported by the National Key R&D Program of China (No. 2018AAA0102100).

# References

1. Cheng, D., Liu, M.: CNNs based multi-modality classification for AD diagnosis. In: 2017 10th International Congress on Image and Signal Processing, BioMedical Engineering and Informatics (CISP-BMEI), pp. 1–5 (2017). https://doi.org/10.1109/CISP-BMEI.2017.8302281
2. De Boer, P.T., Kroese, D.P., Mannor, S., Rubinstein, R.Y.: A tutorial on the cross-entropy method. Ann. Oper. Res. **134**(1), 19–67 (2005)
3. Ge, C., Qu, Q., Gu, I.Y.H., Jakola, A.S.: Multi-stream multi-scale deep convolutional networks for Alzheimer's disease detection using MR images. Neurocomputing **350**, 60–69 (2019). https://doi.org/10.1016/j.neucom.2019.04.023
4. Ge, C., Qu, Q., Gu, I.Y.H., Store Jakola, A.: Multiscale deep convolutional networks for characterization and detection of Alzheimer's disease using MR images. In: 2019 IEEE International Conference on Image Processing (ICIP), pp. 789–793 (2019). https://doi.org/10.1109/ICIP.2019.8803731
5. Girshick, R.: Fast R-CNN. In: Proceedings of the IEEE International Conference on Computer Vision, pp. 1440–1448 (2015)
6. He, K., Zhang, X., Ren, S., Sun, J.: Delving deep into rectifiers: surpassing human-level performance on ImageNet classification (2015)
7. Hon, M., Khan, N.M.: Towards Alzheimer's disease classification through transfer learning. In: 2017 IEEE International Conference on Bioinformatics and Biomedicine (BIBM), pp. 1166–1169. IEEE (2017)
8. Hosseini-Asl, E., Keynton, R., El-Baz, A.: Alzheimer's disease diagnostics by adaptation of 3D convolutional network. In: 2016 IEEE International Conference on Image Processing (ICIP), pp. 126–130. IEEE (2016)
9. Ioffe, S., Szegedy, C.: Batch normalization: accelerating deep network training by reducing internal covariate shift (2015)
10. Jack, C.R., Bernstein, M.A., Fox, N.C., Thompson, P., Alexander, M.W., et al.: The Alzheimer's disease neuroimaging initiative (ADNI): MRI methods. J. Magn. Reson. Imaging **27**(4), 685–691 (2008). https://doi.org/10.1002/jmri.21049
11. Jenkinson, M., Smith, S.: A global optimisation method for robust affine registration of brain images. Med. Image Anal. **5**(2), 143–156 (2001)
12. Kalavathi, P., Prasath, V.B.S.: Methods on skull stripping of MRI head scan images—a review. J. Digit. Imaging **29**(3), 365–379 (2015). https://doi.org/10.1007/s10278-015-9847-8
13. Kingma, D.P., Ba, J.: Adam: a method for stochastic optimization (2017)
14. Li, H., Guo, R., Li, J., Wang, J., Pan, Y., Liu, J.: Joint learning of primary and secondary labels based on multi-scale representation for Alzheimer's disease diagnosis. In: 2020 IEEE International Conference on Bioinformatics and Biomedicine (BIBM), Los Alamitos, CA, USA, pp. 637–642. IEEE Computer Society, December 2020. https://doi.org/10.1109/BIBM49941.2020.9313422
15. Lian, C., Liu, M., Zhang, J., Shen, D.: Hierarchical fully convolutional network for joint atrophy localization and Alzheimer's disease diagnosis using structural MRI. IEEE Trans. Pattern Anal. Mach. Intell. **42**(4), 880–893 (2020). https://doi.org/10.1109/TPAMI.2018.2889096
16. Liu, J., Zeng, D., Guo, R., Lu, M., Wu, F., Wang, J.: MMHGE: detecting mild cognitive impairment based on multi-atlas multi-view hybrid graph convolutional networks and ensemble learning. Cluster Comput. **24**, 103–113 (2021)
17. Niemantsverdriet, E., Valckx, S., Bjerke, M., Engelborghs, S.: Alzheimer's disease CSF biomarkers: clinical indications and rational use. Acta Neurologica Belgica **117**(3), 591–602 (2017). https://doi.org/10.1007/s13760-017-0816-5

18. Pangman, V.C., Sloan, J., Guse, L.: An examination of psychometric properties of the mini-mental state examination and the standardized mini-mental state examination: implications for clinical practice. Appl. Nurs. Res. **13**(4), 209–213 (2000). https://doi.org/10.1053/apnr.2000.9231
19. Paszke, A., Gross, S., Massa, F., Lerer, A., Bradbury, J., et al.: PyTorch: an imperative style, high-performance deep learning library (2019)
20. Sachdev, P.S., Zhuang, L., Braidy, N., Wen, W.: Is Alzheimer's a disease of the white matter? Curr. Opin. Psychiatry **26**(3), 244–251 (2013). https://doi.org/10.1097/YCO.0b013e32835ed6e8
21. Simonyan, K., Zisserman, A.: Very deep convolutional networks for large-scale image recognition. arXiv preprint arXiv:1409.1556 (2014)
22. Smith, S.M.: Fast robust automated brain extraction. Hum. Brain Mapp. **17**(3), 143–155 (2002). https://doi.org/10.1002/hbm.10062
23. Smith, S.M., Jenkinson, M., Woolrich, M.W., Beckmann, C.F., Behrens, T.E., et al.: Advances in functional and structural MR image analysis and implementation as FSL. NeuroImage **23**, S208–S219 (2004). https://doi.org/10.1016/j.neuroimage.2004.07.051. Mathematics in Brain Imaging
24. Szegedy, C., Ioffe, S., Vanhoucke, V., Alemi, A.: Inception-v4, Inception-ResNet and the impact of residual connections on learning. In: Proceedings of the AAAI Conference on Artificial Intelligence, vol. 31 (2017)
25. Thompson, P.M., et al.: Dynamics of gray matter loss in Alzheimer's disease. J. Neurosci. **23**(3), 994–1005 (2003). https://doi.org/10.1523/JNEUROSCI.23-03-00994.2003
26. Yan, J.X., et al.: Identifying imaging markers for predicting cognitive assessments using Wasserstein distances based matrix regression. Front. Neurosci. **13** (2019). https://doi.org/10.3389/fnins.2019.00668
27. Zhang, Y.Y., Brady, M., Smith, S.: Segmentation of brain MR images through a hidden Markov random field model and the expectation-maximization algorithm. IEEE Trans. Med. Imaging **20**(1), 45–57 (2001). https://doi.org/10.1109/42.906424

# Correction to: A Multiple Encoders Network for Stroke Lesion Segmentation

Xiangchen Zhang, Huan Xu, Yujun Liu, Jiajia Liao, Guorong Cai,
Jinhe Su, and Yehua Song

**Correction to:**
**Chapter "A Multiple Encoders Network for Stroke Lesion**
**Segmentation" in: H. Ma et al. (Eds.):**
*Pattern Recognition and Computer Vision*, **LNCS 13021,**
**https://doi.org/10.1007/978-3-030-88010-1_44**

The chapter was inadvertently published with missing acknowledgement which has been included.

---

The updated version of this chapter can be found at
https://doi.org/10.1007/978-3-030-88010-1_44

# Author Index

Printed in the United States
by Baker & Taylor Publisher Services